OFFICIAL REPORT

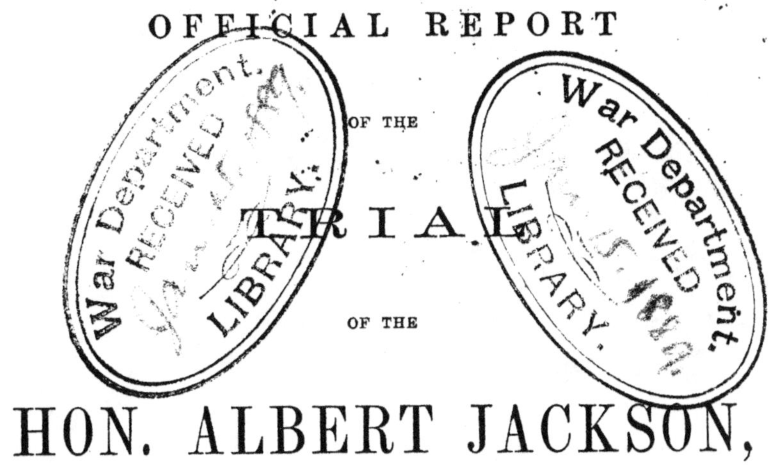

OF THE

TRIAL

OF THE

HON. ALBERT JACKSON,

JUDGE OF THE FIFTEENTH JUDICIAL CIRCUIT,

BEFORE THE SENATE,

COMPOSING THE HIGH COURT OF IMPEACHMENT OF THE STATE OF MISSOURI.

REPORTED BY

THOMAS J. HENDERSON.

JEFFERSON CITY:
W. G. CHEENEY, PUBLIC PRINTER.
1859.

PREFACE.

The report contained in these pages is printed in pursuance of a resolution which passed the Senate on the last day of the session at which Judge JACKSON was tried, and which is as follows:

> *Resolved*, That three thousand copies of the record, evidence; and arguments of the Managers and Respondent in the case of the State of Missouri against Albert Jackson, on articles of impeachment, be printed in bourgeois and minion type; that Thomas J. Henderson be appointed to superintend the printing of the same; and that the Committee on Accounts be required to audit and allow the expenses thereof.

The matter of the whole volume has been carefully prepared for press, and it is believed that a full, fair, and correct report is presented to the reader.

The reporter is greatly indebted to Mr. GEORGE C. STEDMAN, the accomplished phonographer appointed by the Senate to assist in reporting the trial, for his very valuable services. To Mr. S. belongs the credit of the accurate reports of the concluding speeches.

The work has been delayed beyond the time at which it was expected to appear by a pressure of business, and other causes, that prevented the Managers from revising the reports of their speeches as speedily as could have been desired.

Judge JACKSON declined revising his speeches, and they are therefore presented to the world with such corrections only as it is customary for reporters to make.

Hoping that the several objects of this publication may be fully attained, and especially that a reliable precedent for all future cases of the kind may be afforded by it, the report is respectfully submitted.

THOMAS J. HENDERSON.

City of Jefferson, *September* 1, 1859.

RECORD.

IN HOUSE OF REPRESENTATIVES.

TUESDAY, January 11, 1859.

Petitions, memorials and bills being the order of business,

Mr. MURPHY presented the following, which was read:

To the Honorable, the House of Representatives of the State of Missouri:

The petition of Solomon G. Kitchen respectfully showeth: That, as a citizen of the county of Stoddard, which is included in the Fifteenth Judicial Circuit of the State of Missouri, he deems it his duty to bring to the notice of your honorable body official misconduct and misdemeanors of Albert Jackson, as Judge of the Circuit Court of said circuit; and to invoke such action upon the charges herein preferred, as to your honorable body shall seem proper.

Your petitioner represents and charges, that the said Albert Jackson, Judge as aforesaid, has, on divers occasions, and at sundry times, during the last three years, while acting in his capacity as such Judge, been guilty of misconduct and high misdemeanors in office: that is to say, of willful and malicious oppression, partiality, corruption, and other abuses of his authority and official position.

That the said Albert Jackson, Judge as aforesaid, has been guilty of willful oppression, in refusing, without cause, and in violation of the constitution and laws of the land, to persons accused of felony, a speedy trial, in this, to wit: That at the October term, 1856, an indictment was pending in the Circuit Court of the county of Ripley, in said Fifteenth Judicial Circuit, the said Albert Jackson there presiding, against one —— Harris, upon a charge of arson or burglary; and said cause being called, both parties announced themselves ready for trial, and a trial thereof was urged by said defendant; whereupon said court, the said Albert Jackson being Judge, arbitrarily, without cause, and oppressively to said defendant, refused to permit said trial to take place; whereby, and in consequence of such refusal, the confinement of said defendant was prolonged in jail, resulting, as your petitioner is informed and believes, in the death of said defendant, by reason of such confinement, during an inclement winter.

Your petitioner further charges, that the said Albert Jackson, Judge as aforesaid, has, as your petitioner is informed and believes, been guilty of other and further acts of willful oppression, in this, to wit: That at the November term, 1857, of the Circuit Court of Stoddard county, a prosecution was pending in said court, the said Albert Jackson presiding, against one Sarah Buckner, charged with the crime of murder in the first degree; that, upon the trial of said cause, two witnesses were introduced by the State, and testified therein, (which was all the testimony offered,) when the said Judge, (court not being in session,) as your petitioner is informed and believes, advised the Circuit Attorney prosecuting for the State on that behalf to "withdraw" the testimony of one of such witnesses; that said Circuit Attorney accordingly asked leave of said court to "*withdraw*" such testimony, which was granted, and said court refused to permit counsel for said defendant to comment on the same before the jury; that this evidence was competent, relevant, and tended to mitigate the offense with which defendant was charged; that said cause was tried, and defendant convicted of murder in the first degree; that an appeal to the Supreme Court being granted, a bill of exceptions was tendered to said Judge for his signature, omitting the evidence of the witness aforesaid; that said Judge refused to sign such bill of exceptions unless the evidence of such witness was *included therein;* and the same was accordingly made a part of such bill of exceptions.

Your petitioner further represents, that the said Albert Jackson, Judge as aforesaid, has committed other and further acts of willful oppression and tyranny, in this, to wit: That at the May term, 1858, of the Circuit Court of Stoddard county, the said Albert Jackson presiding, a writ of mandamus having been previously issued by said Judge in vacation, directed to one Jonas Eaker, a Judge of District Court of said county of Stoddard, returnable to that term of said court, and said cause being called, said court was advised by counsel for said Eaker that said writ had not been delivered to said Eaker, nor served upon him, and that he was therefore not bound to make return or answer thereto; and your petitioner states that, as counsel for said Eaker, it was his duty to ascertain whether said writ of mandamus had been delivered or served upon defendant, and he avers that it had not been so delivered or served—a fact which said court well knew or might have known by an inspection of the same, which had been returned into court by the Sheriff, and was then in court; that said court, notwithstanding these facts, arbitrarily, oppressively to said defendant, and in violation of the laws of the land, ordered an attachment to issue for his body, caused him to be arrested, held in custody and restrained of his liberty for the space of several hours, and finally released him only on condition that he would surrender himself on the following day, and make return to said writ, which he did accordingly.

Your petitioner further represents and charges, that said Albert Jackson, Judge as aforesaid, has been guilty of official misconduct, abuse of authority, and a usurpation of authority, in appearing in person before grand juries, at sundry times and on various occasions, and urging them to prefer bills of indictment in particular cases and against particular persons, in this, to wit: That at the November term, 1858, of the Circuit Court of Stoddard county, the said Albert Jackson, during said term of court, and while the grand jury was in session, appeared before said jury in their retirement, assumed to instruct, and did instruct, said jury as to their duties, and did urge said grand jury to prefer bills of indictment against a citizen of Stoddard county and your petitioner.

And in this: That at the November term, 1858, of the Butler Circuit Court, said Albert Jackson presiding, before the grand jury had retired, the said Judge instructed them in open court, that certain citizens of said county and your petitioner had been guilty of a violation of the criminal laws, in a certain transaction to which he alluded, and that it was their duty to prefer bills of indictment against them; that upon the retirement of said jury the said Judge, as your petitioner is informed and believes, appeared before them in person, and there again urged said grand jury to prefer bills of indictment against said parties and your petitioner.

Your petitioner further charges, that said Albert Jackson has been guilty of official misconduct and misdemeanor in office, in this: That when grand juries have had under investigation charges of official misconduct against the said Judge, he has appeared before them, and instructed them that it was not their duty, and they had no legal right, to prefer an indictment against *him;* that is to say, that at the May term, 1858, of the Circuit Court of Butler county, the grand jury having, as your petitioner is informed and believes, under investigation acts of official misconduct of the said Albert Jackson, as Judge, he, the said Judge, being advised thereof, appeared in person before said jury and assumed to instruct, and did instruct, said grand jury touching their duties, and *particularly* respecting his own case, then under investigation; that said jury in their retirement were instructed by said Judge that they had no legal authority to prefer a bill of indictment against him.

Your petitioner further represents, that the said Albert Jackson, Judge as aforesaid, has, as such Judge, acted with partiality, corruptly and in gross abuse of his authority and position, in this: That at the special August term, 1858, of the Stoddard Circuit Court, the said Jackson presiding, a Circuit Attorney, *pro tem.*, was appointed by said court (in the absence of the Circuit Attorney) to represent the State, and among other duties to advise and instruct the grand jury touching questions of law arising before them; that said grand jury had before them the case of said Circuit Attorney, *pro tem.*, charged with a felony, to wit, a felonious assault, and they therefore requested said court to appoint another person to act as Circuit Attorney in his stead; that said court, well knowing the facts, (as your petitioner believes,) refused to make the appointment; that said grand jury did prefer a bill of indictment against said Circuit Attorney, *pro tem.*, which he himself prepared; that at the next (November, 1858,) term of said Circuit Court, said Albert Jackson presiding, the Circuit Attorney was again absent, and one D. G. Hicks (the same who acted as such at the former term) was again appointed by said court; that a motion was made at said term, by counsel for said Circuit Attorney, to quash said indictment against him, which motion was by the court sustained, and no person was appointed by said court to represent the State, nor was the State represented in that behalf; all which will more fully appear by a transcript of the record in said cause, which is made a part of this memorial. Also, that at the special August term, 1858, of the Stoddard Circuit Court, an indictment was then and there pending against certain citizens of said county of Stoddard, and the said Albert Jackson, jointly, for a misdemeanor, to wit, gaming; that one of said parties having been put upon his trial under said indictment, and the evidence being heard, said court instructed said jury that they might retire and find a special verdict as to the *fact* charged in the indictment, but refused to permit said jury, and instructed them that they could not find the general issue; that thereupon the Circuit Attorney, *pro tem.*, entered a *nolle prosequi* in said cause; all which will more fully appear by a transcript of the record in said cause, which is made a part of this memorial, and marked *A*.

Your petitioner further represents and charges, that the said Albert Jackson, Judge as aforesaid, has been guilty of other acts of official misconduct as Judge, and has acted corruptly and with partiality, in this: That at the November term, 1858, of the Stoddard Circuit Court, the said Albert Jackson presiding, a certain cause was pending in said court, wherein one Matthew H. Moore, of the county of Cape Girardeau, was plaintiff, and one James Walker, of the county of Stoddard, was defendant; that while said cause was so pending in said court, the parties thereto conferred together with the purpose of effecting a compromise of the same; that while these conferences were going on, and during said term of court, the said Albert Jackson privately advised and counseled said defendant Walker against a compromise of said suit, and gave him, said Walker, to understand, that upon a trial of said cause he could obtain a verdict; whereupon the plaintiff in said cause, being informed of these communications of the said Judge to said defendant, was compelled, in order that justice might be impartially administered, to take a change of venue to another circuit.

Your petitioner further represents and charges, that the said Albert Jackson, Judge as aforesaid, has, as such Judge, acted corruptly, oppressively, and with partiality, in this: That at divers times, and on various occasions, during the last three years, and, indeed, generally, if not habitually, during such period, upon applications before him for changes of venue, he has awarded them to counties and courts remote and inconvenient to parties litigant, instead of awarding them, as was his duty, and as the law of the land required, "to some court as convenient as may be to the opposite party."

Your petitioner states that the foregoing are a few only of the many instances in which the said Albert Jackson has acted in his capacity as Judge, as aforesaid, oppressively, corruptly, and with partiality.

Your petitioner, in conclusion, would respectfully ask at the hands of your honorable body, that the rights of the citizens (which have been outraged by the official misconduct herein alleged) may be vindicated, and the purity of the judiciary preserved, by an investigation into the conduct of the said Albert Jackson, under the power conferred upon you by the constitution; and your petitioner, as in duty bound, will ever pray.

SOLOMON G. KITCHEN.

Mr. Darnes offered the following resolution, which was adopted:

Resolved by the House of Representatives, That the Committee on Judiciary be instructed to inquire into the official conduct of Albert Jackson, Esq., Judge of the Fifteenth Judicial Circuit of this State, and that said committee have full power to send for persons and papers; and that they report to this House by impeachment or otherwise.

Wednesday, February 9, 1859.

Mr. Knott, on leave, from the Committee on the Judiciary, made a report in relation to the charges preferred against Albert Jackson, Judge of the Fifteenth Judicial Circuit of this State, recommending the adoption of the following:

Articles exhibited by the House of Representatives of the State of Missouri, in the name of all the people of the State, against Albert Jackson, Judge of the Fifteenth Judicial Circuit, in support of their Impeachment against him for willful and malicious oppression, partiality, misconduct, abuse of official authority, and other high crimes and misdemeanors.

Article I. That, unmindful of the sacred obligation by which he stood bound to discharge the solemn duties of his office faithfully, impartially, and consistently with the dignity and importance of the trust reposed in him, as Judge of the Fifteenth Judicial Circuit, in the State of Missouri, the said Albert Jackson, at a Circuit Court begun and held at the town of Bloomfield, within and for the county of Stoddard, in the State of Missouri, on the third Monday in May, A. D. 1858, (whereat the said Albert Jackson, by virtue of his office aforesaid, did preside as Judge,) did willfully and maliciously conduct himself in a manner highly oppressive and unjust to one Jonas Eaker, viz:

First. The said Albert Jackson, desiring to harrass and oppress the said Jonas Eaker, did, at the Circuit Court aforesaid, whereat he, the said Albert Jackson, presided as Judge, as aforesaid, cause an attachment to issue against him, the said Eaker, as for a criminal contempt, because said Eaker did not make return to a writ of mandamus, which writ had never been delivered to said Eaker, but of which a *copy* had been delivered to said Eaker; by virtue of which attachment the said Jonas Eaker was arrested and held in custody for several hours, and released finally by said Albert Jackson, on condition that he, the said Jonas Eaker, should make return to the copy that had been delivered to him, said Jackson well knowing that said writ had never been legally served upon him, the said Eaker, and that he was not in contempt for not answering thereto.

Second. In refusing to permit counsel for said Eaker to speak in his behalf, when they proposed to show to the court that said writ of mandamus had never been properly delivered to, or served upon him.

Third. In peremptorily, and in an oppressive, angry and insulting manner, ordering the counsel of said Eaker, to wit, Solomon G. Kitchen and William G. Phelan, *to shut their mouths and sit down*, when they, in behalf of their said client, attempted to suggest an insufficiency in the service of said writ of mandamus.

Fourth. In depriving said Jonas Eaker of the benefit of counsel, and of the privilege of speaking through such counsel in his own defense, as he had a lawful right to.

Art. II. That said Albert Jackson, Judge as aforesaid, regardless of the sacred obligation resting upon him to administer justice faithfully, impartially, and without respect to persons, was, at a Circuit Court begun and held at the town of Bloomfield, in the county of Stoddard, on the third Monday in November, A. D. 1858, whereat he, the said Albert Jackson, presided as Judge, willfully and maliciously guilty of the grossest *partiality* and injustice, to wit:

First. During the Circuit Court aforesaid, whereat said Albert Jackson presided as aforesaid, there was pending before said court the cause of Matthew M. Moore *vs.* James Walker, and the said Albert Jackson, corruptly, partially, and to the utter degradation of the solemn and important functions of his said office, secretly advised the said James Walker, defendant in said cause, not to compromise the same; that the field notes by which the property in dispute between him and the said Moore could be identified, were lost, and that said Walker would be successful in said cause, if he would refuse to compromise the same; and that, in consequence of the prejudice of the said Albert Jackson, the said Moore was compelled to have the venue in said cause changed.

Art. III. That, actuated by a spirit of arbitrary despotism and wanton injustice, totally repugnant to the sacred duties pertaining to his office, and highly dangerous to the rights of the citizens of the State, the said Albert Jackson, Judge of the Fifteenth Judicial Circuit, at a Circuit Court begun and held within and for the county of Wayne, in the State of Missouri, at the town of Greenville, in said county, on the last Monday in September, A. D. 1858, whereat said Albert Jackson, by virtue of his office aforesaid, presided as Judge, was guilty of willful and malicious oppression, misconduct, and abuse of authority in his official capacity:

First. During the Circuit Court aforesaid, at the time and place aforesaid, David M. Fox, one of counsel for plaintiff, in the cause of ——— Limbarger *vs.* ——— Power, then and there pending before said court, presented a petition to said Albert Jackson, then and there presiding as Judge of said court aforesaid, to change the venue of said cause to some other court, because of the prejudice of the Judge, and informed him, the said Albert Jackson, that both parties and their counsel had agreed that said cause might be sent to either the county of Madison or the county of Iron, as either of said counties would be convenient, and easy of access; but the said Albert Jackson, Judge as aforesaid, utterly unmindful of the rights of the parties and counsel in said cause, and totally disregarding the provisions of the statute in such cases made and provided, and willfully and maliciously intending to harrass and oppress the parties aforesaid, and their counsel, awarded a change of venue in said cause to *Mississippi county*, well knowing said county to be remote, difficult of access, and inconvenient to all the parties, counsel, and witnesses in said cause.

Second. When counsel engaged in said cause, to wit, David M. Fox and Philip Pipkin, attempted then and there to prevail upon him, the said Albert Jackson, to change the venue to some other county more convenient to all parties, and informed him that by sending said cause to Mississippi county he would deprive them of the privilege of attending to their clients' cause, as they had been employed to do, he, the said Jackson, replied to each of them in an oppressive, insolent and insulting manner, highly shameful, and derogatory to the dignity of the important position he occupied as Judge, as aforesaid.

Art. IV. That, influenced by a similar spirit of injustice and tyrannous disregard for the rights of the citizens of the State, the said Albert Jackson, at a Circuit Court begun and held within and for the county of Dunklin, at the town of Kennett, in said county, on the second Monday in May, A. D. 1858, whereat he, the said Albert Jackson, presided as Judge, did conduct himself, in his official capacity, in a manner highly oppressive, unjust, and tyrannical, viz:

First. During the sitting of the Circuit Court aforesaid, at the time and place aforesaid, counsel for the defendant, in the cause of —— Smith *vs.* —— Cude, then and there pending before said court, whereof said Albert Jackson was Judge, presented to said Albert Jackson, Judge of said court, a petition to change the venue of said cause to some other court, on account of prejudice on the part of the Judge; whereupon said Albert Jackson, willfully and maliciously intending to harrass and oppress the parties and counsel in said cause, awarded a change of venue in said cause to the *county of Pemiscot*, notwithstanding he was then and there assured by counsel for both parties in said cause, that said county was difficult of access, and inconvenient to both parties and witnesses; that both parties to said cause had agreed that the venue of said cause should be changed to Bollinger or Scott county, either of which would be much more convenient to all parties than the county of Pemiscot, and that if said cause should be sent to the county of Pemiscot, counsel for both parties would be compelled to abandon it; and to the earnest entreaties of counsel for both parties in said cause, that a change of venue therein might be awarded to some other county where it would be possible for them to attend to it, and that would not be so difficult of access, and inconvenient to the parties therein, he, the said Jackson, angrily, rudely, and insultingly replied, in a manner indicating a total disregard for that courtesy toward counsel, and respect for the rights of parties, that common decency and the duties of his office required.

Art. V. That said Albert Jackson, Judge as aforesaid, has, in numerous other instances, been guilty of willful and malicious oppression, misconduct, and abuse of authority, in awarding changes of venue in causes pending before him as Judge as aforesaid, to counties remote, inconvenient, and difficult of access, intending thereby to harrass and oppress counsel and parties, and to deter others from availing themselves of their right to a change of venue under the law; particularly at a Circuit Court begun and held at the town of Kennett, within and for the county of Dunklin, on the second Monday in May, A. D. 1858, whereat said Albert Jackson presided as Judge:

First. In awarding a change of venue in the cause of the Point Pleasant and Dunklin County Road Company *vs.* Moses Farrar, then and there pending, to the county of *Pemiscot*, well knowing said county to be inconvenient and difficult of access to the parties to said cause, and contrary to the earnest request of both parties to said cause, to some more convenient county.

Second. In awarding a change of venue in the cause of said Road Company *vs.* Nathaniel G. Murphy, then and there pending, to the said county of *Pemiscot*, well knowing the same to be difficult of access and inconvenient to both parties and counsel.

Art. VI. That at a Circuit Court begun and held at the town of Poplar Bluff, within and for the county of Butler, on the first Monday in May, A. D., 1858, whereat said Albert Jackson presided as Judge, the said Albert Jackson was willfully guilty of gross and malicious oppression, misconduct, and abuse of official authority, not only unbecoming his high position as Judge, but disgraceful to his character as a man, to wit:

First. During the sitting of the Circuit Court aforesaid, whereat said Jackson presided as Judge as aforesaid, one William G. Phelan, a regularly licensed lawyer, practicing in said court, arose to address a jury that had been empanneled and sworn to try an issue joined in a cause then and there pending, to wit, the cause of Gibson *vs.* Dunn, in which said Phelan had been employed and was acting as counsel; whereupon said Albert Jackson, maliciously intending to oppress said Phelan, and to injure his reputation as a citizen, and diminish his success as a lawyer, in an angry, oppressive, insolent, and insulting manner, ordered him to sit down, and then and there publicly, and in an insulting and contemptuous manner, accused said Phelan of having been guilty of a disgraceful and criminal act, to wit, *tampering with the grand jury*, and that said Phelan was in criminal contempt of court, together with other shameful and insulting expressions.

Second. When said Phelan immediately offered to defend himself against said disgraceful accusations and insulting expressions, said Albert Jackson, under color of his authority as Judge, in an angry, insolent, and oppressive manner, peremptorily ordered said Phelan to shut his mouth and sit down, (or words of that import,) and refused to permit said Phelan to say anything by way of denial, excuse, explanation, palliation, or in any manner to vindicate himself against the disgraceful, criminal charge, thus publicly alleged against him by said Judge in open court.

Art. VII. That said Albert Jackson, Judge as aforesaid, influenced by similar spirit of malicious persecution, was, at a Circuit Court begun and held at the town of Doniphan, within and for the county of Ripley, on the 4th Monday in October, A. D. 1857, whereat said Jackson presided as Judge, guilty of other and similar acts of willful and malicious oppression, misconduct, and abuse of authority:

First. In wantonly, insolently and insultingly accusing one David M. Fox, a regularly licensed lawyer, practicing in said court, of being guilty of the *crime of perjury*, or *subornation of perjury*, and of *lying*, and causing his client to lie; all of which said Albert Jackson, without any provocation, but in a spirit of vindictive persecution, did charge upon said Fox, in open court, whilst he, the said Albert Jackson, was exercising the functions of Judge of said court; tending by these, and innumerable other instances of oppression, contumelious, insolent, and insulting expressions towards lawyers and parties litigant, which he, the said Jackson, almost habitually indulges in the exercise of his official functions, to bring the high and important office he holds into utter degradation and contempt.

Art. VIII. That said Albert Jackson, Judge as aforesaid, forgetting the dignity of his office, and regardless of his sacred obligation to demean himself faithfully and impartially therein, did, on the trial of one Green DePriest, on an indictment for resisting an officer in the exercise of his official duties, had at a Circuit Court begun and held at the town of Thomasville, within and for the county of Oregon, on the third Monday in April, A. D. 1858, whereat he, the said Albert Jackson, presided as Judge, conduct himself willfully *partial* and corrupt, and highly unbecoming and disgraceful to his high official position:

First. In privately advising one James V. Odell, a lawyer, to procure said DePriest to employ him, the said Odell, as his counsel, and to take a contingent fee to defend him; that said DePriest could not be convicted on the indictment pending against him for resisting the officer, because he had already been convicted of disturbing the peace of a family, which was charged to have been done at the same time he resisted said officer.

Second. In officially and voluntarily advising said James V. Odell, as counsel for said DePriest, to plead a former conviction; which said advice said Albert Jackson, presiding as Judge, gave said Odell in open court, upon the trial.

Third. In partially and corruptly transcending his duties as Judge, on the trial of said DePriest, to such an extent that the Circuit Attorney, prosecuting for the State, abandoned said cause, and entered a "*nolle prosequi.*"

Art. IX. That, utterly unmindful of the provisions of the constitution of the State securing to its citizens "the privilege of the writ of *habeas corpus*," which the experience of ages has demonstrated to be one of the chief bulwarks of the liberties of the people, the said Albert Jackson, Judge as aforesaid, willfully and maliciously refused to issue a writ of *habeas corpus* for the purpose of having the body of a man named ——— Atterbury, who was confined in jail in the county of Dunklin, on a criminal charge, brought before him, as a Judge of the Circuit Court of said county, to be admitted to bail, or otherwise dealt with according to law, notwithstanding a petition, in every particular sufficient in law for that purpose, was presented to him, the said Jackson, as Judge as aforesaid, at the county of Stoddard, on the — day of ———, A. D. 1858; he, the said Jackson, well knowing it to be his duty to issue said writ, but refusing to do so because the name of David G. Hicks was necessarily mentioned in the petition.

Art. X. That said Albert Jackson, Judge as aforesaid, was, at the county of Stoddard, in the State of Missouri, on the 15th day of January, A. D. 1859, willfully and maliciously guilty of the most dangerous and reprehensible misconduct, partiality, and abuse of authority:

First. In corruptly and illegally setting at liberty, and discharging from the custody of John J. Jackson, Deputy Sheriff of the county of Stoddard aforesaid, one John R. Maine, who had been regularly arrested, examined, and committed by competent legal authority, on a charge of larceny, and delivered into the custody of said John J. Jackson, to be confined in jail, in default of giving bail; he, the said Albert Jackson, well knowing that said Maine was held in custody for a criminal offense, which was clearly and specifically set forth in the warrant of commitment, by virtue of which he was held in custody, a copy of which was exhibited to said Albert Jackson by the said Deputy Sheriff, in his return to the writ of *habeas corpus*, by which he was compelled to take the body of said Maine before said Jackson.

Second. In corruptly and illegally setting at liberty the said Maine, on account of a pretended informality, insufficiency, or irregularity in the writ or warrant of commitment, by virtue of which said Deputy Sheriff held him, the said Maine, in custody, well knowing that said Maine was held in custody for a criminal offense, and that he was expressly forbidden by the statute to discharge any such prisoner on account of any irregularity, insufficiency, or informality in the warrant of commitment.

Third. In corruptly and illegally discharging said Maine from custody without first having examined any of the evidence taken in support of the criminal charge made against said Maine, by the Justice of the Peace before whom said Maine was examined, as required by the statute in such cases made and provided.

Fourth. In illegally and corruptly setting at liberty, and discharging from the custody of William F. Cryts, a Constable of Stoddard county, one Charles Russell, well knowing that said Russell was held in custody by said Cryts for a felonious, criminal offense, for which he, the said Russell, had been regularly examined before Jonas Eaker, a Justice of the Peace of the county aforesaid, and by him placed for safe keeping until the hour of ten o'clock, (till which time he had been allowed to procure bail,) in the custody of the Constable aforesaid.

Fifth. In willfully, corruptly, and unlawfully having said Charles Russell brought before him, the said Jackson, as Judge of the Fifteenth Judicial Circuit, on a writ of *habeas corpus*, and discharging him from further custody, well knowing that said Charles Russell was at the time he, the said Jackson, issued said writ, lawfully in the custody of a legal magistrate, of competent jurisdiction, before whom he had been brought for examination, upon the charge of passing counterfeit money, and well knowing that said magistrate had found, from the evidence taken before him, that said Russell was probably guilty of said charge, and that said magistrate had allowed him, the said Russell, until a certain hour to procure bail, before he would proceed to commit him to jail, in default thereof; thereby tending to destroy the efficiency of the criminal law, to diminish the confidence of the people in the efficacy and purity of the judiciary of the country, to encourage the commission of crimes, and license every variety of villainy with which it is possible for a civilized community to be cursed.

Art. XI. That at a Circuit Court, begun and held at the town of Bloomfield, within and for the county of Stoddard, on the third Monday of November, A. D. 1858, whereat the said Albert Jackson presided as Judge, the said Albert Jackson, disregarding the duties of his office, did descend from the dignity of a Judge, and stoop to the level of a common informer, by calling the attention of the grand jury, empaneled and sworn for that county, at said court, during his public charge to them, to the fact that he, the said Jackson, had understood that a certain citizen of said county had gone to Jefferson City and pretended to transact some business for said county, in relation to obtaining some certified lists of swamp lands; that he had obtained a warrant upon the County Treasury for one hundred and seventy or seventy-five dollars, and that if the facts were as he understood them, they constituted the crime of obtaining money under false pretenses, which was punishable by imprisonment in the penitentiary, and that it was the duty of said grand jury to make diligent inquiry of said case; that the man to whom he alluded was a lawyer, and that they, the grand jury, could find out who it was by asking the County Treasurer who had obtained a warrant for a hundred seventy or seventy-five dollars; whereby everybody there, and those present, understood him, the said Judge, to mean Solomon G. Kitchen, a citizen of said county.

And by appearing before the said grand jury, in their room where they had retired to consider of presentments, and then and there again telling them it was their duty to make diligent inquiry of said facts; and that if they found the facts to be as he had understood them, they should find an indictment against the person who had obtained the warrant, and that Solomon G. Kitchen was the man who had procured the said warrant; thereby rendering his high functions as a Judge subservient to a low personal malice, and seeking, under color of his official duties, to wreak his own private vengeance, by affixing to the reputation of a personal enemy the imperishable disgrace of a public prosecution for a felonious offense.

Art. XII. That the said Albert Jackson, Judge as aforesaid, at a Circuit Court, begun and held at the town of Poplar Bluff, within and for the county of Butler, on the first Monday in November, A. D. 1857, whereat said Albert Jackson presided as Judge, was willfully and maliciously guilty of gross misdemeanors and abuse of official authority:

First. In refusing to suspend the Clerk of said court and appoint a temporary Clerk thereof, although he well knew that said Clerk was guilty of a misdemeanor in office, in not being present and attending to the duties required of him by law, and should therefore be suspended, and although he was earnestly requested by nearly all of the lawyers present to appoint a temporary Clerk, in order that the business of the court might go on.

Second. In refusing to try any cause pending in said court, civil or criminal, at said term, regardless of the consequences upon the rights of parties litigant and attorneys.

Third. In taking possession of the papers pertaining to causes triable and amenable at said term, and arbitrarily refusing parties and lawyers access thereto.

Fourth. In peremptorily discharging the grand jury, which had been empanneled, sworn and charged to inquire, in and for the body of said county, at said term, notwithstanding members of said grand jury informed said Judge that they had a large amount of business before them; that they had sent out subpenas for witnesses to appear before them, in relation to various matters of which they were inquiring, and did not desire to be discharged; and notwithstanding this was but the second day of the term, and said court was allowed a whole week in which to hold said term: all of which misdemeanors were intended to oppress and harrass the parties and lawyers, and calculated to impair public confidence in the efficacy of the constitutional guaranty "that justice shall be administered without sale, denial, or delay."

Art. XIII. That the said Albert Jackson, unmindful of the dignity of his position as a Judge, and disregarding the restraints imposed by his said office, did, in the month of October, A. D. 1857, privately counsel and advise one William Ringer to sell all the county warrants that should be issued, in payment of a contract which said Ringer had with Stoddard county for the building of a court-house, and put the money in his pocket, and then bring a suit for damages against Solomon G. Kitchen, the commissioner, and assured him he could recover in such suit; endeavoring thereby to incite a vexatious and expensive suit in the court of which he was himself Judge, for the purpose of annoying, harrassing, and oppressing said Solomon G. Kitchen.

ART. XIV. That the said Albert Jackson, Judge as aforesaid, was, at the Circuit Court begun and held at the town of Doniphan, within and for the county of Ripley, on the 4th Monday in April, A. D. 1858, and on the trial of one William Kinsey, for grand larceny, which trial was had at said court, whereat said Albert Jackson presided as Judge, willfully and maliciously guilty of great oppression, misconduct, and abuse of official authority, corruptly intending thereby to embarrass and oppress the counsel of said Kinsey, and procure his conviction:

First. By arbitrarily refusing to allow said Kinsey's counsel time to take down the testimony of the witnesses introduced on said trial.

Second. By repeated interruptions of the counsel for said Kinsey during said trial, tending to harrass and embarrass them.

Third. By the frequent use of rude, insulting, insolent, and discourteous expressions towards said Kinsey's counsel during the trial.

Fourth. By peremptorily stopping one of said Kinsey's counsel in the midst of his argument to the jury, and ordering him to take his seat, although said counsel (David M. Fox) was in the discharge of his proper and lawful duties.

ART. XV. At the same Circuit Court, begun and held in and for the county of Ripley as aforesaid, whereat said Albert Jackson presided as Judge, said Albert Jackson was willfully and maliciously guilty of great partiality, oppression, and abuse of official authority, on the trial of the cause of James Moore *vs.* John Eldridge, administrator of the estate of Wm. Parker, deceased, then and there pending, corruptly intending thereby to injure the rights of said Moore, and to oppress and injure his counsel:

First. In publicly expressing his opinion in relation to the merits of said cause, adversely to the rights of said Moore.

Second. In an unjust, overbearing, and insolent demeanor towards counsel during said trial.

Third. In refusing to sign a bill of exceptions, duly tendered to him by counsel for said Moore, *unless it was made to show that certain facts were proven which were not proven on said trial,* notwithstanding counsel for both parties agreed that the bill of exceptions, as presented, contained all the evidence given on said trial; corruptly intending thereby to deprive said Moore of a fair trial by the Supreme Court.

ART. XVI. That said Albert Jackson, at a Circuit Court begun and held at the town of Bloomfield, within and for the county of Stoddard, on the third Monday in November, A. D. 1858, whereat said Albert Jackson presided as Judge, was willfully and maliciously guilty of much gross oppression, partiality, misconduct, and abuse of authority in his official capacity:

First. In expressing opinions and making assertions relative to the cause of Gustavus Berry *vs.* John Griffie, then and there pending, unbecoming his position as Judge.

Second. In expressing opinions and making assertions relative to the merits of said cause in open court, in the presence and hearing of the jury empanneled and sworn to try said cause, calculated to influence the minds of the jury against the defendant.

Third. In corruptly endeavoring to prevent the defendant in said cause from getting the same fairly before the Supreme Court on appeal, by refusing to sign a bill of exceptions, properly tendered to him by counsel for said defendant, until a large portion of the motion papers had been stricken out, so that a large number of material reasons urged for a new trial in said cause did not appear in said bill.

Fourth. In corruptly refusing to examine and sign the testimony preserved in the bill of exceptions in said cause, although counsel for both parties agreed that all of said testimony was correctly set forth therein, alleging as a reason that there was so much noise in court during the trial of said cause that he did not know what testimony had been given; corruptly intending, by such refusal, to prevent said defendant from getting said cause fairly before the Supreme Court.

Fifth. In corruptly refusing to sign a bill of exceptions properly tendered to him by counsel in the cause of Daugherty *vs.* Whitehead, tried at said term of court, until he had stricken out nearly all the motion papers filed in said cause; so that the greater number of material reasons urged for a new trial and in arrest of judgment did not appear in said bill; corruptly intending thereby to prevent said cause from being fairly presented to the Supreme Court, that his judgment might not be reversed by said court.

Sixth. In hearing and determining a motion to quash an indictment then and there pending, against one David G. Hicks, who was then and there acting as Circuit Attorney, *pro tem.*, without having first appointed some other attorney to represent the State in that behalf.

Art. XVII. That at a Circuit Court, begun and held in the town of Bloomfield, within and for the county of Stoddard, on the 9th day of August, A. D. 1858, whereat the said Albert Jackson presided, the said Albert Jackson was willfully and maliciously guilty of the grossest partiality, corruption, misconduct, and abuse of authority:

First. In visiting the grand jury in their room after they had retired to consider of presentments, and then instructing said grand jury that playing cards for whisky, oysters, etc., did not constitute an offense within the meaning of the statute against gaming; and further instructing said grand jury that they could not find an indictment against him, the said Judge, for anything of which he might be guilty in his official capacity.

Second. Whereas the grand jury empanneled, sworn and charged to inquire in and for the county of Stoddard, aforesaid, at the Circuit Court begun and held in said county, as last aforesaid, found an indictment against the said Albert Jackson and David G. Hicks, who was then and there acting as Circuit Attorney, *pro tem.*, Isaac Brand and Orson Bartlett, for gaming; and whereas, during said Circuit Court, said Albert Jackson presiding, the said Orson Bartlett appeared, plead not guilty to said indictment, and demanded a trial, which was awarded him immediately—the said Albert Jackson, presiding as Judge during said trial, did conduct himself in a manner most shamefully partial and corrupt:

1. In commenting orally at great length upon the case, and declaring in the presence and hearing of the jury, that the fact charged in the indictment and proven before the jury, did not constitute an indictable offense, and illustrating his position by a great variety of illustrations, in order to induce the jury to find the defendant, Bartlett, not guilty.

2. In commenting upon the evidence adduced, and instructing the jury, *orally*, as to the law governing the case, in direct contravention to what he *knew* to be the words of the statute in such cases made and provided.

3. In refusing to allow the jury to find a general verdict, telling them they might find the facts, but he would apply the law, and that if they found a verdict of guilty, he would set the same aside.

4. In endeavoring by various means to influence the jury to find a verdict of not guilty, instead of permitting them to decide impartially whether the defendant was guilty under the law.

5. In manifesting a solicitude for the acquittal, scarcely becoming to an advocate, but highly disgraceful to a Judge.

6. In permitting David G. Hicks, who was acting as Circuit Attorney, *pro tem.*, to enter a *nolle prosequi*, knowing that said Hicks as well as himself was indicted jointly with said Bartlett as *particeps criminis*, and in other shameful acts of partiality and corruption, tending to bring the judicial tribunals of the country into utter obloquy and contempt.

Art. XVIII. At a Circuit Court begun and held at the town of Bloomfield, within and for the county of Stoddard, in the State of Missouri, on the third Monday in November, A. D. 1857, whereat the said Albert Jackson, by virtue of his office of Judge of the Fifteenth Judicial Circuit, presided, and before which one Sarah Buckner was arraigned for trial on an indictment for murder in the first degree, the said Albert Jackson, maliciously and corruptly intending to procure the conviction of said Sarah Buckner, was willfully and maliciously guilty of the most shameful oppression, partiality, misconduct, and abuse of authority in his official capacity:

First. In preventing William C. Grimsley, a witness introduced on the part of the State, who had testified to a certain conversation on the part of the prisoner, from detailing such portions of said conversation as tended to extenuate the crime charged against her; which he, the said Jackson, did on his own motion, without the Circuit Attorney having made any objection thereto.

Second. In privately advising the Circuit Attorney to withdraw the evidence of said Grimsley, and in permitting the Circuit Attorney to withdraw said evidence from the consideration of the jury, and preventing the counsel for the prisoner from cross-examining said witness, Grimsley.

Third. In allowing his partiality and solicitude for the conviction of said prisoner, Buckner, to extend so far as to induce him, the said Judge, to take the examination of the witnesses, and the management of the cause, almost entirely out of the hands of the attorney prosecuting for the State, although counsel for prisoner repeatedly and earnestly protested against such gross abuse of official authority and unprecedented oppression.

Fourth. In refusing counsel for the prisoner any of the usual courtesies due from the bench to the bar, but attempting to oppress, harrass and annoy said counsel during said trial, by making use of the most rude, insolent, contemptuous and insulting expressioas towards them.

Fifth. In refusing to allow said prisoner's counsel to advert to or speak of the testimony of said witness, Grimsley, in their arguments to the jury, even to correct any impression said testimony might have made upon the minds of said jury.

Sixth. In refusing to allow counsel for the said prisoner to make use of illustrations in their arguments in said cause, and by repeatedly and vexatiously interrupting the said counsel for said prisoner, during their arguments to the jury, and so harshly and insultingly as to compel one of said counsel to abandon the defense of said prisoner in the midst of his argument.

Seventh. In imposing such wanton and tyrannical restrictions upon counsel, in arguing said cause for said prisoner, as to effectually defeat her constitutional guaranty of being heard by herself or counsel, and preclude the possibility of her having a fair trial by an impartial jury, which is the ultimate and strongest protection of the rights and liberties of the people.

Eighth. In unjustly, corruptly and cruelly refusing to sign a bill of exceptions, legally tendered to him by counsel for said prisoner, until said bill of exceptions was made to contain the testimony of said William C. Grimsley, notwithstanding he had refused counsel for the prisoner the privilege of cross-examining said Grimsley, and had suffered his testimony to be *withdrawn*, and had refused to allow counsel for prisoner to advert to, or comment on, said testimony, in their argument to the jury.

Ninth. In many other corrupt and oppressive acts, indicating a degree of indecent solicitude on the part of said Jackson, for the conviction of said Sarah Buckner, unbecoming even a public prosecutor, but highly disgraceful to the character of a Judge, as it was contrary to the spirit of our laws, and subversive of justice, and tending to bring the judiciary of the country into utter abhorrence and contempt.

And the House of Representatives, aforesaid, saving to themselves the right of exhibiting at any time hereafter, any other or further articles or accusations or impeachment, against the said Albert Jackson, and also of replying to his answers hereto, or to any of the foregoing articles, or to any that they may hereafter exhibit against him, and of offering proof to all and every of said articles, and to any that may hereafter be exhibited against him, as the case may require, do demand that said Albert Jackson may be put to answer the said crimes and misdemeanors, and that such proceedings, examinations, trials and judgments may be had and given as are agreeable to law and justice.

Mr. Darnes moved to lay the report of the committee on the table till the following day at 10 o'clock, A. M.; which was adopted.

Thursday, February 10, 1859.

The House resumed the consideration of the report of the Committee on the Judiciary, in relation to the charges preferred against Albert Jackson, Judge, etc.; when

Mr. Hardin, of Callaway, offered the following resolutions:

Resolved, That the House of Representatives do now impeach Albert Jackson, Judge of the Fifteenth Judicial Circuit, for misdemeanors in office; and for the purpose of obtaining the trial of the same, adopt the articles of impeachment reported to this House by the Judiciary Committee against said officer, and request that the Senate, in due season, inquire into and try the same.

Resolved, further, That the Clerk of this House transmit to the Senate these resolutions, and the articles of impeachment.

Immediate action on these resolutions was waived, and the reading of the evidence taken before the Judiciary Committee called for; when

Mr. Anderson offered the following resolution:

Resolved, That the further consideration of the report of the Committee on the Judiciary, upon the case of Judge Jackson, be postponed until Wednesday, the 16th day of this month; and that, in the meantime, the report and testimony taken before the committee be published for the use of the members of this House.

Mr. Davis, of Buchanan, moved to lay the resolution last offered on the table; which motion was decided in the affirmative by the following vote, the ayes and noes having been demanded by Mr. Walker, of Cape Girardeau:

Ayes—Messrs. Abney, Baker, Barkley, Barnes, Bedford, Blackwood, Boulware, Bowlin, Briscoe, Burden, Burgess, Clark, Conway, Cordell, Cowgill, Crandall, Cravens, Cullers, Cunningham, Darnes, Davis of Buchanan, Day, Deatherage, Duval, Dyer, Edgar, Ellis, Enloe, Ferry, Gates, Gideon, Glascock, Gooch, Gorham, Gratiott, Halley, Hardin of Callaway, Hardin of Texas, Harris of Boone, Higgins, Hines, Hudgins, Hunter, Jackson, Jameson, Keyser, King of Franklin, King of St. Charles, Knott, Kribben, Lampton, Lenox, McAlister, McGaugh, McSpadden, Mitchell, Moore, Munro, Murphy, Norris, O'Fallon, Parsons, Pulliam, Rayburn, Rives, Roberts of DeKalb, Robertson, Shields, Sitton, Strachan, Sturgeon, Tate, Taylor of Lawrence, Taylor of Lafayette, Turner of Clinton, Turner of St. Louis, Walker of Cedar, Waltman, Wommack, Woolsey, Yager, Young, and Mr. Speaker—88.

NOES—Messrs. Anderson, Anthony, Blanton, Boas, Bowles, Boyd, Caldwell, Chartrand, Chilton, Davis of Nodaway, Dent, Fagg, Guitar, Hampton, Jones of Marion, King of Ray, Letcher, McIlhany, Maguire, Moulder, Nevill, Owen, Parks, Peers, Pilkington, Pitt, Pollard, Polk, Pritchard, Riley, Simpson, Smith, Stone, Walker of Cape Girardeau, Welch, and Woodward—36.

Absent—Messrs. Cox. Edwards, Jones of Webster, and Roberts of Schuyler.

Absent on leave—Messrs. Ament, Dillon, Ferris, Harris of Montgomery, White, Wilcox, and York.

A message from the Governor, and other business, prevented further consideration of the impeachment case until the night session; when Mr. GUITAR offered the following resolutions, which were adopted:

Resolved, That during the reading of the evidence in the matter of the impeachment now pending against Judge Jackson, no one shall be allowed to be present in the hall, except the members and officers of this House, and the accused and his counsel.

Resolved, That the Speaker shall instruct the Doorkeeper and Sergeant-at-Arms to keep the hall clear of all persons, except as provided in the foregoing resolution.

The hall having been cleared of all spectators, in accordance with the above resolutions, the evidence taken before the Judiciary Committee was read, and being concluded, the House adjourned.

FRIDAY, February 11, 1859.

The House having resumed the consideration of the matter of the impeachment of Judge Jackson,

Mr. CLARK offered the following resolution:

Resolved, That the House do now go into secret session, to consider the impeachment case of Judge Jackson.

Mr. YAGER moved to lay this resolution on the table; which was carried.

Mr. ROBERTS, of DeKalb, offered the following resolution, as a substitute for the resolution offered by Mr. Hardin, of Callaway:

Resolved, That after a patient hearing of the testimony in the case of impeaching Albert Jackson, now pending before this House, we find nothing in said testimony to justify this House in sending said case to the Senate; therefore,

Resolved, That we disagree to the report of the committee to whom said case was referred.

Mr. DARNES moved to lay the resolution on the table; which motion was decided in the affirmative by the following vote, the ayes and noes being demanded by Mr. Fagg:

AYES—Messrs. Abney, Baker, Barkley, Barnes, Bedford, Blackwood, Blanton, Boas, Boulware, Bowlin, Briscoe, Burden, Chartrand, Chilton, Conway, Cowgill, Cox, Crandall, Cravens, Cunningham, Darnes, Davis of Buchanan, Day, Deatherage, Dent, Dyer, Edgar, Ferry, Gates, Gideon, Glascock, Gooch, Gorham,

Gratiott, Guitar, Hampton, Halley, Hardin of Callaway, Hardin of Texas, Harris of Boone, Higgins, Hudgins, Hunter, Jackson, Jameson, Jones of Webster, Keyser, King of Franklin, King of St. Charles, Knott, Lampton, Lenox, McAlister, McIlhany, McSpadden, Maguire, Mitchell, Moore, Munro, Moulder, Murphy, Nevill, Norris, Parks, Parsons, Peers, Pulliam, Rayburn, Rives, Robertson, Shields, Simpson, Stone, Strachan, Tate, Taylor of Lawrence, Taylor of Lafayette, Turner of Clinton, Walker of Cedar, Waltman, Wommack, Woolsey, Yager, Young, and Mr. Speaker—83.

NOES—Messrs. Anderson, Anthony, Bowles, Boyd, Clark, Cordell, Davis of Nodaway, Enloe, Fagg, Hines, Jones of Marion, Letcher, Pilkington, Pollard, Polk, Pritchard, Riley, Roberts of DeKalb, Sitton, Sturgeon, Walker of Cape Girardeau, and Welch—23.

Absent—Messrs. Ellis, O'Fallon, Owen, Pitt, Roberts of Schuyler, and Turner of St. Louis.

Absent on leave—Messrs. Ament, Dillon, Duval, Ferris, Harris of Montgomery, Smith, White, Wilcox, and York.

Sick—Messrs. Burgess, Cullers, and Kribben.

Excused from voting—Messrs. Edwards, King of Ray, McGaugh, and Woodward.

Mr. BRISCOE called for the previous question.

The question then being "shall the main question now be put?" it was decided in the affirmative by the following vote, the ayes and noes being demanded by Mr. Edwards:

AYES—Messrs. Abney, Baker, Barkley, Barnes, Bedford, Blackwood, Blanton, Bowles, Boulware, Boas, Bowlin, Briscoe, Caldwell, Chartrand, Chilton, Conway, Cowgill, Cox, Crandall, Darnes, Davis of Buchanan, Day, Deatherage, Dent, Dyer, Edgar, Enloe, Ferry, Gates, Gideon, Glascock, Gorham, Gratiott, Guitar, Halley, Hardin of Callaway, Hardin of Texas, Harris of Boone, Higgins, Hunter, Jackson, Jameson, Jones of Webster, Keyser, King of Franklin, Knott, Kribben, Lampton, Lenox, McAlister, McGaugh, McSpadden, Mitchell, Moore, Munro, Moulder, Murphy, Nevill, Norris, Parsons, Peers, Pilkington, Pulliam, Riley, Robertson, Simpson, Strachan, Sturgeon, Tate, Taylor of Lawrence, Turner of Clinton, Walker of Cedar, Waltman, Wommack, Woolsey, Yager, Young, and Mr. Speaker—79.

NOES—Messrs. Anderson, Anthony, Boyd, Burden, Clark, Cordell, Cunningham, Davis of Nodaway, Edwards, Enloe, Gooch, Hampton, Hines, Hudgins, Jones of Marion, King of Ray, King of St. Charles, Letcher, McIlhany, Maguire, O'Fallon, Owen, Parks, Pitt, Pollard, Polk, Pritchard, Rives, Roberts of DeKalb, Sitton, Taylor of Lafayette, Walker of Cape Girardeau, Welch, and Woodward—34.

Absent—Messrs. Ellis, Rayburn, Roberts of Schuyler, and Stone.

Absent on leave—Messrs. Ament, Cravens, Dillon, Duval, Ferris, Harris of Montgomery, Smith, White, Wilcox, and York.

Sick—Messrs. Burgess and Cullers.

So the House decided that the main question should be put, two-thirds of the members present having voted in the affirmative.

Mr. JONES, of Marion, moved that the record evidence in the case of impeachment of Albert Jackson be read; which was lost by the following vote, the ayes and noes having been demanded by Mr. Hudgins:

AYES—Messrs. Anderson, Anthony, Barnes, Boyd, Burden, Caldwell, Clark, Conway, Cordell, Cunningham, Davis of Nodaway, Dent, Enloe, Fagg, Ferry, Gates, Gooch, Guitar, Hampton, Hardin of Callaway, Hines, Hudgins, King of Ray, King of St. Charles, Knott, Letcher, McGaugh, McIlhany, Maguire, Moore, Nevill, O'Fallon, Owen, Parks, Polk, Pollard, Pritchard, Riley, Rives, Simpson, Sitton, Stone, Taylor of Lafayette, Walker of Cape Girardeau, Welch, Woodward, and Woolsey—47

NOES—Messrs. Abney, Baker, Barkley, Bedford, Blackwood, Blanton, Boas, Boulware, Bowles, Bowlin, Briscoe, Chartrand, Chilton, Cowgill, Cox, Crandall, Cravens, Darnes, Davis of Buchanan, Day, Deatherage, Dyer, Edgar, Gideon, Glascock, Gorham, Gratiott, Halley, Hardin of Texas, Harris of Boone, Hunter, Jackson, Jameson, Jones of Webster, Keyser, Kribben, Lampton, Lenox, McAlister, McSpadden, Mitchell, Munro, Moulder, Murphy, Norris, Parsons, Peers, Pilkington, Pitt, Pulliam, Rayburn, Roberts of DeKalb, Robertson, Shields, Strachan, Sturgeon, Tate, Taylor of Lawrence, Turner of Clinton, Walker of Cedar, Waltman, Wommack, Yager, Young, and Mr. Speaker—64.

Absent—Messrs. Edwards, King of Franklin, Roberts of Schuyler, and Turner of St. Louis.

Absent on leave—Same as before.

Sick—Messrs. Burgess and Cullers.

Excused from voting—Mr. Jones.

Mr. O'Fallon moved an adjournment; which was lost by the following vote, the ayes and noes being demanded by Mr. Bowlin:

Ayes—Messrs. Anderson, Anthony, Barnes, Boyd, Caldwell, Clark, Davis of Nodaway, Fagg, Ferry, Gratiott, Hampton, Harris of Boone, Hines, Jackson, Jones of Marion, Jones of Webster, Letcher, McIlhany, O'Fallon, Peers, Polk, Shields, Taylor of Lafayette, Walker of Cape Girardeau, Welch, and Woodward—26.

Noes—Messrs. Abney, Baker, Barkley, Bedford, Blackwood, Boulware, Bowles, Bowlin, Briscoe, Burden, Chartrand, Chilton, Conway, Cowgill, Cox, Crandall, Cravens, Cunningham, Darnes, Davis of Buchanan, Day, Deatherage, Dent, Dyer, Edgar, Enloe, Gates, Gideon, Glascock, Gooch, Gorham, Guitar, Halley, Hardin of Callaway, Hardin of Texas, Hunter, Jackson, Keyser, King of Ray, King of St. Charles, Knott, Kribben, Lampton, Lenox, McAlister, McSpadden, McGaugh, Maguire, Mitchell, Moore, Munro, Moulder, Murphy, Nevill, Norris, Owen, Parsons, Pilkington, Pitt, Pollard, Pritchard, Pulliam, Rayburn, Riley, Rives, Roberts of DeKalb, Robertson, Simpson, Stone, Strachan, Sturgeon, Tate, Taylor of Lawrence, Turner of Clinton, Walker of Cedar, Waltman, Wommack, Woolsey, Yager, Young, and Mr. Speaker—82.

Absent—Messrs. Blanton, Boas, Burgess, Edwards, Hudgins, King of Franklin, Parks, Roberts of Schuyler, and Sitton.

Absent on leave—Messrs. Ament, Dillon, Duval, Ellis, Ferris, Harris of Montgomery, Higgins, Smith, White, Wilcox, and York.

Sick—Mr. Cullers.

The question then recurring upon the adoption of the resolutions offered by Mr. Hardin, of Callaway, the same were adopted by the following vote, the ayes and noes being demanded by Mr. Pulliam:

Ayes—Messrs. Abney, Baker, Barkley, Barnes, Bedford, Blackwood, Boulware, Bowlin, Briscoe, Burden, Chartrand, Chilton, Conway, Cowgill, Cox, Crandall, Cravens, Cunningham, Darnes, Davis of Buchanan, Day, Deatherage, Dent, Edgar, Ferry, Gideon, Glascock, Gooch, Gorham, Gratiott, Guitar, Halley, Hardin of Callaway, Hardin of Texas, Harris of Boone, Hunter, Jackson, Jameson, Jones of Webster, Keyser, King of St. Charles, Knott, Kribben, Lampton, Lenox, McAlister, McIlhany, McSpadden, Mitchell, Moore, Munro, Moulder, Murphy, Nevill, Norris, Parsons, Pilkington, Pitt, Pulliam, Rayburn, Riley, Rives, Robertson, Shields, Stone, Strachan, Sturgeon, Tate, Taylor of Lafayette, Taylor of Lawrence, Turner of Clinton, Walker of Cedar, Waltman, Wommack, Woolsey, Yager, Young, and Mr. Speaker—78.

Noes—Messrs. Anderson, Bowles, Boyd, Caldwell, Clark, Cordell, Davis of Nodaway, Enloe, Fagg, Gates, Hampton, Hines, Letcher, Peers, Pollard, Polk, Pritchard, Roberts of DeKalb, Simpson, Sitton, Walker of Cape Girardeau, and Welch—22.

Absent—Messrs. Anthony, Blanton, Boas, Burgess, Edwards, Hudgins, King of Franklin, O'Fallon, Parks, Roberts of Schuyler, and Turner of St. Louis.

Absent on leave—Same as before.

Excused from voting—Messrs. Jones of Marion, King of Ray, McGaugh, Maguire, Owen, and Woodward.

Sick—Messrs. Cullers and Dyer.

Mr. Keyser offered the following resolution:

WHEREAS, The House of Representatives have caused articles of impeachment to be preferred against Judge Albert Jackson to be transmitted to the Senate for trial; and, whereas, it becomes the duty of the House to elect managers to prosecute said impeachment before the Senate, as aforesaid; therefore, be it

Resolved, That John B. Henderson and James Proc. Knott be, and they are hereby, appointed such managers, to conduct said impeachment before the Senate.

Mr. RILEY offered the following as a substitute for the resolution offered by Mr. Keyser:

Resolved, That the House do now proceed to elect two managers to conduct the prosecution before the Senate, against Judge Albert Jackson.

Mr. DARNES moved the rejection of the substitute; which motion was decided in the negative.

Mr. HUDGINS moved to amend the substitute by striking out "two" and inserting "five"; which was decided in the negative.

Mr. TURNER, of Clinton, offered the following amendment to the substitute:

Amend by striking out the word "two" and inserting "three";

Which was disagreed to by the following vote, the ayes and noes being demanded by Mr. Sitton:

AYES—Messrs. Abney, Anthony, Baker, Barkley, Barnes, Bedford, Blackwood, Boulware, Bowles, Bowlin, Burden, Chartrand, Conway, Cowgill, Crandall, Davis of Buchanan, Day, Edgar, Ferry, Guitar, Halley, Hardin of Callaway, Hardin of Texas, Harris of Boone, Hudgins, Keyser, King of St. Charles, Kribben, McAlister, McIlhany, Maguire, Mitchell, Munro, Murphy, O'Fallon, Pilkington, Rayburn, Rives, Strachan, Taylor of Lawrence, Turner of Clinton, Turner of St. Louis, Young, and Mr. Speaker—44.

NOES—Messrs. Anderson, Blanton, Boas, Boyd, Briscoe, Caldwell, Chilton, Clark, Cordell, Cox, Cunningham, Darnes, Davis of Nodaway, Deatherage, Dent, Dyer, Enloe, Fagg, Gates, Gideon, Glascock, Gooch, Gorham, Gratiott, Hampton, Hines, Hunter, Jackson, Jameson, Jones of Marion, Jones of Webster, King of Franklin, Lampton, Lenox, Letcher, McGaugh, McSpadden, Moore, Moulder, Nevill, Norris, Owen, Parks, Parsons, Peers, Pollard, Polk, Pritchard, Pulliam, Riley, Roberts of DeKalb, Robertson, Shields, Simpson, Sitton, Stone, Sturgeon, Tate, Taylor of Lafayette, Walker of Cape Girardeau, Walker of Cedar, Waltman, Welch, Wommack, Woodward, and Woolsey—66.

Absent—Messrs. Bowlin, Cravens, Edwards, Knott, Pitt, and Yager.

Absent on leave—Same as before.

Excused from voting—Mr. King of Ray.

Sick—Mr. Cullers.

Mr. NORRIS offered the following amendment to the substitute:

Amend by adding "that the above number be selected from the members of this House";

Which was agreed to by the following vote, the ayes and noes being demanded by Mr. Darnes:

AYES—Messrs. Anthony, Blanton, Boas, Boulware, Bowlin, Boyd, Briscoe, Caldwell, Clark, Conway, Cordell, Cowgill, Cox, Crandall, Cunningham, Davis of Buchanan, Davis of Nodaway, Day, Edgar, Gates, Gideon, Glascock, Gooch, Gorham, Gratiott, Guitar, Hampton, Hardin of Callaway, Hardin of Texas, Harris of Boone, Hudgins, Jackson, Jameson, Jones of Marion, King of St. Charles, Kribben, Lampton, McGaugh, McIlhany, McSpadden, Maguire, Mitchell, Nevill, Norris, O'Fallon, Owen, Parks, Pilkington, Pollard, Polk, Pritchard, Riley, Roberts of DeKalb, Robertson, Shields, Simpson, Strachan, Sturgeon, Taylor of Lawrence, Taylor of Lafayette, Turner of Clinton, Turner of St. Louis, Walker of Cedar, Woodward, Young, and Mr. Speaker—66.

NOES—Messrs. Abney, Anderson, Baker, Barkley, Barnes, Bedford, Blackwood, Bowles, Chartrand, Chilton, Cravens, Darnes, Deatherage, Dent, Dyer,

Enloe, Fagg, Ferry, Halley, Hines, Hunter, Jones of Webster, Keyser, King of Franklin, Lenox, Letcher, McAlister, Moore, Munro, Moulder, Murphy, Parsons, Peers, Pulliam, Rayburn, Rives, Sitton, Stone, Tate, Walker of Cape Girardeau, Waltman, Welch, Wommack, and Woolsey—44.

Absent—Messrs. Burden, Burgess, Edwards, Knott, Pitt, Yager, and Roberts of Schuyler.

Absent on leave—Same as before.

Sick—Mr. Cullers.

The substitute, as amended, was then adopted.

Nominations for managers being in order,

The Chair announced that the vote would be taken for each manager separately.

Mr. Norris put in nomination James Proctor Knott, of Scotland county.

Mr. Anthony nominated Christian Kribben, of St. Louis.

The roll being called, there appeared

For Mr. Knott—Messrs. Abney, Baker, Barkley, Barnes, Bedford, Blackwood, Blanton, Boas, Boulware, Bowles, Bowlin, Briscoe, Burden, Caldwell, Chartrand, Chilton, Clark, Conway, Cowgill, Cox, Crandall, Cravens, Cunningham, Darnes, Davis of Buchanan, Deatherage, Dent, Dyer, Edgar, Ferry, Gates, Gideon, Glascock, Gooch, Gorham, Gratiott, Guitar, Hampton, Halley, Hardin of Callaway, Hardin of Texas, Harris of Boone, Hines, Hunter, Jackson, Jameson, Jones of Webster, Keyser, King of Franklin, King of St. Charles, Kribben, Lampton, Lenox, McAlister, McGaugh, McIlhany, McSpadden, Mitchell, Moore, Munro, Moulder, Murphy, Nevill, Norris, O'Fallon, Parks, Peers, Pilkington, Pritchard, Pulliam, Rayburn, Riley, Rives, Roberts of DeKalb, Robertson, Shields, Simpson, Stone, Strachan, Sturgeon, Taylor of Lafayette, Taylor of Lawrence, Turner of Clinton, Turner of St. Louis, Walker of Cedar, Waltman, Wommack, Woolsey, and Young—90.

For Mr. Kribben—Messrs. Anthony, Boyd, Day, Knott, Owen, and Tate—6.

Absent—Messrs. Burgess, Edwards, Hudgins, Maguire, Parsons, Polk, Pitt, Roberts of Schuyler, Sitton, Walker of Cape Girardeau, Yager, and Mr. Speaker.

Absent on leave—Same as before.

Excused from voting—Messrs. Anderson, Cordell, Davis of Nodaway, Enloe, Fagg, Jones of Marion, King of Ray, Letcher, Pollard, and Welch.

Sick—Mr. Cullers.

Mr. Knott, having received a majority of all the votes cast, was declared duly elected one of the managers.

Nominations being still in order,

Mr. Davis, of Buchanan, nominated Charles H. Hardin, of Callaway county.

Mr. Anthony nominated Christian Kribben, of St. Louis county.

The roll being called, there appeared

For Mr. Hardin—Messrs. Baker, Barnes, Bedford, Blackwood, Blanton, Boas, Boulware, Bowles, Boyd, Briscoe, Burden, Caldwell, Chilton, Conway, Cowgill, Cox, Cravens, Cunningham, Darnes, Davis of Buchanan, Day, Deatherage, Dent, Ferry, Gates, Gideon, Glascock, Gooch, Gorham, Gratiott, Guitar, Hardin of Texas, Harris of Boone, Hunter, Jackson, Jameson, Jones of Webster, King of Franklin, King of St. Charles, Kribben, Lampton, Lenox, McGaugh, McIlhany, McSpadden, Moore, Munro, Moulder, Murphy, Nevill, Norris, Parks, Pulliam, Rayburn, Rives, Roberts of DeKalb, Robertson, Shields, Stone, Taylor of Lafayette, Taylor of Lawrence, Turner of Clinton, Walker of Cedar, Wommack, Woodward, Woolsey, and Young—68.

For Mr. Kribben—Messrs. Abney, Anthony, Barkley, Chartrand, Halley, Hardin of Callaway, Hines, McAlister, O'Fallon, Owen, Pilkington, Riley, Simpson, Strachan, and Waltman—15.

Absent—Messrs. Bowlin, Burgess, Clark, Crandall, Dyer, Edgar, Edwards, Hampton, Hudgins, Jones of Marion, Keyser, Knott, Maguire, Parsons, Peers, Pitt, Polk, Roberts of Schuyler, Sitton, Sturgeon, Turner of St. Louis, Walker of Cape Girardeau, Yager, and Mr. Speaker.

Absent on leave—Same as before.

Excused from voting—Messrs. Anderson, Cordell, Davis of Nodaway, Enloe, Fagg, King of Ray, Mitchell, Pollard, Pritchard, and Welch.
Sick—Mr. Cullers.

Mr. HARDIN, having received a majority of all the votes cast, was declared duly elected as the other manager, under the resolution.

SATURDAY, February 12, 1859.

Mr. BURDEN offered the following resolution, which was adopted:

Resolved, That the managers elected by this House be instructed to repair to the Senate, and, at the bar thereof, in the name of the House of Representatives, and of all the people of the State, to impeach Albert Jackson, Judge of the Fifteenth Judicial Circuit, and acquaint the Senate that the House of Representatives will, in due time, exhibit proper articles of impeachment against him, and make good the same, and to demand that the Senate take order for the appearance of said Jackson, to answer said impeachment.

MONDAY, February 14, 1859.

Mr. COWGILL offered the following resolution, which was adopted:

Resolved, That the managers elected by this House to conduct the impeachment against Albert Jackson, Judge of the Fifteenth Judicial Circuit, do now proceed to present to the Senate the articles adopted by the House of Representatives, in support of such impeachment.

SATURDAY, February 19, 1859.

Mr. WHITE offered the following resolution:

Resolved by the House of Representatives, That the House furnish the Senate with all the original evidence taken by the Committee on the Judiciary, in investigating the charges against Albert Jackson, Judge of the Fifteenth Judicial Circuit, in accordance with the resolution of the Senate, communicated to this House yesterday.

Mr. KNOTT offered the following as a substitute:

Resolved, That the Clerk of this House be required to make out a copy of the testimony supporting the articles of impeachment, preferred by this House against one Albert Jackson, late Judge of the Fifteenth Judicial Circuit of Missouri, now pending, and forward the same to the Senate.

Mr. DAY moved to lay the substitute on the table; which was decided in the affirmative.

The resolution offered by Mr. White was then adopted.

TUESDAY, February 22, 1859.

Message from the Senate by Mr. Murray, Assistant Secretary:

MR. SPEAKER: I am instructed by the Senate to inform the House of Representatives, that the following resolution has passed the Senate:

Resolved by the Senate, the House of Representatives concurring therein, That when the two Houses adjourn on the second Monday in March next, the Senate shall stand adjourned until the first Monday in June next, at which time it shall meet for the purpose of trying the case of Albert Jackson, Judge of the Fifteenth Judicial Circuit, upon the impeachment preferred against him by the House of Representatives; and the House of Representatives shall stand adjourned until the fourth Monday in July next, at which last mentioned day the two Houses shall stand adjourned *sine die,* by virtue of this resolution.

During the evening session,

Mr. COWGILL moved to suspend the rules, in order to take up the foregoing concurrent resolution, which motion prevailed; and the resolution being taken up, was read a first time, and the rule suspended, and read a second time; when

Mr. HARDIN, of Texas, offered the following substitute:

Resolved by the House of Representatives, the Senate concurring therein, That the General Assembly of the State of Missouri adjourn on Monday, the 7th day of March, A. D. 1859, to meet on the first Monday in November thereafter; and that the Senate have leave to meet on the first Monday in June, A. D. 1859, and proceed to the trial of the impeachment of Judge Albert Jackson, and that so soon as such trial be had, the Senate adjourn, to meet the House on the said first Monday in November.

The substitute was read, when

Mr. ANDERSON moved to reject the same; which was decided in the affirmative by the following vote, the ayes and noes being demanded by Mr. Hardin, of Texas:

AYES—Messrs. Abney, Ament, Anderson, Baker, Barkley, Blanton, Boas, Bowles, Boyd, Burgess, Conway, Cordell, Cowgill, Cox, Cravens, Cullers, Cunningham, Davis of Buchanan, Deatherage, Dent, Dillon, Dyer, Edgar, Fagg, Ferris, Ferry, Gates, Gideon, Glascock, Gooch, Halley, Hardin of Callaway, Harris of Boone, Harris of Montgomery, Higgins, Hudgins, Jackson, Jameson, Jones of Marion, Jones of Webster, Keyser, King of Franklin, King of Ray, Letcher, McAlister, McGaugh, Maguire, Munro, Moulder, Nevill, O'Fallon, Parks, Parsons, Peers, Pollard, Pritchard, Riley, Roberts of DeKalb, Robertson, Shields, Simpson, Stone, Strachan, Turner of Clinton, Walker of Cape Girardeau, Welch, White, Wilcox, Wommack, Woolsey, Yager, York, Young, and Mr. Speaker—74.

NOES—Messrs. Anthony, Bedford, Boulware, Burden, Caldwell, Chartrand, Chilton, Clark, Crandall, Day, Enloe, Gratiott, Hampton, Hardin of Texas, Hines, Hunter, King of St. Charles, Knott, Lampton, Lenox, McSpadden, Murphy, Norris, Pilkington, Polk, Smith, Tate, Taylor of Lawrence, Walker of Cedar, and Waltman—30.

Absent—Messrs. Blackwood, Edwards, Ellis, Mitchell, Moore, Pitt, Pulliam, Rayburn, Roberts of Schuyler, Sturgeon, and Turner of St. Louis.

Absent on leave—Messrs. Barnes, Darnes, Guitar, McIlhany, Owen, Gorham, Pilkington, Sitton, and Woodward.

Sick—Messrs. Bowlin, Briscoe, Duval, and Rives.

WEDNESDAY, February 23, 1859.

Mr. KRIBBEN, on leave, (while a resolution touching the question of adjournment was pending,) offered the following resolution:

Resolved by the House of Representatives, That the Attorney General of the State be hereby required to give to this House his legal opinion in regard to the following question: The Senate and House agreeing to adjourn on the second Monday in March next, to meet on the first Monday of November; now, by consent of the House, can the Senate meet in vacation and try the case of Albert Jackson, Judge of the Fifteenth Judicial Circuit?

Mr. HUDGINS moved to lay the resolution on the table, which was lost; and the question being taken on the adoption of the resolution, it was decided in the affirmative.

FRIDAY, February 25, 1859.

The SPEAKER laid before the House the following communication from the Attorney General:

ATTORNEY GENERAL'S OFFICE,
JEFFERSON CITY, February 24, 1859.

The Honorable, the House of Representatives:

GENTLEMEN: You request my opinion upon the question submitted in the following resolution:

"*Resolved by the House of Representatives,* That the Attorney General be required to give to this House his legal opinion in regard to the following question: The Senate and House agreeing to adjourn on the second Monday in March next, to meet on the first Monday of November; now, by consent of the House, can the Senate meet in vacation and try the case of Albert Jackson, Judge of the Fifteenth Judicial Circuit?"

No question arises upon the proposition submitted, as to the right of one House of the General Assembly to sit for legislative purposes, pending the adjournment of the other to a period within the session. The constitutional inhibition upon either House to adjourn without the consent of the other, for more than two days, at any one time, permits, by clear implication, an adjournment for a longer period, *with* such consent. And if the relations of the two Houses to each other, as constituent branches of the General Assembly, are not materially changed after articles of impeachment have been preferred, and the Senate assumes the functions of a court, then that body may proceed with the trial, although the House be not actually in session.

Our constitution provides that the House of Representatives shall have the sole power of impeachment; that all impeachments shall be tried by the Senate, and that the concurrence of two-thirds of the Senators present shall be necessary to convict. Similar provisions are found in most of the State constitutions, and in the constitution of the United States.

All the power possessed by the House of Representatives in cases of impeachment is by virtue of the constitution only; and this is confined to the accusation and preferring articles of impeachment. Our statute concerning impeachments, so far as it prescribes any formula of proceedings and practice, is only declaratory of the common and customary law of parliamentary bodies, especially as it prevails in the British Parliament, and in this country. The prototype of the legislative assemblies of this country is the Parliament of Great Britain, so modified as to make it harmonize with our political system and the genius of our institutions; and the law of proceedings in these bodies, where the constitution and the rules of proceedings which it authorizes, and which are adopted pursuant to it, are silent, is, undoubtedly, the rules and practice of the British Parliament. Precedents in parliamentary practice acquire the force of law, and are regarded with the same respect as those which have been established by courts of justice, and thus become the common law of legislative assemblies; and to this resort must be had for the definition of legal terms, and the construction of legal powers mentioned in our constitution and laws, in connection with parliamentary practice, where no act of Assembly, judicial interpretation, or settled usage, has altered their meaning. An impeachment is a written accusation by the House of Representatives of an officer, in which that body acts solely in the character of complainants or accusers, and the Senate performs the functions of a judicial tribunal. This prosecution, according to the practice of the House of Commons, is conducted by managers previously appointed for the purpose among their own members. The managers sustain to the House the relation of counsel, and proceed with the trial in the same manner as in an indictment; and the trial does not differ in essentials from criminal prosecutions before inferior courts.

The practice of the British House of Commons, however, has given the force of parliamentary law to the custom of attending in a body during the progress of the trial; and this has been followed in this country by the House of Representatives of the United States. If this is essential to the due exercise of the constitutional power of impeachment, or to the prosecution of that impeachment, then the precedent has as much the force of a constitutional obligation as if expressly required. The only practical purpose, it seems, for which this was claimed, as a right, by the House of Commons, is thus stated: In case of conviction, the Commons demand judgment of the Lords, without which they would object to its being pronounced. The necessity for the Commons to demand judgment enables them to spare the accused even after he has been found guilty by the Lords. In the cases of the Earl of Wintoun and Lord Lovat, it was resolved by the Commons "that it was not parliamentary for the Lords to give judgment until the same be first demanded by the House."—[Dwarris.] According to another English authority, the House of Commons have a right to be present, whether they appoint managers or not, that every member may satisfy his conscience whether he will give his vote to demand judgment.—[Strafford's case, Commons Journal 2, 105–8.] It will be observed that this claim of the Commons to demand judgment was based upon the assumed right to arrest the prosecution even after the accused was found guilty, and thus virtually grant him a pardon. Such interposition has never been claimed or exercised in this country, on the part of the prosecutor or body preferring the accusation. It is a power utterly inconsistent with, and subversive of, the jurisdiction of the Senate as a Court of Impeachment. Although the House of Representatives of the United States has followed the precedent of the British House of Commons, in attending in a body upon the trial, yet it has never assumed that it had the right to exercise the power claimed and exercised by the House of Commons in such cases.

It may be assumed that the House has the right to prefer additional articles of impeachment; yet this is not a sufficient reason why it should remain in session, and anticipate the occasion for so doing, or presume that it would be necessary to do so. On the contrary, the presumption would be that the accusation preferred would be sufficient, and that the functions of the House in that behalf had ceased. Besides, an impeachment is not abated by reason of an adjournment of the General Assembly, or the termination of the session. It may be resumed by a succeeding Legislature, and the House may prefer a new accusation, or may add other articles of impeachment at a subsequent session. The question of the effect of a dissolution of Parliament upon a pending impeachment was raised at the trial of Warren Hastings, and it was then determined that the practice in cases of impeachment was analagous and conformable to the invariable course of precedents in all other judicial proceedings, and that the prosecution did not abate by a dissolution of Parliament. Although, then, the precedent referred to may have acquired the force of parliamentary law, yet, like all others that do not affect the substance of the proceeding, it may be disregarded without abridging, or in any wise impairing, the constitutional rights of the House, as the accuser.

The contingencies of a vacancy in the Committee of Managers, by death or from other cause, and a possible failure of the prosecution for that reason, may be provided for by a law authorizing the Governor to appoint other managers; or the House itself may anticipate such contingency by appointing, before its adjournment, alternates.

I have to say, then, in conclusion, that the Senate, by consent of the House, may, in my opinion, meet in vacation and try the case of Judge Jackson. Very respectfully,

E. B. EWING.

The Senate amendment to House resolution in relation to adjournment was taken up, and agreed to by the following vote, the ayes and noes being demanded by Mr. Hudgins:

Ayes—Messrs. Anthony, Baker, Barkley, Boas, Bowles, Boyd, Caldwell, Chartrand, Chilton, Cowgill, Cox, Cunningham, Darnes, Davis of Nodaway, Deatherage, Dent, Dillon, Duval, Edwards, Ellis, Ferris, Gates, Gratiott, Hampton, Halley, Hardin of Callaway, Hardin of Texas, Harris of Montgomery, Higgins, Hines, Hunter, Keyser, Lampton, Lenox, McSpadden, Mitchell, Moore, Moulder, Murphy, Parsons, Pilkington, Shields, Smith, Sturgeon, Tate, Taylor of Lafayette, Taylor of Lawrence, Turner of St. Louis, Walker of Cedar, Waltman, Wilcox, Woodward, Yager, York, Young, and Mr. Speaker—56.

Noes—Messrs. Abney, Ament, Anderson, Boulware, Burgess, Clark, Conway, Cordell, Cravens, Davis of Buchanan, Day, Dyer, Edgar, Enloe, Fagg, Ferry, Gideon, Glascock, Gooch, Harris of Boone, Hudgins, Jackson, Jameson, Jones of Marion, Jones of Webster, King of Franklin, King of Ray, King of St. Charles, Letcher, McGaugh, McIlhany, Maguire, Munro, Nevill, Norris, Parks, Peers, Pollard, Polk, Pritchard, Riley, Rives, Roberts of DeKalb, Robertson, Simpson, Sitton, Stone, Strachan, Walker of Cape Girardeau, Welch, White, Wommack, and Woodward—53.

Absent—Messrs. Blackwood, Blanton, Burden, Kribben, McAlister, O'Fallon, Pitt, and Rayburn.

IN THE SENATE.

SATURDAY, February 12, 1859.

The following message from the House of Representatives was delivered at the bar of the Senate by Messrs. Knott and Hardin, two of the members of said House:

MR. PRESIDENT: In obedience to a resolution of the House of Representatives of the State of Missouri, we now here, in the name of the House of Representatives, and of all the people of the State, impeach Albert Jackson, Judge of the Fifteenth Judicial Circuit, of high crimes and misdemeanors, and apprise the Senate that the House of Representatives will, in due time, exhibit proper articles of impeachment against him, and make good the same; and request the Senate to take order for the appearance of said Albert Jackson to make answer to said impeachment.

On motion of Mr. PARSONS, the message was referred to a select committee of three, consisting of Messrs. Parsons, Richardson, and Wilson, to consider and report thereon.

Thereafter the select committee to whom had been referred the foregoing message, made and submitted the following report, through their Chairman, Mr. Parsons:

WHEREAS, The House of Representatives, on the 12th day of the present month, by two of their members, Messrs. Knott and Hardin, at the bar of the Senate, impeached Albert Jackson, Judge of the Fifteenth Judicial Circuit in the State of Missouri, of high crimes and misdemeanors in office, and acquainted the Senate that the House of Representatives will, in due time, exhibit particular articles of impeachment against him, and make good the same; and likewise demanded that the Senate take order for the appearance of said Albert Jackson to answer the said impeachment; therefore,

Resolved, That the Senate will take proper order thereon, of which due notice shall be given to the House of Representatives.

And the committee further recommend to the Senate, that the Secretary of the Senate be directed to notify the House of Representatives of the foregoing resolution.

PARSONS,
RICHARDSON,
WILSON,
Committee.

The report of the committee was read and agreed to, and the resolution constituting a part of the report was read a first and second time, and adopted.

Afterwards on the same day, on motion of Mr. PARSONS,

Resolved, That the Senate will now resolve itself into a Court of Impeachment, and that the following oath be administered to the President of the Senate by the Secretary, and by the President to each member of the Senate present:

"I solemnly swear, (or affirm, as the case may be,) that in all things appertaining to the trial of the impeachment of Albert Jackson, Judge of the Fifteenth Judicial Circuit in the State of Missouri, I will impartially try and determine the charges, and do justice according to the law and evidence."

Which Court of Impeachment, being thus formed, will immediately thereafter receive the managers appointed by the House of Representatives to exhibit articles of impeachment in the name of themselves, and all the people of the

State of Missouri, against Albert Jackson, Judge of the Fifteenth Judicial Circuit in the State of Missouri, pursuant to the notice this day given to the Senate by the House of Representatives, that they had appointed managers for the purpose aforesaid.

Resolved, further, That the Secretary lay this resolution before the House of Representatives.

On motion of Mr. PARSONS,

Resolved, That after the managers of impeachment shall be introduced to the bar of the Senate, and shall have signified that they are ready to exhibit articles of impeachment against Albert Jackson, the President of the Senate shall direct the Sergeant-at-Arms to make proclamation, who shall, after making proclamation, repeat the words following: "All persons are commanded to keep silence, on pain of imprisonment, while the grand inquest of the State is exhibiting to the Senate articles of impeachment against Albert Jackson, Judge of the Fifteenth Judicial Circuit in the State of Missouri." After which the articles shall be exhibited, and then the President of the Senate will take proper order on the subject of the impeachment, of which due notice shall be given to the House of Representatives.

The required oath was then administered to the President by the Secretary of the Senate, and by the President to the following Senators present, to wit:

Messrs. Brown, Byrne, Churchill, Fox, Frazier, Gullett, Halliburton, Hedgpeth, Horner, Hyer, Johnson, Jones, McFarland McFerran, McIlvaine, Morris, Newland, O'Neil, Parsons, Rains, Richardson, Robinson, Vernon, Wilson, and Wood.

Mr. McFERRAN, before being sworn, gave notice that he would take the oath only under protest, and afterwards presented the following protest, and asked that it be entered upon the Journal of the Senate, which was agreed to:

MR. PRESIDENT: A resolution having passed the Senate requiring the Senators present to be sworn to try the case of impeachment against the Hon. Albert Jackson, Judge of the Fifteenth Judicial Circuit, of which the Senate has been notified by the managers of the House of Representatives; and, whereas, said managers have not, as yet, preferred articles of impeachment against said Jackson, and the Senate has not appointed a day for the appearance of the accused, and no summons has issued, with a copy of the articles of impeachment annexed, requiring the accused to appear on the day appointed for that purpose, and answer the charges exhibited against him, and no answer to said charges, or reply thereto, has been filed, and no issue joined in said case of impeachment, as required by an act, entitled "an act respecting impeachments," approved November 17, 1855; and, whereas, by said act continuing and in force, the members of the Senate are not required to be sworn until the issues are made up, and a time and place appointed for the trial of such impeachment; and, whereas, my name having been called to take the oath to try said cause in accordance with said resolution, and believing the proceedings irregular, premature and unlawful, because in utter disregard of the above recited act, I hereby most respectfully ask leave to enter this my protest against the proceedings, and ask that this may be entered upon the Journals.

JAMES McFERRAN.

The Senate was then resolved into a High Court of Impeachment, and without further proceedings adjourned till Monday morning at 10 o'clock.

HIGH COURT OF IMPEACHMENT.

STATE OF MISSOURI *vs.* ALBERT JACKSON.

MONDAY, February 14, 1859.

The PRESIDENT of the Senate administered the oath prescribed to Messrs. Goodlett, Peyton, Thompson, and Wright.

The Court was opened by proclamation.

The managers on the part of the House of Representatives, viz., Messrs. Knott and Hardin, appeared and were admitted, and

Mr. HARDIN announced that they were now ready, upon the part of the House of Representatives, and all the people of the State, to exhibit particular articles in support of their impeachment of Albert Jackson, Judge of the Fifteenth Judicial Circuit of the State of Missouri, for high crimes and misdemeanors.

Mr. KNOTT arose and read the articles of impeachment,* which were signed by John T. Coffee, Speaker of the House ot Representatives, and attested by William S. Moseley, Chief Clerk.

The PRESIDENT of the Senate then informed the managers that the Senate would take proper order on the subject of the impeachment, of which due notice should be given to the House of Representatives.

The articles of impeachment were then delivered to the Secretary of the Senate to be filed.

On motion of Mr. PARSONS, and by unanimous consent,

Resolved, That the Secretary be requested to issue a summons in the usual form, signed by the President and attested by the Secretary, against Albert Jackson, Judge, etc., with a copy of the articles of impeachment annexed, as exhibited against him by the House of Representatives on this day, requiring him to appear and answer the charges exhibited against him in said articles, on Tuesday, the 15th instant, and that it be served by the Sergeant-at-Arms, the day before the return day thereof.

Ordered, That the Secretary be requested to lay this resolution before the House of Representatives.

On motion of Mr. PARSONS, and by unanimous consent, it was further

Resolved, That one hundred copies of the articles of impeachment exhibited against Albert Jackson, Judge of the Fifteenth Judicial Circuit, be printed for the use of the Senate.

On motion of Mr. PARSONS, the Court then adjourned until 3 o'clock, P. M., on Tuesday next.

---

*The articles of impeachment do not appear here because they are embodied in the House proceedings. *Vide* pp. 8-18, *ante*. REPORTER.

TUESDAY, February 15, 1859.

The PRESIDENT of the Senate administered the oath prescribed to Messrs. Harris and Coleman.

The Court was then opened by proclamation.

The summons issued to Albert Jackson, and the precept endorsed thereon, are as follows:

STATE OF MISSOURI, SS:

The State of Missouri to ALBERT JACKSON, *Judge of the Fifteenth Judicial Circuit of Missouri, Greeting:*

WHEREAS, The House of Representatives of the State of Missouri did, on the 14th day of February, A. D. 1859, exhibit to the Senate articles of impeachment against you, the said Albert Jackson, Judge, etc., in the words following: [Here follows the articles of impeachment, for which *vide* pp. 8-18, *ante*.] And did demand that you, the said Albert Jackson, should be put to answer the accusations as set forth in said articles, and that such proceedings, examinations, trials and judgments might be thereupon had as are agreeable to law and justice; you, the said Albert Jackson, are, therefore, hereby summoned to be and appear before the Senate of the State of Missouri, at their chamber in the City of Jefferson, on the 15th day of February, A. D. 1859, then and there to answer to the said articles of impeachment, and then and there to abide by, obey and perform such orders and judgments as the Senate of the State of Missouri shall make in the premises, according to the constitution and laws of the State of Missouri.

Hereof you are not to fail.

Witness, HANCOCK JACKSON, President of the Senate thereof, at the City of Jefferson, this 14th day of February, in the year of our Lord one thousand eight hundred and fifty-nine.

ATTEST: WARWICK HOUGH, [L. S.]
Secretary of the Senate.

STATE OF MISSOURI, SS:

The State of Missouri to WILLIAM L. THRAILKILL, *Sergeant-at-Arms of the Senate of the State of Missouri, Greeting:*

You are hereby commanded to deliver to, and leave with Albert Jackson, if to be found, a true and attested copy of the within writ of summons, together with a like copy of this precept, and the articles of impeachment herewith, showing him the same; or, in case he cannot, with convenience, be found, you are to leave true and attested copies of the said summons and precept, and articles of impeachment, at his dwelling-house or usual place of abode, with some free white member of the family, over the age of fifteen years; and in whichsoever way you perform the service, let it be done at least one day before the appearance day mentioned in said writ of summons. Fail not, and make return of this writ of summons and precept, with your proceedings thereon endorsed, on or before the appearance day mentioned in the said writ of summons.

Witness, HANCOCK JACKSON, President of the Senate of the State of Missouri, at the City of Jefferson, this 14th day of February, in the year of our Lord one thousand eight hundred and fifty-nine.

ATTEST: WARWICK HOUGH, [L. S.]
Secretary of the Senate.

The return of the Sergeant-at-Arms of the foregoing summons and precept was read, as follows:

I, WILLIAM L. THRAILKILL, Sergeant-at-Arms of the Senate of the State of Missouri, in obedience to the within writ of summons, to me directed, did proceed to the City Hotel, in the City of Jefferson, on Monday, the 14th instant, and did then and there deliver to and leave with the within named Albert Jackson, a true copy of the within writ of summons and articles of impeachment, and a like copy of the precept thereon endorsed, and did show him both.

W. L. THRAILKILL.

CITY OF JEFFERSON, Feb. 15, 1859.

The Secretary then administered the following oath to the Sergeant-at-Arms:

You, WILLIAM L. THRAILKILL, Sergeant-at-Arms of the Senate of the State of Missouri, do swear that the return made and subscribed by you upon the process issued on the 14th day of February, instant, by the Senate of the State of Missouri, against Albert Jackson, Judge of the Fifteenth Judicial Circuit, is truly made, and that you have performed the services as therein described; so help you God.

Proclamation was then made, as follows:

Oyez! Oyez! Oyez! ALBERT JACKSON, Judge of the Fifteenth Judicial Circuit of the State of Missouri, come forward and answer the articles of impeachment exhibited against you by the House of Representatives of the State of Missouri.

Mr. PARSONS offered the following resolution, which was unanimously adopted:

Resolved, That the Doorkeeper of the Senate procure seats within the bar for Judge Jackson and his counsel, (if any,) and also for the managers appointed on the part of the House of Representatives.

ALBERT JACKSON then appeared in person, and presented reasons why he should not be required to answer the articles of impeachment preferred against him by the House of Representatives, and asked that they be filed. After debate,

On motion of Mr. JONES, the Court adjourned until 9 o'clock to-morrow morning.

WEDNESDAY, February 16, 1859.

The Court having been opened by proclamation, the managers on the part of the House of Representatives attended.

ALBERT JACKSON, respondent, also attended.

Mr. PARSONS offered the following resolution:

Resolved, That the President appoint a committee of three to draft rules for the government of the Senate while sitting as a Court of Impeachment.

Which was, upon ballot, adopted: all the Senators present voting in the affirmative.

Absent—Messrs. Gullett, Halliburton, and Robinson.
Absent on leave—Mr. Scott.

The respondent, on leave, withdrew his reasons why he should not be required to answer the articles of impeachment preferred against him by the House of Representatives, which he had asked to be filed, and asked further time in which to file his answer.

On motion of Mr. PARSONS,

Ordered, That Albert Jackson file his answer and plea with the Secretary of the Senate, to the articles of impeachment preferred against him by the House of Representatives, on Thursday evening at 2 o'clock.

On motion of Mr. PARSONS,

Resolved, That the House of Representatives be informed that the Hon. Albert Jackson, against whom articles of impeachment have been exhibited, has appeared to the summons issued against him, and that, upon his motion, leave is given him until to-morrow at 2 o'clock, P. M., to file his answer, and at which time the Senate will take further order on said impeachment, of which the House of Representatives will be duly informed.

On motion of Mr. PARSONS, the Court adjourned until 2 o'clock to-morrow evening.

THURSDAY, February 17, 1859.

The PRESIDENT of the Senate administered the oath prescribed to Mr. Scott.

The Court was opened by proclamation, and the managers on the part of the House of Representatives attended, as also the respondent, Albert Jackson.

ALBERT JACKSON being called upon to make answer to the articles of impeachment exhibited against him by the House of Representatives, appeared, without counsel; and having been asked by the President of the Senate whether he was prepared to answer the said articles, he replied in the affirmative, and requested that his answer might be read by the Secretary.

The PRESIDENT of the Senate then directed the Secretary to read the answer, and it was accordingly read, and is as follows:

Answer of Albert Jackson, Judge of the Fifteenth Judicial Circuit, to Articles of Impeachment exhibited against him in the Senate of the State of Missouri, on February twelfth, eighteen hundred and fifty-nine.

ARTICLE I. The said Albert Jackson, Judge of the Fifteenth Judicial Circuit, saving and reserving to himself the benefit of all mistakes and irregularities which now exist, which have been or may be made, in any and all the proceedings, the proceedings heretofore had, or which may hereafter be had, and denying to the House of Representatives the right to alter, amend, modify, or withdraw any part or portion of said articles, or at any time hereafter to exhibit any other or further articles of impeachment herein; for answer to so much of said articles as he deems it necessary for him to answer or respond to, says that:

First. He wholly and fully denies that at the May term of the Circuit Court of Stoddard, begun on the third Monday in May, 1858, in said county, in his official capacity, or under color of his office, he did willfully and maliciously conduct himself in a manner highly oppressive and unjust to one Jonas Eaker.

To specification *first* of said article, said Albert Jackson says that he did not desire to oppress and harrass said Jonas Eaker, and did not maliciously and unjustly cause to be issued against said Eaker an attachment as for a *criminal* contempt; that, in his official capacity, he knew nothing about the manner in which said writ of mandamus had been executed on said Eaker. The said Eaker admitted said writ had been *served* on him, but refused to make return to said writ; then an attachment was issued against said Eaker for contempt of court, by refusing to make a proper return on said writ, as will appear by the papers and record in relation thereto.

For answer to specification *second*, he says he did not refuse to hear counsel speak for said Eaker after his *appearance*, but when Eaker made return to the writ he was discharged from the attachment without a penalty; does not know that said Eaker was in custody several hours;

thinks he was not; but that he came into court and asked for time to answer, which was granted.

Third. Said Jackson did not peremptorily, and in an insulting and oppressive manner, order the counsel of said Eaker, to wit, Solomon G. Kitchen and William G. Phelan, to shut their mouths; said Jackson did not know they were counsel for Eaker; they said they were not, but claimed the right to appear as the *next friend of the court.*

Fourth. Did not deprive said Eaker of counsel, and of the privilege of speaking through counsel, in his own defense.

Said Jackson says that article first, and specifications 1, 2, 3, and 4, are insufficient in law, and do not contain charges of a nature and degree that would warrant a conviction in an impeachment. The said Jackson has the right, by virtue of his office, to issue writs of mandamus to an inferior court, and enforce by attachment the return of every writ or process sent out of said Circuit Court.

ART. II. Said Albert Jackson says that at a Circuit Court begun at Bloomfield, on the third Monday in November, 1858, he was not guilty of the grossest partiality and injustice:

First. That he did not know that there was then pending a suit by Matthew H. Moore against James Walker, in said court, and that he did not corruptly, partially, and to the utter degradation of the *solemn* duties of his office and important functions thereof, secretly advise said Walker not to compromise the same, and say that said Walker would be successful if he would refuse to compromise. Does not know for what reason Moore took a change of venue; knows he was not compelled to do so; thinks he had applied for a change of venue on the first or second day of court, which application for a change of venue was the first said Jackson knew about Moore having sued Walker.

This article and its specifications are not sufficient in law to warrant impeachment. It does not allege that the said Jackson did what he did do in his official capacity or under color of his office, but, on the contrary, says he did it in his private capacity.

ART. III. Said Jackson says that he was not actuated by a spirit of arbitrary despotism and wanton injustice, totally repugnant to the *sacred* duties pertaining to his office, and highly dangerous to the rights of the citizens of the State, at a court begun and held in the county of Wayne, on the last Monday in September, 1858, and by virtue of his office was not guilty of malicious oppression, misconduct, and abuse of authority, in his official capacity:

First. Does not know that during the Circuit Court aforesaid, David M. Fox, counsel for plaintiff in the case of Limbarger *vs.* Power, presented a petition to said Albert Jackson to change the venue in said case to some other court, because of prejudice of the Judge. Said Fox did not then inform said Albert Jackson that *both* parties and their counsel had agreed to send said cause to either Madison or Iron counties, and the said Albert Jackson was not utterly unmindful of the rights of the parties and counsel in said cause, and did not totally disregard the provisions of the statute in such case made and provided. The said Jackson did not willfully and maliciously then and there intend to harrass and oppress the parties aforesaid, by awarding a change of venue to Mississippi; and said Jackson did not well know that said county was of difficult access to the parties, and counsel, and witnesses, (but believed there were good counsel residing in Mississippi county.)

Second. Said Jackson does not know that D. M. Fox and P. Pipkin tried to prevail on him to send the case to some other county, and that parties would be deprived of counsel if he did not; and the said Jackson did not reply to each of them in an oppressive, insolent, and insulting manner, highly shameful and derogatory to the dignity of the important office he holds. Said Jackson says the law is, that the Judge, and not the lawyers, must decide where a case must be sent on a change of venue.

Art. IV. Said Jackson says he was not influenced by a similar spirit of injustice and a *tyrannous* disregard of the rights of the citizens of the State, at a Circuit Court, begun and held within and for the county of Dunklin, on the second Monday in May, 1858; did not conduct himself in a manner highly oppressive, and unjust, and tyrannical:

First. At the time and place aforesaid the said Albert Jackson did not know that counsel for defendant, in the case of Smith *vs.* —— Cude, then pending, presented to said Albert Jackson a petition to change the venue in said case to some other court, on account of prejudice of said Judge. The said Albert Jackson did not then and there willfully and maliciously intend to harrass and oppress the parties and their counsel, by awarding a change of venue in said case to Pemiscot county, (that being the proper county to send it to.) Said Jackson did not know that said counsel for both parties assured him that said county was difficult of access and inconvenient to both parties and witnesses. Said Jackson did not know that the parties to said cause had agreed that said case could be sent to Bollinger or Scott counties. Said Jackson did not know that either of said counties would be more convenient than Pemiscot county (that being only twenty-five miles distant, and Bollinger about ninety miles, and Scott about eighty miles distant.) Said Jackson did not know that said parties could not get counsel to attend to their cause, if it was sent to Pemiscot county. Said Albert Jackson did not know of the earnest entreaties of the counsel of both parties to get the cause sent to some other county. The said Jackson did not angrily, and insultingly, and rudely reply, in a manner indicating a total disregard for that courtesy towards counsel, and respect for the rights of parties, that common decency and the duties of his office require. Said Jackson further says that the law is, that in cases of change of venue the Judge, and not the parties nor their counsel, has the right to designate the county to which a cause should be sent; and that, therefore, it is not willful and malicious oppression, partiality, misconduct, or abuse of authority in his official capacity, or under color of his office, to send a case, on change of venue, from Dunklin county to Pemiscot county, or from Wayne county to Mississippi county.

Art. V. Said Albert Jackson has not, in numerous other instances, been guilty of willful and malicious oppression, misconduct, and abuse of authority, in awarding changes of venue in cases pending before him to counties remote, inconvenient, and difficult of access. Said Albert Jackson never did intend thereby to harrass and oppress counsel and parties, nor to deter others from availing themselves of their right to a change of venue under the law, nor particularly at a Circuit Court begun and held in the county of Dunklin, on the second Monday in May, 1858:

First. In awarding a change of venue in the case of the Point Pleasant and Dunklin County Road Company *vs.* Moses Farrar, from Dunklin to Pemiscot county. Said Jackson did not well know said county to be inconvenient and difficult of access to said parties, and contrary to the earnest request of both parties to the cause, to send said cause to some more convenient county. Said Jackson further says, that in cases of change of venue, the Judge, not the parties nor their counsel, has the right to designate the county to which a cause shall be sent; therefore it is not willful and malicious oppression, partiality, misconduct, or abuse of authority in his official capacity, or under color of his office, to send a cause, on a change of venue, in this case, from Dunklin county to

Pemiscot, by the Judge, however difficult of access said county may be, or however much parties or counsel may desire it to be sent to some other county.

Second. Nor in sending or awarding a change of venue in the cause of said Road Company *vs.* Nathaniel Murphy, then and there pending, to the said county of Pemiscot, the said Jackson not well knowing that to be difficult of access and inconvenient to both parties and counsel, was the said Jackson guilty of willful and malicious oppression, partiality, misconduct, or abuse of authority in his official capacity, or under color of his office; the law in this case being that the Judge, not the parties or their counsel, has the sole right to designate the county to which a cause shall be sent on a change of venue.

ART. VI. Said Jackson was not, at a Circuit Court begun and held at the town of Poplar Bluff, within and for the county of Butler, on the first Monday in May, 1858, willfully guilty of gross and malicious oppression, misconduct, and abuse of official authority, not only unbecoming his high position as Judge, but disgraceful to his character as a man:

First. During the sitting of the Circuit Court aforesaid, one William G. Phelan was not a regularly licensed lawyer, practicing in said court. The said William G. Phelan did not arise to address a jury that had been empanneled and sworn to try an issue joined in a cause then and there pending, to wit, the cause of Gibson *vs.* Dunn; said Phelan had not been employed, and was not acting as counsel. The said Jackson did not maliciously intend to oppress said Phelan, nor to injure his reputation as a citizen, nor to diminish his success as a lawyer; nor did the said Albert Jackson, in an angry, oppressive, insolent, and insulting manner, order him to sit down. The said Jackson did not then and there publicly, and in an insulting and contemptuous manner, accuse said Phelan of having been guilty of a disgraceful and criminal act. Said Albert Jackson did not accuse said Phelan with tampering with the grand jury; nor did he say that said Phelan was in criminal contempt of court, together with other shameful and insulting expressions.

Second. Said Phelan did not immediately offer to defend himself against disgraceful accusations and insulting expressions. Said Albert Jackson did not, under color of his office as Judge, in any angry, insolent, and oppressive manner, order said Phelan to shut his mouth and sit down, nor words to that import. The said Phelan did not offer to say anything by way of denial, excuse, explanation, palliation, or in any manner to excuse himself against the disgraceful criminal charge alleged against him.

ART. VII. Said Albert Jackson was not influenced by a similar spirit of malicious persecution at a Circuit Court begun and held at the town of Doniphan, in Ripley county, on the fourth Monday in October, 1857; and was not guilty of other and similar acts of willful and malicious oppression, misconduct, and abuse of authority:

First. Said Albert Jackson did not wantonly, insolently, and insultingly accuse one David M. Fox, who was not a regularly licensed lawyer, and who was not practicing in said court, of being guilty of the crime of perjury, nor of subornation of perjury, nor did he accuse him of lying (though he thinks said Fox was often guilty of doing so;) nor of causing his client to lie, the said Albert Jackson did not, without provocation, nor in a spirit of vindictive persecution, charge upon said Fox, in open court. The said Albert Jackson did not by innumerable other instances of oppression, contumelious, insolent, and insulting expressions toward lawyers and parties litigant; nor does the said Jackson almost habitually indulge in such expressions, to bring the high and important office he holds into utter degradation and contempt.

ART. VIII. Said Albert Jackson did not forget the dignity of his office, and was not regardless of his sacred obligations to demean himself faithfully and impartially therein; did not, on the trial of Green DePriest, in an indictment for resisting the officer, there being no such indictment and trial against said DePriest at a Circuit Court held in the town of Thomasville, in the county of Oregon, on the third Monday in April, 1858; did not conduct himself willfully partial and corrupt, and highly unbecoming and disgraceful to his high official position:

First. Said Albert Jackson did not privately advise James B. Odell (James B. Odell was not a lawyer) to procure said DePriest to employ him, the said Odell, as his counsel; did not advise him to take a contingent fee to defend him; did not say that said DePriest could not be convicted on the indictment (there being no indictment then and there pending against him,) pending against him for resisting the officer, because he had already been convicted of disturbing the peace of a family, which was charged to have been the same act as when he resisted the officer; did not officiously and voluntarily advise said James B. Odell, as counsel for DePriest, to plead a former conviction; did not give said advice in open court upon the trial; did not partially and corruptly transcend his duties as Judge, on the trial of said DePriest, to such an extent that the Circuit Attorney abandoned said cause, and entered a *nolle prosequi.*

ART. IX. Said Albert Jackson was not utterly unmindful of the provision of the constitution of the State securing to its citizens the privilege of the writ of *habeas corpus.* Said Jackson does not know that the experience of ages has demonstrated that the writ of *habeas corpus* is one of the chief bulwarks of the liberty of the people; joins issue and takes the negative of the proposition. Said Albert Jackson did not willfully and maliciously refuse to issue a writ of *habeas corpus* for the purpose of having the body of a man named Atterbury, who was confined in jail in Dunklin county, on a criminal charge, brought before him as Judge of the Circuit Court, to be admitted to bail or otherwise dealt with according to law. Said Albert Jackson says there was not a petition, in every particular sufficient in law for that purpose, presented to him at the county of Stoddard, on the ——— day of 1858. Said Jackson did not well know it to be his duty (under the circumstances) to issue said writ. Said Jackson did not refuse to do so for the reason that the name of David Hicks was necessarily mentioned in the petition.

ART. X. Said Albert Jackson was not, at the county of Stoddard, on the 15th day of January, 1859, willfully and maliciously guilty of the most dangerous and reprehensible misconduct, partiality, and abuse of authority:

First. In corruptly and illegally setting at liberty, and discharging from the custody of John N. Jackson, one John R. Maine. Said Albert Jackson did not well know that said Maine was held in custody on a criminal charge. Said Jackson says that the cause for commitment was not clearly and specifically set forth in the warrant of commitment, a copy of which was not exhibited to said Albert Jackson, by said Deputy Sheriff.

Second. Said Albert Jackson did not corruptly and illegally set at liberty on account of a pretended informality, insufficiency, or irregularity in the writ of commitment. Said Jackson did not well know that said Maine was held in custody for a criminal offense; did not know he was by statute expressly forbidden to discharge said Maine on a writ of *habeas corpus.*

Third. Said Jackson did not corruptly and illegally discharge said Maine from custody. There was no evidence produced before said Jackson whatever, nor did said Jackson know that any evidence had ever been taken against said Maine.

Fourth. Said Albert Jackson did not willfully and corruptly set at liberty, and discharge from the custody of William Cryts, one Charles Russell; said Jackson did not know that said Russell was held in custody on a criminal charge, for a felonious offense, for which said Russell had been examined and committed. Said Jackson did not know from the evidence that said magistrate had found said Russell guilty of said charge. Said Jackson did not know that Russell had been given time to get bail. The course said Jackson pursued in this matter was just and proper, and did not tend to destroy the efficiency of the criminal law, nor diminish the confidence of the people in the efficiency and purity of the judiciary of the country, nor does it tend to encourage the commission of crime, and license every variety of villainy with which it is possible for a civilized community to be cursed. The case of Maine and the case of Russell transpired since the institution of this impeachment.

ART. XI. At a Circuit Court begun and held at the town of Bloomfield, on the third Monday in November, 1858, said Albert Jackson did not disregard the duties of his office, nor did he descend from the dignity of a Judge, nor did he stoop to the level of a common informer, (does not know, though, exactly what kind of character that is,) by charging the grand jury in relation to their duties, nor to direct their attention to any particular offense which may have been committed within the limits of the county. Said Albert Jackson does not know that every body then and there present thought he alluded to S. G. Kitchen when he publicly charged the grand jury that obtaining money under false pretenses was an indictable offense. The said Jackson did not, by informing the grand jury, after they had retired to their room to consider of their presentment, that it was their duty faithfully to discharge their duties, thereby render his high functions as Judge subservient to a low personal malice, and did not thereby seek, under color of his official duties, to wreak his own private vengeance, by affixing to the reputation of a personal enemy the imperishable disgrace of a public prosecution for a felonious offense.

ART. XII. Said Albert Jackson was not, at a court of Butler county, on the first Monday in November, 1857, willfully and maliciously guilty of gross misdemeanor and abuse of his official authority:

First. In refusing to suspend the Clerk of said court and appoint a temporary one, because said Clerk was sick and unable to attend to business. Said Jackson did not know that said Clerk had been guilty of a misdemeanor in office, by getting sick during a term of court. Said Jackson was not willfully and maliciously guilty of gross misdemeanor and abuse of official authority, and regardless of the rights of parties litigant and attorneys, by refusing to try causes when there was no Clerk to take minutes or make up the record, nor in taking possession of the papers pertaining to cases and placing them in safety; nor in discharging the grand jury under these circumstances, and adjourning court; nor was such course intended and calculated to impair public confidence in the efficacy of the constitutional guaranty that justice shall be administered without sale, denial, or delay.

ART. XIII. That said Albert Jackson was not unmindful of the dignity of his position as Judge, and did not disregard the restraints imposed by his said office, in the month of November, 1857. The said

Jackson did not privately counsel and advise one William Ringer to sell all the county warrants that should be issued in payment of a contract which said Ringer had with Stoddard county, for the building of a court house, and put the money in his pocket, (though he believed it would be good advice.) Said Jackson did not advise said Ringer to bring suit against Solomon G. Kitchen, the commissioner, for damages; nor did he assure him he could recover in such suit. Nor did said Jackson endeavor thereby to incite a vexatious and expensive lawsuit, in the court of which he was Judge, for the sake of annoying, harrassing, and oppressing said Solomon G. Kitchen.

ART. XIV. Said Jackson was not, at a Circuit Court of Ripley county, on the fourth Monday of April, 1858, on the trial of William Kinney for grand larceny, willfully and maliciously guilty of oppression, misconduct, and abuse of official authority, and corruption; nor did he intend thereby to embarrass and oppress the counsel of said Kinney, and procure his conviction:

First. Said Albert Jackson did not arbitrarily refuse to allow said Kinney's counsel time to take down the testimony of the witnesses introduced at said trial.

Second. Did not, by repeated interruption of the counsel for prisoner, try to harrass and embarrass them.

Third. Did not frequently use such insulting, insolent, and discourteous expressions toward said counsel, during the trial.

Fourth. Did not peremptorily stop one of said Kinney's lawyers in the midst of his argument to the jury, and order him to take his seat. Said David M. Fox was not in the discharge of his proper and lawful duties.

ART. XV. At the same court, said Albert Jackson was not willfully and maliciously guilty of great partiality, oppression, and abuse of official authority, on the trial of James Moore *vs.* John Eldridge. Said Jackson did not corruptly intend thereby to injure the rights of said Moore, and to oppress and injure his counsel:

First. Said Jackson did not publicly express his opinion in relation to the merits of said case, adversely to the right of said Moore. Said Jackson did not refuse to sign a true, and proper, and just bill of exceptions, duly tendered to him by counsel for defendant, unless it was made to show that certain facts were proven, which were not proven on said trial by witnesses, though said facts were proven by the appearance and condition of a certain paper then and there produced before said jury, and which facts would be proven by occular inspection of said paper only, and not by a copy; counsel for both parties did know that the bill of exceptions, as presented, contained all the *evidence* given on said trial. Said Jackson did not corruptly intend thereby to deprive said Moore of a fair trial by the Supreme Court. Said Jackson was not unjust, overbearing, and insolent in his demeanor toward counsel during said trial.

ART. XVI. Said Albert Jackson, at a Circuit Court in Stoddard county, on the third Monday in November, 1858, was not willfully and maliciously guilty of any gross oppression, partiality, misconduct, and abuse of authority, in his official capacity:

First. Said Jackson did not express opinions, and make assertions, unbecoming his position as Judge, in relation to the cause of Gustavus Berry *vs.* John Griffiths, (said Jackson does not know that such cause was then and there pending.)

Second. Said Jackson did not express opinions, and make assertions, relative to the merits of said cause, in open court, in presence and hearing of the jury empanneled and sworn to try the case, calculated to influence the minds of the jury against the defendant.

Third. Said Jackson did not corruptly endeavor to prevent the defendant in said cause from getting the same fairly before the Supreme Court, on appeal. Said Jackson did not refuse to sign a bill of exceptions, properly made out and tendered to him by counsel for defendant, until a large portion of the motion papers had been stricken out. Said Jackson says that a number of material reasons were not urged for a new trial in said cause, which did not appear in said bill.

Fourth. Said Jackson did not corruptly refuse to examine and to sign the testimony presented in the bill of exceptions in said cause; counsel for both parties did not agree that all of said testimony was correctly set forth in the bill of exceptions. Said Jackson did not allege that there was so much noise in court during the trial of said cause that he did not know what testimony had been given. Said Jackson did not intend, by such refusal, to prevent the said defendant from getting said cause fairly before the Supreme Court.

Fifth. Said Jackson did not corruptly refuse to sign a bill of exceptions, properly made out, and tendered to him by counsel, in the cause of Daugherty *vs.* Whitehead. Said Jackson does not know that said cause was tried at said term of court. Said Jackson did not strike out nearly all papers filed in the cause. Said Jackson says that the greater number of material reasons urged for a new trial, and in arrest of judgment, did not appear in the bill correctly. Said Jackson did not intend thereby to prevent said cause from being fairly presented to the Supreme Court, that his judgment might not be reversed by said court.

Sixth. Said Jackson did not hear and determine a motion to quash an indictment then and there pending against one David Hicks, then acting as Circuit Attorney, *pro tem.*, without having first appointed some other Circuit Attorney to represent the State in that behalf.

Art. XVII. Said Jackson says that there was no regular Circuit Court begun and held at the town of Bloomfield, in Stoddard county, on the 9th day of August, 1858. Said Albert Jackson was not willfully and maliciously guilty of the grossest partiality, corruption, misconduct, and abuse of authority. Said Jackson did not visit the grand jury in their room, after they had retired to consider of their presentments, and there instruct said grand jury that betting at cards, whisky, oysters, etc., did not constitute an offense within the meaning of the statute against gaming. Said Jackson did not further instruct said grand jury that they could not find indictment against him, said Judge, for anything of which he might be guilty in his official capacity.

Second. Said grand jury did not find an indictment against Albert Jackson, David G. Hicks, Isaac Brand, and Orson Bartlett, jointly, for gaming. Said Albert Jackson did not conduct himself in a manner most shamefully partial and corrupt. Said Jackson did not comment at great length on the testimony in said case. Said Jackson did not declare, in the presence and hearing of the jury, that the fact charged in the indictment before the jury did not constitute an indictable offense; said offense was not proven. Said Jackson did not illustrate to the jury his views, by a great variety of illustrations, in order to induce the jury to find defendant not guilty.

Third. Said Jackson did not comment on the evidence to the jury, and instruct the jury as to the law governing the case, in direct contravention to what he knew to be the words of the statute, in such case made and provided; did not refuse to allow the jury to find a general verdict; did not tell the jury that if they found a verdict of guilty, he would set it aside. Said Jackson did not, by various means, endeavor to influence the jury to find a verdict of not guilty.

Fourth. Did not manifest a solicitude for the acquittal scarcely becoming an advocate, nor highly disgraceful in a Judge; did not permit said

Hicks, who was acting as Circuit Attorney, *pro tem.*, to take a *nolle prosequi* in the cases against Hicks and Jackson; did not know that said Hicks and Jackson were indicted jointly with said Bartlett; said Hicks and Jackson were not *particeps criminis.* Said Jackson was not guilty of other acts of shameful partiality and corruption, tending to bring the tribunals of the country into utter obloquy and contempt.

ART. XVIII. At a Circuit Court begun and held in Stoddard county, on the third Monday in November, 1857, one Sarah Buckner was not *arraigned* on an indictment for murder in the first degree. The said Albert Jackson did not maliciously and corruptly intend to procure the conviction of said Sarah Buckner. Said Jackson was not maliciously guilty of the most shameful oppression, partiality, misconduct, and abuse of authority in his official capacity:

First. Said Albert Jackson did not prevent William C. Grimsley, a witness on the part of the State, from detailing any legal and competent testimony he might be possessed of, whether that testimony was in favor, or whether it was against, the defendant or the plaintiff.

Second. Said Jackson did not exclude competent testimony, on his own motion, nor on the motion of any one else. Said Jackson did not privately advise the Circuit Attorney to withdraw the evidence of said Grimsley; did not permit the Circuit Attorney to withdraw the evidence of Grimsley from the consideration of the jury. Said Jackson did not prevent counsel for defendant from cross-examining said Grimsley.

Third. Said Jackson showed no partiality or solicitude for the conviction of said Sarah Buckner. Said Jackson did not take the examination of witnesses on himself; did not take the management of the cause out of the hands of the Circuit Attorney; counsel for prisoner did not except to the course pursued in this matter by the Judge. Said Jackson was not guilty of gross abuse of official authority and unprecedented oppression.

Fourth. Said Jackson did not refuse counsel for the prisoner any courtesies due them; did not attempt to oppress, harrass, and annoy said counsel during the trial; did not use insolent, contemptuous, and insulting expressions towards them.

Fifth. Said Jackson did not refuse to allow prisoner's counsel to advert to, or speak of, any evidence that was properly before the jury, in their arguments in the cause.

Sixth. Said Jackson did not refuse to allow prisoner's counsel to make illustrations in their arguments; did not repeatedly and vexatiously interrupt said counsel during their arguments. Said Jackson was not so harsh and insulting as to compel any of said counsel to abandon his duties in this cause.

Seventh. Said Jackson did not impose wanton and tyrannical restrictions on counsel in arguing said cause for said prisoner; did not defeat her constitutional guaranty of being heard by herself and counsel; did not preclude the possibility of her having a fair trial by an impartial jury. Said Jackson does not know that trial by jury is the ultimate and strongest protection of the rights and liberties of the people—demands proof thereof.

Eighth. Said Jackson did not unjustly, corruptly, and cruelly refuse to sign any true bill of exceptions legally tendered to him by any counsel. Said Jackson did not refuse counsel for prisoner the privilege of cross-examining Grimsley to the whole extent of the rules of evidence in such cases. Said Jackson did not suffer said Grimsley's testimony to be withdrawn; did not refuse to allow counsel for prisoner to advert to, or comment on, any testimony which was legitimately before the jury.

Ninth. Said Jackson is guilty of no corrupt and oppressive acts. Said Jackson showed, nor had, any solicitude whatever for the conviction of Sarah Buckner; did not act in a manner unbecoming to the character of a Judge; nor was his course contrary to the law, nor subversive of justice, nor tending to bring the judiciary of the country into abhorrence and contempt.

The said Albert Jackson says that, for the purpose of having a full and fair investigation of the whole of the charges, specifications, suppositions, and insinuations contained in said articles of impeachment, he has denied and negatived each and all of the said charges, specifications, suppositions, conclusions, inferences and inuendoes, or intended to do so; and if, by oversight or otherwise, he passed over some one or more of any of the said charges, specifications, conclusions, inferences, suppositions, or arguments, and not denied them, he claims the right, when it shall be ascertained, to supply or amend the defect.

And the said Albert Jackson, Judge of the Fifteenth Judicial Circuit of the State of Missouri, hereby claims the right to further answer these accusations against him, if this should be found defective and not sufficient for the purpose of enabling him to introduce testimony in his defense to each and every charge, article, specification, declaration, averment, insinuation, inuendo, hypothesis, or argument contained in said impeachment or accusation against him.

The said Albert Jackson here denies to the House of Representatives the right to alter, amend, modify, change in any manner, or to withdraw the said articles of impeachment against him. The said Albert Jackson here denies the right of the House of Representatives to exhibit the said articles of impeachment against him. The House of Representatives have not the right to exhibit articles of impeachment against a Judge of the State of Missouri for errors, omissions, and mistakes, and irregularities committed in the discharge of his official acts and duties, whether the same be of practice, of law, of fact, or of judgment, but for misdemeanor in office only. By the constitution of Missouri, a Judge can only be impeached for misdemeanors in office, and those misdemeanors must first be declared, and the penalty affixed therefor by an act of the Legislature.

The said Albert Jackson here says, that the said articles of impeachment exhibited against him are not for misdemeanor in office, but for supposed errors, and mistakes, and omissions, and irregularities of judgment, of law, of fact, or of practice.

The said Albert Jackson therefore says, that the House of Representatives has not the right, and he here, in the name and on the behalf of the constitution and the laws of the State of Missouri, protests against their offering proof to all or to any portion of said articles of impeachment or accusation, for the reason that they do not charge corruption, or fraud, or misdemeanor in office, but allege error, mistake, omission, or irregularity only.

ALBERT JACKSON.

Mr. Knott, on behalf of the managers, moved that they have time to consult the House of Representatives on a replication, and that they be furnished with a copy of the answer of the respondent; which motion was agreed to.

On motion of Mr. Parsons, and by unanimous consent, it was

Resolved, That one hundred copies of the answer of Albert Jackson to the articles of impeachment exhibited against him, be printed for the use of the Senate, the managers and the respondent.

On motion of Mr. HEDGPETH, and by unanimous consent, it was

Resolved, That the House of Representatives be requested to transmit to the Senate all the evidence, or a copy thereof, in the possession of the House, taken by the Committee on the Judiciary of the House, in investigating charges against Albert Jackson, Judge of the Fifteenth Judicial Circuit, prior to preferring articles of impeachment against him.

On motion of Mr. PARSONS, and by unanimous consent, it was

Resolved, That the House of Representatives be informed that Albert Jackson has this day filed his answer to the articles of impeachment exhibited against him by the House of Representatives, and that time has been given the managers until Saturday evening at 2 o'clock to consult with the House of Representatives on a replication, and that they will be furnished with a copy of said answer.

And further, That the Secretary be requested to communicate the foregoing resolution to the House of Representatives.

On motion of Mr. PARSONS, the Court adjourned until Saturday evening at 2 o'clock.

SATURDAY, February 19, 1859.

The Court was opened by proclamation.

The managers on the part of the House of Representatives attended, as also the respondent, Albert Jackson.

The PRESIDENT of the Senate inquired of the managers if the House of Representatives had agreed upon a replication to the answer of Albert Jackson. They replied in the affirmative, and the replication of the House of Representatives was read by Mr. KNOTT, one of the managers, as follows:

Replication by the House of Representatives of the State of Missouri to the Answer of Albert Jackson, Judge of the Fifteenth Judicial Circuit in said State, to the Articles of Impeachment exhibited against him by said House of Representatives.

The House of Representatives of the State of Missouri have considered the answer of Albert Jackson, Judge of the Fifteenth Judicial Circuit of said State, to the articles of impeachment exhibited against him, by them, in the name of the people of the State, and reply:

That said Albert Jackson hath, in his said answer, endeavored to palliate the enormity of the high crimes and misdemeanors laid to his charge, by affecting to treat them with indifference, and to evade the just consequences of his high-handed infractions of law, and violations of justice, by an ill-timed exhibition of frivolous levity; that each and every of said articles is, in every particular, sufficient in law, and true in fact; that each of said articles specifically charges said Albert Jackson with one or more act of willful and malicious oppression, misconduct, or abuse of authority, in his official capacity; and that said Albert Jackson is guilty of each and every of the said high crimes and misdemeanors of which he, by said articles, stands accused; and that the House of Representatives, in full confidence of the truth and justice of their accusation, and of the necessity of vindicating the purity of the Judiciary, the majesty of the law, and the honor of the State, by bringing said Albert Jackson to exemplary punishment, do aver their charges against the said Albert Jackson to be true; and that said Albert Jackson is guilty in manner, as he stands impeached; and that the House of Representatives will be ready to prove their charges against him at such convenient time and place as shall be appointed for that purpose.

Signed in behalf of said House:

JAS. PROC. KNOTT,
CHARLES H. HARDIN,
Managers.

The replication was then handed to the Secretary to be filed.

Mr. PARSONS thereupon submitted the following motion, which was considered:

Resolved, That when the High Court of Impeachment, now convened for the trial of Albert Jackson, Judge of the Fifteenth Judicial Circuit, on articles of impeachment exhibited against him by the House of Representatives, shall adjourn, it shall be until the first Monday in March next, at 10 o'clock, A. M., then to proceed with the trial of said impeachment.

Mr. McFERRAN offered the following amendment to the motion:

Resolved, That the Senate will proceed with the trial of the Hon. Albert Jackson, Judge of the Fifteenth Judicial Circuit in this State, on the first Monday in June next, until which time said cause is continued.

Afterwards, Mr. McFERRAN moved to postpone further consideration of motion and amendment until 2 o'clock this evening; which was decided in the affirmative, the ayes and noes being taken in pursuance of law:

AYES—Messrs. Brown, Byrne, Churchill, Coleman, Fox, Frazier, Gullett, Harris, Horner, McFerran, McIlvaine, Newland, O'Neil, Richardson, Scott, Thompson, Vernon, Watkins, Wilson, and Wood—20.

NOES—Messrs. Goodlett, Hedgpeth, Hyer, Johnson, Morris, Parsons, and Rains—7.

Absent—Messrs. Halliburton, McFarland, and Wright.

Absent on leave—Messrs. Jones and Robinson.

Sick—Mr. Peyton.

Mr. PARSONS, from the select committee appointed to draft rules and forms for the government of the Senate in the trial of the impeachment case now pending, submitted the following, and recommended their adoption:

Rules for the Conduct and Management of Cases of Impeachment before the Senate of the State of Missouri.

1. Whensoever the Senate shall receive notice from the House of Representatives that managers are appointed on their part to conduct an impeachment against any person, and are directed to carry such articles to the Senate, the Secretary of the Senate shall immediately inform the House of Representatives that the Senate is ready to receive the managers, for the purpose of exhibiting such articles of impeachment, agreeably to the said notice.

2. Before the articles of impeachment shall be exhibited to the Senate by the managers, the Secretary shall administer to the President the following oath or affirmation: "You solemnly swear, (or affirm,) that in all things pertaining to the trial of ——— ———, you will impartially try and determine the charges, and do justice according to law and evidence." The President shall then administer the said oath or affirmation to each Senator present.

3. When the managers of an impeachment shall be introduced to the bar of the Senate, and shall signify that they are ready to exhibit articles of impeachment against any person, the President of the Senate shall direct the Sergeant-at-Arms to make proclamation; who shall, after making proclamation, repeat the following words: "All persons are commanded to keep silence on pain of imprisonment, while the Grand Inquest of the State is exhibiting to the Senate of the State of Missouri articles of impeachment against ———." After which the articles shall be exhibited, and then the President of the Senate shall inform the managers that the Senate will take proper order on the subject of the impeachment, of which due notice shall be given to the House of Representatives.

4. A summons shall issue, directed to the person impeached, in the form following:

STATE OF MISSOURI, SS:

The State of Missouri to ——— ———, Greeting;

WHEREAS, The House of Representatives of the State of Missouri did, on the ——— day of ———, exhibit to the Senate articles of impeachment against you, the said ———, in the words following:

(*Here insert the articles.*)

And did demand that you, the said ———, should be put to answer the accusations as set forth in said articles; and that such proceedings, examinations, trials, and judgments might be thereupon had as are agreeable to law and justice; you, the said ———, are, therefore, hereby summoned to be and appear before the Senate of the State of Missouri, at their chamber in the City of Jefferson, on the —— of ———, then and there to answer to the said articles of impeachment, and then and there to abide by, obey, and perform such orders and judgments as the Senate of the State of Missouri shall make in the premises, according to the constitution and laws of the State of Missouri.

Hereof you are not to fail.

Witness, ———, President of the Senate thereof, at the City of Jefferson, this —— day of ———, in the year of our Lord ——.

Which summons shall be signed by the Secretary of the Senate, and sealed with their seal, and served by the Sergeant-at-Arms to the Senate, or by such other person as the Senate shall specially appoint for that purpose, who shall serve the same pursuant to the directions given in the form next following:

5. A precept shall be endorsed on the said writ of summons, in the form following, viz:

STATE OF MISSOURI, SS:

The State of Missouri to ———, Greeting:

You are hereby commanded to deliver to, and leave with ———, if to be found, a true and attested copy of the within writ of summons, together with a like copy of this precept, and the articles of impeachment herewith, showing him the same; or, in case he cannot, with convenience, be found, you are to leave true and attested copies of the said summons and precept, and articles of impeachment, at his dwelling-house or usual place of abode, with some free white member of the family, over the age of fifteen years; and in whichsoever way you perform the service, let it be done at least —— days before the appearance day mentioned in said writ of summons. Fail not, and make return of this writ of summons and precept, with your proceedings thereon endorsed, on or before the appearance day mentioned in the said writ of summons.

Witness, ———, President of the Senate of the State of Missouri, at the City of Jefferson, this —— day of ———, in the year of our Lord ——.

Which precept shall be countersigned by the Secretary of the Senate, and sealed with their seal.

6. Subpenas shall be issued by the President of the Senate, upon the application of the managers of the impeachment, or of the party impeached, or of his counsel, in the following form, viz:

THE STATE OF MISSOURI,

To ———, *Greeting:*

You, and each of you, are hereby commanded to appear before the Senate of the State of Missouri, on the —— day of ———, at the Senate Chamber in the City of Jefferson, then and there to testify your knowledge in the cause which is before the Senate, in which the House of Representatives have impeached ———; and hereof fail not.

Witness, ———, President of the Senate of the State of Missouri, at the City of Jefferson, this —— day of ———, in the year of our Lord ——.

Which shall be countersigned by the Secretary of the Senate, and sealed with their seal. Which subpena shall be directed, in every case, to the Sergeant-at-Arms of the Senate, or to any special messenger appointed by the Senate.

7. The form of direction to the Sergeant-at-Arms, for service of a subpena, shall be as follows:

SENATE OF THE STATE OF MISSOURI,

To the Sergeant-at-Arms of the State of Missouri:

You are hereby commanded to serve and return the within subpena, according to law. Dated at Jefferson City, this —— day of ———, in the year of our Lord ——.

——— ———, *Secretary of the Senate.*

8. The President of the Senate shall direct all the necessary preparations in the Senate Chamber, and all the forms of proceeding while the Senate are sitting for the purpose of trying an impeachment; and all forms during the trial, not otherwise specially provided for by the Senate.

9. On the day appointed for the return of the summons against the person impeached, the legislative and executive business of the Senate shall be suspended for the time being, and the Secretary of the Senate shall administer the oath to the returning officer, in the form following, viz: "I, ———, do solemnly swear that the return made and subscribed by me, upon the process issued on the —— day of ———, by the Senate of the State of Missouri, against ———, is truly made, and that I have performed said services as therein described; so help me God." Which oath shall be entered at large on the records.

10. The person impeached shall then be called to appear and answer the articles of impeachment against him. If he appear, or any person for him, the appearance shall be recorded, stating particularly if by himself or by agent or attorney, naming the person appearing and the capacity in which he appears. If he do not appear, either personally or by agent or attorney, the same shall be recorded.

11. On the day appointed for the trial of an impeachment, the legislative and executive business of the Senate shall be postponed for the time being.

12. Counsel for the parties shall be admitted to appear, and be heard, upon an impeachment.

13. All motions made by the parties, or their counsel, shall be addressed to the President of the Senate, and if he shall require it, shall be committed to writing, and read at the Secretary's table; and all decisions

shall be had by ayes and noes, and without debate, which shall be entered on the records.

14. Witnesses shall be sworn in the following form, to-wit: "You ——— ——— do swear, (or affirm, as the case may be,) that the evidence you shall give in the case now pending between the State of Missouri and ——— ———, shall be the truth, the whole truth, and nothing but the truth; so help you God." Which oath shall be administered by the Secretary.

15. Before the examination of the witnesses against the accused commences, the accused shall, by himself or counsel, have the right to require all the witnesses in attendance, who shall be called upon to testify, to be sworn, and be excluded from the court, except the witness who shall be placed upon the stand to testify; and thereupon no witness, who has thus been sworn, shall be present during the examination of another witness, unless the defendant or his counsel shall consent thereto; and it shall be the duty of the President of the Senate to advise all the witnesses of this rule; and if any witness, in violation of said rule, shall enter the court, he shall be deemed to be in contempt of the court, and shall be punished as the court shall adjudge. And in like manner, before the witnesses for the accused are examined, they shall, upon demand of the managers, be sworn and excluded as provided above, in the case of the witnesses against the accused, and shall in like manner be dealt with.

16. Witnesses shall be examined by the party producing them, and then cross-examined in the usual form.

17. If a Senator is called as a witness, he shall be sworn, and give his testimony standing in his place.

18. If a Senator wishes a question to be put to a witness, it shall be reduced to writing, and put by the President.

19. At all times, while the Senate is sitting upon the trial of an impeachment, the doors of the Senate Chamber shall be kept open.

20. No person shall be admitted within the bar of the Senate, during the trial, except the managers, the respondent and his counsel, and witnesses when they are called to testify. This rule shall not apply to the reporters and officers of the Senate.

21. In all cases not provided for in the foregoing rules, the rules adopted for the government of the present Senate shall apply.

Ordered, That one hundred copies of the rules, together with one hundred copies of the replication, be printed for the use of the Senate, the managers, and the respondent.

On motion of Mr. Richardson, the Court adjourned to 2 o'clock, Monday evening next.

Monday, February 21, 1859.

The Court was opened by proclamation.

The managers on the part of the House of Representatives attended, as also the respondent, Albert Jackson.

The President of the Senate announced the further consideration of the resolution in reference to the postponement of the trial to some future day, offered by Mr. Parsons on February 19th, together with the substitute offered by Mr. McFerran, to be in order; when

Mr. Frazier offered the following amendment to the substitute:

Amend by striking out "June," wherever it occurs in the substitute, and inserting "November."

This amendment was considered and rejected by the following vote, a ballot being had in pursuance of law:

Ayes—Messrs. Byrne, Frazier, Gullett, Thompson, and Vernon—5.
Noes—Messrs. Brown, Churchill, Coleman, Fox, Goodlett, Halliburton, Harris, Hedgpeth, Horner, Hyer, McFarland, McFerran, McIlvaine, Morris, Newland, O'Neil, Parsons, Peyton, Rains, Richardson, Scott, Watkins, Wilson, Wood, and Wright—25.
Absent on leave—Messrs. Johnson, Jones, and Robinson.

The question then recurring upon Mr. McFerran's amendment by way of substitute, it was agreed to by the following vote, the yeas and nays being taken in pursuance of law:

Yeas—Messrs. Brown, Byrne, Churchill, Frazier, Gullett, McFarland, McFerran, McIlvaine, O'Neil, Richardson, Scott, Thompson, Vernon, Watkins, Wood, and Wright—16.
Nays—Messrs. Coleman, Fox, Goodlett, Halliburton, Harris, Hedgpeth, Horner, Hyer, Morris, Newland, Parsons, Peyton, Rains, and Wilson—14.
Absent on leave—Messrs. Johnson, Jones, and Robinson.

Mr. Morris then moved to indefinitely postpone the original resolution as amended; which motion was decided in the negative by the following ballot:

Yeas—Messrs. Brown, Fox, Harris, Hedgpeth, Horner, McFarland, Morris, Parsons, Peyton, Rains, and Wilson—11.
Nays—Messrs. Byrne, Churchill, Coleman, Frazier, Goodlett, Gullett, Halliburton, Hyer, McFerran, McIlvaine, Newland, O'Neil, Richardson, Scott, Thompson, Vernon, Watkins, Wood, and Wright—19.
Absent on leave—Messrs. Johnson, Jones, and Robinson.

The question then recurring on the original resolution as amended, after discussion,

On motion of Mr. Parsons, the Court adjourned until 2 o'clock tomorrow evening, by the following vote:

Yeas—Messrs. Brown, Byrne, Fox, Goodlett, Harris, Hedgpeth, Horner, Hyer, McIlvaine, Morris, Newland, Parsons, Peyton, Rains, Richardson, Vernon, and Wilson—17.
Nays—Messrs. Churchill, Coleman, Frazier, Gullett, Halliburton, McFarland, McFerran, O'Neil, Scott, Thompson, Watkins, Wood, and Wright—13.
Absent on leave—Messrs. Johnson, Jones, and Robinson.

Tuesday, February 22, 1859.

The Court was opened by proclamation.

The managers on the part of the House of Representatives attended, as also the respondent, Albert Jackson.

After deliberation, on motion of Mr. Parsons, and by unanimous consent, the Court adjourned until 2 o'clock, p. m.

WEDNESDAY, February 23, 1859.

The Court was opened by proclamation.

The managers on the part of the House of Representatives attended, as also the respondent, Albert Jackson.

On motion of Mr. PARSONS,

The resolution offered by him on the 17th inst., in reference to a postponement of the trial of the impeachment, and subsequently amended on the 21st, by way of substitute, was taken up and considered; when,

On motion of Mr. WATKINS, the Court adjourned to 9 o'clock on Friday morning next, by the following vote, a ballot being had:

AYES—Messrs. Brown, Byrne, Churchill, Coleman, Frazier, Goodlett, Gullett, Harris, Johnson, Jones, McFerran, McIlvaine, O'Neil, Thompson, Watkins, Wood, and Wright—17.

NOES—Messrs. Fox, Halliburton, Hedgpeth, Horner, Hyer, McFarland, Morris, Newland, Parsons, Peyton, Rains, Richardson, Robinson, Vernon, and Wilson—15.

Absent—Mr. Scott.

FRIDAY, February 25, 1859.

The Court was opened by proclamation.

The managers and respondent attended.

The PRESIDENT of the Senate announced the further consideration of the amended resolution, in reference to the postponement of the trial of Albert Jackson, to be in order; which was, on motion of Mr. RICHARDSON, informally passed over.

The rules reported by the select committee, on February 19th, for the government of the Senate, when sitting as a High Court of Impeachment, were then taken up and adopted by the following vote:

AYES—Messrs. Brown, Byrne, Churchill, Coleman, Fox, Frazier, Goodlett, Gullett, Halliburton, Harris, Hedgpeth, Horner, Hyer, Johnson, Jones, McFerran, McIlvaine, Morris, Newland, O'Neil, Parsons, Peyton, Rains, Richardson, Scott, Vernon, Watkins, and Wood.

NOES—Messrs. Robinson and Wright.

Absent—Messrs. McFarland and Wilson.

Sick—Mr. Thompson.

Mr. RICHARDSON offered the following resolution:

Resolved, That James L. Jones is hereby appointed a special messenger to serve subpenas, and such other process as may be required of him by the Senate, in the case of the impeachment against Albert Jackson, now pending before the Senate.

For which, after it was read,

Mr. JONES offered the following substitute:

Resolved, That Benjamin F. Jeffries be appointed a special messenger, whose duty it shall be to serve and execute all subpenas and other process that may be issued in the case of impeachment now pending in the Senate against Judge Albert Jackson, Judge of the Fifteenth Judicial Circuit.

Mr. PARSONS moved to amend the substitute by inserting the name of William Vanover after that of Benjamin F. Jeffries.

Mr. Newland moved to lay both the original resolution and substitute on the table; which motion was decided in the affirmative by the following vote:

Ayes—Messrs. Byrne, Churchill, Coleman, Frazier, Harris, Horner, Hyer, Johnson, McFerran, McIlvaine, Morris, Newland, Rains, Scott, Vernon, Watkins, Wood, and Wright—18.

Noes—Messrs, Brown, Fox, Goodlett, Gullett, Halliburton, Hedgpeth, Jones, McFarland, O'Neil, Parsons, Peyton, Richardson, and Robinson—13.

Absent—Mr. Wilson.

Absent on leave—Mr. Thompson.

The amended resolution, postponing further proceedings in the trial until the first Monday in June next, which had been informally passed over, was then taken up and passed by the following vote:

Ayes—Messrs. Brown, Byrne, Churchill, Frazier, Gullett, Hedgpeth, Horner, Johnson, Jones, McFarland, McFerran, McIlvaine, Rains, Scott, Vernon, Watkins, and Wood—17.

Noes—Messrs. Coleman, Fox, Goodlett, Halliburton, Harris, Hyer, Morris, Newland, Parsons, Peyton, Robinson, and Wright—12.

Absent—Messrs. O'Neil, Richardson, and Wilson.

Absent on leave—Mr. Thompson.

On motion of Mr. Newland, the High Court of Impeachment adjourned until the first Monday in June next.

IN THE SENATE.

SATURDAY, February 19, 1859.

On motion of Mr. RICHARDSON, it was

Resolved, That the Committee on the Judiciary be instructed to inquire whether, under the constitution, the Legislature can pass an act authorizing the Senate to try the case of impeachment of the Hon. A. Jackson after the Legislature shall have adjourned *sine die*, and report to the Senate by bill or otherwise.

MONDAY, February 21, 1859.

Mr. PARSONS, from the Judiciary Committee, to whom had been referred a resolution of the Senate directing said committee to inquire in relation to the constitutional power of the General Assembly to pass a law authorizing the Senate to remain in session to sit as a Court of Impeachment after the adjournment, *sine die*, of the House of Representatives, submitted the following report in relation thereto:

MR. PRESIDENT: The Committee on the Judiciary, to which was referred a resolution of inquiry in relation to the constitutional power of the General Assembly to pass a law authorizing the Senate to remain in session to try the case of impeachment, now pending against the Hon. Albert Jackson, after the adjournment, *sine die*, of the House of Representatives, have had the same under consideration, and have instructed me to report. The committee have investigated the question, and are somewhat divided as to whether, under the constitution, the Legislature has any power to pass a law authorizing the Senate to remain in session after a final adjournment of the House of Representatives; and as the question is one of importance, the committee are of opinion that it would be most prudent not to undertake to exercise a doubtful right.

PARSONS, *Chairman*.

The report was read and made the special order for to-day, at 2 o'clock, P. M.

TUESDAY, February 22, 1859.

On motion the regular order of business was dispensed with; when Mr. RICHARDSON offered the following concurrent resolution:

Resolved by the Senate, the House of Representatives concurring therein, That when the two Houses adjourn on the   Monday in March next, the Senate shall stand adjourned until the first Monday in June next, at which time it shall meet for the purpose of trying the case of Albert Jackson, Judge of the Fifteenth Judicial Circuit, upon the impeachment preferred against him by the House of Representatives; and the House of Representatives shall stand adjourned until the fourth Monday in July next, on which last mentioned day the two Houses shall stand adjourned *sine die*, by virtue of this resolution.

The resolution was read a first and second time; when

Mr. WATKINS proposed to fill the blank with "first."

Mr. WILSON proposed to fill the blank with "second;" which was agreed to by the following vote, the ayes and noes being demanded by Mr. Halliburton:

AYES—Messrs. Fox, Halliburton, Harris, Hedgpeth, Horner, Hyer, McIlvaine, Morris, Newland, Peyton, Rains, Richardson, Thompson, Wilson, and Wright—15.

NOES—Messrs. Brown, Byrne, Coleman, Frazier, Gullett, McFarland, McFerran, Scott, Vernon, Watkins, and Wood—11.

Absent—Messrs. Churchill, Goodlett, O'Neil, and Parsons.

Absent on leave—Messrs. Johnson, Jones, and Robinson.

Mr. MORRIS then offered the following amendment to the resolution:

Strike out "first Monday in June," and insert "third Tuesday in March."

The amendment was read a first and second time, and disagreed to by the following vote, the ayes and noes being demanded by Mr. McFerran:

AYES—Messrs. Churchill, Coleman, Fox, Goodlett, Halliburton, Harris, Hedgpeth, Hyer, Morris, Newland, Peyton, and Wilson—12.

NOES—Messrs. Brown, Byrne, Frazier, Gullett, Horner, McFerran, McIlvaine. O'Neil, Rains, Richardson, Scott, Thompson, Vernon, Watkins, Wood, and Wright—16.

Absent—Messrs. McFarland and Parsons.

Absent on leave—Messrs. Johnson, Jones, and Robinson.

Mr. THOMPSON then offered the following amendment to the resolution:

Strike out "first Monday in June," and insert "first Monday in November."

The amendment was read a first and second time, and disagreed to by the following vote, the ayes and noes being demanded by Mr. Halliburton:

AYES—Messrs. Byrne, Fox, Frazier, Gullett, Halliburton, Hyer, Newland, Rains, Scott, Thompson, and Vernon—11.

NOES—Messrs. Brown, Churchill, Coleman, Goodlett, Harris, Hedgpeth, Horner, McFarland, McFerran, McIlvaine, Morris, O'Neil, Peyton, Richardson, Watkins, Wilson, and Wood—18.

Absent—Mr. Parsons.

Absent on leave—Messrs. Johnson, Jones, and Robinson.

The question then being upon the adoption of the resolution,

It was decided in the affirmative by the following vote, the ayes and noes being demanded by Mr. Halliburton:

AYES—Messrs. Brown, Byrne, Churchill, Coleman, Frazier, Gullett, Hedgpeth, Horner, McFarland, McFerran, McIlvaine, O'Neil, Richardson, Scott, Thompson, Vernon, Watkins, Wilson, Wood, and Wright—20.

NOES—Messrs. Fox, Goodlett, Halliburton, Harris, Hyer, Morris, Newland, Peyton, and Rains—9.

Absent—Mr. Parsons.

Absent on leave—Messrs. Johnson, Jones, and Robinson.

[The foregoing resolution in relation to the adjournment and trial was laid upon the table in the House of Representatives, on Wednesday, February 23d.]

THURSDAY, February 23, 1859.

The following message from the House of Representatives was received, through Mr. Love, Assistant Clerk:

Mr. PRESIDENT: I am instructed by the House of Representatives to inform the Senate that the House has adopted the following resolution:

Resolved by the Senate and House of Representatives, That the two Houses will adjourn on the second Monday in March next, and stand adjourned until the fourth Monday in November of this year.

On motion of Mr. WILSON, the above resolution of the House was taken up, read a first and second time, and, the question being on its adoption,

Mr. ROBINSON demanded the ayes and noes. Before the vote was taken,

Mr. MORRIS moved its postponement until to-morrow morning, at 9 o'clock; which motion was disagreed to.

The question then recurring upon the adoption of the resolution, it was decided in the negative by the following vote:

AYES—Messrs. Churchill, Coleman, Gullett, Hedgpeth, Hyer, Johnson, Jones, McFerran, McIlvaine, O'Neil, Thompson, and Vernon—12.

NOES—Messrs. Brown, Byrne, Fox, Frazier, Goodlett, Halliburton, Harris, Horner, Morris, Newland, Peyton, Rains, Richardson, Robinson, Watkins, Wilson, and Wood—17.

Absent—Messrs. McFarland, Scott, and Wright.

Absent on leave—Mr. Parsons.

Mr. MORRIS moved to reconsider the vote rejecting the resolution, and moved to lay the vote to reconsider on the table; and, after debate on point of order, Mr. Morris withdrew both motions.

Mr. WILSON then renewed the motion to reconsider the vote.

Mr. MORRIS moved to lay Mr. Wilson's motion on the table; which was decided in the negative by the following vote, the ayes and noes being demanded by Mr. McFerran:

AYES—Messrs. Brown, Fox, Goodlett, Halliburton, Harris, Morris, Peyton, and Robinson—8.

NOES—Messrs. Byrne, Churchill, Coleman, Frazier, Gullett, Hedgpeth, Horner, Hyer, Johnson, Jones, McFerran, McIlvaine, Newland, O'Neil, Rains, Richardson, Thompson, Vernon, Watkins, Wilson, and Wood—21.

Absent—Messrs. McFarland, Scott, and Wright.

Absent on leave—Mr. Parsons.

The question then being on the reconsideration of the vote rejecting the resolution, it was decided in the affirmative by the following vote, the ayes and noes being demanded by Mr. Robinson:

AYES—Messrs. Byrne, Churchill, Coleman, Frazier, Gullett, Hedgpeth, Hyer, Johnson, Jones, McFerran, McIlvaine, Newland, O'Neil, Richardson, Thompson, Vernon, Watkins, Wilson, and Wood—19.

NOES—Messrs. Brown, Fox, Goodlett, Halliburton, Harris, Horner, Morris, Peyton, Rains, and Robinson—10.

Absent—Messrs. McFarland, Scott, and Wright.

Absent on leave—Mr. Parsons.

The Senate having agreed to the reconsideration of the resolution, the question then was on its adoption; when

Mr. WILSON offered the following amendment:

Provided, however, That when the Senate adjourn on the socond Monday in March, it shall stand adjourned until the first Monday in June next, and proceed with the trial of the case of impeachment now pending against the Hon. Albert Jackson, Judge of the Fifteenth Judicial Circuit, and continue in session from day to day until said trial shall be completed, and then adjourn over until the fourth Monday in November next.

The amendment was read a first and second time, and agreed to; and the resolution, as amended, was then passed by the following vote, the ayes and noes being demanded by Mr. Halliburton:

AYES—Messrs. Byrne, Churchill, Coleman, Frazier, Gullett, Hedgpeth, Hyer, Johnson, Jones, McFerran, McIlvaine, O'Neil, Scott, Thompson, Watkins, Wilson, and Wood—17.

NOES—Messrs. Brown, Fox, Goodlett, Halliburton, Harris, Horner, Morris, Newland, Peyton, Rains, Richardson, Robinson, and Vernon—13.

Absent—Messrs. McFarland and Wright.

Absent on leave—Mr. Parsons.

MONDAY, March 14, 1859.

Mr. HEDGPETH offered the following resolution:

Resolved, That during the session of the Senate as a Court, they will only require the services of the Secretary, Assistant Secretary, Doorkeeper, and Sergeant-at-Arms.

The resolution was read a first and second time; when

Mr. JOHNSON offered the following substitute for the resolution:

Resolved, That when the Senate shall meet in June, to try the impeachment case of Judge Jackson, it shall retain the following officers, to wit: Secretary, Assistant Secretary, Sergeant-at-Arms, Doorkeeper, and Pages. The Senate, when met as a Court, shall have the right to appoint two stenographers, or phonographic reporters, and to order the printing of such matter as it may deem necessary.

The substitute was read a first and second time, and adopted.

TRIAL.

HIGH COURT OF IMPEACHMENT.

STATE OF MISSOURI *vs.* ALBERT JACKSON.

FIRST DAY.

MONDAY, June 6, 1859.

The Court having met pursuant to adjournment, the roll was called, when the following Senators answered to their names: Messrs. Brown, Byrne, Churchill, Frazier, Goodlett, Gullett, Halliburton, Harris, Hedgpeth, Horner, McFarland, McFerran, Newland, Rains, Richardson, Scott, Vernon, Wilson, Wood, and Wright.

A quorum being present, the Court was opened by proclamation, and the Journal of the previous proceedings read.

Mr. HARDIN, on behalf of the managers, moved that attachments issue against Messrs. Davis, Bedford, Pipkin, and Fox, witnesses subpenaed on the part of the State and not appearing; and that an *alias* subpena issue for Matthew H. Moore; and that a special messenger be immediately dispatched to execute said attachments and subpena; which was ordered by the following vote, a ballot being had in pursuance of law:

AYES—Messrs. Brown, Byrne, Churchill, Frazier, Goodlett, Gullett, Halliburton, Harris, Horner, McFarland, McFerran, Newland, Rains, Richardson, Scott, Vernon, Wilson, Wood, and Wright—19.

NOES—Mr. Hedgpeth.

Absent—Messrs. Coleman, Fox, Hyer, Johnson, Jones, McIlvaine, Morris, O'Neil, Parsons, Peyton, Robinson, Thompson, and Watkins.

The respondent, on leave, filed the following objections against further proceedings against him:

In the Case of Impeachment of Albert Jackson, Judge of the Fifteenth Judicial Circuit, before the Senate of Missouri, June 6th, 1859:

There having been thirty-three Senators present and sworn in this case, and there being but twenty now in attendance, the said Albert Jackson, Judge of the Fifteenth Judicial Circuit, objects to any proceedings which may be taken until the whole number present shall answer to their names.

[Signed,] ALBERT JACKSON.

SENATOR CHURCHILL offered the following resolution:

Resolved, That the President of the Senate is hereby authorized and required to appoint two stenographers, or phonographic reporters, to report the proceedings and testimony in the trial now pending before the Senate.

This resolution was adopted by the following vote:

AYES—Messrs. Brown, Byrne, Churchill, Goodlett, Halliburton, Harris, Hedgpeth, Horner, McFerran, Newland, Rains, Richardson, Scott, Vernon, Wilson, Wood, and Wright—17.

NOES—Messrs. Frazier, Gullett, and McFarland—3.

Absent—Messrs. Coleman, Fox, Hyer, Johnson, Jones, McIlvaine, Morris, O'Neil, Parsons, Peyton, Robinson, Thompson, and Watkins.

On motion of SENATOR NEWLAND, it was

Resolved, That the Senate adopt, as its regular hours of meeting while sitting as a High Court of Impeachment, 8 o'clock in the forenoon, and 3 o'clock in the afternoon.

On motion of SENATOR SCOTT, the Court then adjourned until 8 o'clock to-morrow morning.

SECOND DAY.

TUESDAY, June 7, 1859.

The Court met pursuant to adjournment, and was opened by proclamation.

The managers and respondent attended.

On motion of SENATOR GOODLETT, the roll was called, and the following Senators, noted as being absent yesterday, answered to their names: Messrs. Coleman, McIlvaine, Morris, O'Neil, and Thompson.

The PRESIDENT of the Senate announced that two stenographers could be procured, in pursuance of the resolution passed on yesterday, empowering him to employ them, and requested the Senate to fix the compensation; whereupon

SENATOR WRIGHT moved a reconsideration of the vote adopting said resolution; which motion was agreed to by the following vote:

AYES—Messrs. Brown, Byrne, Coleman, Frazier, Goodlett, Gullett, Horner, McFarland, McFerran, Morris, O'Neil, Parsons, Rains, Richardson, Scott, Vernon, Wilson, Wood, and Wright—19.

NOES—Messrs. Churchill, Halliburton, Harris, Hedgpeth, McIlvaine, Newland, Peyton, and Thompson—8.

Absent—Messrs. Fox, Hyer, Johnson, Jones, Robinson, and Watkins.

SENATOR CHURCHILL then moved to amend by striking out the word "two," where it occurs in the resolution, and inserting "one."

This amendment was agreed to by the following vote:

AYES—Messrs. Brown, Byrne, Churchill, Coleman, Goodlett, Halliburton, Horner, McIlvaine, Morris, O'Neil, Parsons, Peyton, Rains, Richardson, Scott, Thompson, and Wilson—17.

NOES—Messrs. Frazier, Gullett, Harris, Hedgpeth, McFarland, McFerran, Newland, Vernon, Wood, and Wright—10.

Absent—Messrs. Fox, Hyer, Johnson, Jones, Robinson, and Watkins.

The question then being upon the passage of the resolution as amended, it was decided in the affirmative by the following vote:

AYES—Messrs. Brown, Byrne, Churchill, Coleman, Halliburton, Harris, Hedgpeth, Horner, McIlvaine, Morris, O'Neil, Parsons, Peyton, Rains, Richardson, Scott, Thompson, and Wilson—18.

NOES—Messrs. Frazier, Goodlett, Gullett, McFarland, McFerran, Newland, Vernon, Wood, and Wright—9.

Absent—Messrs. Fox, Hyer, Johnson, Jones, Robinson, and Watkins.

The PRESIDENT of the Senate, in pursuance of the resolution thus passed, employed Thomas J. Henderson to make the required report of the proceedings and evidence, and announced the same from the chair.

SENATOR SCOTT moved a call of the Senate, which was ordered, and the following Senators noted as being absent without leave: Messrs. Fox, Hyer, Johnson, Jones, Robinson, and Watkins.

On motion of SENATOR SCOTT, further proceedings under the call were dispensed with.

JUDGE JACKSON said he wished the following to be filed and acted upon:

Case of Albert Jackson, Judge of the Fifteenth Judicial Circuit, before the Senate, sitting in Impeachment:

The said Albert Jackson asks that the managers in this case be ordered to specify, in writing, the cause or causes, or in other words, the offense or offenses, in plain, distinct, and legal language, upon which they intend to offer evidence in this case. [Signed,]

ALBERT JACKSON.

MR. HARDIN said that such a motion as this was without precedent or authority of law; was out of order, and he did not think it should be, or could be, entertained. The articles of impeachment, the answer and replication thereto, having been filed, it certainly was unnecessary to make a synopsis of the offenses charged; and since such a motion was without any precedent, authority, or utility, he must object to its being sustained.

JUDGE JACKSON proceeded to discuss his motion at length. He did not know, he said, that an argument based upon precedent would apply in this case. He believed the history of the world could not furnish a parallel for its inception and progress thus far. Notwithstanding he was arraigned before the Senate, no offense was charged against him—at least no offense cognizable before this body. If he had done anything that the constitution or laws prohibited him from doing, he wanted to know it—what it was exactly—and the triers of the cause should also be thus informed. Take the constitution and laws, and if a single infraction of them could be found in his official conduct, let that infraction be pointed out specifically. He held that this had not been done. A most egregious mistake had been made, both in the paper drawn up at the starting of this proceeding, and in the articles of impeachment—they were twin children, and had a strongly marked paternity. It seemed to have been the object merely to hurt his feelings by abusive epithets, rather than to charge him with any offense against the laws. He should find an opportunity to speak of the vituperation heaped upon him, and should speak of it without being mealy-mouthed himself; but at present it was necessary to find some question of fact or some issue of law to try. The gentlemen claimed that their pleadings were backed by precedent. On the contrary, he thought them unprecedentedly abusive. Every charge, whether it constituted a legal offense, if proved or not, was stated in the strongest terms possible, and was intensified by adjectives *ad libitum.* He asked Senators to look at the language of the instrument paraded here against him. On every page he was charged with *high* crimes and misdemeanors, but the specifications to support these general allegations consisted simply in personal abuse. Neither the Judiciary Committee, nor the House, nor managers, had any right to thus speak of and treat him. When they undertook to prepare charges against him, they could not do anything more without transcending their powers, and this last they had certainly done.

He had heard, last winter, in the House of Representatives, a member of that body claiming that, in this case, either the House was a grand jury, or the Judiciary Committee was a grand jury. This was certainly a silly position. Yet it had been assumed to be correct, and it had been acted upon. Now, what right had the House of Representatives to sit as a grand jury? He read the second article of the constitution of the State of Missouri concerning the distribution of the powers of government, and claimed that it plainly prohibited the exercise of any such power by either branch of the Legislature. The functions of a grand jury were *judicial* to all intents and purposes; and yet the Legislature, or a branch of it, had presumed to exercise these judicial functions, notwithstanding each member of the General Assembly had taken a solemn oath to support the constitution, which prohibited it. What was that oath for? If there was anything in the oath taken by a member of the House, it was an obligation not to interfere with the coördinate branches of the government; and it must forbid the House, or any portion of it, to sit as a grand jury. The gentleman to whom he had alluded—Mr. Fitz, he believed, was his name—

SENATOR SCOTT. I must call the gentleman to order. I conceive it out of order for the gentleman now to go into a history of either the case, the constitution, or any such matter. And I think it out of order to use language here derogatory to the coördinate branch of this Legislature. I call him to order now, and I expect to do so again, when I see a similar course pursued by him, in derogation of legal and parliamentary principles. Here, he has not only started an argument on his motion, but seems to be going into a general exposition of his views of the constitution and government, besides giving us a history of the case in hand. I expect both him and the managers to treat the Senate with more respect than such a course implies, and I shall consider them in contempt if they fail to do so.

[The Senator was here interrupted by Judge Jackson, and a short colloquy occurred, which is omitted for want of relevancy.]

JUDGE JACKSON continued his remarks. He had not, he said, intended any disrespect, and did not think he was in contempt of the tribunal before which he was to be tried. He wanted to talk plainly. He was charged with grave offenses, and he was not to be intimidated in defending himself against them. It was necessary for him to speak of the constitution, for by it he ought to be and wished to be tried. And what did that constitution say in regard to impeachments? It said that "all Judges of the courts of law and equity shall be liable to impeachment for any misdemeanor in office." Now, as he was arraigned here under proceedings styled impeachment, was it too much to ask that those who thus arraigned him should specify, in plain and precise terms, the particular misdemeanor for which he was to be tried?

He could conceive of but two classes of impeachable offenses. It was well to remember that our present law on the subject was made when Judges held their offices almost by life tenures. Now the people had it in their power to remove any Judge almost at their pleasure, and this was a good reason for relaxing the old laws on the subject. Our constitution, however, still permitted Judges to be impeached for misdemeanors in office. The constitution of the United States provided that Judges and all civil officers could be impeached for treason, bribery, or other high crimes and misdemeanors. There, he said, was the only substantial basis for this proceeding against him, and it was a wrong basis. There, and not from the constitution of our own State, was where the words "high crimes and misdemeanors" were found. There was to be found all that portion of the articles not derived from the trial of Warren Hastings,—whence most school-boys got their ideas about impeachments. It must be evident, as he had before said, that a most egregious blunder had been made here. In this State, under the constitution of Missouri, a Judge could be impeached only for misdemeanors. Does this document (the articles of impeachment) set forth any misdemeanors? It is profuse in general and vague charges of *high crimes;* but does it charge and set forth any misdemeanors? What violation of constitutional or statute law is complained of? The constitution provides that Circuit Judges shall reside within their circuits; that they shall be at least thirty and not over sixty-five years of age; that they shall take an oath of office, and do other particular things mentioned. Now, if a Circuit Judge were to disregard any of these provisions, although it would be no high crime,—no crime at all in itself considered, —it would be a misdemeanor, and would be ground of impeachment. Nothing of this kind, however, is charged. But go further,—take the statutes, and in them we find a law prohibiting the Judge from practicing law. Now it is no sin or crime to practice law, as, in like manner, it is no heinous matter to be under thirty or over sixty-five years of age. But these things have been supposed to be incompatible with the office of Judge; and hence, if they are disregarded or violated, the Judge can be arraigned for a misdemeanor. If any charge of this nature was to be brought against him, now, in his opinion, was the time to do it.

He could admit but one other class of offenses punishable by impeachment. If a Judge were *convicted* of an infamous crime, he might afterwards be impeached. In all such cases, the intervention of a jury was necessary. In this State, every man, be he Judge or what not, had an inviolate right to a trial by jury of every infamous crime charged upon him. Our own State constitution not only provides generally that the right of trial by jury shall remain inviolate, but further says that no person can, for an indictable offense, be proceeded against criminally by information,—with certain exceptions which could not by any possible construction include the case in hand. He asked the Senators if they could in the face of this plain constitutional provision proceed to try him for an *indictable* offense,—for an infamous crime? Certainly they could not. The Senate was not, in contemplation of law, a jury. There might be in some of its exercises a remote semblance to the functions of a jury; but the Senate was not and could not be such a jury as was contemplated by the constitution. If they were to adjudicate an impeachment case in which an infamous crime was involved, they could only examine the record of some criminal court to ascertain whether a *conviction* for this offense had taken place. They could not try the fact whether a crime had been committed. They could only inquire whether there was a *conviction.* If so, that conviction incapacitated the accused for office, and the impeachment could be sustained—otherwise it could not. It was true that in operating under the laws of our general government, against United States officers, the same rule might not apply. The constitution of the United States provided that "the trial of all crimes, *except* in cases of impeachment, shall be by jury." But in the constitution of the State of Missouri no such exception existed, and there was no provision for trying the question as to the guilt or innocence of a man accused of an infamous crime, except by presentment and indictment in a regularly constituted criminal court. If it was alleged that he had been guilty of an infamous crime, and that he had been convicted of the same, let those allegations appear in plain and distinct language, and he would meet them with a defense. But if all the allegations against him turned out to be upon matters not in themselves impeachable, he would clear his hands at once of the iniquity of protracting this trial. For his own part, leaving out of view his duty as Judge, and laying aside his regard for the organic law of the land, he would be willing to accept any issue tendered him. He was ready for a trial of the question whether his conduct had been proper or improper, decorous or indecorous; but he did not conceive that the public weal demanded that the differences of opinion and personal animosities existing between himself and his enemies should be passed upon in this manner; and he would only be a party to such a proceeding, illegal and void in itself, for the protection of his reputation as a man and a Judge.

In his official capacity he had made certain decisions. Would it be pretended that the Senate could review them, or must the Supreme Court do that? It might be that in some instances he had done wrong. Errors he may have committed. But the question was whether he had committed any wrong knowingly, willfully, and corruptly. In short, was any *corruption*, not error, charged. He contended that none was, and he now called upon the managers to state plainly wherein he had been guilty of corruption. The Senate could try that question. It could not undertake to say whether he had committed errors. Senators were no more to be the judges of his official conduct than he was to be of theirs. It would be no greater usurpation of power to indict a Senator for passing or assisting to pass an unconstitutional law, than to impeach a Judge for errors in his judgments. How he had changed *venues*, told lawyers to sit down, discharged prisoners under writs of *habeas corpus*, attached parties for contempt, caused bills of exceptions to be prepared, and so on—what was all that to Senators? What was it to this court whether he had been polite or impolite while on the bench? For all such things he was responsible to the people of the Fifteenth Judicial Circuit alone. If they did not like his manner of doing business, they had an easy and expeditious means of ousting him from the bench. They had only to express their preference for another at the polls. But it was unreasonable and unjust to arraign him for such things before the Senate of Missouri. He could admit all that was alleged against him here with safety. If the things said about him in the articles of impeachment were in fact true, he would be perfectly willing to admit them. Something more was required for the purposes of the trial, and for that something he now asked. No issue could be made upon the articles of impeachment, and he was unacquainted with the legal procedure to be denominated a trial unless there was an actual, substantial, and palpable issue. He asked, then, that the motion which he had filed be sustained.

Mr. HARDIN said that he had listened with patience to the gentleman's speech; but he was not able, even with much charitable construction, to admit a single one of his positions to be tenable. As he had before remarked, the motion was without precedent. The respondent here was asking something which no one ever before asked, and which would do him no good if granted. Neither under our constitution nor law, nor under any other system, could authority for this procedure be found. The respondent could not in this manner, or in any other, demur to the articles of impeachment. It was, in his view, an exclusive constitutional prerogative of the House of Representatives to impeach. It was the duty of the Senate to try the impeachment, and it could not prescribe the form or substance of the charges preferred against any respondent. The whole of the gentleman's argument, if argument it could be called, rested upon the presumption that the Senate had the power of an ordinary court trying a civil action to direct the manner in which an issue should be made up, when the bare statement of this proposition would be a sufficient refutation. The objections to the motion, he said, were so palpable that he would simply ask that it be voted down, and that the cause proceed.

JUDGE JACKSON commenced a reply to the remarks of Mr. Hardin, but was interrupted by the latter, and a question raised as to his right to speak on the subject at this time. He finally yielded the floor; when

Mr. KNOTT said that he had refrained from the discussion of this point up to the present time, because he wished to avoid even the appearance of captiousness. But he wished it understood that the managers simply took this impregnable position in regard to the question raised by the paper filed by the respondent; namely, that the motion was out of order, irregular, unauthorized by law or precedent, uncalled for by any facts or circumstances, and void even if sustained by this court. The House of Representatives had impeached the respondent, and in support of that impeachment had filed here articles with specific and detailed allegations of high crimes and misdemeanors. In due time and form the respondent was brought to the bar of this court. When asked for his answer, he produced a statement of reasons why he should not be held to answer, asked that they be filed, and argued his propositions at length. They were subsequently overruled, or rather withdrawn, upon an intimation that they would be overruled. He then answered, and in his answer traversed the material allegations of the articles of impeachment, in some instances affecting to treat them with indifference and levity, and averring their insufficiency in law to support an impeachment. Then came the replication, in which the House of Representatives averred the sufficiency of the articles as well as their truth. Here, then, the issue was completely made up. Certain offenses were alleged and denied. Nothing more explicit was desirable or could be attained. That the respondent had seen the force of the charges preferred against him, and that he was fully apprised of their nature, was evidenced by his admission this morning that serious charges were made against him.

JUDGE JACKSON. I never admitted, this morning nor at any other time, that *serious* charges had been made against me. I have been careful not to make such an admission.

MR. KNOTT. I repeat, and can substantiate what I say, that the respondent stated in his reply to the Senator from Buchanan, [SCOTT,] that serious or grave charges—perhaps *grave* was the word—were alleged against him. Be this as it may, however, it is too plain for argument, that, after the replication in this case was filed, the issue was made up. At that point all the law and reason bearing upon the case demanded that the pleadings should be concluded, and they were so concluded. I regard the gentleman's motion as nothing more nor less than a pin upon which to hang a harangue, the substance of which has been already delivered before this Court upon one or two other occasions. I would be willing to grant all he asks, if I did not know, from an examination of all the precedents, not only that such a thing was never contemplated by the law, but that in this case we already have a most elaborate statement of the charges against the respondent, infinitely better, for the purposes of this trial, than any such summary or synopsis as is called for by his motion. Holding the motion to be irregular and wholly out of order, I can only ask that it be voted down at once, without further discussion.

MR. PRESIDENT. The motion must be sustained or overruled by the Senate. Is the Senate ready for action upon it?

SENATOR PARSONS. For the purpose of bringing the matter to issue at once, I move that the motion filed by the respondent be overruled.

JUDGE JACKSON. The Senate will bear with me a moment. This is it: I have filed the motion not for my own advantage. I don't care whether you proceed in this way or not. But if this is to be a trial, you will have to have something to try, and as yet there is nothing of the kind here. I do not want to take advantage of this to stop the prosecution, for I want it to go on; but I must do my duty in objecting to what is wrong and illegal. And I may say here that the same motives governed me in filing the objection yesterday to the Senate proceeding with the case without all the Senators who have been sworn. The law expressly says that no member shall sit or give his vote until he has been sworn, and the plain implication is that all who are sworn must try the case. The managers seemed to be tender-footed on this point. How much it interferes with their plans I won't undertake to say.

Mr. Knott tells us that the articles of impeachment, the answer, and the replication have all been successively filed, and the issue is made up. If it is made up, I want them to point out what it is. The law says that after all this which we know has been done, "*and when* the issue shall be joined on any such impeachment, the Court shall appoint a time for the trial thereof." Now, what are the issues? I hold that none are presented, and although they should have been made up before this time, I am willing to waive this irregularity and make up an issue now. The law in this case explicitly requires issue to be joined. It has not been done. Now if they have anything to allege against me—if they can at this late day hatch up anything—I am ready to meet it. I am ready to answer for every judicial and every private act of my life, if it is necessary, before any tribunal having jurisdiction. While I, being fallible, like other men, may have, as I said before, committed many errors, yet what I have done I stick to, and am proud of. Impeach as much as you please—convict as much as you please: I maintain the honesty and justice of my official conduct. As to all these complaints about harsh treatment of lawyers, and the like of that, if it must all be investigated, I expect to show that if I had gone off the bench occasionally and inflicted personal chastisement upon some of those lawyers, ninety-nine out of every hundred who might learn all the facts would say I did right. I deny that any of these charges against me are serious, because they can all be disproved. I admit that they are *grave* charges, because they affect my private character as a Judge and as a gentleman. They are not *grave* in any other sense. In fact, the truth of the whole matter is, there is no issue for this Court to try. The contract of these gentlemen did not extend so far as the making of an issue, and they have made none. Their only contract was for ruining my character by a proceeding of this kind. It did not extend to this stage of the game.

SENATOR WRIGHT. I would like to know, Mr. President, if I can state my position on this question? I want to know whether the discussion of these matters is to be left entirely to Judge Jackson and the honorable managers, and whether there is no means of stopping it when it goes wrong?

Mr. HARDIN. I would say in answer to the honorable gentleman, that from an examination of the precedents in the British Parliament and the United States Senate, there seems to be no authority for Senators participating in the discussion of legal questions raised during the trial, except it be in secret session.

JUDGE JACKSON. The gentleman is always in error in referring to the English Parliament and Congress. Under the constitution of this State, Judges are not subordinate to the legislative power, as they are in England, and our constitution is essentially different from the constitution of the Federal government. It might do, perhaps, in Massachusetts, to hunt up parliamentary precedents, for there they call the Legislature the General Court of last resort. But in this State it is entirely different.

Mr. PRESIDENT. I will read, in answer to the Senator from Warren, the rule upon this point, adopted by the Senate for its government during the progress of the trial. It is the 13th, and reads thus:

All motions made by the parties, or their counsel, shall be addressed to the President of the Senate, and if he shall require it, shall be committed to writing, and read at the Secretary's table; and all decisions shall be had by ayes and noes, and without debate, which shall be entered on the records.

The vote was then taken upon the motion of Senator Parsons to overrule the motion of the respondent, and stood as follows:

AYES—Messrs. Brown, Byrne, Churchill, Coleman, Frazier, Goodlett, Gullett, Halliburton, Harris, Hedgpeth, Horner, McFarland, McFerran, McIlvaine, Morris, Newland, O'Neil, Parsons, Peyton, Rains, Richardson, Scott, Thompson, Vernon, Wilson, Wood, and Wright—27.

NOES—None.

Absent—Messrs. Fox, Hyer, Johnson, Jones, Robinson, and Watkins.

So the respondent's motion was overruled.

Mr. HARDIN, on behalf of the managers, moved the Court to enter the following order:

Ordered, That the witnesses on behalf of the State and accused be sworn and charged to leave the chamber, and not to be present whilst any witness shall be testifying, under penalty of attachment and punishment as for contempt.

Mr. PRESIDENT suggested that the object of this motion was, perhaps, already provided for by the 15th rule adopted for the government of the Court, which he read as follows:

Before the examination of the witnesses against the accused commences, the accused shall, by himself or counsel, have the right to require all the witnesses in attendance, who shall be called upon to testify, to be sworn, and be excluded from the Court, except the witness who shall be placed on the stand to testify; and thereupon no witness, who has thus been sworn, shall be present during the examination of another witness, unless the defendant or his counsel shall consent thereto; and it shall be the duty of the President of the Senate to advise all the witnesses of this rule; and if any witness, in violation of said rule, shall enter the Court, he shall be deemed to be in contempt of the Court, and shall be punished as the Court shall adjudge. And in like manner, before the witnesses for the accused are examined, they shall, upon demand of the managers, be sworn and excluded as provided above, in the case of the witnesses against the accused, and shall in like manner be dealt with.

Mr. HARDIN. Our motion is not inconsistent with the rule, but in furtherance of its requirements.

After some discussion by Senators Rains, Wilson, and Gullett, in relation to copies of the Rules and the Journals of the Senate, the motion made by Mr. Hardin was agreed to.

Whereupon the following named witnesses upon the part of the State were called, and the President of the Senate administered to them the following oath, to wit:

You, and each of you, do solemnly swear that the evidence you shall give in the present case, wherein the State of Missouri is plaintiff and Albert Jackson is defendant, shall be the truth, the whole truth, and nothing but the truth; so help you God.

WITNESSES' NAMES.

Jonas Eaker,	Joseph Miller,	Wm. Ringer,
Wm. C. Harty,	J. A. Walker,	David Manning,

WITNESSES' NAMES — *Continued.*

S. G. Kitchen,
Moses Harvey,
Lemuel Kittrell,
Daniel Eppes,
Wm. Vandiver,
B. Thornburg,
Wm. O. Hull,
James Hale,
Daniel McCloud,
J. J. Jackson,
Mr. — Whitehead,
M. H. Tyrell,
James B. Odell,
Hamilton Scott,
James Walker,
Thomas A. Mooré,
W. F. Cryts,
A. J. Ruff,
Daniel L. Jennings,
N. W. Sites,
Wm. G. Phelan,
Washington Carlisle,
Chris. C. Green,
James Cooper.

Witnesses subpenaed, but not appearing.

Wm. Grimsley,
John R. Woodside,
John P. Conrand,
James M. Dunn, (not found,)
Richard Wall, (not found,)
M. McCormick, (not found,)
C. A. Davis, (attachment issued,)
David M. Fox, (attachment issued,)
M. H. Moore, (alias subpena issued,)
Philip Pipkin, (attachment issued,)
H. H. Bedford, (attachment issued.)

Those of the foregoing witnesses on the part of the State who appeared, having been sworn as above stated, were charged in accordance with the rule by the President of the Senate, and the Secretary of the Senate was proceeding to call the witnesses on the part of the defendant, when

Judge Jackson objected. He did not understand the rule as requiring his witnesses to be called, sworn, and charged at this stage of the trial.

Mr. Knott said that the rule requiring the exclusion of witnesses should be made to operate so as to prevent any imputation of unfairness or collusion; and this could not be done unless all the witnesses were put under the rule alike. The motion just acted upon was intended to carry out this view.

Judge Jackson thought the gentlemen only intended to exclude their own witnesses, to which he had no objection. He read the rule (above cited by the President of the Senate) to show that the witnesses summoned on his part were not to be excluded, upon the motion of the managers, until he entered upon his defense, and in further support of his position alleged that he did not know what witnesses he would introduce, and could not know until the testimony for the State was closed. He should most probably have to use one or both of the managers for the purposes of evidence, and they with the others would come under the rule if it was enforced now. He should certainly insist upon using Mr. Knott, at least, as a witness. He wished this matter to be regulated by the rule adopted for the purpose of regulating it, and thought there could be no difficulty about it.

Mr. Knott replied, urging that the object of the rule would be defeated by the course which the respondent seemed desirous of taking, and that the question raised by him had already been determined by the Court, in ageeeing to the motion of Mr. Hardin. If there was any propriety in excluding the State's witnesses, the same propriety existed for excluding the witnesses on the other side. What if the respondent did not know the exact number of witnesses he would wish to use, and who they were? If any of those he had subpenaed were not needed, their being excluded from the Senate Chamber would not necessitate their examination, and could do neither them nor the respondent any harm. It was not proposed by the managers to cut off the respondent from his right to summon new witnesses, if he deemed it expedient, during the trial. Hence there was no force in this objection.

After some further and desultory discussion on this point, during which the propriety of reporting and printing the evidence was adverted to and debated at some length, and which discussion was participated in by Senators Richardson, (in the chair,) Rains, Thompson, Parsons, Halliburton and Scott, and by Messrs. Hardin and Knott, and the respondent, the question was decided by a vote of the Senate, as follows:

For calling respondent's witnesses, and putting them under the rule now—Messrs. Brown, Byrne, Churchill, Coleman, Frazier, Goodlett, Gullett, Halliburton, Harris, Hedgpeth, Horner, McFarland, McFerran, McIlvaine, Morris, O'Neil, Parsons, Peyton, Rains, Richardson, Scott, Thompson, Vernon, and Wood—24.

Opposed—Messrs. Newland, Wilson, and Wright—3.

Absent—Messrs. Fox, Hyer, Johnson, Jones, Robinson, and Watkins.

The following named witnesses were then called, sworn, and charged in accordance with the rule:

WITNESSES' NAMES.

George W. Creath,
Adams Dalton,
Horace Bailey,
Chas. Henderson,
Henry Miller,
John D. Smith,
Sanders Walker,
David G. Hicks,
John Beasley,
John Marsh,
Henry Noble,
Dr. Russell,
C. M. Dowdy,
William B. Cone,
James Hodges,
John C. Walker,
Lewis Chandler,
David Cryts,
Frank Lawson,
A. Lowe,
J. Proc. Knott,*
Moses Harvey, (sworn for State)
Dabney S. Cooper,
John S. Gallaway,
Jacob Miller,
Pinkney Powers,
Alex. Ward,
A. J. Ruff, (sworn for State,)
Lemuel Kittrell, (sworn for State,)
Wm. Vandiver, (sworn for State,)
James Dennis,
Richard Spencer,
James A. Atkins,
Thos. Walker,
William Culbertson,
H. A. Shook,
W. H. Horner,
James Dowdy,
Samuel H. Flournoy,
J. W. Souther,
Alex. Sloan,
Chas. H. Hardin.*

Witnesses subpenaed, but not appearing.

Reuben P. Owens,
Jacob Catron,
Barnabas Bledsoe,
Orson Bartlett,
Miles Ponder,
W. W. Norman,
Joseph Davis,
Robert Miller,
Wm. Henley,
Joseph White,
Frank Lee,
Jacob Blount,
J. H. Board,
John Yarber,
W. B. Howell,
Stephen Rice.

Witnesses subpenaed, but not found.

John Dillon,
Reuben Harper,
James J. Gardiner, (alias subpena issued,)
John Lax,
Wm. Morrow,
Albert Reaves,
Thos. A. Lovelace.

On motion of SENATOR HALLIBURTON, the Court adjourned till 3 o'clock in the afternoon.

* Managers on the part of the House of Representatives.

EVENING SESSION.

TUESDAY, June 7, 1859.

The Court met at 3 o'clock.

The following witnesses on the part of the defendant appeared, and were sworn and charged according to the rule: Isaac Hobbs, Joseph Davis, W. B. Howell.

Mr. PRESIDENT. Are there any further preliminary matters to be attended to before proceeding with the trial? If not, the managers on the part of the House will proceed with their case.

MR. KNOTT'S OPENING SPEECH.

Mr. KNOTT rose and said:

Mr. PRESIDENT: It devolves upon me to present to this honorable Court the grounds upon which the House of Representatives predicated, and confidently expects to sustain the impeachment, for the determination of which we are at present convened; and I trust I will not be suspected of a trifling affectation when I express the very great degree of embarrassment under which I approach the discharge of that duty. I do not appear at this bar merely as the advocate of an individual demanding, at the hands of those who have it in charge to administer the laws, redress for a violation of his personal rights; nor am I here to plead the cause of the State against an ordinary offender, charged with some petty infraction of the criminal code; but at the command of the Grand Inquest of the State, made by the constitution the guardians of the purity and integrity of the government, to present in behalf of all the people of the State, and make good their accusation against one occupying a distinguished official position, for a long catalogue of high crimes and misdemeanors; to establish against one whom the people have honored with one of the most sacred and important trusts pertaining to the government, the deep guilt of disregarding that distinguished trust; of trampling under his feet the laws he was bound by his solemn oath to maintain and administer in their purity, integrity and justice; and of outraging the rights he was sworn to protect, in a series of abuses of official authority unparalleled, at least in the annals of this country.

I appear, too, before the highest court known to our constitution,—a tribunal of statesmen, before which that magistracy which tries all others else is brought to account for the fidelity of its deportment in the distinguished position to which public confidence has elevated it; while I am fully sensible that consequences of the most portentous character must necessarily attend the result of the investigation upon which we are about to enter. As the illustrious Burke remarked in his celebrated speech upon the bill for the taxation of the American colonies, I know our people "augur misgovernment from afar, and snuff the approach of tyranny in every tainted breeze." I know that public attention is directed from every portion of the State to the proceedings in which we are now engaged, the result of which I am confident will either demonstrate the efficacy of the barriers erected by the constitution against the abuse of that authority necessarily delegated by the people to those in power, or it will tend to destroy public confidence in the securities provided by the State against the encroachments of arbitrary oppression.

A proper appreciation of all these circumstances excites within me a painful distrust of my ability to present this case in a manner commensurate with its importance,—that will justify the generous partiality of those at whose instance I am here on this occasion, and comport with the dignified character of the tribunal at whose bar I now have the honor to stand.

But, sir, the duty devolving upon me is not less disagreeable than onerous. The human mind possesses the same instinctive repugnance, and perhaps even more readily revolts at the contemplation of moral degradation, than at a spectacle of physical decay, particularly when associated with endowments of intellect and advantages of mental culture from which better results might reasonably have been anticipated. When we behold a mind endowed by nature with every faculty that can constitute it a source of benefaction to our kind, and sufficiently cultivated to render it a sparkling gem in the coronet of society, rendered subservient to the most ignoble passions of the human heart, a slave to all the dark, malignant emotions of man's baser nature, we can but pity its unfortunate possessor, while we deprecate the monstrous perversion of his splendid gifts. But when we see a man, thus endowed, elevated in consequence of that very endowment, by a confiding country, to a distinguished participation in its government, rendering the power incidental to his position subsidiary to the gratification of the worst impulses of his soul, betraying the generous confidence of those who were instrumental in his elevation, and bringing disgrace, obloquy, and evil of every description upon a country of which he might have been the benefactor, the ornament, and pride, every other emotion gives place to unmitigated abhorrence and disgust. In the one instance, sir, we may be said to experience something like the same feelings we would in gazing upon the ruins of some splendid temple, where the hyena's horrid laugh echoes through the "long-drawn aisle and fretted vault,"—where owls flit at noon day, the loathsome toad distils its venom beneath each slimy stone, and the deadly night-shade waves its noxious foliage around the altar where once arose grateful incense to the living God; in the other, we feel as if in the presence of the grim demon of destruction himself, who, folding his dusky pinions above the broken arches and mouldering columns, broods in fiendish ecstacy over the desolation his baleful breath has scattered around him.

But, sir, onerous and disagreeable as this duty is, it is likewise inevitable. The same dire necessity that impels the application of the surgeon's knife to rid the body of the mangled, gangrened, putrescent member, to preserve the balance from putrefaction and death, induced the institution of this impeachment, and requires its present prosecution. No ends of private vengeance are to be attained by it,—I thank God this tribunal is far above the approach of causes instituted for any such purposes,—but it is designed to vindicate the purity and integrity of the institutions of our State; to admonish those with whom the people have committed that degree of power necessary for the good government of society, that they cannot abuse that power with impunity; that when they pervert their authority to the gratification of their own passions, they shall be held to strict and speedy retribution. And, sir, onerous and disagreeable as is the duty devolving upon me, in connection with this case, and illy capacitated as I know I am for its proper discharge, as a representative of the people, I would not shrink from it if I could. For, sir, I hold that as this government is instituted for the benefit of the governed, to protect them in their lives, liberties, reputation, property, and the pursuit of happiness, it becomes the especial duty of the representative selected from the general mass, under the most solemn pledges of fidelity to their interests, to see that no foul pollutions are permitted to contaminate this great fountain-head of popular happiness.

It is an axiom incorporated in the constitution of our State that all political power is vested in the people,—that they are sovereign, the ultimate and sole repository of all political authority,—and that they delegate to those in the various departments of government only so much of that power as is necessary for the protection of all and the promotion of the general welfare; and hence, sir, the representative of the people, the immediate acting agent of the whole, is under every obligation that gratitude, patriotism, honor, morality, and religion impose, to watch the exercise of that delegated power with the most jealous vigilance, to see that it is not perverted to personal aggrandizement, or arbitrary oppression.

Influenced, sir, no doubt, by such considerations as these, the wise framers of our State constitution, as well as the patriotic sages who framed the constitution of the United States, vested the sole power of impeachment in the House of Representatives, composed of members coming directly from among the popular masses, understanding their wills, participating in their feelings and interests, and immediately responsible to them for the manner in which they discharge the important trust committed to their hands. But, sir, whatever may have been the reasons that influenced the investment of the House of Representatives with the power of impeachment, I hold its exercise to be one of the most sacred and important duties devolving upon them, and one from which I trust in Almighty God they may never be disposed to shrink, whenever circumstances may exist demanding its exercise. And such, I make no doubt, were the views and sentiments of the gentlemen of the House of Representatives, when, with a unanimity unparalleled in the legislative annals of this country, they impeached the respondent at this bar of that extraordinary catalogue of high crimes and misdemeanors to which I now propose to invite the attention of this honorable Court,—which it is expected we shall be able to establish by the most incontrovertible evidence, and which, moreover, if so established, it is as confidently expected this Court will stamp indelibly with the seal of unqualified condemnation. But, sir, if the proofs we shall offer shall be insufficient to fix upon the respondent the deep guilt of which he stands charged in these articles, none will acquiesce more cordially, or rejoice more sincerely at his honorable acquittal, than those who have it in charge to conduct this prosecution.

In order to determine the exact points in controversy,—that you may be enabled to properly appreciate and apply the testimony as it will be adduced,—it is necessary that I should enter upon a specific examination of the several matters of complaint alleged against the respondent. I will premise, however, that, as it has pleased the respondent to urge something in the nature of a demurrer to the articles exhibited against him, I am compelled to offer a more elaborate commentary upon the several charges preferred against him than I had intended.

Permit me to read to the Court the first article:

ARTICLE I. That, unmindful of the sacred obligation by which he stood bound to discharge the solemn duties of his office faithfully, impartially, and consistently with the dignity and importance of the trust reposed in him, as Judge of the Fifteenth Judicial Circuit, in the State of Missouri, the said Albert Jackson, at a Circuit Court begun and held at the town of Bloomfield, within and for the county of Stoddard, in the State of Missouri, on the third Monday in May, A. D. 1858, (whereat the said Albert Jackson, by virtue of his office aforesaid, did preside as Judge,) did willfully and maliciously conduct himself in a manner highly oppressive and unjust to one Jonas Eaker, viz:

First. The said Albert Jackson, desiring to harrass and oppress the said Jonas Eaker, did, at the Circuit Court aforesaid, whereat he, the said Albert Jackson, presided as Judge, as aforesaid, cause an attachment to issue against him, the said Eaker, as for a criminal contempt, because said Eaker did not make return to a writ of mandamus, which writ had never been delivered to said Eaker, but of which a *copy* had been delivered to said Eaker; by virtue of which attachment the said Jonas Eaker was arrested and held in custody for several hours, and released finally by said Albert Jackson on condition that he, the said Jonas Eaker, should make return to the copy that had been delivered to him, said Jackson well knowing that said writ had never been legally served upon him, the said Eaker, and that he was not in contempt for not answering thereto.

Second. In refusing to permit counsel for said Eaker to speak in his behalf, when they proposed to show to the court that said writ of mandamus had never been properly delivered to, or served upon him.

Third. In peremptorily, and in an oppressive, angry, and insulting manner, ordering the counsel of said Eaker, to wit, Solomon G. Kitchen and William G. Phelan, *to shut their mouths and sit down*, when they, in behalf of their said client, attempted to suggest an insufficiency in the service of said writ of mandamus.

Fourth. In depriving said Jonas Eaker of the benefit of counsel, and of the privilege of speaking through such counsel in his own defense, as he had a lawful right to.

A celebrated philosopher of antiquity being asked what was the best government, is said to have replied, "that in which the whole power of the State is pledged to avenge an injury done to its humblest citizen." But, whilst this is no doubt true, it is not the object of the present prosecution to make reparation to Mr. Eaker for any injury he may have sustained. It is intended to wipe out the odium brought upon the law and the judiciary of the country, by the illegality of his imprisonment and the malice with which it was inflicted, and to prevent the recurrence of such abuses of power, in future, by the prompt condemnation of the party guilty in this instance.

It is not denied that courts having the power to issue writs of mandamus are also clothed with power to enforce return to such writs, by attachment; but we do contend that before a court can lawfully cause an attachment to issue to compel a return to such a writ, it must appear that the writ of mandamus has been legally served upon the person required to make return thereto, and that there is reason to believe such person is in contempt. The law compels no man to answer to process that has not been legally served upon him. This principle is so clearly understood, so universally acknowledged, that it requires neither argument nor illustration.

The statute founded upon a recognition of this palpable principle of common sense has prescribed a definite mode in which process must be served, and until executed in the manner prescribed by law, the person upon whom it should have been served is neither compelled to appear, nor answerable for contempt in not appearing. Were this not true, you would have no security for the enjoyment of a single right you possess. The same authority that would justify a court in compelling a party to appear and answer where there had been an insufficient service of process, would authorize it to assume a jurisdiction where there had been no service at all. So, sir, your rights might be adjudicated upon in your absence,—your property might be swept away, your liberty declared forfeited, your person seized and hurried away to the dungeon, ultimately to dangle at the arm of the gibbet, without your ever knowing a syllable of the cause, or being permitted to speak a single word in your own defense. It needs no argument to demonstrate that a disregard of this principle would at once destroy all permanency and certainty in the operation of our laws, and render them entirely dependent upon the whim and caprice of those who are to administer them,—thus establishing a tyranny of the most dangerous and detestable character. If, therefore, it shall appear that the writ of mandamus issued by the respondent in this instance had not been legally served upon Mr. Eaker,—that the respondent was apprised of this want of a proper service, and, notwithstanding his knowledge of that fact, caused a writ of attachment to issue against him, by virtue of which he was taken in custody and restrained of his liberty,—the conclusion is inevitable, he is guilty of a double wrong—a willful and dangerous perversion of the law, and an outrage upon the personal liberty of a citizen, perpetrated under color of his official authority, and for which he is properly held to answer at this bar.

I grant, sir, that the courts are very properly endowed with power to imprison for contempt, under certain circumstances; but if they are not responsible for abuses of that power,—if they are permitted to tear the citizen from the bosom of his family, and the demands of his business, upon an alleged contempt, and shut him up like a malefactor in the jail, whether guilty or not, and still be amenable to no tribunal for such high-handed oppression,—we are under a despotism far more despicable than the autocracy of Russia, for we are subject to all the arbitrary injustice and cruelty that characterizes that government, while we blindly cherish the illusion that we are in the full enjoyment of a blood-purchased liberty. Establish the doctrine, sir, that a Judge of the Circuit Court may imprison the citizen without the authority of some definite rule of law, but merely to gratify his own malignant passions, and who is safe? at what moment may the storm not break forth, and who may not be the victim? Have you a guaranty that *you* may not be torn from your business and your family, and thrust into jail, to glut the hate of some petty despot, mantled by the "judicial ermine?" But, thank God! so far from this horrible doctrine being true, our laws place the liberty of the citizen upon the same footing with his life, his property, and his reputation, and gives the Judge no more power over the one than he has over the other. He is not authorized to trample upon either. Sir, this is no new doctrine that I enunciate. Hundreds of years ago, our English ancestry, properly estimating the propriety of erecting as many bulwarks as possible against infringements of their rights by those in power, assembled upon the "grassy plain of Runnemede," and, at the point of the sword, forced from their unwilling sovereign a guaranty that *no subject should ever be deprived of his liberty, except by the judgment of his peers and the law of the land!* And, sir, the framers of our constitution, impressed with the inestimable importance of the right of personal liberty, ingrafted the provision of Magna Charta I have just quoted into our own bill of rights,—incorporated it in our constitution,—in order that all who might be endowed with power to violate it should take a solemn oath to maintain it inviolate. Nor is it remarkable that the preservation of this right should have been made a special subject of constitutional enactment; for it is upon the preservation of this that the enjoyment of all other rights depends. What to you, sir, were all the wealth of Peru or Golconda, if, immured in the damp walls of the prison, you were unable to accumulate around you any of the appliances of ease, elegance, and luxury, that go to make up the sum of refined enjoyment? What enjoyment could life itself afford you, if chained down and made to breathe the noisome vapors of a dungeon, where the glad smile of friendship could never beam around you, nor the sweet voice of affection break the gloomy monotony of your horrible solitude?

But, sir, I go even farther than this: I maintain that the vigilance of the people should be more constantly awake to infringements of their personal liberty than of any other right they enjoy, and that violations of this right should of all offenses be most promptly and energetically condemned; for while it is upon the preservation of this that the enjoyment of all other rights depends, it is of all others most easily violated with impunity by unprincipled and arbitrary officials. To bereave a man of life, or strip him of his property, without warrant of law, but under color of official authority, would be an outrage so glaring, so palpable, that public justice would instantly arouse and vindicate itself, by visiting upon the offender immediate and exemplary vengeance; but a man may be hurried, under pretext of lawful authority, to the damp, loathsome vaults of the prison, whence no wailing cry for help can ever reach the ear of pitying justice, and his wrongs are either unknown or soon forgotten by all beyond the confines of his living tomb, except those to glut whose malice he is buried there! But more, sir: the judiciary is intended to *protect* our rights, not trample them under foot; and the Judge upon the bench, so far from possessing a license to trifle with our liberties, is under the obligations of a solemn oath to preserve and secure them from violation. He has no more right to deprive you of your liberty without proper warrant of law, than he has to confiscate your estate, apply the incendiary's torch to your dwelling, or plant the assassin's dagger in your bosom.

Yet, sir, palpable as these considerations are, we have here one of the pillars of the law,—a man professedly learned in all departments of human wisdom,—asserting without a blush that he can, without authority of law, deprive a citizen of his most inestimable right, and still be held amenable to no authority,—still be guilty of no crime against the laws of his country!

In his answer the respondent says specifications one, two, three, and four, of article first, charging as they do a willful and malicious outrage upon the constitutional rights of a citizen of Missouri, are insufficient in law!

But, sir, let it not be urged in extenuation of the crime charged in this article, that the imprisonment of Eaker may have been but of a few hours' duration. It is immaterial, so far as this action is concerned, whether it was accompanied with that duration and other circumstances that in a private prosecution for false imprisonment would go in aggravation of damages, or whether it was not. Every curtailment of the liberty of the citizen is an *imprisonment*, whether it be in the dungeons of a Bastile, or the custody of a ministerial officer of a court of justice,—whether it be of but an hour's duration, or poison the happiness of a whole existence; and it is of the illegality of this imprisonment of Eaker, and its malicious infliction, of which complaint is here made. But granting this imprisonment of Mr. Eaker *was* of but an hour's duration: who gave the respondent control over that single hour of his existence? who will undertake to determine with what consequences upon the destinies of Eaker, and those dependent upon him, that single hour may have been pregnant? "Where," remarks a profound thinker of the present age, "can a place be found to hang the scales on which to weigh the results of a single human action?" The destinies of a whole life may turn upon the fulcrum of a moment; and yet a learned Judge will tell this Court that he can rob you of your freedom without authority of law,—that he can usurp control over the destinies of your life, and of the lives of all dependent upon you,—and still be guilty of no wrong! Sir, has it come to this—can an American Judge, in this land, where freedom was purchased with the blood of so many martyred heroes, deliberately tell a Court of the dignity and learning of the one I now have the honor to address, that, without any authority save the caprices of his own licentious passions, he can violate the dearest right of a free-born man, and be guilty of no offense?

But, sir, I forbear to comment further upon this article, for I am confident, with whatever indifference the respondent may affect to treat it, every member of this honorable Court is satisfied that the offense alleged in it is, by no means, the most trivial that could be charged against him; and, if established by the evidence, it will be sufficient to dismiss him in disgrace from a position he has shown himself intellectually and morally disqualified to occupy longer.

In the second article the respondent is charged with the most unjust, improper, and disgraceful conduct as Judge,—a willful partiality between certain parties litigant before him, clearly manifested in his officiously advising and counseling one of the parties not to compromise an action in which he was defendant, pending before the respondent, assuring him he would be successful, and giving him the reasons why.

It is not because, if the charge alleged in this article is true, the respondent has violated an express statute, that I rely upon its sufficiency to sustain an impeachment; but because it exhibits a degree of partiality entirely at variance with every duty of a Judge, disgraceful to the judicial character, and utterly inconsistent with the proper administration of justice.

The Judge, sir, from the very nature of his office, is bound to yield a blind obedience to the law as he finds it, regardless of the tender sentiments of friendship, or the malignant promptings of animosity and hate. He is to know no friend, no foe; but with the integrity of an Aristides, and the disinterested fidelity of a Brutus, to deal out even and exact justice to all under the law, as he finds it, without endeavoring to swerve it a single hair's breadth from its legitimate course. From such a course alone can community derive from the judiciary that protection which its establishment was designed to give, and by such a course alone can the judicial character secure that veneration so essential to a full and proper discharge of all its functions.

I have frequently thought, sir, that human nature can afford no more splendid spectacle,—that the image of deity never shines with more unclouded lustre,—than in the honest, upright Judge, who, sacrificing every personal feeling and sentiment of his own bosom, holds the scales of justice with a steady, impartial hand, uninfluenced by any consideration save the purest love of truth and right.

> With an equal scale
> He weighs the offenses betwixt man and man;
> He is not soothed with adulation,
> Nor moved with tears, to wrest the course of justice
> Into an unjust current.

Upon the other hand, it seems to me that if there is a living proof of the utter depravity of our race,—if there is a fitting portraiture of the arch enemy of man,—it must be he who, elevated by a confiding country to one of the most sacred, important, and distinguished trusts that can be conferred upon the citizen, basely betrays the confidence reposed in him,—renders the power incidental to his position subservient to the gratification of his own passions, the promotion of his own interests, and the accommodation of those he may see proper to favor, irrespective of law, justice, or any of the duties of his place.

I will not now trespass upon the forbearance of the Court, by attempting a full exposition of the utter inconsistency of a course of conduct, such as is charged in this article, with the duties of this respondent as Judge, nor cite any of the numerous authorities within my reach by which such conduct is unqualifiedly denounced, not only as being unbecoming his character as Judge and inconsistent with his official duties, but as a misdemeanor in office for which he is liable to indictment. The respondent himself has not had the hardihood to contend that such conduct would not be highly improper in him as Judge; but sets up in his answer the very singular palliation that the advice complained of was given in his *private capacity*, and not as Judge.

Friar Tuck, I believe, was in the habit of making a distinction between himself as the Holy Clerk of Copmanhurst, and as the Merry Outlaw of Harthillwalk; but the delicate distinction was always beyond my comprehension. I never could understand how he could divest himself of all his unholiness with his suit of Lincoln green, and take on the purity of the priesthood with his grey friar's frock; and I am as much at a loss to understand how the respondent can make a difference between counsel given as Judge and that imparted as a private individual, when the effect upon the rights of the parties is precisely the same in both instances. Indeed, sir, it appears to me, if a Judge *must* give way to his feelings,—if he *cannot* resist the inclination to act partially,—it would be more reprehensible in him to cloak that partiality in public, and only give his favorite the advantage of it privately, than to make an open exhibition of it upon the bench; for in the latter instance, the opposite party having an opportunity of seeing the influences operating against him, might remove his cause to some court where he could obtain justice; while in the other, he goes like the unsuspecting lamb to the slaughter, not dreaming that his cause has not only been already judged, but that the very Judge to whom he looked with the most implicit trust for right and justice has been enlisted as counsel for his adversary. Let this Court imagine an unsuspecting citizen, confiding in the justness of his cause and the integrity of the laws of his country, approaching a tribunal of justice in full confidence that ample justice will be done him, while that same court is secretly closeted with his competitor, advising him how to conduct his cause, what advantages to avail himself of, and what he may rely upon as the result; and tell me if the human heart can conceive a more odious, disgusting, sickening picture of corruption and iniquity!

But, sir, the instance of corrupt partiality complained of in the second article is by no means the only one alleged against the respondent in this impeachment. Turn to the eighth article, and you will find a similar accusation, or perhaps rather broader, since he is there charged with advising Mr. Odell publicly as well as privately how to conduct his cause, and assuring him his client could not be convicted. Again, if you will turn to the thirteenth article, you will find him accused of advising Mr. Ringer to bring suit against Mr. Kitchen, assuring him that Kitchen was personally liable to him, and there could be no doubt of his recovering a judgment,—endeavoring thereby, as the language of the article expresses it, "to incite a vexatious and expensive law suit in the court of which he himself was Judge, for the purpose of harrassing said Kitchen."

Turn again to the sixteenth article, and you behold him charged with hearing and determining a motion to quash an indictment pending against one David G. Hicks, who was acting as Circuit Attorney, without appointing some other attorney to represent the State in that behalf; intending thereby to screen Mr. Hicks from a prosecution for a serious offense against the laws of the country, for which he had been regularly indicted. You will perceive, also, in the seventeenth article, he is charged with permitting his partiality to exhibit itself in a variety of ways; but I will not comment upon it now, as it will recur upon an examination of the articles in the order in which they are presented.

I will not trouble the Court with a further discussion of the character of the crimes charged in the allegations to which I have just directed your attention. There will be occasion for that hereafter, for I entertain no doubt the evidence will establish them indubitably,—that all the circumstances will show that the respondent did all of which he stands charged *mala animo*, totally regardless of the duties of his office, the rights of the parties, or the law of the land.

But, sir, improper, disreputable, and unbecoming as it is to a Judge to exhibit the slightest degree of partiality in the exercise of his official functions,—disastrous as that partiality may be to the rights and interests of parties litigant before him,—it really assumes the character of a *virtue*, when compared to its opposite extreme—willful, wanton, heartless, arbitrary oppression. The one may result from a redundancy of good feeling, that, under some circumstances, would reflect credit upon our nature—an overweaning desire to confer a benefit upon a friend; the other is always the offspring of the most malignant passions of the human soul—the revenge of an ignoble spirit, pinioned down by the grossness of its own innate corruption in the lowest depths of depravity, and made, like Milton's portraiture of Sin, the perpetual prey of its own fiendish whelps—envy, hate, and malice.

It is upon this reckless spirit of wanton oppression that the House of Representatives has based a charge against the respondent in almost every article they have exhibited against him; and surely, if he is guilty of them all, he must have taxed his invention for a variety of ways in which to manifest that despotic inclination. I will read one of them to the Court:

ARTICLE III. That, actuated by a spirit of arbitrary despotism and wanton injustice, totally repugnant to the sacred duties pertaining to his office, and highly dangerous to the rights of the citizens of the State, the said Albert Jackson, Judge of the Fifteenth Judicial Circuit, at a Circuit Court begun and held within and for the county of Wayne, in the State of Missouri, at the town of Greenville, in said county, on the last Monday in September, A. D. 1858, whereat said Albert Jackson, by virtue of his office aforesaid, presided as Judge, was guilty of willful and malicious oppression, misconduct, and abuse of authority in his official capacity:

First. During the Circuit Court aforesaid, at the time and place aforesaid, David M. Fox, one of counsel for plaintiff, in the cause of —— Limbarger *vs.* —— Power, then and there pending before said court, presented a petition to said Albert Jackson, then and there presiding as Judge of said court aforesaid, to change the venue of said cause to some other court, because of the prejudice of the Judge, and informed him, the said Albert Jackson, that both parties and their counsel had agreed that said cause might be sent to either the county of Madison or the county of Iron, as either of said counties would be convenient and easy of access; but the said Albert Jackson, Judge as aforesaid, utterly unmindful of the rights of the parties and counsel in said cause, and totally disregarding the provisions of the statute in such cases made and provided, and willfully and maliciously intending to harrass and oppress the parties aforesaid, and their counsel, awarded a change of venue in said cause to *Mississippi county*, well knowing said county to be remote, difficult of access, and inconvenient to all the parties, counsel, and witnesses in said cause.

Second. When counsel engaged in said cause, to-wit, David M. Fox and Philip Pipkin, attempted then and there to prevail upon him, the said Albert Jackson, to change the venue to some other county more convenient to all parties, and informed him that by sending said cause to Mississippi county he would deprive them of the privilege of attending to their clients' cause, as they had been employed to do, he, the said Jackson, replied to each of them in an oppressive, insolent, and insulting manner, highly shameful, and derogatory to the dignity of the important position he occupied as Judge, as aforesaid.

The law allowing changes of venue in causes was enacted out of the tenderest regard to the rights of parties, and to secure the administration of the strictest justice.

If from any cause the people of a county where any case is pending, or the Judge before whom it is to be tried, is liable to be biased by favor, affection, or prejudice, so that the strictest impartiality and the fairest trial cannot be confidently relied upon, it is provided that such case may be removed to some county where such impediments to the proper administration of justice do not exist; and it is true that, in granting changes of venue, the court is clothed with a certain discretion as to what county the case may be sent to; but that discretion must be guided by reason, and is, as far as practicable, circumscribed by positive statutory enactment, in order to secure to the parties, counsel, and witnesses the cheapest, speediest, and most convenient trial; and it follows as an unavoidable conclusion, if a Judge send a case upon a change of venue to a court, knowing that it is remote and cannot be attended by the parties, counsel, or witnesses without great expense, trouble, and inconvenience, while there are other courts to which it might be sent far more suitable and convenient to all concerned, such Judge, in imposing such a hardship, is guilty of oppression in office,—an offense at common law, and by statute indictable and impeachable. It is necessary for you to understand that, in the case complained of in this article, the cause was pending in Wayne county, in the northern part of which both Limbarger and Power resided; that immediately contiguous on the north is situated the county of Iron in the Ninth Judicial Circuit, the county seat of which is about twenty or twenty-five miles from the residence of the parties, the county of Madison in the Tenth Judicial Circuit, with Fredericktown, the county seat, about eighteen or twenty miles from the parties, and the county of Bollinger in the Tenth Judicial Circuit, the county seat of which is some twenty or thirty miles from the residence of the parties; that, when the application was made for a change of venue, these facts were suggested to the court, and further, that the parties had both agreed, through their counsel, that the cause might be sent to either Iron or Bollinger, as either of them would suit the convenience of all concerned; and that the respondent, in full view of all these things, sent the case through Bollinger, Cape Girardeau, and Scott,—all in the Tenth Judicial Circuit, —to Mississippi county, over one hundred miles distant: more than five times as far from the parties as either of the counties suggested to him as being suitable, proper, and agreed upon by the parties. And the circumstances will show, moreover, that this outrage upon the rights of the parties was perpetrated with the malicious design of harrassing and oppressing them and their counsel. But the respondent, in his answer to this article, announces the astounding doctrine, *that the court has the right to send a case on change of venue to any county, however remote and inconvenient it may be to the parties.*

Now, sir, if he is really sincere in this position, he will no doubt say he can with perfect impunity send a case from the county of Dunklin to the extreme northwestern county in the State; nay, that he can send every cause in which an application for a change of venue may be presented to him, to the most remote and difficult county that can be found in the State, and still be guilty of no impropriety. If he make this admission, he is also forced to contend that he has a perfect right to inflict upon parties all of the outrageous wrongs that must result from such a course of conduct,—he must claim that he can force them to absent themselves from their business and their families for weeks; that he can impose upon them the difficulties, the dangers, inconvenience, expense, and fatigue of hundreds of miles travel; that he can deprive them of the evidence of their witnesses, and compel them to engage strange counsel, who neither know anything of the witnesses or the facts at issue; in short, that he, by an arbitrary and oppressive ruling, may *compel* them to try their causes before himself, and still be guiltless of any wrong. Yet, who is here so blind as not to see the extreme absurdity of such a position? But, sir, the Legislature of our State, in its wisdom foreseeing that there might possibly be a Judge who would entertain the dangerous and despotic doctrine advanced by the respondent here, or who, to gratify some feeling of vengeance against a personal enemy, might be tempted to subject him to as much trouble and expense as possible, to guard against such a disgraceful abuse of authority, has provided that, in granting changes of venue, the courts *shall* consult the convenience of parties; and it is somewhat astonishing to me that a gentleman so well experienced as this respondent is said to be, in granting changes of venue, should have overlooked this provision of the statute.

In articles four and five similar outrages are charged; but I will not trouble the Court to read them at this time. I am instructed, however, to say to the Court, that, in all these instances, the evidence will show that the respondent, so far from consulting the convenience of the parties, the promotion of their rights, or the furtherance of justice, seemed to exert his ingenuity in ascertaining the particular counties that would be most inconvenient, particularly to the counsel presenting the petition for a change of venue, so as to drive him entirely out of the case; and furthermore, that he spared no pains to insult, annoy, and perplex them, when they ventured to speak in defense of their own rights, and the right of their clients.

The House of Representatives, sir, complains in almost every article of the rude, insulting, tyrannical, and oppressive demeanor of this respondent, towards lawyers practicing in his courts; and the respondent has not only by numerous inuendos in his answer, but whenever he has had occasion to make any remarks to this court, attempted to excite a prejudice against those gentlemen who compose his bar, as well as the profession generally, and to create the impression that, because a man is a practicing lawyer, he is justly subject to all the galling oppression and villainous abuse the Judge under whom he practices may see proper to heap upon him. I am not here, however, to vindicate the profession of which I am an humble member from such insidious and unnecessary attacks—such a thing is not necessary before this honorable court; nor is it my province to pronounce a panegyric upon its character—it needs none at my hands: its panegyric is the history of human civilization. The common law and the constitution of our country, those wonderful achievements of human wisdom, are the monuments that will secure to it the admiration and gratitude of mankind, when the respondent and I shall be known only as common dust.

I claim for the profession of the law no other immunities than are due to the private citizen. They are entitled to no more, but they are entitled to as much. I claim for them as citizens, under the protection of the law, the same respect to which every other citizen is entitled in appearing before the tribunals of his country, and no more; but I do contend that a Judge should not be permitted to shelter himself behind his official authority to insult even the meanest and most obscure. It is unbecoming the character of a gentleman, under any circumstances, wantonly to offer an insult to another, particularly when that other is unable to defend himself; how, then, does it comport with the position of a Circuit Judge, shielded by the panoply of his office, to convert the bench into a theatre for the enactment of such disgraceful scenes as are set forth in the sixth article? Permit me to read it:

ARTICLE VI. That at a Circuit Court begun and held at the town of Poplar Bluff, within and for the county of Butler, on the first Monday in May, A. D. 1858, whereat said Albert Jackson presided as Judge, the said Albert Jackson was willfully guilty of gross and malicious oppression, misconduct, and abuse of official authority, not only unbecoming his high position as Judge, but disgraceful to his character as a man, to wit:

First. During the sitting of the Circuit Court aforesaid, whereat said Jackson presided as Judge as aforesaid, one William G. Phelan, a regularly licensed lawyer, practicing in said court, arose to address a jury that had been empanneled and sworn to try an issue joined in a cause then and there pending, to wit, the cause of Gibson *vs.* Dunn, in which said Phelan had been employed and was acting as counsel; whereupon said Albert Jackson, maliciously intending to oppress said Phelan, and to injure his reputation as a citizen, and diminish his success as a lawyer, in an angry, oppressive, insolent, and insulting manner, ordered him to sit down, and then and there publicly, and in an insulting and contemptuous manner, accused said Phelan of having been guilty of a disgraceful and criminal act, to wit, *tampering with the grand jury,* and that said Phelan was in criminal contempt of court, together with other shameful and insulting expressions.

Second. When said Phelan immediately offered to defend himself against said disgraceful accusations and insulting expressions, said Albert Jackson, under color of his authority as Judge, in an angry, insolent, and oppressive manner, peremptorily ordered said Phelan to shut his mouth and sit down, (or words of that import,) and refused to permit said Phelan to say anything by way of denial, excuse, explanation, palliation, or in any manner to vindicate himself against the disgraceful, criminal charge, thus publicly alleged against him by said Judge in open court.

But, sir, shocking and atrocious as the conduct charged in this article must be to every man of correct principles, it dwindles into utter insignificance when compared to that attributed to the respondent in the one succeeding it, where he is charged with deliberately accusing Mr. Fox of one of the most odious and detestable felonies known to the calendar. I will not venture now to give my opinion upon such conduct, or of a man that would be guilty of it; nor is it necessary for me to remind this Court that, had either of these gentlemen dared to retort upon the respondent in such terms as the character of his assaults upon them justified, entrenched as he was behind his official authority, he would have added injury to insult by fining or sending them to jail. But there must be some redress for this,—some remedy for an evil so gross and palpable,—some protection against a despotism as dangerous as it is mean, petty, and despicable. Where is it? It is here, in the tribunal that protects the purity and integrity of the government,—it is in the High Court of Impeachment that such violence to the rights of the private citizen, by the elevated official, must be tried and punished. The question is submitted to you, whether your judiciary may be made the theatre for the enactment of scenes that would disgrace the lowest resort of vice and blackguardism? whether the bench is to be degraded to the meanest purposes of personal vituperation? whether the citizen who approaches the courts of his country must tamely crouch beneath a burden of abuse and insult that would gall the most servile slave or vilest dog, and the tyrant who heaps these grievous wrongs upon him go unscathed? And this question you must answer to your consciences, your country, and your God.

I now ask leave to call the attention of the Court to the ninth article:

ARTICLE IX. That, utterly unmindful of the provisions of the constitution of the State securing to its citizens "the privilege of the writ of *habeas corpus,*" which the experience of ages has demonstrated to be one of the chief bulwarks of the liberties of the people, the said Albert Jackson, Judge as aforesaid, willfully and maliciously refused to issue a writ of *habeas corpus* for the purpose of having the body of a man named ——— Atterbury, who was confined in jail in the county of Dunklin, on a criminal charge, brought before him, as a Judge of the Circuit Court of said county, to be admitted to bail, or otherwise dealt with according to law, notwithstanding a petition, in every particular sufficient in law for that purpose, was presented to him, the said Jackson, as Judge as aforesaid, at the county of Stoddard, on the — day of ———, A. D. 1858; he, the said Jackson, well knowing it to be his duty to issue said writ, but refusing to do so because the name of David G. Hicks was necessarily mentioned in the petition.

In his answer to this article the respondent becomes exceedingly facetious. I will read the splendid corruscation of wit it occasions:

Said Albert Jackson was not unmindful of the provision of the constitution of the State securing to its citizens the privilege of the writ of *habeas corpus*. Said Jackson does not know the experience of ages has demonstrated that the writ of *habeas corpus* is one of the chief bulwarks of the liberty of the people; *joins issue, and takes the negative of the proposition!*

It is said, sir, that Nero fiddled whilst Rome was in flames, and we can account for the brutal indifference of this cruel tyrant to the suffering, ruin, and misery transpiring around him, on the hypothesis that he was not himself immediately involved in it; but the spectacle of a dignified official, when his own character is made the cynosure of all eyes, making a serious accusation exhibited against him, involving his reputation as a man and as an officer, the subject of a pitiful, puny jest, is a phenomenon in moral science I can only account for upon the theory of mental aberration, or total insensibility to every sentiment of self-regard. It may not, perhaps, be entirely proper for me at this time to remark upon the character and tone of the respondent's answer; but it does seem to me from this response, and others of a kindred nature to be found in his answer, he has either intended it as a matter of contempt to the House of Representatives, who preferred these articles, or to bring this honorable Court into ridicule, by making it the arena for an exhibition of low buffoonery.

He "does not *know* that the experience of ages has demonstrated that the privilege of the writ of *habeas corpus* is one of the chief bulwarks of the liberty of the people!" Perhaps, for his especial edification, I had better cite some authorities that possibly he has overlooked. If he will take the trouble to read Hallam's History of the English Constitution, he will be informed that, in one of the oldest British Year-Books, the writ of *habeas corpus* is denominated "one of the *chief bulwarks* of the English constitution." The gentleman will also find a distinguished essayist upon civil society characterizing the writ of *habeas corpus* as "the *keystone of liberty*, the writ that forces the secrets of all prisons to be disclosed, and the cause of every commitment to be exhibited." Or if he will even recur to the days when he read Blackstone's Commentaries, (for I presume he has at least read that author,) he will remember that distinguished writer names it the "bulwark of the English constitution."

JUDGE JACKSON. Will you please give me the volume and page?

Mr. KNOTT. Fourth book, page 359, I think. And, sir, any English authority upon the subject will teach you that the privilege of the writ of *habeas corpus* was coeval with the common law, and that it was ever esteemed—long before the enactment of the statute of Charles II., known as the "*habeas corpus* act"—one of the most sacred rights of the citizen. And now that it occurs to me, there is another item of intelligence that I would impart to the gentleman, for his special delectation. This celebrated statute of Charles II., so much esteemed by every true friend of human liberty, enacted one hundred and eighty years ago, resulted from the imprisonment of a man as humble as this man Atterbury, confined in jail for contempt of a court over which the king himself presided in person! The unjust refusal of a corrupt, venal court, to issue a writ of *habeas corpus* for the relief of that obscure man, aroused public indignation to such a degree that Parliament found it necessary to embody the salutary provisions of the common law upon this subject, which had been recognized for ages, into a plain statute, that none might, under a pretense of ignorance of them, refuse to grant the relief guarantied by those provisions of law.

But, sir, if the respondent is as ignorant upon this subject as he pretends, and desires to be enlightened as to the esteem in which the citizens of our own country have held this inestimable writ, I will inform him that in 1774, in the passage of the celebrated "Quebec bill," the British Parliament refused to extend to that province the privilege of the writ of *habeas corpus;* and that our Revolutionary Fathers, in their enumeration of grievances for which, in the Declaration of Independence, they declared they no longer owed any allegiance to the British crown, alleged that the citizens of a sister province were deprived of the privilege of this writ. They not only considered it grounds for a revolution, to be accomplished by a sanguiniary and protracted war, but when they came to erect a new government of their own upon the ruins of their colonial allegiance, fearing that men endowed with power might be tempted to deprive the citizen of this cherished right, they provided in the constitution of the United States that the privilege of the writ of *habeas corpus* should never be suspended, except in cases of rebellion or invasion, when the public safety might require it. And the framers of our State constitution, desiring to throw additional safeguards around this privilege of the citizen, incorporated in that constitution the very same provision. When the respondent took upon himself his official obligation, he made a solemn oath to support and maintain both these constitutions in all their purity and force; and yet, when he is charged with a willful violation of one of the plainest and most vital principles they contain, he seeks to insult this dignified tribunal by making a jest of the accusation. I hope, sir, I have vindicated the rhetoric of this article to the satisfaction of the respondent.

But, sir, inestimable as the privilege of the writ of *habeas corpus* is,—indispensable as it is to the complete security of the liberty of the citizen,—and notwithstanding every Judge of the Circuit Court in the State is bound by his oath of office to issue such a writ whenever a proper petition is presented to him therefor, it by no means follows that he has power to turn every prisoner brought before him, on such process, loose upon the community, irrespective of his character, and regardless of his guilt or the legality of his imprisonment.

The Judge is compelled by his oath under the constitution to issue writs of *habeas corpus*, upon the presentation of sufficient facts; and his action in relation to the prisoner, when brought before him, is clearly and definitely defined by law. Were it not so, there would be no certainty or efficacy in our criminal code whatever. The corrupt Judge, guided alone by his own inclinations, and those inclinations influenced by the basest considerations, could with perfect impunity inflict the deadliest injuries upon the well-being of society, by arbitrarily turning loose in its midst the worst of felons, reeking with the most revolting and dangerous crimes. To guard against such a contingency,—such a dangerous assumption of power by the courts,—it is provided in the *habeas corpus* act of this State that,

> When the imprisonment is for a criminal or *supposed* criminal matter, the court or magistrate before whom the prisoner shall be brought under the provisions of this act shall not discharge him for any *informality, insufficiency,* or irregularity of the commitment; but if from the examination taken and certified by the committing magistrate, or *other evidence,* it appear that there is sufficient legal cause for commitment, he shall proceed to take bail, if the offense be bailable, and good bail be offered; if not, he shall commit the prisoner to jail.

Again, sir, it is provided in the very next section that,

> When the offense is clearly and specifically set forth in the warrant of commitment, no evidence other than the examination taken and certified thereunto, shall be received for or against the prisoner, unless such examination has not

been taken and certified according to law, in which case the committing magistrate may be examined, if desired by the prisoner, as to the evidence on which the commitment was found; and thereupon the court or magistrate shall proceed to bail, discharge, or remand the prisoner, as the circumstances of the case may require; and in *the absence of all such evidence the prisoner shall not be discharged, but may be bailed or remanded,* according to the circumstances of the case.

Now, sir, under these provisions of the statute, the duties of a Judge or court, before whom a prisoner may be brought on a writ of *habeas corpus*, are made so plain as to utterly preclude the possibility of mistake.

He is first to examine the warrant of commitment: if that is sufficiently specific to notify him clearly of the charge resting against the accused, he is precluded from the right to examine any testimony for or against the prisoner, except that which is taken and certified with the warrant. If, however, the committing magistrate has failed to reduce the evidence to writing and certify it according to law, the Judge before whom the prisoner is brought may, upon the application of the prisoner, examine the *committing magistrate* as to the evidence upon which he found the commitment; but he can only do this on the application of the prisoner; and if the prisoner do not desire it, the Judge can do no more than examine the warrant, and, if he is charged with a bailable offense, bail him, or if the offense be not bailable, or sufficient bail be not offered, commit him to jail. The statute is plain; there is no discretion.

But, sir, our committing magistrates, as a general thing, are men engaged in the various industrial avocations of life, and being unaccustomed to drafting legal documents, are not to be presumed to be at all times capable of doing so with perfect accuracy. Must every villain charged with crime go unpunished because the magistrate before whom he is examined fails to draft his commitment with perfect formality? or even fails to certify his examination according to law? By no means. The statute I have just read clearly forbids it; yet, notwithstanding these positive enactments of law, it is charged in the tenth article, and I expect it to be clearly proven that, on the 9th day of January, 1859, this respondent, willfully disregarding these plain provisions of the statute, and reckless of the good order and welfare of community, discharged from the custody of the Sheriff of Stoddard county a man who had been arrested and found guilty of grand larceny, simply upon the pretense of an informality in the warrant of commitment by which he was held in custody by the officer; and more, that even this pretext was groundless; that the Sheriff, or Deputy Sheriff, Mr. John J. Jackson, I believe it was, held the prisoner by virtue of a regular warrant of commitment, sufficient in every particular, and clearly and specifically setting forth the crime of which he was charged, a copy of which was not only exhibited to the respondent by Mr. Tyrell, when he presented the petition for a writ of *habeas corpus*, but also by Mr. Jackson, in his return to the writ. You will be shown, by the very order discharging Maine from custody, that the respondent did not predicate that discharge upon a want of reasonable grounds to believe the prisoner guilty, but simply upon a pretended omission or mistake of the magistrate before whom he was examined. But this is not all, sir. It will be shown that upon the very same day the respondent, in open violation of law, turned loose upon that community another felon, who had been examined and committed in default of bail. I feel assured, sir, that the circumstances attending this last case will preclude every other conclusion than that the respondent acted willfully and maliciously corruptly.

A man had been arrested upon a charge of passing counterfeit money, taken before a competent magistrate, and examined. Upon the conclusion of the examination, the magistrate was of opinion there were sufficient grounds to believe him guilty, and held him to bail in the sum of three hundred dollars; but desiring to afford him every opportunity to obtain bail, he placed him in the keeping of Mr. Cryts, Constable of his township, to be secured until the next day at ten o'clock, at which hour he determined to deliver him, with a proper warrant, into the custody of the Sheriff, in case he should fail to obtain security. Before the hour of ten o'clock arrived, however, the respondent issued a writ of *habeas corpus* and discharged the prisoner, *with a full knowledge of all the facts*, simply because Mr. Cryts had not in his possession a warrant of commitment and the examinations. But what makes this case still more glaring, Mr. Cryts procured the examinations and commitment, brought them and presented them to respondent before he had discharged the prisoner, and he refused to look at them; but, bent upon liberating him, regardless of his guilt, turned the scoundrel loose, to curse the country with the commission of additional crimes.

I cannot consistently with what yet remains for me to do in presenting this case to you, dilate upon the outrageous character of the conduct charged in this article, or the consequences of permitting it to go unchecked. Nor will I now advert to the numerous authorities I have before me, touching the law in relation to it; but I will ask this court to contrast the unbecoming leniency to criminals, the recklessness of crime exhibited in these cases, with the disgusting zeal for the enforcement of the criminal law manifested in his conduct before the grand jury of Stoddard county, as shown in the next article:

ARTICLE XI. That at a Circuit Court begun and held at the town of Bloomfield, within and for the county of Stoddard, on the third Monday of November, A. D. 1858, whereat the said Albert Jackson presided as Judge, the said Albert Jackson, disregarding the duties of his office, did descend from the dignity of a Judge, and stoop to the level of a common informer, by calling the attention of the grand jury, empanneled and sworn for that county, at said court, during his public charge to them, to the fact that he, the said Jackson, had understood that a certain citizen of said county had gone to Jefferson City and pretended to transact some business for said county, in relation to obtaining some certified lists of swamp lands; that he had obtained a warrant upon the County Treasury for one hundred and seventy or seventy-five dollars, and that if the facts were as he understood them, they constituted the crime of obtaining money under false pretenses, which was punishable by imprisonment in the penitentiary, and that it was the duty of said grand jury to make diligent inquiry of said case; that the man to whom he alluded was a lawyer, and that they, the grand jury, could find out who it was by asking the County Treasurer who had obtained a warrant for a hundred seventy or seventy-five dollars; whereby everybody there, and those present, understood him, the said Judge, to mean Solomon G. Kitchen, a citizen of said county.

And by appearing before the said grand jury, in their room where they had retired to consider of presentments, and then and there again telling them it was their duty to make diligent inquiry of said facts; and that if they found the facts to be as he had understood them, they should find an indictment against the person who had obtained the warrant, and that Solomon G. Kitchen was the man who had procured the said warrant; thereby rendering his high functions as a Judge subservient to a low personal malice, and seeking, under color of his official duties, to wreak his own private vengeance, by affixing to the reputation of a personal enemy the imperishable disgrace of a public prosecution for a felonious offense.

Sir, throughout this entire catalogue of disgusting and disgraceful malversations in office, none strikes me as more detestable or dangerous than this. Certainly no spectacle more humiliating, and at the same time more alarming, can be presented to the patriotic citizen, than that of a Circuit Judge using his office—that office which of all others should exhibit the most spotless purity—that office to which all should look for safety and protection in the rights guarantied by law—as an engine of private vengeance, as a means of glutting his fiendish hate, his demoniac malice against a personal enemy. How easily, too, he accomplishes his diabolical design, and that without incurring the universal detestation his infamous conduct so justly merits. On the contrary, whilst he is cowardly assassinating the character of an unoffending citizen, he is applauded as a zealous advocate for the supremacy of the law he ruthlessly tramples beneath his unhallowed feet. In his public charge to the grand jury, in the presence of hundreds, he signalizes his victim by name; or, by some damning inuendo more destructive to his reputation, tells them he has been informed that certain facts exist, in relation to the conduct of the object of his vengeance, for which he should be indicted. He dilates upon the information until he is certain the public ear has caught the poison of his breath, and the unhappy man goes forth the object of a thousand furtive glances of suspicion, shunned and avoided by his former friends and neighbors as though he were infected with the deadly plague. Not content with having set in motion the simoon of slander, whose baleful fires will blast the fair fame and consume the happiness of his victim, he follows the grand jury to the privacy of their retirement. There, with the influence his position gives him, by perverting the law and magnifying the facts, he succeeds in fixing upon the devoted object of his hate the imperishable odium of a public prosecution for a felony,—a disgrace that will poison his whole existence, and even survive the premature grave that opens its hospitable portals to hide his sorrows; and when he beholds his weeping wife and little ones, left to wander through a friendless life with the leper-spot of suspicion upon them, with a chuckle of fiendish exultation he folds the "pure ermine of justice" about him and laughs, "ha! ha! revenge is sweet." My God! is there no help for this? May a Judge thus demean himself and there be no remedy? You must answer that question to your constituency.

Sir, when Mr. Kitchen was employed by the County Court of Stoddard county to visit this city on business for that county,—when he had spent his time and money in its service, and had accepted pay for his time and reimbursement of the money he had paid out for the county,—Argus, with his hundred eyes, could not have been more watchful than this respondent. He could permit his zeal for the majesty of the criminal code not only to induce him to condescend to the level of a common informer, but to violate the law both in the manner and substance of his charge to the grand jury. But how different was his conduct at the November term, 1857, of the Butler Circuit Court, when he refused to prefer charges against the Clerk and suspend him from office and appoint a temporary Clerk in his place, notwithstanding he knew the Clerk was in a state of total drunkenness, and in the entire neglect of every duty of his office. Sir, if you will read the twenty-first section of the "act regulating Clerks," you will find that any Clerk, willfully neglecting any duty of his office, shall be deemed guilty of a misdemeanor in office. Read the very next section, and you will see that is the duty of the Judge or court, when he has reason to believe of his own knowledge that a Clerk has been guilty of any misdemeanor in office, to give information to the Attorney General of the charges against the Clerk, suspend him from office, and appoint a temporary Clerk in his place. Now, it is charged in the twelfth article, and we *expect to establish it beyond a doubt, that the respondent knew this* Clerk was guilty of a gross misdemeanor in office; that he was completely intoxicated, and not present at all to keep the minutes of the court, take charge of papers, swear juries, or to perform any of the duties of his office; that the respondent was earnestly requested to exercise the prerogative the law gives him, to suspend the Clerk and appoint a temporary one, but that notwithstanding all this he refused to do so; but on the second day of the term he dismissed the grand jurors against their wills while they were inquiring into important matters, continued all the causes pending, adjourned court, and took possession of the papers pertaining to causes triable and answerable at that term; and when lawyers requested permission to see them, he insultingly refused them, alleging that he was afraid they would be purloined; and that the excuse he gave for this neglect to perform a positive duty enjoined upon him by the statute was, that Mr. Blount, the Clerk, was a *good fellow, and it would be a pity* to turn him out of office! Sir, in this instance an officer willfully neglects his duty, involving the rights and interests of an entire community,—indeed, there is no calculating the real extent of the injury resulting from his misdemeanor,—and the very Judge whose sworn duty it is to see that such derelictions of duty are brought before the proper legal authorities, screens him from justly merited punishment because he is a *good fellow!*—not because he is innocent of any wrong, but because he is a *good fellow!* I suppose, sir, the respondent, from this example of his philanthropy, will justify this Court in concluding that, if one of his friends were arraigned of a brutal assassination, he would endeavor to protect him from the vengeance of the law on account of his being a *good fellow.* A short time since we see him publicly and privately engaged in hounding the grand jury on to a peaceable citizen, because he had made an honorable contract with his County Court—I presume he did not consider Mr. Kitchen a *good fellow!* But, sir, shall this respondent be held guiltless of any offense in thus disregarding the rights and interests of an entire community? I had thought I would not advert to any authorities at this time; but there is one that answers this important question so much better than I can, that I ask leave to read it. I will read from Hawkin's Pleas of the Crown.

SENATOR PARSONS. Will you give the volume and page, that I may save the citation in my notes?

MR. KNOTT. Yes, sir. Book first, chapter sixty-seven. The copy I have in my hand is divided by chapters, but not paged so as to be of easy reference by that means.

In the grant of every office whatsoever, there is this condition implied by common reason, that the grantee ought to exercise it diligently and faithfully; for since every office is instituted, not for the sake of the officer, but for the good of some other, nothing can be more just than that he who either *neglects* or refuses to answer the end for which his office was ordained should give way to others who are both able and willing to take care of it. And therefore *it is certain* that an officer is liable to a forfeiture of his office, not only for doing a thing directly contrary to the design of it, but also for *neglecting to attend to his duty at all usual, proper, and convenient times and places, whereby any damage shall accrue to those by or for whom he was made an officer.*

Sir, the distinguished writer of this could have made no more perfect commentary upon the article under consideration had it been directly referred to him, and I shall attempt no other.

My present strength, and a proper regard for the patience of the Court, will not allow me to attempt an elaborate examination of the remaining articles, even were any remark necessary to convince this learned body of the highly dangerous and reprehensible conduct attributed in them to the respondent. I take it for granted that no amount of argument could possibly heighten the condemnation with which this Senate would regard a Judge of the Circuit Court who, to prevent his decisions from being reviewed, or to oppress a party and deprive him of his rights, would resort to such means to prevent him from getting his cause fairly before the Supreme Court as the respondent is charged with in the fifteenth and sixteenth articles. I need not say that, if the Judges of the Circuit Courts are to be permitted thus to act and be held guiltless,—if they are to be licensed to falsify their records so as to present a case with entirely different features from the one actually tried,—the provision of the constitution providing for the establishment of a Supreme Court and the statute regulating its powers and duties are entirely nugatory; nay, sir, it is worse than useless to maintain such a tribunal at all,—learned, honest, and capable, as I am proud to say those distinguished gentlemen are who now do so much honor to its bench,—if parties are to be prevented from bringing their causes fairly before it, by a corrupt and officious Judge.

But, sir, there are some offenses charged in the seventeenth article that deserve at least a passing notice; and I feel constrained to ask the indulgence of the Court while I briefly direct attention to them. In the first place, he is charged with having visited the grand jury, at the August term, 1858, of the Stoddard Circuit Court, during their retirement, whilst they were considering of presentments, and then and there instructing them that playing cards for whisky, oysters., etc., was not an indictable offense under the statute to prohibit gaming.

Mr. Parsons. I would ask whether you insist that the offense charged in the first paragraph consists in entering the grand jury room, or in giving the charge after entering?

Mr. Knott. I had intended, after enumerating the acts charged in the article, to point out in what the illegality of each consists; but I thank you for calling my attention particularly to the point in passing, for I might have omitted something connected with it. I hold, in the first place, that the respondent was guilty of an offense in visiting the grand jury, in their retirement, for the purpose of instructing them as to their duties. He had no more right to enter the grand jury room to instruct them as to the law, or their duties, than he has to go into a petit jury room and give them instructions privately as to the law governing the particular case they may have under consideration. I claim, also, that he misstated the law; but that is immaterial in my estimation, or at least would be if it were not true, as will be shown, that the grand jury was engaged in the investigation of a charge against the respondent for that very identical offense, when he instructed them that playing cards for whisky, oysters, and so forth, did not constitute an indictable offense.

Judge Jackson. Is it not also charged that I said playing for money?

Mr. Knott. No, sir. You may have given such an instruction, but it is not so charged. In the second place, I maintain that he was guilty of an offense in telling the grand jury that they should not find an indictment against him for anything of which he might be guilty as Judge. This instruction, in direct contravention of law, and revolting to common sense, given not in the face of a scrutinizing public, but in the secrecy of the grand jury room and under the circumstances of personal interest, is of itself a sufficient indication of corruption to condemn him in the estimation of every citizen of correct notions of official duty. But the grand jury, in spite of his charge to the contrary, find a bill against the respondent and others for gambling. One of the parties, claiming a separate trial, is immediately arraigned; and upon this trial the respondent, by no means dispirited by his discomfiture in the grand jury room, takes up the cudgels for the defendant, comments upon the evidence and the nature of the offense, argues the case and illustrates his position by a variety of illustrations, and finally puts the climax to his outrageous misconduct by invading the province of the jury, taking possession of their consciences, and telling them they should not find a general verdict,—that they might find the facts, but he would take upon himself to say whether the defendant was guilty or not under the law; that finally, when the accommodating Circuit Attorney, who was indicted as "*particeps criminis*," proposed to enter a *nolle prosequi*, he opposes no objection whatever. Now, sir, I aver that this conduct is not only disgraceful to the judicial character, but in direct violation of two plain provisions of the statutes. It has always been the custom of the English courts, and is customary for the courts of several of the States of this Union, to sum up and comment upon the evidence adduced before the jury; but this practice, so fraught with wrong, or, to say the least, so dangerous to the rights of parties, has been wisely and justly condemned in our statute, which expressly forbids a Judge to do so, and further provides that the court shall not instruct the jury orally, but in writing, in order that he shall have no power to bias the law without being liable to exposure. Yet, sir, this respondent, in open defiance of provisions of law plain as it is possible for human language to render them, permits his partiality and solicitude for the cause of his friend to precipitate him into abuses of official authority not merely calculated to bring disgrace and the con tempt of all good men upon himself, but to bring the judiciary of the country into disrespect, obloquy, and derision.

I will not enlarge upon the charges contained in the eighteenth article. If the bare recital of them does not send a thrill of horror through every bosom here, I despair of any power I possess as being capable under the most auspicious circumstances, of conveying any adequate impression of their atrocity. Yet, sir, to all these charges, exhibiting an array of crime as various as diabolical ingenuity can invent, and as dark as human depravity can conceive, this respondent avers in answer that they are not sufficient in law to warrant an impeachment! He seeks to soften the horrid aspect of this dark catalogue of crime by giving to it the milder appellations of *errors*, *omissions*, *mistakes*, and *irregularities*; and concludes with the annunciation that, "by the constitution of Missouri, a Judge can only be impeached for misdemeanors in office, and those misdemeanors must first be declared, and the penalty affixed by an act of the Legislature." Here, sir, is the great point of the respondent. It has been the burden of his defense since he made his first appearance at this bar, that the House of Representatives could only impeach him for misdemeanors in office, and that such misdemeanors should first be declared by statute; in other words, that a Judge can only be impeached for a statutable offense, and that offense must relate to his official conduct. It is said to be the prerogative of great men to differ; and certainly, sir, there is a remarkable difference between this respondent and Mr. Story, Mr. Sergeant, and Mr. Rawle, who have all given it as their opinion that, to constitute an impeachable offense, it need not be a statutable or even an indictable one, but, on the contrary, that the greater number of offenses for which an officer may be impeached are such as are not indictable. These are denominated political offenses, and may consist of any misconduct tending to bring the offices of the country into obloquy and disrespect, or to diminish their adaptation to the objects they were designed to accomplish. The involutions of society are so intricate and numerous, and the variety of forms this species of misconduct may assume is so great, that it is impossible to define them by statutory enactment, and consequently it has never been attempted by our Legislatures. For these offenses an officer may be impeached, whilst he cannot be indicted.

For instance, under the constitution of the United States, certain Federal officers may be impeached for "bribery, treason, or other high crimes and misdemeanors." There is no law of the Federal government under which a man may be indicted for drunkenness or profane swearing, even though he be a Judge upon the bench; yet a Judge has been successfully impeached before the Senate of the United States, and broken of his office, for these very offenses. I allude to the case of Judge Pickering, with which every member of this court is doubtless familiar.

Again, sir, if the doctrine laid down by the respondent is true, that a Judge can only be impeached for offenses committed in the discharge of his official duties, he can leave the bench and go upon the street, and there, without cause or provocation, blow out the brains of an unoffending citizen; he may steal his neighbor's horse, or lay his dwelling in ruins with the incendiary's brand, and you cannot impeach him, because he didn't commit the murder, theft, or arson, in the discharge of his official duties! The process of impeachment in this country is merely to remove a man from office, and to disqualify him from holding office,—and it is the only process by which some officers can be removed from office; and if you can only impeach such as have been guilty of some official misconduct, you may have your judiciary polluted with murder, arson, theft, robbery, and every other description of villainy you can imagine, without the power of correcting the evil! I must really ask pardon of Court for pretending to combat a position so ridiculously absurd.

But, sir, grant the respondent the full benefit of his position,—admit that a Judge can only be impeached for official misconduct,—and I am prepared to show, not only by the common law authorities which I have now here before me, but by the statutes of the State, that in every article he is accused of one or more offenses—statutable, indictable offenses, if you please—for which, if established, he should be hurled in disgrace from the seat he has so foully polluted. Read the sixteenth section of the sixth article of the act concerning crimes and their punishments:

Every person holding or exercising any office or public trust, who shall be guilty of willful and malicious oppression, partiality, misconduct, or abuse of authority in his official capacity or under color of his office, shall on conviction be punished by imprisonment in a county jail for a term not exceeding one year, and fine not exceeding one thousand dollars.

So, sir, wherever this respondent is accused of willful and malicious oppression,—wherever he is accused of partiality,—wherever he is accused of abuse of authority under color of his office,—wherever he is accused of any official misconduct, he is accused of an indictable, statutable offense, for which, according to his own showing, he is properly impeached at this bar.

Sir, the House of Representatives have discharged their duty in relation to this matter. They investigated the charges here submitted to you, calmly and dispassionately, as honest, earnest men, in full view of the obligation under which they rested to themselves and their country, and deliberately determined that this respondent should be put upon his trial for the offenses I have enumerated. In doing so, they entertained the highest confidence that this distinguished tribunal would receive this cause in a spirit commensurate with its importance, and investigate it with that dignity, ability, and justice you are known to possess; and I am satisfied this Court will justify this distinguished confidence upon the part of the House of Representatives, by doing full and complete justice both to the State and to the respondent; that, if the respondent is guilty, whatever may be his position or influence in the social circle, you will strip him of the robes of office he has polluted; if innocent, you will give him the plaudit, "well done, thou good and faithful servant,"—there is no spot in thee.

The opening speech of Mr. Knott having been concluded, on motion of SENATOR SCOTT, the Court adjourned.

THIRD DAY.

WEDNESDAY, June 8, 1859.

The Court met at 8 o'clock, and was opened by proclamation.

The managers and respondent attended.

SENATOR WILSON moved a call of the Senate, which was ordered, and the following named Senators were noted as being absent without leave: Messrs. Fox, Hyer, Johnson, Jones, Rains, Robinson, Thompson, and Watkins.

Several of the absentees appearing directly after the call, on motion of Senator Wilson, further proceedings under the call were dispensed with.

MR. PRESIDENT. Are the parties ready to proceed in the examination of witnesses?

JUDGE JACKSON. In my list of witnesses are J. Proc. Knott and Chas. H. Hardin. As a rule has been adopted requiring the exclusion of all my witnesses while the State's witnesses are on the stand, and as the managers themselves urged this rule, I can only ask that it be enforced, and they be excluded. It is for the Senate to say whether it will enforce its rule. I cannot be held responsible for a violation of the rule if the Senate permits it after I call attention to the fact that any of my witnesses are present.

MR. PRESIDENT. I suppose the rule cannot be held to apply to the managers sent here by the House of Representatives.

SENATOR SCOTT. I concur with the opinion expressed by the Chair. Messrs. Knott and Hardin are not here by virtue of any process, by subpena or otherwise, of this Court. They are here in discharge of a duty imposed upon them by the House of Representatives, and the Senate has no power to expel them, although it may have adopted a rule on the subject which may seem to include them. If this Senate had the power and could be called upon in this way to exclude the managers, the ends of justice could be most readily defeated, and this trial would be a perfect farce. Senators might with the same propriety and by the same means be excluded from all participation in the trial. It is my opinion that this question ought not to have been raised here, and I hope it will not be urged.

SENATOR WILSON. I agree, entirely, Mr. President, with the Senator from Buchanan, in the views he has just expressed. The rule adopted by the Senate for the exclusion of witnesses is of the same nature as the common ruling of courts of justice on the point, and could have no greater effect or operation. It certainly was never the practice to exclude attorneys of record from courts by means of a subpena. If the Senate were now to attempt an exclusion of the managers, it would seem that this body was in contempt of the coördinate branch of the Legislature. There can be but one opinion on this subject, and I hope it will be dropped, and the case proceed.

JUDGE JACKSON. It is no affair of mine if the Senate cannot and will not enforce its own rulings. The gentlemen have laid a trap, and it turns out that they have caught themselves in it. The position may be embarrassing to them, but it is no fault of mine.

SENATOR PARSONS. Are Messrs. Knott and Hardin your witnesses, Judge Jackson?

JUDGE JACKSON. Yes, sir. They have been subpenaed for me. And they have asked and obtained a rule for the exclusion of all the witnesses on both sides from the start. It is the first time I ever heard of such a course. It would be right, I admit, to separate the witnesses of the State, while they are giving testimony, and equally right to separate my witnesses when the time comes for them to testify. That is the way the thing is done in the courts, and it's the way the Senate provided by rule at the start. But the managers have altered it so as to exclude all the witnesses all the time, and if their own rule works hard with them, they have only themselves to blame. I merely ask for the operation of their own rule. If the Senate does not enforce it, I shall simply think it a hard case, and say, as I said before, that it would be better to go back to the rule at first adopted by the Senate.

SENATOR GOODLETT. For the purpose of saving time, Mr. President, I offer this resolution:

Resolved, That the managers be excepted from the rule requiring the exclusion of witnesses.

I do not hold that a resolution of this kind is necessary to except the managers, because I believe they are already expressly excepted by law. But there is no telling to what length this and similar discussions may be spun out if some decisive action is not taken.

Senators McFerran, McFarland and others, said that the resolution was the unanimous sense of the Senate, and it was unnecessary to vote upon it; whereupon it was withdrawn.

Mr. PRESIDENT. There being nothing before the Court, I presume we are ready to proceed with the examination of witnesses.

Mr. KNOTT. We are ready to proceed.

TESTIMONY OF M. H. TYRELL.

M. H. TYRELL called on the part of the State, and examined by Mr. Knott:

Question. Mr. Tyrell, where do you reside?

Answer. In Bloomfield, Stoddard county, Missouri.

Q. What is your profession?

A. I am a lawyer.

Q. Are you acquainted with Judge Jackson, and have you practiced in his courts?

A. I am acquainted with Judge Jackson, and have practiced in his courts.

Q. Were you present at a Circuit Court held by Judge Jackson in Bloomfield, commencing on the third Monday in May, 1858?

A. I was.

Q. Were you present in that court during the proceedings in a case of mandamus against Jonas Eaker? Did you witness the proceedings when the case was called?

A. I am not certain that I was present when the writ of mandamus issued, but I was present when Mr. Eaker was brought in by attachment, and I understood the attachment to have issued in consequence of his failure to make a return to the mandamus.

Q. You will please state to the Court what you may know in relation to the acts and conduct of Judge Jackson upon that occasion?

JUDGE JACKSON. I object. When any evidence of the acts or doings of a court of record are sought to be used, no oral testimony is admissible.

Mr. KNOTT. Well, sir, produce your authorities. We hold that there are thousands of matters which occur in a court of record, which are not matters of record, and which can be proved by oral testimony.

JUDGE JACKSON. Are you through? If so, I will proceed to make my concluding argument on the objection.

Mr. KNOTT. My understanding of the rules governing the argument of objections to testimony is this: The party making an objection states his reasons and cites the authorities and law upon which he relies in asking that his objection be sustained. The other party then answers; and the objecting party is entitled to the conclusion without a right to introduce any new matter. Now, in the case in hand, if the respondent has any objection to the testimony sought to be elicited by the question propounded to the witness, let him state it distinctly and specifically, together with the authorities which he conceives will support his position. We will reply as we think proper, and he can conclude. Such is the rule and the operation of the rule in every court I have ever known anything about, and such I presume is the rule here.

JUDGE JACKSON. I don't admit the right of the gentleman to prescribe the manner in which I shall make my argument. I am going to suit myself about that. I say that you can't offer oral testimony of the acts and doings of a court of record. Mr. Knott says I must not make this objection without the authorities. But authority for such a position as that is hardly needed. But if the Senate wants to have authorities, they are abundant.

Mr. KNOTT. If Judge Jackson will give way a moment, I propose to take the sense of the Senate in regard to this matter of opening and closing arguments. It would be as well to settle the matter at once, and prevent delay and dispute hereafter.

JUDGE JACKSON. I was proceeding to do just what Mr. Knott says he wants. I will rely upon the case of Bompart *vs.* Boyer, 8 vol. Supreme Court Reports, page 234. Also a case in 12 Missouri Reports, page 598. I have stated my objection to the question.

Mr. KNOTT. In order to prevent any future difficulty or misunderstanding, I offer for the action of the Senate an order which I will read:

Ordered, That whenever the managers or the respondent shall make any objection to the introduction of any testimony, the admissibility of evidence, or to any other proceeding whatever, during the trial, the party so objecting shall, in his opening, state distinctly the grounds of such objection, together with his authorities. The opposite party shall then be heard in reply, and the party making the objection shall be entitled to conclude; but in his conclusion he shall not be permitted to introduce any new matter.

After some little explanation, the foregoing order was made and entered on the record by the following vote:

AYES—Messrs. Brown, Byrne, Churchill, Coleman, Frazier, Goodlett, Halliburton, Harris, Hedgpeth, Horner, McFarland, McFerran, McIlvaine, Morris, Newland, O'Neil, Peyton, Rains, Richardson, Scott, Wilson, Wood, and Wright—23.

NOES—Messrs. Gullett, Parsons, and Vernon—3.

Absent—Messrs. Fox, Hyer, Johnson, Jones, Robinson, Thompson, and Watkins.

Mr. Knott. That we may proceed in this matter regularly, I have reduced to writing the question to which Judge Jackson objects, as follows:

Question. State what occurred in court during the pendency of the case of mandamus to Jonas Eaker; all the facts and circumstances you observed touching the behavior of the Judge and others concerned in the case.

To this question, (continued Mr. Knott,) we ask that the respondent state specifically his objections, and the grounds of it, with his authorities, under the rule just adopted by the Court.

Judge Jackson. Well, I object to this question because it asks for oral testimony concerning my acts and doings as a court. Of such things the only admissible evidence is the record. If they want anything of the kind, they must bring the record. I refer to the statutes. By reference to the twenty-third section of the "act to establish courts of record, and prescribe their powers and duties," it will be seen that a Circuit Court is a court of record, and in the twenty-fourth section a very full record of all the proceedings and rulings of such a court is provided for. Now let us see what the Supreme Court has said in regard to evidence of doings of a court of record. I have referred to the case of Bompart *vs.* Boyer, in 8 Mo. Rep., page 234. I will read the opinion of Judge Tompkins in that case:

Pelagie Boyer sued Louis Bompart in the Court of Common Pleas of St. Louis county, where judgment being given for her, Bompart appealed to this court.

Much evidence was given on each side, and two instructions asked by the appellant were refused. No exception was taken to the refusal of the court to give these instructions.

The court, after the evidence was given in, gave several instructions, none of which were excepted to. After the jury had brought in their verdict, the defendant moved the court for a new trial, for the usual reasons: First, that the verdict is against evidence, and against the instructions of the court; and the court gave erroneous instructions, and refused the defendant's instructions.

In the first place, as these instructions given were not excepted to, and as the refusal to give the defendant's instructions was not excepted to, it must not now be expected to reverse the judgment of the Court of Common Pleas on that account.

There was much conflicting evidence, and all the instructions given by the court were hypothetical.

It is impossible for this court to know what the jury believed. They might well have believed facts to justify their finding, under the instructions of the court. The verdict of the jury appearing to be supported by the evidence in the cause, and no exceptions being taken to the giving or refusing of instructions by the Court of Common Pleas, the judgment must be affirmed.

This case is not so directly in point as the one which follows it. I believe I meant to read the following case, and will now do so. It is the case of Medlin *vs.* Platte county:

1. A., as principal, and J. and M., as securities, executed their note to Platte county, for money borrowed. It appeared, upon the trial, that the name of J., one of the securities, had been erased from the note, and M., the other security, offered to prove that the County Court of that county, while in session, *verbally* ordered the name of J. to be erased, without the consent of M. *Held:* That this evidence was inadmissible; that the records of the County Court are the evidence of their official acts; and that all orders not entered of record, are extra-judicial and void.
2. There is a distinction betweed the *alteration* and the *spoliation* of an instrument, as to the legal consequences. The first is usually applied to the act of the party entitled under the instrument, and imputes some fraud or design, on his part, to change its effect; the other refers to the unauthorized act of a stranger, and does not change the legal operation of the writing, so long as the original remains legible, and, if it be a deed, any trace remains of the seal.

TOMPKINS, Judge, delivered the opinion of the court.

The State of Missouri sued Hall Medlin and others in debt.

The action was brought on an instrument of writing by which Medlin and two others promised to pay to the State $500. There were several counts in the declaration, in some of which the plaintiff declared on the instrument of writing sued on, as a sealed instrument, and in others as an unsealed writing. The two other co-defendants being otherwise disposed of, a verdict and judgment went against Hall Medlin in said count, and to reverse it he appealed to this court.

The bill of exceptions shows, that the instrument of writing sued on was given to the county of Platte for so much money borrowed from it by the defendants, of whom John Allen was principal, and Stephen Johnson and Hall Medlin, the present defendant, were securities, and that Johnson's name was erased.

James H. Johnson, the first witness, introduced by the plaintiff below, states, that by request he wrote the instrument of writing sued on, and saw said Allen and Johnson sign it, and that immediately after they went to the court-house, the court being then in session; that he was Treasurer of the county; that a day or two afterwards the note was handed to him by the Deputy Clerk, and that about a week after he gave the Clerk of the County Court a receipt for said note or writing. He further states, that his recollection is not distinct, but he thinks the name of Johnson was erased from said note at the time he received it. The Deputy Clerk, who handed the writing to the Treasurer, thought that Johnson's name was not erased when he passed said writing to James H. Johnson, the Treasurer; and the Treasurer succeeding to Johnson stated that he never heard of the erasure of Johnson's name till he parted with the possession, and that he did not believe it was erased before he parted with it. No order was found on the records of the County Court to authorize either the loan to Allen, on the security of Johnson and Medlin, or the erasure of the name of Stephen Johnson.

John B. Collier, a witness of the defendant, stated, that when said instrument of writing was accepted by the County Court of Platte county, he was a member of that court; that when the writing was handed to the court the names of the three makers were signed and affixed thereto; that he did not recollect how long, after its reception by the court, it was until the name of Johnson was erased; that no order was made accepting said Medlin and Johnson as securities for Allen, but they were received verbally by the court.

The defendant then offered to prove, by this witness, that the said County Court, whilst in session, and in open court, agreed verbally that the name of said Johnson might be erased from said note, and that it was erased accordingly by the authority of said court, without the knowledge or consent of Medlin. This testimony was rejected by the Circuit Court, and the decision of the court was excepted to.

The evidence being closed, the Circuit Court, on the motion of the plaintiff, instructed the jury that the erasure of the name of Johnson could not release Medlin unless it were made by the order of the County Court, while in session. This is the substantial part of four instructions demanded by the plaintiff.

The defendant asked the four following instructions:

1. That if the name of the said Johnson has been erased from said writing since the execution and delivery thereof, it is incumbent on the plaintiff to prove that it was done by accident or mistake, or by the consent of Medlin, and that in the absence of such proof they must find for Medlin.

2. That if the County Court of Platte county, whilst in session, gave leave to said Johnson, or to any other person, to erase the name of said Johnson from said writing, and that it was in pursuance of such leave erased therefrom, and that it was done without the consent of Hall Medlin, then the jury will find for said Medlin; and that it is not necessary that the order of the court, in order to be binding on the plaintiff, should have been entered on the record book of the court, and that the same may, at any subsequent term of said court, be entered, *nunc pro tunc.*

3. That if the County Court of Platte county, whilst in session, ordered Johnson's name to be erased from the note, and the erasure was made in pursuance of such order, and without Medlin's consent, then they will find for him, said Medlin, whether that order was entered of record or not, and that it is the duty of the plaintiff to show that the alteration was not made by the plaintiff, or by any of the agents of said plaintiff.

4. That if the jury believe the name of said Johnson has been erased from said note, since its execution and delivery to the plaintiff, and that it was done either by the plaintiff, or by any other person than Medlin, and without his consent, then the note as to him is void, whether the erasure was made with or without the consent of the plaintiff. These instructions were refused, and exceptions were taken to the decision of the court.

A new trial was moved for, for several reasons, which may be resolved into one—that the court refused to give the instructions.

The defendant also moved in arrest of judgment.

Even had the defendant stood on his demurrer to the declarations, (which he withdrew,) there could have been no reason to reverse the judgment for a misjoinder. Chitty, in the first volume of his pleading, says, that debt on a bond, or other specialty, may be joined in the same action with debt on simple contract.

With regard to the instructions charged to have been erroneously given by the Circuit Court, it may be observed, that, like other bodies corporate, and also like persons, it will be presumed to accept whatever is for its interest to receive, until it in some way signifies its dissent; but it will be presumed to part with none of its rights till it has expressed its will on its records: the evidence then offered, *i. e.*, the testimony of one of the Judges, to prove that the several members of that court, while in session, assented to the erasure of Johnson's name, &c., was inadmissible. The Judges of the County Court could express their assent to such an act on their record only; and it will then only be in season for this court to decide whether such an entry of assent can be made *nunc pro tunc*, when such an entry shall have been made by the County Court, but no such entry being now made, this court must proceed as if it had never heard anything of the assent of the Judges in open court.

The only question remaining, then, for this court to decide, is, whether the instrument here sued on became void in consequence of the erasure of Johnson's name.

In Greenleaf on Evidence, it is said, that the early decisions establish the general proposition, that written instruments which are altered, in the legal sense of that term, are thereby made void. The grounds of this doctrine are two-fold. The first is, that of public policy, to prevent fraud, by not permitting a man to take the chance of committing a fraud, without running any risk of losing by the event when it is detected. The other is, to insure the identity of the instrument, and prevent the substitution of another, without the privity of the party concerned.

A distinction, however, is to be observed, between the alteration and spoliation of an instrument, as to the legal consequences. The term alteration is, at this day, usually applied to the act of the party entitled under the deed, or instrument, and imports some fraud or improper design on his part to change the effect. But spoliation or mutilation of the instrument, not changing its legal operation, so long as the original writing remains legible, and, if it be a deed, any trace of the seal remains. If, by the unlawful act of a stranger, the deed is mutilated or defaced, so that its identity is gone, the law regards the act, so far as the rights of the parties to the instrument are concerned, merely as the accidental destruction of primary evidence, compelling a resort to that which is secondary. Thus, if it be a deed, and the party would plead it, he cannot plead it with a profert, but the want of profert must be excused by an allegation that the deed, meaning its legal identity as a deed, has been accidentally, and without the fault of the party, destroyed; and whether it be a deed, or any other instrument, its original tenor must be substantially shown, and the alteration or mutilation accounted for.—See pages 600, 601.

The old doctrine, that every material alteration of a deed, even by a stranger, and without the privity of either party, avoided the deed, was strongly condemned by Story, Judge, in United States *vs.* Spalding, (2 Mason, 478,) as repugnant to common sense and justice; as inflicting on an innocent party all the losses occasioned by mistake, by accident, by the wrongful acts of third persons, or by the providence of heaven; and which ought to have the support of unbroken authority, before a court of law was bound to surrender its authority to what deserved no better name than a technical quibble.—See note to the same page of Greenleaf.

Under this law, as declared in the authority cited, (and there are many others cited,) the county cannot be called on to prove the erasure of Johnson's name. The County Court, the representative of the county, has entered up no order to that effect; it has made no order even, commanding its agent, the Treasurer, to do so; the Deputy Clerk, who delivered the writing sued on to the Treasury, says he does not believe that the erasure was made when he delivered the writing to the Treasurer, Johnson, and although Johnson says he believes the name was erased when he received the instrument from the Deputy Clerk, yet the Treasurer who succeeded to Johnson testifies that the name was not erased, as he believes, when the instrument of writing passed from his hands. More satisfactory evidence could not be required of a person; but in this case the plaintiff is a body corporate, speaking by its record only, and none of its agents have authority to make such an erasure; two of those agents testify that the writing passed from them undefaced.

But if those agents ever had defaced this instrument of writing, their act could have been no other than the act of a stranger, they having no authority to do the act, and no interest in the money due by the writing. The note was, then, admissible evidence, and the judgment must be affirmed.

Senators will see (continued Judge Jackson) the application of this law without any comment from me. I will now turn to the case in 12 Mo. Reports, page 598. It is directly in point. It was here decided that "what a court of record does is known alone by its record; its doings and proceedings cannot be established by parol testimony." Judge Ryland delivered the opinion of the Court, which I will read:

This was a proceeding commenced originally in the Marion County Court, taken thence by appeal to the Marion Circuit Court, and now brought before this court by writ of error.

From the record it appears that on the 23rd day of April, 1847, the plaintiff, James V. Milan, as administrator of the estate of Anthony Crockett, deceased, caused a notice in writing to be served on the defendant, Richard Pemberton, as the executor of Jane Wilcox, deceased, informing him that on the first Monday, being the third day of May next, he, as administrator as aforesaid, would make application to the County Court of said county for an allowance against the estate of Jane Wilcox, deceased, on a note of which the following is a copy, (viz:) "Twelve months after date we or either of us promise to pay Col. Anthony Crockett, or order, two hundred dollars for value received. Witness our hands and seal, this 3rd day of October, 1833.

October, 1833. JANE WILCOX.

Witness: A. Crockett."

At the July term of said County Court in 1847, judgment was rendered on this application for allowance in favor of the defendant. The plaintiff appealed therefrom, and the proceedings were duly certified to the Circuit Court, and at March term, 1848, judgment in that court was again rendered in favor of defendant.

From the evidence preserved in the bill of exceptions, it appears that Jane Wilcox being anxious to obtain the sum of $200, prepared the note of which the above is a copy, and applied to Col. Anthony Crockett for the loan of that sum. Col. Anthony Crockett did not lend the money to her, but William R. Crockett did, and took the note, which she had thus prepared as above, from her, from the payment, without any alteration; that is, took the note payable to Col. Anthony Crockett, instead of to himself, being the note first prepared.

Thus the matter remained for several years. In 1838 Col. Anthony Crockett died. Jane Wilcox died in the early part of the year 1843. Letters testamentary were granted on her estate, dated 20th March, 1843, and notice calling upon the creditors to exhibit their demands for allowance against her estate, was duly published in pursuance of the statute in such case provided, dated March 30th, 1843, and appeared on that day in the *Missouri Courier*, a public newspaper.

This application for allowance was made at the May term, 1847, of Marion County Court, and notice thereof was served on the 23d day of April, 1847, after a lapse of more than *four years*, from the date of the letters testamentary, and from the publication of the notice to creditors. On the trial in the Circuit Court, the plaintiff, in order to show that his claim was not barred by the statute which requires claims and demands to be exhibited within three years, proved "that on the 7th day of July, 1845, the note now sued on was presented to the County Court for allowance; that it was so presented at the instance of William R. Crockett; that Richard Pemberton, administrator of Jane Wilcox, the defendant, appeared therein before said court and waived notice, and several witnesses were examined to prove the signature of the said Wilcox, but not being able to prove the signature, the attorney, John D. S. Dryden, suffered a nonsuit, and withdrew the claim; *that no trace of said proceeding before the County Court appears of record.*"

The defendant objected to all the evidence touching the presentation of said claim to the County Court; but the court overruled the objection and heard the evidence, and the defendant excepted to this opinion of the court. The plaintiff showed his letters of administration granted on the estate of Col. Anthony Crockett, deceased, dated 23rd day of November, 1846, eight years after the death of said Crockett.

The plaintiff moved the court to decide, that if it appeared from the evidence in the cause that the note sued on was presented for allowance to the County Court in July, 1845, and that Pemberton, as administrator of Wilcox, appeared there, and waived notice of the demand; and the claim was subsequently withdrawn; that this constituted a legal exhibition of the demand. That the limitation of three years did not commence running till the date of the letters of administration on Anthony Crockett's estate; and that an administrator is not barred by the statute of limitations. All of which the court overruled: the plaintiff excepted. The court found a verdict for defendant. The plaintiff moved to set aside the verdict and grant him a new trial, which the court overruled; and now plaintiff seeks to reverse this judgment of the Circuit Court.

In our statutes concerning executors and administrators, article 4th, sections 5, 6, 12, 13, and 14, we shall find what the law contemplates as an exhibition of a demand. Section 5th is in these words: "Every person may exhibit his demand against such estate by serving upon the executor or administrator a notice in writing, stating the nature and amount of his claim, with a copy of the instrument of writing or account upon which the claim is founded, and such claim shall be considered legally exhibited from the time of serving such notice."

Section 6. "Every executor and administrator shall keep a list of all demands thus exhibited, classing them, and make return thereof to the County Court every year, at the term at which he is to make settlement."

Section 12. "Every person desiring to establish a demand against any estate, shall deliver to the executor or administrator a written notice, containing a copy of the instrument of writing or account on which it is founded, and stating that he will present the same for allowance at the next term of the County Court."

Section 13. "Such notice shall be served on the executor or administrator ten days before the beginning of such term of the court, and may be served by any Sheriff or Constable, or by any competent witness, who shall make affidavit to such service."

Section 14. "The executor or administrator may appear in open court and waive the service of any such notice."

From the testimony in this case, it is apparent that the plaintiff relied upon what was done by him under the last cited clause of the statute. He proved before the court, that he had offered this claim for allowance in the County Court at July term, 1845, and that the defendant waived the notice in open court. That the claim was not sufficiently proved and was withdrawn. There was an objection to this proof by parol; there was no trace of any such proceeding on the record of the County Court. The testimony was offered before the court, and as there was no jury, it was right and proper for the court to hear the testimony first before it could determine upon its legality. The effect of this testimony, its admissibility, its competency, were brought before the court by the plaintiff's instruction. We have no doubt that such evidence was improper; it was entirely inadmissible. No case has been found, where a party has been permitted to prove before one court of record what he did, what proceedings were had and done before another court of record in a judicial investigation, by mere parol testimony. The acts, doings, judgments and proceeding of courts of record are known by the records of these courts. Such proceedings may often be amended; may be altered to suit the true state of facts; but there is always something to alter or amend by. Here there is an attempt not to alter or amend, but to make out a new subject matter altogether, and that too by the testimony of witnesses. It is admitted that there is no trace of any such proceeding as the one here proved by witnesses upon the records of the County Court.

There is no proof of the waiving of notice but by parol. Why does the statute permit this waiver of notice only to be done in open court? Because it then is put on record among the proceedings of the court in adjudicating upon the claim. Had this waiver of notice been made in open court, and put on the records of the court, or on the back of the note, or on any part of the demand or claim, we should feel inclined to receive it as evidence of such an exhibiting of the claim as might warrant the court in taking it out of the statute of limitations.

I feel satisfied that there was no evidence (that is, legal evidence) of any such exhibition of this claim, as is required by law, before the County Court of Marion in July, 1845; and consequently the Circuit Court committed no error in refusing the instructions first asked for by the plaintiff.

I see no reason why the statute of limitations should not run against an executor or administrator.

But in this case William R. Crockett might have presented this claim against the estate of Mrs. Wilcox at any time he might have thought proper. He was the bona fide holder of the note, and the real owner. He loaned the money to Jane Wilcox, and he might have used the name of Anthony Crockett any time before his death in order to collect this money; and from the parol evidence which was offered, we see that in 1845, after his death, and before administration, was presented the note in the County Court.

He waived and delayed too long. The Circuit Court committed no error in finding for the defendant, no error in overruling the motion for a new trial, and the judgment is affirmed.

I rely upon the law as decided by the Supreme Court in these cases. It leaves no room to question the propriety of my objection to the attempt made here to prove by parol testimony my acts as a court, in the face of the declaration of the Supreme Court that what a court of record does is known alone by its record, and that its doings and proceedings cannot be established by parol testimony. I shall leave the matter here till I hear from the managers.

Mr. Knott. May it please the Court, I can hardly deem the positions assumed by the respondent as worthy of a serious reply. It is true that as long as a court keeps itself within the scope of its legitimate functions as a court, any act or fact which is made a matter of record must be evidenced by the record. But this principle can have no application in the present case. The conduct of the Judge in court, concerning which we are inquiring, is not a matter of record. It cannot properly be made a matter of judicial record, and for this simple reason it is not to be proved by record evidence. Now, for instance, if the fact were in issue whether a writ of mandamus to Jonas Eaker had ever issued, or if the inquiry was as to what judgment was entered by the court, there would be some point in the objection of the respondent. But we are investigating a matter of a very different nature, the history of which could not be detailed in the record. We want to know something of the conduct of the Judge upon the bench—his demeanor, his bearing and language. Suppose that in this or any other State a Judge were impeached for appearing on the bench in a state of beastly intoxication, and that he had been acting as Judge while in that disgraceful condition; would the fact that a statement of that condition did not appear on the records of the court estop the prosecution? Will it be said that a Judge may arise in his seat and pour a volley of villainous vituperation upon the devoted head of some unoffending party, and yet that the only evidence of the fact in a Court of Impeachment would be the record of the court where such a thing was done? I repeat that if the respondent had, by his answer or otherwise, put in issue the fact of the issuing the mandamus, we would go to the record for proof on that point. Nobody controverts the position, and every reasonable man must be confident, that a judicial proceeding can be proved alone by the record. But suppose a charge of the obliteration of the record were under investigation; suppose the

7

Judge was charged with burning it up—who will tell us that the only competent evidence must be found in that very record? Such a thing is absurd in the extreme. The existence of a certain judgment, the filing of an answer, or demurrer, the disposition of the same—all such proceedings are made a part of the record, and to such the authorities cited by the respondent refer. But there are a thousand other matters which have no place on the record; and in a proceeding of this kind it becomes necessary to establish more or less of them. The facts alleged by us concerning the matters appearing of record are not controverted by the respondent; if they were, we would seek record proof. In the cases of Judges Peck and Chase, all questions of this nature—concerning the conduct of the accused—were investigated by means of parol testimony. In fact that is the only legitimate source of evidence on such points. In almost every impeachment case that ever occurred, it is not so much the irregularity of the action of the accused which has been complained of, as the malice involved in that irregularity; and the existence or non-existence of malice is the vital point upon which the bare record of judicial proceedings will generally be silent. To sustain the objection of the respondent in this instance would not only be a palpable violation of the plainest rules governing the admissibility of evidence, but would be a virtual denial of the right to impeach a Judge at all, for it would render a successful impeachment almost impossible. But I will leave my colleague to discuss this matter further if he sees proper. As for myself, I think it too plain for argument.

Mr. Hardin. May it please the Court, I do not think it at all necessary to debate the question raised now by the respondent. He demands record evidence, and of what? There is nothing as to the record involved in the question propounded to the witness. We have alleged that he oppressed Judge Eaker willfully and maliciously. We desire to show his malevolence by his acts, and to this end the question is directed. It is true that the record is evidence of the facts appearing of record, and we expect to have use for such proof. We may even have to show that the records in some cases do not state facts, because they have been mutilated or falsified. But all that has nothing to do with the present testimony, to which I cannot see that there is the shadow of a sensible objection. I entirely concur with my colleague in the view expressed by him of the authorities cited by the respondent. They establish the principle that a record fact must be proved by the record, and not by parol testimony. They go no farther, and they have no application to the case in hand.

Senator Parsons. Before the respondent proceeds with his concluding remarks on the question now before the Court, I would like to turn his attention to a question arising in my mind, and which I conceive has some bearing upon the matter in controversy. I find in the answer of the respondent, under the head of Article I, the following:

First. He wholly and fully denies that at the May term of the Circuit Court of Stoddard, begun on the third Monday in May, 1858, in said county, in his official capacity, or under color of his office, he did willfully and maliciously conduct himself in a manner highly oppressive and unjust to one Jonas Eaker.

To specification *first* of said article, said Albert Jackson says that he did not desire to oppress and harrass said Jonas Eaker, and did not maliciously and unjustly cause to be issued against said Eaker an attachment as for a criminal contempt; that, in his official capacity, he knew nothing about the manner in which said writ of mandamus had been executed on said Eaker, etc.

Now, the question I ask Judge Jackson is, whether he intended by this to set up the plea of *nul tiel record*, or whether he only intended to negative the allegation of *malice* and oppression set forth in the articles of impeachment?

JUDGE JACKSON. Yes, sir. I will speak of that directly. I can't help but admit that I feel very much embarrassed, not so much by anything here to be done, as by the way the proceedings against me are conducted. Now, I am charged with *official* misconduct. I have labored from the start to find out what *official* misconduct I am charged of being guilty of. The articles did not tell me, and nothing told me, and in the whole speech of Mr. Knott I was not told what official acts were complained of. It did come out, though, that this whole thing is founded upon a little section of the criminal code about misdemeanors in office. There it is held I am liable to indictment for misdemeanors in office. I don't suppose that any Judge would look at this little statute like Mr. Knott. He advances the most astounding doctrine. You Senators, for your official acts, are indictable, according to Mr. Knott. But that is not all. How would he prove you guilty of official misconduct? Not by the statutes you pass—not by your journal of proceedings—but by oral testimony. He would arraign you and prove by oral testimony all about your tone of voice, demeanor, and personal acts. He can do this just as well as he can arraign a court of record with oral testimony for official misconduct. What are the official acts of a Judge? Why, they are the doings, acts, and judgments that are recorded in the records of the court. But Mr. Knott says the acts he complains of are not in the record. That is the truth at last. I knew all the time that it would turn out so; it is not in the record. All these accusations are really about things that were not official—personal and individual objections to me. Not a single witness and not a juror complains; but it is only some dissatisfied persons who dislike me personally, and they are brought up here to swear against me, in some instances I doubt not for pay. Now the question is, can you try me for things that are not official, and not on the record? They want to go outside of the record to come at my tone of voice. If I have been guilty of any improper, indecorous, or impolite conduct, I would not shrink from an investigation of it. Guilty or not guilty, I wouldn't shrink from an investigation, if I had a fair chance to defend myself. But no man's conduct, let alone any Judge's, will stand a test of this kind, unless he knows beforehand what he must defend. I shrink from such an investigation more than I would shrink from death. But I have never had any fear of your proceedings. Outside of the wishes of persons whom I know have been kind to me, I care nothing for this trial. They want to bring persons here whom I know have been hired to swear against me to prove my conduct. I simply object that my official conduct is all matter of record, and you have no jurisdiction of any charge against me, except official misconduct. Now what is this charge? I will read it:

ARTICLE I. That, unmindful of the sacred obligation by which he stood bound to discharge the solemn duties of his office faithfully, impartially, and consistently with the dignity and importance of the trust reposed in him, as Judge of the Fifteenth Judicial Circuit, in the State of Missouri, the said Albert Jackson, at a Circuit Court begun and held at the town of Bloomfield, within and for the county of Stoddard, in the State of Missouri, on the third Monday in May, A. D. 1858, (whereat the said Albert Jackson, by virtue of his office aforesaid, did preside as Judge,) did willfully and maliciously conduct himself in a manner highly oppressive and unjust to one Jonas Eaker, viz:

First. The said Albert Jackson, desiring to harrass and oppress the said Jonas Eaker, did, at the Circuit Court aforesaid, whereat he, the said Albert Jackson, presided as Judge, as aforesaid, cause an attachment to issue against him, the said Eaker, as for a criminal contempt, because said Eaker did not make return to a writ of mandamus, which writ had never been delivered to said Eaker, but of which a *copy* had been delivered to said Eaker; by virtue of which attachment the said Jonas Eaker was arrested and held in custody for several hours, and released finally by said Albert Jackson, on condition that he, the said Jonas

Eaker, should make return to the copy that had been delivered to him, said Jackson well knowing that said writ had never been legally served upon him, the said Eaker, and that he was not in contempt for not answering thereto.

Second. In refusing to permit counsel for said Eaker to speak in his behalf, when they proposed to show to the court that said writ of mandamus had never been properly delivered to, or served upon him.

Third. In peremptorily, and in an oppressive, angry, and insulting manner, ordering the counsel of said Eaker, to-wit, Solomon G. Kitchen and William G. Phelan, *to shut their mouths and sit down,* when they, in behalf of their said client, attempted to suggest an insufficiency in the service of said writ of mandamus.

Fourth. In depriving said Jonas Eaker of the benefit of counsel, and of the privilege of speaking through such counsel in his own defense, as he had a lawful right to.

Now, here they charge a breach of the "solemn duties" of my office. I will now read my answer:

ARTICLE I. The said Albert Jackson, Judge of the Fifteenth Judicial Circuit, saving and reserving to himself the benefit of all mistakes and irregularities which now exist, which have been or may be made, in any and all the proceedings, the proceedings heretofore had, or which may hereafter be had, and denying to the House of Representatives the right to alter, amend, modify, or withdraw any part or portion of said articles, or at any time hereafter to exhibit any other or further articles of impeachment herein; for answer to so much of said articles as he deems it necessary for him to answer or respond to, says that:

First. He wholly and fully denies that at the May term of the Circuit Court of Stoddard, begun on the third Monday in May, 1858, in said county, in his official capacity, or under color of his office, he did willfully and maliciously conduct himself in a manner highly oppressive and unjust to one Jonas Eaker.

To specification *first* of said article, said Albert Jackson says that he did not desire to oppress and harrass said Jonas Eaker, and did not maliciously and unjustly cause to be issued against said Eaker an attachment as for a *criminal* contempt; that, in his official capacity, he knew nothing about the manner in which said writ of mandamus had been executed on said Eaker. The said Eaker admitted said writ had been *served* on him, but refused to make return to said writ; then an attachment was issued against said Eaker for contempt of court, by refusing to make a proper return on said writ, as will appear by the papers and record in relation thereto.

For answer to specification *second,* he says he did not refuse to hear counsel speak for said Eaker after his *appearance,* but when Eaker made return to the writ he was discharged from the attachment without a penalty; does not know that said Eaker was in custody several hours; thinks he was not; but that he came into court and asked for time to answer, which was granted.

Third. Said Jackson did not peremptorily, and in an insulting and oppressive manner, order the counsel of said Eaker, to wit, Solomon G. Kitchen and William G. Phelan, to shut their mouths; said Jackson did not know they were counsel for Eaker; they said they were not, but claimed the right to appear as the *next friend of the court.*

Fourth. Did not deprive said Eaker of counsel, and of the privilege of speaking through counsel, in his own defense.

Said Jackson says that article first, and specifications 1, 2, 3, and 4, are insufficient in law, and do not contain charges of a nature and degree that would warrant a conviction in an impeachment. The said Jackson has the right, by virtue of his office, to issue writs of mandamus to an inferior court, and enforce by attachment the return of every writ or process sent out of said Circuit Court.

Now, I would ask how my official doings in this case are to be investigated? The statutes provide that the decisions of the Supreme Court have the force of law, and must govern all similar cases. I have shown you that the Supreme Court has decided that the acts and doings of a court of record can be known only from the record. My acts and doings as a Circuit Judge can only be known then in that way, and you can't try me for anything else. But if the Supreme Court had not decided this way, the law of evidence would be enough. I appeal to every lawyer on this floor to know if it isn't the universal rule of law that the best evidence must always be produced. Now, what is the best evidence of the solemn acts of a court of record? Why the record itself. I am always ready to meet my record. Well, but they say, if you did not do the things mentioned in the record in a smooth, silvery voice, we want to prove that by oral testimony. Well, I can't think it matters to this Court whether I did or not. But, says Mr. Knott, suppose the records were burnt up. Well, if they were, there is a way to supply their loss. If the record is burnt up or destroyed, they can call in the Clerk and other officers of the court to prove the loss and contents. I here assert that all my official acts must appear on the record and do appear there. All acts not appearing there are individual acts; and if these acts complained of were individual, and not judicial, I am responsible for them as an individual and not as a Judge. If I oppressed Eaker in this way, why didn't he bring suit against me? I am not publicly answerable if I am not privately. But no, they couldn't annoy me enough by a private suit. Besides, they didn't wish to become liable for costs. I have dwelt this long on this point because it is an important one in this trial. I leave it now for the action of the Senate.

The question to which Judge Jackson had objected was then decided pertinent and proper by the following vote:

AYES—Messrs. Brown, Byrne, Churchill, Coleman, Frazier, Goodlett, Gullett, Halliburton, Harris, Horner, McFarland, McFerran, McIlvaine, O'Neil, Parsons, Peyton, Rains, Richardson, Scott, Thompson, Vernon, and Wright—22.

NOES—Messrs. Hedgpeth, Morris, Newland, Wilson, and Wood—5.

Absent—Messrs. Fox, Hyer, Johnson, Jones, Robinson, and Watkins.

The question being read to the witness, he was proceeding to answer, when

JUDGE JACKSON objected to the witness making any statement about the attachment. The question he said was upon the mandamus.

The question was then re-read to the witness, and he answered as follows:

Mr. Eaker was brought into court by an officer, and the Judge informed him that he was in contempt for not making a return to the mandamus. I may as well state that I had no knowledge of the mandamus before this conversation between the Judge and Mr. Eaker. I had no knowledge of the original writ. Eaker replied that he had never been served. Then followed some conversation between the Judge and Mr. Eaker in relation to the service, which I cannot repeat exactly. Mr. Eaker said in effect, that only a copy of the writ had been given him, and that he had never seen the original. The Judge told him that he should have made a return anyhow. Some more conversation took place, when Mr. Kitchen and Mr. Phelan, I think, arose, and attempted to address the court on the subject. Judge said it was not a case for argument; that it was not a case for counsel. One of them said something about appearing as the next friend of the court. Judge Jackson ordered them to sit down, and to stop addressing the court. They did so. After some time, Mr. Eaker stated that he would make a return on the copy of the writ of mandamus, or whatever it was, (I cannot state from my own knowledge the character of the instrument.) Mr. Eaker then went away somewhere, and that was the last I saw of it. What further was done I cannot state.

Q. What was the conduct or manner of Judge Jackson during this affair?

A. It was like that of any other Judge on the bench, or at least his usual conduct. He was urbane as usual, and I saw no manifestation of anger or ill-will until some pretty sharp words passed between Mr. Kitchen, Mr. Phelan, the court, and Mr. Eaker. Then they all four seemed to be excited and angry, and the Judge spoke in a very harsh tone—not in his usual manner. He seemed very much provoked, very much out of temper, and I think he ordered them to shut their mouths.

Q. You say you knew nothing about the original process in this case?

A. I knew nothing about it previously. My understanding was had from what took place after Mr. Eaker was brought in by attachment.

Q. Did Messrs. Kitchen and Phelan appear as counsel for the respondent to the mandamus?

A. They did. I do not recollect that they announced themselves as counsel, but from their proceedings one lawyer would understand another as doing that.

JUDGE JACKSON. Didn't they say they were not counsel in the case?

A. Yes, they stated something to that effect.

MR. KNOTT. That was after the Judge had informed them that it was not a case for argument, or in which counsel could appear?

A. Yes, sir, it was after that.

Q. Were you at the Wayne county Circuit Court, September term, 1858?

A. I was.

Q. Was Judge Jackson there presiding?

A. He was.

Q. Were you present in court when the case of Limbarger *vs.* Powers was tried?

A. I was there part of the time, and witnessed a portion of that trial; cannot say that I witnessed it all.

Q. Please state to the Court what you know in relation to that trial, and the conduct of Judge Jackson in connection with an application for a change of venue in the case.

A. An application was made by one of the parties for a change of venue. Messrs. Fox and Pipkin, the counsel engaged in the cause, suggested Madison or some other county as convenient to all parties. Madison county adjoins Wayne. As to the other county, I am not certain. It was in my mind at the time that it was not remote. Judge Jackson told the counsel that it was the province of the court to fix the county to which the cause should be sent. After some debate about the matter he sent it to Mississippi county.

Q. In what part of the State is Mississippi county?

A. In the south-east.

Q. How far from the county seat of Wayne?

A. I cannot state the exact distance; by the usual mode of travel it is more than one hundred miles.

Q. Was this fact represented to the court?

A. It was. Both parties protested against the case being sent there. Among other objections urged, I think Mr. Pipkin remarked that he couldn't attend the Mississippi court, and that if the case was sent there he would be compelled to abandon the cause of his client. Judge Jackson remarked in reply that he believed there was counsel in Mississippi county; that there was good counsel there, or something to that effect.

SENATOR PARSONS. I want to understand if the case was sent there against the consent of counsel on both sides?

WITNESS. It was objected to by both counsel.

JUDGE JACKSON. Who were the counsel engaged in the case?

A. Mr. Fox and Mr. Pipkin.

JUDGE JACKSON. Were they not both on the same side of the case?

A. That was not my understanding of the fact.

Mr. KNOTT. What case was this?

A. The case of Limbarger *vs.* Powers.

Q. Were you present at a Circuit Court held for Dunklin county, commencing on the second Monday of May, 1858, during the pendency of applications for change of venue in the cases of Smith *vs.* Cude, and of a certain road company *vs.* Moses Farrar?

A. I am not certain I was in court during the trial or evidence upon those cases.

Q. Were you present at a Circuit Court in Butler county, held at Poplar Bluffs, in May, 1858?

A. I was.

Q. Were you present at the trial of the case of Gibson *vs.* Dunn?

A. I do not remember that I was.

Q. Well, Mr. Tyrell, state to the Court, if you please, what you may know in relation to a habeas corpus writ in the case of the State *vs.* John R. Maine, before Judge Jackson in January last?

A. I drew the petition in that case. I presented it to Judge Jackson. The writ was issued, and the prisoner brought before the Judge by an officer. I call him an officer; I presume he was. His name was Sutfirm. The prisoner, John R. Maine, was in his custody. The writ was served upon J. J. Jackson, the Deputy Sheriff of Stoddard county, who said the prisoner was in his custody. But he was in the actual manual custody of Sutfirm. He was brought before the Judge in my office. Think at that time, according to the best of my recollection, the return to the writ showed no written examination of witnesses against the accused. That at least was one of my reasons for suing out the writ, and as well as I recollect, that was the character of the return. After the return was made, J. J. Jackson came in and left the mittimus. I am not able to state precisely the facts. I never saw the prisoner until he was brought into the office in custody of the officer, and I then talked to him for the first time pending the proceedings. Afterwards, or about this time, the Judge examined the mittimus, and pronounced it insufficient.

[Judge Jackson here handed the witness a paper, requesting him to examine it, and pronounce upon its authenticity. The managers demanded an inspection of the paper before it was subjected to the examination of the witness. Considerable discussion ensued, which is here omitted.]

When the Deputy Sheriff came in, perhaps I wrote the return to the writ for him. I believe it is my handwriting, signed James Dowdy, Sheriff, by J. J. Jackson, deputy. I could not state the exact nature of the return without looking at it. I think it was as I have stated.

Q. What reason was assigned by Judge Jackson for discharging the accused?

A. It was some insufficiency in the mittimus, but I am not able to say positively what it was. I remember distinctly his remarking that the warrant was not sufficient, for the reason that the accused had been before the Justice on a charge of larceny, but there was no showing that the Justice had found there was sufficient reason to believe that an offense had been committed. I remember this, because one of the reasons I urged for the discharge of the prisoner was that the mittimus did not show that there had been an examination, and that the testimony was not reduced to writing. That is my recollection of it, and I only state the substance. The Judge said that such a defect might be cured; that the point I urged concerning the absence of an examination would not be good if the mittimus showed that the Justice had found there was sufficient reason for a commitment.

Q. Did the Judge make any rule or order upon the officer to produce the papers in the case, or any papers?

A. He did not, that I know of. He may have done so.

Q. Did he inquire if there had been an investigation of the facts of the case by the Justice?

A. He may have made such an inquiry. I am inclined to think he did.

Q. What reply was made?

A. I can't say.

Q. Did you detail the facts to the Judge?

A. I did detail to him my understanding of them. I was counsel for the accused.

Q. Were you present when one Charles Russell was brought before Judge Jackson by writ of habeas corpus?

A. I was.

Q. When was that?

A. It was on the same day—in the morning of the same day.

Q. Detail if you please the facts in that case.

A. As well as I can remember them. Russell was arrested and brought before Jonas Eaker, a magistrate, the day before the occurrences we have been speaking of. An examination of the usual character was had, and at its conclusion, Judge Eaker announced that he would commit the accused; or rather said he would hold him to bail. He was asked to give the accused till 10 o'clock the next morning to get bail in the amount required. To this Judge Eaker assented, and the prisoner was placed in charge of the Constable, to hold till that time. That evening I presented to Judge Jackson a petition for a writ of habeas corpus; a writ was accordingly issued, and returned served, at my office, the next morning. Cryts, the Constable, in whose custody the prisoner was, returned that he held him by virtue of parol or verbal orders from the magistrate, Eaker. I do not remember that there was anything in the return about an examination. After some time, and considerable talk, the purport of which I cannot now state, I believe the return of the Constable was amended, or corrected, once or twice. Cryts went out, and after being gone a short time, brought in some papers, and gave them to the Judge, or laid them before him. The Judge examined them, and I think I did the same.

Q. What were those papers?

A. I think they were a mittimus and an original warrant for the arrest of the prisoner.

Q. What did the Judge do with them?

A. Judge Jackson told the officer he was too late; I think he added something to the effect that the papers brought in contradicted the return made to the writ of habeas corpus; that the officer's acts contradicted his return, or something of that kind.

Q. Was the discharge of the prisoner before or after this?

A. It was afterwards. I remember that I was somewhat disturbed upon seeing the papers come in; it startled me somewhat, and I remarked that it was too late after the return already made.

Judge Jackson. Hadn't the prisoner been discharged before the papers came in; and wasn't I engaged in writing out the discharge at the time?

A. I am pretty clear, Judge, that the prisoner was not discharged until after the papers came in.

Judge Jackson. Didn't I discharge the man before, and simply wait to write the discharge with that of the other case?

A. Such is not my recollection; I am pretty clear to the contrary.

Mr. Knott. How long before the discharge of both these men were the papers you speak of brought in?

A. It may have been half an hour, or an hour.

Q. Well, what reason was assigned by the Judge for the discharge of Russell?

A. I believe it was that the return showed no cause for holding him in custody.

Q. Was the nature of the accusation against Russell known to the Judge?

A. I think it was. At least it was known to the Judge that the man had been before Judge Eaker on a charge of passing counterfeit half dollars, or of passing counterfeit money. On the evening before the discharge I may have stated the facts myself, when I presented the petition.

Q. I refer particularly to the facts of the arrest, the charge, the examination, and placing the prisoner in custody till he should procure bail. Were they detailed to the Judge?

A. I am quite clear that all the facts concerning the case were communicated to him.

Q. Where was this?—the hearing upon the return to the writ, I mean.

A. In my office, in Bloomfield.

Q. Where was the examination before the committing magistrate had?

A. Judge Eaker held his court in the same building.

Q. Did Judge Jackson, when the return was made, inquire of the officer concerning the examination and commitment?

A. I think so. The Judge had a conversation with Cryts about the papers.

Q. What was that conversation? What did Cryts tell him?

Judge Jackson objected to this question, alleging that it would elicit hearsay testimony. A short discussion ensued, during which the question was reduced to writing, as follows:

Did the Constable, William F. Cryts, communicate to Judge Jackson the circumstances under and the authority by which he held the body of Charles Russell in custody? If so, what was it Mr. Cryts said to Judge Jackson in your presence and hearing?

The question was ruled to be proper by the following vote:

Ayes—Messrs. Brown, Byrne, Churchill, Coleman, Frazier, Goodlett, Gullett, Halliburton, Harris, Hedgpeth, Horner, McFarland, McFerran, McIlvaine, Morris, Newland, O'Neil, Parsons, Peyton, Rains, Richardson, Scott, Thompson, Vernon, Wilson, Wood, and Wright—27.

Noes—None.

Absent—Messrs, Fox, Hyer, Johnson, Jones, Robinson, and Watkins.

Witness. In the conversation I heard, Cryts stated, in substance, that he held Russell by reason of a charge or order of Judge Eaker, before whom he was accused of passing counterfeit money. That was the substance of his communication; I cannot give his words. At the time I had something to say about it myself, and was, in fact, a party to the conversation. Cryts had but little to say before he went out and brought in the papers.

Q. You say the accused was discharged after this?

A. That is my impression.

Q. Well, Mr. Tyrell, were you present at the Ripley Circuit Court, held on the fourth Monday in April, 1858?

A. I was.

Q. Were you present at the trial of one William Kinsey, on an indictment for grand larceny?

A. I was present at that trial.

Q. Who acted as counsel for the defendant then?

A. Mr. Fox and Mr. Phelan; I do not now recall the other counsel of the prisoner.

Judge Jackson here presented a paper to the Court of the nature of a bill of exceptions, excepting to the ruling of the Court on the question above to which he had objected.

The managers opposed the filing of this bill of exceptions, taking the ground that there was no law providing for any appeal from this Court, and asserting that it would be a useless expenditure of time to file exceptions during the progress of the trial.

The question then being, shall the respondent be allowed to file the paper? the vote stood as follows:

Ayes—Messrs. Gullett, Hedgpeth, Morris, Newland, Scott, Wilson, and Wood—7.

Noes—Messrs. Brown, Byrne, Churchill, Coleman, Frazier, Goodlett, Halliburton, Harris, Horner, McFarland, McFerran, McIlvaine, O'Neil, Parsons, Peyton, Rains, Richardson, Robinson, Thompson, Vernon, and Wright—21.

Absent—Messrs. Fox, Hyer, Johnson, Jones, and Watkins.

So the motion to file the paper was overruled, and the examination of the witness proceeded as follows:

Q. You will please state, Mr. Tyrell, what you know in relation to the demeanor of Judge Jackson during that trial—his conduct to counsel and parties—so far as you observed it.

A. The only things out of the regular and usual course of such trials that I observed, I will state: A witness for the prosecution was placed on the stand; one of defendant's counsel, (I cannot say which, though it was Mr. Phelan, I think,) desired the witness to narrate the circumstances to which he was testifying, slowly, in order that he might have an opportunity of writing them down. Judge Jackson said the witness was not brought there for the purpose of having his testimony written out, or something to that amount; he said the counsel, if they desired it, could take the testimony down afterwards, or that he had no objection to taking the testimony after the examination was concluded.

Q. Is it customary in your courts for counsel to save the testimony as it is delivered, or is it the practice to wait till the trial is concluded?

A. I have seen a great many cases both ways. It is not usual, I believe, in the cases of minor importance to write out the evidence as the trial progresses; in important cases the other practice prevails.

Q. Were you present throughout the trial of this Kinsey case?

A. I was present most of the time.

Q. You will please tell the Court what you observed of the deportment of the Judge and lawyers, during the argument.

A. There was what I would call a considerable squabble among them. There were many harsh words used on both sides.

Q. Can you tell us what was said?

A. I do not recollect.

Q. I will call your attention to what occurred between the Judge and Mr. Fox, particularly. Were you present when Mr. Fox made his argument to the jury?

A. I was. He was several times interrupted by the court, with harsh comments on his remarks. Finally the Judge ordered him to sit down, in a severe, imperious manner.

Q. Was Mr. Fox in the discharge of his lawful duties as an attorney?

A. I so considered it. He was presenting the case of his client to the jury.

Q. What was his manner, before interrupted?

A. It was certainly respectful, sober, and I saw no objection to it. When interrupted by the court, he retorted; and, as I said before, sharp words passed between them, which I could not pretend to give.

Q. Did Mr. Fox sit down when ordered to do so?

A. He did.

Q. Do you recollect, particularly, any remark made by him on the occasion?

A. I do not.

Q. Who was acting as Circuit Attorney at that time?

A. I think it was Mr. Woodsides—John R. Woodsides.

JUDGE JACKSON. You say, Mr. Tyrell, my manner on this occasion was very hard or harsh; could you tell the Court in what the harshness consisted? Was it in looks, words, tone, or what was it?

A. I cannot better describe it than by calling it harsh; the word is English; I suppose it is understood.

JUDGE JACKSON. Couldn't you tell us what it was? Could you imitate my actions and looks then?

A. I could not undertake to do so. Your manner was imperious and commanding.

Mr. KNOTT. We would like to proceed with the examination of the witness without interruption. Mr. Tyrell, were you present at the November term of the Stoddard Circuit Court, 1858, pending the case of Gustavus Berry *vs.* John Griffie?

A. I was.

Q. Will you please state the conduct of the Judge during the pendency of that suit, what he said and did, as succinctly as possible?

A. I was one of defendants counsel in that case. It was, if I remember rightly, an action for damages, and something was alleged about an agreement to work on land, and a breach of the contract. A question was asked by counsel on the opposite side, in substance, as to who was the owner of the land in question. I objected to the question, and some discussion was had over it. I cannot now state the precise ruling of the court in regard to it, but the Judge about that time turned round, while I was excepting to the witness or attorney talking on the subject to the jury, and remarked that very likely the defendant had no interest in the land that he could convey. I objected to an instruction from the court in that form and manner, as improper and unfair, and received some harsh reply. The cause went on, but was several times interrupted by remarks from the Judge; and from the character of those remarks, it was very evident to the defendant and his counsel that the Judge had made up his mind in regard to the case, and that we could not have a fair trial. I so remarked at the time.

JUDGE JACKSON. Didn't I order you to jail for it? If I didn't, I ought to have done so.

WITNESS. I do not wish to be understood as saying that I spoke to you of your prejudice at the time.

Mr. KNOTT. Well, what was the result of the case?

A. The jury rendered a verdict for the plaintiff for considerably more than the petition asked. I filed a motion for a new trial, stating among other reasons in support of the motion, that the jury had been influenced by the remarks and comments of the court, in making up their verdict. As to the remarks, I proposed to adduce the affidavit of myself and others, to prove that the verdict was based on them. I will not be understood as saying that such affidavits were made; I merely proposed to take them in support of the motion. This motion, however, was overruled, the court refusing to consider the affidavits. I then filed a motion in arrest of judgment. One of the reasons on which this motion was based was, that the verdict was for more than the plaintiff had alleged to be due him. This last motion was five or six days after the trial of the cause. It was overruled. After this, the same day, or the day after, Mr. Bedford filed a motion to enter a remitter for the excessive verdict; but before this was entered, I presented a bill of exceptions. The Judge signed it, but not till after striking out of the bill of exceptions a part of the reasons stated in the motion papers for a new trial and in arrest.

Q. You say the Judge signed the bill of exceptions?

A. Yes, sir; but I was compelled to strike out most of the reasons urged in the motion papers.

Q. Was the evidence incorporated in your bill of exceptions?

A. It was not. I presented the evidence agreed upon by Mr. Bedford and myself, as the testimony had in the case. The Judge refused to examine the paper. I urged the matter upon him as well as I could. I called his attention to several points in the testimony which I thought he would recollect. But he said that as he couldn't get up the whole testimony, on account of there having been so much noise, or because he did not know what it all was, he would not sign any.

Q. Did the testimony you presented embody the facts in evidence before the jury as they were detailed on the trial?

A. It did, sir.

Q. And you say the court refused to look at, or examine it, and refused to let it become a part of the bill?

A. He did so refuse.

Q. I believe you stated that the counsel on both sides were agreed as to the correctness of this evidence?

A. If I did not, I say so now.

Q. When did you say a motion to enter a remitter was filed?

A. I believe it was the next day. At any rate, it was after this time of which we have just been speaking.

Q. What became of your case?

A. It is now pending before the Supreme Court.

Q. Did you get the evidence before that court at all?

A. We were not able to do so.

Q. You will please explain the manner of preparing bills of exception in the courts of your circuit generally,—whether each exception is made the subject of a separate bill, drawn and signed at the time, or whether all the exceptions or points saved during the trial are embodied in a single bill and presented at the conclusion of the trial.

A. So far as my limited practice has enabled me to observe, the exceptions are generally all embodied together. In preparing a bill the attorneys usually refer to matters that they are not able to introduce in brackets, writing, "here insert testimony," or, "here insert a certain motion," as a direction to the Clerk. The testimony is usually prepared separately, and signed separately by the Judge. This is the practice so far as I have examined.

Q. Were you present at the same term of the court when the case of Daugherty *vs.* Whitehead was tried?

A. I was.

Senator Parsons desired to ask the witness a question before leaving the point upon which he had just been examined. The question propounded was as follows:

What part of the bill of exceptions did the Judge require you to strike out?

A. Some of the reasons urged in support of the motions in arrest and for a new trial. By reasons, I mean causes assigned in the motion papers.

SENATOR PARSONS. I wanted to know what the reasons were.

A. I can give them by refreshing my memory from papers in my possession.

JUDGE JACKSON objected to the witness being allowed to read any papers pertaining to this case, unless the papers were proved genuine and relevant.

The managers asserted the right of the witness to refresh his memory by any private writing or memorandum of his own making.

JUDGE JACKSON persisted in his objection, and after some explanations of the point presented by his objection by Senators Richardson, Scott, Wilson, and Goodlett, the question being, shall the respondent's objection be overruled? the vote stood as follows:

AYES—Messrs. Brown, Byrne, Churchill, Coleman, Frazier, Goodlett, Gullett, Halliburton, Harris, Hedgpeth, Horner, McFarland, McFerran, McIlvaine, Morris, Newland, O'Neil, Parsons, Peyton, Rains, Richardson, Scott, Thompson, Vernon, Wilson, Wood, and Wright—27.

NOES—None.

Absent—Messrs. Fox, Hyer, Johnson, Jones, Robinson, and Watkins.

So the objection was overruled, and the witness having examined the papers as he desired, proceeded to answer as follows:

A. One of the reasons stricken out was that the jury had been misled by the remark of the court, and by the testimony tending to show who was the owner of the land in question. Another, that this testimony should have been excluded. Another, that the jury were misled by remarks of the court. I think, in the motion for an arrest of judgment, I urged that the jury had given damages for more than the plaintiff claimed, and that these damages were given on excluded matter. I remember that I and others were of opinion at the time that the jury could not have based their excessive verdict on anything but the excluded matter. I did not see how they had reached the amount without taking into account the excluded matter.

MR. KNOTT. Did you argue these motions before the court with these causes assigned?

A. I did.

JUDGE JACKSON. You call it argument, I suppose.

MR. KNOTT. How did the language or remarks of the court, which you have mentioned, occur? In what stage of the trial were you then?

A. The language of the court arose after some conversation between the counsel and the court about the right of the man, the defendant, to convey the land. As I said before, I cannot repeat the exact words used, but he said that he didn't see that he (the defendant) was the owner of the land, that he had any right to convey it, or something to that effect.

Q. In your motion for a new trial you say you offered to adduce affidavits to prove that the verdict of the jury was founded on this remark?

A. Yes, sir, I did offer to do so. I did not adduce the affidavits, because there was no intimation from the court of a wish or willingness to hear them.

Q. And this matter was stricken out of the bill of exceptions?

A. Yes, sir, it was.

The hour of twelve having arrived, the Court adjourned till 3 o'clock, on motion of Senator Rains, by the following vote, the ayes and noes having been demanded by Senator Morris:

AYES—Messrs. Brown, Churchill, Frazier, Goodlett, Gullett, Halliburton, Harris, Hedgpeth, McIlvaine, Peyton, Rains, Scott, Thompson, Vernon, Wilson, Wood, and Wright—17.

NOES—Messrs. Byrne, Coleman, Horner, McFarland, McFerran, Morris, Newland, O'Neil, Parsons, and Richardson—10.

Absent—Messrs. Fox, Hyer, Johnson, Jones, Robinson, and Watkins.

EVENING SESSION.

WEDNESDAY, June 8, 1859.

The Court met pursuant to adjournment.

The managers and respondent attended.

SENATOR RICHARDSON moved a call of the Senate, when the following Senators were noted as being absent without leave:

Messrs. Brown, Churchill, Coleman, Fox, Halliburton, Hyer, Johnson, Jones, McFerran, Parsons, Rains, Robinson, Scott, Thompson, and Watkins.

Several of the absentees appearing, on motion of Senator Newland, further proceedings under the call were dispensed with.

JOSEPH S. WHITE, a witness on the part of the respondent, appeared, and was sworn and charged under the rule.

The examination of Mr. M. H. TYRELL on the part of the State was then resumed.

Mr. KNOTT. Mr. Tyrell, I will call your attention to the cause of Daugherty *vs.* Whitehead, at the trial of which you say you were present, and get you to state your knowledge in relation to that trial, and the conduct of Judge Jackson and the parties to it, respectively, while it was pending.

A. I came into the case but a little time before the examination of the witnesses was concluded: all the knowledge I have in relation to the case was acquired after that time. The most I did was to prepare a bill of exceptions. First, however, I filed a motion for a new trial, which was overruled. I then filed a motion in arrest, which was also overruled. Then I tendered a bill of exceptions, which Judge Jackson declined signing till I struck out some of the grounds for one of the motions as they appeared in the motion paper. If I remember correctly, he had no objection to the motion paper in arrest, but objected to the motion paper for a new trial. When the striking out was done to suit him, he signed the bill.

Q. Did the bill of exceptions embody the reasons as urged in the argument of the motion for a new trial?

A. Yes, sir.

Q. You say he refused to sign the bill till several of the reasons urged were stricken out?

A. Yes, sir.

Q. Mr. Tyrell, there is one other matter that I wish to call your attention to. You were present, I believe, at the last January term of the Stoddard Circuit Court. Did you hear the charge of the Judge to the grand jury at that time?

A. I did hear the charge, or at least I was present part of the time, and heard part of the charge.

Q. Did you hear anything about a citizen of the county coming to this city on business for the county, or anything said by the Judge in relation to such an event?

A. I did. I distinctly heard some remarks in the charge to the effect that he was informed some person had gone to Jefferson City as a pretended agent for the county; that this person had no right or authority to pretend to represent the county; and that if the grand jury found from an investigation that such a thing had been done, and that the person alluded to had received pay for this, he had received money under false pretenses, the punishment for which was imprisonment in the penitentiary.

Q. Did he in any manner designate the particular person alluded to?

A. I don't think he mentioned any name in that connection. Whether he mentioned any circumstances by which the grand jury would be enabled to say who was meant, I do not now remember. I couldn't say that he did not, nor that he did.

Q. Were you present at the Circuit Court held in Bloomfield in August last?

A. I was.

Q. Were you in court when the case of the State *vs.* Orson Bartlett was tried or called?

A. I was there. I was asked by Mr. Bartlett's counsel, I believe, to take a part in the trial. A jury was empanneled.

Q. Who was acting as Circuit Attorney at that time?

A. David G. Hicks was Circuit Attorney *pro tem.* After some conversation between the Circuit Attorney and Mr. Kitchen, counsel for the defendant, the court stated that it was not necessary to state or argue such a case to the jury.

Q. What were the circumstances of the case?

A. Bartlett, with others, was indicted for playing cards for something; I cannot at this moment say what, positively. The Judge said he would not allow the jury to find a general verdict. He went on to say that the offense set forth in the indictment was not statutory; that it was not the offense of gambling described in the statutes, or something to that effect; that if the jury were to find a general verdict, he should set it aside. He said that playing cards under such circumstances was not gambling, any more than the competition for the rewards or premiums of agricultural societies and schools was gambling, and that it was not indictable. He spoke words of this meaning, and illustrated his position at some length.

Q. Were his remarks in the form of written instructions?

A. They were not. They were orally stated. There were no written instructions in the case, to my knowledge.

Q. Well, what became of the case?

A. The Circuit Attorney, I think, entered a *nolle prosequi*, and there it ended.

Q. Did he give any reason for entering the *nolle?*

A. I do not remember that he did.

Q. Was this an indictment against Orson Bartlett alone?

A. It was not; according to my recollection, Isaac Brand, David G. Hicks, Bartlett, and Judge Jackson himself, were all presented in the same indictment.

Q. What was the demeanor of the Judge while the case was before the court? Did he manifest any solicitude about it?

A. I could hardly say, definitely. His language indicated that he was satisfied that the facts stated in the indictment were not sufficient, or did not constitute an offense, and he remarked, if I mistake not, that it was useless to put the county to the expense of trying such cases, or finding such bills. I thought from his whole manner, that he seemed to think that there was something personal to himself in the finding of the bill. He disclaimed any personal interest, or, rather, said that if his own name was not mentioned in the same indictment, he would quash it.

CROSS-EXAMINATION BY JUDGE JACKSON.

Q. Mr. Tyrell, how long have you resided in this State?

A. I came to Missouri in the latter part of November, 1857, and have resided here ever since, except a short absence in Illinois last summer.

Q. Did you not leave the State once?

A. I left as I just stated; but I did not move out of the State. My family was here.

Q. Did you not announce your intention to leave?

A. I think perhaps I did.

Q. Didn't you leave when you announced your intention of going?

A. I did not.

Q. Where did you see me first?

A. I think, Judge, that I first met you at Ripley Circuit Court, in the spring of '58. I have no recollection of seeing you before that time.

Q. Didn't you come to that part of the State first?

A. That was the first court I attended.

Q. How many courts in the Fifteenth Circuit have you attended?

A. One in Ripley, two in Butler, two regular and one special term in Stoddard, and one in Wayne.

Q. Have you ever been round the circuit?

A. Only in the counties I have mentioned.

Q. What was the first case you ever saw me try?

A. I do not recollect.

Q. Were you an attorney in the Kinsey case at Ripley Circuit Court?

A. I was in the case, but not as an attorney. I had no license to practice at that court; no license to practice in this State, I mean.

Q. When did you get license?

A. Got it sometime in the month of May, 1858. It is dated May 8, 1858, I believe.

Q. When was the court in Ripley county held?

A. I do not remember; I could easily ascertain.

Q. Wasn't it the last Monday in April?

A. I could easily ascertain, so as to speak positively. I would not undertake to do so now.

Q. Who were Mr. Kinsey's lawyers in the case you have been talking about?

A. I think they were Mr. Fox, Mr. Kitchen, and Mr. Phelan.

Q. Haven't you given testimony in relation to this matter before?

A. I have.

Q. Didn't you swear then that you were an attorney in the case?

[Mr. Hardin objected to the question. The objection was discussed, and finally withdrawn by Judge Jackson, to be stated differently.]

Q. I will ask you to look over that paper, (showing manuscript to witness,) and see if you made that statement.

A. I will not say positively. I may have made it as it is, and I may have made it with the addition of a single little word, which would materially change the meaning of the paragraph.

[Question repeated here several times in slightly modified form, eliciting the same reply substantially.]

Q. Well, what had you to do with the Kinsey case?

A. I had nothing much to do with it. I expressed opinions on the points rendered, and perhaps did some writing; but I did not appear in court as an attorney for Kinsey, simply because I did not have license at that time.

Q. I understood you to say that I had told the witnesses in that case to go on, and had refused to let the counsel take down the testimony as the examination progressed. Now didn't you hear this in a conversation with the witnesses afterwards?

A. I don't so remember the fact.

Q. Wasn't it that I told them they might have any reasonable time to take down a single statement of the witness, as soon as the statement was completed?

A. I didn't remember it as you say. To the best of my recollection the facts occurred as I related them before.

[Question repeated, with same answer.]

Q. I think you used the term squabbling in regard to some difficulties with the lawyers in this case. Will you tell us what you mean by that?

A. I referred to the harsh expressions used by you.

Q. Couldn't you give us an example of one of those harsh expressions?

A. I couldn't undertake to do it, sir. I might if I remembered them particularly enough, but I do not.

Q. Well, I want to know what you mean by harsh expressions?

A. I couldn't undertake to repeat exactly what you said.

Q. Perhaps you could if you had any disposition to do so; come, now, give us an example; couldn't you let off a blank shot or two by way of example? No one will take any offense of course, knowing the purpose for which it is done.

A. I am not skilled in such practice.

Q. Well, did Mr. Fox use any sharp expressions?

A. I think both of you did.

Q. Can you tell us any of Mr. Fox's sharp expressions?

A. I don't remember them.

Q. Are you certain that what I said was sharp?

A. I am well assured that it was.

Q. Well, do you think there were any blunt expressions used? Were those you speak of sharp at the point—were they two-edged? Have you ever seen a tri-angular expression?

A. I will answer that question if required to do so.

Q. Well, tell us if my expressions were improper?

A. Some of them were very improper, in my judgment.

Q. Well, what were they?

A. I have answered that.

Q. What did I say to Mr. Fox?

A. I do not remember the expression used. I think you stopped him once or twice—two or three times—while he was speaking.

Q. I believe you said that he was in the regular discharge of his duties. Wasn't I, also?

A. I think I said "arguing his cause," instead of regular discharge of duties.

Q. Well, wasn't I in the discharge of my duties as Judge?

A. Sometimes you were—at other times, in my judgment, you were not. I don't know about the matter. I could only give you my opinion.

Q. Do you think that I thought I was not in the discharge of my duty?

A. I couldn't give an opinion as to what you thought.

Q. Why do you say that my conduct was improper?

A. In saying so, I only gave my opinion.

Q. Well, Mr. Tyrell, about this celebrated mandamus case. I believe you said you were not present all the time. At what stage of the case did you come in?

A. I was present when Mr. Eaker was brought into court.

Q. How was he brought in? What was the stage of the case then?

A. I do not know of my own knowledge whether he was brought in by an attachment, or how. I learned that, or rather inferred it, from the conversation which took place when he came in.

Q. Now, wasn't it that Mr. Kitchen and Mr. Phelan were both trying to prevent an attachment from being issued, and wasn't this talk that you heard before the attachment was issued?

A. I can't say when the attachment issued.

Q. Wasn't all the matter about issuing an attachment?

A. I have stated the facts according to my best recollection and knowledge.

Q. Didn't they assert that there had been no service of the writ, and that there was no case in court?

A. I think so.

Q. Well, didn't I then ask them if they appeared as attorneys?

A. You did ask them if they appeared in that capacity. They said they did not; that they would not appear as attorneys.

Q. Well, didn't one of them, or both, say he appeared as the next friend of the court?

A. I think Mr. Kitchen used some expression like that.

Q. Did you ever hear of an attorney appearing as next friend of the court before?

A. I can't say that I ever heard of such a proceeding before.

Q. Well, wasn't it after this that the attachment was issued?

A. I decline swearing upon facts not within my own knowledge. All that I know is that Mr. Eaker was brought into court, and when his attorneys attempted to speak, you said if he was not in court, or not served, you would not hear an argument. I remember distinctly your saying that it was not a proper cause for argument.

Q. Well, did I refuse to hear counsel after there was a case in court?

A. I don't know. I only know that Mr. Eaker was brought in by the officer before this conversation that I have related.

Q. Was there any disposition on my part, before this difficulty about the argument, to oppress anybody?

A. I saw nothing in the beginning of the matter that I thought any one could object to, on your part.

Q. Did you say you were at the town of Greenville, in court, when the change of venue in the case of Limbarger *vs.* Powers was awarded?

A. I was there at that time.

Q. Were you present when the matter was under discussion?

A. I was. Do not know that I was there all the time, but think I was.

Q. Well, wasn't Mr. Fox trying to have the case sent to a particular county, and wouldn't it have been wrong to have sent it just where he wanted it?

A. I cannot answer.

Q. Well, what is your opinion in regard to changes of venue? What ought to be the rule in regard to awarding them?

[Question objected to and withdrawn.]

Q. How far is the county seat of Madison from Greenville?

A. I could not give the precise distance. It is called forty or forty-five miles, I believe.

Q. How far to the county seat of Mississippi?

A. I cannot speak more positively about that; I believe it is considerably over one hundred miles.

Q. You don't know the distance from Greenville to Charleston?

A. No.

Q. Isn't the way to go there by Nigger Wool?

A. I never traveled from Greenville to Charleston. I never was at Charleston. All I know about it is from common inquiries.

Q. Well, what have you always heard to be the route?

[The witness here described the route, during which he was so frequently interrupted by Judge Jackson that the reporter's account is not intelligible.]

Q. You say the attorneys requested the case to be sent to one of two adjoining counties: did the attorneys on both sides do this?

A. That is my impression.

Q. Where does Mr. Fox reside?

A. I think in Madison county.

Q. What other lawyers were in the case?

A. Mr. Pipkin was the other. There may have been others. I do not recollect.

Q. Where does Mr. Pipkin reside?

A. I believe he lives in Iron county.

Q. Which do you think would have been the proper county to have sent the case to?

[Question objected to, debated at some length, and finally withdrawn.]

Q. Do you know whether business had accumulated so that it was almost impossible to get a case tried?

A. I do not know; I have heard something of the kind.

Q. Would it be proper to send a case there under such circumstances?

A. Perhaps it would.

Q. Were not Mr. Bedford and Mr. White employed in this case?

A. I am not certain. I think one, Mr. Bedford, and perhaps both were?

Q. Were not Mr. Fox and Mr. Pipkin both on the same side of the case?

A. I believe not, though I may be mistaken.

Q. Is not there business relations between the counsel named and counsel in Mississippi county?

A. Perhaps there is; I wouldn't undertake to say. I believe Mr. Bedford and Mr. White used to live in Mississippi county.

Q. Hasn't Mr. Bedford a brother living in Mississippi county, who is a lawyer?

A. I have so understood.

Q. How far is it from Pemiscot county to Dunklin county?

A. I think they are adjoining counties.

Q. How far from the county seat of one to that of the other?

A. I am unable to tell you. Think it is called sixty miles from Bloomfield to Kennett, the county seat of Dunklin, and Pemiscot is beyond, adjoining Dunklin.

Q. Is there not a plank road or roads leading from Kennett to Pemiscot county?

A. I have heard that there was; I don't know anything about it.

Q. Well, which would be the most convenient to travel to attend a case, one hundred miles or forty miles; or is the distance the only thing to be considered?

A. Under some circumstances it might be more convenient to go one hundred miles than to go forty in another direction.

Q. Well, did you see anything improper in my conduct in sending cases from Dunklin to Pemiscot?

A. At the time, and with my knowledge of the facts, I thought it was very improper.

Q. Well, when would it be proper to send a case to a court one hundred miles distant rather than to one forty miles distant?

A. I could only tell from a full knowledge of the facts.

Q. I thought so, and if I thought I knew best, and sent a case to Mississippi county, I reckon there would be no great harm in it. And now, if the parties, if both sides, were agreed to take the case to a particular county, instead of the one it was sent to, what harm would be done? Couldn't they, by consent, withdraw the application and take it where they pleased?

[Mr. Knott protested against this manner of arguing the case with the witness. Judge Jackson defended his course for a time, and then proceeded with the cross-examination.]

Q. Well, Mr. Tyrell, we will go to this Griffie and Berry case. Can you tell me who was the plaintiff's attorney in that case?

A. I think it was Mr. Bedford. I am sure it was.

Q. Who was on the other side?

A. I have forgotten one of the defendant's attorneys. Mr. Griffie employed me.

Q. Was there a jury in the case?

A. Yes, sir.

Q. Were you in the case at the commencement?

A. I think I was.

Q. What was the action about?

A. I think it was brought to recover damages, and there was an allegation of the failure of a conveyance. There was something in it about a horse.

Q. Did the petition claim anything in relation to a conveyance?

A. I am not certain that it did. But the matter or controversy about the conveyance was the principal question at issue on the trial.

Q. Now, Mr. Tyrell, wasn't it all about an improvement?

A. Yes, sir, I believe it did in the end turn out to be an improvement matter.

Q. Was there any instructions asked or given in the case?

A. I am not certain. I do not remember any written instructions.

Q. Isn't it admissible, under the statutes, for a Judge to give instructions to a jury?

A. It is hardly necessary for me to answer that.

Q. What were the causes assigned in your motion for a new trial in this case?

A. I do not remember all of them. Most of them were directed by you to be struck out.

Q. Well, what reason did I give for doing so?

A. I do not remember that you gave any.

Q. Wasn't it that I objected to your motion, showing that I had *instructed* the jury when I had not? Didn't it go on to say that the Judge had *misinstructed* the jury, and didn't I tell you that I had not instructed the jury at all?

A. I don't think any such word was used in the motion paper.

Q. Didn't I tell you that if I had instructed the jury, you must incorporate the instruction in your bill of exceptions?

A. I think the expression misinstructed was not in the motion papers at all. I think *misdirected* was the word used in that connection.

Q. Well, what did that refer to?

A. To your words to the effect that the defendant had no interest in the land which he could convey.

Q. Well, what else was there that you say I made you strike out?

A. An allegation that the jury had been misled by testimony going to show that the defendant was not the owner of the land.

Q. And you say I overruled your motion for a new trial?

A. Yes, sir, you did; and the motion in arrest also.

Q. Now, wasn't it that you wanted your way as an attorney, and I thought my way was right, and you couldn't get your way about it,—wasn't that what was the matter?

A. I cannot testify as to your thoughts.

Q. Whose duty was it to decide when there was a difference between us?

[Mr. Knott objected to this style of examination, and after some discussion the Judge continued.]

Q. Did you say I refused to sign the testimony in this case because there was so much noise I couldn't hear it?

A. You did give that as your reason for refusing to sign it.

Q. During the trial, didn't I ask Mr. Bedford to remove his seat, because I couldn't hear what was going on?

A. I think you did.

Q. Well, was there much noise?

A. During a portion of the testimony there was too much noise.

Mr. Knott. Whose duty was it to keep order?

A. It was not mine. I was not the court.

Judge Jackson. I'll ask you, Mr. Tyrell, if you have ever seen me exercise arbitrary power—if you have seen me oppress—that is, I mean, that I have exercised power that I didn't think I possessed or should exercise?

A. I have never seen you act arbitrarily in that sense.

Q. Did you ever know me to fine an attorney?

A. I never did.

Q. Did you ever know me to send one to jail?

A. No. I have heard of your ordering an attorney to be taken to jail, and I have heard of your fining attorneys; but I don't know of any cases.

Q. How often have you heard of my fining attorneys?

A. I don't know.

Q. Have you heard that such things were of frequent occurrence?

A. They have not been of frequent occurrence within the past year or so. There are frequent disturbances in court between you and the lawyers, but I cannot say that you often take that course with them.

Q. Couldn't you give an instance?

A. The case that occurred in Ripley court, the Kinsey case, I suppose would do for one.

Q. In this case of Bartlett, I believe, you say that Bartlett was tried for gaming?

A. I did not say there was a trial. He was indicted, and a jury was sworn—I can't say whether any evidence was submitted to the jury. After your statements in regard to the law of the case, a *nolle* was entered by the Circuit Attorney.

Q. Did you state the substance of what I said then about the law?

A. To the best of my ability I did.

Q. Wasn't what I said more to the lawyers than to the jury? Didn't I address myself to the lawyers?

A. I cannot say for whose ears you intended your remarks. They were in open court, and in the hearing of the jury.

Q. Didn't I say that betting, and not playing for property, oysters, or anything of that kind, was the offense known to our statutes; that the statutes punished betting, and not such things; and were not the illustrations I used going to show that playing cards where there was no bet was not indictable?

A. I stated before the full extent of my recollection about it. I have heard you speak of the point out of court, and you may have discussed it this time in the way you represent: I cannot say.

Q. Did you ever hear me say that betting was not indictable?

A. I never heard you say that betting was not indictable in this State.

[Mr. Knott here objected that the Judge's construction of the law was not a matter relevant to the issue, and a discursive debate sprung up which continued some time. The Judge returned to the examination of the witness, saying that he had been "butted off the track" by the gentleman.]

Q. In speaking of this case, wasn't I talking more to the Circuit Attorney, to yourself and the other lawyers, than to the jury?

A. I cannot say, I am sure.

Q. Were you not employed in the case?

A. I had been spoken to, but I had nothing more to do than to listen, and give my opinion occasionally.

Q. Is that the way you do business for your clients?

A. Not usually.

Q. Well, Mr. Tyrell, we will go back to those habeas corpus cases. Do you recollect where you presented the petition in the first case?

A. It was at your own house.

Q. When was the writ issued?

A. It was issued that evening.

Q. Do you recollect what time that was? Wasn't it some time early in January?

A. I think it was. I think it must have been near the ninth of January. I saw you in the street, and had some talk to you about the case.

Q. At what time was the other case presented?

A. Believe they were both presented together. Some of the causes alleged in both petitions were the same.

Q. Didn't I tell you the causes alleged were not sufficient?

A. I believe you did, and I think I made an alteration or two at your suggestion.

Q. When Mr. Cryts made his return to the writ, didn't I tell him the prisoner was discharged?

A. I believe you did tell him that the prisoner was or would be discharged.

Q. When did I write the discharge? Didn't I write the discharge in both cases at the same time?

A. I cannot say positively; my attention was not particularly given to that matter; but it may have been so.

Q. When was it that the papers were brought in by the Constable? Was it before or after the discharge?

A. I believe the papers came in before the discharge of the prisoner.

Q. Did you say that you had told me the character of the examination taken before the Justice?

A. I do not remember saying so.

Q. Well, what was your opinion about the making of that order?

[Objected to and withdrawn.]

Q. Do you say that the facts were told to me by Mr. Cryts?

A. Yes, sir. He had a conversation with you before or at the time he made his return, and I think that he then related them. He did not have much to say about it, however. There was something wrong about his return, and he amended it once or twice.

Q. In what particular did he amend it?

A. I don't remember.

[Witness proceeded here to relate the facts, his statement not differing materially from that given upon the examination in chief.]

Q. Is it customary to take the testimony of by-standers in relation to such cases, instead of the record?

[Objected to and withdrawn.]

Q. Do you think I had any corrupt motive in discharging the prisoner?

[Objected to and withdrawn.]

Q. What was the ground of the discharge?

A. I do not remember the ground stated in the order.

Q. Well, had the Constable Cryts any authority for holding the prisoner in custody?

A. I can only give an opinion. I believe when the mittimus and other papers were in his hands, and my belief was at the time when I saw them, that he had authority to hold the prisoner.

Q. Do you say that the papers brought in by the Constable were the identical papers in the cause?

A. The only thing I know about that is, that the papers were claimed by Cryts to be the papers in the cause. He brought them into the office and said there was the papers.

Q. Well, how about the other case?

A. The case of John R. Maine?

Q. Yes. What authority had the officer to hold him in custody?

A. Well, he had a mittimus.

Q. How do you know it was a mittimus?

A. I know it purported to be one. It was directed to the Jailer, and commanded him to keep the body of Russell. It was the usual warrant of commitment.

Q. Would any person's writing a paper of that kind make it a mittimus?

A. Of course not.

Q. Well, what was in this paper?

A. There was statement that the man, John R. Maine, had been brought before the magistrate charged with larceny. It then directed the officer to keep him—to commit him to jail.

Q. Did that mittimus state that there had been an examination as to the probable guilt or innocence of the accused?

A. It is my impression that it did not, and I believe that was one of the reasons I urged for the discharge. You said that if it had only gone so far as to state that sufficient evidence to believe an offense had been committed was adduced, it would have been good.

Q. Mr. Tyrell, what is the state of your feelings towards myself?

A. At present I have no particular admiration or respect for you. A few months ago I did respect you very much.

Q. What has produced the change?

A. Your conduct towards me.

Q. In what respect?

A. One cause that I can name now is, that you stated that on my examination before the Judiciary Committee of the House, last winter, I had committed perjury. You told me so, and others have informed me that you made the statement.

Q. Did I not tell you that I did not know whether you had been sworn to, or had stated certain things, or not, but that if you had stated certain things that I understood you had stated, you were falsifying? Didn't I ask you whether you had sworn to those things?

A. I believe you did.

Q. Were you sworn here?

A. I was.

Q. Did not you and myself go to St. Louis on the same train together, and were we not perfectly friendly at that time?

A. Yes, sir.

Q. Did you not then tell me that I need not expect justice at the hands of the committee?

A. I don't remember, but think I did not; though I had serious doubts on the subject at the time.

Q. Where was your home then?

A. Bloomfield.

Q. Hadn't you changed your residence before you came up here? Were you not living in Jackson, then?

A. My wife was there, temporarily.

Q. Didn't you make a contract for board there with that understanding?

A. I made a contract for board, but not with any such understanding.

Q. Didn't you make an affidavit that you had traveled a good many miles, and didn't you draw more mileage than you were entitled to?

A. I drew mileage, but do not know that I made any claim for it, or made any affidavit.

Q. Haven't you said repeatedly that these proceedings against me were hellish, were devilish, and so on?

[Objected to and withdrawn.]

Q. When you told me about the committee, didn't you tell me there were too many who wanted to wear the ermine, and that that was what was the matter?

The managers objected to this question on the ground that it was irrelevant; and arguing that if the question were asked for the purpose of laying a foundation to contradict the witness, it was improper for the reason that a witness could not be examined for the purpose of contradiction on an immaterial point. Thereupon a confused and colloquial debate sprung up, a report of which would not be intelligible. The question was finally reduced to writing by Judge Jackson, as follows:

Did you not, at the time you told me in Jefferson City that I need not even expect justice from that committee, state that there were too many who wanted to wear the ermine, and that was what was the matter?

The question before the Court being, shall the respondent be permitted to ask the question? it was decided in the negative by the following vote:

AYES—Messrs. Goodlett, Gullett, Harris, Hedgpeth, McFarland, Morris, Newland, Peyton, Scott, Wilson, and Wood—11.

NOES—Messrs. Brown, Byrne, Churchill, Coleman, Frazier, Halliburton, Horner, McFerran, McIlvaine, O'Neil, Parsons, Rains, Richardson, Thompson, Vernon, and Wright—16.

Absent—Messrs. Hyer, Johnson, Jones, Robinson, and Watkins.

Excused from voting—Mr. Fox.

The cross-examination then proceeded.

Q. Haven't you been very active in spreading rumors about me, since the commencement of these proceedings?

A. Never.

Q. Were you not the author of an article in the ——— ———, signed "Plus?"

[A long debate ensued about whether the witness should be allowed to answer the question. It was finally decided that he might do so. The witness stated that he could not tell who was the author of the piece (which was shown to him,) and after a long debate as to whether he should be compelled to give a more definite answer, the Senate adjourned.

FOURTH DAY.

THURSDAY, June 9, 1859.

The Court met pursuant to adjournment, and was opened by proclamation.

The managers and respondent attended.

On motion of SENATOR McILVAINE, leave of absence was granted to Senator O'Neil.

DAVID M. FOX, a witness on the part of the State, against whom an attachment had issued, was sworn as a witness, and charged under the rule by the President of the Senate; and on motion of SENATOR SCOTT, was excused from any further proceedings against him in pursuance of the attachment, all the Senators present voting in the affirmative.

Absent—Messrs. Hyer, Johnson, Jones, and Watkins.
Sick—Mr. Vernon.

The cross-examination of Mr. M. H. TYRELL was resumed.

[The question, an answer to which Judge Jackson was urging at the adjournment yesterday, was waived.]

Q. Where did you say you reside?

A. I reside at Bloomfield, Stoddard county. I call that my home, at least. My family has been boarding at Jackson latterly. I have been at home very little during the last two months.

Q. Where have you been during that time?

A. In Butler county.

Q. What have you been doing there?

A. Laying out a road.

Q. Haven't you represented yourself as an engineer?

[Question objected to and passed without answer.]

Q. Mr. Tyrell, you have answered as to your own feeling and opinion about me; now tell us what is the opinion of the people of Stoddard county with regard to me, as a Judge?

[Question objected to, and then put in a different form. An objection being still urged, it was waived.]

Q. Did you ever hear me accuse Mr. Fox of perjury, of subornation of perjury, or of lying, on the bench?

A. I cannot say that I ever did.

Q. Is that my general conduct towards lawyers?

This question was objected to by the managers, reduced to writing, (as below given,) and decided proper by the following vote:

AYES—Messrs. Churchill, Coleman, Goodlett, Gullett, Harris, Hedgpeth, McFerran, McIlvaine, Morris, Newland, Parsons, Peyton, Rains, Richardson, Robinson, Scott, Thompson, Wilson, Wood, and Wright—20.
NOES—Messrs. Brown, Byrne, Fox, Frazier, Halliburton, Horner, and McFarland—7.
Absent—Messrs. Hyer, Johnson, Jones, and Watkins.
Absent on leave—Mr. O'Neil.
Sick—Mr. Vernon.

Q. As far as your observation extends, has my conduct as Judge, towards lawyers and parties litigant, been habitually oppressive, contumelious, insolent, and insulting?

A. To some lawyers and some litigants your conduct and language have been as described.

Q. Couldn't you give an instance?

A. I think on some occasions your conduct towards Mr. Kitchen, Mr. Phelan, and Mr. Fox, has been of this character.

Q. How many times have you ever been present in courts with Mr. Fox?

A. I don't know the number of times. Not very often. Perhaps not more than three.

Q. Well, now in regard to Mr. Phelan; how many times have I treated him in that way?

A. I couldn't tell.

Q. In what cases was it?

A. I couldn't give the particular cases, either.

Q. Well, prior to my treating Mr. Fox, and Phelan, and Kitchen this way, was there not an understanding that these men would hold a meeting against me at Butler Circuit Court?

[Objected to and question not answered.]

Q. At the April term, was there not some kind of plan gotten up to hold a meeting of the bar at Butler court?

[Objected to, debated some time, and withdrawn.]

Q. You stated that some lawyers and some litigants had been treated in that bad manner by me. Now I want you to give an instance of some parties.

A. I believe I have already remarked that it occurred in two instances. The case of Griffie and Whitehead would perhaps do for one.

Q. Well, what was it that I did then?

A. I don't remember exactly what.

Q. Well, did my bad conduct consist in my decisions or my words?

A. Sometimes in both.

Q. What was it that was oppressive?

A. I will not undertake to detail.

Q. What was it that was contumelious, insolent, and insulting?

A. I said that to some lawyers and to some litigants your conduct had some of those characteristics.

Q. Well, what was the contumelious matter?

A. I gave yesterday your expression in regard to Mr. Fox. I think perhaps that would do for an instance.

Q. What did I say to him?

A. You told him to sit down, in a harsh manner.

Q. Well, what made my conduct towards Griffith and Whitesides bad? What was the matter there? Was it anything I said to them, or was my ruling oppressive?

A. The effect of your ruling was oppressive, in my judgment.

Q. Did you ever hear me address any party out of the way?

A. Think I have, sir, repeatedly. I have heard it in nearly every court-house that you have held court in while I was present.

Q. Did you ever hear anything of the kind in Ripley court?

A. Yes, sir.

Q. Well, what was it you heard?

A. I can't now undertake to give names or precise expressions. I might, perhaps, by a little investigation.

Q. Did I ever do it in Wayne court?

A. Yes, sir.

Q. In Stoddard?

A. Yes, sir.

Q. In Dunklin?

A. In all your courts that I have attended.

Q. And after hearing all these things at all these places, you can't now give a single instance?

A. Not at present—not here, I would have to refresh my memory by a reference to papers.

Q. Well, now, Mr. Tyrell, haven't you said, at various times and to various persons, that all you had against me as a Judge was, that I ought to have sent Mr. Phelan and Mr. Kitchen, and others, perhaps, to jail, or words with that meaning?

A. I think I never said that I approved your course as Judge.

Q. That is not answering my question. If you ever said anything about me as a Judge, let us hear it.

A. Perhaps by limiting your question you would be able to get a definite reply.

The managers objected to this question as irrelevant, and as opening a door for collateral issues. The respondent reduced his question to writing, (as given below,) and it was decided proper by the following vote:

AYES—Messrs. Goodlett, Gullett, Harris, Hedgpeth, Morris, Newland, Parsons, Peyton, Rains, Richardson, Robinson, Scott, Wilson, and Wood—14.

NOES—Messrs. Brown, Byrne, Churchill, Coleman, Fox, Frazier, Halliburton, McFarland, McFerran, McIlvaine, and Wright—13.

Absent—Messrs. Hyer, Johnson, Jones, and Watkins.

Absent on leave—Mr. O'Neil.

Sick—Mr. Vernon.

Q. Have you not, in the presence of David G. Hicks, in the county of Stoddard, since you gave your testimony before the Committee of the Judiciary last winter, in this case, stated that you mostly approved my course as Judge; that had you been in my place you would have sent some of the attorneys to jail?

A. I am unable to say. Perhaps I did,—perhaps I did not. Had a good many conversations with several persons on the subject, and perhaps I used that language, though I don't recollect it, while I am not sure that I did not. A part of that was often in my mind, and I was convinced ——

Q. Was it the part relating to the jail?

[Not answered.]

Q. Now, Mr. Tyrell, I want to ask you one question in regard to your getting license to practice. When did you say your license was dated?

A. On the 8th of May.

Q. Didn't you get it in Butler county?

A. The license was issued in Stoddard county. The Clerk of the Stoddard court's certificate to the affidavit on the license is on it.

Q. But mightn't that have been put there at a different time. Mightn't the license have been given you in Butler, and the affidavit made afterwards?

A. The *jurat* and the license have the same date.

Q. Well, it don't matter. Do you recollect a conversation that you and I had about my not giving you license at Doniphan?

[Objected to and question waived.]

RE-EXAMINED BY MR. KNOTT.

Q. I understood you to say, Mr. Tyrell, that in one of the habeas corpus cases, about which you testified, the Judge suggested an alteration of your petition, in reference to some of the causes assigned for the application for the writ of habeas corpus. Did you alter it then?

A. Yes, sir, I think I made the alteration pursuant to his suggestion. I endeavored, by an interlineation, I think, at least, to make the petition conform to his opinion in regard to the law.

JUDGE JACKSON. Wait a moment about that. Wasn't the petitions both alike?

A. I think some of the same causes were alleged in both.

Q. Is that it? (showing witness a paper.)

Mr. KNOTT. Let me see it, Mr. Tyrell, before you answer.

JUDGE JACKSON. No, that is not it. It is not offered in evidence. Mr. Tyrell, didn't you consider those petitions sufficient?

Mr. KNOTT. That is a matter of law, and you needn't give your opinion.

JUDGE JACKSON. Well, didn't you, Mr. Tyrell, present those petitions in good faith?

A. Of course I did.

Mr. KNOTT. Please state the words interlined by you at the suggestion of the Judge, by refreshing your memory from any memorandum that you may have.

A. To the best of my recollection they were these words: "That the said warrant of commitment is insufficient and defective;" "that said magistrate has not certified an examination of the accused," and "that there is no testimony to warrant the commitment." I can't say that the Judge suggested those very words, but they were inserted in pursuance to his suggestion.

Mr. HARDIN. Were the interlineations made before the petition was signed? Were they sworn to with the balance?

A. I don't remember.

The examination of Mr. Tyrell here closed.

TESTIMONY OF JONAS EAKER.

JONAS EAKER called for the State and examined by Mr. Hardin.

Q. Where do you reside?

A. I reside near Bloomfield, in Stoddard county, Missouri.

Q. What is your occupation?

A. I am a farmer.

Q. What offices in that county have you held or do you now hold?

A. Judge, or one of the Judges, of the County Court, and Justice of the Peace.

Q. Were you a Judge of the County Court in May, 1858?

A. I was.

Q. Well, Mr. Eaker, Judge Jackson is charged here with issuing an attachment against you for a criminal contempt, at the spring term of the Circuit Court in Stoddard county, because you did not make a return to a writ of mandamus issued from his court. I will get you to state the facts, what occurred between you and the Judge, and all you may know about the matter, as nearly as you can recollect?

A. Well, I'll tell all about the business as near as I remember. Sometime prior to the May term of the Circuit Court, the Deputy Sheriff, J. J. Jackson, told me he had a mandamus for me, and presented a copy of it, or something purporting to be a copy, and I knew it to be a copy from the handwriting of the Sheriff, or Deputy Sheriff, rather. I didn't consider it a service, and let the matter run on, and didn't appear in court to answer. I had spoken to Mr. Kitchen and Mr. Phelan about it, and when the case came up, they moved to quash the return or the writ, or something of that kind, but the Judge told them to hush up, or to take their seats, or something to that amount; I couldn't pretend to give his exact words; and he ordered the Clerk to issue an attachment for me. The Clerk issued one. I was sitting near by at the time, and it was served on me by the officer in the room where the court was held. When I heard what they were doing, I got up from where I was sitting and went back and took a position on a work bench that was there. After I was arrested, I was held in custody about an hour by the principal Sheriff. When the case was called up again, I went in, and the Judge told me I was in contempt. I told him I was not, because I hadn't been served. It was talked about some; the Judge said if I was not in contempt I didn't know my duty. I told him I thought I did. After that he said he would release me if I would answer under the copy. I took it out and answered, and brought it in to the Judge, and he dismissed the case at the prisoner's cost.

Q. Did you say Mr. Kitchen and Mr. Phelan were your attorneys in the case?

A. Yes, sir, I spoke to them as attorneys to attend to it for me.

Q. Well, did they attend to it for you?

A. They tried to, but the Judge required them to shut their mouths and sit down, and wouldn't allow them to speak about the matter.

Q. You say, then, that they made an effort to speak to the court in your behalf?

A. Yes, sir, they did.

Q. When the Judge told them to shut their mouths and sit down, what did they do?

A. Well, Mr. Kitchen rather contended that he had a right to speak for his client; he said he was a lawyer, or a member of the bar, and had a right to be heard.

Q. Mr. Eaker, I will call your attention to another matter. Were you present at the August term of the court?

A. I was in and about there.

Q. Were you in court during the trial of Orson Bartlett?

A. Yes, sir. I was present during the trial of Col. Bartlett.

Q. You will please commence and go through with what occurred then—what you noticed of the way that case turned out, and what you heard the Judge say.

A. Well, in the first place, I think Col. Bartlett, and David G. Hicks, and Isaac Brand, and the Judge himself were all returned in the same indictment for playing cards, or for gaming. I am not certain how it was, but I think they had a jury, and a witness or two was brought in to testify in the case. While the matter was up the Judge undertook to define the law on the case. If I understood it right, the charge was for playing cards for a watermelon worth ten cents; it was something like that I know. The Judge told the jury to take the case and find the facts, and he would apply the law. Just about that time some one tapped me or beckoned me that he wanted to see me, and I went out; and that is all I know about it of my own knowledge.

Q. Have you seen the articles of impeachment in this case?

A. I don't know; I believe I have. I think some one read them to me.

Q. Do you know anything about any other charges than the ones you have spoken of?

A. Well, you mean the charges here to be tried? I do not know that I do.

Q. Do you know anything about Judge Jackson's going before the grand jury of Stoddard county and giving them some instructions?

A. Not of my own knowledge.

Q. Did you hear the charge of the Judge to the grand jury at this term of the court?

A. I wasn't present.

CROSS-EXAMINED BY JUDGE JACKSON.

Q. Mr. Eaker, wasn't it this way about that mandamus matter: on the application for the mandamus didn't we have a conversation about the matter, and wasn't it then you told me about the service ?

A. I don't know, Judge. I believe I was talking to you and told you I expected there would be an application made, some weeks before court.

Q. Now wasn't it in this conversation I said some of the things you say I said about it?

A. I don't know. I have told the circumstances according to my best recollection.

Q. Well, at the time you say I told them to take their seats and shut their mouths, now who was that language addressed to ?

A. It was first, or you talked first in that style, to Mr. Kitchen.

Q. Well, what did Mr. Kitchen say ? Didn't he say he was not an attorney in the case ?

A. I don't recollect. When you said it was not a case for an attorney, I think may be he did.

Q. Didn't I tell them I wouldn't hear them because there was no case in court ?

A. I believe I recollect that you said it was not a case in court for argument.

Q. You say you were in the court-house when I was talking to Mr. Kitchen and Mr. Phelan ?

A. Yes, sir.

Q. Well, didn't I then tell you, or didn't I ask you if you were ready to make a return, and wasn't that before the attachment was issued ?

A. All the conversation I had with you about it in the court-house was when I was brought in under the attachment.

Q. Did'nt I tell you I couldn't do anything in the case till you made a return ; that you could make your return, and if the writ hadn't been served, I intimated my willingness to dismiss the proceeding ?

A. Yes, you did say something like that after I was brought in under the attachment.

Q. At the time the Sheriff served the writ upon you, or copy you call it, do you know whether you saw the original ? Did you ever see the original ?

A. I think, perhaps, I did see the original at some time, though I couldn't now say it was then.

Q. Did you see the copy ?

A. I did, sir.

Q. How did you know it was a copy if you didn't see the original ?

A. I knew it wasn't the original from the hand-writing. I was tolerably familiar with your hand-writing.

Q. How did you know it was a mandamus ?

A. I knew it from the reading, and I saw it was in the hand-writing of somebody else.

Q. And you knew it was a copy, because it wasn't in my hand-writing? Now couldn't there be an original mandamus, without my writing it out myself? In your opinion does the law require the Judge to write a writ of mandamus himself?

[Mr. Knott objected to the witness giving an opinion upon a matter of law.]

A. I knew well enough that you, Judge, was not in the habit of getting other people to sign your name to writs.

[Some little discussion about this question, between Judge Jackson and Mr. Knott, ensued here. When it was through, the Judge proceeded with the cross-examination.]

Q. Have you told all you know about this matter? Wasn't it merely a difference of opinion of it as to the law?

A. About all I recollect, Judge. I was afraid of misunderstanding the law, and examined it about the service. I had my view about it, and didn't expect to have any trouble.

Q. Didn't you ask me to wait till the next morning for an answer, and you would answer then, if I would release you under the attachment?

A. That was the arrangement made in the end about the matter.

Q. Well, did you answer?

A. I did.

Q. How did the case turn out?

A. It was dismissed at the prisoner's cost.

Q. Didn't Mr. Dowdy hand in the return to one of the papers?

A. No, the return was not handed in by Uncle Jimmy.

Q. Didn't you, or do you recollect anything that he had to do with the matter?

A. I have no recollection about it if he had. I was a little excited at the time, and it may have escaped my memory.

Q. What excited you?

A. Well, I thought, Judge, that you spoke to me pretty short.

Q. What did I say?

A. Well, I have told, I believe, as near as I can recollect. You told me that if I was not in contempt, I didn't know my duty. I told you I thought I did, and we talked awhile about it.

Q. Didn't I make that observation after you was called up under the attachment, or wasn't it before?

A. Yes, sir, it was after I was called up under the attachment.

Q. And have you no recollection of Dowdy saying anything about the affair?

A. None.

Q. Now I wish I had an attorney. I want to ask some questions about personal matters, and don't like to do it myself. Mr. Eaker, how long have you lived about Bloomfield?

A. Near twenty-two years.

Q. What offices have you held in that county?

A. The first office I held there was Clerk of the Circuit and County Courts. I was Clerk about seven years. I have held no other offices but Justice of the Peace and Justice of the County Court.

Q. Have you ever signed what is commonly called a lie-bill?

A. No, sir, I never did. I know what you refer to, and I can tell you all about it, and prove what I say, by plenty of men from south-east Missouri. I would like to explain.

Q. Never mind; just answer my questions. Didn't you state, under oath, once, that what you had said on a former occasion was false?

[This question was objected to by Mr. Hardin. After discussion, the objection was withdrawn, and the witness was proceeding to answer in his own style, but was so frequently interrupted by the Judge, in the course of his narration, that the reporter could make nothing of it. Senator Rains objected to the altercations between the witness and the respondent, and after stating his objections, the matter was dropped.]

JUDGE JACKSON. I am through with the witness for the present.

MR. KNOTT. Mr. Eaker, before this attachment was issued against you, was the Judge distinctly informed that you had been served with the mandamus only by copy?

A. I cannot say that I so informed him myself. There was nothing said about it that I remember, in our conversation before the court, between the County Court and Judge Jackson's court. At that time I told my counsel about it, and they, my lawyers, represented the matter to the Judge.

Q. What was the manner of the Judge in court during the pendency of the matter?

A. He appeared to be angry. He seemed as if he thought I was trying to get the advantage of the court.

Q. You say you did yourself apprise him of the fact that you had not been properly served after the attachment issued?

A. Yes, sir.

Q. In making answer to the copy, did you plead to the service?

A. Yes, sir. After I was compelled to answer on the copy, I was discharged.

JUDGE JACKSON. You said, I believe, there was considerable contention about the matter. Wasn't it principally by your lawyers?

A. Well, I believe Mr. Kitchen did contend that he had some rights there; that he was a lawyer, and so on.

TESTIMONY OF JAMES WALKER.

JAMES WALKER called for the State and examined by Mr. Knott.

Q. Mr. Walker, where do you reside?

A. In Stoddard county, at Bloomfield.

Q. Are you acquainted with Matthew Moore?

A. Yes, sir. I am acquainted with him.

Q. Were you present at the November term of the Stoddard Circuit Court, 1858?

A. Yes, sir.

Q. Had you a suit pending in that court?

A. No, sir. Well, I recollect I was expecting one to be there, between Moore and myself, but whether it was in court then, I don't remember.

Q. Did Judge Jackson, here, and you have any conversation in regard to the controversy between you and Moore?

A. Yes, sir. I had some chat with the Judge about it.

Q. Well, sir, please state to the Court the time and place, and what the conversation was—what he said to you in relation to that suit. Tell all you know about it, as succinctly as you can.

A. I will, as nigh as I can recollect. Me and Mr. Moore was disputing about some property. He was claiming my lots in Bloomfield. I thought he had no right to them; and that was the matter that the suit was to be about. Me and Mr. Jackson talked about it. He asked me how had we come out with our difficulty, if we had fixed it up, or something like that. I told him we hadn't fixed it up, and I didn't know as we would. Then he told me it didn't matter; that the field-notes of Bloomfield had got lost, and, says he, they can't hurt you anyhow. I told him that I thought not, and he said, that's my opinion about it. That was about all there was of it.

Q. Where did this conversation take place?

A. It was at my stable. I had met the Judge and we had talked about it there.

Q. Do you recollect the time of the month?

A. No, sir. I don't recollect the time of the month, nor what day of the week it was. It was last November court.

Q. Had the Sheriff served a writ upon you?

A. No, sir, he had not. The Sheriff didn't serve me. He sent it down by a man. I recollect that the Sheriff had notified me before this that he would send it down. I recollect now there was a suit there.

Q. How did the suit turn out?

A. Well, they took a change of venue to Scott county.
Q. Has it been tried yet?
A. No, sir, I believe not. It was to have been tried in Benton at the last term, but I think they told me that it wasn't tried, because the papers were not sent up in time.
Q. Was this conversation before court?
A. Well, I believe it was; or now I come to think about it, I think it was during the session of the court.
Q. Did you mention the fact that you had had this conversation to any body?
A. It's likely I did. I think I spoke of it afterwards to several in talking about the case.
Q. Did the Judge tell you not to mention what he had told you?
A. No, sir, he didn't. I spoke about it to any person that asked. I didn't consider it any secret, or anything of that kind, and I just said there was no danger of my losing the lots, for Mr. Jackson had told me this.
Q. When you say Mr. Jackson, you mean the Judge here?
A. Yes, sir.
Mr. KNOTT. You can take the witness.

CROSS-EXAMINED BY JUDGE JACKSON.

Q. Do you remember the time of the week this conversation between you and me took place?
A. I do not.
Q. Do you remember we walked down together from a store, as you were going on to your place; wasn't it the last part of the week?
A. I can't recollect whether it was or not.
Q. How did the conversation come up?
A. I think you asked me about the matter, and I told you as I said.
Q. Didn't I observe that if the south-west corner of the town was moved, it would affect my property? Isn't that the way we came to talk about it?
A. Yes, you had that chat to me.
Q. Didn't I say it might change my lines? Was it more than a casual observation?
A. I don't know, Judge.
Q. How long were we talking?
A. I don't recollect. Not many minutes.
Q. Had Moore talked to you any about a compromise, and didn't I ask you whether you *had* compromised your difficulty with him? Wasn't that the way of it?
A. Mr. Moore had talked to me about a compromise, but he got mad and said he wouldn't compromise; or, at any rate, he said it could be made up, but it would take more than before.
Q. When did you say this was?
A. I think it was before court.
Q. Had he withdrawn his proposition?
A. No, sir. He sent down word that he would compromise for $1,000.
Q. Was that before or since the conversation with me?
A. It has been since. There has been a good deal of chat before and since, and I don't remember precisely about it.
Q. Well, Mr. Walker, did I give you any advice about your suit?
A. The only advice you gave me was what I have said. You told me the field-notes was lost, and he couldn't hurt me about the matter.
Q. Didn't I speak to you about my own property; or how did I approach you on the subject?

9

A. Well, I could hardly say.

Q. Did I tell you how you could get ahead of him and beat him in the suit?

A. No, you didn't tell me that.

Q. Did I tell you what lawyer to get, or what course to pursue about the matter?

A Not that I recollect.

Q. Are you certain it was during court week that we had this conversation?

A. Yes, sir, I am pretty certain.

Q. Hadn't court adjourned?

A. I don't think it had.

Q. Don't you recollect that it was in the latter part of the week?

A. I do not.

RE-EXAMINED BY MR. KNOTT.

Q. Where does Matthew H. Moore live?

A. In Cape Girardeau.

Q. What is his business? Isn't he a lawyer?

A. Yes, sir.

Mr. Knott. That is all. You can go.

RECALLED BY JUDGE JACKSON.

Q- If the south corner, or the south-east corner of the town was moved, wouldn't it change my lots? Wouldn't the change affect my property in town then by changing my lines? From the way the lots are laid off, wouldn't a change have materially affected my property?

A. Yes, I suppose if the corner was moved either way, north or south, it would affect your lines.

Senator Goodlett. I want to understand the witness whether a suit was pending between him and Moore at this time?

A. Yes. Notice had been served upon me.

Judge Jackson. How long was it after this conversation before you told any one anything about it?

A. I don't remember. I told several about it shortly after that. I was just as apt as not to have told it the same day, and if any one asked me, perhaps I did.

Senator Parsons. Was the notice served on you a notice to quit, or a notice to appear and defend the suit?

A. I forget. I don't recollect that.

Mr. Hardin. The record will show.

TESTIMONY OF J. J. JACKSON.

John J. Jackson called and examined for the State by Mr. Knott.

Q. Where do you reside, Mr. Jackson?

A. In Stoddard county, Missouri.

Q. Were you acting as Deputy Sheriff of Stoddard county in January last?

A. Yes, sir. I have been acting as Deputy Sheriff for better than two years—it will be three years next August.

Q. Did you, some time in January last, have in your custody the body of one John R. Maine? If so, state how he came into your custody, what become of him, and all about it, as briefly as you can?

A. Well, sir, he came into my custody—was delivered to me by the Constable, with a mittimus. There was no other papers but the mittimus that I saw. As far as the mittimus was concerned, I can't say now for what it said he was charged. I believed at the time that it was a good mittimus.

Q. Well, how did he get out of your custody?

A. He was taken by me before Judge Jackson by a writ of habeas corpus. I do not know that I can recollect the time exactly; it was, though, I think, about the middle of January. I made a return to the writ the same day it was served upon me, in an hour or two afterwards. I returned that I had the man in custody, and took in the papers, or rather I took in the warrant of commitment, or mittimus, for there was no other papers in my hands. I took it to the office where the Judge was, and after a while he was discharged.

Q. Did the Judge ask you for any other papers than the mittimus?

A. I think he did. I told him I had no others.

Q. Did he make any rule upon you or anybody for the production of other papers in the case?

A. I think not. If he did, I do not know it.

Q. Did he make any inquiry as to the facts?

A. I believe he made no inquiry for further facts than the mittimus showed. He asked me if I had any other papers, and I told him I had not. I think that was about all he asked me.

Q. For what purpose did you have Maine in custody?

A. The warrant commanded me to safely hold him to answer some charge. I was going with him to jail at Greenville, as our jail had been condemned. I received him the evening before, and left him with my son, while I went out home (I live five miles out of town) to make preparations to go the next day to Greenville. When I came back next morning I found the writ of habeas corpus had been issued, and I made my return to it.

Q. What time of day was it when you took the prisoner before the Judge?

A. I don't recollect exactly; it was along about 10 or 12 o'clock.

Q. Did you see anything of one Charles Russell that day?

A. Yes, sir; I had seen him the day before under trial before Jonas Eaker. After an examination, he was held to bail. My son was prosecuting him.

Q. What was done with him?

A. Wm. F. Cryts had him in custody, holding him to see if he could give bail. They told me a writ of habeas corpus had been taken out for him.

Q. Were you in the room when the writ of habeas corpus was returned?

A. Yes, sir.

Q. Well, tell us what took place—tell the details as near as you can?

A. I cannot detail all that took place. I heard no conversation except that this Mr. Cryts came in with a bunch of papers, and either handed them to the Judge, or laid them down before him. The Judge picked them up, and said he might falsify his return, or he would falsify his return if he wasn't careful. After that, both Russell and Maine were released.

Q. Did the Judge read the papers that were handed to him, or did he look at them to see what they were?

A. I cannot say whether he did or not. I don't think he opened them. I only know the Judge made some remark like that I have repeated.

Q. What was the charge against this man?

A. Russell was charged with passing counterfeit money.

Q. Were you in the examining court at the time of the examination?

A. Yes, sir; my son was the prosecutor in the case, and I was there looking on. It was before Jonas Eaker.

Q. Where was this trial?

A. Well, Judge Eaker lives out of town, or three-quarters of a mile from the court-house. He held his court then in the court-house, in the court-room.

Q. Well, where was this room in which Judge Jackson heard and determined these cases?

A. It was in the same building, up stairs. It was a room used as a law office by Mr. Tyrell.

Q. Did Judge Jackson make any rule upon Mr. Eaker, or any one, to produce any papers?

A. I cannot say—not to my knowledge.

JUDGE JACKSON. I made none. It's not necessary to trouble yourself about that.

Mr. KNOTT. Did you observe Mr. Cryts or any one go out after papers?

A. I think I recollect Mr. Cryts went out of the house once or twice, and once he brought in the papers as I have said.

Q. Do you recollect whose name was signed to the mittimus for the man in your custody?

A. It was signed by James Creary, a Justice of the Peace in our county. That is my recollection of it.

Q. You will please look at that instrument and say whether your signature is attached to it?

[Paper shown to witness.]

A. Yes, sir; I think that is my signature.

Q. Do you recollect at any time of having or serving a writ of mandamus for Judge Eaker, returnable at the May term of the Stoddard Circuit Court?

A. Yes, sir. I recollect that I had such a writ. I do not know that I can state now, positively, what it is about, of my own knowledge. On the streets I heard about it, but I do not recollect the reading of the mandamus.

Q. How did you serve it?

A. I served it by delivering to Judge Eaker a copy, and made my return on the original. I returned the manner in which I had served the writ.

Q. Were you in court on the return day of the writ?

A. Yes, sir; I was.

Q. Do you know anything about an attachment issued for Mr. Eaker for not answering this mandamus?

A. Yes, sir. I served it on Jonas Eaker.

Q. Do you know upon what conditions Mr. Eaker was discharged under that attachment?

A. No, sir; I do not. I may have heard, but I did not hear anything of what took place in court myself. Just about the time I returned the attachment I was called off to attend to something or other.

Q. Do you recollect who was foreman of the grand jury at the August term, 1859?

A. Yes, sir. I believe it was Mr. James Hale.

Q. Do you know anything about Judge Jackson going before the grand jury at that term of the court for any purpose?

A. Well, sir, I did not see Judge Jackson before the grand jury, myself; I heard some conversation between the Judge and David G. Hicks in regard to something that was before the grand jury—a paper, I think it was—and the Judge then said he would go and see about it. I can't say of my own knowledge where he went, but he went out and came back with a paper. Mr. Hicks said that was the paper alluded to. It was a paper citing to some sections of the law and some decisions of the Supreme Court.

Q. Where was this interview?

A. It was in the court-room. Judge Jackson had, I think, adjourned court for the day; the court was not in session, anyhow. The Judge and myself were walking about there in conversation about something, I couldn't say what it was now. Mr. Hicks came up and said to the Judge something about the paper circulating before the grand jury. The Judge remarked that he would go and see about it, and he went and came back with the paper. It was handed to me. I can't say what I did with it. Mr. Hicks said that was the paper alluded to.

Q. Was the grand jury in session at that time?

A. Yes, sir, I think so. So far as I know it had not been discharged; though whether they were doing business at that moment I couldn't say of my own knowledge, because I didn't see them. I never visit the grand jury when it is in session unless I am called to do it on business.

Q. Did you hear the charge to the grand jury at this term of the court?

A. No, sir; I may have heard a part of it as I was passing in and out of the court-room; but I couldn't say that I listened to it particularly.

CROSS-EXAMINATION BY JUDGE JACKSON.

Q. What you did hear of that charge—was it pretty good? Did I get it off tolerably well?

Mr. Knott. May it please the court, I must object to the respondent's asking questions and making Buncombe speeches in the same breath. We have had enough of it already. The gentleman has heretofore displayed his wit sufficiently, and it is now time for him to settle down to a proper and legal examination of witnesses.

Judge Jackson. You, Mr. Knott, examine witnesses in your own style, and I'll do the same. I object, too, to your jumping up with your objections so often. If you would hold still we would get along faster. Don't get into a stew. There, now, I have forgotten what my question was. You have knocked me off the track again. Let it go now. (To witness:)

Q. Mr. Jackson, you speak of Wm. Cryts being a Constable. When was he elected?

A. I cannot say exactly. I suppose he was elected in August last. I couldn't say, except from my understanding from others.

Q. Wasn't there considerable difficulty about his election? Wasn't there a number of reports about it, or about a former election being illegal?

A. Do you mean the contested election case? I know nothing about it, except what I heard from others.

Q. Well, at a former election, wasn't it reported that there had been a good deal of illegal voting done, by which Isaac Brand was elected?

A. I heard something of the kind.

Q. Well, wasn't that election set aside, and a new election ordered, and wasn't it then that Mr. Cryts was elected?

A. I believe that was the way of it.

Q. What relation is Isaac Brand to Judge Eaker?

A. He is son-in-law to the Judge, I believe.

Mr. Knott here objected to the course of the cross-examination, saying that these questions and answers all related to things outside of the issues to be tried in this Court.

Judge Jackson explained his reasons for asking the questions in relation to the Constable's election. He had told Cryts that his return was contradicted by his statements, for what seemed to him, with his intimate knowledge of the facts, a very good reason. He and many others in that community knew that Judge Eaker was a little disappointed at the manner in which the election for Constable had finally resulted, and he thought, and others thought, that when Judge Eaker and his friends had heard there was a writ of habeas corpus got out for this man, they had kept the papers back as a little trap to catch Cryts in, hoping that he would thereby contradict his return, or make a false return, and they could break him of his office for it. These things, he said, Senators could not understand or know without an explanation, and therefore he wanted to go into this matter fully. If the truth was fully stated, it would be seen that this matter of the election of Isaac Brand, Judge Eaker's son-in-law, and his being ousted by Cryts, prompted the course pursued by Judge Eaker in keeping back the papers, and he had prevented Cryts from a contradiction of his return to keep him out of the little trap set for him by the cunning Judge.

Mr. Knott. I cannot but object and protest against Judge Jackson testifying his suspicions about this election case, but—

Judge Jackson. No matter. I waive the question. I am sorry I asked it.

Mr. Knott. Yes, you no doubt are now. You see the predicament that your remarks get you into.

The cross-examination was here resumed.

Q. In the examination in the Russell case you said you attended, I believe?

A. Yes, sir, I was there.

Q. Well, how did you know Russell was held to bail or committed? Was it by the simple say-so of the Justice, in the court-room, or did you see any papers in the hands of the officer?

A. He handed him no paper that I saw. After the examination was through, he told Russell he would hold him to bail in some amount, $300 I think it was, and Russell, or some one for him, asked the Judge to give him till 10 o'clock the next day to get the bail; and then he said he would do it.

Q. But how did the man come into the hands of the Constable? Was there any written order to hold him?

A. None that I know of. I heard him tell Cryts to hold him over till 10 o'clock.

Mr. Hardin. You say you heard the magistrate tell the Constable that he must hold him over till 10 o'clock the next day, and heard him say that he found him guilty, and demanded a bond in the sum of $300, and then gave him till 10 o'clock the next day to fill the bond?

A. That's the way of it as well as I recollect.

Judge Jackson. Was I about there that day?

A. I have no recollection of seeing you there.

On motion of Senator Thompson, the Court adjourned till 3 o'clock.

EVENING SESSION.

Thursday, June 9, 1859.

The Court met pursuant to adjournment.

The managers and respondent attended.

James Walker, witness on the part of State, was by consent of parties discharged from further attendance.

After some little delay occasioned by the absence of witnesses, the taking of testimony was resumed.

TESTIMONY OF WILLIAM F. CRYTS.

William F. Cryts called and examined by Mr. Knott.

Q. Mr. Cryts, you will please state to the Court where you reside.

A. I live in Stoddard county, Missouri.

Q. What is your occupation?

A. At present I am acting as Constable in Castor township, Stoddard county.

Q. How long have you held that position?

A. Since last September, if I am not mistaken.

Q. Were you acting in that capacity in January last?

A. Yes, sir.

Q. Did you, in that month, have in your custody a man named Charles Russell? If so, please state to the court how he came into your hands, and what you did with him.

A. Well, a writ for him was placed in my hands, and I arrested him. He was charged with passing counterfeit money. The writ was issued by Mr. Eaker. I brought him before the Justice.

Q. Was there a trial before the Justice? Tell us about that.

A. Well, sir, there was a trial, and he was committed or bound over. At the conclusion of the trial he was bound over till the next day, to give bail. He was placed in my custody to keep till then.

Q. Were you in attendance at Mr. Eaker's courts?

A. Yes, sir. I usually attended his courts, and was then there.

Q. After the Judge or Justice found there was probable cause to believe him guilty, and he was placed in your hands to hold till he got bail, what became of him then?

A. There was a writ of habeas corpus served on me, and I gave him up.

Q. Who issued that writ?

A. Judge Jackson.

Q. Well, go on and state all the facts about that writ.

A. I don't know that I can state all the facts, but I will as near as I can. I made a return on the writ that I had him in custody, and took him before Judge Jackson. I returned that I had him in custody by verbal orders from Jonas Eaker.

Q. Did the Judge make any inquiry for the papers in the case?

A. I don't recollect that he did.

Q. Did he make any order for you or the Justice to produce the papers?

A. I can't say that he made any order for the papers. I left my return in the room, and went down after the balance of the papers. I got them and brought them in, and laid them on the table.

Q. What were those papers?

A. They were the papers in the case; I think there was several of them. I won't undertake to say what they were. Russell was discharged.

Q. Where did you go after the papers?

A. I went to Miller's store-house.

Q. Who did you get the papers from?

A. From Judge Eaker.

Q. What did you do after laying down the papers on the table?

A. I left the room; when I came back he was discharged.

Q. Don't you know what the papers were?

A. I don't recollect reading them. They were the papers in the case.

Q. Was the testimony taken in the trial among them?

A. Yes, sir, I believe it was.

Q. And the writ—the warrant for his arrest?

A. Yes, sir.
Q. What was Judge Jackson doing at the time you brought the papers in?
A. I don't recollect. He was at the table, I believe.
Q. Do you recollect whether Russell was arrested and tried before the Justice the same day?
A. I don't think it was the same day. The writ of habeas corpus was issued the next day after the trial.
Q. Did any part of the trial take place the same day that Russell was arrested?
A. I think not. I think it was over two days from the time I made the arrest till the trial. I wouldn't say positively, from the fact that I don't recollect.
Q. Did you hold him in custody during the night before the trial?
A. I did hold him in custody by virtue of the orders given me by Judge Eaker.
Senator Parsons. About how long were you absent at Miller's store after the papers?
A. But a short time. I couldn't state how long. Probably two or three minutes.

CROSS-EXAMINED BY JUDGE JACKSON.

Q. Is Jonas Eaker a Justice of the Peace?
A. Yes, sir. I suppose he is. I believe he was elected by the people to that office.
Q. How do you know he is Justice of the Peace?
A. I think I know it, because he was a candidate for the office, and was elected.
Q. Do you know whether he has ever been sworn as a Justice of the Peace?
A. I do not.
Q. Do you know whether the examination in this Russell case was reduced to writing?
A. I could not say positively whether it was or not.
Q. Didn't you talk to me about the case before the hearing of the habeas corpus application?
A. I think you spoke to me about making my return. You met me in the street, and asked me if I had done it.
Q. How long was this before you had made your return?
A. It was at least an hour, or half an hour.
Q. Didn't I ask you about it on the square, when we met the first time?
A. I couldn't say. I believe it was some time before.
Q. When you did make your return, the papers, you say, were not delivered to me. How did you come to make a return without the papers?
A. I allowed you were a waiting on me, and I thought I could step down and get the papers afterwards.
Q. Well, how did you come to bring up the papers after making a return? Had I seen the papers before, or did you tell me what they were?
A. I don't know how it was.
Q. Did you have a warrant when you arrested him?
A. Yes, sir. I had a writ, of course, when I took him in custody.
Q. Do you make returns under oath?
A. I suppose I do.
Q. Did any person tell you to go and get the papers?
A. I don't recollect.
Q. Had he written out the papers when you went after them?

A. I don't recollect.

Q. Is that your signature? (showing witness a paper.)

A. Yes, that is my name, signed in my handwriting.

Q. Did you hear the examination of the witnesses before Judge Eaker?

A. Yes, sir, I did hear the examination.

Q. Well, what did the witnesses say?

A. I can't say what the witnesses said.

Q. Now tell me, when Jonas Eaker told you to take this man, Russell, and keep him until the next morning, which do you consider it was, that you had him in custody, or that Jonas Eaker had just set him at liberty?

Mr. KNOTT objected that this question could only elicit the opinion of the witness upon a matter of law, and was therefore incompetent and irrelevant.

JUDGE JACKSON claimed that he was not allowed the latitude of ordinary cross-examinations, and stated that he was treated more severely than the man who was, a day or two previously, arrested for the murder of Mr. Charless in St. Louis. He wanted record evidence to be produced in the case, and then it would not be necessary to seek the reasons of his official acts from parol testimony. Finally, however, he waived the question.

SENATOR WILSON. At the time the writ of habeas corpus was served on you, requiring you to produce the body of Russell before Judge Jackson, by what authority did you hold said Russell in custody? Was it written, or verbal?

A. It was a verbal order.

Mr. KNOTT. Which did you do first, make your return or bring in the papers?

A. I made my return first.

JUDGE JACKSON. Do you recollect what I said when you brought them in?

A. No, sir.

Q. Didn't I ask you if those were the papers in the case? and didn't I say, "now, if you don't be careful you will contradict your return?"

A. I believe you did.

Q. What became of the papers?

A. I returned them to Mr. Eaker. I did not do anything with my return.

Q. Did you ever bring the papers to me afterwards?

A. I don't think I ever brought them to you any more.

Q. Did you ever hear anything about Mr. Moore suing Mr. Walker?

[The witnessed answered that he didn't know anything of his own knowledge, and the statement made by him was for that reason excluded.]

SENATOR PARSONS. Did you at the time of making return to the writ of habeas corpus, or at any time before the discharge of Russell, inform Judge Jackson that the Justice had ordered you to hold the prisoner in your custody to give him an opportunity to give bail?

A. I never informed him about it that I recollect.

Mr. KNOTT. Did you deliver all the papers, that Judge Eaker gave you as the papers in the case, on the table before Judge Jackson?

A. Yes, sir.

Q. Did I understand you as stating that the Judge had asked you if those were the papers in the case?

A. Yes, sir.

JONAS EAKER recalled and examined by Mr. Knott.

Q. Were you an acting magistrate in January last?

A. Yes, sir, I was.

Q. Did you issue a warrant for Charles Russell on any day in that month?

A. Yes, sir, I did issue a warrant for him to answer a charge of passing counterfeit money.

Q. Please state, Mr. Eaker, the circumstances attending the investigation you gave of the case, whether there was an examination of witnesses against the accused, and what became of the papers in the case?

A. After investigating the case, I gave him until 10 o'clock the next morning to file a bond for his appearance at court to answer the charge. The next morning, while I was completing writing out the papers, Mr. Tyrell, or Mr. Cryts, informed me that the accused had been taken out of Mr. Cryts' custody by writ of habeas corpus. I went on writing the papers. I think, now, it was Mr. Cryts told me about the writ, and that he said he had left Mr. Tyrell writing out a return. While waiting on me, he remarked, "I will go and see whether he is done, or what he is doing." He hadn't the papers at that time. He came back and informed me that Russell was discharged. I then gave him all the papers. I was not in Mr. Tyrell's office while the matter was before the Judge there. I know nothing about what took place there.

Q. In the hearing of the case before you, did you reduce the testimony to writing?

A. I took the examination of witnesses in writing, and gave it to Mr. Cryts, and he took it with the other papers.

Q. Did Mr. Cryts tell you that the prisoner had been discharged, before you gave him the papers?

A. I think he did.

CROSS-EXAMINED BY JUDGE JACKSON.

Q. What time of day did these occurrences take place?

A. It was something near about 10 o'clock.

Q. Didn't you write out the mittimus before?

A. No, sir. I thought I could do what writing I had to do at the time I fixed for him to give bail.

Q. Do you think you have authority to order men into the custody of an officer, without any written warrant?

A. Yes, sir. I believe that is customary among Justices of the Peace. It has been my practice.

Q. What was the state of your feelings towards me before this mandamus proceeding we have talked about?

A. I don't think there were any unkind feelings between us. There was not on my part.

Q. What is the state of your feelings now towards me?

A. I have nothing very particular against you. There is one thing, Judge; when you come back from Jefferson City, last winter, you didn't speak to me.

The witness was interrupted in his statements of some private matters, and his examination here closed.

TESTIMONY OF JAMES L. HALE.

James L. Hale called and examined by Mr. Knott.

Q. Mr. Hale, will you state where you reside?

A. I reside in Stoddard county, near Bloomfield, Missouri.

Q. Have you ever been a member of the grand jury in your county?

A. Yes, sir. I was foreman of the grand jury at the last August term of the Circuit Court.

Q. State if you know anything about Judge Jackson's going into the grand jury at that time.

Judge Jackson objected to allowing grand jurors to testify concerning what occurred before them; and to give an opportunity for the production of authorities, and for arguments on the objection, the witness was withdrawn, to be introduced next day.

TESTIMONY OF WILLIAM RINGER.

William Ringer called and examined by Mr. Hardin.

Q. Mr. Ringer, Judge Jackson is charged here with having had some conversation with you, and with giving you some advice in relation to certain county warrants. You will please state whether you ever had any such conversation, and if so, what it was, when it was, and all about it.

A. I think it was after the election in 1857, some time in September or October, in Bloomfield. I was complaining a good deal about not getting my pay for building a court-house. The Judge asked me if I had any warrants. I told him that I had, or that I had spoken to Mr. Kitchen to draw them for me. The Judge said that I'd better sell them, and use the money; that the whole thing was illegal, and that I couldn't get my pay out of the county. I think that about what I said in reply was, that the court-house was already up, and the amount of the money I could get for the warrants would not pay me for the work done. He said then that Kitchen was liable to me.

Q. What was his language, as near as you can state it?

A. I don't recollect his exact words. He said I could move against Kitchen instead of the county. He said I could recover against Kitchen, and not off from the county.

Q. What had Mr. Kitchen to do with the matter?

A. I contracted with him as Superintendent of the court-house. I don't say that he acted as Superintendent, but our contract was that way. The warrants were issued to Kitchen for my benefit. He was to get the money and pay it to me.

Q. How did this conversation with the Judge begin?

A. I can hardly say. I think he asked me what I had done with my warrants, or something of that kind. I had been complaining, as I said before, about not getting my pay. I thought the Judge had some say in it, and perhaps I asked him about it. This time he told me that he had no connection with the business, and told me I had better sell the warrants; that the whole transaction about the court-house was illegal. He advised me that the County Court was no court at all. I don't remember what reason he stated.

Q. Where did this take place?

A. It all took place in Bloomfield.

CROSS-EXAMINED BY JUDGE JACKSON.

Q. Did you sue him? Kitchen, I mean.

A. No, sir.

Q. How did we happen to get into this conversation that you speak of?

A. You came by Owen's, Judge, and called me to step aside, if I am not mistaken, and then we talked about it.

Q. Didn't you tell me that they were selling county warrants at a large discount, and that you were about to lose a great deal?

A. I don't know; it is likely I did.

Q. Was not that conversation in Miller's store?

A. I think not.

Q. Was not what I said this: that if you wouldn't give up the county warrants, you had no business to talk against the people of the county; that so far as the county was concerned, it had paid?

A. I don't recollect that.

Q. Was not Eaker elected County Court Judge before the time when you say we had this conversation?

A. I think so.

Q. Had he held any court?

A. I don't know. The election was held in August, I believe, and this was in September or October.

Q. Was not it as late as November?

A. It may have been.

Q. Did you repeat this to Mr. Kitchen?

A. Yes, sir; I told Mr. Kitchen what took place between you and myself.

Q. What did he say he was going to do about it? Did he say he would tell the Legislature?

[Question objected to and waived.]

Q. You say you didn't sue him?

A. Yes, sir; I didn't sue him.

Q. What was the reason?

A. I don't like to state the reason unless I am bound to do it.

Q. Well, didn't I ask you if you had warrants to sell? Didn't I propose to buy your warrants, or something of that kind, and was not that the way the conversation came up?

A. If it was so, I don't remember.

Q. Did I advise you what lawyer to employ?

A. I don't think you did.

Q. How did you come to make this contract with Kitchen?

A. He was the Superintendent, or he signed his name to the contract as Superintendent.

Q. When was the contract made?

A. It was made in June, 1857, if I am not mistaken.

Q. When did you get the house up?

A. I got it up the next fall some time. The brick work was done at the time we had this talk.

Q. You say this conversation was in October, 1857?

A. Yes, sir. I can't be exact about the time, but I think it was then.

Q. Who was in your bond as contractor?

[Question objected to and not answered.]

Q. Was not Kitchen and you in partnership?

[Objected to and not answered.]

Senator Wilson. I wish to understand the witness upon one point. In the outset, I understood him to say that he had some warrants for sale, or that he had some warrants, and the Judge advised him to sell the warrants. What does he say about that now?

A. Judge Jackson did tell me to sell the warrants. I did not have any warrants at that time, but I thought that I could get them. Kitchen told me that he could get the warrants, and they were to be drawn by Kitchen for my benefit. Judge Jackson told me that Judge Eaker's court was no court, or that there was no County Court, and that Kitchen was not legally an agent or Superintendent of the county. He said the only course I could take would be to hold Kitchen liable, and that if I sued the county I couldn't recover. He said Kitchen was responsible to me.

Judge Jackson. Were you and I tolerably intimate when this conversation took place?

A. I think we were at that time.

Q. Hadn't we a difficulty about settlement for some plastering, and didn't you bring suit against me about it?

A. Not since that time, Judge; all the lawing of your's and mine was long before that.

Q. How long?

A. I couldn't tell.

Q. Mr. Ringer, are you certain this conversation was in the year 1857?

A. Yes, sir, I am satisfied it was in the fall after the election.

Q. What disposition did I tell you to make of the money?

A. We had some more conversation, but about that I don't recollect.

TESTIMONY OF JAMES B. ODELL.

JAMES B. ODELL called and examined by Mr. Knott.

Q. Mr. Odell, where do you live?

A. I live in Bloomfield, Stoddard county, Missouri.

Q. What is your occupation?

A. Well, I am part of a lawyer. I practice a little sometimes.

Q. Were you at Thomasville on the third Monday of April, 1858?

A. I was there.

Q. Were you in court during the trial of the case of the State *vs.* DePriest?

A. Yes, sir. I was counsel for the defendant.

Q. Mr. Odell, did you have any conversation with Judge Jackson in regard to that case?

A. Yes, sir, I had a conversation. I don't know that I had a conversation with the Judge about it, but he had with me.

Q. Well, what was it? what was said?

A. Mr. DePriest had been convicted of disturbing the peace of a family; well, I don't know, he was either convicted or plead guilty, and at the same time was indicted for resisting an officer. The conversation the Judge had with me was this: He observed to Mr. Hull, or myself, that we could safely take a conditional fee in the case; that there were two distinct indictments, and only one offense, and that that would be a good plea. I did take the case, but being quite young in the practice, I didn't make a plea of a former conviction, but moved to quash the indictment, giving the former conviction as a reason for the motion. The motion to quash was overruled, and the Judge said that was not the way to do it. The Circuit Attorney entered a *nolle prosequi.* I got the fee.

Q. Were you employed at the time of the conversation?

A. No, sir. DePriest came to me afterwards. It was his son that employed me. Solomon DePriest, the old man, was not there.

Q. You took the case then after this conversation with the Judge?

A. Yes, sir. I took it, as the doctors say, on the principle of "no cure no pay."

Q. Was the Circuit Attorney by at the time the Judge had this conversation with you?

A. I don't remember.

Q. Did the Judge make that remark, that you could safely take a conditional fee, when the Circuit Attorney was not present?

A. Yes, sir. I recollect now that he was not there.

Q. Who was the Circuit Attorney?

A. John R. Woodsides.

Q. After your motion to quash was overruled, did the Judge advise you to plead a former conviction?

A. Yes, sir, I think he did.

Q. Who was in the case with you?

A. I was alone.
Q. How did the conversation with the Judge come up?
A. Mr. Hull, and the Judge, and I were in a room, and I don't know how it came up.
Q. Did you suggest the facts to the Judge, or did you commence the conversation about the case?
A. No, sir, I did not.
Q. Was the nature of the two offenses charged in the two indictments the same?
A. I don't remember much about that.

CROSS-EXAMINED BY JUDGE JACKSON.

Q. Was that the first court you attended? Did we get together there the first time?
A. No, sir. We got together first at Greenville.
Q. Was not Mr. Hull with you when we met at Greenville?
A. No, sir. Mr. Hull joined us at Eminence. We then went with you through to Thomasville.
Q. Was not Woodsides in the company going from Eminence to Thomasville?
A. I do not remember.
Q. Well, at the time the conversation occurred, were not you and Mr. Hull talking and complaining that business was dull, and then didn't I say, "now, young men, here is Green DePriest is indicted twice for the same offense, and you might get a fee from him?"
A. I don't know that the conversation came up that way. It might have been so.
Q. Didn't I tell you my impressions were that the two indictments were for the same offense, and that if I was correct in my impressions about the facts, you might safely take a fee in the case?
A. It is likely you are right, Judge.
Q. Didn't you say DePriest wouldn't employ you, and wasn't it then I told you you might take a conditional fee?
A. We had a long conversation about it, and it may be as you say, though I don't remember.
Q. Didn't you make a motion to quash on the ground that there was no legal offense charged, or something of that kind?
A. I don't recollect.
Q. Was not Mr. Hull with you in the case?
A. That was not my understanding.
Q. How much did you charge him?
A. I charged him five dollars, but it was not enough.
Q. Didn't you divide the fee with Mr. Hull?
A. No, sir. He claimed the right to half of it. He pretended like I agreed to divide with him, because he was present when the conversation took place, but I told him it was not enough to divide, and that if I had to give any of it to him, I would give it all.
Q. Well, when you made your motion to quash on the ground that there was a former conviction, was it not then that I suggested that that would be a good ground of acquittal?
A. Yes, sir, you did say that that would be a good ground of acquittal.
Q. When we were talking about it, didn't I tell you that if my impressions about the facts were correct, you might go into the case whether you got a fee or not, and that you would get the glory of acquitting him, which would be worth as much as the fee?
A. I think you did tell me something like that.
Q. And you did get the fee?

A. Yes, sir. I know I got it, and Hull raised a fuss with me because I wouldn't divide. [Laughter.]

Mr. Knott. Was it in consequence of advice given you by the Judge that you undertook the defense of the case?

A. Yes, sir; it was.

The Court adjourned.

FIFTH DAY.

Friday, June 10, 1859.

The Court met pursuant to adjournment, and was opened by proclamation.

The managers and respondent attended.

Senator Churchill offered the following resolution, which was thereupon considered:

Resolved, That the testimony in the case now pending before the Senate be published daily for the use of the Senate, and that thirty-five copies be published; thirty-three for the Senate, and one for the managers, and one for the respondent; and that copies be given to no other persons.

Senator Parsons offered the following substitute for this resolution:

Resolved, That as soon as the evidence is closed on the part of the State, the same shall be printed for the use of the Senate. And in like manner, when the evidence is closed on the part of the respondent, that shall be printed for the use of the Senate.

This substitute was agreed to by the following vote:

Ayes—Messrs. Brown, Byrne, Fox, Frazier, Goodlett, Gullett, Harris, Hedgpeth, Horner, McFarland, McIlvaine, Parsons, Peyton, Rains, Richardson, Thompson, and Vernon—17.

Noes—Messrs. Churchill, Coleman, Halliburton, McFerran, Morris, Newland, Robinson, Scott, Wilson, and Wood—11.

Absent—Messrs. Hyer, Johnson, Jones, and Watkins.

Absent on leave—Mr. O'Neil.

Senator Gullett then moved to lay the substitute on the table, which was disagreed to by the following vote:

Ayes—Messrs. Gullett, Harris, Morris, Robinson, Scott, and Wright—6.

Noes—Messrs. Brown, Byrne, Churchill, Coleman, Fox, Frazier, Goodlett, Halliburton, Hedgpeth, Horner, McFarland, McFerran, McIlvaine, Newland, Parsons, Peyton, Rains, Richardson, Thompson, Vernon, Wilson, and Wood—22.

Absent—Same as before.

Senator McFerran then offered the following amendment to the substitute:

Strike out all after the word "*Resolved,*" and insert as follows:

That no part of the testimony in this case shall be published until the entire evidence is taken, and then thirty-six copies shall be printed; thirty-three for the use of the Senators, one for the respondent, and one for each of the managers.

This amendment was disagreed to by the following vote:

AYES—Messrs. Byrne, Coleman, Halliburton, Harris, McFerran, McIlvaine, Morris, Rains, Robinson, and Wright—10.

NOES—Messrs. Brown, Churchill, Fox, Frazier, Goodlett, Gullett, Hedgpeth, Horner, McFarland, Newland, Parsons, Peyton, Richardson, Scott, Thompson, Vernon, Wilson, and Wood—18.

Absent—Same as before.

The question then being upon the adoption of the substitute, it was adopted by the following vote:

AYES—Messrs. Brown, Byrne, Churchill, Coleman, Fox, Frazier, Goodlett, Gullett, Halliburton, Hedgpeth, Horner, McFarland, McIlvaine, Newland, Parsons, Peyton, Rains, Richardson, Scott, Thompson, Vernon, Wilson, and Wood—23.

NOES—Messrs. Harris, McFerran, Morris, Robinson, and Wright—5.

Absent—Same as before.

The examination of witnesses for the State was then resumed.

TESTIMONY OF JAMES L. HALE.

JAMES L. HALE recalled and examined by Mr. Knott.

[The witness testified to his residence, and to his having been foreman of the grand jury at the last August term of the Stoddard Circuit Court, in reply to interrogatories similar to those propounded yesterday. He was then asked the following:]

Q. You will please state whether Judge Jackson visited the grand jury room, where the grand jury had retired to consider of presentments, during the session of the grand jury. If so, did he there give, or undertake to give, any instructions or opinions to the grand jury, upon any matter of law or fact, touching or concerning their duties? If so, what were the instructions or opinions given by him at that time?

JUDGE JACKSON objected to the witness answering this, and argued the question of its pertinency at some length. He took the ground that a grand juror could not, under his oath and the law, be allowed to disclose what transpired in the grand jury room, except in cases of indictments for perjury. He further argued that he had, as a Circuit Judge, a legal and moral right to go to a grand jury room while they were considering presentments, and to instruct them as he saw proper upon questions of law; and that the instructions thus given constituted a part of "the counsel of the State" mentioned in a grand juror's oath, which he was bound to keep secret. To support the position that cases of indictments for perjury afforded the only exception to the rule requiring grand jurors to keep secret all that transpires in the jury room, he cited and read sections 15, 16, and 17, 3d article, Revised Statutes, p. 1169; also section 65, "act to establish courts of record, and prescribe their powers and duties," p. 542, Rev. Stat. Mo.; also Tindle *vs.* Nichols, p. 326, and State *vs.* Baker, p. 338, 20 Mo. Rep.

Messrs. HARDIN and KNOTT replied briefly. They reviewed the authorities cited by Judge Jackson, endeavoring to show that they did not establish the principles for which he contended. They argued that a crime or misdemeanor, committed before a grand jury, whether it be murder, assault, perjury, or misdemeanor of a Judge, was not thereby protected from punishment; that all the functions of a Judge were public, and that he had no legal or moral right to give secret instructions or charges to a grand jury; that a Judge could not ignorantly mistake his duty and charge a grand jury secretly, for no law nor practice could be found to warrant such a proceeding; that the charge of a

Judge was not part of the "counsel of the State," which grand jurors were sworn to keep secret; that it was not the design or effect of the question proposed to the witness to elicit from him *evidence* given before the jury, and that the cases cited by the respondent related to such a question as that, and hence were not pertinent in the present issue; that it was a dangerous and inexcusable usurpation of power for a Judge to assume the functions of a Circuit Attorney, and visit the grand jury room for the purpose of discharging those functions, or for the purpose of suppressing any indictment against himself or others, or for the worse purpose of instigating a criminal prosecution against a personal enemy; and in support of the various positions assumed by them, they cited 1 Chitty's Criminal Law, pp. 313-317, together with the cases cited by the respondent.

JUDGE JACKSON replied, combatting the positions taken by the managers, and rearguing those taken by himself in his opening remarks.

The question for the action of the Court being, is the question propounded by the managers pertinent and proper? the vote stood as follows:

AYES—Messrs. Brown, Byrne, Churchill, Coleman, Fox, Frazier, Goodlett, Gullett, Halliburton, Harris, Horner, McFarland, McFerran, McIlvaine, Newland, Parsons, Peyton, Rains, Richardson, Thompson, Vernon, Wilson, and Wright—22.

NOES—Messrs. Hedgpeth, Robinson, Scott, and Wood—4.

Absent—Messrs. Hyer, Johnson, Jones, and Watkins.

Absent on leave—Mr. O'Neil.

Excused from voting—Mr. Morris.

So the question was decided proper, and the witness answered as follows:

A. The Judge came into the room, and we were talking with him. We asked him several questions upon points we had been considering. I can't say as to what the points were now, but they were something similar to the public charge he gave us.

Q. Did he say anything in regard to the law about gaming?

A. I don't know whether it was the first or second time he talked about the law of gaming.

Q. Well, what did he say about gaming either time?

A. We had been talking about gaming, and we asked him if he considered it gambling to play for watermelons, oysters, and the like of that. As I said, we had been considering that matter, and had found one or two bills, I believe.

Q. Was there anything in the public charge on that subject?

A. I disremember whether he said anything about playing for whisky and watermelons.

Q. Had you at that time a charge against him for such an offense?

A. Yes, sir. And we found a bill, I think. Whether we gave it in before his visit to the grand jury or after, I don't recollect.

Q. What did he say with regard to the law of gaming?

A. He stated that he did not consider it gaming to play in this way, on this ground, that it was not betting. He said if we played for money it was a different case.

Q. Did he apply his exposition of the law to any particular case?

A. I don't recollect.

Q. How did the conversation commence?

A. I don't recollect that either—whether it was that we commenced by asking questions, or whether he spoke about it first himself. Mr. Carlisle asked some questions, and I asked some myself.

Q. What did he say his object was in coming there first?

A. I don't know whether it was the first or second time, but once when he came in he said that he had understood some person or persons had been engaged in tampering with the grand jury, and he inquired about that.

Q. Do you know who he referred to?

A. I do not, though I thought at the time it was to Mr. Eaker and Mr. Phelan, from some circumstance, I cannot now say what.

Q. Did he instruct the grand jury whether they could find an indictment against him for any act of his as Judge?

A. I don't recollect of his saying that it was not competent for the grand jury to find an indictment against him. There was an instrument of writing which had been handed around, and whether he named it first, or we did, I can't now tell.

Q. What was that paper?

A. It was a paper referring to some part of the law.

Q. Do you know what law it was that the paper referred to?

A. I don't recollect, though I think at the time we took it as referring to a case about an attachment against Jonas Eaker.

Q. Had there been any complaint of oppression under consideration to which the law cited in this paper seemed to apply?

A. Yes, sir. There had been a complaint made, and we supposed it was founded on the law that this paper referred to.

Q. What did the Judge say about the paper?

A. He demanded it—we gave it to him; whether he called for it, or whether some one mentioned it to him, I won't say.

Q. Did he say it referred to his conduct, and that he was not indictable for his official acts?

A. I don't recollect that.

Q. Did he ask for the paper the first thing when he came into the room?

A. I don't think he did.

Q. Did he explain what it was that brought him there?

A. I don't remember.

Q. Did he express any opinion in relation to the law referred to in the paper?

A. Well, I believe he did, though I can't now say what it was.

Q. What time was it that he got the paper; was it at the first or second visit?

A. I don't recollect.

Q. Well, do you recollect whether both visits were on the same day?

A. I think one visit was in the afternoon, and the other was in the forenoon.

Q. Had you consulted the Circuit Attorney in regard to the matters concerning which the Judge instructed you?

A. I rather think we had.

Q. Was he in the grand jury room before the Judge came?

A. It is my impression that he was.

Q. Who was acting as Circuit Attorney at that time?

A. David G. Hicks was acting as Circuit Attorney.

Q. Had he seen this paper that you have mentioned?

A. Yes, sir. He had seen it.

Q. Don't you know whether Judge Jackson spoke of the paper before any one in the room mentioned it to him?

A. I don't recollect. It is altogether likely it was that way.

Q. Were you considering the question of his presentment for any act of oppression previous to this conversation?

A. I don't think we were.

SENATOR WILSON. I do not consider it competent to inquire so particularly as to what the grand jury was doing.

Mr. KNOTT. We only desire to show the motive of the respondent in his instructions to the grand jury, and to elicit the facts necessary to explain that motive.

CROSS-EXAMINED BY JUDGE JACKSON.

Q. Didn't I tell you not to hesitate to find a bill against me for any act not done as a court, if there was any testimony going to show my connection with any act that you thought indictable, though my opinion was that you could not indict me for my official conduct?

A. I so understood you.

Q. Wasn't that paper that you have spoken about an intimation that there would be a case of that kind presented?

A. I think that case was under investigation at the time.

Q. Mr. Hale, as far as your knowledge goes, am I in the habit of using contumelious, insolent, and insulting expressions towards lawyers and parties litigant?

A. I never saw anything that I thought much out of the way.

The witness was here dismissed, and on motion of SENATOR HALLIBURTON, the Court adjourned.

EVENING SESSION.

FRIDAY, June 10, 1859.

The Court met pursuant to adjournment.

The managers and respondent attended.

On motion of JUDGE JACKSON, the Court awarded an attachment against John R. Woodsides, a witness who had been subpenaed for the defendant, and was not in attendance.

TESTIMONY OF MOSES HARVEY.

MOSES HARVEY called and examined by Mr. Knott.

Q. You will state if you please, Mr. Harvey, whether you were a grand juror at the last term of the Stoddard Circuit Court.

A. I was.

Q. You will state if you please whether Judge Jackson was up in the grand jury room while it was in session, at that term of the court.

A. Yes, sir, he was there once or twice.

Q. Did he give the grand jury any instructions?

A. I consider that he did.

Q. What day of the court was that?

A. I won't say; I don't recollect.

Q. You speak of the August term?

A. Yes, sir, I do.

Q. What did he say his business was in visiting the grand jury room?

A. I don't know that I could tell. He came in, and some chat got up between the grand jurors and him. He went on to state what constituted gaming; what would be considered betting. The idea conveyed was this: that playing cards for watermelons and oysters was not considered betting.

Q. Did he apply that opinion of the law to any particular case?

A. Well, he seemed to be talking about gaming cases generally. I won't say that I give his opinion of the law, but that is what I understood.

Q. Do you know what brought up the conversation?

A. Well, I don't know precisely what it was. In the grand jury we had found I don't know how many bills, but I think we had included twelve or fifteen, or twenty, all in the same bill, for such betting as he was talking about.

Q. Well, tell us what Judge Jackson did and said.

A. I don't recollect what else he said.

Q. What time of day was it when he came?

A. I can't say. I never expected to be called on to swear about it, and I don't remember.

Q. Had you received any paper referring to certain points of law?

A. Yes, sir. There was a memorandum of certain sections of the law that had been handed round among the jurors.

Q. Was the Judge in the grand jury room more than once?

A. Yes, sir. I recollect of his being there twice.

Q. Did he give you either time any instructions regarding this paper?

A. Yes, sir, he gave us some instructions about it. I don't know as I can tell just how it was, but the idea was that if the person who did it was known, he was liable to indictment.

Q. Indictment for what?

A. For sending it before us.

Q. What case had the paper connection with?

A. I don't recollect.

Q. Do you recollect what the law was that the paper referred to?

A. To some sections of law in the statutes. It was something about oppression in office.

Q. What became of the paper?

A. I don't know what became of it. I don't know whether the Judge took it away or not.

Q. Did the Judge say anything about the law that the paper referred to?

A. I think he did, but I can't say what it was.

Q. Was this conversation about the paper had the second time that Judge Jackson visited the grand jury room?

A. It is likely it was.

Q. Who was charged with oppression?

A. It was Judge Jackson.

Q. What did he say about that charge?

[Question objected to and discussed for some time, when the objection was withdrawn.]

A. This charge we had against the Judge was for some kind of oppression, I believe. The paper had reference to the law in such cases.

Q. Did the Judge say anything about the charge, and the power of the grand jury to indict him?

A. I recollect of his making some statement, upon which he went on to say that he was not liable to indictment for any of his official acts.

CROSS-EXAMINED BY JUDGE JACKSON.

Q. Was not there other officers mentioned by me at this time? Didn't I instance Justices of the Peace, County Court Judges, Judges of the Supreme Court, and other judicial officers; and didn't I point out the distinction between officers of trust and judicial officers? Didn't I say that the County Court Judge was not like the Judge of the

Circuit Court; that he was a trust officer; and wasn't it then that I said that the Judge of the Circuit Court was not indictable for his official acts?

A. I won't say about the others, but you said the Judge of the Circuit Court was not indictable for his official conduct.

Q. Was not something said about Judge Eaker being indicted for issuing county warrants without authority?

A. Perhaps there was. I don't recollect.

Q. Was this at the August term of the Circuit Court?

A. Yes, sir. It was at the August term.

Q. Was the Circuit Attorney, Woodsides, not there?

A. I think not. I think Mr. D. G. Hicks was acting as Circuit Attorney.

Q. Well, wasn't I sent for, or did I go to the grand jury room without being sent for?

A. You were sent for, I think.

Q. Wasn't there something said about David Hicks being young, and that you wanted me sent for, for that reason?

A. There was something of that kind said, though what it was I do not recollect.

Q. Well, about this paper. When I came up and asked about it, didn't I say whoever sent it in was in contempt of court, and liable to indictment? Wasn't that what I said?

A. Well, you said that he was liable to indictment. I don't think you said that he could be indicted for contempt. I may have forgotten.

Q. Wasn't it that word had been sent in that a case of this kind would be presented—I mean that there would be a charge against me—and wasn't the paper sent in before the charge was made?

A. I don't recollect about that.

Q. How did I come to know that this paper was before you?

A. I can't say. You didn't know from me.

Q. Who was it that made the complaint against me?

A. I don't know, but I suppose it was Judge Eaker.

Q. What was it about?

A. It was something about a mandamus. That was what I heard it was about, if I recollect aright, and your issuing an attachment against him.

Q. Have you been in court much?

A. I have been in every Circuit Court in the county since I have been in the State, which has been for about three years.

Q. What has been my general course in relation to lawyers, litigants, and others?

A. I don't know, hardly. If I ever knew you to do anything wrong, I was not sensible that it was wrong.

Mr. Knott. Had David Hicks been attending on the grand jury before this visit of the Judge?

A. Yes, sir. He had.

Q. Did he see this paper?

A. Yes, sir. He did.

Q. And you say the Judge was in the grand jury room twice?

A. Yes, sir. I think he was there twice.

Q. When you say you have been in every Circuit Court that has been held since you have been in the State, do you mean that you have been there incidentally, from time to time, or that you were there all the time?

A. I have only been in each court occasionally.

Q. Did you have an opportunity to observe closely the conduct of the Judge towards lawyers and litigants?

A. No, sir. I can't say that I had.

TESTIMONY OF WILLIAM VANDIVER.

WILLIAM VANDIVER called and examined by Mr. Knott.

Q. Mr. Vandiver, state to the Court where you reside?

A. I reside in Butler county, Missouri.

Q. Were you a member of the grand jury, at the April term of the Circuit Court, 1857, in that county?

A. I was foreman of the grand jury at that term.

Q. On what day of the week did the Circuit Court commence?

A. On Monday.

Q. On what day was the grand jury discharged?

A. On Tuesday, the next day.

Q. You will please state to the Court the circumstances under which you were discharged.

A. On Tuesday, some time after dinner, the Judge asked me if we had any business before us, and he observed that he wished we would finish, and hand in a report that evening. I told him that we had a good deal of business before us. I don't know that he said anything more at that time. As I went out I saw the Circuit Attorney. We conferred about the business, and held over until sundown. We completed what business we could, made some reports, and told the court we had business on hand unfinished. Says he, "gentlemen, you are discharged."

Q. How long a time is allowed to the Circuit Courts in that county?

A. A week.

Q. Did the Judge assign any reason for discharging the grand jury?

A. There was no reason assigned to me.

Q. Was there anything said in relation to what you were to do with the unfinished business?

A. Not that I recollect of.

Q. Had there been any presentments made when the Judge first spoke to you about finishing your business?

A. I believe not.

Q. Have you any idea of the amount of unfinished business on hand at the time you were discharged?

A. I have no idea. We had a good deal.

Q. Where was the Clerk of the court at that time?

A. I couldn't tell you. I didn't see him.

CROSS-EXAMINED BY JUDGE JACKSON.

Q. Was it Tuesday morning or Wednesday that the grand jury was discharged?

A. It was Tuesday evening, I think.

Q. Didn't I tell you that we had no Clerk, and that that was the reason why the grand jury would have to be discharged?

A. I think that perhaps you did.

Q. Did you hear me tell any person else that we had no Clerk, and couldn't proceed with the business?

A. Not as I recollect.

Q. Did you hear me say that there was no Clerk, and that that was the reason you would have to be discharged?

A. That was the general chat; I don't know whether you told me so or not.

Q. What was the matter with the Clerk?

A. Report said that the Clerk was sick, but I did not see him myself.

Q. Were you in court all the time?

A. I was there a part of Monday.

Q. Did you see the Clerk in court Monday?

A. I believe I did. I think he was reported sick the next morning.

Q. Did you hear me give any reason why the grand jury was discharged?

A. No, sir, I didn't hear you give any that I now recollect.

Q. When the grand jury came in, and I asked you if you had any returns to make, did you make any returns?

A. Yes, sir, and reported further unfinished business.

Mr. KNOTT. Wasn't it the general understanding about town that the Clerk was drunk?

A. Yes, sir, that was the general understanding, though I didn't know him to be drunk, not having seen him myself.

JUDGE JACKSON. That was my understanding of the matter.

Q. Is there any person here who was on the grand jury?

A. Yes, sir. Mr. Ruff, Hamilton Scott, and Daniel Epps were all on the grand jury, and they are here.

Q. Wasn't it you that I had the conversation with in relation to what you should do with reference to the witnesses summoned to appear before the grand jury?

A. No, sir, I think not.

Q. Well, it seems it was not with him that I had the conversation. What became of the bills of indictment that you handed in?

A. I don't know. We came in, and just left three or four indictments, and reported unfinished business on hand, and then were dismissed.

TESTIMONY OF DANIEL EPPS.

DANIEL EPPS called and examined by Mr. Knott.

Q. Where do you live, Mr. Epps?

A. I live in Butler county, Missouri.

Q. Where you a member of the grand jury at the November term of the Circuit Court in April, 1857?

A. I believe I was.

Q. How long was the grand jury in session at that court?

A. I don't recollect. It has been some time, and I have forgotten.

Q. Were you discharged before the business was finished?

A. Yes, sir. I think we were discharged before we got through.

Q. Do you know whether it was represented to the court that you could not get through with the business before you were discharged?

A. I don't know. I know we couldn't do anything because we had no Clerk.

Q. How did you come to be without a Clerk?

A. Well, sir, I suppose the Clerk was drunk. I didn't see him myself, but that was my understanding from what I heard.

CROSS-EXAMINED BY JUDGE JACKSON.

Q. Do you remember whether it was the second or third day of the court when the grand jury was discharged?

A. I couldn't say. It was either Tuesday or Wednesday.

Q. Wasn't it the second day of court when the Clerk was reported sick or drunk?

A. I think it was, though I couldn't be positive.

Mr. KNOTT. Did any member of the grand jury inform the Judge that they had unfinished business which it would be impossible to dispose of before they were discharged?

A. All that I know about that is only hearsay.

TESTIMONY OF WILLIAM G. PHELAN.

William G. Phelan called and examined by Mr. Knott.

Q. Where do you reside, Mr. Phelan?

A. I reside in Bloomfield, or convenient to it, Stoddard county, Missouri.

Q. What is your profession?

A. I am a lawyer, and a farmer by courtesy. I have a farm at least.

Q. Were you at a Circuit Court held at Bloomfield, in May, 1858?

A. Yes, sir, I was there.

Q. Do you know whether there was pending, at that term of the court, a proceeding against Jonas Eaker by a mandamus?

A. Yes, sir. Judge Eaker spoke to me as counsel.

Q. You will please state the case, and what occurred when it was called up for trial in court?

A. It was a mandamus against Judge Eaker, requiring him to show cause why he had not done something in regard to a road, or the reason for some act as County Judge. I am not able to state definitely the act complained of in the application for a mandamus, though I have reflected upon it, and have endeavored to make myself able to do so. I desired to appear as *amicus curiæ*. There has been some reflection upon the technical expression, as I used it, and I repeat it here for that reason. Judge Jackson would not allow me to appear in this capacity, and when I attempted to do so, he ordered me to shut up, or to hush up, I will not be positive as to the exact expression; perhaps he used both. He also refused to allow my associate in the case, Mr. Kitchen, to appear in this capacity. I had been out of court for some purpose, and as I came in, Mr. Eaker whispered to me that the court had refused to allow Mr. Kitchen to suggest that there had been no service of the writ. I could hardly believe it at the time, and attempted to speak, but the Judge stopped me as I have stated.

Q. What was the manner of the Judge upon this occasion?

A. It was harsh and severe in the extreme. He was evidently laboring under great excitement.

Q. When you attempted to speak, what was your object?

A. My object was to state to the court that there never had been any service of the writ of mandamus.

Q. Did you make that statement?

A. I endeavored to do so. We were both speaking at once. I no doubt used the words; but whether I succeeded in getting that fact before the court is doubtful, owing to the violence of his manner.

Q. Do you attend the Dunklin Circuit Courts?

A. Yes, sir, I do.

Q. Were you at the Circuit Court held at the county seat of Dunklin county, on the second Monday of May, 1858?

A. I am satisfied that I was.

Q. Were you connected in any manner with the cause of Smith *vs.* Cude, pending at that term of the court?

A. Yes, sir. I was lawyer for Smith, indirectly. Mr. Cude, or his attorney, filed an application for a change of venue in the case. Mr. Bedford, I think, was representing Mr. Cude, and made the application. The court sent the cause to Pemiscot county.

Q. What are the relative positions of Dunklin and Pemiscot counties?

A. They are adjoining counties, but during the greater portion of every year it is almost impossible to get from one to the other. I could get from one to the other if I had a good steamboat.

Q. What is the difficulty?

A. The difficulty consists in a large swamp, which lies between the two counties.

Q. Was it convenient to the parties and to the counsel engaged in the cause?

A. As far as convenience is concerned, I will only state that I would have had to travel two or three hundred miles. It was necessary to go something like that distance to get around the swamp, and go down to Pemiscot county.

Q. At what season of the year is it necessary to take this circuitous route, in order to pass from one county to the other?

A. About the time of the fall and spring terms of the court. I was never there myself, and consequently I state these facts merely from my knowledge of the country, and as I have always understood them to be.

Q. Which side of the case were you on?

A. I was counsel for Smith.

Q. Were the attorneys or the parties agreed that the case should be sent to any other county?

A. Yes, sir, the lawyers on both sides fully concurred. We wanted the case sent to Bollinger county, I think it was.

Q. Was this fact represented to the court?

A. Yes, sir. It had been agreed between the lawyers and the parties, and it was so stated to the court. When I speak of parties, understand me, Mr. Smith, the plaintiff in the cause, was not in the country. He had assigned his interest in the suit to a Mr. Johnson, and Mr. Johnson employed me.

Q. What reason was assigned besides the agreement for requesting the cause sent to Bollinger county?

A. It was more convenient, and more suitable in every respect.

Q. What was the Judge's reply when these facts were represented to him?

A. It was very brief, brief in the extreme, and anything but courteous. It was indicated more by his arm, (witness illustrating by his own arm,) saying that he would have nothing said about it. We understood very well what it meant, and I could not convey that meaning by repeating his exact language, even if I were able to do so, which I am not. It was utterly impossible to get his whole meaning from what he said. It was more by looks and gestures than by language.

Q. Were you present at the same term of the court when a change of venue was awarded in the case of the Point Pleasant and Dunklin County Road Company *vs.* Moses Farrar?

A. I may have been present, but I know nothing about that case.

Q. Were you present when a change of venue was awarded in which the same company was plaintiff and Nathaniel G. Murphy was defendant?

A. I was not present when the application was made, and I did not draw the petition.

Senator Parsons. What were the causes assigned in the application for a change of venue in the first case you mentioned?

A. I saw the petition, and I waived the usual notice. It was for prejudice on the part of Judge Jackson.

Q. Which side took the change of venue?

A. Mr. Cude. I was representing the other side.

Mr. Knott. Who were the attorneys in the case of the road company against Murphy?

A. Mr. Watkins, I think, represented the road company. Mr. Murphy took the change. The cause alleged was the same—prejudice on the part of the Judge.

Q. Who were the opposing attorneys in the case of the road company *vs.* Murphy?

A. I think Mr. Bedford, Mr. Arthur, and Mr. Hull, and perhaps others. My impressions are not distinct. I paid no marked attention to the case.

Q. Were you at the Circuit Court held at Poplar Bluff, Butler county, in May, 1858?

A. Yes, sir. I have attended every Circuit Court held in Butler county during the past five years. I was there at that time.

Q. Were you in court during the trial of the cause of Gibson *vs.* Dunn?

A. I was counsel in the case.

Q. You will please state what occurred during the trial of that cause; whether you observed anything unusual in the conduct of the Judge, and if so, what it was.

A. I noticed nothing unusual in the trial of this cause—nothing that had any particular connection with it. The trial of the cause was commenced in the forenoon, and I cannot tell the exact stage of the case when the court took a recess for dinner. After dinner, Judge Jackson came in apparently very much excited. I made a motion—I am unable to say now what it was, whether it was addressed to the court, or whether it was the commencement of my argument of the case before the jury: I am inclined to think it was the latter. The Judge stopped me. He said that I couldn't go on; that I was in contempt of court, and that I had been tampering with the grand jury. I don't recollect what my reply was, though I recollect being astonished at the manner in which the charge was brought against me. I think I said, "I believe not, Judge," and I wished to defend myself. I cannot state exactly what occurred. There were some little altercations between us, and I demanded to know what the charge was. The Judge told me to sit down. I did sit down, but got up again directly, and he told me to go on with the case, but he wished me to understand that I was in contempt of court, and that I would have to answer for it—understand me that I do not pretend to give his exact phraseology. I was under the impression at the time that a certain man who was a particular friend to the Judge had betrayed the secrets of the grand jury, and I still think he did. I proposed to myself to take some steps in regard to the matter; however, that leads me into outside matter, and it is not necessary to mention it further here.

Q. When you attempted to rebut the charge brought against you, did you succeed in getting an opportunity?

A. I endeavored to do so, but I never got leave to say a single word. His reply to my inquiries concerning the charge, and to my offers to exculpate myself, was, in effect, that I might go on with the case then on hand.

Q. What was the character of his address to you?

A. It was very severe, very severe, indeed, and his manner showed much excitement.

Q. Were you excited yourself at the time?

A. I was not excited at that moment. Afterwards I was, when he told me to "sit down," to "hush up," "take your seat." I do not pretend to give the words exactly, though it was one or the other, and made an impression upon me as very severe and insulting.

Q. What was the motion you had made in the case of Gibson *vs.* Dunn, just prior to this interruption?

A. I have endeavored, from reflection, to ascertain, but I have not been able to recollect it.

Q. Had you done anything to excite the Judge in the manner that you speak of, in the trial of this cause?

A. I think not. I think his excitement proceeded from another matter, a matter having nothing to do with this case.

Q. Were you present at the Ripley Circuit Court, November term, 1857?

A. I was.

Q. Did you see Mr. Fox there?

A. I did.

Q. Does he practice there?

A. Yes, sir. He attends that court as a lawyer.

Q. Were you present in court at that term when any difficulty occurred between the court and Mr. Fox?

A. I was there when the Judge called attention to a paper. I think it was an answer. I do not remember the case at this moment; but it is my impression that whatever it was, I was on the other side. When he called Mr. Fox's attention to the paper, he said to him, "you have either sworn to a lie, or caused your client to do so."

Q. What was Mr. Fox doing at the time?

A. I think he was talking to some other lawyers. He was not addressing the Judge.

Q. Mr. Phelan, I will call your attention to the case of a man named Atterbury, and an alleged application by you for the privilege of a writ of habeas corpus, made before Judge Jackson, and get you to state the circumstances of the case, as they occurred.

A. Yes, sir, I will state the facts to the best of my ability. The man Atterbury had been arrested, and was held in custody in Dunklin county. It is not needful to enter into all the details of the case. He was detained by a warrant from a Justice of the Peace. I do not remember the charge, though my impression was at the time that it was made simply with the intention of getting time, and detaining him, until a party could reach the residence of the Judge, and take him on a capias. Be that as it may, I applied or drew up a petition for a writ of habeas corpus, and it was sworn to by Atterbury's son. There were several parties mixed up in the affair, and bearing in mind one section of the law requiring such petitions to give a full statement of the cause, in doing this I found it necessary to use the name of David G. Hicks. It was averred in the petition that Atterbury was first taken by Hicks, without any shadow of right. The petition further stated that he could not give bail in Dunklin county, where he was a comparative stranger, and that he was able to give bail in Stoddard county. I may not state correctly the allegations of the petition, but I recollect that I found it necessary to use the name of Mr. Hicks, and when I presented the petition, the Judge refused to issue the writ, giving as a reason that the name of Mr. Hicks was used. He wrote "refused," and made a memorandum of a certain section of the law on the petition.

JUDGE JACKSON. Is that mark on the petition now?

A. I do not know.

JUDGE JACKSON. What became of the man?

A. I do not know. I suppose he escaped. He broke jail, or something of that kind.

[Mr. Knott objected to the interruption, and after some discussion, the examination of the witness was resumed.]

MR. KNOTT. Do you say that the writ of habeas corpus was refused Atterbury?

A. Yes, sir.

Q. Can't you remember the offense with which he was charged?

A. I cannot; though if offense at all it would have been triable in the Circuit Court of Dunklin county. He could give security or bail in Stoddard county, though he was not able to procure it in Dunklin.

Q. Is Dunklin county in the Fifteenth Judicial Circuit?
A. Yes, sir.

SENATOR PARSONS. Did the Judge assign any other reasons for refusing the writ except that David G. Hicks was mentioned in the petition?

A. It is my impression that he did not. The cause of the imprisonment was not presented at that time, for a reason stated in the petition.

Q. Were you present at a Circuit Court held at the town of Poplar Bluff, in November, A. D. 1857?
A. I was.
Q. What day did the court commence that term?
A. I believe it was at the time set—the first Monday in November.
Q. What day did the court adjourn?
A. In accordance with the law a week is allowed for this court, but to the best of my recollection, at this term court adjourned on Tuesday night.

Q. You will please detail to the Court what you observed unusual in the conduct of Judge Jackson—how it came that the court adjourned so soon, and what you may know about the matter generally.

A. It is not easy to detail the incidents that occurred at that court. The first day business went on as usual, but on that evening or afternoon the Clerk got on a "bust," or little spree, and the next morning he was incompetent to the discharge of his duties; in fact he was incapable of moving in his bed. Court called at the usual hour, but we had no Clerk. I had some business in court that I deemed very important, and being anxious for business to proceed, I proposed to the court to act as Clerk myself. He said I could do so if I would not act as lawyer during the term. That did not suit me, and afterwards I found an excellent pensman, Mr. Donaldson Walker, and requested the court to appoint him Clerk, *pro tem.* He said he could not do so, because the Clerk had not requested it. I do not know that that is exactly what he said, but it was something tantamount to that. Not being willing to abide by that, I waited till noon, and got the Clerk to sign a paper requesting the Judge to appoint Mr. Walker Clerk, *pro tem.*, by the assistance of his wife, who helped me or some other person to hold him up in bed while he signed it. I took the paper to Judge Jackson, and he still refused to make the appointment, and the consequence was we had no Clerk at all at that term of the court after the first day, and no business of any consequence was done.

Q. Did Judge Jackson assign any reason for refusing to make the appointment of a Clerk?

A. I cannot say that he stated anything which would be accounted a reason. He said that Blount was a good fellow, or something of that kind.

Q. Was the Judge apprised of the condition of the Clerk?

A. I cannot doubt but that he was. I was present when others told him of it, and I told him myself. It was a notorious fact also, and I suppose everybody about the Court knew it.

Q. Did any serious detriment to the business of court result from this turn of affairs?

A. I cannot speak for others. I must have lost myself some three or four hundred dollars in consequence of a failure to proceed with one case—a St. Louis claim for $1,300 or $1,400, upon which I expected judgment at that term.

Q. What became of the papers pertaining to the causes set for trial at that court?

A. The lawyers in attendance were trying to fix up their business as well as they could. The Judge took all the papers, I suppose all that he could find—took the key of the office, turned everybody out, and put the papers under his arm.

Q. Do you know whether any one applied to him for the papers in any cause for any purpose?

A. I do not remember seeing any one do so. I would not like to do it myself under such circumstances.

Q. Did he assign any reason for taking possession of the papers?

A. The only one I heard was that he was fearful the papers might be purloined. I only give the substance, or my understanding of the statement.

Q. Were any causes tried on the second day of the term?

A. I do not remember. If so, the Judge acted as Clerk.

Q. Was any order made suspending the Clerk for neglect of duty?

A. I think not. None that I know of.

Q. Was any charge of misdemeanor in office preferred against him?

A. Not up to the time of the last County Court. I understand that he is beyond your jurisdiction now—that he has left the State.

Q. Were you in court at the time the grand jury was discharged?

A. I was.

Q. What occurred at that time?

A. The usual questions were asked, and the foreman of the grand jury replied that they had more business unfinished. I do not recollect whether they made any presentments or not; I think they made one.

Q. Did the grand jury go home as soon as they were discharged?

A. No, sir. The most of them remained in town a day or two.

Q. Were you at the April term of the Ripley Circuit Court?

A. I was.

Q. Were you present at the trial of William Kinsey?

A. I cannot say. In some case at that term of the court I was desirous to take down the testimony. Whether it was the Kinsey case or not I don't know. I am totally unable to recollect in what cause it was that the difficulties in regard to taking down the testimony occurred. Well, when we asked for time, the Judge said that the witnesses were not brought there for counsel to write down their testimony. He refused to allow time for this purpose, and we were not able to accomplish it.

Q. What was the manner of the Judge upon that occasion?

A. It was very severe and harsh. There were a number of counsel engaged in the cause. The Judge was on one side, and most of the lawyers on the other My recollection of the case, however, is not distinct.

[The witness was here interrupted and made to repeat, several times, portions of his testimony.]

Q. Were you, at the April term of the Ripley Circuit Court, 1858, present pending the cause of James Moore *vs.* John Eldridge, administrator of the estate of William Parker?

A. I was counsel in that case.

Q. Please state the conduct of Judge Jackson in that trial.

A. His conduct on that occasion was very kind to me. I suppose that on the other side they could not say so much. I do not remember that any difficulty occurred during the trial. I agreed to the testimony which counsel for the other side prepared to incorporate in a bill of exceptions. I understood that they had a severe time about this bill of exceptions. I believed the testimony as prepared by counsel set forth the facts in evidence before the jury substantially as they were.

Q. You will please state the practice in Judge Jackson's courts in regard to saving exceptions. When exceptions are taken, are they written out and signed at the time, or do you wait and incorporate all the exceptions to the ruling of the court, during the progress of the trial, in one bill?

A. The practice in Judge Jackson's courts has varied in this particular. I believe the latter course is the one now generally pursued.

Q. Were you present at a Circuit Court held at Stoddard county, on the third Monday of November, 1857, during the trial of Sarah Buckner, on an indictment for murder?

A. Yes, sir. I was present, and was one of defendant's counsel.

Q. You will please give the court a succinct history of the manner in which Judge Jackson conducted that trial?

A. There were but two witnesses examined for the prosecution in this case. One was defendant's son, and the other William C. Grimsley, ex-Sheriff of Stoddard county. Mr. Grimsley went on to give in his testimony at considerable length. He was under examination two or three hours. Mr. Woodsides, the Circuit Attorney, finally asked leave to withdraw the witness, which was granted, and the trial went on.

Q. Did you object to the withdrawal of the witness?

A. We made what objection we could. I cannot say whether any exception was entered of record. We were not allowed to speak of Grimsley's testimony, and when Judge Jackson announced that the testimony of the witness was withdrawn, we knew well enough it was useless to make objection. He is very decided. When he has once made a decision, it is impossible to get him to review it. You may talk of the laws of the Medes and Persians, but they were not more unalterable than Judge Jackson's decisions. Mr. Davis alluded to the statements of Grimsley not as testimony, but by way of illustration. He was stopped in his argument by the court. I being the oldest attorney in the cause, tried to conclude the argument for the defense; and in my argument before the jury, I wished to allude to the statements of Grimsley for the purpose of removing any impressions they might have made on the minds of the jury. The Judge stopped me, also, and reiterated that the evidence of Grimsley was withdrawn from the jury. I was not willing that the verdict of the jury should stand, and wished to have a chance to take the case to the Supreme Court; but I had not time then to prepare a bill of exceptions. In this matter the Judge treated me with more than kindness. However, I am anticipating; I will come to that directly. I filed a motion for a new trial, and Judge Jackson adjourned the court to a day one or two weeks subsequent. I was compelled to leave the place, and while I was gone, I was taken sick and was unable to attend on the day to which Judge Jackson had adjourned the court. He continued his kindness to me, however, and adjourned the court a second time to a day perhaps three weeks subsequent to the day of trial. After I returned home, on the day appointed I presented a bill of exceptions. In making out the bill of exceptions, I believe I put in the motion for arrest of judgment (I inserted it then, because it was the first time I thought about it,) the point that the testimony of one witness, uncorroborated, was not sufficient to support a conviction for a capital offense. In discussing this, the Judge persisted in saying that the testimony of Grimsley was not withdrawn. When I adverted to the fact that I was not permitted to comment upon the testimony of Grimsley, and that we had not been allowed the benefit of a cross-examination, the Judge took offense, and made some threat. He said that he was going to do something. I asked him was it fine? He said, "no, worse than that." I asked him was it go to jail? He said, "no, worse than that," again. "Then," I said, "I suppose you mean to strike me from the roll."

Q. When did this occur?

A. I have not, perhaps, made myself understood. This was in my argument of the cause before the jury. I adverted to these facts and others, but the Judge persisted in saying that the testimony had not been withdrawn, and refused to sign the bill of exceptions until it was incorporated.

Q. Did you say that Grimsley was a witness on the part of the State?

A. Yes, sir. While he was on the stand under examination, the Judge observed, "Mr. Circuit Attorney, I would withdraw that witness." He made use of some expression tantamount to that, if it was not those very words. The Circuit Attorney did not seem to take the hint given him, and the examination continued until the adjournment at noon. As soon as court convened after dinner, the Circuit Attorney asked leave to withdraw the testimony of this witness. The Judge said "well," and the testimony was accordingly withdrawn. When Mr. Davis, my associate in the case, spoke of it by way of illustration, and not as testimony, the conduct of the Judge was then harsh in the extreme, so much so that Mr. Davis gave up the case, saying that if he could not act for the defendant without the dictation of the court, he would abandon his cause. As I said before, when I came to argue the case, I spoke of Grimsley's testimony to divest the minds of the jurors of any impression that it was testimony. The Judge told me I must not speak of it —that it was not testimony. I endeavored to explain to him my purpose. He seemed to get angry, and threatened me. Then it was that I asked would he fine? and he told me "worse than that;" was it go to jail? and when he told me it was worse than that, I said, "I reckon you intend to strike me from the roll." The point about the testimony of one witness, uncorroborated, not being sufficient, never struck me until I came to prepare the motion in arrest of judgment. It is proper to observe that the prosecution rested the case on the testimony of the prisoner's son alone, after the testimony of Grimsley was withdrawn. When I presented the bill of exceptions, as I before stated, he refused to sign the bill until Grimsley's testimony was incorporated.

Q. Was Mr. Grimsley examined in the presence of the jury?

A. Yes, sir. The examination lasted an hour or two; and his testimony was withdrawn from the consideration of the jury as I have stated.

Q. What was the conduct of the Judge during the examination of the witnesses?

A. As regards his conduct towards myself it was as it should have been,—as usual I did not take a very active part. He and Mr. Davis conducted the examination of the witnesses principally. He seemed to be more the State's attorney than Mr. Woodsides.

Q. What was the nature of Grimsley's testimony so far as you heard it?

A. I recollect that it was confined to a conversation with the accused, in which it was alleged she made certain confessions. All that was given of it was against her. We relied upon the cross-examination to bring out the fact of the admission of a daughter of the accused that she had killed Buckner. This daughter was his step daughter, and it was alleged that he had committed a rape upon her, and that she had either killed him herself, or assisted in killing him. Her admission to Grimsley, of this kind, we were anxious to get before the jury.

Senator Parsons. Did the prosecuting attorney comment before the jury on Grimsley's testimony?

A. To the best of my recollection, I think not, nor advert to it in any manner.

On motion of Senator Wilson, the Court adjourned.

SIXTH DAY.

SATURDAY, June 11, 1859.

The Court met pursuant to adjournment, and was opened by proclamation.

The managers and respondent attended.

WILLIAM G. PHELAN recalled and his examination resumed.

Q. Mr. Phelan, do you know the place of residence of this man Atterbury?

A. At this time I do not. At the time when the petition for the writ of habeas corpus was presented to Judge Jackson, I am of the impression that he resided in Stoddard county. He had moved from the county of Dunklin, had gone back there for some purpose, and was arrested on some pretext, as I understood, for the purpose of allowing the Sheriff to get there and take him with a capias.

Q. You will please look at this paper (handing it to the witness) and see whether it is the petition presented by you to Judge Jackson?

A. Yes, sir. I know this to be the paper. It is my handwriting, and I observe the memorandum made by Judge Jackson. I am truly happy that the paper is here.

Mr. KNOTT. We are done with the witness.

CROSS-EXAMINED BY JUDGE JACKSON.

Q. Mr. Phelan, you say that you are a farmer and lawyer?

A. Yes, sir. I am a lawyer, and a farmer I hope. I have a farm at least.

Q. Do you work it yourself?

A. Occasionally I do.

Q. In which of the two capacities are you most expert?

A. I endeavor to fulfill both to the best of my ability.

Q. Have you more than one farm?

A. Yes, sir, I own several.

Q. Do you carry on more than one yourself?

A. I cannot say that I do.

Q. Well, Mr. Phelan, are you a religious man?

[The managers here objected to the course of the cross-examination, but the witness stating that he would like to answer, he was permitted to proceed.]

A. I cannot say that I am particularly religious. I am no spiritualist, but I do not contemn religion.

Q. Do you not approve of the Mormon doctrine and practices?

A. No, sir, I do not.

Q. Have not you a house near by your own, where there are some females that you stay with about as much as you stay at home?

A. No, sir. Nothing of the kind.

Q. Don't you often stay two or three days at that house without going home at all?

[Senator Parsons objected that the character of this cross-examination was probably improper, and below the dignity of the Court, whereupon Judge Jackson withdrew the question.]

Q. Mr. Phelan, state if you please, whether this is the paper (handing it to witness) that you told about holding Blount up to sign?

A. Yes, sir. I think it is the paper. I know it more from Blount's signature than from any recollection of its contents.

Q. Mr. Phelan, I will inquire about this celebrated mandamus case. I believe you stated you were present when it was up in court?

A. Yes, sir. I was not present at the outset. When I came in the case was called.

Q. How did you come in? Did you appear as an attorney?

A. I was just going to state, Mr. Eaker had spoken to me before, and when I came in, he whispered to me that the case was called, and that the court had refused to allow Mr. Kitchen to appear for him. I could not really believe that I could not be permitted to appear as *amicus curiæ.* When I made the attempt, however, I learned better.

Q. Now, Mr. Phelan, wasn't it to prevent an attachment being issued that you and Mr. Kitchen were a talking?

A. No, sir, an attachment was issued after I got in.

Q. Well, but what did you appear in the case for? Wasn't it to prevent the attachment?

A. No, sir. I wished to present to the court the fact that there had been no service of the writ of mandamus. I had so advised Judge Eaker.

Q. If there had been no service of the mandamus, why did you wish to appear? Wasn't it to prevent an attachment?

A. I have stated the facts according to my best recollection. Mr. Eaker had spoken to me, and I had promised to attend to the case for him.

Q. Did you appear in the defense of Mr. Eaker after the attachment issued?

A. I cannot say. I don't think I did.

Q. After the attachment, did you try to prevent him from answering, on the ground that there was no service?

A. I do not understand you. Judge Eaker was then in court, and I cannot state precisely what occurred between you and him in regard to the attachment. I think you made the arrangement yourself that he should answer, and I cannot remember that there were any suggestions of counsel in relation to it.

Q. Did you see Mr. Kitchen in court?

A. Yes, sir. He was then in court.

Q. When Judge Eaker spoke to you as you came in, hadn't an attachment already issued against him?

A. If any had issued, I have no knowledge of it.

Q. And you say Mr. Kitchen was there. Did you hear him say anything about appearing as the next friend of the court?

A. Were I to speak from circumstances, I could not answer; I do not know. I have no recollection of anything of the kind, and I don't believe that Mr. Kitchen would use such an expression.

Q. Now, Mr. Phelan, if you were the attorney of Judge Eaker, why did you not act as his attorney?

A. When spoken to by Judge Eaker, I told him there was no service, and he requested me to attend to the matter in court. I concluded the only way to get at it was to appear as the friend of the court, and not as an attorney, and suggest the failure of the service. You will recollect, Judge Jackson, that you picked me up on that point once at Butler Court, and I knew you too well to take a course for which you had once, as it were, reprimanded me. I didn't want you to get me again in a matter of that kind, and I thought the course I did pursue was the only one you would regard as proper. Mr. Eaker asked my opinion as to the matter prior to this term of the court.

Q. How long before the court was it?

A. I am unable to say exactly; several days.

Q. Was it more than two days before?

A. Perhaps. I think it was more than one day.* I have been Mr. Eaker's lawyer for a long time, and every lawyer knows when he is in the habit of attending to cases for a client generally, it is hard to remember the precise time when a particular case is mentioned to him. Be that as it may, Judge Eaker had spoken to me to attend to this case.

Q. Did you tell him you would attend to it as an attorney?

A. I did not.

Q. Didn't I ask you if you entered an appearance for him?

A. I cannot say now, Judge, what you asked me.

Q. Well, what made you want to act as his attorney?

A. I considered that what I did was within the line of my duty, and supposing it my privilege, as a lawyer, practicing at that bar. I was one of the lawyers on the other side in the origin of the matter, though my connection with the other side ceased before the application for a mandamus.

Q. Was I excited, and do you think my manner betrayed this excitement?

A. I have no earthly doubt of it, on that occasion more particularly.

Q. Which, Mr. Phelan, do you think it was: was I acting oppressively in the matter, or was it that you thought you had a right to do something, and that I thought you had no right to do it, and you wanted your way, and I wanted mine? Wasn't that what was the matter?

A. In that respect there might be a difference of opinion.

Q. Well, when there is a difference of opinion occurring in court, between lawyers and the Judge, whose province is it to decide?

A. The Judge's, of course.

Q. Might not the Judge make a wrong decision honestly? Couldn't he be honestly mistaken, and do you think such a mistake would be a fraud?

A. No, sir, there can be no question on the point whether an honest mistake is a fraud.

Q. Didn't you get excited on that occasion, and talk a good deal, as you are apt to do?

A. Annoyed is the utmost term I can use to express my feelings at the time. There was a good deal of hard feeling excited by your course.

Q. Wasn't this hard feeling with the lawyers because they thought certain things ought to have been done which the court thought was not right to do?

A. I will not undertake to say what others thought.

Q. Did you and Mr. Kitchen have a consultation about the matter?

A. There was no conversation between Kitchen and myself. I cannot fully understand your question.

Q. Never mind, you have answered. Did you not hear Mr. Kitchen disclaim being an attorney in the case?

A. I did not. It is my impression that he said nothing after the attachment issued.

Q. Didn't I tell Mr. Eaker, after the attachment was issued, that, if there was no service, to make that return, and he would be discharged?

A. I think perhaps you did. After Mr. Eaker was already a prisoner, he said he would make a return, and I suppose he did so. I did not advise him about it. I think he said you offered him until the next morning.

Q. What was it you said about my manner while this matter was up in court?

A. I believe I spoke of it as harsh, uncourteous, and severe in the extreme. It would be hard to convey, in words, any idea of your manner.

Q. Couldn't you give us a specimen of it? Couldn't you stand out there on the floor, now, and show the Court how I gesticulated, and manage to convey in that way some notion of your meaning?

A. I do not wish, Judge, to perform a pantomime, and the attempt would fail if I were to undertake it.

Q. Well, what did I do? Did I turn a summerset?

A. You ordered me, in the harshest terms, to sit down; and your looks spoke more than your words.

Q. Couldn't you give us one of those looks?

A. It would be impossible.

Q. We will now travel to Doniphan. Let us inquire about the Kinney or Kinsey case. I believe that is the case. Were you engaged in that cause?

A. I was an attorney on the last occasion when the case was tried. I don't know positively, but I think there were two trials, or rather, one mistrial, in which there was a hung jury. This is my impression; I am not certain; perhaps the jury hung both times.

Q. Wasn't the Circuit Attorney in that case?

A. I have no distinct recollection about it.

Q. I believe you stated that I told Mr. Fox, in this case, (or was it in another?) that he lied, or had caused his client to lie. What I want to know is, did I use the word lie, or falsehood?

A. I will give you my recollection of it. You had a paper in your hands at the time; I suppose the paper was an answer. You called Mr. Fox's attention to the paper, asked him if he wrote it, and told him that if he did, he either lied or caused his client to lie. That is my best recollection of the terms used by you. You may have used the term falsehood, as you say.

Q. Was it that time you say I told Mr. Fox to sit down?

A. That time? Well, I don't think I gave any testimony on that point. I did on one occasion, in Ripley Court, hear you tell Mr. Fox to sit down. Whether it was on that occasion I am not now prepared to say.

Q. Well, now, Mr. Phelan, I will ask you whether previous to that time there wasn't an understanding between you, Kitchen, Fox, and others, that you would hold a meeting against me?

[Mr. Knott objected to the question, and after discussion it was withdrawn.]

Q. Mr. Phelan, we will now go to your story of what happened at the trial of the Gibson and Dunn case. What was it you said in relation to it?

A. I have no very distinct recollection of the case itself. You had been out—had been to dinner, I think. When you came in, I arose, either to address the jury, or to make some motion for the consideration of the court, in connection with the cause, when you stopped me with the accusation of having tampered with the grand jury. I attempted to defend myself, and you told me to sit down; and afterwards told me to go on with the case. It is not necessary, I presume, to repeat further what I said.

Q. How did you characterize my manner on this occasion?

A. I have said, and I repeat, that it was harsh and very severe. You seemed to be angry.

Q. How did you know I was angry?

A. I knew it from your appearance, as well as from your language. Your face was inflamed.

Q. Isn't it usually somewhat inflamed when I speak earnestly?

A. On this occasion it was very much inflamed, and betokened anger.

Q. Couldn't you add that my cheeks were puffed out, that my eyes were rolling, that I blowed like a porpoise?

A. I can say, at least, Judge, that you were angry. I have seen you so a hundred times, and I could not be mistaken about it.

Q. Well, you said something about some one betraying the secrets of the grand jury. Who did you refer to?

A. It was William Henley. It was my impression that you were presented to the grand jury for oppression in office, and that the fact had been communicated to you by Mr. Henley. I really knew nothing about it at that time, but afterwards I was confirmed in my opinion by the fact that you claimed that if William Henley had told you, he had a right to do so. I presented him to the grand jury for this act. Henley was a member of the grand jury.

Q. What made you think that William Henley rather than any other person had told me?

A. I knew that you boarded with Henley; that when he was sued you befriended him; and I thought you were upon such terms with him as would induce him to communicate the fact to you, especially if you instructed him that he had a right to do so.

Q. How did you know that we were such particular friends?

A. I knew it from your acts. You are one of the best men to your friends in the world. When you are a friend at all you are a strong friend. Besides, I had heard you express feelings of friendship towards Mr. Henley, and heard similar expressions made by him concerning you.

Q. You say, then, that I am a good man towards my friends?

A. Yes, sir, and a good friend you have been to me. I don't deny that.

Q. Well, how am I towards my enemies?

A. I think you are a very bad enemy.

Q. Towards whom did you ever see me act as an enemy?

[Mr. Knott objected to the question. The witness, however, answered as follows:]

A. If I am not permitted to answer directly, I may perhaps state that when friendly with you I had an excellent chance. You assisted me all that you could. What you would do for one with whom you are not upon good terms, I will not now say, if, in doing so, I would violate the rules.

Judge Jackson. Let him go on. His statement is made for effect.

[Some little discussion here ensued in relation to the substance of the cross-examination, in which the witness participated, and which is here omitted.]

Q. Have we ever had any difficulty calculated to embitter your feelings towards me?

A. We had a little difficulty in Ripley once; also in Butler county. You insulted me there, as I thought, and afterwards you discovered that you were wrong, and apologized.

Q. Where was this difficulty? Was it in court?

A. It was in court. You wouldn't allow me to draw up a ——. The facts were, that a man had sold land, and perhaps warranted the title. Afterwards a difficulty arose in regard to the matter. The land was attached before a Justice of the Peace for a large amount, at least largely over the amount of the jurisdiction of the Justice of the Peace—three or four hundred dollars I think it was—and the Justice gave judgment. The Sheriff employed me for the defendant. He had a power of attorney authorizing him to attend to the land in absence of the owner, and the man had gone away in the interval. You would not allow me to act, because I was not employed by the man himself. I can give the names, and state all the facts in connection with the transaction more definitely, if it is desired.

[The witness was proceeding to make some further statement in regard to this matter, when he was stopped.]

Q. I will ask you, Mr. Phelan, if, at this term of the Butler court, you did not say to several persons, that if I said anything to you that was out of the way, you would shoot me?

[A discussion as to whether the witness should answer this question arose, and after some altercation between Judge Jackson, the witness, and the managers, it was dropped without being answered.]

Q. You say I told you, after coming in, in the excited manner that you describe, that you had been tampering with the grand jury. Now, wasn't it that I told you, after you got through with that case, you should answer for a contempt, and that you might go on with the case?

A. That is partially in accordance with my statement and recollection of the matter.

Q. Was it ever called up after that?

A. No, sir, it was not.

Q. You said a moment ago that I had insulted you, and apologized. Now, didn't you come to my room, say you were sorry for what you had done and said, and promise that you would never be guilty of the like again?

A. I have no recollection of making an apology of that character. Mr. Chandler came to me as a mutual friend, and stating that he was sorry to see any hard feelings existing between us, and that he was certain it had originated in a mistake, prevailed upon me to go to you, and when I did so, explanations were asked and given, and our difficulty, for the time, settled. My impressions are, however, that this had nothing to do with the Butler court matter.

Q. Well, speaking of this Eaker matter. Was it in reference to that that you said you had been excited, that you were ashamed of what you had done, and would never be guilty of the like again?

A. I have no recollection of anything of the kind.

Q. I will call your attention again to another Butler county matter. You stated, in speaking of the adjournment of the court, owing to the absence of the Clerk, you had suffered a great loss. To what case did you refer?

A. To the case of Ewing & Co. *vs.* ——. I cannot now recall the names of the other parties. There were several of them, I believe.

Q. So far from any chance of the suit being disposed of, at that term, wasn't the suit wrongly brought, and were you able to get judgment even at the next term of the court?

A. I will explain.

Q. Never mind the explanation, answer the question. Hadn't you brought the suit wrong? and would you have been able to get judgment at that term, even if we had had a Clerk?

A. I had leave to amend. I had brought the suit without being able to insert the full names of the persons composing the firm of Ewing & Co., and relied upon obtaining privilege to amend before I brought the suit. Before court I had got them through Daniel S. Miller.

Q. Didn't you have to get alias summonses for the parties? Had you any service upon Jennings, Thomas Price, Lawson, and Judge Lenoir?

A. I am not prepared to state as to that fact.

Q. Had you had no chance to amend, would the cause have been ready for trial at that term of the court?

A. I believe I would have been entitled to judgment. Of course I cannot say what the action of the court would have been. I had not the names at the time I had brought the suit, and knew that I would have to amend. I had sent by Daniel Miller and got them, and I do not know any obstacle that would have prevented me from getting judgment, if the business of the term had been gone through with as usual.

Q. On what day did the court adjourn?

A. I think it was on Tuesday night. Perhaps it was not till Wednesday morning, and only the grand jury were discharged on Tuesday night. I would not say that you did not on Tuesday night state that you would wait till the next morning to see if Blount would be able to attend to business.

Q. On Tuesday morning didn't I announce that I would keep the minutes, and that we could go on with such business as did not absolutely require a Clerk?

A. I do not recollect any announcement of that kind.

Q. Do you recollect anything said about the papers?

A. I do not call to mind anything in particular.

Q. Did I not state that as the papers were in rather a disorderly condition, or had been badly kept, when there was no Clerk that knew anything about them, it would be impossible to do business which required the hunting up of papers; but that I would keep the minutes, and we would transact such business as was possible under the circumstances? and wasn't it just after this announcement by me that Mr. Bedford came in with an application for a rule upon the Clerk to produce the papers in a certain cause, knowing that there was no Clerk to get the papers?

A. It is very probable that you state the facts correctly.

Q. And didn't I then say that if that was the course that lawyers would pursue, I could do nothing, and must adjourn the court for want of a Clerk?

A. I think you did make some such statement.

Q. What did you say became of the papers?

A. You put them under your arm, after wrapping them up in a newspaper.

Q. Do you know what was done with them afterwards?

A. I did not observe particularly.

Q. When you stated that Mr. Blount requested me to appoint a deputy, had you seen him?

A. Not till the time I spoke of, when he was assisted in signing a paper for that purpose.

Q. Had not you had a pretty severe bite from the "critter" yourself, about that time?

A. I have been very often under the influence of liquor, but I was not at that time; perhaps I was—well as I am now. I may have been more affected by liquor in the evening, but I was certainly not out of the way.

Q. Haven't you for years taken about a quart a night? Hasn't it taken about that quantity to do you?

A. I have been tight with you many a time, Judge, but I never in my life drank after going to bed. I have no recollection of it, if I ever did.

Q. Do you say that you were never drunk after night?

A. I understand you. I thought you meant if I drank after going to bed. Yes, sir, I have occasionally got on sprees in the evening, and after night.

Q. Well, to return to the point, didn't I take charge of the papers, lock them up in the office, give the key to some one there, and tell him what to do?

A. I do not know.

Q. Do you know whether there were any witnesses summoned to appear before the grand jury?

A. As to that I cannot make any positive statement; I only know that they were discharged while in the midst of their business, and that they were, or at least some of them were, very indignant at your conduct.

Q. How do you know? What manifestation was there of this?

A. I heard some of them make a motion to put you in Black river.

Q. Who made that motion?

A. I do not know that I could state positively who it was.

Q. Is there any one here who was on that grand jury?

A. Yes, sir, Mr. Ruff, William Vandiver, and perhaps others, who will know more about it than myself. I know the proposition was made.

Q. By whom?

A. I do not remember. Several members of the grand jury, I recollect, used very severe language in reference to your conduct.

Q. Well, I want you to state what the language was, and who used it.

[Mr. Knott objected to the question, and it was not answered.]

Q. Wasn't you and some others talking about this affair, endeavoring to excite the people against me by remarks in connection with it, and saying that it was about as good a matter as you could get up to break me of my office?

SENATOR McFERRAN. Mr. President, I know that we have tied ourselves up with rules, and that it is not in order for me to raise a question as to the pertinency of evidence in this cause. But by the leave of the Senate I would like to make a suggestion.

I do think that, for one, I am willing to give to the respondent here all proper latitude in the examination of witnesses. But I understand the rules of evidence to limit the subjects of examination to matters relevant to the issue, and I cannot see any propriety in departing from that course here now. I know that very great latitude must be given in cross-examination, but I think many of the questions proposed by Judge Jackson extend that latitude beyond all limit. The question just asked can only elicit facts relating to a wholly collateral issue; and if asked merely for the purpose of laying a foundation to impeach the witness, it is still improper, because a witness cannot be impeached upon an irrelevant point. Nothing can be attained by asking such questions. In view of the fact that this trial is a very important one, and a very costly one to the State, if for no better reason, I would urge upon the parties conducting it that they confine themselves as strictly as possible to the course prescribed by the plain rules of evidence.

JUDGE JACKSON. Well, the gentleman has stated the law as I always understood it. But he might have applied it at another point. I was astonished yesterday while they were giving oral testimony of the record. If they hadn't done that, I wouldn't have to run over all these little things, trying to get a full statement of the facts upon which the reasons for my conduct in various cases rested. I know that this trial is expensive; and when Senators think of that, they should think of the source of it. I am not responsible for its starting. Besides, I have something at stake which is above the question of value. For the full amount of the State debt, now over $20,000,000 I understand, I wouldn't have my official conduct unfairly and falsely dealt with. But I withdraw the question. If they would only introduce competent testimony, I would have no occasion to introduce any other kind myself.

The cross-examination of the witness was then resumed.

Q. Well, Mr. Phelan, you informed us that you were an attorney. Where do you practice?

A. In the Fifteenth Circuit. I cannot say that I am enrolled in all the courts in that circuit. I have never taken the trouble to attend to the matter. In fact I cannot say that I ever thought about it.

Q. Is your name enrolled as an attorney in any county?

[In answer to this question the witness went on to enumerate the counties in which he had practiced. The names of the counties, and the remarks made in connection with his enumeration, were lost by the reporter, owing to the fact that two Senators just at this point seated themselves on his table and commenced an undertoned conversation which prevented him from hearing.]

Q. In what county was it that the Smith and Cude case was tried?

A. In Dunklin.

Q. What did you say was done with that case?

A. A change of venue was awarded to Pemiscot county.

Q. Did you say there was any agreement that the case should go to any other county, and that this agreement was made known to the court?

A. Yes, sir. The parties and attorneys had an understanding, and they wanted the case to go to either Scott or Bollinger county. I think now that it was Bollinger.

Q. On what side of the case were you?

A. I was on the side of Mr. Johnson. I was the attorney of Smith's representative, Mr. Johnson.

Q. Did he wish the case sent to Bollinger county?

A. I cannot say that he wished it to go there, or anywhere, but it is my impression that I had a consultation with him, and that he was willing for the case to go to Bollinger.

Q. Where did Mr. Cude want the case to go?

A. I cannot say. I understood from his lawyers that he was willing, and I know they were willing for the case to be sent to Bollinger.

Q. Who were his attorneys?

A. Mr. Horner, I think, was one of them, and there were others.

Q. Did Mr. Horner consent that the case should go to Bollinger?

A. I think he consented. It is my impression that he did.

Q. Was any proposition made to take the case to New Madrid by Mr. Horner?

A. I think not. If there was, I have no knowledge of it.

Q. Where does Mr. Johnson reside?

A. In Dyer county, Tennessee, opposite Pemiscot.

Q. Would not Pemiscot county have been as convenient to Mr. Johnson as any other?

A. For the purpose of attending the trial alone it would have been the most convenient to him.

Q. In the case of the State *vs.* Sarah Buckner, I believe, you stated that the testimony of Grimsley was withdrawn?

A. Yes, sir. In the progress of the trial the Judge gave an intimation, or what I took to be an intimation, that that would be the best course for the Circuit Attorney to pursue. He said, "Mr. Circuit Attorney, if I were you, I would withdraw that testimony," or something of that kind. As I have stated before, the Circuit Attorney did not seem to notice this suggestion at the time. Afterwards, however, he made the motion to withdraw the testimony, and the Judge said, "well."

Q. Was it the testimony or the witness that was withdrawn?

A. I do not know which it would be considered. The witness was withdrawn.

Q. Was there any order given to the jury at that time not to consider Grimsley's testimony as before them?

A. It is my impression that such an order was not given at that time, but it was a conceded fact by the lawyers throughout the remainder of the trial that Grimsley's testimony was not evidence before the jury.

Q. Was any motion filed in regard to the matter?

A. I think not. I believe it was a mere verbal motion assented to by the court, as I have stated.

Q. Who moved to instruct the jury that Grimsley's testimony was not in evidence?

A. If any such instruction was asked or given, I am not apprised of it.

Q. Now, Mr. Phelan, wasn't it this way: while Grimsley was proceeding with his testimony, when he came to speak of what Sarah Buckner had told him that the daughter had told her, didn't I stop him, and wasn't that what was excluded, and not the whole of the testimony of Grimsley?

A. I think it was not that.

Q. Did you ask any instructions to the effect that no part of Grimsley's testimony was before the jury?

A. To the best of my recollection I did not.

Q. Did you ask any instruction to the effect that the evidence of but one witness was not sufficient?

A. No, sir. I thought of that for the first time on the spur of the moment in the argument of the motion for a new trial. This cause was alleged in the motion for arrest of judgment.

Q. Who made that suggestion?

A. I believe it was first made by me.

Q. Wasn't it this—when the woman's trial was talked about out of court, and a contention arose concerning the testimony of Grimsley, and I, hearing that the course of the court had been commented on pretty severely, said that if what the woman's lawyers claimed to be true was true, she must blame them for her conviction, and suggested the point that you say was inserted in your motion for arrest of judgment—wasn't it after hearing of this, that you put it in?

A. I was not indebted to you for the suggestion.

Q. Why didn't you try to keep out the testimony of Grimsley?

A. I relied upon the cross-examination to bring out such facts as I thought would acquit the defendant. I could, perhaps, give another reason for the course which I took, though it may not have been a good one. Gen. Watkins had been employed, and was represented in the case by Mr. Davis, who tried to take the lead in the case, and I was obliged to, or did, take a little to the back ground in conducting the defense.

Q. Well, I will ask why wasn't the instructions in relation to Grimsley's testimony asked for by the counsel of the defendant?

A. I can only answer, I doubt if we ever thought of it at that time. It will be remembered, as I stated before, that Judge Jackson very kindly adjourned the court to give me an opportunity of preparing the case for action in the Supreme Court, and some twenty or thirty days intervened from the trial to the time of fixing up the bill of exceptions. The cross-examination was what we relied upon, and——

Q. Did you ever cross-examine at all?

A. No, sir. We did not.

Q. Do you say the testimony of Grimsley was withdrawn, or was it the witness himself?

A. It was the witness, I think.

QUESTION BY A SENATOR. What was it you expected to get from the cross-examination of Grimsley?

A. We expected to prove that Susan, the daughter of the defendant, had admitted that she killed the deceased, and that though Mrs. Buckner admitted that he had been killed, she said that Susan did it.

JUDGE JACKSON. What was it you said was done with Grimsley's testimony in the bill of exceptions?

A. I said that you would not sign unless Grimsley's testimony was incorporated.

Q. Who wrote out the testimony of Grimsley?

A. I believe you did it yourself. I think it is in the office now, in your own handwriting.

Mr. Knott. In this case, in which a change was awarded from Dunklin to Pemiscot, were the counties to which you were willing the case should be sent situated on the same side of the swamp as Dunklin?

A. Yes, sir.

Q. In what county do the witnesses in that case reside?

A. Mostly in Dunklin county. There may have been some in Tennessee. I am not prepared to say.

Q. What are the means of conveyance from Dunklin to Pemiscot county? How is the traveling between the two counties usually done?

A. In going around the swamp, all ordinary conveyances are used. In going across the swamp, I am told they sometimes go in skiffs and canoes.

Judge Jackson. Is there not a plank road down there that is traveled a good deal?

A. I have heard of one, but I disbelieve in it. How far it is finished, if there is any, I am not prepared to say. I believe I would be safe in saying there is no plank road there at all.

Mr. Knott. Do you know, Mr. Phelan, how the papers in Butler county are kept?

A. It would be hard to say that they are kept at all.

Q. Was the court apprised of the manner in which the Clerk transacted his business?

A. Yes, sir, he was well apprised of it, and has been for two or three years.

Senator Wilson. In the bill of exceptions, as signed by the Judge, in the case of the State *vs.* Sarah Buckner, was the testimony of Grimsley set out in full with the action of the Judge in relation to said testimony?

A. No, sir. There was nothing in it about his excluding the testimony. That is in Jackson's own handwriting, and will show.

Senator Parsons. I will ask of the managers if this bill of exceptions will be introduced?

Mr. Hardin. The record is here.

TESTIMONY OF WASHINGTON CARLISLE.

Washington Carlisle called and examined by Mr. Knott.

Q. Where do you reside, Mr. Carlisle?

A. I live in Stoddard county, Missouri.

Q. What is your occupation?

A. I am a farmer.

Q. Were you ever a member of the grand jury in Stoddard county? If so, please state when.

A. I was a member of the grand jury at the last August term of the Circuit Court.

Q. Please state to the Court if you know anything about Judge Jackson visiting the grand jury in their room at that time.

A. Yes, sir, he did.

Q. On how many occasions?

A. I don't recollect, exactly. Once or twice, I think.

Q. Do you recollect his giving the grand jury any instructions upon points of law?

A. Well, I don't know but he did, some.

Q. State what they were—what you remember about them. I will call your attention first to whatever he may have said about gambling.

A. In regard to that, it seems to me all a little like a dream. As well as my memory serves me, there had been some presentments for this.

[The witness was going on with a statement of some immaterial matters, when he was stopped, and afterwards proceeded as follows:]

I think the Judge named some certain offenses which he said were not indictable. He said they could not be considered in law as gaming. One was the case of a watermelon; as well as my memory serves me, it was this: There had been a watermelon lying on a porch. It was not yet bought. I don't know whether the persons knew this or not. They knew the price, and they played to see who should pay for it. The Judge said such instances as this were not indictable; that in cases where they merely played for something, to see who should pay for it, it wouldn't be considered gambling because it wasn't betting. He talked about it considerable; I couldn't pretend to say what all he said.

Q. You will now please state the circumstances attending the other visit, and particularly anything in relation to the circulation of a paper among the jurors.

A. I don't recollect, and I wouldn't be positive as to which visit it was when the paper was mentioned. There was a paper before the grand jury with some writing on it. I think it cited to some law. I don't pretend to say where it came from, though I think I know the page referred to. It also referred to some report or law book. It was page 613, vol. 1, of the Statutes.

Q. How did the Judge happen to come to the grand jury room? What was the first thing he said or did?

A. Well, he came to the door and knocked. The door was opened, and he stepped in, and, if I remember rightly, there was quite a silence for a few minutes. Directly he spoke, and said he learned that there were some persons tampering or trying to tamper with the grand jury, and he called for the paper. The paper was looked for. At first it was thought to be lost, but eventually, on opening the book, it was found just where the paper spoke of the law; that is, it was at the page referred to in the paper. The Judge read the page, I think, or may be it was only a section, and he said that law did not apply to him. I think he went on to state that this law referred to a Sheriff or guard, or some officer of that kind, and that it didn't apply to judicial officers. Then the conversation turned up whether a Judge was indictable for oppression in office. I think may be some one of the grand jurors asked him whether any Judge—I don't believe he was spoken of alone—but whether the grand jury had power to find an indictment against any Judge. He said that a Judge was subject to indictment for any act like another man, but he couldn't be indicted for any act done under color of his office. He said that if he did wrong, there was a higher tribunal to take the matter to.

Q. Had you at that time under investigation a charge against the Judge for oppression in office?

[Question objected to and waived.]

Q. You will state, then, whether the grand jury had under consideration any charge for oppression in office to which this law cited in the paper had been supposed to refer?

A. Well, yes. There had been such a presentment made against Judge Jackson. When the paper came in, it was before the presentment had been made to the grand jury, but somehow we knew that the paper referred to a charge of this kind that would be made.

CROSS-EXAMINED BY JUDGE JACKSON.

Q. Do you know whether I was sent for either time I went to the grand jury?

A. I think you was sent for but once.

Q. Now, at the time when I was not sent for, when I came in, didn't I say that I came to inquire if any one had been tampering with the grand jury?

A. I think perhaps that was the way of it.

Q. Didn't I ask if there was not such a paper before the grand jury, saying that I had learned there was, and that if there was, the man that sent it should be indicted?

A. Yes, sir. It was something like that.

Q. Did the paper come into the grand jury through the Circuit Attorney?

A. No, sir, I think not.

Q. Did one of the grand jury bring it in?

A. I don't think I know. There was considerable chat about that—as to how the paper got there; and it was my understanding that we all wanted to find who it was that brought it there, or sent it.

Q. Were you one of the jury in the case of the State *vs.* Sarah Buckner?

A. No, sir. I was never but once or twice on a petit jury in your court.

[The cross-examination here ended, and the managers consulted a few minutes, at the conclusion of which consultation the witness was recalled by Judge Jackson.]

Q. You stated that I told you in the grand jury room that the section of law to which you had been referred by this paper was not for a Judge—that you could not indict a Judge for an official act. Now, Mr. Carlisle, don't you recollect that I made a distinction between judicial officers and officers of trust, and that I pointed out the distinction between a County Court Judge and a Circuit Court Judge?

A. I won't be positive, but I think you did.

TESTIMONY OF LEMUEL KITTRELL.

LEMUEL KITTRELL called and examined by Mr. Knott.

Q. Where do you reside?

A. I reside in Doniphan, Ripley county, Missouri.

Q. Were you present at the Circuit Court in April, 1858, pending the trial of the case of James Moore *vs.* John Eldridge, administrator of the estate of William Parker?

A. Yes, sir. I was a witness in that case.

Q. Did you hear Judge Jackson express any opinion in relation to the merits of the cause? Did you hear him say how it should go, or who he thought would succeed in the trial?

A. During the court there was a good deal of contention. Judge Jackson made some observation, and Moore told me that he supposed he was bound to lose the case, as Jackson had already decided it against him. There was an instrument of writing in the case, and it was to testify about that instrument of writing that I was a witness. It was considered by some that this writing in one part contradicted another part, and the contention was as to which side the paper would support. In a conversation which happened before court, Judge Jackson decided it against Moore.

Q. Were you present during that conversation? If so, state what you heard the Judge say—how the conversation came up.

A. Well, there had been a partnership of Moore and Parker. This instrument of writing was an agreement between them, and it read that Parker on his part would pay James Moore a certain sum of money a month. The question was whether this meant that Parker must pay this himself, or rather whether his estate should pay it, or the firm of Moore and Parker pay it. The matter came up in the conversation, and Judge Jackson said that the firm must pay it. He said the firm ought to pay Moore, which would make Moore pay half himself, as he was a member of the firm of Parker and Moore. That was the opinion expressed by the Judge.

Q. Did you say that you were a witness?

A. Yes, sir. I was a witness on this instrument to prove whether it was a genuine article of agreement.

Q. Do you remember any difficulty arising after the trial about your evidence?

A. Yes, sir. I was in court after the trial was over. The parties disagreed about my testimony concerning this instrument of writing. I was called in to say what I had said about it.

Q. You will please state the substance of what occurred when you were called in, as well as you recollect it.

A. Well, there was a difference about the instrument. The date of the instrument was blotted. I don't think in my testimony I had said anything about it. After the trial was concluded, they called me in to know if I had said anything about the defect or blot on the paper. I said that I did not think that I had testified anything about that, but I believed the instrument was just as I had always seen it. If I did say anything during the trial it was just that.

Q. Do you know what they were doing when you were called in?

A. I understood that they were endeavoring to get up a bill of exceptions, and that the part of my testimony to which they called my attention was whether I had said that the date of the instrument had been altered. I replied that that instrument was as I had always seen it. I had seen it for a long time on the books. Parker had died very suddenly, and there was a contention between Moore and the administrator of Parker's estate. Moore had several witnesses to prove what he wanted to establish about the instrument.

Q. Did you say when you were called back that you had made any statement, upon your examination during the trial of the cause, in reference to the alteration of the instrument of writing?

A. I told them that to the best of my recollection I had not.

Q. Did you see the bill of exceptions after it was drawn up?

A. No, sir. I have no recollection of seeing it. I may have seen it; but I am pretty certain that I didn't read it, if I did see it.

Q. When was this conversation when the Judge expressed an opinion as to who should pay?

A. I think it was the day before the trial. If I recollect rightly a jury had been called the evening before the trial, and this conversation happened either at noon or at night.

CROSS-EXAMINED BY JUDGE JACKSON.

Q. Hadn't that case been in a different shape, and been tried once or twice before the trial at this term of the court that you speak of?

A. Yes, sir. I think so.

Q. Didn't the question come up in the former trials whether the money should be paid out of the firm or out of the estate?

A. I suppose it did.

Q. Wasn't I present when the case was tried in the County Court?

A. I don't recollect.

Q. Did Mr. Moore ask my opinion in regard to the matter?

A. I can't say. I don't recollect hearing him ask it.

Q. Hadn't there been a suit on one view of the paper in which there was a non-suit? and then wasn't there two or three views or ways in which the paper could be construed?

A. There was a good deal of difference about the paper.

Q. Wasn't there two suits in which it was involved in the Circuit and County Courts?

A. They were, I know, lawing about it a good deal.

Q. Well, when the matter came up one way, don't you recollect that there was a non-suit, and when it came up on another view, there was an appeal taken and the appeal dismissed?

A. It is my opinion there was a non-suit once, and then they commenced anew. I don't recollect exactly how it was.

Q. Wasn't that instrument talked about all over town. Wasn't it the common talk, and the people generally had two ways of construing the instrument?

A. Yes, sir. It was talked about pretty generally, and a good many thought it ought to go one way, while others thought it ought to go the other.

Q. Didn't I say that neither party was right, and that there was a third way of construing it?

A. No, Judge, there couldn't be but two ways.

Q. I know most persons thought so; but I believe the instrument would show that I was right. What did you say the difference was about when you were called back after the trial?

A. I suppose I was called back to say what I had stated about the instrument—whether I had said so and so. That was my understanding of it at least.

Q. What did you say?

A. I said that I didn't think I had said anything about it before when I was giving in my testimony, and that the instrument was just as I had always seen it.

Q. But wasn't there a controversy whether there was a defect in the instrument which couldn't be perceived without examining it?

A. Well, as I said before, there was a blot on the date of the paper. I think the contention was about what I had said.

Q. Will you state whether the instrument was in evidence before the jury?

A. Well, as I said before, I was a witness there to testify about the instrument.

Q. That is not what I want. Wasn't this instrument before the jury?

A. Yes, sir. If I recollect aright it was handed around amongst the jurors.

Q. Didn't there exist on the instrument itself a blot or erasure, a defect in the writing, which you would have to examine before you would see what it was?

A. Yes, sir. It was.

Q. Wasn't it matter of inspection—an obscuration of the date that could only be known by looking at it? and wasn't that what we were contending about?

A. I believe that was it.

Mr. Hardin. Where was this conversation that you speak of before the trial?

A. It was in the town of Doniphan, on the wood-pile before my yard. There were five or six of the neighbors in company, and we were all sitting down talking, when the Judge came up. We were disputing whether the verdict would be against Moore. They were all talking about this when he came up, and not thinking there was anything wrong about it, I believe I asked the Judge his opinion.

JUDGE JACKSON. Had not I given an opinion upon that question when the case was up before? Wasn't the same question involved in the other trials?

[Question objected to and withdrawn.]

JUDGE JACKSON. Did you hear me say anything about which way I thought the case ought to go? Wasn't it simply an expression of my opinion about the paper?

A. Yes, sir. That was it. We asked you who should pay,—Moore or the firm? Your opinion was that the firm should pay.

Q. Wasn't my attention directed solely to that piece of writing?

A. I believe that was what we asked you about.

Q. Were there not other matters involved in the suit?

A. Yes, sir. I supposed there were, though that was the principal matter. You took a different view of the paper from what I did.

MR. KNOTT. Did any person coincide with the view that the Judge took of the matter?

A. Well, we were arguing about it some. I think one or two said they believed the Judge was right.

JUDGE JACKSON. Who beside yourself was in this company?

A. I don't recollect who all was there.

Q. Was Mr. Arthur present?

A. I don't recollect. I believe he was.

TESTIMONY OF DAVID M. FOX.

DAVID M. FOX called and examined by Mr. Knott.

Q. Where do you reside, Mr. Fox?

A. I reside in Fredericktown, Madison county, Missouri.

Q. What is your profession?

A. I am an attorney at law.

Q. Have you been practicing in the Fifteenth Judicial Circuit?

A. Yes, sir. I have practiced in some counties in that Circuit.

Q. Do you practice in Wayne county?

A. Yes, sir.

Q. Please state if you were present at the September term of the Wayne Circuit Court in 1858.

A. Yes, sir.

Q. Were you engaged in any manner in the cause then pending of Limbarger *vs.* Powers?

A. Yes, sir. I was counsel in that case. There was another case of Powers *vs.* Limbarger. Perhaps I was in both cases. I was counsel for Limbarger.

Q. Please state to the Court what was done in this case.

A. There was a change of venue awarded. I believe the application was in my handwriting. The cause alleged was prejudice against the plaintiff.

Q. Please state to the Court what occurred on the presentation of the petition for change of venue?

A. The change was granted, and the case sent to Mississippi county.

Q. How far is it from the county seat of Wayne (Greenville) to Charleston, the county seat of Mississippi?

A. I don't know the exact distance. I think it would be a hundred miles or more.

Q. How many counties of the Tenth Circuit intervene between Wayne and Mississippi?

A. By the usually traveled route, Bollinger, Cape Girardeau, and Scott counties intervene. The route through these counties forms a kind of angle.

Q. Can you describe the relative position of these counties?

A. I would like to examine the map. [After an examination,] I think Greenville is nearly north of Charleston. The direct road at some seasons of the year is somewhat swampy, and it is necessary to go through the counties I have named, at such times.

Q. At what seasons of the year is this direct road swampy?

A. Generally about the time of the spring terms of the courts.

Q. At such times is any additional travel necessary?

A. Yes, sir. I suppose so.

Q. How far is the county seat of Madison from Greenville?

A. I think it is called forty miles.

Q. What are the relative positions of Madison and Wayne counties?

A. They are contiguous; Madison lies north of Wayne.

Q. Is Madison in a different circuit?

A. Yes, sir. Madison is in Judge Hough's circuit.

Q. How far from the county seat of Wayne to the county seat of Iron?

A. The county seats of Madison and Iron are equi-distant from the county seat of Wayne. Forty miles I think it is.

Q. In what circuit is Iron county.

A. Judge Stone presides there. I believe the law does not include it in either the Fifteenth or Tenth.

Q. How far is the county seat of Bollinger county from Greenville?

A. About the same distance as Fredericktown—forty or forty-five miles.

Q. Whereabouts do the parties in this suit of Limbarger *vs.* Powers reside?

A. At the time the petition for a change of venue was presented, they resided about half way between Greenville and Fredericktown, about twenty-one miles each way. The parties lived in sight of each other, and were formerly partners in trade. The witnesses lived in the neighborhood of the parties generally.

Q. Who was engaged with you in the cause?

A. I was, sir, the senior counsel. I had as my junior Mr. Phillip Pipkin.

Q. Who was on the other side?

A. My recollection is that Messrs. White and Bedford were counsel for Mr. Powers.

Q. Was there any conference or agreement, as to what would be a suitable county for the trial of the cause, among the attorneys?

A. My impression is that there had been such a conference.

Q. What counties were fixed upon?

A. I think there was an agreement that the case should go to either Iron, Madison, Bollinger, or Cape Girardeau.

Q. Why were these counties selected?

A. They were selected because of their convenience to the parties concerned, and to the witnesses.

Q. How would it have suited the convenience of counsel in the cause to try the case in Mississippi?

A. As to myself I have never been in Mississippi county at court. I live in Madison. Either of the other counties would have suited me better. Mr. Pipkin lives in Iron county, at Arcadia. It would have been much more convenient to him to attend court in any county named than in Mississippi. Mr. White lives in Greenville; Mr. Bedford in Bloomfield.

Q. When the award was made to Mississippi county, what occurred in court?

A. If you will merely lead the way, by directing my attention to any particular fact, I can perhaps tell you better.

Q. Was anything said by counsel to the court, in relation to the inconvenience to which the parties and attorneys would be subjected by sending the case to Mississippi county?

A. Mr. Pipkin said something in regard to it. He remarked that by sending the case to Mississippi he would be thrown out of the case entirely, as it would be impossible for him to attend there. I couldn't quote the reply of the Judge.

Q. Did you make any representation of the facts to the court?

A. Yes, sir. I made this remark: when I presented the petition, and a change was awarded to Mississippi, I said that it would be inconvenient to attend down there. The Judge did not make any reply immediatly that I recollect, but turned to the law, and after reading it, said that he found that the party presenting a petition for a change of venue in any case had no right to designate the county to which it should be sent; and he then said, "if I did not think you would consider it a personal matter, I would fine you for a contempt of court."

Q. What was your manner in addressing the court upon the subject?

A. It was in the same style of coolness, candor, and respectful address, in which I am now speaking.

Q. What was the manner of the Judge in his replies to yourself and Mr. Pipkin?

A. It was unjudicial, unparliamentary. That was the idea I formed of it.

SENATOR SCOTT. Tell us what he said and did, and leave us to judge of whether it was unjudicial and unparliamentary.

A. I couldn't repeat it verbatim. I only quote from memory. His language towards me was, as nearly as I can state it, that if he didn't think I would look upon it as a personal matter, he would fine me for contempt of court. Towards Mr. Pipkin I cannot state exactly his demeanor. When he was told that sending the case to Mississippi county would throw Mr. Pipkin out of the case, he said he didn't care about that, or something of the kind. I suggested to the court that either of the other counties named would be more convenient to all the parties, and in answer to that he used the expression I have quoted.

Q. You can state whether his manner indicated any feeling in regard to the matter.

A. Yes, sir. His manner was angry, tumultuous, and stormy—that is, if I am to judge of those feelings.

Q. Was it represented to the court that counsel had consulted in regard to the matter, and wished the case sent to some other county?

A. As to that I cannot speak from the card. I think Mr. Bedford did say something about it, but I would not be positive.

On motion of SENATOR PARSONS, the Court adjourned.

EVENING SESSION.

SATURDAY, June 11, 1859.

The Court met pursuant to adjournment.

The managers and respondent attended.

On motion of SENATOR GULLETT, leave of absence was granted to Senators Thompson and Wood until Monday.

On motion of SENATOR CHURCHILL, leave of absence was granted to Senator Coleman until Monday.

A call of the Senate was then ordered, and the following Senators noted as being absent without leave: Messrs. Hedgpeth, Johnson, Jones, Newland, Rains, Scott, Watkins, and Wright.

Sick—Mr. Halliburton.

On motion of SENATOR MCFERRAN, further proceedings under the call were dispensed with.

The examination of DAVID M. FOX was then resumed.

Q. Mr. Fox, you will state, if you please, whether you were at the Butler Circuit Court in May, 1858?

A. I was.

Q. Were you in court during the trial of the case of Gibson *vs.* Dunn?

A. I was, sir.

Q. Did you see Mr. Phelan at that court?

A. I saw him during the trial.

Q. Please state what occurred between the court and Mr. Phelan at any stage of that case.

A. In what particular?

Q. Any irregularity or unusual conduct of either party that you may have noticed.

A. Upon the trial of that cause, I heard Judge Jackson tell Mr. Phelan that he was in contempt of court. The court had adjourned for dinner. Immediately after dinner, when the Judge came in, he told Mr. Phelan that he was in contempt of court, saying that he had been tampering with the grand jury, and endeavoring to injure him. Mr. Phelan seemed somewhat excited when the charge was made, and I think he said he would see him again, or that he would settle the matter elsewhere.

Q. Did Mr. Phelan offer to vindicate himself then?

A. That was my impression.

Q. What was the Judge's conduct towards him?

A. I thought it was rather out of place,—out of the usual order. I never saw a Judge conduct himself in such a manner before.

Q. When Mr. Phelan attempted to vindicate himself, what did the Judge say to him?

A. He told him to hush up, or to shut his mouth. It was some expression of that kind. I do not undertake to give his precise language.

Q. What was the charge alleged against Mr. Phelan?

A. A charge of tampering with the grand jury to interfere with him, the Judge.

Q. Do you attend Ripley Circuit Court?

A. I have attended there.

Q. Were you in Ripley Circuit Court, at the October term, 1857?

A. I think I was.

Q. Judge Jackson is charged with certain irregular conduct towards you at that court. You will please state the facts, if any such thing occurred.

A. To what case do you refer?

Q. I don't know what case it was, but I refer to a charge of lying alleged against you.

A. There was a case pending in which I think the firm of Lacey & Gale was plaintiff. If I recollect rightly, the suit was brought against Ponder & Co.—Ponder & Barrendon—or something of that kind; I don't recollect the style of the firm. The suit was founded on a note. Mr. Ponder employed me. I filed an answer, denying the execution of the note as far as Ponder was concerned,—a regular plea of *non est factum*, so far as he was concerned in the note. A demurrer or motion to strike out was filed by the other party. This motion or demurrer was sustained. On motion I obtained leave to amend. My client lives 7, 8, 10, or 15 miles from the place, and was not at court. In the meantime I filed an amended answer, to which I made affidavit myself. The purport of the affidavit was that the matters and things set forth in the amended answer were true to the best of my knowledge, as I understood them from my client. The court examined this paper and asked me the question, "is this your writing?" There was no necessity for this question, for he was perfectly familiar with my handwriting. When I replied that I believed it was, or something of that kind, he said, "you must either have sworn a lie yourself, or caused your client to swear a lie." He further observed that the grand jury was in session, (pointing with his finger towards the grand jury room.) I was angry enough. In my opinion it was intended as an insult.

Q. Was this in open court?

A. Yes, sir. It was in open court. He was on the bench, and I suppose it would be fair to say that he was acting officially.

Q. Are you a practicing lawyer at that bar?

A. I am.

Q. At the time this conversation occurred, did you say anything to provoke this language from the court?

A. I had not been saying anything. I do not remember that I was doing anything at the time. My demeanor towards the court then, and to all courts at all times, so far as I know, was respectful.

Q. Were you at the April term, A. D. 1858, of the Ripley Circuit Court?

A. I was.

Q. Were you in court during the trial of William Kinsey on an indictment for grand larceny?

A. Yes, sir, I was.

Q. You will please relate what occurred pending the trial of that cause in regard to taking down the testimony of the witnesses.

A. There had been another trial at the same term in which the jury hung, and at the second trial we took every precaution to prepare the case for an appeal. Almost the whole bar volunteered for the defense, Mr. Tyrell among others, and wishing to take the precaution of having the whole testimony, we assigned to him, (I am not positive, but I think it was Mr. Tyrell,) the work of reducing the testimony to writing. Upon propounding a question, we asked for time to reduce the answer to writing. We wished the witness to stop for this purpose, but the court would not give us the time, and he then and there observed that the witness was not there for the purpose of having his testimony written down by lawyers, but that he was there for the benefit of court and jury. We were not able to take it down as reporters do, and because we were not so able, we could not accomplish our purpose of reducing the whole of the testimony to writing, owing to the refusal of the court to allow time for that purpose.

Q. Was it customary in the courts of that country to keep minutes of the depositions of witnesses in that way?

A. It has been so in every court I have practiced in.

Q. Was there any interruption of counsel by the court during this trial?

A. Yes, sir. Upon this second trial of the Kinsey case, Mr. Joseph White volunteered to prosecute. The evidence in the case was altogether circumstantial. In my argument for the defense, before the jury, I took occasion to comment or reflect upon Joseph. It had leaked out during the progress of the trial that this Joseph had volunteered his services in the prosecution. In my remarks I played upon the name of Joseph some. I said that I supposed that he was named after Joseph of old, and that out of respect for his great prototype, who was himself the victim of circumstantial evidence, he ought not to undertake to forward the perpetration of a similar wrong. I carried this allusion to some extent; spoke of the fact that the father of Joseph the prototype, when he heard that his son was in Egypt, could not believe that it was true; and in some manner which I am not now able to detail, I instituted a comparison between the father of the prototype Joseph and the prosecutor in the case, saying that as the one could not believe in the existence of his son, so the other, when he heard of his hog, would not believe it to be the same. In my further remarks I spoke in an ironical strain of a grand inquisitorial body sitting in judgment upon this hog matter, and in this connection I did refer to Judge Jackson. Before this, however, I should have observed that my time had been limited to an hour and forty-five minutes. When I came to speak, in the ironical strain that I have mentioned, of the grand inquisitorial body, the Judge interrupted me and asked me to explain myself, and say whether I meant him. I replied that if he would not discount or offset my time, I would not explain. Afterward,—I don't know what gave rise to it,—he abruptly told me to sit down. Whether this grew out of what I had been saying in my speech I will not undertake to say, but he did order me to sit down. I then told the jury to see what a poor chance my unfortunate client had, and that my only dependence for getting justice was in them, and complied with the order of the court by taking my seat. And, gentlemen, I believe it was the best speech I ever made in my life.

CROSS-EXAMINED BY JUDGE JACKSON.

Q. Wasn't your ironical allusion, that you have just been speaking of, to a person in authority, whom you described as trying to get a conviction against your client? and was it not there that I interrupted you and asked you if you meant me? and did I not have to repeat my demand, in order to know if you meant me, before you stopped? Didn't you tell me that it was me? and wasn't it then that I told you to sit down?

A. I don't recollect that it occurred in that way.

Q. Have you a pretty good memory?

A. In some respects my memory is very good. It is not so good in retaining dates and names, but ordinarily I may speak of my memory as good.

Q. Couldn't you repeat that fine speech for us?

A. It would not be interesting.

Q. That depends upon your auditory. But let me inquire about what you said concerning my pointing to the grand jury. Didn't the affidavit attached to that amended answer contradict the answer itself?

A. I can't say that it did.

Q. Didn't you have it in your head to get your client indicted for perjury, and then come in to defend him from the charge?

A. I had nothing of the kind in my head or heart.

Q. Didn't you testify concerning this matter once before?

A. Yes, sir; before the Judiciary Committee of the House last winter.

Q. Didn't you then say that Lacey and Sturdivant was the firm that brought the suit, and not Lacey and Gale?

A. If so, I was not positive then as to the style of the firm, nor am I now. I think I stated it then as now, however.

Q. If your memory is defective on that point, would it not be very safe to suppose that it was equally defective in other respects?

A. It would show that my memory was not clear upon that point, and I leave others to draw such inferences as they please. As to the style of the firm, or the exact turning of a phrase, a man might have a poor recollection and yet have a very clear and distinct one touching the the idea to be conveyed.

SENATOR PARSONS. I would inquire of the managers if the testimony taken before the Judiciary Committee was subscribed by the witnesses?

MR. HARDIN. It was.

JUDGE JACKSON. You admit then, Mr. Fox, that you are apt to make mistakes about words?

A. Yes, sir. All men are fallible in that respect.

Q. Well, now then, did I really use the word lie or falsehood, in speaking of your contradictory answer and affidavit?

A. In speaking of what you call my contradictory answer and affidavit, it is my impression that you used the word lie. If you did not, it was a harsh word conveying that idea.

Q. Is it your impression from the fact itself, or from the recollection of the accusation?

A. I have stated my best recollection.

Q. Well, now about this Joseph matter. Wasn't you intoxicated when you were going through that long rigmarole?

A. I won't answer that question. He sometimes gets drunk himself. I will say that I was not drunk then.

Q. Well, now, Mr. Fox, what was it you said I stated to Mr. Phelan at Butler court? Didn't I tell Mr. Phelan he was in or had been in contempt, and must answer? and didn't he then insist upon going into that matter immediately?

A. I don't recollect that occurrence differently from my statement on examination in chief. I state things from memory.

Q. But you say that your memory is bad sometimes?

A. Whether it is bad or good, I set up that in answer.

Q. But it does not answer my question.

A. I have given a truthful statement of the occurrence. If it does not suit you, you can seek another statement elsewhere. Like every other true lawyer, I adopt the maxim, "*fiat justitia, ruat cœlum.*"

SENATOR SCOTT objected to the style of the witness' answer.

Q. Were you and Mr. Pipkin the attorneys on both sides in the case of Limbarger *vs.* Powers?

A. We were on the same side of one case. In the other, a change of venue was not taken. On account of a want of the completion of the pleadings a change was not granted.

Q. Is there not a great deal of business at the Madison Circuit Court?

A. The docket is nearly clear now.

Q. Wasn't the docket crowded at that time, owing to the time that the Phillips trial took?

A. Yes, sir. The docket was crowded then.

Q. Was it not the same way at Bollinger court?

A. I understand so, on account of changes of venue from the Fifteenth Judicial Circuit.

Q. Shouldn't the advantages for procuring a trial as early as possible be considered by a Judge in awarding changes of venue?

A. That is argumentative, sir.

Q. Where does Mr. Bedford reside?

A. At Bloomfield.

Q. How far is it from Bloomfield to Greenville?

A. Forty or forty-five miles.

Q. Wouldn't it be as advantageous for Mr. Bedford to have the case sent to Mississippi as to Bollinger or Madison?

A. I decline making an argument for you, sir.

Q. I understood you to say that the distance from Greenville to Charleston was about one hundred miles. How would you go to make that distance out of it?

A. I would go the usually traveled route.

Q. You spoke this morning of representations made to the court in relation to the inconvenience resulting from sending the case to Mississippi county. Were not those representations made after the order for the change was entered of record?

A. I don't recollect that they were. I think that you looked at the law at the time, and stated substantially that it was adverse to allowing lawyers to designate the place to which the case should be sent.

Q. You said the other party as well as yourself made representations concerning where the case should go. Who was the other party?

A. I think that Mr. Bedford spoke to you in relation to the matter, and he was on the other side.

Q. How far is it to the county seat of St. Francois county from Greenville?

A. I do not know that I could give you the exact distance.

Q. How far is it from Farmington to where these parties reside—Limbarger and Powers?

A. I would estimate the distance at about thirty-eight miles.

Q. How far is it from Limbarger's to Ironton?

A. It is about the same distance.

Q. How far would Mr. Bedford have to come, if the case were to be tried at either Farmington or Ironton?

A. I couldn't tell you, sir.

Mr. Knott. What was Mr. Phelan's manner before the assault on him about tampering with the grand jury?

Judge Jackson. That is not a proper question. I committed no assault upon him.

Mr. Knott. We will change the word *assault* to *charge.*

A. Immediately before, it was reserved. The relations existing between him and Judge Jackson were such as to make impossible any cordiality between them. No lawyer could treat a Judge very kindly who was subjected to such treatment as Mr. Phelan received from Judge Jackson.

Q. I mean to ask if Mr. Phelan's deportment towards the court was respectful immediately before the charge made in open court against him?

A. I think it was. I don't think he was in contempt from anything that passed before. I could not have inferred that he had been in contempt.

TESTIMONY OF JOSEPH J. MILLER.

Joseph J. Miller called and examined by Mr. Knott.

Q. Mr. Miller, what is your profession?

A. I sometimes practice law. I am a lawyer by profession; at least I have license.

Q. Were you at the November term, 1858, of the Stoddard Circuit Court?

A. Yes, sir. I was.

Q. Do you know who was counsel for David G. Hicks on the trial of an indictment then pending against him for an assault with intent to kill?

A. I was counsel for him.

Q. Who was acting as Circuit Attorney when that case came up in court?

A. I don't know as any person was acting as Circuit Attorney in connection with that case.

Q. What was done with the case?

A. I filed a motion to quash. It was on the fifth or sixth day of the term. I can't say either that I filed the motion. I went into court and observed that I wished to file the motion. The Judge asked me what was the matter with the indictment. I told him the words "on purpose" were left out. He just turned to the docket and observed to the Clerk that that indictment was quashed.

Q. You didn't file your motion, then?

A. No, sir. I suppose it was a mere verbal motion to the court to quash.

Q. Who was acting as Circuit Attorney at that term of the court?

A. David G. Hicks.

Q. Was any person appointed to represent the State in the matter of the indictment pending against Hicks?

A. Not to my knowledge.

Q. If any person had been appointed would you have known it?

A. Yes, sir. Nobody was appointed, I think. Allow me to state further, that, on the first day of court, there was an indictment against Lewis W. Chandler. At that time a young lawyer was appointed to defend. Whether he could have been acting as Circuit Attorney I won't say. If he was, I did not know it.

Q. Was he called into court when you made the motion to quash?

A. No, sir. No one was called.

Q. Do you know the nature of Judge Jackson's feelings towards David Hicks?

A. They are good, I believe.

JUDGE JACKSON. Yes, sir. I wish it understood that I am particularly partial to David Hicks.

Mr. KNOTT. Were you at the August term of the Stoddard Circuit Court?

A. Yes, sir.

Q. Was you in court when the case of Orson Bartlett was called?

A. I think I was.

Q. Did you hear Judge Jackson give the jury any instructions in that case?

A. Yes, sir. I heard the Judge instruct the jury orally. It was an indictment for gaming. One of the attorneys in the case asked the court to give the jury some instructions. He then told the jury that playing for whisky was not an offense. He said that it was necessary to stake property against property; and he went on at some length to show that playing for whisky and the like of that was simply an inducement to show who should beat, and that it was similar to fairs and schools, and so on. He said the jury might find a special verdict, and it was the only verdict they could find from the testimony.

Q. Who was Bartlett's counsel?

A. I think it was Mr. Kitchen, and others; perhaps Mr. Tyrell and Mr. Phelan.

Senator Parsons. Who drew the indictment against Hicks?

A. I think Mr. Hicks' name was signed as Circuit Attorney, *pro tem.*

Q. What were the alleged defects of the indictment?

A. The words "on purpose" were left out. That is all that I recollect.

CROSS-EXAMINED BY JUDGE JACKSON.

Q. You say that you prepared a motion to quash, but did not file it. What was the reason you did not file it?

A. Hicks told me to let the motion lie over. I told Mr. Hicks on Friday that I would file a motion, and he then told me to let it lie over. After I had prepared the motion, I came into court and observed that I wished to file it. You asked me if it was similar to the case of the State against others that had been quashed, and I replied that it was precisely similar.

Q. Didn't I ask you if the same defect existed in this indictment that I had quashed others for at the same term of the court?

A. Yes, sir, I think you did; and when I said yes, you remarked that it ought to be quashed. You then observed that the indictment would be quashed.

Q. If the indictment was quashed for reasons filed, would not the record show that?

A. Yes, sir; if I understand what a record is, I suppose it would. Mr. Hicks spoke himself, and said he didn't want it done.

Q. How came it to be done, then?

A. I drew a motion.

Q. How did your motion come not to be filed?

A. Well, I remarked that I wished to file a motion, and the court never said whether I should file it or not. So it wasn't filed.

Q. Was it then that I asked the question about the indictment?

A. Yes, sir. You just asked that question, and then told the Clerk that the indictment was quashed.

Q. Do you know whether the grand jury had found another bill against Hicks?

A. I don't know anything about that.

Q. Wasn't the remarks that I made in the Orson Bartlett case more to the attorneys than to the jury?

A. Well, sir, I understood from the request of the attorneys, that your address was to the jury.

Q. Didn't I tell the jury that they might find a special verdict—that, from the testimony, they could only find a special verdict—and if they found a general verdict of guilty or not guilty, I would have to set it aside?

A. Yes, sir; I think you did.

Q. Didn't I tell the Circuit Attorney that if he wished to test the question, that the jury might find a special verdict—I would then declare the law, and he could then take the case up?

Mr. Knott. When you were told by Mr. Hicks that he wanted your motion to lie over, what reason did he give?

A. He didn't say what his reason was. I only drew the inference that he wanted the grand jury to pass over before it was done.

Q. Had the grand jury been discharged when you made the motion to quash?

A. Yes, sir; it had, I think.

On motion of Senator Wilson, the Court adjourned.

SEVENTH DAY.

MONDAY, June 13, 1859.

The Court met pursuant to adjournment, and was opened by proclamation.

The managers and respondent attended.

On motion of SENATOR GOODLETT, leave of absence was granted to Senator Wright.

On motion of SENATOR CHURCHILL, it was

Resolved, That the President of the Senate is hereby authorized to employ any assistance that he may deem proper for the present reporter of the Senate.

On the adoption of this resolution the Senators present voted as follows:

AYES—Messrs. Brown, Byrne, Churchill, Fox, Goodlett, Halliburton, Harris, Hedgpeth, Horner, Hyer, Jones, McFarland, McFerran, McIlvaine, Morris, Newland, O'Neil, Parsons, Peyton, Rains, Robinson, and Watkins—22.

NOES—Messrs. Frazier, Gullett, Scott, Vernon, and Wilson—5.

Absent—Messrs. Johnson and Richardson.

Absent on leave—Messrs. Coleman, Thompson, Wood, and Wright.

The examination of witnesses for the State was then resumed.

TESTIMONY OF HAMILTON SCOTT.

HAMILTON SCOTT called and examined by Mr. Knott.

Q. State, Mr. Scott, whether you were a member of the grand jury at the Butler Circuit Court, November term, 1857.

A. Yes, sir; I was.

Q. On what day were you discharged?

A. I think it was on Tuesday evening.

Q. Was there any unfinished business when you was discharged?

A. There was business that we did not get through with.

Q. State whether this fact was communicated to the Judge, if you know.

A. I think Mr. Vandiver told the Judge that we had more business on hand, and the Judge said there was no Clerk; and the grand jury was discharged that evening.

Q. Were you a member of the grand jury at the next term?

A. I was.

Q. Do you know whether the Judge visited the grand jury that term, during their retirement?

A. I know of the Judge being called in before the grand jury.

Q. State whether he gave any instructions as to offenses you were then inquiring into.

A. I don't recollect exactly. I think Mr. Henley was brought before the grand jury for revealing the secrets of the grand jury. The Judge said, if Mr. Henley had told him, it was not an offense; that he had a right to do so.

Q. Was this in connection with anything for which the Judge had been presented?

JUDGE JACKSON objected to the question, and it was withdrawn.

CROSS-EXAMINED BY JUDGE JACKSON.

Q. Are you positive about the time that the grand jury was discharged? Was it Tuesday night or Wednesday morning?
A. I can't be right positive, but to the best of my recollection I think it was on Tuesday evening.
Q. Did you stay at the Bluff after you were discharged?
A. I don't recollect whether I did or not.
Q. When I told Mr. Vandiver that there was no Clerk, and that you could go on and finish what business you had on hand, didn't he then tell me that the grand jury wanted subpenas?
A. I don't know what passed between you and Mr. Vandiver.
Q. Did the grand jury remain in session after it was discharged?
A. I think not.
Q. Did they do anything?
A. Do you mean did they do any business?
Q. Did anybody make a motion to put me in Black river?

[Question objected to, but before a decision of the objection witness answered.]

A. I heard nothing of that kind.

Mr. Knott. When did you leave after being discharged?
A. I left on Wednesday.
Q. Do you know whether it rained that day?
A. Yes, sir. It rained hard.
Q. Of course you don't know what transpired after you left?
A. No, sir, I don't.

TESTIMONY OF J. G. RUFF.

J. G. Ruff called and examined by Mr. Knott.
Q. State, Mr. Ruff, if you were a member of the grand jury at the November term of the Circuit Court of Butler county, in 1857.
A. Yes, sir, I was.
Q. When were you discharged?
A. On Tuesday evening.
Q. Had you completed the business before the jury before you were discharged?
A. No, sir. We had some very important business on hand, and it was against my feelings.
Q. State what occurred when you were called into court and discharged.
A. As well as I recollect, we were called in on Tuesday evening, and made some reports. Then the Judge told us to consider ourselves discharged.

CROSS-EXAMINED BY JUDGE JACKSON.

Q. Didn't I state that there was no Clerk, and for that reason no subpenas could be issued for witnesses before the grand jury?
A. Yes, sir, I think you did.
Q. Didn't you need subpenas?
A. Yes, sir, we did.

Mr. Knott. What was the matter with that Clerk?
A. The report was that the Clerk was drunk.
Q. Do you know Donaldson Walker?
A. No, sir. I don't know him.

TESTIMONY OF HENRY H. BEDFORD.

HENRY H. BEDFORD called and sworn, and examined by Mr. Knott.

Q. Where do you reside, Mr. Bedford?

A. In Bloomfield, Stoddard county, Missouri.

Q. What is your profession?

A. I practice law.

Q. In what counties do you practice?

A. I practice in all the counties of the Fifteenth Judicial Circuit.

Q. How long have you been practicing in that circuit?

A. Ever since it was established.

Q. Were you at Wayne Circuit Court when a change of venue was awarded in the case of Limbarger *vs.* Powers?

A. Yes, sir. I was attorney for Mr. Powers.

Q. Who were attorneys on the other side?

A. Mr. Fox and Mr. Pipkin were the attorneys for Mr. Limbarger; Mr. White and myself for Mr. Powers.

Q. State, if you please, if you were present when a change of venue was awarded in this case, and whether there was any understanding between the parties and the attorneys as to what counties the case should be sent.

A. I do not know that I can relate everything that occurred, but I can give the substance of it. Mr. Fox, attorney for the plaintiff, filed a petition for a change of venue. I believe there were two cases,—one Limbarger *vs.* Powers, and the other Powers *vs.* Limbarger, and the petitions were prepared in both cases. When Mr. Fox presented the petition in the first case, he asked me if we could agree upon a county, and I think suggested Fredericktown. I asked Mr. Powers, and I do not recollect what his response was. He or I observed that the case could go to Bollinger or Iron. Mr. Fox said that either would suit him. I think this was the understanding between Mr. Fox and myself. Upon the agreement being consummated, Mr. Fox presented the fact to the court, as well as I recollect, at the time the petition was presented, saying that the case could go to either Iron or Bollinger. I believe there was no immediate reply, but when Mr. Fox handed up the petition and affidavit, the Judge dropped the papers, and said the case should go to Mississippi county. He spoke in an unkind tone. His language as near as I can give it was: "Mr. Clerk, a change of venue is awarded in this case to Mississippi county." Mr. Pipkin then stated that if the court persisted in sending the case there, he would be thrown out of the case. The Judge replied that that was no business of his, saying that it was for the Judge to determine where a case should be sent to.

Q. How far is Mississippi county from Wayne?

A. Well, sir, I couldn't be positive about the distance. I would estimate it between seventy-five and one hundred miles from the county seat of Wayne to the county seat of Mississippi, by the usually traveled route going through Bollinger, Cape Girardeau, and Scott counties.

Q. In what circuit are these counties?

A. They are all in the Tenth Judicial Circuit.

Q. Where do Limbarger and Powers live?

A. In the north part of Wayne.

Q. Do you know whether the county of Mississippi was convenient to these parties?

A. It was more inconvenient than any of the counties mentioned.

Q. Do you know whether they wished the case sent to Mississippi?

A. I can say that my client was opposed to it.

Q. How far is it from the county seat of Wayne to the county seat of Iron county?

A. They say it is about forty miles. Ironton I think is pretty nearly north of the county seat of Wayne. The two counties are contiguous.

Q. What are the relative positions of Wayne and Bollinger?

A. They join. Wayne is bounded on the north by Iron, Madison, and a part of Bollinger.

Q. What was the demeanor of the Judge towards the counsel upon this occasion?

A. I thought it manifested an unkind spirit. He said but little, and I could not give his precise language.

Q. Do you practice in Dunklin county?

A. Yes, sir. I do.

Q. Were you at the May term of the Dunklin Circuit Court in 1858?

A. Yes, sir.

Q. Were you connected in any manner with the case of Smith *vs.* Cude?

A. That case was sent on change of venue to Pemiscot county. I represented Cude.

Q. Do you know who the attorneys on the other side were?

A. I do not know that I recollect all the attorneys on the other side. I think Mr. Kitchen, Mr. Horner, and a young gentleman from Dyer county, Tennessee, were on that side. Mr. Richardson was perhaps the principal counsel, though I believe he was not present at the Dunklin Circuit Court.

Q. Were you in court when the change was awarded in this case?

A. I may have been, but I have not any distinct recollection about it.

Q. Were you connected with the cases of the Point Pleasant and Dunklin County Road Company *vs.* Moses Farrar, and the same *vs.* Nathaniel G. Murphy?

A. I was representing the road company. I don't recollect which of the counsel took the change of venue.

Q. Was there any understanding between the counsel on both sides and the parties as to where the case should be sent?

A. It is my impression that there was. If I am not mistaken, we understood that the suit should be taken to Cape Girardeau. When this was represented to the court, the Judge then said, I think, that the counsel had no right to say where a case should be sent; that it was the business of the court to say; and he sent the case to Pemiscot county.

Q. Why did you prefer Cape Girardeau county to Pemiscot?

A. Our preference could only be understood by a knowledge of the peculiar geography of that country. Although Pemiscot and Dunklin are adjoining counties, there is a large swamp, commonly called "Nigger Wool," which separates them, and generally at the spring of the year it is impassable; at least the only travel is by means of dug-outs, canoes, and the like. To go from Dunklin to Pemiscot we have to travel out by the Levee, and I think it is over a hundred miles from the county seat of Dunklin to the Levee, and thence to the county seat of Pemiscot the distance is about the same, so that altogether it is 200 miles.

Q. How many counties do you pass through in going from one place to the other?

A. You would have to go through Cape Girardeau, Scott, and New Madrid counties. As I said before, Pemiscot and Dunklin are adjoining counties, but this swamp operates a barrier, so that they are completely cut off from direct communication throughout the greater part of each year.

Q. Was any representation of these facts made to the court?

A. At the time the petition was filed, I do not know that anything was said to the court about the inconvenience to which the parties would be subjected should they have to go to Pemiscot, though I think when the petition was prepared the counsel agreed upon Cape Girardeau, and after the award was made they remonstrated with the court, endeavoring to induce a different award.

Q. Which party took a change of venue?

A. It was the defendants in both cases, I believe.

Q. Where does Mr. Murphy live?

A. In Dunklin county. He was the Representative from that county in the Legislature last winter.

Q. Where does Moses Farrar live?

A. He lives close to the county seat of Dunklin county.

Q. Did any of the counsel engaged in the causes at Dunklin court follow them to Pemiscot county?

A. They never have to my knowledge. I have not, and I have not heard that any of the others did.

Senator Parsons. What were the causes assigned in the petitions for change of venue?

A. My recollection is that the change was asked on the ground of prejudice against the persons presenting the petitions.

Mr. Knott. Were you at Butler Circuit Court in May, 1858?

A. Yes, sir, I think I was.

Q. Were you present at the trial of Gibson *vs.* Dunn?

A. I cannot be positive that I was present during the whole of that trial.

Q. Did you see William G. Phelan there?

A. I did.

Q. Please state what occurred, during the pendency of the suit, between the court and Mr. Phelan.

A. My recollection is that the case was called in the morning and progressed as such trials usually do till noon. The argument of the case was deferred till afternoon session.

Q. Were you present in the afternoon?

A. Yes, sir, I was.

Q. Please state what transpired between the court and Mr. Phelan at that time.

A. I don't recollect the precise point at which the trial had arrived, but I think the case was ready for argument. Mr. Phelan arose at the time I expected him to address the jury, and made some motion addressed either to the court or the jury, I am not prepared to say which. The court stopped him, saying that he wanted him to understand that he was in contempt of court, and that he would have to answer for that in an alleged charge of tampering with the grand jury. The court ordered him to set down. Mr. Phelan said something, whatever it was I couldn't repeat it. He waited a few minutes, and the court told him he might proceed with the case then on hand. There was a great deal of unkind expressions passed between them. I do not recollect them with sufficient accuracy to repeat.

Q. How did Mr. Phelan demean himself before this?

A. So far as I saw, he demeaned himself with becoming courtesy to the court. Nothing of which I have any knowledge transpired in the forenoon, or immediately after noon, to disturb the usual course of proceedings.

Q. Did you observe any indication of ill feeling on the part of Mr. Phelan before the charge brought against him of tampering with the grand jury?

A. No, sir, I did not. It was not until after the charge was made that he exhibited any feeling, but then he seemed somewhat excited. I am not certain whether it was on this occasion, but I think the Judge, in his remarks to Mr. Phelan, made some threat, or intimated that Mr.

Phelan would have something to dread. Mr. Phelan asked if it was a fine. The court said it was not. He then asked if it was confinement in jail, and receiving a negative response, he said, "ah, perhaps it is to strike me from the roll."

Q. Were you at Ripley county Circuit Court, November term, A. D. 1857?

A. I don't know that I could testify as to the date. I presume that I was there.

Q. Are you acquainted with D. M. Fox?

A. Yes, sir. He is a lawyer practicing in the Tenth and Fifteenth Circuits. I have known him for the last ten or twelve years.

Q. The point I wish to direct your attention to is some conversation between Judge Jackson and Mr. Fox, involving a charge of lying.

A. If I recollect rightly, the circumstance happened at Ripley court. I wouldn't undertake to testify as to the term. Probably it was the fall term, 1857. Some firm in Cape Girardeau sent out a note to Ripley county, and sued somebody on it. Mr. Fox filed an answer. I don't recollect the filing, and do not speak from my own knowledge as to the character of the paper. The Judge examined it in court, and while doing so, turned to Mr. Fox and asked him if he wrote that, whether it was in his handwriting, or something of that kind. Mr. Fox replied, "yes, sir, I believe so, it looks like my handwriting," and inquired what was the reason for the question. The Judge replied as well as I can recollect, "nothing much, only whoever wrote it either swore a lie himself or made his client do so."

Senator Watkins. What was Mr. Fox doing at that time? Was he addressing the court?

A. I don't think Mr. Fox was doing anything in the way of business. It is my impression that he and I were sitting together, and we were all waiting for the decision of some question submitted to the court. Perhaps it was the sufficiency of the answer filed by Mr. Fox. I don't recollect anything going on at that time, except that the Judge was examining the paper.

Q. Were you at the Butler Circuit Court, November, 1857?

A. Yes, sir. I think I was.

Q. What time did court there convene?

A. Under the statute we are allowed one week for court there, commencing on the first Monday of November. I think court convened then at the usual time.

Q. When did court adjourn?

A. On the second day of the term—about the middle of the day, on Tuesday, I think.

Q. Were you present when the grand jury was discharged.

A. I think I was.

Q. State what occurred when they were called in and discharged?

A. Well, they were asked the ordinary question whether they had any returns to make. They replied that they had some, and I believe they did make some presentments. I am not clear about that, however. They were then asked if they had any further business on hand, and the foreman replied that they had unfinished business on hand. I don't think anything more was said. The Judge dismissed them then.

Q. Was there any business done on the second day of court?

A. I don't think there was any trial. Some efforts were made to dispose of cases and business not requiring a trial.

Q. What occasioned the disturbance in the usual business of the court?

A. The absence of the Clerk.

Q. What was the matter with the Clerk?

A. Those who went to see him said that he was drunk. I did not see him myself.

Q. Do you know whether any proposition was made to the court by which this difficulty could be obviated?

A. Yes, sir. There was some proposition to allow the lawyers to keep the minutes and make up the record in turn, in such cases as they were not severally interested in.

Q. Do you know of any other plan proposed by which to get on with the business?

A. There may have been, but I do not recollect it.

Q. Was the plan which you mentioned, of allowing the lawyers to make up the record in such cases as they were not engaged, in turn, an unusual thing? Had such a thing ever been done before?

A. Yes, sir, it was very customary. I think that at least one-half of the minutes and one-half of the record of that court for the last few years have been made by the lawyers. I have done a good deal of recording there myself.

Q. What did the Judge reply when this proposition was made to him?

A. I don't recollect precisely what it was. He did not acquiesce.

Q. What became of the papers pertaining to the causes then pending in court, after the failure of the Clerk to go on in the discharge of his duties?

A. I could hardly say. I think the Judge made some remarks to the effect that there had been a good deal of complaint about the papers being lost. It is a fact that they are very badly kept at best. In the course of the day, he took what papers he could find, and wrapped them in a newspaper, and put them under his arm.

Q. What became of them after that?

A. I only know from what the rest say. I did not see anything more of them.

Q. Was Judge Jackson apprised of the manner in which the papers were usually kept by the Clerk?

A. He must have been.

Q. Have you any recollection of a request made to the Judge to appoint a Deputy Clerk, or to approve an appointment made by the Clerk?

A. I believe I do recollect now that a gentleman named Donaldson Walker was proposed by some one, and I think there was a written application made for his appointment.

Q. Who made that application?

A. It purported to be written or was signed by the Clerk.

Q. What was the Judge's reply to this application?

A. The reply, as well as I recollect it, was, that unless Mr. Blount was in court himself, and would ask for the appointment of this deputy, he didn't deem that he had any right or authority to make it. He wouldn't appoint him.

Q. Were you at Ripley Circuit Court in April, 1858?

A. Yes, sir.

Q. Were you concerned in the case of James Moore *vs.* John Eldridge, administrator of the estate of Parker?

A. Yes, sir. I was engaged as attorney for Mr. Moore.

Q. You will please give the Court a statement of any unusual or irregular incidents of that trial that you may recollect.

A. I will as well as I can. There had been a non-suit taken by Moore. The case was then in the Circuit Court on an appeal from the County Court. It was an application for an allowance from the estate of Parker to Moore of charges as clerk of the firm of Parker and Moore, and the charges were predicated upon an article of agreement entered into between Moore and Parker in Parker's lifetime.

Q. Were you present at the trial of the cause?

A. Yes, sir. I was.

Q. Do you know anything in relation to a bill of exceptions prepared after this trial?

A. Yes, sir. It was prepared by Mr. Kitchen, who was on the same side of the case with me. He presented the bill of exceptions, and the Judge objected to signing it, and pointed out an alleged defect in the testimony. He said the bill didn't contain the testimony of a witness named Kittrell as it had been given before the jury on the trial. There was a difference of opinion as to what the testimony of this witness was, and to settle it, the proposition was made to have Kittrell called in. He was accordingly called. The Judge had objected to signing the bill of exceptions unless Mr. Kittrell's testimony was made to contain a statement as to the fact of an erasure existing, upon the article of agreement, of a certain date. Mr. Kitchen insisted that the witness, Kittrell, hadn't said anything about this erasure. When Kittrell was called in he said that he didn't say any such thing, and added that the mark or erasure upon the paper was just as it had always been. Then I understood the court to say that whether Mr. Kittrell had said so or not, it was a fact that the erasure did exist upon the instrument, and that he wouldn't sign a bill of exceptions until this fact was made to appear in the testimony. He then interlined the bill and signed it.

Q. Did the interlineation make Kittrell's testimony contain a statement of this fact which he said he had not testified to before the jury?

A. That was my understanding of it. He made Kittrell's testimony state the fact of the erasure upon the instrument by means of the interlining.

[Several Senators did not fairly understand the witness in his relation of the circumstances as above, and at their request he repeated this portion of his testimony once or twice, without any substantial variance.]

Q. Were you present at Bloomfield, at the Stoddard Circuit Court, November, 1858?

A. I was.

Q. Were you present in court during the pendency of the case of Gustavus Berry *vs.* John Griffie?

A. Yes, sir. I was connected with that case as counsel. I represented Mr. Berry.

Q. Who was on the other side? what attorneys?

A. Mr. Tyrell for one, Mr. Wasson, perhaps, and others. I do not remember distinctly.

Q. Do you know whether there was a bill of exceptions prepared in that case?

A. Yes, sir, there was.

Q. Who prepared it?

A. Mr. Tyrell, I think.

Q. Did you examine it?

A. I did.

Q. Did you find it correct and in accordance with the facts as they should have appeared of record?

A. I don't know that I noticed it very particularly.

Senator Watkins suggested that the record would now be the most appropriate and most acceptable evidence in connection with that charge.

Mr. Knott stated that they were going in the light of precedent, and that after the parol testimony on this point was concluded, they would complete the proof they wished to lay before the Court with the record.

SENATOR PARSONS stated his view of the law, and the examination proceeded.

Q. You will please go on and state whether you examined the bill, and whether you found it correct.

A. If the Court sees proper to hear my statement in regard to this matter, I will say that I did examine it, and I found it to contain the testimony substantially as it was introduced upon the trial.

Q. Did you examine the bill with a view to ascertaining whether the motion papers were correctly set forth?

A. I do not remember to have noticed very particularly as to that.

Q. Did you hear his motions argued?

A. Yes, sir, I did. I saw his motion.

Q. What was it?

A. It was two-fold; first, in arrest of judgment, and then for a new trial.

Q. What were the causes alleged as the basis of these motions?

A. I do not remember them all. Among others was the cause that the jury had given more damages than the plaintiff had claimed.

Q. Had there been a remitter entered?

A. Yes, sir. I entered a remitter. But I don't recollect whether it was before or after the motion. I believe Mr. Tyrell had argued his motion before the remitter was made, and I think the remitter was made sometime between the argument of the motion and the decision upon it.

Q. Were you present when the bill of exceptions was presented to the court for signature?

A. I don't think I was. It was presented to me by Mr. Tyrell, and he asked me to examine it. It was with a view to ascertaining whether the testimony was correctly set forth that I examined it. When he asked me if I was satisfied, I think perhaps I made some few corrections, and gave it back to him.

Q. Did you consent to that being a sufficient statement of the evidence had in the cause?

A. Yes, sir, I did. And I recollect now that I was present when the bill was presented. There was a good deal said by both the Judge and Mr. Tyrell, which I could not now repeat.

Q. Did you hear anything said about the motion papers?

A. I did, but I could not now state what it was. I felt very indifferent about it. I thought Mr. Tyrell was trying to get a good many immaterial points in his case, and feeling confident that I had the strong side, I paid very little attention.

Q. Did the court sign the bill as it was presented?

A. I think, after a good deal of discussion, he ultimately refused to sign it until something was stricken out.

Q. Did he then sign it?

A. It is my impression that he did.

Q. Did he sign the evidence?

A. No, sir, he did not. I believe the evidence was on a separate paper.

Q. What reason did he assign for refusing to sign the evidence?

A. Well, I think he said that the counsel had spoken so low that he didn't know what their questions were, and he didn't know what the testimony in the cause had been.

Q. Was it represented to him that you had consented to the testimony as prepared?

A. Yes, sir, it was.

Q. What is the practice in your courts, Mr. Bedford, in relation to the saving of exceptions? Do you prepare the record matter for a bill of exceptions, leaving blanks where you say, "here insert the testimony," and prepare the testimony as a separate document, or do you copy it all out together?

13

A. When Judge Jackson came on to the circuit, it was the practice, I think, to sign the bill of exceptions and the testimony separately; the first being prepared with blanks, and directions to insert the testimony, in parenthesis. I think he has changed that rule, and in some instances would not sign a bill of exceptions unless it was filled out with the testimony, and all other matter necessary to make it out.

Q. Were you present at Stoddard Circuit Court pending the trial of Orson Bartlett on an indictment for gaming?

A. Yes, sir, I was present. I don't know that I was in when the case was called, but I think I was.

Q. You will please give us an account of what occurred in court during that trial.

A. The indictment embraced Col. Bartlett and others. A jury was empanneled. David G. Hicks was acting as prosecuting attorney.

Q. You say that the indictment embraced Col. Bartlett and others. Who were the others?

A. Judge Jackson, David G. Hicks, and some one else, I do not know that I remember. The charge was for betting, or playing for whisky, or oysters. Perhaps it was for a watermelon; I don't recollect. On the trial, perhaps there were three or four attorneys for the defense—Mr. Kitchen, Mr. Tyrell, and two or three others. When it came up to be tried, James B. Odell was called as a witness, and testified that the parties charged had played and bet for some article. The court, or some one of the attorneys, asked Mr. Hicks what he was going to do in the case. He replied that he was going to argue it, and submit it to the jury. The court objected, saying that there were no facts to base an indictment upon. He said the Legislature never intended, nor had not made indictable such playing as the facts of this case showed it to be; that where parties played, and whoever lost the game merely had to pay some penalty, it was not betting, or such betting as the statute made punishable; and he went on with a somewhat elaborate opinion to show what a contrary notion would lead to. He went on to state that where the loser in such games paid for the property, it became his, and that if he saw fit to allow others to participate in its enjoyment, it certainly was not betting on their part, or the part of the loser. He referred to two or three instances in which, if a contrary doctrine prevailed, the State of Missouri might be considered as gaming, and in this connection spoke of the division of the State into agricultural districts, and the premiums which it was customary to offer for the best stock, and the best machinery, and the like. He further illustrated his position by an allusion to the premiums offered in schools and academies to the pupils who would beat the others learning. I could not repeat his language, and do not pretend to do so.

Q. Well, what did he say in relation to the action of the jury in the case on hand?

A. He told the jury they should find a special verdict; that there was no testimony to prove a betting, and that they could find a special verdict, or find the facts, and he would apply the law. After the enunciation of this opinion, Mr. Hicks entered a *nolle prosequi*.

Q. The case was not argued to the jury at all then?

A. No, sir. It was not.

Q. Were any instructions asked by the attorneys on either side?

A. I do not recollect that there was.

Q. Was any proposition made to send the case to the Supreme Court?

A. Not that I know of.

Senator Parsons. Did I understand you to say that the Judge and the Circuit Attorney were presented in the same indictment with this man?

A. That was my understanding.

Q. Were you at the Stoddard Circuit Court, November, 1857, at the trial of Sarah Buckner?

A. I wasn't there the whole time, though I was present a good part of the time.

Q. Were you present when William C. Grimsley was on the stand as a witness?

A. I was there during a portion of that time, not all. I know nothing of my own knowledge about his testimony, except that he was on the stand as a witness.

Q. Were you present when Mr. Davis was arguing his case before the jury?

A. I was.

Q. Will you please give a detailed account of what you saw transpire during the delivery of Mr. Davis' argument?

A. I don't know that I can give an intelligent one, but from the argument I understood that the testimony of the witness Grimsley had been withdrawn from the consideration of the jury. Mr. Davis was counsel for the accused. Whenever in the course of his argument he alluded to the evidence of Grimsley, he was interrupted by Judge Jackson. On one occasion the Judge told him not to make his argument on outside matter, but to confine himself to the facts in evidence. Mr. Davis replied that he was proceeding to do so, and the Judge rejoined that the testimony of Grimsley was withdrawn. Mr. Davis proceeded, saying it was true this testimony was withdrawn, but the defendants had excepted to it. He went on to state a hypothetical case, and spoke of the girl, a daughter of the accused, who was connected with the murder. There had perhaps been some intimation that the deceased attempted to violate the person of this girl; and Mr. Davis, in stating his hypothetical case, was calling upon the jury to think of what would be the consequence, and what the feelings of the mother, if this tale of woe was poured into her ears. I think in the form of a supposition he pictured the girl as "pouring this tale of woe into her mother's ears." At this point he was stopped by the court in an abrupt manner. I can't pretend to say what it was the Judge said to him. It was something expressing dissatisfaction as to the manner in which the argument was proceeding.

Q. Did you hear all of Mr. Davis' argument?

A. Yes, sir, I believe I did.

Q. Do you say he was stopped more than once?

A. Yes, sir, several times; as often as three times, at least.

Q. Was he in the proper line of his duty when stopped?

A. I do not know that I could decide. I saw nothing in Mr. Davis' demeanor that I would have designated as improper. He seemed disposed to manage the case as well as he could for his client.

Q. In this hypothetical case that you speak of, was there anything disrespectful to the Judge?

A. Nothing, that I saw.

Q. What happened after the last interruption that you mentioned?

A. Mr. Davis said that if he couldn't argue the case without being told what he was to say, or if he couldn't be permitted to argue it as he thought best, he would give it up. The reply was that if parties didn't see fit to get attorneys who were competent to attend to their business, they would not lose much when the attorneys that they did employ gave up their cases.

Q. I understood you to say that Mr. Davis spoke of Grimsley's testimony as having been withdrawn, and not as evidence before the jury?

A. Yes, sir. He spoke of it, and in his allusions to it he only brought it in, by way of supposing that the facts were so and so. I thought he was building his hypothesis on Grimsley's testimony as a basis. Before he had fairly submitted his supposed case, the court interrupted him, and said that he had been told often enough that that was not testimony, and that it had been withdrawn.

Q. Were you present during the argument of Mr. Phelan in this same case?

A. I was not.

SENATOR VERNON. Were you in court when the motion for a new trial, or the motion in arrest in the Buckner case, was under consideration?

A. I don't think I was present. According to the best of my recollection, leave was given to file a motion, and it was not decided until some time afterwards.

CROSS-EXAMINED BY JUDGE JACKSON.

Q. Did you say you were present throughout the trial?

A. I was not present a great deal—not all day. I don't know how much of the trial I witnessed.

Q. Was there more than one witness besides Grimsley?

A. I never saw more.

Q. Did you hear the testimony of Grimsley?

A. I did not. I may have heard detached portions of it, as I was passing in and out, but I could not say that I heard his testimony.

Q. Do you know whether they excepted to the withdrawal of Grimsley's testimony?

A. I don't know, indeed. I inferred so from what I heard of Mr. Davis' speech.

Q. Wasn't it only that part where he undertook to tell what Mrs. Buckner said her daughter had said? Wasn't that the part that was objected to on the ground that it was hearsay?

A. I don't know.

Q. With regard to my stopping Davis, wasn't it when he undertook to comment on the part of Grimsley's testimony what the girl told her mother?

A. Not having heard Mr. Grimsley's testimony, I cannot say. First, he went on to state that if the facts were as this girl had represented them, and the man Buckner had violated her person, and the girl then "poured this tale of woe," and then you stopped him.

Q. Well, now, wasn't it his object in going on with this supposition to get Grimsley's testimony before the jury?

A. I wouldn't undertake to say precisely what his object was.

Q. Well, what had they excepted to? what did Davis say, in talking to the jury, that they had excepted to in regard to Grimsley's testimony?

A. What was done during the trial, prior to what I have related, I do not know. I understood or inferred that they had objected to the withdrawal of the witness.

Q. You state that my interruption of Mr. Davis was abrupt?

A. Yes, sir; on the third occasion I thought it quite abrupt.

Q. What do you mean by abrupt? What would be called an abrupt interruption?

A. When I said that you had interrupted him abruptly, I meant that you did it with more vehemence, energy, and force than you ordinarily speak. I do not know that I could describe it otherwise. It seemed that you thought he was doing wrong, and felt incensed at him. I think you observed to Mr. Davis that the testimony had been withdrawn, and that he had been so informed often enough.

Q. Did I say that the testimony had been withdrawn, or that what he was going over was not testimony?

A. The language used conveyed to my mind the idea that he was commenting on what was not testimony.

Q. Well, we will go back to Wayne. In this case of Limbarger *vs.* Powers, which party did you represent?

A. I was for Mr. Powers. He had employed me.

Q. Did he tell you that he wished the case sent to Madison or Iron county?

A. I think he did tell me he would prefer going to Ironton rather than to Madison county.

Q. Did he prefer Iron to any other county?

A. I do not know.

Q. When Mr. Fox presented the petition for the change of venue, did he tell me that there was any agreement as to where the case should go, or did you or any other attorney make any such statement?

A. I think Mr. Fox simply stated the fact of such an agreement having been made.

Q. Did any other attorney know it was an agreement?

A. I cannot say that any one did. My impression is that Mr. Fox and I were standing together, and he told you that the counsel for both parties had agreed that the case should be sent to Iron or Bollinger.

Q. How far do you live from the county seat of Mississippi county?

A. Straight through from Bloomfield to Charleston is about forty-five miles. During the winter and spring we cannot go that way, and it is farther then.

Q. How far would you have to go from where you live going to Iron or Madison?

A. It would be nearer to Mississippi if the waters were not up. I do not know that I could give you the exact distance to either Ironton or Fredericktown.

Q. Do you attend the courts in Iron county?

A. I never did attend there.

Q. If the case had been sent to Iron county wouldn't it have cut you out of the case?

A. I suppose, sir, it would.

Q. Isn't it difficult in Madison Circuit Court to get a case tried? Isn't there an accumulation of business in both Madison and Bollinger counties, so that it would have been wrong to have sent the case there?

A. I think there is always a good deal of margin not disposed of in both those counties. That is a general thing in the Tenth Circuit. They have one or two days more than is necessary for the trial of the causes.

Q. Was it not more convenient to you to have the case in Mississippi than it would have been if it had been sent to either of these counties?

A. As an individual it would have been more convenient, because if I wanted to have a case attended to there, and could not attend to it myself, I have some relatives living in that county, and could send to some individuals who would be more attentive to my business for me than I could expect others to be.

Q. Do you attend the courts of Madison?

A. I have not recently attended the Circuit Courts in that county.

Q. If the case had been sent there would you have attended?

A. No, sir, I should not have attended. As far as that is concerned, I don't attend the courts in either county named.

Q. In speaking of this array of counties, do you pretend to say that there is not a nearer way to go straight through from Greenville to Charleston?

A. Yes, sir; at some seasons it is possible to go through by way of Dallas, but to say that there is any travel on that route I could not. There is no road which is passable any great portion of the year.

Q. What kind of a route is it to go from Greenville to Bloomfield?

A. Very good.

Q. Did you ever hear of persons going through by way of "Nigger Wool?"

A. Very rarely. I never went that way myself, and I have seldom heard of others doing so. It is possible that there may be some travel on that road when the swamps and ponds are frozen over.

Q. Well, now, in regard to this Dunklin county case of Smith *vs.* Cude. Where does Cude live?

A. Mr. Cude lives in ——

Q. Where does the other party live?

A. Mr. Smith is a Tennesseean. I understood that he lived in Dyer county, Tennessee.

Q. Would not Pemiscot county be the most convenient for him?

A. I suppose it would be the most convenient for that party under any kind of circumstances.

Q. Didn't Smith take the change of venue?

A. I cannot say. I don't know which one of them it was.

Q. Wasn't there a proposition to take the case to Jackson, or to the county seat of Scott?

A. I don't recollect.

Q. Well, about the other two cases—the Dunklin plank road cases. Which party did you represent?

A. I was employed by Mr. Clark.

Q. Who are the officers of that company?

A. I think Messrs. Richardson and Clark are the principal men.

Q. Where do they live?

A. Mr. Richardson lives in Memphis; Mr. Clark, I think, in New Madrid.

Q. Who is President of the road?

A. Mr. Clark, I think.

Q. Which will be the most convenient county for him?

A. Pemiscot, I suppose.

Q. Who compose the company?

A. It is composed of citizens of Pemiscot, New Madrid, and Dunklin counties.

Q. Which party took the change of venue?

A. The defendants, in both cases.

Q. Hasn't that company built a road by which you can go through on a direct route from Greenville to Pemiscot county?

A. I do not know how it is now. Before that court I think there was no road there for ordinary traveling.

Q. Well, don't the citizens of that county go through direct across the swamp the year round?

A. I think not. I know there is a great deal of travel from Pemiscot to Dunklin, and from Dunklin to Pemiscot, going around through our place; while it is possible perhaps to go through that way, I don't know any person who does so.

Q. Haven't they got within three miles of —— with that plank road?

A. I don't think any road is finished yet. How much of it is finished I can't say. When this change of venue was taken at the spring term a year ago, it is my impression that no part of the work was done.

Q. At what time does the court come on in Madison county?

A. On the first Monday of March.

Q. And when is the court in Wayne?

A. I believe it is the last Monday in March.

Q. Then they come on pretty near together, and when the court in Wayne was held, the court in Madison was over.

A. Yes, sir, the court was over there.

Q. How long would it be from the Wayne Circuit Court to the court in Mississippi county?

A. I don't know.

Q. Wasn't there time to take the papers, and have the case ready for trial at the next term?

A. I can't say.

Q. In the other two cases didn't the plank road company want the cases sent to Pemiscot?

A. No, sir. We wanted them to go to New Madrid or Scott.

Q. What kind of suits were those?

A. Suits were brought before a Justice of the Peace to recover subscriptions of stock, I believe. The defendants took the change of venue.

Q. You say you were at the Butler court when this Gibson *vs.* Dunn matter transpired. When I told Mr. Phelan he was in contempt, wasn't it that I had just notified him that he was in contempt of court, and would have to answer?

A. I inferred from what was said that something had transpired which you considered contempt of court, and you did notify him that he was in contempt.

Q. Well, don't you think I had just cause?

A. I only know from others what your cause was, and it is perhaps needless to express an opinion about it.

Q. When he got up and said he wanted to vindicate himself from the charge of contempt of court, didn't I tell him to go on with the case? and when he insisted after that on going into an exculpation of himself, wasn't it then I told him to hush up and go on? Wasn't it when he still insisted upon vindicating himself after I told him that I didn't want to hear a vindication of himself then,—wasn't it then that I told him to go on with the the case?

A. It is true that you notified him he was in contempt of court, and that he wanted to vindicate himself immediately. I didn't understand the circumstances to transpire exactly in the order in which you relate them. When you said that he had been tampering with the grand jury, he replied by asking why you said so, and a good deal of talk passed between you which I don't pretend to relate with exactness.

Q. Was Mr. Phelan very mild in the remarks he addressed to the court?

A. He was not, but just the reverse. The harsh manner in which you spoke to him was met by a corresponding harshness on his part.

Q. Well, what further did you see there?

A. I didn't see anything further of an unusual character after the trial of the cause then pending was resumed.

Q. Did you see anything improper in my treatment of Mr. Phelan in notifying him that he was in contempt, and that at the proper time I would hold him to answer?

A. If I was to give an opinion, I would say that you were wrong all around.

Q. In what way?

A. In the harsh expressions used on both sides.

Q. What were those harsh expressions that you think wrong?

A. I have said that it was out of my power to rehearse the conversation.

Q. Don't you think you could imitate my harshness?

A. I am not here for that purpose.

Q. Couldn't you give a single instance of a harsh expression?

A. I can only describe your manner and expressions generally. Your whole manner and tone was excited and vehement.

Q. Which was the worst, the tone or the language? You say you can't give the manner; couldn't you give us an instance of the tone in which I addressed Mr. Phelan?

A. I don't know that I could. As to your tone and language, I think they were about on a par.

Q. Wasn't it simply a warm discussion on matters about which we happened to differ?

A. That may or may not be. I should say you showed too much hard feeling to make that a good description.

Q. Well, how were these hard feelings shown?

A. In various ways; on his part in his attempts to rebut the charge against him, and on your part in bidding him hush up, take his seat, and so on.

Q. Did I fine him, or send him to jail?

A. Not to my knowledge.

Q. Let me now inquire about this Ripley county case, in which it is alleged that I told Mr. Fox he lied. What did you say was the origin of that matter?

A. I said that to the best of my recollection there had been some difficulty about a pleading drawn up by Mr. Fox. I think it was some difficulty about an answer filed by him.

Q. Wasn't it an answer filed in the same case on a former term, which had been demurred to and the demurrer sustained?

A. I don't know.

Q. Didn't you hear him say that he had filed an amended answer?

A. If I did, I don't recollect it.

Q. When I took the paper and compared it with the other, and asked him if this was his handwriting, wasn't my expression that one or the other was false?

A. My recollection is that you asked him if this was his handwriting; and when he answered affirmatively, you said that the draftsman had either sworn a lie, or had made his client swear to a lie.

Q. Do you think that was the way of it?

A. I do. That is your language as nearly as I can repeat it.

Q. You say, then, that I said that the draftsman had lied. Is that the way you mentioned it before?

A. Yes, sir, it is substantially as I stated it before.

Q. Do you think I used the word draftsman at all?

A. I cannot be positive that you did.

Q. How do you happen to be more positive that I used the term lie than that I used the term draftsman?

A. I do not know that I have been very positive as to any part of your phraseology.

Q. Don't you think that your memory would change the term falsehood or false into lie?

A. Whatever my memory may do, I have stated your language as well as I recollected it.

Q. You say you were at the Butler court at the May term, A. D. 1857. When did you say the grand jury were discharged?

A. It was on the first or second day. I am inclined now to think it was on the first day.

Q. Wasn't it on the second day the Clerk was reported sick?

A. I am not certain.

Q. Didn't we empannel a jury on the second day?

A. I think not.

Q. Was the record made up the first day?

A. I think not. I don't know whether any record was made up at all.

Q. Was there any other reason assigned for a failure to do business than the absence of the Clerk?

A. None that I recollect.

Q. Were you present when the grand jury was discharged?

A. I think I was. I am not positive, but I think it was just before dinner on the second day.

Q. Did you leave court before they were discharged?

A. No, sir, not till afterwards.

Q. Was it not nearly night?

A. My recollection is that it was just before dinner.

Q. Is your memory pretty good?

A. Ordinarily so.

Q. Were there any returns made by the grand jury?

A. I don't know.

Q. Did you say before that they did make returns?

A. I think not. I think I said that I didn't know, and I say still that I don't know.

Q. Where were the papers belonging to the cases on the first day?

A. Well, I can't say that they were in any particular place. Some were in the hands of the lawyers, some in possession of the Clerk, and they were scattered here and there, according as they were wanted by interested parties.

Q. Were any answers filed the second day?

A. I can't say whether any were filed the second day or not. It is likely that application was made to file some answers, but whether you received them or not, I don't recollect.

Q. Don't you remember that after I announced that I would keep the minutes of the business myself—don't you recollect that the first thing after this was, that you came in, asking for an order for a supply of records, and to get some lost papers, and then I said if lawyers, seeing the condition of affairs, would pursue such a course as this, it would be impossible to do any business?

A. My impression is that I did, on the second day, endeavor to get hold of some papers. As to the rest, I don't recollect.

Q. And you say the grand jury was discharged about noon on the second day?

A. I think so.

Q. On what day did you start home?

A. On the same day.

Q. Do you know what was done with the papers finally?

A. I have no positive knowledge.

Q. Where were they usually kept?

A. In a room adjoining the court room, separated by a partition.

Q. Whose duty was it take charge of the papers in the absence of a Clerk?

A. I thought it my duty to look after such as pertained to cases in which I was employed.

Q. You say you had acted as Clerk at this court. Were you ever a deputy there?

A. No, sir; but I have done a good deal of recording which I was compelled to do, on account of having a very inefficient Clerk.

Q. Wasn't there a suit there of Davis and Horner, a case there on change of venue, in which there was a paper not found, after diligent search, until the second day, and it turned up mysteriously in your possession?

A. I recollect that there was inquiry made for a paper, and somebody brought it into court. Don't know whether it turned up mysteriously or not.

Q. Mr. Bedford, about this adjournment. Are you satisfied it was on the second day?

A. That is my impression.

Q. And you started home the same day, did you?

A. Yes, sir.

Q. Did you go all the way home that day?

A. I cannot say. I may have stopped at night, at my usual stopping place, on my way home. My recollection is pretty clear that the adjournment was about noon.

Q. If it should turn out that the grand jury were not discharged till night, and that the court did not adjourn till the next morning, what would you say to that?

A. Simply that I was mistaken. It is possible that I may be mistaken about it.

Q. Well, if it should turn out that you were mistaken in this matter, would it not be safe to conclude that you have been mistaken in a good many other things?

A. It would be safe to conclude that in a good many other things of this nature my recollection is imperfect.

Q. And you are certain that just after the grand jury was discharged you started home. On what day was it that the Clerk was reported sick? What does your recollection tell you about that?

A. My recollection is that it was on the first day, when court first opened.

Q. You think he didn't attend one day?

A. I think so.

Q. Well, what do you recollect about a request to the court to appoint a deputy?

A. I recollect seeing a paper requesting the court to appoint Donaldson Walker as Deputy Clerk.

Q. Was it a request that the court should appoint Donaldson Walker, or requesting the court to approve the appointment of Donaldson Walker made by the Clerk?

A. I am not sure which it was.

Q. Wouldn't there be a great deal of difference?

A. Under such circumstances I should think not.

Q. Are you acquainted with Mr. Blount's handwriting?

A. I am.

Q. Can't you say whether he requested me to appoint a deputy, or appointed one himself, and requested me to approve?

A. I can say that I think the legal effect would be about the same under the circumstances.

Q. We will now go to the Ripley Circuit Court, May term, 1858, and inquire about this Parker and Moore case. I understood you to say that I stated that the instrument which evidenced the debt seemed to have a defect upon it, an erasure of date, marked with different ink. Now I wan't to know if that wasn't a material question in the case?

A. I believe that the fact that such an erasure existed was not an altogether immaterial one upon the trial.

Q. Wasn't it necessary to make it appear in the bill of exceptions, and wasn't it that a copy would not show that such a thing had been considered by the jury?

A. I don't recollect the connection that the paper had with the matter in controversy with sufficient distinctness to say.

Q. Was the date of the instrument important?

A. My recollection is that the date was not in issue. The instrument was used as an evidence of a contract, and I think the only question about it was whether it had been executed by the parties.

SENATOR JONES. Was there any allegation as to the alteration of the date of the instrument?

[Judge Jackson answered this question himself, and went on to give a statement of the matter, which is here omitted.]

SENATOR PARSONS. I will inquire of the witness if the erasure was a matter of controversy upon the trial?

A. It was a matter of controversy, though I don't know how it affected the suit. There were no pleadings, as the case was in court upon an appeal.

JUDGE JACKSON. Are you sure it wasn't two suits?

A. This was the case, I think, that originated in the County Court. This was the second of the two, if there were two.

Q. Wasn't both suits in the County Court?

SENATOR WATKINS requested the witness to repeat what he had stated in regard to this matter, and he did so, relating the facts, substantially, as he had before done in the examination in chief.

On motion of SENATOR PARSONS, the Court adjourned.

EVENING SESSION.

MONDAY, June 13, 1858.

The Court met pursuant to adjournment.

The managers and respondent attended.

The cross-examination of Mr. BEDFORD was resumed.

Q. Mr. Bedford, about this Moore case, state if you haven't given testimony concerning it before.

A. Yes, sir. I wrote out a statement to be used before the Judiciary Committee of the House, last winter.

Q. I will ask you if you didn't swear "that Kittrell had stated that there was an erasure in a certain instrument of writing to which he had referred," meaning the instrument which we have spoken of, and referring to my version of Kittrell's testimony?

A. I don't know whether I did or not.

Q. Did you not call it an erasure?

A. I don't recollect whether I did or not.

Q. What do you call it now?

A. I say now that there was a defect in the instrument, which made it look as if it had been dated and then redated. It had that appearance at least.

Q. Do you call it an erasure?

A. I suppose it would be called an erasure, or a blot.

Q. What do you say I said in regard to this erasure?

A. I say that you said the fact did exist, and that you refused to sign the bill of exceptions unless the testimony of Kittrell was made to show it.

Q. Didn't you say that I said that, whether Kittrell said so or not, it was a fact?

A. I may have used that phraseology, or I may not. I don't recollect. It is something very like that.

Q. When was it that you wrote a statement for the Judiciary Committee?

A. Sometime in February last, I believe.

Q. If you can't recollect what you said yourself then, and committed to writing, how do you come to recollect what I said more than a year ago—nearly two years ago?

A. When the thing to be recollected consists of phraseology, I do not know there would be any difficulty in distinguishing that from remembering an idea.

Q. Haven't you pretended to give my exact phraseology in this instance, when you say that you are unable to recollect your own?

A. I pretend to give my idea then and now, in the same language, or in language not materially different.

Q. Didn't you say that "the Judge then asked Kittrell to there state if such was not the fact, whereupon Kittrell stated that the heading or date of said instrument did look as if it were altered or blotched, but did not know but that it was done at the time of writing said instrument?" and didn't you state that I then said, "if the witness did not say so, yet it was the fact?"

A. As I said before, I don't recollect my phraseology. I suppose I made similar statements, and I reckon I could now adopt them to express the same idea with safety.

Q. In the case of Berry *vs.* Griffie, in stating that I refused to sign the bill of exceptions, did you say that the testimony was incorporated in the bill?

A. I think you required them to be together.

Q. Did you say that I refused to sign the testimony?

A. Yes, sir. You refused to sign it, and alleging as a reason that it was impossible for you to tell what the testimony was, owing to the fact that during the trial the counsel spoke so low, and there was so much noise, that you could not hear.

Q. Had you agreed that this should be the testimony in the case?

A. Yes, sir. I made some few corrections in the testimony written out by Mr. Tyrell, to which he assented.

Q. Did I refuse to sign the bill because there was so much noise, or was it because I had no perfect understanding of what the testimony had been?

A. I cannot say why you refused; I only know that you said the reason was that the attorneys spoke so low, and the testimony was so indistinct, that you couldn't tell what it was.

Q. Well, don't you recollect that you were setting where I couldn't see you, and that it was hard for me to hear what you said?

A. Yes, sir. There was a large cornice on the platform where you were, and I was sitting under it; and I recollect that you asked me to move my seat, saying that you couldn't hear what I said.

Q. Now let us go to this Bartlett case. What did I say about that case? Didn't I state that playing cards for money or liquor, or any thing else, was not gaming within the meaning of the statute, unless there was betting? Did you ever hear me say that betting was not an indictable offense?

A. I have often heard you speak of it, and give your views upon that question. I don't think I ever heard you say that betting was not indictable; but I suppose you can express your opinion upon the subject with more definiteness than I can.

Q. In all that I said upon that occasion, wasn't it more of a conversation with the lawyers than to the jury?

A. I understood it to be addressed principally to the attorneys.

[Judge Jackson here went into a somewhat elaborate statement of his views concerning the law of gaming, at the conclusion of which he asked the witness if that was not the substance of his remarks upon the occasion referred to, which question the witness answered affirmatively, and the cross-examination here closed.]

Mr. KNOTT. In this conversation which you say was addressed principally to the lawyers, did the Judge talk loud enough to be heard by the jury?

A. Yes, sir. Though I understood him to be addressing the lawyers principally, the latter part of his remarks were addressed to the jury; the part I mean in which he told them that if they were a mind to do so, they could find a special verdict, and he would apply the law.

JUDGE JACKSON. Was there any other person than Orson Bartlett on trial at this time?

A. No, sir. No other person, I believe.

SENATOR FOX. In the case that you have spoken of, where there was something said about the testimony being withdrawn, did the Circuit Attorney speak of it as withdrawn?

A. I say that I understood from what occurred between Mr. Davis and the court, during the argument of Mr. Davis, that the testimony was withdrawn from the jury.

Q. Who took the exceptions that you spoke of?

A. I understood Mr. Davis as not referring to it as evidence; and he stated that although it was withdrawn there were exceptions taken. Of course, I could only understand that exceptions were taken by defendant's counsel.

SENATOR CHURCHILL. When Mr. Davis was proceeding with his argument, was he commenting in the form of a supposition upon what he admitted was not testimony?

A. Well, sir, he stated his proposition about thus: "Now if this man has violated the person of the girl, and she has gone and poured this tale of woe,"—just there he was stopped.

Q. Did he make the application of this supposed case to the case in hand before saying that the testimony was withdrawn, or that it was not testimony?

A. I think he just stated that the testimony had been withdrawn, and that the defendant had excepted.

JUDGE JACKSON. Were you present when Mr. Davis stopped his speech?

A. Yes, sir, I was.

Q. How far were you from him?

A. I was about the distance from Mr. —— to the wall there. When he stopped he walked off.

Q. Do you remember the expression he used at that time—what he said he would or would not do?

A. He made some unkind expression. Perhaps he used some oath. I cannot undertake to repeat it.

Q. In this Griffie case, what was it in the motion for a new trial that was stricken out?

A. I don't know.

Q. Wasn't it that the court had instructed the jury by telling them that if the defendant had no title to the land he had nothing to convey?

A. I don't know.

Q. Were there any instructions given to the jury?

Mr. KNOTT. It is not pretended there was an instruction. A remark in the presence and hearing of the jury, calculated to influence their verdict, was the thing complained of.

JUDGE JACKSON. Isn't it usual to merely state, as a reason for a motion of this kind, because the court misinstructed the jury, and in this case was not the misinstruction entered the same as if it had been given?

A. I don't recollect.

Q. Wasn't it that way, that the motion contained a statement that the court had misinstructed the jury, and the misinstruction set out in the motion, thereby conveying the idea that such an instruction had really been given?

A. I don't think that I paid enough attention to make any definite reply to that question.

Q. You stated that in the motion there was more there than you thought belonged to it. What was there that shouldn't have been in the motion?

A. I believe there were reasons assigned that I didn't think had anything to do with the case. I thought he had alleged reasons that had no legitimate bearing in a motion of that kind.

Mr. Knott. When Mr. Tyrell filed his motions, I understand he assigned a variety of reasons in support of them. Do I understand you to say that he misstated any facts?

A. I didn't intend to convey that idea. I thought he had put a good many reasons in that had no connection with the case, and could have no bearing upon its decision.

Q. Did the facts, set out in the motion papers, actually exist, whether they had any connection with the case or not?

A. I have no reason to think that they did not. There was no misstatement. He had simply inserted reasons not necessarily connected with his case, in my opinion.

Q. Do you recollect what the Judge said about these reasons?

A. No, sir. I cannot now recall it.

Q. Do you know whether the bill of exceptions contained the reasons of the motion papers, copied fully in the bill?

A. I think that in place of leaving the space, and directing the insertion of the motions, they were copied in with the causes set out fully.

Q. Were not the motion papers, as copied in the bill, identical with the motion papers filed in the cause?

A. I have not any distinct recollection of any difference.

Senator Churchill. Did you, or not, understand the Judge to say that the whole of Grimsley's testimony was excluded?

A. I heard him say that the testimony was excluded. I do not know that I stated that he had stated the whole of the testimony was withdrawn. Not having heard the testimony of Grimsley, I could not tell, from what I heard the Judge say, whether there was any limitation to a portion of this testimony. I can't recollect whether he stated that the whole of it was withdrawn or not.

Senator Parsons. Was the Judge in the habit of striking out formal reasons, assigned in motions for new trials, before signing bills of exceptions?

A. I don't think he was. My recollection is that he is in the habit of taking the motions just as they are filed. I don't think I ever knew the Judge to strike out any reason assigned for any motion.

Judge Jackson. Did you ever see that tried before? Did you ever see motions filed, with reasons assigned that were immaterial, and had no existence as facts?

A. I don't recollect ever having seen a motion presented by any one in the same way exactly as Mr. Tyrell's.

Hamilton Scott recalled and examined by Judge Jackson.

Q. You say, Mr. Scott, that you were at Butler court, in 1857? Was the Clerk there on the first day?

A. Yes, sir. And on Tuesday he was not at his post, but was reported sick.

Q. When did you say that the grand jury was discharged?

A. On Tuesday evening, late.

Mr. Bedford recalled and examined by Judge Jackson.

Q. Who was counsel besides Mr. Tyrell, in this Berry *vs.* Griffie case?

A. I think Mr. Wasson had managed the case principally until after the verdict of the jury. My recollection is that he was the active attorney during the progress of the trial.

Q. Was Mr. Tyrell an attorney in the case at all?

A. Yes, sir. I think he was an attorney in the case. He acted in that capacity.

Mr. J. G. Ruff recalled and examined by Judge Jackson.

Q. You say you were on the grand jury, May term, 1857?

A. No, sir. I was not at the May term. I was there at the November term, 1857, and also at the May term, 1858.

Q. Well, at the November term, 1857, was the Clerk there the first day?

A. He was there every time I passed in and out.

Q. Did the grand jurors, or a portion of them, after they were discharged at the November term, A. D. 1857, in Butler county, remain some two or three days; and did they then say that they would put me (the Judge) in Black river; and did you say that you would, for one?

The managers objected to this question, alleging that its design was evidently to contradict the statement of Mr. Phelan upon an irrelevant point in his testimony, and which the respondent himself had drawn out upon the cross-examination.

Judge Jackson persisted in asking an answer to the question. He contended that Mr. Phelan had made a statement against him for effect which he had a right to disprove by this witness if he saw proper.

The question for the action of the Court then being, shall the respondent be permitted to ask the question? the vote stood as follows:

Ayes—Messrs. Churchill, Fox, Gullett, Harris, Hedgpeth, Horner, McIlvaine, Morris, Newland, Peyton, Robinson, Scott, and Wilson—13.

Noes—Messrs. Brown, Byrne, Frazier, Goodlett, Halliburton, Hyer, McFarland, McFerran, O'Neil, Parsons, Rains, Richardson, and Vernon—13.

Absent—Mr. Johnson.

Absent on leave—Messrs. Coleman, Thompson, Wood, and Wright.

Excused from voting—Messrs. Jones and Watkins.

There being an equal number of the Senators present voting affirmatively and negatively on the question, the President of the Senate was called to the chair to give the casting vote, (the chair having been filled during the ballot by Senator Richardson, President *pro tem.*) Upon taking his seat, the President asked the Senators to show him what authority he had for voting in such a case. This gave rise to a spirited discussion, which lasted till the hour of adjournment, and at the conclusion of which the President announced that he had no authority to vote in such a case; and hence that the proposition was lost for want of a plurality.

Thereupon, on motion of Senator Wilson, the Court adjourned.

EIGHTH DAY.

TUESDAY, June 14, 1859.

The Court met pursuant to adjournment, and was opened by proclamation.

The managers and respondent attended.

The examination of witnesses for the State was resumed.

TESTIMONY OF BENJAMIN THORNBERG.

BENJAMIN THORNBERG called and examined by Mr. Knott.

Q. Where do you live?

A. In Bollinger county.

Q. Please state if you were at the town of Bloomfield, in Stoddard county, during the trial of Sarah Buckner, on a charge of murder.

A. I was there and in the court house a part of the time. I was in after the witnesses were examined, and Mr. Davis was speaking.

Q. State, if you please, what occurred while Mr. Davis was speaking—whether he was interrupted, and by whom.

A. While Mr. Davis was speaking of the evidence of Mr. Grimsley, Judge Jackson stopped him, and told him he should not allude to Grimsley's evidence,—that it was withdrawn from the jury.

Mr. KNOTT. You can take the witness.

JUDGE JACKSON. I don't want him, and never did want him. He can stand aside. I will, however, ask one question: Are you sure I told him that all of Grimsley's testimony was withdrawn from the jury?

A. I didn't understand it that way.

[A discussion as to the manner in which the cause should proceed, growing out of the absence and sickness of several witnesses, here occupied some time, during which, at the suggestion of Senator Parsons,]

Mr. PHELAN was recalled, and examined as follows:

SENATOR PARSONS. It was at my suggestion, Mr. Phelan, that you have been recalled, that I might have a more definite understanding of some points of your testimony. I will now request you to state what the substance was of Grimsley's testimony in this Buckner trial. I do not want the legal effect of it, but the substance of the testimony itself.

A. My answer must be very indefinite. His testimony was in regard to a conversation had with Sarah Buckner, the defendant, in which she was stated to have made certain admissions.

Q. What was that conversation, and what were those admissions?

A. As far as he was allowed to testify, it was concerning connections had with her prior to the trial. The general effect was antagonistic to Mrs. Buckner.

Q. That is the legal effect of the testimony; we want the substance.

A. I confess I am unable to say what it was. I am unable to give anything like the substance of this testimony. The impression was on my mind vivid enough at the time.

Mr. HARDIN. Who wrote out this testimony?

A. Judge Jackson, I think.

Q. Did you examine it after it was written out?

A. I believe I did, and I think it was about the same in substance that the witness stated when on the stand. I don't remember any material deviation. This was the testimony incorporated in the bill of exceptions.

JUDGE JACKSON. Didn't you draw up the bill of exceptions yourself ?

A. Yes, sir. I think, however, that Mr. Moore and Mr. Davis did something of the kind before I did so. You kindly adjourned court to give me an opportunity to prepare the case for an appeal. I drew up a bill of exceptions, and you rejected it because Grimsley's testimony was not included.

Q. Isn't the testimony, as saved in the bill of exceptions, in the handwriting of Mr. Davis ?

A. I am not prepared to say. The testimony of Grimsley is, I think, in your own handwriting.

Q. Well, now, when he was stopped, wasn't he beginning to tell what Mrs. Buckner had told him her daughter had said ?

A. I think he was not stopped at all. The Circuit Attorney asked permission to withdraw the testimony.

Q. That is what I mean. When you contended that this conversation should be introduced, wasn't that the part that the Circuit Attorney withdrew, or wasn't that the part of the testimony that was excluded ?

A. You did not permit me to contend for the introduction of any part of Grimsley's testimony.

Q. Didn't you wait for the cross-examination, expecting to bring out this hear-say testimony, and wasn't that all that was excluded ?

A. I think the whole of the testimony was withdrawn.

Q. Wasn't the witness under cross-examination when he was stopped ?

A. My impression is that the witness was never in the hands of the defendant's counsel. I know that we relied upon the statements of the girl. It may be that Mr. Grimsley incidentally alluded to it, and that it was objected to when he did so.

Q. Didn't the argument about Grimsley's testimony spring up at that stage ?

A. If we had any argument at all, I suppose it was then.

Q. Did either party withdraw all the testimony of Grimsley ?

A. Yes, sir. I understood the Circuit Attorney to withdraw both the witness and his testimony.

SENATOR CHURCHILL. I would ask the witness to repeat the conversation between Judge Jackson and Mr. Davis, at the time of the alleged interruption of the latter by the Judge. I want to know, particularly, what the Judge then claimed in regard to this testimony of Grimsley ?

A. Yes, sir. Mr. Davis was addressing the jury. In the course of his remarks, he referred to Grimsley's testimony by way of illustration. The Judge interrupted him, and told him that Grimsley's testimony was not for the consideration of the jury. Afterwards he prevented me from alluding to it, even for the purpose of removing any impression that it might have made on the minds of the jurors, stating, again, that the testimony of Grimsley was not in evidence. Our next conversation on the subject was some three weeks subsequent, when we were preparing the case for an appeal. Then when I, on the spur of the moment, sprung the point that the testimony of one witness uncorroborated was not sufficient to support a conviction for a capital offense, the Judge changed his ground, and claimed that Grimsley's testimony had been evidence in the case. It should be known that the body of the deceased was not found.

SENATOR WATKINS. Did I understand you to say that the testimony of the witness Grimsley was positively and entirely withdrawn from the jury, when a motion was made to that effect by the Circuit Attorney ?

A. That was the understanding of all parties at the time of the trial.

Q. Did the Judge afterwards insist that this testimony should be incorporated in the bill of exceptions?

A. Yes, sir. The testimony, as originally prepared by the bill of exceptions, embraced simply the evidence of the only other witness, and he refused to sign it until the testimony of Grimsley was added.

Q. Was there any regular motion made to withdraw the last witness?

A. It was a motion made orally during the progress of the trial.

Q. Was there any exception taken by either party to the exclusion of this testimony?

A. I cannot remember that there was.

Q. And you say the whole of it was withdrawn, and that there was no cross-examination whatever?

A. Yes, sir.

Q. Did you ask an instruction to tell the jurors that they were not to consider any portion of Grimsley's statements?

A. We did not, that I recollect.

[The witness here repeated what he had before stated concerning the whole trial, some of the Senators not having heard his previous statements.]

Mr. KNOTT. Why didn't you object when the Circuit Attorney made the motion to withdraw the testimony of Grimsley?

A. Because I knew when the Judge ever made a decision it was final; and I didn't want that testimony to remain as a part of the evidence in the cause.

JUDGE JACKSON. Could you not have excepted, and had your exception entered of record?

A. I suppose it could have been done.

DANIEL EPPS recalled and examined by Judge Jackson.

Q. Are you acquainted with the handwriting of Jacob C. Blount?

A. Yes, sir, I am.

Q. From your knowledge of his handwriting, would you say that was his signature? (showing to the witness the paper signed by Mr. Blount, and requesting the appointment of a Deputy Clerk.)

A. I think not. It don't imitate it. It don't look to me that it is his handwrite.

Mr. HARDIN. Did you ever see him write his name when he was so drunk that he had to be held up for the purpose?

A. I never did.

SENATOR FOX. In what respect is it different? Is it better? Is it worse? Is it smoother?

A. Well, sir, this writing is not so good as Mr. Blount usually does. This handwrite is different. It is a more open handwrite. He writes a running hand, and this is more open-like.

TESTIMONY OF SOLOMON G. KITCHEN.

SOLOMON G. KITCHEN called and examined by Mr. Knott.

Q. Mr. Kitchen, please state where you reside, and what is your occupation.

A. I live in Stoddard county, Missouri, and have been practicing law nine or ten years, and farming a little.

Q. Were you at the November term, 1858, of the Circuit Court of Stoddard county?

A. Yes, sir.

Q. Were you present when the grand jury was charged?

A. Yes, sir; I heard it.

Q. You will please go on and state the substance of that charge, and particularly anything in reference to an alleged offense said to have been committed by a lawyer, to which the especial attention of the grand jury was directed.

A. I couldn't undertake to state the entire charge. In the course of it the Judge alluded to some offense which he said had been committed by a citizen of that county, a lawyer. He said this lawyer had some business here in Jefferson City; he didn't know what it was, and didn't know whether the individual himself knew what it was; that while here he had procured from an office plats of certain swamp lands; that he had received from the county for this $100 or $170, which he had no right to receive; and that such an offense was punishable by imprisonment in the penitentiary, because it was receiving money under false pretenses. He also spoke of courts at some length, and their accountability for official acts. He said that some Judges, the Judge of the Circuit Court and Justices of the Peace, were exempt from indictment for official acts; but that the County Court was of a different nature, and when it transcended its powers, it ought to be indicted. He said that if the County Court had paid this money to this individual without any legal authority for so doing, the person composing that court should be indicted. I was the person that had come to this city and obtained a certified list of the swamp lands. For this list I paid the Secretary of State $65 for clerk hire, and I paid my expenses. I was here some time on this business. For this service the County Court struck a warrant for $177. All the town knew that I was the individual alluded to. The whole transaction was well known. Judge Eaker was then the only Judge of the County Court.

Q. In this charge, in speaking about the lawyer who had committed this offense, did he indicate any means of ascertaining who the person was?

A. He referred them to the Clerk's office and to the Treasurer, saying that they could find information at either office.

Q. What was the manner of the Judge in delivering this charge?

A. From appearances, he seemed angry or exulting, one of the two—I was unable to decide which. He threw up his hands, gesticulated with some energy, and spoke in a declaiming style. I was in the court house at the time and paid marked attention.

Q. Do you practice in the Ripley Circuit Court?

A. I have practiced there some from the time the new circuit was organized. I think I was there at court once or twice before. I have practiced there all the time for the last three years.

Q. Were you a member of the Senate when this new circuit was organized?

A. Yes, sir, I was.

Q. Were you at Ripley court in the fall of 1857, and in April, 1858?

A. I was.

Q. Were you connected in any manner with the case of James Moore *vs.* John Eldridge, administrator of the estate of Parker?

A. Yes, sir. I was attorney for Mr. Moore. I believe Moore was plaintiff, though I can't speak positively as to that. The suit was about a note, and in it was involved an investigation about a copartnership between Moore and Parker. The suit was between the administrator of Parker, Mr. Eldridge, and Moore.

Q. Do you know anything about a bill of exceptions in that case?

A. Yes, sir. I drew it up.

Q. Who was the counsel on the other side?

A. Mr. Phelan. He looked at my bill of exceptions; and we agreed upon the testimony. The Judge refused to sign unless it appeared in the evidence that one of the witnesses, a Mr. Kittrell, had stated a certain fact which I contended that he had not stated. Mr. Kittrell was called on to settle the dispute, and when called in, he said that he had not stated, in giving in his testimony, the fact in question; that he had not made such a statement. The Judge, notwithstanding this, said he would include the statement in brackets; and I think he interlined it, and I believe he did make a scrawl around it.

Q. What was the Judge's demeanor towards counsel at this time?

A. Towards some, it was kind; towards others, it was abrupt.

Q. Can you specify who it was he treated kindly?

A. He seemed to treat the attorney of Mr. Eldridge very kindly. Towards myself, his demeanor was different.

Q. What was your demeanor towards him?

A. I was as mild as I could be.

Q. Did you hear Kittrell testifying in this case at the time of the trial?

A. Yes, sir.

Q. Had he made such a statement as the Judge wished to make a part of the testimony in the bill of exceptions?

A. No, sir, he had not. He interlined the bill himself.

Q. Were there any other witnesses in the case besides Kittrell?

A. I am not sure whether Kittrell was the only witness or not—I don't recollect; but I believe Kittrell knew more about the things in controversy than any other witness.

Q. Were you at Ripley Circuit Court in April, 1858, pending the trial of William Kinsey for grand larceny?

A. Yes. I assisted in the defense of Kinsey, at that court. There were four or five attorneys on the side of the defense. I can now mention Mr. Fox and Mr. Tyrell as having been thus engaged. I am not sure whether Mr. Bedford was engaged in it or not.

Q. State if you please whether any difficulty occurred during the trial of this case in regard to taking down the testimony.

A. About the time we made an arrangement to take down the testimony—

Q. Why did you want the testimony taken?

A. We wanted to have it taken down as it was delivered. We had had a good deal of trouble to get a verdict in the case, and it was not unusual to have unpleasant difficulties as to what the testimony was in cases. When the first witness came on to be examined, some one spoke to him and told him not to be too fast, but to make his statement so as to give time to have it written down. The Judge remarked that the witness was not put there for the lawyers to reduce his testimony to writing, but to give evidence for the court and jury. After the testimony had been gone through with, he then remarked that it could be reduced to writing, if the attorneys saw proper to do so.

Q. Had there been a previous trial of the same case?

A. I don't know now whether there had been or not.

Q. What was Judge Jackson's demeanor to the counsel during this trial?

A. I thought it quite rude to some. Mr. Fox was stopped in the course of his argument once or twice, I think; I don't recollect the cause. He was making some illustration when the Judge interrupted him, and they had some words; after which he was proceeding to argue his case, when the Judge ordered him to take his seat.

Q. Did you observe any other manifestation of harshness then?

A. Not that I recollect, at this trial.

Q. Were you at the October term, 1857, of the Ripley Circuit Court?

A. I was.

Q. Did you see David M. Fox there?

A. Yes, sir. He has been there every term that I have been there.

Q. Did you observe at that term any transaction between the Judge and Mr. Fox, involving a charge of perjury or lying?

A. Either at that term or some other of the same court—I cannot now be positive as to the time—Mr. Fox had filed an answer or a replication in some cause in which he was interested. The Judge was examining the paper, and asked Mr. Fox if he had written it. Mr. Fox advanced up very near to where the Judge was sitting, near enough to have a sight at the paper, and he perhaps made an affirmative reply, when the Judge told him that if he wrote it, he had sworn a lie himself, or made his client do so.

Q. Was this in open court?

A. Yes, sir. There were a good many persons in the court house at the time. It was about the middle of court.

Q. What was Mr. Fox doing?

A. I don't recollect. He wasn't addressing the court. The case involving the paper had just been called.

Q. Were you at Butler Circuit Court, May term, A. D. 1858?

A. Yes, sir.

Q. Were you in court during the trial of Gibson *vs.* Dunn?

A. I was in court when the case was first opened, and in after dinner.

Q. Who were the counsel for the parties engaged in that suit?

A. I think Mr. Phelan, Mr. Bedford, and Mr. Walls appeared for Dunn. Mr. Fox and Mr. Dennis, if I recollect rightly, were for the plaintiff. Immediately after dinner the Judge came in very much excited; walked on to the bench, took off his hat, and remarked that Mr. Phelan was under charges, and would be held to answer, or would be expelled from the bar, or something of that kind. He notified him that he would be held to answer for tampering with the grand jury. Mr. Phelan got up, and as he rose, the Judge told him to sit down, and go on with his case. I think he stated that the charge was either false or a lie, as he got up from his chair.

Q. Do you practice at Dunklin Circuit Court?

A. Yes, sir, sometimes.

Q. Were you counsel in the case of the Point Pleasant and Dunklin County Plank Road Company *vs.* Moses Farrar?

A. Yes, sir. I was for defendant.

Q. What became of that case?

A. It was sent on change of venue to Pemiscot county. The grounds of the petition were prejudice on the part of the Judge. I am not certain who presented the petition, but it is my impression it was Mr. Bedford. It may have been some one else. Mr. James Walker, I believe, was representing the road company, and I think Dr. Horner was in the case, on one side or the other.

A. Do you know whether there was any agreement of counsel as to where the case should be sent?

A. Yes, sir. There was an agreement that the case should go to either Scott or Bollinger county.

Q. Why?

A. Because either county was easier of access, going by horseback, and much more convenient to all parties.

Q. Why would either be more convenient? Is there any difficulty in going from Dunklin to Pemiscot?

A. Yes, sir. There is a very large swamp, which is impassable the greater part of every year. From the time the fall rains set in, until the following July, in order to get from Dunklin to Pemiscot, horseback, one has to go around by way of Cape Girardeau, a distance of two hundred miles, or more.

Q. Where do the witnesses in that case reside?

A. I think their only witness lives in Kennett. Mr. Walker is the agent of the company, and perhaps the only witness of the company. Counsel for the company is Mr. Walker, and, I believe, Mr. Arthur. He was then staying at Bloomfield. There was a Mr. Richardson in the case, but I don't think he was there at the time it was moved.

Q. Were you counsel in the case of Smith *vs.* Cude?

A. Yes, sir. That case was also sent to Pemiscot county.

Q. Was anything said in relation to the inconvenience that would result from sending the case there?

A. Yes, sir. Mr. Phelan and I were present, and we both insisted on the case going to Scott or Bollinger county. We stated our reasons, so far as the court would hear them; that we couldn't attend there, because the court in that county conflicted with the courts in our own circuit, and the difficulty of access, also. Defendant's counsel urged very strongly that they couldn't attend there, on account of the swamp, and because they would have to be at another court at the same time. None of us are in the habit of attending court in Pemiscot county, except Mr. Bedford, who has perhaps gone there occasionally.

Q. Was the court apprised of these facts?

A. Yes, sir. I can say that he was well apprised of them.

Q. Were you at the Circuit Court in Stoddard county, at the November term, 1858?

A. Yes, sir. I was there.

Q. Were you connected with the case of Berry *vs.* Griffie?

A. I didn't appear in the case, though I was spoken to. I was in court part of the time only during the trial.

Q. Well, Mr. Kitchen, I will now ask you to state, as succinctly as you can, the facts within your knowledge in connection with the writ of mandamus *vs.* Jonas Eaker, made returnable to the May term of this court?

A. Yes, sir. I saw the writ of mandamus against Judge Eaker. It was concerning a road. When the case was called by the court, I was in, and suggested that the writ had not been served. I made this suggestion as the friend of the court. He appeared to get excited, and said that he didn't want my friendship. I replied that he wanted mine about as bad as I wanted his. About that time Mr. Phelan came in, and we had some discussion about the matter. I wanted to prevail upon him to look at the writ himself. I was assured he must see there was no service. Not being able to accomplish anything, I left Mr. Phelan and him contending about the matter, and directly he ordered Mr. Phelan to sit down. He then went on to say it was a kind of proceeding in which parties could not appear by attorney. He said a good many things, which I couldn't attempt to repeat, and appeared to be excited and angry.

Q. What did he do with the case?

A. He ordered an attachment, after making some remarks about its being a matter between the two courts. After the attachment was issued, Mr. Eaker was arrested and kept in the custody of the Deputy Sheriff about half an hour, or perhaps an hour. The Judge then ordered the Sheriff to bring him into court, and after this was done, he remarked that, if he was not in contempt, he was ignorant of his duty. Mr. Eaker told him he didn't intend any contempt of court. After talking a while about it, the Judge told him he could come in the next morning and answer upon the copy of the writ with which he was served, and he was then released. He made the return the next morning, I believe.

Q. Do you know what return he made of the copy?

A. I do not; I never saw it afterwards.

Q. Were you at the November term, 1857, of the Stoddard Circuit

Court, at the time Sarah Buckner was tried on an indictment for murder?

A. I was not there at the time of the trial. After the verdict, the court was adjourned to some time in December. I was present when the bill of exceptions was presented to the court for signature.

Q. Please state what occurred between the court and attorneys in regard to that bill of exceptions.

A. The Judge said he would not sign the bill unless it was made to contain the testimony of a witness that Mr. Phelan contended was excluded. Mr. Phelan said the evidence was not commented on by attorneys in the argument of the case; that it ought to to have been excluded, and that it certainly was excluded. Whether the Judge made any reply I do not know. He took an opposite ground, and refused to sign the bill of exceptions until it was made to conform to his representations of the facts.

Senator Parsons. At the time the Judge delivered his charge to the grand jury of Stoddard county, at the November term, A. D. 1858, had there been, or was there then, any unfriendly feeling between you and the Judge?

A. There had been for some time—for over a year.

CROSS-EXAMINED BY JUDGE JACKSON.

Q. Mr. Kitchen, you said that in my charge to the grand jury I was angry—about that county warrant, I mean?

A. Yes, sir, it seemed to me you were either angry or exulting.

Q. How did it seem so? What cause had you to think so?

A. It seemed to me that such was the case, from the flush in your face, and your throwing up your hands.

Q. Don't I gesticulate always in every charge, more or less?

A. I believe you generally gesticulate some.

Q. Don't I speak with more energy at some times than at others? and can't I do that without being angry?

A. I have seen you speak with more zeal upon some occasions than upon others.

Q. Did you not hear me, at the August term of the Stoddard court, charge the grand jury?

A. Yes, sir; I believe so.

Q. Did I not then single out a particular offense, and comment at length upon its character and the punishment connected with it?

A. Yes, sir; I—

Q. Did I not gesticulate then? and did I not go into the particular points likely to be presented in a certain case? and did I do anything more, or was I more excited or angry, in this warrant matter? Did I even do as much gesticulating, or was my face as much flushed then, as when I was charging the grand jury in the Davis case?

A. In the Davis case you commented at length upon circumstantial evidence; and that was a special term of the court, held for a special purpose.

Q. Did I as pointedly speak about the warrant matter as I did then? Did I not tell them that it was their duty to indict if the facts were as I had understood them to be?

A. I don't know that you made any particular reservation on that score.

Q. Did I state how I understood them to be?

A. You said you had reason to believe that the individual referred to had procured the plats without any proper authority, and had received

$170 for pretended services to the county, while he was transacting his own business, which was obtaining money under false pretenses.

Q. Did I not state that he had gone to Jefferson City on his own business, or on business for Dunklin county, and that he had not gone on business for that county?

A. What I heard on that subject was, that you didn't know what my business was here, and you said, "I don't know whether he knows himself."

Q. Who employed you to come here and get those plats?

A. There had been an order for a sale of the swamp lands belonging to that county, and it was necessary to have a certified list of the swamp lands patented. A number of citizens of the county had farms made on these lands, and the whole business was in such a condition that it required some man acquainted with it to come up here and attend to it. I agreed to come if they would pay me my expenses and for my time.

Q. Did you not intend to come up here anyhow, on business for Dunklin county?

A. I stated that I was going to look into some business for that county.

Q. What was the amount of the warrant you received?

A. One hundred and seventy-seven dollars.

Q. Hadn't you and Phelan been attorneys for Dunklin county? and wasn't this warrant issued to you jointly?

A. It was. He said that he would attend to my business at Poplar Bluff, and in consideration of this, the warrant was issued to us jointly.

Q. Were you not partners in the Dunklin county swamp land business?

A. We were. Mr. Eaker said that he wished one of us to come up—that he didn't care which one it was; and by agreement I came.

Q. Was there any order made by the County Court before you came?

A. Not that I know of. I procured them on my own name.

Q. Did you get plats for yourself?

A. I did not get any plats. I got certified lists of the county.

Q. Well, had you got them before any order was made for procuring them?

A. I think it was a week or so after the order was made. I had received them before I drew the warrant.

Q. Well, now with regard to this Eldridge and Moore matter. What did you say that suit was about?

A. About a note involved in some copartnership transactions between Moore and Parker, whose estate Eldridge was administering.

Q. You say there was a difference in regard to the testimony of Kittrell, as to whether he had stated anything about a certain erasure or blot upon an instrument which was a part of the evidence in the cause?

A. Yes, sir.

Q. Well, now, as to Kittrell, after he came in and said that the instrument was just as he had always seen it, wasn't it necessary to show that fact in the bill of exceptions? Wasn't the paper in testimony before the jury?

A. Yes, sir; it was.

Q. Well, then, wasn't it necessary in making up the testimony for a bill of exceptions that the fact of this erasure, which was a matter of inspection by the jury and a matter of evidence, should go into the bill?

Mr. Knott objected to the question.

Judge Jackson reduced it to writing, as follows:

Was it not necessary to state in the bill of exceptions, or in the evidence, for the purpose of making a full bill of exceptions, the fact of the erasure existing in the instrument of writing?

The question was decided improper by the following vote:

AYES—Messrs. Harris, Hedgpeth, Jones, Morris, Newland, Peyton, Robinson, Scott, Wilson, and Wood—10.
NOES—Messrs. Brown, Byrne, Churchill, Fox, Frazier, Goodlett, Gullett, Halliburton, Horner, Hyer, McFarland, McFerran, McIlvaine, O'Neil, Parsons, Rains, Richardson, Thompson, Vernon, and Watkins—20.
Absent—Mr. Johnson.
Absent on leave—Messrs. Coleman and Wright.

The cross-examination then proceeded.

Q. Why was it put in brackets?

A. When Mr. Kittrell came in he said that he had not made any statement when upon the witness stand; you stated that you would make the fact show in the evidence, anyhow. I didn't hear any reason for putting it in brackets.

Q. Was not that instrument of writing copied into the bill, and would the erasure appear on the copy?

[Mr. Knott objected to this question as argumentative, and after some little discussion it was waived.]

Q. In this Kinsey case you say the attorneys wished to take down the testimony, and that I told them the witness had not been brought there for that purpose. Now, if that was my first statement, did I not then go on and say that they could let the witness make his statement of any particular fact—that when he was through the attorneys should have ample time to take it down?

A. After the State got through, you told us we might take down the testimony if we wished. I don't remember that you made any proposition such as you describe.

Q. Did you ask for more time to take down the testimony?

A. If I did not, some one else did, and you replied at first as I have before stated. After the witness was through, I think, perhaps you said, "now you can reduce it to writing, if you want to."

Q. Well, wasn't the testimony written down?

A. Mr. Tyrell had reduced as much of it to writing as he could, though it was not taken down as fully as we wished it.

Q. Don't you recollect that I said that the general practice of making witnesses repeat the words of their statements slowly, so as to have them written down, was embarrassing, and that the better way was to let the witness proceed to the conclusion of his statement, and then stop him until it was written out?

A. I don't recollect that you said anything about the general practice, or about the effect of taking down the testimony of a witness.

Q. You state that my conduct on this occasion was harsh to Mr. Fox. What was it that was harsh? What was he saying at the time to provoke harshness on my part?

A. He was making his speech, and you stopped him. He proceeded a little further, and you stopped him again, and ordered him to sit down.

Q. Wasn't he making an assertion then that the court was using its influence to bring about a conviction?

A. I don't recollect what it was he was saying.

Q. When I stopped him, didn't he claim a credit on his time for the interruption, saying that he should extend over his time on account of it? and the second time when I spoke to him, didn't he say he was alluding to me?

A. I don't recollect anything of the kind. I thought on that occasion he was mild enough.

Q. Well, if he was mild enough on that occasion, how is he on others?

At the other time, when you say I told him that he lied, or caused his client to lie, how did he behave then? What did you say he was doing?

A. I stated upon my examination in chief, that when you called his attention to the paper you had been examining, he walked up towards where you were sitting, and about that time you said that, if he had written the paper, he had either lied or caused his client to lie.

Q. Didn't I tell him that the paper and the affidavit contradicted one another?

A. I don't recollect that you did.

Q. Are you sure I used the word lie? Wasn't it falsehood, or some word less opprobrious than lie?

A. I am sure you said he had sworn a lie, or made his client do it.

Q. You state that I had used very rough words, and very harsh words. How do you distinguish between rough and harsh terms?

A. I aimed to convey the same idea with both words.

Q. Well, what would you mean by a smooth word?

A. I would mean a word having in its connection a conciliatory effect.

Q. Did you ever hear me use a sharp word?

A. I think I have repeatedly.

Q. Well, what does it take to make a sharp or a rough word, or a harsh word? What effect does a sharp word have on a man? Does it make him jump or shrink?

A. If it comes in anger, it makes me angry, and I am apt to reply with words of the same kind.

Q. How do you think it is about others? Would it make a similar impression upon others, do you think, if you were to use harsh words? How do you tell when a word is sharp?

A. In various ways. I tell from gestures, looks, and the connection in which they are used.

Q. Are you not something of a mathematician?

A. Not much of a one.

Q. Did you ever see an angular word, a word with three corners?

SENATOR FOX. I must remonstrate against this kind of proceeding, as a waste of time, capital and dignity.

JUDGE JACKSON. It must be remembered that great latitude is allowed on a cross-examination.

Q. At this Butler case, the Gibson *vs.* Dunn case, you state that when Mr. Phelan came in after dinner—

A. No, when *you* came in. I didn't say anything about Mr. Phelan coming in.

Q. Well, don't you know that I notified him that he was in contempt, and that at a proper time he would be called upon to answer?

A. You notified him that he was under charges—that he had been tampering with the grand jury. He jumped up and said something, what it was I am not prepared to state exactly; I think it was that the charge was false, or that it was a lie. Then I think you told him to sit down and go on with the case.

Q. What did he do then?

A. He set down and wrote an affidavit charging Mr. Bill Henley with divulging the secrets of the grand jury.

Q. Had he not done this before?

A. No, sir. I know that he made an affidavit before the Clerk immediately after this.

Q. What time of day was this?

A. It was directly after dinner. It happened immediately on your return from dinner.

Q. Did I fine him?
A. I don't think you did.
Q. Did I allow him to go on with his case?
A. You told him he should have an opportunity to defend himself afterwards, and that he might then go on with the case.
Q. In these Dunklin county road cases, which party applied for a change of venue?
A. I don't know which.
Q. Where did the plaintiff live?
A. The plaintiff was a road company.
Q. Well, then, for whose use was the suit prosecuted? Was it not for the use of Mr. Clark?
A. Mr. Clark was a contractor. I don't know that he was more particularly interested than others.
Q. Well, where do the stockholders of that company live?
A. Dunklin county is one; and they live in Pemiscot and New Madrid, and scattered about over the country there.
Q. Wouldn't it have been as convenient for them to have the case—those on the east side of the swamp? Was not Mr. Moore in the road case?
A. I don't recollect.
Q. Wouldn't it be as convenient for him to go from Cape Girardeau to attend the trial, as to attend it at Kennett?
A. He would have about the same distance.
Q. You say that yourself and Mr. Phelan told me you wanted the case to go to Scott or Bollinger. Now, wasn't there a proposition that the case should go to the Cape or to Bollinger, and then Horner suggested New Madrid? and wasn't it because none of these counties seemed to suit all parties that I sent the case to Pemiscot?
A. I have no recollection that such was the case.
Q. Wasn't Phelan, Walker, and Horner, all on the same side? and wasn't they glad when the case was sent to Pemiscot?
A. If the others were in the case, Mr. Phelan took the lead, and he was not glad, I am sure.
Q. Well, in this other case. Where does Johnson or Smith live? Did not the party conducting the suit live in Tennessee?
A. I am not prepared to say. If he did live in Tennessee, the most convenient county was probably Pemiscot.
Q. Well, we will now go to this mandamus case. When you suggested that there was no return, what was my first expression in reply?
A. I suggested that there was no service, and asked you to look at the return, and satisfy yourself that there was no legal service. As to your first expression after this, I don't recollect what it was; but I know that after some considerable jowering, you said that it was not an attorney's business, and that it was a matter exclusively between the two courts.
Q. Well, who did this jabbering that you speak of?
A. You did your share.
Q. What do you call jabbering?
A. I presume it is not necessary to give a definition.
Q. Well, did you appear in the case as an attorney? Did you do any of this jabbering as an attorney?
A. I did what I did as Solomon Kitchen.
Q. Well, what occurred after the jabbering you speak of?
A. I wished you to see how the writ was served, and after some considerable contention, you said the case was one in which counsel could not appear.

Q. Didn't I state that whatever his case was, he should not keep it to himself, but he must come in and make a return to the writ?

A. You said it was a matter between you and him, with which an attorney should have nothing to do.

Q. Didn't I state that in reply to your first expression that you appeared in the case as the next friend of the court?

A. I didn't put in that word "next friend" of the court. I claimed an undoubted right to make a suggestion of the failure of service, and that seemed to anger you.

Q. Did you do anything else? I believe you said a moment ago that you jabbered?

A. You may call it as you please.

Q. When Mr. Eaker came in, didn't he offer to make a return on the copy?

A. You had him brought in by an officer, and proposed to release him yourself upon this condition.

Q. Well, when he was brought in on the attachment, didn't he ask till the next morning, and I told him he could have it? And wasn't this matter of disturbance (I mean all the conversation) before an attachment issued? Wasn't you and Mr. Phelan trying to prevent an attachment from being issued?

A. No, sir. We were trying to show that there was no service of the writ of mandamus. You had just called the case.

Q. Did you enter an appearance for Mr. Eaker?

A. You said I shouldn't do it. You said I had nothing to do with the matter; that it was a peculiar kind of a case; that lawyers had nothing to do with it; and in talking to Mr. Phelan, you told him to shut his mouth and sit down.

Q. Didn't I ask him if it wasn't possible for him to keep his mouth shut? and wasn't that what I said, instead of saying to him to keep his mouth shut?

A. You made the remark I have repeated.

Q. Had there been any unkind feelings between us before this occurrence?

A. Yes, sir, there had been.

Q. What gave rise to them?

A. Your treatment of me.

Q. My treatment in court or out? In what cases?

A. In a number of cases. I can name the case of Johnson *vs.* Sness; in the mandamus; in the case of Johnson and Dickens, and in a good many others.

Q. In the case of Johnson and Dickens, what did I do to give rise to hard feelings?

A. You threw me entirely upon the mercy of the opposing counsel in the matter of preparing the testimony in that case for a bill of exceptions. Such had not been your practice in any other instance. After the testimony was prepared, you wouldn't even look at it until the opposing counsel had consented that it was correctly set out; and when there was a difference between us, you wouldn't decide.

Q. Didn't I say this: that I wouldn't sign the testimony for you, in this Johnson and Dickens case, while the other party was protesting that the testimony was not correctly set out? and when I learned that you made a good many remarks out of court in regard to my course, didn't I remark then that until I was satisfied you had the testimony correct, I wouldn't sign it?

A. I recollect it as I have stated it.

Q. Well, in court what was the difficulty?

A. A part of the difficulty was in getting an appeal.

Q. Didn't it grow out of your obstinate manner of pressing points that I had decided against you?

A. No, sir. You wouldn't decide when there was a difficulty between myself and other counsel as to what the testimony was, and still stronger, after we had agreed upon it, you put things in there that didn't belong. The first difficulty was because you wouldn't decide; and the second because, after writing out the testimony and agreeing upon it with the other counsel, you wouldn't sign the bill till you had put things in there that the witnesses said that they had never stated.

Q. Well, now, don't you think that I was right, or that I thought I was right?

A. My thoughts about that matter were, that you wanted to support your judgment with testimony which had not been before the jury.

Q. Didn't the jury decide the case?

A. Yes, sir.

Q. Were there any instructions given to the jury?

A. No, sir. And you wouldn't grant a new trial, although the judgment was against the weight of evidence. The Supreme Court thought so too, for the judgment was reversed, and the case remanded.

[Judge Jackson here commented at some length upon the facts stated by the witness; but as his remarks were not in the form of questions, they are here omitted.]

Q. Have you any unkind feelings towards me now?

A. I have such unkind feelings as are naturally occasioned by wrongs done me without cause. Our personal relations are unfriendly.

Q. Have these feelings not grown out of personal matters that happened out of court?

A. I have heard things out of court which I never paid any particular attention to. All hard feelings between us have grown out of what I considered an erroneous course on your part.

Q. Have you not expressed yourself as favorable to me as a Judge? During the fall of 1855, and the spring of 1856, during the two first rounds on the circuit, didn't you pass high encomiums on my course?

A. Yes, sir. Up to the third round on the circuit, I saw nothing in you to censure.

Q. Well, Mr. Kitchen, don't you urge your views with a good deal of zeal?

A. Yes, sir, I believe I do.

Q. Don't you get excited, and when you are thwarted, go to extremes?

A. When I think I am badly treated, I get excited. I don't think I ever went to extremes but once in my life.

Q. Well, Mr. Kitchen, these unpleasant feelings—was it what you conceived to be errors on my part?

A. I thought it was bad treatment. I thought at some times your errors were willful, and sometimes I didn't know. They were so often against me, and not against others, that I concluded I was a particular object of spite.

Mr. Knott. Tell us about this Davis case. Was he in custody when the Judge charged the grand jury concerning the charge alleged against him?

A. Yes, sir; he was then under recognizance. The court was especially called for the purpose of trying him, and he was either in jail or in custody.

Mr. Hardin. In reference to this interlineation in the bill of exceptions, made by Judge Jackson in Kittrell's testimony, was there anything there to show it was not a part of Kittrell's testimony?

A. Nothing but a scrawl. I didn't see the bill afterwards. I took it that the scrawl only showed that the interlineation was not a necessary part of the sentence.

SENATOR WATKINS. Did I understand you to say that this was an interlineation affecting the date of the instrument?

A. The interlineation was in reference to an obscuration of the date.

The testimony of Mr. Kitchen was here concluded.

On motion of Mr. KNOTT, and by unanimous consent, it was

Ordered, That the managers be permitted to discharge such witnesses on the part of the State as they may deem proper, with the consent of the respondent.

Benjamin Thornberg, Hamilton Scott, A. J. Ruff, and Daniel Epps, witnesses, were discharged under the foregoing rule.

The managers not being ready to proceed with the case, and having announced the fact,

SENATOR CHURCHILL moved to adjourn till to-morrow morning at 8 o'clock, which was decided in the negative by the following vote, the ayes and noes having been demanded by Senator McFerran:

AYES—Messrs. Brown, Byrne, Churchill, Halliburton, Harris, Hedgpeth, Hyer, Jones, McIlvaine, Parsons, Peyton, Rains, Robinson, Scott, and Watkins—15.

NOES—Messrs. Fox, Frazier, Goodlett, Gullett, Horner, McFarland, McFerran, Morris, Newland, O'Neil, Richardson, Thompson, Vernon, Wilson, and Wood—15.

Absent—Mr. Johnson.

Absent on leave—Messrs. Coleman and Wright.

[RICHARDSON in the chair.]

SENATOR SCOTT then moved to adjourn until 4 o'clock in the afternoon, which was decided in the negative by the following vote:

AYES—Messrs. Brown, Byrne, Harris, McIlvaine, Parsons, Peyton, Robinson, and Watkins—8.

NOES—Messrs. Churchill, Fox, Frazier, Goodlett, Gullett, Halliburton, Hedgpeth, Horner, Hyer, Jones, McFarland, McFerran, Morris, Newland, O'Neil, Rains, Richardson, Scott, Thompson, Vernon, Wilson, and Wood—22.

Absent—Mr. Johnson.

Absent on leave—Messrs. Coleman and Wright.

SENATOR GOODLETT then moved to adjourn until the regular hour, which was lost.

On motion of SENATOR WATKINS, the Court then adjourned until 8½ o'clock to-morrow morning, by the following vote, the ayes and noes being demanded by Senator O'Neil:

AYES—Messrs. Brown, Byrne, Churchill, Gullett, Halliburton, Harris, Hedgpeth, Hyer, Jones, McIlvaine, Parsons, Peyton, Rains, Robinson, Scott, Vernon, and Watkins—17.

NOES—Messrs. Fox, Frazier, Goodlett, Horner, McFarland, McFerran, Morris, Newland, O'Neil, Richardson, Thompson, Wilson, and Wood—13.

Absent—Mr. Johnson.

Absent on leave—Messrs. Coleman and Wright.

NINTH DAY.

WEDNESDAY, June 15, 1859.

The Court met pursuant to adjournment, and was opened by proclamation.

The managers and respondent attended.

On motion of Mr. HARDIN, it was

Ordered, That Eugene Donnelly, special messenger appointed to serve the attachment against the witnesses, Davis and others, be required to make return to this Court how he has discharged his duty under the same.

J. P. Conrand, witness on behalf of the State, was discharged under the rule.

Mr. EUGENE DONNELLY stated orally in Court the manner in which he had served, or attempted to serve, the attachment placed in his hands.

It appearing that two witnesses for the State, Messrs. Davis and Moore, would not probably be in attendance before Thursday evening, a short discussion ensued as to the manner in which the trial of the cause should proceed. It was finally determined that the managers should now offer what documentary evidence they had, and that the respondent should thereupon proceed with his opening remarks and his evidence, with the understanding that when the absent witnesses for the State arrived, they should be examined.

Mr. HARDIN, in accordance with the arrangement, offered in evidence the following copies of several records, which were read by the Secretary of the Senate from his desk:

THE STATE OF MISSOURI *vs.* ORSON BARTLETT.

Record of the pleas, proceedings, orders, and judgments of a special term of the Circuit Court, begun and held at the court house, in the town of Bloomfield, in Stoddard county, in the Fifteenth Judicial Circuit of the State of Missouri, on Monday, the 9th day of August, A. D. eighteen hundred and fifty-eight, before the Hon. Albert Jackson, Judge of the Circuit Courts for the circuit aforesaid, which said court was ordered to be held by the Judge thereof, in conformity to law.

Be it remembered, that on the 14th day of August, A. D. 1858, at said special term of said Circuit Court, held in August, 1858, before the Hon. Albert Jackson, of said court, among others, the following proceedings were had, to wit:

The grand jury returns here into court the following bill of indictment, to wit:

The State of Missouri,
versus
Orson Bartlett, Albert Jackson, Isaac Brand, and David G. Hicks. } Indictment for Gaming.

A True Bill.

Which said indictment is in words and figures following, to wit:

The State of Missouri,
Fifteenth Judicial Circuit, } *ss.*

In the Circuit Court of Stoddard county, August term, in the year of our Lord one thousand eight hundred and fifty-eight.

The grand jurors of the State of Missouri, empanneled and sworn to inquire within and for the body of the county of Stoddard, upon their oath present: That Col. Orson Bartlett, Hon. Albert Jackson, Isaac Brand, and David G. Hicks, all late of the county of Stoddard, in the State of Missouri, not having the fear of God before their eyes, but being moved and seduced by the instigation of the devil, on the first day of May, in the year of our Lord one thousand eight hundred and fifty-eight, with force and arms, in the back room of Thomas Ligget's grocery, at the county of Stoddard, in the State of Missouri, did willfully, deliberately, and of their malice aforethought, then and there bet whisky; to wit, four glasses or drinks, of the value of five cents; but for [which] whisky they the said Col. Orson Bartlett, Hon. Albert Jackson, Isaac Brand, and David G. Hicks paid twenty cents, at and upon a certain game of chance then and there played, called cards, or at and upon a certain gambling device then and there being, called cards, adapted, devised, and designed for the purpose of playing games of chance for money and property. And so, the grand jurors aforesaid, upon their oath aforesaid, do say that Col. Orson Bartlett, Hon. Albert Jackson, Isaac Brand, and David G. Hicks, then and there, in manner and form aforesaid, willfully, deliberately, premeditatedly, and of their malice aforethought, did, in the back room of Thomas Ligget's grocery, bet four glasses of whisky or good grog, of the value of five cents, against the forms of the statute in such case made and provided, and against the peace and dignity of the State of Missouri.

D. G. HICKS, *Circuit Attorney.*

On the back of which said indictment is the following endorsements, to wit:

"(10.) State of Missouri *vs.* Col. O. Bartlett *et. al.* Gaming. A True Bill. James L. Hale, foreman of the grand jury. Witnesses—James V. Odell, Thomas Liggett. Filed August 14th, 1858. Reuben P. Owen, Clerk."

And afterward, to wit, on the 16th day of August, A. D. 1858, at the August term, 1858, of the Circuit Court of said county of Stoddard, before the Hon. Albert Jackson, Judge, the following proceedings were had in said cause in court, to wit:

The State of Missouri, *versus* Orson Bartlett. } Indictment for Gaming.

The Circuit Attorney and the said defendant appears, and the said defendant having heard the said indictment read to him, says of the said indictment and the matters and things therein charged against him, he is not guilty, and of this he puts himself upon the country for trial, and the Circuit Attorney doth the like; whereupon comes a jury, to wit, 1 George C. Neill, 2 Rear B. Hickman, 3 Jiles J. Harvey, 4 B. G. Womble, 5 Robert McCollvine, 6 James Hodges, 7 Samuel Gibson, 8 Francis M. Hodges, 9 James W. Childress, 10 Thomas J. Walker, 11 R. C. Boyd, 12 John S. Galaway, twelve good and lawful men, who being duly elected, tried, and sworn to well and truly try this cause, and having heard all the testimony offered; whereupon the Circuit Attorney says he will not further prosecute this indictment. It is therefore considered and adjudged by the court that the said defendant of the said indictment and the matters and things therein charged against him be hence discharged, and go thereof without day.

State of Missouri, County of Stoddard, } *ss.*

I, Reuben P. Owen, Clerk of the Circuit Court in and for the county of Stoddard, in the State of Missouri, do certify that the foregoing is a true and perfect transcript of the record and proceedings in the foregoing case of the State of Missouri *vs.* Orson Bartlett, indicted with Albert Jackson *et. al.*, as the same appears now remaining in my office.

{ L.S. } In testimony whereof I have hereunto signed my name and affixed the seal of said Circuit Court, at office in Bloomfield, county and State aforesaid, this 24th day of January, A. D. 1859.

REUBEN P. OWEN, *Clerk.*

JOHNSON *et al. vs.* JONAS EAKER.

Be it remembered, that on the 22d day of March, A. D. 1858, was filed in the office of the Clerk of the Circuit Court of Stoddard county, in the State of Missouri, the following papers in the case of Larkin Johnson, and others, against Jonas Eaker, Judge of the District County Court of Stoddard county, on mandamus, which papers are in words and figures following, to-wit:

To Jonas Eaker, Judge of the District County Court within and for the county of Stoddard:

You are hereby notified that an application will be made to Hon. Albert Jackson, Judge of the Circuit Courts for the Fifteenth Judicial Circuit, at the Clerk's office, in the county of Stoddard, on Monday, the 22d day of March next, at 10 o'clock in the forenoon, for a writ of mandamus, touching the proceedings in said County Court relating to the viewing and marking out the road leading from the town of Bloomfield, in said county, to John Kitchen's mill, on Castor river.

HIRAM WASSON, *Attorney for the Petitioners.*

To the Hon. Albert Jackson, Judge of the Circuit Courts for the Fifteenth Judicial Circuit, in the State of Missouri:

Your petitioners respectfully represent, that at the December term of the District County Court for the county of Stoddard, in the State of Missouri, a petition, signed by William L. Kelley, *et al.*, was presented to said court, asking for a road to be located, leading from the town of Bloomfield, in said county, to John Kitchen's mill on Castor river, in Duck Creek township in said county; that after due proceeding had upon said petition, John Kitchen, Robert Hill, and William Culbertson were appointed by said County Court, Commissioners, to view and mark out the line of said contemplated road; that said Commissioners viewed said route, marked out the line of said contemplated road, and made report of their doings at the March term thereof, 1858. Your petitioner further represents, that at said March term of said court, and before final hearing had on said report, your petitioners presented to said court a remonstrance against the report of said Commissioners, signed by ten householders, residents within the township through which said contemplated road was to pass and had been marked out by said Commissioners, praying said court to reject said report of said Commissioners, and to dismiss all proceedings under said petition; and further asking said court, that if said court did not so reject said report and dismiss said proceedings, to appoint other Commissioners to view and mark out said road, in conformity with the law, and locate the same; which petition, report, and remonstrance are now on file in the office of the Clerk of said court, and are made a part of this petition. Your petitioners further represent, that said County Court refused either to reject the report of said Commissioners, or dismiss the proceedings under said petition, or to appoint other Commissioners to view and mark out said road and locate the same, as the law required, and as your petitioners prayed; but on the contrary, did pass an order for the opening of said road, as located by said Commissioners. Your petitioners, therefore, pray your Honor to order a writ of mandamus to issue in conformity with law, directed to Jonas Eaker, Judge of the District County Court of Stoddard county, aforesaid, returnable at the next Circuit Court, to be held within said county of Stoddard, commanding said Eaker to show cause why a peremptory writ of mandamus should not issue to compel said Judge to appoint said Commissioners to view and mark out said road, as prayed for in the remonstrance presented to said County Court by your petitioners, and for such further and other orders as law and justice may require.

Larkin Johnson,	William D. Taylor,	Henry E. Sifford,
J. R. McLane,	Marquis Williams,	William H. Hickman,
T. J. Walker,	William G. Lincoln,	Daniel B. Miller,
	William Griffin.	

By their attorney, HIRAM WASSON.

I, Hiram Wasson, on behalf and as agent of the plaintiffs, make oath and say, that the foregoing petition, and the matters and things as therein stated, are true, to the best of my knowledge and belief.

HIRAM WASSON.

15

Subscribed and sworn to before me this 18th day of March, 1858.

REUBEN P. OWEN, *Clerk*,
by his Deputy, JOHN W. LEACH.

And afterwards, to wit, on the 17th day of May, 1858, the following writ or instrument of writing was filed in the office of said Clerk, to wit:

State of Missouri, County of Stoddard, } *ss.*

The State of Missouri to Jonas Eaker, Judge of the District County Court of Stoddard county, Greeting:

Whereas, it has been represented to me, Albert Jackson, Judge of the Fifteenth Judicial Circuit in the State of Missouri, that at the March term of the said District County Court a remonstrance, signed by ten householders of the township through a certain contemplated road, leading from the town of Bloomfield to Kitchen's mill, on Castor river, was presented to said District County Court, protesting against the location of said contemplated road, in accordance with the provisions of the law in such cases made and provided; and whereas, it is represented that the Judge of said District County Court, refusing to entertain or take any steps, or make any order in relation said remonstrance, and left the said remonstrants without remedy: These are, therefore, to command you to be and appear before the Circuit Court of Stoddard county on the first day of the next term thereof, to be held at the court house in the town of Bloomfield, in said county, on the third Monday in May next, to show cause why the relief asked in said remonstrance should not be granted.

Given under my hand, March the 22d, A. D. 1858.

ALBERT JACKSON, *Judge*.

On which said writ or instrument of writing the Sheriff of Stoddard county, aforesaid, made the following return or endorsement, to wit:

Served the within writ and summons on the within named Jonas Eaker, on the 25th day of March, 1858, by delivering him a true copy of the same. Served in Stoddard county, Missouri.

JAMES DOWDY, *Sheriff*,
by his Deputy, JOHN J. JACKSON.

And afterwards, to wit, on the 20th day of May, A. D. 1858, at the May term, A. D. 1858, of the Circuit Court of said county of Stoddard, before the Hon. Albert Jackson, Judge of said court, the following proceedings were had in said cause in said Circuit Court, to wit:

Larkin J. Johnson, *et al.*, *versus* Jonas Eaker, Judge of the District County Court. } Mandamus.

Ordered by the court that an attachment issue in this cause against Jonas Eaker, returnable immediately.

Which said writ of attachment is in words and figures following, to wit:

State of Missouri, County of Stoddard, } *ss.*

The State of Missouri to the Sheriff of Stoddard county, Greeting:

We command you to take the body of Jonas Eaker, if he be found in your county, and him safely keep, so that you have his body before our Honorable Circuit Court, now in session, at the court house in the town of Bloomfield, in and for the county aforesaid, then and there to answer for a contempt; and also to show cause why he does not make answer to a writ of mandamus, issued from this court, in favor of Larkin J. Johnson and others, against Jonas Eaker, Judge of the District County Court of Stoddard county; and that you certify to our said court how you execute this writ; and have you then and there this writ.

{L.S.} Witness, Reuben P. Owen, Clerk of said Circuit Court, with the seal thereof hereunto affixed, at office in Bloomfield, this 20th day of May, A. D. 1858.

REUBEN P. OWEN, *Clerk*.

On which writ of attachment the Sheriff of said county of Stoddard made the following return, to wit:

Served the within attachment by taking or arresting the body of Jonas Eaker, on the 20th day of May, 1858. Served in Stoddard county, Missouri.

JAMES DOWDY, *Sheriff*,
by his Deputy, JOHN J. JACKSON.

And afterwards, to wit, on the 21st day of May, A. D. 1858, was filed with the Clerk of said court, during the sitting of said Circuit Court, the following instrument of writing, to wit:

State of Missouri,
County of Stoddard, } *ss.*

The State of Missouri to Jonas Eaker, Judge of the District County Court of Stoddard county, Greeting:

Whereas, it has been represented to me, Albert Jackson, Judge of the Fifteenth Judicial Circuit in the State of Missouri, that at the March term of said District County Court a remonstrance, signed by ten householders of the township through a certain contemplated road, leading from the town of Bloomfield to Kitchen's mill, on Castor river location, presented to said District County Court, protesting against the location of said contemplated road, in accordance with the provisions of the law in such cases made and provided; and whereas, it is represented that the Judge of said District County Court refused to entertain, or take any steps, or make any order in relation said remonstrance, and left the said remonstrants without remedy: These are, therefore, to command you to be and appear before the Circuit Court of Stoddard county, on the first day of the next term thereof, to be held at the court house in the town of Bloomfield, in said county, on the third Monday in May next, to show cause why the relief asked in said remonstrance should not be granted.

Given under my hand, March the 22d, A. D. 1858.

ALBERT JACKSON, *Judge.*

On which instrument of writing, filed as aforesaid, is the following endorsement, to wit:

Now comes the within named Jonas Eaker, and for answer to the within copy of writ of mandamus says, that the within writ was served by the Sheriff by a copy of the original upon him, and declines to make further answer.

May 21st, 1858.

JONAS EAKER,
Judge of the District County Court, Mo.

I, Reuben P. Owen, Clerk of the Circuit Court in and for the county of Stoddard, in the State of Missouri, do certify the foregoing to be a true and perfect transcript of the record and proceedings in the case of Larkin J. Johnson, *et al.*, against Jonas Eaker, Judge of the District County Court of Stoddard county, on petition for a writ of mandamus, as the same appears now remaining on file and of record in my office.

{ L.S. } In testimony whereof, I have hereunto signed my name and affixed the seal of said Circuit Court, at office in Bloomfield, county and State aforesaid, this 22d day of January, A. D. 1859.

REUBEN P. OWEN, *Clerk.*

THE STATE OF MISSOURI *vs.* JOHN R. MAIN.

Be it remembered, that on the 7th day of January, A. D. 1859, was filed in the office of the Clerk of the Circuit Court of Stoddard county, in the State of Missouri, the following papers in the case of the State of Missouri *versus* John R. Main, which papers are in words and figures following, to wit:

To the Honorable Albert Jackson, Judge of the Fifteenth Judicial Circuit in the State of Missouri:

John R. Main, the undersigned petitioner, humbly shows, that he is restrained of his liberty by one John J. Jackson, at the town of Bloomfield, in the county of Stoddard, in the State of Missouri. That on or about the 5th day of January, 1859, he was arrested on a warrant or process issued by one James Cravey, Justice of the Peace in the county of Stoddard aforesaid, charged with grand larceny, and taken before the said Justice, who made and issued the warrant or process, a copy of which is hereto annexed; and by virtue of which, your petitioner is restrained of his liberty as aforesaid. That the property charged as having been stolen by your petitioner, your petitioner held in possession by reason of a contract made with the owner thereof. That said restraint is illegal in that the said magistrate who made the said warrant, by virtue of which your petitioner is restrained of his liberty, did not at any time before committing your petitioner as aforesaid, take the examination of your petitioner, in relation to the offense charged as provided by law; but when your petitioner asked leave to make a statement in relation thereto, said magistrate refused to hear the same, and told your petitioner that what your petitioner could say would make no difference. That the said warrant of commitment is insufficient and defective, and that said magistrate has not certified the examination of your petitioner as by law commanded, and there is no testimony to warrant such restraint. Therefore your petitioner humbly prays that your honor will inquire respecting said restraint, and your petitioner as in duty bound will ever pray, &c.

JOHN R. MAIN.

John R. Main, petitioner above named, makes oath that the above petition and the matters therein are true to the best of his knowledge and belief.

JOHN R. MAIN.

Subscribed and sworn to before the undersigned, Clerk of the Circuit Court of Stoddard county, Missouri, this 7th day of January, 1859.

REUBEN P. OWEN, *Clerk*.
By VAN W. HALE, *Deputy Clerk*.

State of Missouri, }
County of Stoddard, } *ss.*

The State of Missouri to the Constable of Richland Township and the keeper of the Jail of said county of Stoddard, Greeting:

These are to command you, the said Constable, forthwith to convey and deliver into the custody of the keeper of the jail of the county of Stoddard aforesaid, the body of John R. Main, taken and brought before me, a Justice of the Peace within and for the county aforesaid, and charged before me, upon the oath of Robert Whitehead of Stoddard county, with grand larceny; and you the said keeper of the said jail, are hereby required to receive the said John R. Main into your custody into the said jail, and him there safely keep until he shall thence be discharged by due course of law.

Given under my hand this 5th day of January, A. D. 1859.

JAMES CRAVEY, *Justice of the Peace*.

State of Missouri, }
County of Stoddard, } *ss.* "By the Habeas Corpus Act."

The State of Missouri to John J. Jackson, Deputy Sheriff of Stoddard county, Greeting:

You are hereby commanded that the body of John R. Main, under your custody detained as it is said, under safe and secure conduct, together with the day and cause of his being imprisoned and detained, by whatsoever name the said John R. Main may be known, you have before me, Albert Jackson, Judge of the Fifteenth Judicial Circuit of the State of Missouri, at the court house in the town of Bloomfield, in said county, on the —— day of January, 1859, to do and receive what shall then and there be considered concerning the said John R. Main, so imprisoned and detained as aforesaid; and hereof fail not at your peril.

Witness my hand this 7th day of January, 1859.

ALBERT JACKSON, *Judge*.

I do hereby certify and return that the above named John R. Main is in my custody, by virtue of a warrant made and issued by James Cravey, Justice of the Peace in the county of Stoddard, a copy of which is hereto annexed and filed. That I have not in my possession, and never had, any certified examination of said John R. Main, in relation to the offense stated in said warrant, and no testimony in relation thereto.

JAMES DOWDY, *Sheriff*,
by his Deputy, JOHN J. JACKSON.

The State of Missouri *versus* John R. Main. } Charged with Grand Larceny.

The defendant being brought before me in obedience to the within writ, and there being no charge brought against him, nor any evidence produced against him, and there being no evidence that he had been legally arrested and tried before a committing magistrate, or before any one having authority to commit him to the custody of the Jailor of Stoddard county, and the paper herewith presented as a mittimus not being sufficient in form and substance to authorize the Jailor of Stoddard county to hold him, the said John R. Main, in custody, it is ordered that he be forthwith discharged.

January 7th, 1859. ALBERT JACKSON.

State of Missouri,
County of Stoddard, } *ss.*

I, Reuben P. Owen, Clerk of the Circuit Court in and for the county of Stoddard, in the State of Missouri, do certify the foregoing to be a true copy of the petition and affidavit for a writ of habeas corpus, writ of commitment, writ of habeas corpus, and the Sheriff's return thereon, and also the order of the Judge of the Circuit Court discharging the defendant in the case of the State of Missouri against John R. Main, as the same appears now on file in my office.

{ L.S. } In testimony whereof I have hereunto signed my name and affixed the seal of said court, at office in Bloomfield, this 8th day of February, A. D. 1859.

REUBEN P. OWEN, *Clerk.*

MATTHEW H. MOORE *vs.* JAMES WALKER.

Record of the proceedings, orders, and judgments of the Circuit Court for the county of Stoddard, in the Fifteenth Judicial Circuit of the State of Missouri, begun and held at the court house, in the town of Bloomfield, in said county, on Monday the fifteenth day of November, in the year of our Lord eighteen hundred and fifty-eight, before the Hon. Albert Jackson, Judge of the Circuit Courts for the circuit aforesaid.

Be it remembered, that on the 15th day of October, A. D. 1858, was filed in the office of the Clerk of the Circuit Court of said county of Stoddard, a petition in writing, in the case of Matthew H. Moore against James Walker, which said petition is in words and figures following, to wit:

Matthew H. Moore *versus* James Walker. } Circuit Court of Stoddard county, November term, A. D. 1858.

Plaintiff states that on the first day of December, A. D. 1857, he was entitled to the possession of the following described premises, situate in the county of Stoddard, in the State of Missouri, to wit: A tract of land of three and 129-160 acres, purchased by said plaintiff of and from Isaac Hobbs, of said county, beginning at the south-west corner of the town of Bloomfield, and running north, with the west boundary of the town of Bloomfield, twenty-nine poles; thence west twenty-one poles; thence south twenty-nine poles; and thence east twenty-one poles, to the place of beginning; which said tract was by said plaintiff laid out into blocks and lots, and a plat thereof filed in the Recorder's office of said county, on the 17th day of May, A. D. 1858, as an addition to said town of Bloomfield; and being so entitled to the possession thereof, that the defendant, afterwards, on the first day of April, A. D. 1858, entered into that part of said premises known and described as follows, to wit: Beginning at a point twenty-seven feet south of the north-east corner of said tract, and running thence west parallel with the northern boundary line of said tract, to the western boundary line of said tract; thence south, along said line last mentioned, sixty-three feet; thence east to the eastern boundary line of said tract; and thence north sixty-three feet, to the place of beginning; and being sixty-three feet in depth of the southern part of lots numbers one, two, three, four, and five, of block A, as said premises are laid down and described on said plat, filed in said Recorder's office, as aforesaid, and fronting on the north side of Shawanee street, of said addition; and unlawfully withholds from the plaintiff the possession thereof, to his damage in the sum of two hundred dollars. He further avers that the monthly value of the rents and profits of said premises is fifteen dollars. Therefore the plaintiff demands judgment for the recovery of said premises, and two hundred dollars damages for the unlawfully withholding of said premises from said plaintiff, and fifteen dollars for monthly rents and profits, from the day last aforesaid until the possession of said premises be delivered to the plaintiff, and for other proper relief. M. H. MOORE, *Plaintiff.*

State of Missouri, }
Bollinger county, } *ss.*

Matthew H. Moore, the plaintiff named in the foregoing petition, makes oath and says that the foregoing petition, and the matters and things therein as stated, he believes to be true. M. H. MOORE.

Sworn to and subscribed before me this 15th day of September, 1858.

J. C. NOELL,
Clerk Circuit Court, Bollinger county, Mo.

Annexed to said petition, the Clerk of said Circuit Court of Stoddard county issued the following summons, to wit:

State of Missouri, }
County of Stoddard, } *ss.*

The State of Missouri to the Sheriff of Stoddard county, Greeting:

We command you to summons James Walker to be and appear at the Circuit Court of said county of Stoddard, on the first day of the term thereof, to be begun and held at the court house in the town of Bloomfield, in said county and State, on the third Monday of November next, to answer the foregoing petition of Matthew H. Moore, and that you testify to our said court how you execute this writ; and have you then there this writ.

Witness Reuben P. Owen, Clerk of said Circuit Court of said county of Stoddard, with the seal thereof hereunto affixed, at office in Bloomfield, this 15th day of October, A. D. 1858. REUBEN P. OWEN, *Clerk,*
by his Deputy, VAN W. HALE.

On which said petition and summons, the Sheriff of said county of Stoddard made the following return:

Served the within petition and summons on the within named James Walker by delivering him a copy of the same, on the 18th day of October, 1858. Served in Stoddard county, Missouri. JAMES DOWDY, *Sheriff,*
by his Deputy, JOHN J. JACKSON.

And afterwards, to wit, on the 22d day of November, A. D. 1858, at the November term, A. D. 1858, of said Circuit Court, before the Hon. Albert Jackson, Judge, the following proceedings were had in said cause, in said court, to wit:

Matthew H. Moore }
versus } Civil action.
James Walker. }

And now comes the defendant, by his attorney, and files his answer to the plaintiff's petition herein.

Which said answer, filed by said defendant, as aforesaid, is in words and figures following, to wit:

Matthew H. Moore }
against } Civil action, in the Circuit Court of Stoddard county,
James Walker. } Missouri, November term, A. D. 1858.

Defendant, for answer to plaintiff's petition, says, he denies that he (plaintiff) was, on the first day of December, 1857, entitled to the possession of three and

129-160 acres of land, beginning at the south-west corner of the town of Bloomfield, and running north, with the west boundary of said town of Bloomfield, twenty-nine poles; thence west twenty-one poles; thence south twenty-nine poles; thence east twenty-one poles, to the place of beginning; as is set forth in plaintiff's petition. Defendant further answers and says, that he has not sufficient knowledge to form a belief as to whether the plaintiff laid out into blocks and lots three 129-160 acres, and filed plat thereof in the Recorder's office of the county of Stoddard, or not, and therefore requires proof. Defendant denies that he, on the first day of April, A. D. 1858, or any other day, entered into any lands or possessions belonging to plaintiff, as is alleged in plaintiff's petition. Defendant denies that he unlawfully withholds the possession of said lands or other possessions, the property of plaintiff, as is alleged in his petition. Defendant denies that he has damaged plaintiff to the amount of two hundred dollars, or any other amount, by unlawfully withholding the possession of any premises, as is alleged in plaintiff's petition. Defendant denies that the monthly value of the rents and profits of any premises belonging to said plaintiff is worth fifteen dollars, as is alleged in plaintiff's petition.

Defendant states that he is the owner of a certain tract or parcel of land adjoining the west boundary of the town of Bloomfield, in the county of Stoddard, in the State of Missouri, as follows, to wit: Beginning twenty-one poles north of the south-west corner of the town of Bloomfield, in Stoddard county, aforesaid; thence west forty poles; thence north thirteen poles; thence east forty poles; thence south thirteen poles; situated and lying immediately north of the northern fence of the premises occupied by Isaac Hobbs, which said premises has been owned and occupied by defendant and those under whom he claims for more than twenty years, which defendant is ready to verify.

S. G. KITCHEN, *for Defendant.*

James Walker, defendant, makes oath and says that the matters and things as stated in the foregoing answer, he believes to be true.

his
JAMES ⋈ WALKER.
mark.

Sworn to and subscribed before the undersigned, Clerk of the Circuit Court of Stoddard county, Missouri, the 22d day of November, A. D. 1858.

REUBEN P. OWEN, *Clerk.*

And afterwards, to wit, on the said 22d day of November, A. D. 1858, at the November term, A. D. 1858, of said Circuit Court, before the Hon. Albert Jackson, Judge, the following proceedings were had in said cause, in said Circuit Court, to wit:

Matthew H. Moore *versus* James Walker. } Civil action.

And now comes the parties, by their attorneys, and the plaintiff files his petition and affidavit, praying for a change of venue herein. It is therefore ordered that a change of venue be awarded herein to the Circuit Court of Scott county, and that the Clerk of this Court make out a full, true, and perfect transcript of the record in this cause, and transmit the same duly certified to the Clerk of the Circuit Court of said county of Scott, with all convenient speed. Which said petition and affidavit for a change of venue in this cause, is in the words and figures following, to wit:

Matthew H. Moore, Plaintiff, *versus* James Walker, Defendant. } Circuit Court of Stoddard county, November term, 1858.

To the Honorable Circuit Court of Stoddard county:

The undersigned petitioner, plaintiff in the above entitled action, respectfully prays this Honorable Court to award a change of venue herein, because the Judge of said court is prejudiced against him.

M. H. MOORE, *Petitioner.*

Matthew H. Moore, the plaintiff and petitioner above named, makes [oath] and says that the above petition is true, and that he has just cause to believe that he cannot have a fair trial in this action, on account of the prejudice of said Judge.

M. H. MOORE.

Sworn to and subscribed before me this 18th day of November, 1858.

REUBEN P. OWEN, *Clerk.*

State of Missouri, }
County of Stoddard, } *ss.*

I, Reuben P. Owen, Clerk of the Circuit Court in and for the county of Stoddard, in the State of Missouri, do certify that the foregoing is a true and perfect transcript of the record and proceedings in said cause of Matthew H. Moore against James Walker, as the same appears now remaining in my office.

{L.S.} In testimony whereof, I have hereunto signed my name and affixed the seal of said Circuit Court, at office in Bloomfield, county and State aforesaid, this 21st day of January, A. D. 1859.

REUBEN P. OWEN, *Clerk.*

GUSTAVUS BERRY *vs.* JOHN GRIFFIE.

Record of the pleas, proceedings, orders, and judgments of the Circuit Court for the county of Stoddard, in the Fifteenth Judicial Circuit of the State of Missouri, begun and held at the court house, in the town of Bloomfield, in Stoddard county aforesaid, on Monday, the 17th day of May, A. D. 1858, (eighteen hundred and fifty-eight,) before the Honorable Albert Jackson, Judge of the Circuit Courts for the circuit aforesaid.

Be it remembered that on the 1st day of January, A. D. 1858, was filed in the office of the Clerk of the Circuit Court, a petition, bond, and affidavit in writing, in the case of Gustavus Berry against John Griffie, which said petition, bond, and affidavit are in words and figures following, to wit:

Gustavus Berry, Plaintiff, against John Griffie, Defendant. } Civil action by attachment in the Stoddard Circuit Court, to the May term thereof, A. D. 1858.

Plaintiff states that the above named defendant is indebted to plaintiff in the sum of two hundred and eleven dollars, on account of moneys advanced and paid to said defendant upon contract to sell to plaintiff one certain piece or parcel of land, and to build a house thereon for plaintiff, said land situated in the county of Stoddard and State of Missouri, which the said Griffie has failed to do and perform, to the damage of said plaintiff in the sum of two hundred and eleven dollars, for which he asks judgment. The evidence of the indebtedness is herewith filed.

BEDFORD, *for Plaintiff.*

Gustavus Berry makes oath and states that the above petition and the matters and things therein as stated he believes to be true.

GUSTAVUS BERRY.

Sworn to and subscribed before the undersigned, Clerk of the Circuit Court of Stoddard, Missouri, this, the 1st day of January, A. D. 1858.

REUBEN P. OWEN, *Clerk,*
by his Deputy, JOHN W. LEACH.

Gustavus Berry *versus* John Griffie. } Attachment—civil action.

We, Gustavus Berry, as principal, and Moses Neill, Philip P. Neill as his securities, acknowledge ourselves to be indebted to the State of Missouri in the sum of five hundred dollars, for the payment whereof we bind ourselves, our heirs, and executors, and administrators, firmly by these presents, sealed with our seals, this December 31st, A. D. 1857.

The conditions of the above obligation is that whereas Gustavus Berry, as plaintiff, is about to commence a suit by attachment in the Circuit Court of Stoddard county, Missouri, against John Griffie, defendant, returnable to the next term thereof, wherein the sum sworn to is two hundred and eleven dollars: Now, if the said plaintiff shall prosecute his action without delay and with effect, refunding all sums of money that may be adjudged to the defendant, or found to have been recovered by the plaintiff and not justly due him, and pay all damages that may occur to any defendant, or garnishee by reason of the attachment, or any process or proceeding in the suit, or by reason of any judgment, or process thereon, then this obligation to be void, otherwise to remain in full force. Witness our hands and seals this the 1st day of January, A. D. 1858.

GUSTAVUS BERRY, [SEAL.]
his
MOSES ⋈ NEILL, [SEAL.]
mark.
P. P. NEILL, [SEAL.]

Approved the 1st day of January, A. D. 1858.

REUBEN P. OWEN, *Clerk,*
by his Deputy, JOHN W. LEACH.

Gustavus Berry, Plaintiff, against John Griffie, Defendant. } Attachment in civil action, in the Circuit Court of Stoddard county, Missouri, to May term, A. D. 1858.

This affiant, Gustavus Berry, states, that in the above entitled cause he has a just demand against the defendant therein now due, and that the amount which he (the plaintiff) ought to recover after allowing all just credits and set-offs is two hundred and eleven dollars; and that plaintiff has good reason to believe, and does believe, that the defendant is about to remove his property or effects out of this State, with the intent to defraud, hinder, or delay his creditors.

GUSTAVUS BERRY.

Sworn to and subscribed before me this 31st day of December, A. D. 1857.

REUBEN P. OWEN, *Clerk,*
by his Deputy, JOHN W. LEACH.

Annexed to said petition and affidavit the Clerk of said court issued the following writ, to wit:

State of Missouri, County of Stoddard, } *ss.*

The State of Missouri to the Sheriff of Stoddard county, Greeting:

We command you to attach John Griffie by all and singular his lands and tenements, goods, chattels, rights, moneys, credits, evidences of debt and effects, or so much thereof as shall be sufficient to satisfy two hundred and eleven dollars, with interest and costs of suit, in whose possession soever the same may be found in your county, and that you summons the said John Griffie that he be and appear before our Circuit Court of the county of Stoddard, on the first day of the next term thereof, to be held at the court house in Bloomfield, in the said county of Stoddard, on the 3rd Monday of May next, then and there to answer the petition of Gustavus Berry, wherein he asks judgment for two hundred and eleven dollars. And that you summons all persons that you shall find in the possession of goods, moneys, or effects of the defendant not actually seized by you, and all debtors of the defendant, and such other persons as the plaintiff or his attorney shall direct as garnishees, to be and appear before our said court, at the time and place aforesaid, then and there to answer such allegations and interrogatories as may be exhibited against them; and have you then and there this writ.

{L.S.} In testimony whereof, the undersigned Clerk of the Circuit Court has hereunto signed his name and affixed the seal of said court at office, this 1st day of January, 1857.

REUBEN P. OWEN, *Clerk,*
by his Deputy, JOHN W. LEACH.

On which said writ and petition the Sheriff of said county of Stoddard made the following return, to wit:

Executed the within writ of attachment upon the within named defendant, John Griffie, by reading the same in his presence and hearing, January 2nd, A. D. 1858, in Stoddard county, Missouri, and by levying upon and taking into actual [possession] one sorrel horse, about four years ot age; also bridle and saddle, martingales, and one pile of rails, supposed to be one thousand, on the 3rd of January, A. D. 1858. Levied upon the 6th of same month, at same county and State, one ox wagon, and one yoke of oxen, colored, one red, with a white face, the other a brown, with a white face; all of which was levied upon as above stated, as the property of the above named John Griffie.

JAMES DOWDY,
Sheriff of Stoddard county, Mo.

The evidence of indebtedness, filed with said plaintiff's petition, is in words and figures following, to wit:

Know men by these presents, that I, John Griffie, have *sould* all my *wright* and title, *bouth* in law equity, to *Gustavtus* Berry, of a pre-emption made 11th of November, A. D. 1856, one 40, lying section 34; one 80 in section 33. Received payment in full, this the 26th day of November, 1856.

JOHN GRIFFIE.

Know men by these presents, that I, John Griffie, agree to build Mr. *Gustavtus* Berry a *hous* as follows: 18 by 20, I *hugh* the logs, put it up, and under a three foot board *ruf*, and put the chimney to it, 43 hundred rails to be made and put up, for one hundred dollars *payed* in hand; thear is a 11 dollars more payed, which is to be satisfied by labour done on the house, the labour to be completed by the first of May.

November 26th, 1856. JOHN GRIFFIE.

And afterwards, to wit, on the 17th of May, A. D. 1858, at the May term, A. D. 1858, of the Circuit Court of said county of Stoddard, before the Hon. Albert Jackson, Judge, the following proceedings were had in said cause in said Circuit Court, to wit:

Gustavus Berry, *versus* John Griffie. } Civil action—attachment.

And now comes the defendant and moves the court to rule the plaintiff to give security for the costs of this suit.

Which said motion is in words and figures following, to wit:

Gustavus Berry *versus* John Griffie. } Civil action by attachment in the Stoddard Circuit Court, to the November term, A. D. 1858.

John Griffie, defendant in the above cause, moves the court to rule the plaintiff to give new and better security, on the grounds that the security in his bond is wholly insufficient, being insolvent or likely to become insolvent.

C. DAVIS & WASSON,
Attorneys for Defendant.

And afterwards, to wit, on the 20th day of May, 1858, at the May term, A. D. 1858, of the Circuit Court of said county of Stoddard, before the Hon. Albert Jackson, Judge, the following proceedings were had in said cause in said Circuit Court, to wit:

Gustavus Berry *versus* John Griffie. } Civil action—attachment.

The defendant by his attorney comes and files a plea in the nature of a plea in abatement.

Which said plea is in the words and figures following, to wit:

Gustavus Berry *versus* John Griffie. } In the Circuit Court of Stoddard county, State of Missouri, May term, A. D. 1858.

The defendant, John Griffie, denies the matters as alleged in plaintiff's affidavit, and says that he was not at any time before the suing out of the writ of attachment, and filing the affidavit in the same, about to remove his property or effects out of the State of Missouri with the intent to defraud, or hinder, or delay his creditors, as set forth in the said affidavit of plaintiff.

JOHN GRIFFIE.

Sworn to and subscribed in open court this 17th day of May, A. D. 1858.

REUBEN P. OWEN, *Clerk.*

And afterwards, to wit, on the said 20th day of May, A. D. 1858, at the said May term, A. D. 1858, before the Hon. Albert Jackson, Judge, the following proceedings were had in said cause in said Circuit Court, to wit:

Gustavus Berry *versus* John Griffie. } Civil action—attachment.

The parties by their attorneys appear, whereupon comes a jury, to wit: 1 William L. Boyd, 2 Thomas Kenney, 3 Francis M. Smith, 4 Thomas Lingo, 5 Cader Dement, 6 Jesse B. Griffin, 7 Daniel Bridges, 8 James Simmons, 9 William P. Wright, 10 Joseph Mooney, 11 James K. Cook, 12 Thomas J. Walker—twelve good and lawful men, who being elected, tried and sworn to well and truly try the issue joined in the plea in abatement in this cause, and having heard all the testimony offered and argument of counsel, retire to consult of their verdict. When they return here into court, and say, we the jury find that the defendant, John Griffie, was about to remove his property or effects out of this State, with the intent to defraud, hinder, or delay his creditors.

And the defendant files his answer to the plaintiff's petition herein, and this cause is continued until the next term of this court.

Which said answer filed by said defendant as aforesaid, is in words and figures following, to wit:

Gustavus Berry *versus* John Griffie. } In the Circuit Court of Stoddard county, State of Missouri, May term, A. D. 1858.

Defendant denies that plaintiff ever paid him the sum of two hundred and eleven dollars. Defendant says that he sold to plaintiff his pre-emption right, or whatever right, title, both in law or equity, he had to forty acres in section thirty-four, (34;) also eighty acres in section thirty-three, for the sum of two hundred and eleven dollars in goods, and believed by the false and fraudulent representations of plaintiff that he had received the same, but that upon examining said goods he ascertained that they did not amount to the said sum at the prices agreed upon between plaintiff and defendant, but to the amount of one hundred and eighty-six dollars. Defendant further answers that he built said house as he contracted on said land in the county of Stoddard, and the same was ready for delivery. Defendant further says that he has not damaged plaintiff in the sum of two hundred and eleven dollars, or in any other sum, but that he has performed in full his said contract made with said plaintiff.

WASSON & DAVIS, *for Defendant.*

John Griffie, defendant, makes oath and says that the above answer and the matters as therein stated he believes to be true.

JOHN GRIFFIE.

Sworn to and subscribed in open court, May 20th, 1858.

REUBEN P. OWEN, *Clerk.*

And afterwards, to wit, on the 22nd day of May, A. D. 1858, at the May term, A. D. 1858, of the said Circuit Court, before the Hon. Albert Jackson, Judge, the following proceedings were had in said cause, in said Circuit Court, to wit:

Gustavus Berry *versus* John Griffie. } Civil action—attachment.

Ordered by the court that James Dowdy, Sheriff of this county, be allowed the sum of twenty-one dollars, to be taxed as other costs in this cause, for expense of keeping the property attached in this cause.

And afterwards, to wit, on the 18th day of November, A. D. 1858, at the November term, A. D. 1858, of the Circuit Court of said county of Stoddard, before the Hon. Albert Jackson, Judge, the following proceedings were had in said cause, in said Circuit Court, to wit:

Gustavus Berry *versus* John Griffie. } Civil action—attachment.

The parties by their Attorneys appear, whereupon comes a jury, to wit: 1 Henry Miller, 2 Amstead Dowdy, 3 Charles G. Hawkins, 4 Andrew J. Dewblin, 5 James

Cravens, 6 John D. Warren, 7 William C. Randal, 8 Cader Dement, 9 Lemuel H. Jackson, 10 Carter T. Welburn, 11 Jacob Wilfong, 12 Jesse Purtle—twelve good and lawful men, who being duly elected, tried, and sworn, to well and truly try this cause.

And afterwards, to wit, on the 19th day of November, 1858, at the November term, A. D. 1858, of the Circuit Court of said county of Stoddard, before the Hon. Albert Jackson, Judge, the following proceedings were had in said cause, in said Circuit Court, to wit:

Gustavus Berry *versus* John Griffie. } Civil action—attachment.

The parties by their attorneys come, and the jurors in this cause appear all here in court, and having heard all the testimony offered and argument of counsel, retire to consult of their verdict. When they return here into court and say, "We, the jury, find that the defendant is indebted to the plaintiff in the sum of two hundred and twenty-one dollars, and interest from the date of contract."

And afterwards, to wit, on the 19th day of November, A. D. 1858, at the November term, A. D. 1858, of the said Circuit Court, before the Hon. Albert Jackson, Judge, the following proceedings were had in said cause, in said court, to wit:

Gustavus Berry *versus* John Griffie. } Civil action—attachment.

The defendant by his attorney comes and moves the court to grant a new trial herein on reasons filed.

Which motion, filed as aforesaid, is in the words and figures following, to wit:

Gustavus Berry *versus* John Griffie. } Circuit Court, Stoddard county, November term, 1858.

Defendant moves for a new trial in this action; because, first, on the trial plaintiff totally failed to prove any cause of action alleged in the petition. Second, the jury were misled by testimony to prove who was the owner of the land in question at the time of trial. Third, the testimony introduced which tended to prove who was the owner of the land in question at the time of trial should have been excluded. Fourth, the jury were misled by the opinion of the court, that defendant had no interest susceptible of conveyance in the land mentioned in the petition. Fifth, plaintiff on the trial proved no damages. Sixth, on the trial defendant proved performance of the contract alleged in petition. Seventh, the verdict is greater than the testimony warrants.

WASSON, *Defendant's Attorney.*

And afterwards, to wit, on the 20th day of November, A. D. 1858, at the November term, A. D. 1858, of the Circuit Court of said county, before the Hon. Albert Jackson, Judge, the following proceedings were had in said cause, in said court, to wit:

Gustavus Berry *versus* John Griffie. } Civil action—attachment.

The parties by their attorneys appear, and the court having sufficiently advised of the motion to grant a new trial herein, doth consider that said motion be overruled. And the said defendant moves the court in arrest of judgment in this cause on reasons filed; which motion is overruled by the court. To which opinion and decision of the court in refusing to grant a new trial herein, and overruling the motion in arrest of judgment, the defendant objects and excepts.

Which said motion in arrest of judgment, filed as aforesaid, is in words and figures following, to wit:

Gustavus Berry *versus* John Griffie. } Circuit Court of Stoddard county, November term, 1858.

Defendant moves the court to arrest the judgment in this action for this: That, first, the verdict is inconsistent with the plaintiff's demand of relief, in that it is greater in amount than the relief demanded. Second, the jury gave damages for an item in plaintiff's account, which the plaintiff was not allowed to prove, to wit: the item of rails, for which plaintiff claimed one hundred dollars.

WASSON, *Defendant's Attorney.*

And afterwards, to wit, on the 22nd day of November, A. D. 1858, at the November term, A. D. 1858, of the said Circuit Court, before the Hon. Albert Jackson, Judge, the following proceedings were had in said cause, to wit:

Gustavus Berry *versus* John Griffie. } Civil action—attachment.

The defendant by his attorney comes and files his affidavit, and prays an appeal herein to the Supreme Court, which appeal is here granted.

Which said affidavit, filed as aforesaid, is in the words and figures following, to wit:

Gustavus Berry *versus* John Griffie. } Circuit Court, Stoddard county, November term, 1858.

This affiant states that the application for an appeal by John Griffie, defendant in the above entitled action, is not made for vexation or delay, but because this affiant believes that the appellant is injured by the judgment of the court in said action.

JOHN GRIFFIE.

Subscribed and sworn to before me this 20th day of November, 1858.

REUBEN P. OWEN, *Clerk.*

And afterwards, to wit, on the 23rd day of November, A. D. 1858, at the November term, A. D. 1858, of the Circuit Court of said county of Stoddard, before the Hon. Albert Jackson, Judge, the following proceedings were had in said cause, in said court, to wit:

Gustavus Berry *versus* John Griffie. } Civil action—attachment.

And now at this time comes the parties with their respective attorneys, and on motion of the plaintiff he has leave to remit all that sum of in the verdict of the jury in this cause, which exceeds two hundred and eleven dollars, the amount claimed by said plaintiff. It is therefore considered and adjudged by the court, that said plaintiff recover against said defendant his debt aforesaid, in form aforesaid, to the sum of two hundred and eleven dollars, together with his costs and charges by him laid out about his said suit in this cause expended, to which opinion and decision of the court in allowing said plaintiff to remit, and in rendering judgment herein, the defendant objects and excepts. And on motion of the plaintiff, it is ordered that the Sheriff of this county pay over to the plaintiff herein the money arising from the sale of the property attached in this cause, or so much thereof as will pay off and satisfy the judgment in this cause. And the said defendant files his bill of exceptions herein, which is allowed and signed, and made part of the record in this cause.

Which said bill of exceptions is in the words and figures following, to wit:

Gustavus Berry *versus* John Griffie. } Circuit Court, Stoddard county, November term, 1858. Bill of exceptions.

Be it remembered, that in the trial of this cause, a jury was empanneled and sworn to try the issue, and (here insert the testimony,) and the jury (here insert posted.)

Defendant then and there moved for a new trial, for the following reasons: First, on the trial plaintiff totally failed to prove any cause of action alleged in the petition. Fourth, plaintiff in the trial proved no damages. Fifth, on the trial defendant proved performance of the contract alleged in the petition. Sixth, the verdict is greater than the testimony warrants. Which motion was overruled by the court, and defendant then and there objected and excepted to the decision of the court.

Defendant afterwards moved in arrest of judgment for the following reasons, to wit: The verdict is inconsistent with the plaintiff's demand of relief, in that it is greater in amount than the relief demanded. Which motion was overruled by the court, and to which decision by the court defendant then and there objected and excepted and prayed an appeal, which was granted.

On the seventh day of the term plaintiff filed the following motion: Now at this time comes the plaintiff by his attorney herein and moves the court to permit him to remit all of that sum in the verdict which exceeds two hundred and eleven dollars, the amount claimed by said plaintiff in his petition, which motion is granted by the court, and to which decision defendant objects and excepts. The defendant tenders this bill of exceptions, and prays the same may be signed, sealed, and made part of the record in this cause, which prayer is granted.

ALBERT JACKSON.

State of Missouri,
County of Stoddard, } *ss.*

I, Reuben P. Owen, Clerk of the Circuit Court within and for the county of Stoddard, in the State of Missouri, do certify that the foregoing is a full, true, and perfect transcript of the record and proceedings in the foregoing cause of Gustavus Berry *versus* John Griffie, as the same appears now remaining in my office.

{L.S.} In testimony whereof, I have hereunto signed my name and affixed the seal of said court, at office in Bloomfield, county and State aforesaid, this 24th day of January, A. D. 1858.

REUBEN P. OWEN, *Clerk.*

THE STATE OF MISSOURI *vs.* DAVID G. HICKS.

Record of the pleas, proceedings, orders, and judgments of a special term of the Circuit Court, begun and held at the court house in the town of Bloomfield, in Stoddard county, in the Fifteenth Judicial Circuit of the State of Missouri, on Monday, the 9th day of August, A. D. eighteen hundred and fifty-eight, before the Hon. Albert Jackson, Judge of the Circuit Courts for the circuit aforesaid, which said court was ordered to be held by the Judge thereof, in conformity to law.

Be it remembered, that on the 14th day of August, A. D. 1858, at said special term of said Circuit Court, held in August, A. D. 1858, before the Hon. Albert Jackson, Judge of said court, among others, the following proceedings were had, to wit:

The grand jury returns here into court the following bill of indictment, to wit:

The State of Missouri
versus
David G. Hicks. } Indictment for an assault with a deadly weapon, with intent to kill.

A True Bill.

Which said bill of indictment is in words and figures following, to wit:

The State of Missouri,
Fifteenth Judicial Circuit, } *ss.*

In the Circuit Court for Stoddard county, August term, in the year of our Lord one thousand eight hundred and fifty-eight.

The grand jurors of the State of Missouri, empanneled, sworn, and charged to inquire within and for the body of the county of Stoddard, upon their oath do present: That David G. Hicks, late of the county of Stoddard, in the State of Missouri, on the first day of July, in the year of our Lord one thousand eight hundred and fifty-eight, at the county of Stoddard aforesaid, with force and arms, unlawfully, then and there with a certain pistol, which he, the said David G. Hicks, held in his right hand, attempt to shoot one John Conran, with intent him, the said John Conran, to kill, against the peace and dignity of the State of Missouri.

D. G. HICKS, *Circuit Attorney.*

On the back of which said indictment is the following endorsements, to wit:

"(3.) State of Missouri *vs.* David G. Hicks. Attempting to shoot. A True Bill. James L. Hale, foreman of the grand jury. Witnesses—Joseph J. Miller, John P. Conran, H. A. Shook. Filed August 14th, A. D. 1858. Reuben P. Owen, Clerk."

And afterwards, to wit, on the 20th day of November, A. D. 1858, at the November term, 1858, of the Circuit Court aforesaid, before the Hon. Albert Jackson, Judge, the following proceedings were had in said cause in said court, to wit:

The State of Missouri *versus* David G. Hicks. } Indictment for an assault with a deadly weapon, with intent to kill.

The defendant, by his attorney, comes and moves the court to quash the indictment in this cause, on reasons filed, which motion to quash is sustained by the court. It is therefore considered and adjudged by the court, that said defendant of the said indictment and the matters and things therein charged against him be hence discharged, and go thereof without day.

State of Missouri, County of Stoddard, } *ss.*

I, Reuben P. Owen, Clerk of the Circuit Court in and for the county of Stoddard, in the State of Missouri, do certify the foregoing to be a true and perfect transcript of the record and proceedings in the case of the State of Missouri *vs.* David G. Hicks, as the same appears of record now remaining in my office.

{ L. S. } In testimony whereof I have hereunto signed my name and affixed the seal of said court, at office in Bloomfield, county and State aforesaid, this 24th day of January, A. D. 1859.

REUBEN P. OWEN, *Clerk.*

APPOINTMENTS OF DAVID G. HICKS.

Record of the proceedings, orders, and judgments of the Circuit Court for the county of Stoddard, in the Fifteenth Judicial Circuit of the State of Missouri, begun and held at the court house in the town of Bloomfield, in said county, on Monday, the fifteenth day of November, A. D. eighteen hundred and fifty eight, before the Hon. Albert Jackson, Judge of the Circuit Courts for the circuit aforesaid.

Be it remembered, that on the 15th day of November, A. D. 1858, at the said November term, A. D. 1858, of the Circuit Court aforesaid, before the Hon. Albert Jackson, Judge as aforesaid, among others, the following proceedings were had in said court, to wit:

"Ordered by the court that David G. Hicks, Esq., be appointed Circuit Attorney for the time being."

I, Reuben P. Owen, Clerk of the Circuit Court in and for the county of Stoddard, in the State of Missouri, do certify that the foregoing is a true copy of the order of said court, appointing David G. Hicks Circuit Attorney, as the same remains of record now in my office.

{ L.S. } In testimony whereof I have hereunto signed my name and affixed the seal of said Circuit Court, at office in Bloomfield, this 24th day of January, A. D. 1859.

REUBEN P. OWEN, *Clerk.*

Record of the proceedings, orders, and judgments of special term of the Circuit Court, begun and held at the court house in the town of Bloomfield, in Stoddard county, in the Fifteenth Judicial Circuit of the State of Missouri, on Monday, the ninth day of August, A. D. eighteen hundred and fifty-eight, before the Hon. Albert Jackson, Judge of the Circuit Courts for the circuit aforesaid, which said court was ordered to be held by the Judge thereof, in conformity to law.

Be it remembered, that on the 9th day of August, A. D. 1858, at a special term of the said Circuit Court of said county of Stoddard, before the Hon. Albert Jackson, Judge, among others, the following proceedings were had in said Circuit Court, to wit:

"Ordered by the court that David G. Hicks be, and he is hereby, appointed Circuit Attorney, for the time being."

I, Reuben P. Owen, Clerk of the Circuit Court in and for Stoddard county, State of Missouri, do certify the foregoing to be a true copy of the order of said court, appointing David G. Hicks Circuit Attorney, as the same appears of record, now remaining in my office.

{L.S.} In testimony whereof I have hereunto signed my name and affixed the seal of said court, at office in Bloomfield, this 24th day of January, A. D. 1859.

REUBEN P. OWEN, *Clerk.*

PETITION OF WM. M. ATTERBURY FOR WRIT OF HABEAS CORPUS.

To the Honorable Albert Jackson, Judge of the Fifteenth Judicial Circuit in the State of Missouri:

The undersigned, your petitioner, respectfully makes known to your Honor, that one William W. Atterbury is restrained of his liberty at this time by, he believes, Henry Noble, Sheriff of Dunklin county, and *ex officio* Jailor of said county; and he believes that said Atterbury is imprisoned in the jail of said county; that said Atterbury was taken and delivered to said Jailor by one David G. Hicks, on the pretense that he had a capias for him on the charge of embezzlement, which petitioner well knows said Hicks never had, though he believes that said Atterbury is indicted in the Circuit Court of said county for embezzlement; that he prays your Honor to issue a writ of habeas corpus to bring said Atterbury before your Honor, that he may give bail, which he is able and willing to give in Bloomfield, as two good and solvent men will go his bail, but is unable to do so in Dunklin county. Petitioner does not present a copy of the cause of detention, from the fact that he has had no opportunity to apply for the same.

And, in duty bound, he will ever pray.

WILLIAM M. ATTERBURY.

[The 5th section of article 1st is not complied with sufficiently.*]

William M. Atterbury, the above named petitioner, makes oath, and says that the foregoing petition, and the matters therein, as stated, he believes to be true.

WILLIAM M. ATTERBURY.

Sworn to and subscribed before me, this first day of February, 1858.

REUBEN P. OWEN,
Clerk Circuit Court of Stoddard county, Missouri.

On motion of SENATOR VERNON, the Court adjourned.

*The memorandum made by Judge Jackson, and alluded to by Mr. Phelan in his testimony.

EVENING SESSION.

WEDNESDAY, June 15, 1859.

The Court met pursuant to adjournment.
The managers and respondent attended.
The reading of the record evidence offered by the State was resumed.

STATE OF MISSOURI *vs.* SARAH BUCKNER.

Record of the pleas, proceedings, orders, and judgments of the Circuit Court, for the county of Stoddard, in the Fifteenth Judicial Circuit of the State of Missouri, begun and held at the court house in the town of Bloomfield, county aforesaid, on Monday, the 21st day of May, in the year of our Lord eighteen hundred and fifty-five, before the Hon. Albert Jackson, Judge of the Circuit Courts for the circuit aforesaid.

Be it remembered, that on the 7th day of March, A. D. 1855, was filed in the office of the Clerk of the Circuit Court of said county of Stoddard, a transcript of the record and proceedings of the Circuit Court of Bollinger county, in the case of the State of Missouri *versus* Sarah Buckner, which said transcript is in words and figures following, to wit:

State of Misssouri, }
County of Bollinger, } *ss.*

Be it remembered, that at the March term of the Circuit Court, for the year A. D. eighteen hundred and fifty-five, commenced on the first day of March, in the said year, and held at the court house in the town of Dallas, in the county of Bollinger, and State of Missouri, among other proceedings the following were had, viz:

Circuit Court of the county of Bollinger, in the State of Missouri, March term, A. D. 1855.

Thursday, March 1st, A. D. 1855, first day of the term. Court met pursuant to adjournment. Present H. Hough, Judge.

William C. Grimsley, Sheriff of Bollinger county, Missouri, returns the following named persons summoned to serve at this term of this court as grand jurors of said county, viz: Samuel Ramsey, 1; Samuel Whylark, 2; Andrew Seabaugh, 3; George W. Smith, 4; Daniel Seabaugh, 5; Garrett Tidwell, 6; Washington Slinkard, 7; William Stevens, 8; James Check, 9; Caleb Eaker, 10; Drury J. Williams, 11; Alfred Slaugh, 12; Richard H. Winters, 13; William Youngblood, 14; Shadrick Warren, 15; James Step, 16; George Wiggins, 17; Samuel Merida, 18. When Samuel Ramsey was appointed foreman, and the jury having been duly sworn and charged, retire to consult of their duties.

And afterwards, to wit, on the third day of March, A. D. 1855, being the third day of the term, among others, the following proceedings were had:

The grand jury returns into court the following bill of indictment:

The State of Missouri *versus* Sarah Buckner and Susan P. Seabaugh. } Indictment for the murder of Whitson Buckner.

And the grand jury having no further business before them, are discharged.

And whereas, afterwards, to wit, on the said 3d day of March, A. D. 1855, it being the third day of the term, among others, the following proceedings were had on the aforesaid indictment against Sarah Buckner and Susan P. Seabaugh, for the murder of Whitson Buckner; and which said indictment is in the following words and figures, to wit:

State of Missouri,
Tenth Judicial Circuit, } ss.

In the Circuit Court for the county of Bollinger, in the State of Missouri, commenced on the Thursday before the first Monday of March, in the year of our Lord one thousand eight hundred and fifty five.

The grand jurors of the State of Missouri, empanneled and sworn to enquire in and for the body of the county of Bollinger, upon their oath do present, that Sarah Buckner and Susan P. Seabaugh, late of the county of Bollinger, in said State of Missouri, on the tenth day of January, in the year of our Lord one thousand eight hundred and fifty-five, with force and arms, at the county of Bollinger, in said State of Missouri, not having the fear of God before their eyes, but being moved and seduced by the instigation of the devil, upon the body of one Whitson Buckner, in the peace of God and the said State of Missouri then and there living, feloniously, willfully, deliberately, premeditatedly, and of their malice aforethought, did make an assault. And the said Susan P. Seabaugh, with a deadly weapon, to wit, one axe, which she, the said Susan P. Seabaugh, then and there had and held in both her hands, upon the head of him, the said Whitson Buckner, then and there feloniously, willfully, deliberately, premeditatedly, and of her malice aforethought, did strike and beat, giving to the said Whitson Buckner, with the axe aforesaid, divers mortal wounds and contusions upon the side of the head of the said Whitson Buckner, of which said mortal wounds and contusions he, the said Whitson Buckner, did, on the said tenth day of January, in the year of our Lord one thousand eight hundred and fifty-five, at the time and place aforesaid, instantly did die. And the said Sarah Buckner feloniously, willfully, deliberately, premeditatedly, and of her malice aforethought, present, aiding, assisting, abetting, comforting, and counselling her, the said Susan P. Seabaugh, at the time and place aforesaid, him, the said Whitson Buckner, feloniously, willfully, deliberately, premeditatedly, and of her malice aforethought, to kill and murder. And so the jurors aforesaid, upon their oath aforesaid, do say that the said Sarah Buckner and the said Susan P. Seabaugh, the said Whitson Buckner, upon the said tenth day of January, in the year of our Lord one thousand eight hundred and fifty-five, in manner and form aforesaid, at the time and place aforesaid, feloniously, willfully, deliberately, premeditatedly, and of their malice aforethought, did kill and murder, contrary to the forms of the statute in such case made and provided, and against the peace and dignity of the State of Missouri.

H. H. BEDFORD, *Circuit Attorney.*

And on the back of which said indictment are the following endorsements and memorandums, viz:

State *vs.* Sarah Buckner and Susan P. Seabaugh, indictment for murder. A true bill. [Signed] Samuel Ramsey, foreman of the grand jury. Filed 3d March, 1855. O. E. Snider, Clerk Circuit Court. Witnesses—Belinda Bollinger, John Seabaugh, jr., Joseph Gramds, Samuel McDowell, Frederick Wolford, Wm. C. Lee, Susan E. Thornburgh, Anthony Leakafer. Indict. No. 3.

[The transcript in this cause is very lengthy, and we present here only the portions of it which were read at the desk of the Secretary. The omitted portion of the transcript sets out the proceedings in connection with the change of venue to Stoddard county, and the first trial of the accused in that court, setting aside judgment, etc.—REPORTER.]

And afterwards, on the 18th day of November, A. D. 1857, at the November term, A. D. 1857, of said Circuit Court of Stoddard county, before the Hon. Albert Jackson, Judge, the following proceedings were had in said cause, in said court, to wit:

The State of Missouri
versus
Sarah Buckner. } Indictment for Murder.

"Ordered that a *venire facias* issue in this cause, directing the Sheriff of this county to summons a panel of thirty-six good and lawful men from which to select a jury in this cause."

And afterwards, to wit, on the said 18th day of November, 1857, at the November term, 1857, of said court, before the Hon. Albert Jackson, Judge, the following proceedings were had in said cause, in said court, to wit:

The State of Missouri *versus* Sarah Buckner. } Indictment for Murder.

The Circuit Attorney comes, and the defendant, in the custody of the Sheriff, appears in her proper person, and the Sheriff returns the *venire facias* in this cause, with the names of the persons by him summoned as jurors. Whereupon the following jury is selected, to wit: 1 Calvin J. Lester, 2 John S. Galaway, 3 Caleb Hopkins, 4 John B. McPheters, 5 William Rogers, 6 Moses Harvey, 7 Dabney S. Cooper, 8 William B. Cone, 9 Henry E. Sifford, 10 John Singleton, 11 John Thomasson, 12 William Culbertson; twelve good and lawful men, who being duly elected, tried, and sworn to well and truly try this cause; and during the trial of this cause, the defendant's counsel proposed to ask John Seabaugh, a witness on the part of the State, a question, which question was overruled by the court, to which opinion and decision of the court in overruling said question, the defendant excepts, and tenders her bill of exceptions, which is allowed and signed, and made part of the record herein.

Which said bill of exceptions is in the words and figures following, to wit:

State of Missouri *versus* Sarah Buckner. } Indictment for the murder of Whitson Buckner. In the Circuit Court of Stoddard County, State of Missouri, November term, A. D. 1857.

Be it remembered, that on the trial of the above cause, the following proceedings were had: John C. Seabaugh, being introduced as a witness by the State, the following questions were asked of said witness: "Did you ever hear Whitson Buckner say that he had used force and committed a rape upon the person of Susan Seabaugh, the daughter of Sarah Buckner, the defendant?" which question was overruled by the court. To this defendant excepts, and herewith tenders her bill of exceptions, and prays that it may be made a part of the record.

ALBERT JACKSON.

And afterwards, to wit, on the 19th day of November, A. D. 1857, at the said November term, 1857, of said Circuit Court, before the Honorable Albert Jackson, Judge, the following proceedings were had in said cause, in said Circuit Court, to wit:

The State of Missouri *versus* Sarah Buckner. } Indictment for Murder.

The Circuit Attorney comes, and the said defendant, in the custody of the Sheriff, appears; and the jurors in this cause being all present, and during the progress of the trial herein, the defendant's counsel asked Emma Hartle, a witness, a question, which was objected to by the Circuit Attorney, which objection was sustained by the court; to which opinion of the court in sustaining said objection, defendant excepts, and tenders her bill of exceptions, which is allowed and signed, and made part of the record herein; and the jury, having heard all the testimony, retire to consult of their verdict. Which said bill of exceptions, filed by said defendant, is in words and figures following, to wit:

State of Missouri *versus* Sarah Buckner. } Indictment for Murder.

Be it remembered, that on the trial of this cause defendant introduced Emma Hartle as a witness, and, among others, asked the witness this question: "What part of it did you hear him (John Seabaugh) state was true?" to which question the State's attorney objected, which objection was by the court sustained; to which opinion of the court in sustaining said objection defendant excepts, and tenders this her bill of exceptions, and prays that the same may be signed, sealed, and made part of the record in this cause.

ALBERT JACKSON. [SEAL.]

And afterwards, to wit, on the 21st day of November, A. D. 1857, at the November term, 1857, of said Circuit Court, before the Hon. Albert Jackson, Judge, the following proceedings were had in said cause, in said Circuit Court, to wit:

The State of Missouri *versus* Sarah Buckner. } Indictment for Murder.

And now comes the Circuit Attorney, and the said defendant, in the custody of the Sheriff, appears; and the jurors in this cause, to wit, Calvin J. Lester, John S. Galaway, Caleb Hopkins, John B. McPheters, William Rogers, Moses Harvey, Dabney S. Cooper, William B. Cone, Henry E. Sifford, John Singleton, John Thomasson, William Culbertson, all appear here in court, and, being polled, upon their oath do say: "We, the jury, find the defendant, Sarah Buckner, guilty of murder in the first degree, in manner and form as charged in the indictment." And the jurors in this cause are discharged. Whereupon the plaintiff, by her attorney, moves the court to grant a new trial herein on reasons filed.

And afterwards, to wit, on the 14th day of December, 1857, at the said November term, 1857, of said Circuit Court, before the Hon. Albert Jackson, Judge, the following proceedings were had in said cause, in said court, to wit:

The State of Missouri *versus* Sarah Buckner. } Indictment for Murder.

The Circuit Attorney comes, and the said defendant, in the custody of the Sheriff, appears; and the court, having sufficiently advised of the motion to grant a new trial herein, doth consider that said motion be overruled; and the said defendant moves the court to arrest the judgment in this cause, which motion is overruled; to which opinion and decision of the court in refusing to grant a new trial herein, and overruling said motion in arrest of judgment, the defendant excepts, and files her bill of exceptions, which is signed and allowed, and made part of the record herein. Which said bill of exceptions is in words and figures following, to wit:

State of Missouri *versus* Sarah Buckner. } Indictment for Murder. Venue from Bollinger county, Missouri.

Defendant comes and presents her motion for a new trial, which motion is in words and figures following:

State of Missouri *versus* Sarah Buckner. } Indictment for Murder. Venue from Bollinger county.

Defendant, by her attorneys, comes and moves the court for a new trial in this cause for the following reasons: 1st. The verdict is against the testimony; 2d. It is against the weight of testimony; 3d. It is against law; 4th. The court erred in rejecting testimony offered by defendant; 6th. The court erred in instructions given to the jury; 7th. The court erred in refusing to give instructions to the jury asked for by defendant.

PHELAN, MOORE & DAVIS,
Attorneys for Defendant.

Which motion was overruled. She, the said defendant, then presented her motion for an arrest of judgment, which motion in arrest of judgment is in words and figures following:

State of Missouri *versus* Sarah Buckner. } Indictment for Murder. Venue from Bollinger county, Missouri.

Defendant comes, by her attorney, and moves the court to arrest the judgment in this cause, for the following reasons: 1st. Because the court, by overruling questions put in cross-examination to John C. Seabaugh, the only witness introduced by the State, rendered defendant unable to make a defense; 2d. Because no judgment of capital punishment ought to be rendered on the testimony of one witness, without corroborating circumstances tending to prove the offense charged.

WATKINS & PHELAN,
Attorneys for Defendant.

Which is also overruled; to which overruling defendant excepts, which exceptions she prays may be signed, sealed, and made part of the record in the above cause.

ALBERT JACKSON.

And the said defendant, Sarah Buckner, being asked if she has anything to say why sentence of the law should not be passed upon her, answers that she has nothing to say but what she has heretofore said; and the said defendant having been convicted by the verdict of the jury of the crime of murder in the first degree, it is therefore considered and adjudged by the court that said defendant, Sarah Buckner, be taken by the Sheriff of this county to the jail of this county, and there be kept until the fifth day of February, and that she be taken on said day, between the hours of ten o'clock in the morning and three o'clock in the evening, and by said Sheriff hung by the neck until she be dead, and that said plaintiff recover against said defendant her costs and charges in this prosecution expended. Whereupon said plaintiff prays an appeal to the Supreme Court, which is granted. It is, therefore, ordered that execution of the sentence in this cause be staid until the opinion of the Supreme Court can be had in the premises.

The following instructions on the part of the State were given by the court, to wit:

It is the province of the jury to weigh the testimony, and they are the judges of the testimony adduced before them. It is evidence of malice in all cases of willful killing when a deadly weapon is used. If a human being is killed by lying in wait, or by any other willful, deliberate, and premeditated means, the person who struck the fatal blow, and all who are present aiding, abetting, and giving counsel to the perpetrators of the crime are equally guilty; it makes no difference which struck the fatal blow. If the testimony proves that Susan Seabaugh struck the fatal blow, and Sarah Buckner was present aiding and abetting, or present with the intention of assisting Susan Seabaugh, though she rendered no assistance, she is equally liable as if she had struck the fatal blow herself.

The following instructions were asked for by defendant:

1. Before the jury can convict, they must be satisfied, beyond a reasonable doubt, from the evidence, that the accused deliberately, willfully, premeditatedly, and of her malice aforethought, was present aiding and abetting Susan Seabaugh in the murder of said Whitson Buckner.
2. If the jury believe that the witness John Seabaugh swore falsely in any one material part of his testimony, it should go to the discredit of the whole.

The second instruction refused.

The following is the testimony preserved and on file in the foregoing case of the State of Missouri *vs.* Sarah Buckner:

John C. Seabaugh, a witness on the part of the State. Knows Sarah Buckner. Knows Whitson Buckner. Don't know what time it was I last saw Whitson Buckner. I don't know the season of the year. When I saw him last, he came up there where we lived in Bollinger county. I don't know how long it has been since he came there, and I saw him. It must have been about three years since I last saw him. Buckner was burnt up. How did he come to be burnt up? Well, he was burnt up in the house. Suse struck him with an axe. Suse threw down the axe, and mam went and picked it up, and gave him a couple of licks. When I say Suse, I mean Susan Seabaugh. When I say "Mam," I mean Sarah Buckner. Mam told Suse to go and get the axe. Suse then went and got the axe and brought it in the house. Mam then told Suse to do it and strike him. Suse then went and struck him, and then he fell over, and Suse flew back and dropped the axe, and then mam went and gave him a couple of licks. Then we took up the boards and put him under the floor, and then mam tried to wash up the blood and couldn't. Then we went to bed and laid there a little while, and mam said we should get up and set the house a fire. By "we" I mean Suse, mam, and I. We took out some of the things and set the house a fire. Mam set down and commenced crying, and said I should go over to uncle Joe's and tell him to come over. Joe Hahn come over then. I think Suse went over to aunt Malinda's, and then Malinda's two gals come over, and they staid there until morning. That morning Belinda moved mam over to her house. We staid there I think one night and a couple of days. Then one morning uncle Joe come over to aunt Belinda's and said he had dreamt a dreadful dream last night. And he and Whitener went over to where the house was burnt and looked for the man, and found him. Then we went over and built a fire on him and burnt him up. I am speaking of Whitson Buckner. That fire we built would not burn him up, and then we built another and put some of the pieces in the fire. Then we went back to aunt Belinda's and staid there a couple of days. That was the last of it. The house was set on fire and then mam went out and commenced crying. We put him under the floor. I mean by "we," mam, Suse, and me. He was dead when we put him under the house. He was struck on the back of his head, (describing it.) When mam struck him he was lying on his back. I don't know where mam struck him. I reckon she struck him two or three times. He didn't do anything after mam struck. He fell backwards when Suse struck him. When he fell down he sorter grunted, and that was all he done. Mam struck him pretty quick after Suse did. I don't know how long it was after mam struck him before we put him under the floor. It may have been ten minutes or more. (Venue proven.) This took place in Bollinger county, Missouri.

CROSS-EXAMINED.

I said may be it was three years, but I don't know how long. I saw some pieces of him where the fire was, the day we went back to burn him up. It was in the night when we sot the house on fire. I was three or four steps from Suse when she struck him. It was in the night when she did it. I don't know whether there was any light in the house at the time or not—there was a fire. When Suse struck Buckner, he was setting on a chair, before the fire. I saw him a little before she struck, and he was sorter leaning backward. She held the axe with both hands. She went up behind him and struck him. Buckner was in one house, and we were in the other part, when mam told Suse to get the axe. There was a partition or some logs between the rooms, but a [door] to go through. She spoke tolerably loud. I was right again her, and Buckner some distance from her, when she told Suse to strike him. Suse made no fuss when she went up to strike him. When mam struck him, I was three steps from him. I don't know where mam struck him, but along the side of his neck, I believe. She stood at the side of him when she struck him. I didn't count the wounds I saw on Buckner. I saw three I think—one on the back of his head, and the other two about his throat. I don't know how long the wounds were. I saw them whilst we were putting him under the floor. I don't recollect in what position we put him under the floor. I didn't see him turned over after Suse struck him. Did not see Sarah Buckner turn him over. I was in the same house with mam when she struck him—I was three or four steps from her, but don't remember how I stood in relation to "mam." I think the fire was blazing at the time of the occurrence. Susan Seabaugh was the daughter of Sarah Buckner.

Question by Wm. G. Phelan for defense: Did you ever hear Whitson Buckner say that he had used force, and committed a rape upon the person of Susan Seabaugh, the daughter of Sarah Buckner, the defendant. *Question overruled and excepted to; bill of except. filed.* Did you not in the county of Bollinger, about three years ago, the time you speak of, tell Emma Hartle, that it was you and Suse who killed him. That you struck him, and that your mother had nothing to do with it?

Answer. I did not. The occurrence took place at mam's house. He left mam—have no idea how long he was gone from her. I don't know how long he was at mam's before the occurrence. He came in the evening. I forget who was there when Buckner came to the house. I don't know whether mam was at home or not when Buckner came. Mam and aunt Belinda were there, but whether before he came or not I don't know. I don't know whether he had any knife or not; I did not see any knife. Buckner wanted the child, and mam said she wanted it, and he said he 'lowed to have it. He said he 'lowed to take it away. They had parted. The child was sucking.

Did not Whitson Buckner, in your presence, threaten to kill your mother and Susan Seabaugh? I did not hear him make any threats. Did you not communicate this to them? I did not. Did you not swear before Daniel Wolford, a Justice of the Peace, that you struck a blow on Whitson Buckner? (Court adjourned to 9 o'clock.)

STATE RECALLS WITNESS—THURSDAY MORNING.

I can't say how long after they parted before Buckner was killed. They just left and quit living together. They were just married together, and the child I spoke of was mam's child and Buckner's. I think mam had the child when the lick was struck with the axe. I believe that mam sorter give up that Buckner might have the child. Mam just said he might have it then. When she *apeared* to give up the child Buckner was in the house. This was may be an half hour before Buckner was killed, but I don't know.

WILLIAM C. GRIMSLEY.

Knows Sarah Buckner when he sees her. Didn't know Whitson Buckner. I know nothing about the killing of Buckner, except what Sarah Buckner and Susan told me after the trial before the Justice of the Peace, and they were put in my custody as Sheriff of Bollinger county. Sarah Buckner asked me what I thought of her case. I replied, I did not hear the evidence. She then said, I can tell you the whole circumstance; and then she up and related it. She said Buckner came to her house in the evening drunk, and abused her twice by using bad language, and cursing her, and swearing. He wanted the child, and she didn't want to give it up, and they couldn't come to any conclusion at that time. Buckner started to leave, and Malinda Bollinger, her sister, who was then at the house, said I would give him the child *that to* [rather than] have such a difficulty. She said she consented to give him up the child, and told her little son, John (here) to call him back. John called to Buckner and told him to come back, mam wanted to see him. Buckner came back then into the house, and took a chair and set down before the fire. After setting down before the fire, he drew a knife out of his pocket and opened it, and looked around at her while setting in that position. I don't think she said that he said anything—her daughter, Susan Seabaugh, came in with an axe, and came up behind him and then struck him with an axe on the back part of his head, and he fell over dead. She was put in my charge, February, 1855, I think.

CROSS-EXAMINATION.

Mr. J. Pringle and Susan Seabaugh were present at the conversation, and Susan said neither yea or nay about it. She told the same tale several times in my presence, but never varied in the substance of her story. She gave as her reasons for Susan Seabaugh killing Buckner was, that Buckner tried to have intercourse with Susan.

Question. How old is Susan Seabaugh?

JOHN C. SEABAUGH.

Was sworn in the trial before. Did you not swear on a former trial that Whitson Buckner was leaning forward in his chair with his head down when Susan struck him with the axe? Don't recollect whether he did or not. Did you not swear that you saw the eyes of Buckner after he was struck? I don't know as I did. Did you not swear that when Susan struck him he fell upon his face towards the fire? I did not. She struck Buckner with the blade of an axe. I saw blood flow from the wound made on Buckner's head when Suse struck him.

FOR DEFENSE—DAVID R. CONRAD.

I knew Whitson Buckner. The last time I saw him he was at my house. Did you have a conversation with Whitson Buckner charged to have been killed by Sarah Buckner, concerning his seducing or having sexual intercourse with her daughter, Susan Seabaugh? Question objected to and objection sustained. Opinion excepted.

EMMA HARTLE.

State what John Seabaugh said to you in Bollinger county about three years ago, or about the time of the killing of Whitson Buckner took place. Question overruled and excepted to.

Did you hear John Seabaugh say about three years ago, about the time of the killing of Whitson Buckner, in Bollinger county, that it was he and Susan who killed him, and his mother, Sarah Buckner, had nothing to do with it? Answer. I heard him say part of it, and part I did not. Question. What part of it did you hear him state? Overruled by court.

The foregoing is the testimony of John Seabaugh, W. C. Grimsley, and for defendant, David R. Conrad and Emma Hartle.

ALBERT JACKSON.

W. CARLISLE.

Are you acquainted with John Seabaugh? I know him when I see him. Did you hear him swear in this cause? I did. Did you not hear him say in the town of Bloomfield, county of Stoddard, hear him say that he, Buckner, was leaning forward? I did. Did you not at the same time and place hear witness say that he saw his eyes? I did. Did he not say that he fell forward when he was struck. Answer. I am not sure.

The foregoing is the testimony of Carlisle.

ALBERT JACKSON.

State of Missouri, } ss.
County of Stoddard, }

I, Reuben P. Owen, Clerk of the Circuit Court in and for the county of Stoddard, in the State of Missouri, do certify the foregoing to be a true and perfect transcript of the record and proceedings in the case of the State of Missouri *versus* Sarah Buckner, as the same appears now remaining in my office.

{ L.S. } In testimony whereof I have hereunto signed my name and affixed the seal of said court, at office in Bloomfield, county and State aforesaid, this 20th day of January, A. D. 1859.

REUBEN P. OWEN, *Clerk.*

STATE OF MISSOURI *vs.* CHARLES RUSSELL.

Be it remembered that on the 7th day of January, A. D. 1859, was filed in the office of the Clerk of the Circuit Court of Stoddard county in the State of Missouri, the following papers in the case of the State of Missouri against Charles Russell, which said papers are in words and figures following, to wit:

To the Honorable Albert Jackson, Judge of the Fifteenth Judicial Circuit in the State of Missouri:

Your petitioner, the undersigned, Charles Russell, respectfully shows that he is restrained of his liberty by William F. Cryts, in the town of Bloomfield, in the county of Stoddard, and State of Missouri: That, on the 4th day of January, 1859, your petitioner was arrested upon a warrant or process issued by Jonas Eaker, a Justice of the Peace in Stoddard county, and charged with passing a counterfeit half dollar to one Thomas Jackson, and ever since the day aforesaid your petitioner has been, and still is, restrained of his liberty by said Cryts. That, on the 6th day of January, 1859, the said James Eaker, Justice of the Peace aforesaid, examined witnesses touching the matter charged in said warrant or process, but the said Justice of the Peace did not examine nor take the statement of your petitioner touching said matter, and commanded said Cryts to take your petitioner into custody, and in want of bail in the sum of three hundred dollars, your petitioner to keep in custody until the next term of the Circuit Court of said county. That said restraint is illegal, because the said magistrate, the said Jonas Eaker, Justice of the Peace aforesaid, who issued said warrant or process, and committed to custody your petitioner as aforesaid, did not, at any time, take the examination of your petitioner in relation to the offense charged as provided by law. That your petitioner has demanded a copy of the warrant, order, or process, by virtue of which he is restrained as aforesaid of said Cryts, and such copy was refused by said Cryts.

his
CHARLES ⋈ RUSSELL.
mark.

Charles Russell, petitioner above named, makes oath that the foregoing petition and the matters therein are true to the best of his knowledge and belief.

his
CHARLES ⋈ RUSSELL.
mark.

Subscribed and sworn to before the undersigned, Clerk of the Circuit Court of Stoddard county, this 6th day of January, 1859.

REUBEN P. OWEN, *Clerk*,
by his Deputy, VAN W. HALE.

State of Missouri,
County of Stoddard, } *ss*.

The State of Missouri to William F. Cryts, Constable of Castor township, Stoddard county, Greeting:

You are hereby commanded that the body of Charles Russell, under your custody detained as it is said, under safe and secure conduct, together with the day and cause of his being imprisoned and detained, by whatever name the said Charles Russell may be known, you have before me, Albert Jackson, Judge of the Fifteenth Judicial Circuit of the State of Missouri, at the court house in the town of Bloomfield, in said county, on the — day of January, 1859, to do and receive what shall then and there be considered concerning the said Charles Russell, so imprisoned and detained as aforesaid; and hereof fail not at your peril.

Witness my hand this 6th day of January, A. D. 1859.

ALBERT JACKSON, *Judge*.

I do hereby certify and return that I have in custody the above named Charles Russell, by virtue of a verbal order of Jonas Eaker, a Justice of the Peace in and for Stoddard county, Missouri, and that no certified copy of said examination has been delivered to me.

W. F. CRYTS, *Constable*.

State of Missouri
versus
Charles Russell.

The defendant being brought before me by the said William Cryts, and he showing no authority, or mittimus, or warrant, for holding in custody, it is ordered that the said Charles Russell be discharged from the custody of said William Cryts.

January 7th, 1859.

ALBERT JACKSON.

[The Secretary was proceeding to read the remainder of this transcript, when Judge Jackson objected to its being admitted as evidence, on the ground that the portion already read set out fully all his action and proceedings, and that the remaining papers set forth in the transcript were not filed by him, and were not a part of the record in the cause. Mr. Knott stated the nature of the remaining portion of the transcript, argued its admissibility briefly, and called Reuben P. Owen, Clerk of the Stoddard Circuit Court, who testified as to the manner in which the matter to which Judge Jackson objected was filed. The question for the decision of the Court then being, shall the whole transcript be admitted as evidence? the vote stood as follows:

AYES—Messrs. Brown, Byrne, Churchill, Frazier, Goodlett, Gullett, Halliburton, Harris, Horner, Hyer, McFerran, McIlvaine, Newland, O'Neil, Parsons, Peyton, Richardson, Thompson, and Vernon—19.

NOES—Messrs. Fox, Hedgpeth, Morris, and Wood—4.
Absent—Messrs. Johnson, McFarland, Rains, Robinson, Scott, and Wilson.
Absent on leave—Messrs. Coleman and Wright.
Excused from voting—Messrs. Jones and Watkins.

So the question was decided in the affirmative, and the reading of the transcript proceeded as follows:]

And afterwards, to wit, on the 8th day of January, 1859, the following transcript of a Justice's docket was filed in the office of the Clerk of the Circuit Court of said county of Stoddard, to wit:

State of Missouri }
versus }
[Charles Russell. }

Suit brought before the undersigned Justice of the Peace, upon the affidavit of Thomas Jackson, for passing counterfeit money. Writ issued on the 4th day of Jan'y, 1859, delivered to W. F. Cryts, Constable of Castor township, made returnable forthwith. On the said 4th day of January, 1859, said Constable returned said writ executed, by bringing the body of said Charles Russell into court. On the 5th day of January, 1859, the cause *calld*, and the defendant not being ready for trial, for the want of witness, this cause is continued until the 6th day of January, 1859. On said day the *partes* by *ther* attys. *apper* and defendant puts in plea of not guilty; the testimony in the cause being produced, and their testimony reduced to writing, and the court after *hering* the testimony—it is considered by the court that Charles Russell is guilty in manner and form as alleged in the affidavit filed, and that he be held to bail in the sum of three hundred dollars for his appearance at the Circuit Court to be held on the 3rd Monday of May, 1859, and that he have until 10 o'clock, the 7th of January, 1859, to fill his bond for his appearance as aforesaid; and it is further *consided* that judgment be *rended* for the sum of thirty-seven *dolls* and fifty cents, cost accrued in said suit. Judgment *rend* on the 6th day of January, 1859.

JONAS EAKER,
Justice of the Peace.

State of Missouri, }
County of Stoddard. }

I, Jonas Eaker, a Justice of the Peace of Castor township, *with* and for said county and State, do hereby certify the foregoing to be a true transcript of the judgment in said cause, as more fully *apprs* from my docket.

Given under my hand this the 7th day of January, 1859.

JONAS EAKER,
Justice of the Peace.

State of Missouri, } *ss.*
County of Stoddard, }

I, Reuben P. Owen, Clerk of the Circuit Court in and for the county of Stoddard, in the State of Missouri, do certify the foregoing to be a true transcript of the petition and affidavit, writ of habeas corpus, and officer's return thereon, and the order of the Judge discharging the defendant, in the cause of the State of Missouri against Charles Russell, and also a copy of the transcript of the Justice's docket in said cause filed in my office.

{ L.S. } In testimony whereof, I have hereunto signed my name and affixed the seal of said court at office, in Bloomfield, this 9th day of February, A. D. 1859.

REUBEN P. OWEN, *Clerk.*

On motion of SENATOR JONES, the Court adjourned.

TENTH DAY.

THURSDAY, June 16, 1859.

The Court met pursuant to adjournment, and was opened by proclamation.

The managers and respondent attended.

Mr. KNOTT announced that they had no further testimony to offer on behalf of the State until the arrival of absent witnesses; whereupon

JUDGE JACKSON rose and said:

MR. PRESIDENT, AND SENATORS: In going on with this case, it is proper now for me to give you my opinion of the law governing it, as it exists in the State of Missouri, in support of my answer to the charges against me, and to show what the other party must confine themselves to. I will first call your attention to certain constitutional provisions, certain provisions of the constitution of the United States and of the constitution of the State of Missouri. There has been a good deal said about the law and precedents in cases of this kind in the Congress of the United States. But you will see that there is a wide difference between the law of our State, and the law of the United States. Under the laws of the United States, Congress may try a Judge for many things that he would not be answerable for by impeachment in our State. In this State, it is only in certain cases can a Judge be impeached, and we shall see what those cases are. Under the laws of the United States, *all* crimes *and* misdemeanors, when a Judge commits them, he can be impeached for it. In this State, every man must be tried by a jury for a criminal offense, and there is no exception, like there is under the United States law, of cases for impeachment. And there's the great difference that the prosecutors in this case it seems couldn't or wouldn't understand. I will read from the constitution, where it says that the right of trial by jury shall remain inviolate, and that no person can be proceeded against criminally by information or otherwise, except by indictment. These constitutional provisions make certain rules which must guide you in this case. But first, you will see that there is but two classes of offenses that you can try a Judge for. One is, for doing something, or omitting to do something—some official act, which the constitution or law says he shall do. That is one kind of misdemeanor in office. Then there is another class of cases, where a Judge is indicted and convicted by a jury, like another man, for some infamous crime. But first always he must be indicted and convicted of some such crime before you can impeach him. Then it may be that you can go ahead upon the record of that conviction to say he has misdemeaned in office. You all know that the way to proceed against a Judge whom you may think incapacitated for his office by ignorance or imbecility, or peculiarities of temper, is by address, and not by impeachment. The two classes of impeachable offenses, the proceeding by address, and the right of appeal, are sufficient restrictions upon the power of Judges. These provisions of the constitution were inserted when it was the law that the Judges should be appointed by the Governor, and they may have been needed then; but now they are, or some of them are, of very doubtful utility. Now, you know, if a Judge behaves badly, and the people, in whose name all proceedings against him are to be conducted, don't want him in office, they can just turn him out, and put some one in his place who will suit them better. The people select the Judges. Still, they might make a very bad selection; and they might find it out, and want to get clear of him before his time would be out; and then, if he has been guilty of any crime, it would be the duty of the Senate, as the law now stands, to try him, when the House impeached. The House should specify what particular crime he had been convicted of, or what particular act he had done which was a misdemeanor in office, and then it would be the duty of the Senate to turn to the record and see if the thing was so, and then they would pass judgment upon him. The Senate cannot look into his judgments and rulings to see whether they were legal or illegal. That is the Supreme Court's business, and the Senate cannot look into such things.

Now turn to the constitution of the State, Art. II, page 65, 1 vol. Rev. Stat., and what do we find there? I will read:

The powers of government shall be divided into three distinct departments, each of which shall be confided to a separate magistracy; and no person charged with the exercise of powers properly belonging to one of those departments, shall exercise any power properly belonging to either of the others, except in the instances hereinafter expressly directed or permitted.

Now isn't that plain and distinct? I ask you if the Legislature isn't one of these separate and distinct magistracies, and the Judiciary another? Then it says, "no person charged with the exercise of powers properly belonging to one of those departments, shall exercise any powers properly belonging to either of the others." Now, gentlemen, if you investigate the legality or illegality of my official acts, ain't you acting in the judiciary capacity? Didn't they contend, in the House of Representatives, that they were a grand jury? A grand jury cannot exist out of the Judiciary department. Yet they all took an oath that they would observe the constitution of Missouri. Now if this Art. II of the constitution means anything, it must mean that when you act as legislators, you shan't act as judiciary. What right, then, had they to act as a grand jury?

A Judge, like everybody else, may make mistakes in his acts. Now his acts—if they are wrong, how is that provided for? If he has done anything wrong, any party may appeal to the Supreme Court and be righted. That is the way the constitution has provided for such cases. How then can the Legislature take the place of the Supreme Court? How can the Senate undertake to decide with regard to the legality of my official disposition of bills of exceptions, applications for changes of venue, and the like of that? Now, you will remark that they don't say that I did any of this for bribery. Admit that I sent cases on changes of venue to counties remote and inconvenient, and that it was illegal for me to do so. Could they not appeal? My action was not final. They could take all such cases to the Supreme Court, and if what I did was wrong, that is the way to get at it. They,—the Supreme Judges,—would rectify any errors I might make. Though you may think I was wrong, that is not the way to get at it, for you to pass judgment upon it. In that you exercise powers not belonging to your department, which the constitution says you shan't do, except in certain instances in it directed and permitted. Now, what are these exceptions? Why they are only in cases of impeachment. But, then, let me turn to that clause in the constitution which empowers the Legislature to impeach, and see what it is for:

The Governor, Lieutenant Governor, Secretary of State, Auditor, Treasurer, Attorney General, and all Judges of the courts of law and equity, shall be liable to impeachment for any misdemeanor in office; but judgment in such case shall not extend farther than removal from office, and disqualification to hold any office of honor, trust, or profit, under this State.

That is the constitution of Missouri. Now, the constitution of the United States provides:

The President, Vice President, and all civil officers of the United States, shall be removed from office on impeachment for, and conviction of, treason, bribery, or other high crimes and misdemeanors.

You must see the difference. In one the impeachable matter must be "any misdemeanor *in office*." In the other it is "conviction of treason, bribery, or other high crimes and misdemeanors." Misdemeanors *in office* and high crimes and misdemeanors are very different things. Now, what are misdemeanors *in office?* Where will you look for what misdemeanors in office are? You must look to the constitution and laws. What does the constitution say about it? We will look to that first. Well, the constitution says that a Circuit Judge must reside and be a conservator of the peace in the circuit for which he is Judge. Now suppose a Circuit Judge doesn't reside in his circuit. He is not indictable for that, because it couldn't be a crime in itself. But he could be impeached; and suppose he was, then you would inquire into that matter,—whether he did live in his circuit or not,—and not into his official conduct. You would have nothing to do with that. Again, the constitution says that no person shall be appointed Judge of the Circuit Court before he has attained the age of thirty years. Now if a man does act as Judge before he is thirty, he can be impeached, and you would inquire into his age, not into his official conduct. So it is if he holds the office after he is sixty-five years of age. For that he would be impeachable; but you couldn't examine into his conduct on the bench. That is not your province.

The judiciary can't examine into the manner you discharge your duties. If you are sent here faithfully to represent the people, and you don't discharge your duties, or discharge them improperly, can they,—the judiciary,—enter your province and arraign you for that? If they were to attempt it, you would tell them "no, you can look at the laws we pass,—you must be the judges of whether they are constitutional,—but that is all you can do. You are not the judges whether they are good or bad laws, and our behavior while we were making those laws, is none of your business." The reason for all this is that the two departments of the government are distinct and separate, and one is not to infringe on the other. Like any other officers of the government, you may be arraigned for treason and bribery, and you can be indicted for your own individual, personal crimes. So with a Circuit Judge. He is as free as you. And his personal official demeanor is no more a matter for your courts than yours is for his.

Suppose the President of the Senate raps on his desk when he thinks some captious member is out of order, is that insolence? Suppose the President happens to think a member is out of order when he is in order, and he tells him he is out of order and must sit down. Is that oppression in office? Most certainly not. So, too, it is with the Judge in court. It is his duty to keep order, and whenever he thinks an attorney out of his place, he may call him to order, and to enforce obedience to his orders, he may send the attorney to jail. If the Judge mistakes his duty,—if he abuses it,—it is not oppression in office. For his decisions, if wrong, they can be rectified by the Supreme Court, and for all else he is responsible alone to his constituents—the people who placed him in office, and can remove him if they see proper. If he is not corrupt in office, he can't be impeached. But, so much for the constitution, and all that can be learned from it about misdemeanors in office.

Now let us turn to the statutes on the same point. In the act concerning courts, in sec. 58, p. 541, it is provided that "no Judge shall practice, or act as counsellor or attorney, in any court within this State." Further, in sec. 60, it is provided that "no Judge shall have a partner practicing in the court of which he is Judge." Now, there are some cases in which a Judge might commit some misdemeanors in office. If I have acted as an attorney, or if I have had a partner practicing in any of my courts, then I am guilty of a misdemeanor in office, and I can be impeached.

In section sixty-three it is provided that any person violating the provisions of this act, shall be deemed guilty of a misdemeanor in office. Now, then, in this case, are either of these charges alleged against me? If so, you can try it. If not, so far you have nothing to do.

But this is one of the two classes of impeachable offenses. We will, now, examine into the other, and see how it affects me in this case. I read from the constitution, article three, a section found on page 67:

SECTION 14. The General Assembly shall have power to exclude from every office of honor, trust or profit, within this State, and from the right of suffrage, all persons convicted of bribery, perjury, or other infamous crime.

There is the constitutional clause upon which this last class of impeachable cases is founded. Mark you, it says "all persons *convicted* of bribery, perjury, or other infamous crime." Here, in the section which follows, is another:

SECTION 15. Every person *who shall be convicted* of having, directly or indirectly, given or offered any bribe to procure his election or appointment, shall be disqualified for any office of honor, trust, or profit, under this State; and any person who shall give or offer any bribe, to procure the election or appointment of any other person, shall, *on conviction* thereof, be disqualified for an elector, or any office of honor, trust, or profit, under this State, for ten years after such conviction.

Can anything be plainer than that the first thing to be done in any case of this kind is to procure the conviction, and that no man, under this clause of the constitution can be disqualified for office until he is convicted. If it is a Judge against whom such a charge is made, and he is impeached, you have nothing to do but to go to the record and see if any conviction is set down there. The record is all you can examine. If the party making the charge happened to be mistaken as to the existence of the conviction, the Judge would have to be acquitted. If it were otherwise, although you might think that the conviction was an unjust one, the mere fact of the record showing there was a conviction would sustain the impeachment. There is the provisions, and I hope the Senators will examine them carefully for themselves. I conceive the constitution on this point to be very clear. I believe I read before that clause which says, the right of trial by jury shall remain inviolate. I will come to that again, though, after awhile, in commenting upon what Mr. Knott said in his opening remarks. I will read this:

That, in all criminal prosecutions, the accused has the right to be heard by himself and his counsel; to demand the nature and cause of accusation; to have compulsory process for witnesses in his favor; to meet the witnesses against him face to face; and, in prosecutions on presentment or indictment, to a speedy trial by an impartial jury of the vicinage; that the accused cannot be compelled to give evidence against himself, nor be deprived of life, liberty, or property, but by the judgment of his peers, or the law of the land.

And here is another section bearing on the same point:

That no person can, for an indictable offense, be proceeded against criminally by information, except in cases arising in the land or naval forces, or in the militia, when in actual service in time of war or public danger, or by leave of the court, for oppression or misdemeanor in office.

You will see that you cannot proceed against me, in indictable matters, by information of oppression or misdemeanor in office, except by leave of the court. If the House ever proceeds in this way, it must be in cases not indictable. Now, turn to that part of the law providing for impeachments, and you will understand this, perhaps, better than I do. That law says, that when a party is convicted or acquitted in an impeachment proceeding, he shall, notwithstanding such conviction or acquittal, be subject to indictment, trial, judgment, and punishment for any indictable offense, according to the law of the land. I hold that if he can be indicted as well as impeached, I hold that the indictment must precede the impeachment, and be the basis of it. If this statute has any other construction, it is clearly unconstitutional.

There are provisions in the constitution of the United States similar to those of our State constitution, which I will here pause to read, that you may not only see what governing effect they must have in this case, but that you may mark the difference. I read the fifth and sixth articles of the amendments to the constitution:

ARTICLE V. No person shall be held to answer for a capital, or otherwise infamous crime, unless on a presentment or indictment of a grand jury, except in cases arising in the land or naval forces, or in the militia, when in actual service in time of war or public danger; nor shall any person be subject for the same offense to be twice put in jeopardy of life or limb; nor shall be compelled in any criminal case to be a witness against himself, nor be deprived of life, liberty, or property, without due process of law; nor shall private property be taken for public use, without just compensation.

ARTICLE VI. In all criminal prosecutions, the accused shall enjoy the right to a speedy and public trial, by an impartial jury of the State and district wherein the crime shall have been committed, which district shall have been previously ascertained by law, and to be informed of the nature and cause of the accusation; to be confronted with the witnesses against him; to have compulsory process for obtaining witnesses in his favor, and to have the assistance of counsel for his defense.

I will refer you back now to the provision of our own State constitution, which provides that the General Assembly shall have power to exclude from every office of honor, trust, or profit, all persons convicted of bribery, perjury, or other infamous crime, and also to the one providing for impeachments, for misdemeanors in office. You see that the cases of bribery, perjury, and other infamous crimes are all provided for, in a certain way, and that when it is sought to disqualify a man for office for one of these things, he must first be convicted. Now, let us look after these misdemeanors in office. It is clear that mere mistakes of a Judge are not misdemeanors. There is another provision for them.

Now I want to illustrate the effect of the doctrine maintained here by the managers in this case. They will admit that everybody else but Judges can always avail themselves of the right of trial by jury. But when any one thinks a Judge can do wrong, what can he do? Why, he can try to get him indicted; and if he don't succeed in that, he can go up to the Legislature, drag the Judge after him, and there cut him off from the means of defending himself before an impartial jury of the vicinage. If he commits any offense, it would be better, under this view of the law, not to try to indict him. No, you could inflict on him a much worse punishment. He may have acquired a name that he was proud of; but cutting him off from the means that other men have to defend their fair names, you tell him to go forth disgraced, and that he is not worthy of any trust or honor. And this is to be done, not by the people who elected him, but by the Legislature. The statutes have laid it down that the people have a right to choose their own Judges. But here it seems that this is a mere cheat. After they have elected a Judge, if he does not suit the Legislature, they dismiss him with disgrace. This is the kind of doctrine that the managers are maintaining here. They say, to be sure, if a Judge has committed a crime, he may be indicted; but we won't do that. He is a stain upon the judiciary of the whole State. We must select a mode of trial for him where he will have no chance. He must be tried, not in a court,—not in a proper tribunal accustomed to the protection of innocence and the punishment of guilt,—but you take him without indictment or sufficient specific charges and try him in the Legislature. If he were indicted, like others, he would have a hand in the selection of a jury. Here it is different, and he can do nothing of the kind. You recollect that the constitution says a man cannot be deprived of life, liberty, or property, but by the judgment of his peers, or the law of the land. Now haven't I, as a Circuit Judge, a property in this office. It was given me for a time by the people. Most certainly I have a property in it. And will you take it away from me without the judgment of my peers? Who are my peers? I tell you plainly that you are not. My compeers are higher than Senators, or Governors, or Representatives. A Judge does not cease to be a citizen, and as a citizen, citizens are his compeers. He has a right to select the best of them, and when he does, he selects higher than Senators or Representatives. I mean no disrespect. Your capacity of citizen is higher than your capacity of Senator, and higher than any other capacity. A good citizen is nothing more nor less than an honest man, and "an honest man is the noblest work of God."

I have thus given you my views of the constitutional aspect of this case, not because I wanted to be technical, but because I wanted you to get at the foundation of the law on this subject. I would not avail myself of a merely and exclusively technical defense. I will now pass to this law which they say these articles are particularly founded upon. You will readily see that the whole or nearly the whole of this article in the criminal code of our State, rests on the provision of the constitution to which I referred you. I will read several sections to get at the connection of the section that they claim as giving authority for the proceedings here against me, giving you my comments as I go on:

SECTION 1.—Every person who shall, directly or indirectly, give any money, goods, right in action, or any other valuable consideration, gratuity or reward, or any promise, undertaking or security therefor, to any officer of this State, or of any county: *First,* With intent to influence his vote, opinion, judgment or decision, on any question, matter, cause or proceeding, which may be then pending, or may, by law, be brought before him in his official capacity, or to induce him to neglect or omit the performance of any official duty, or to perform such duty with partiality or favor, otherwise than is required by law; or, *Second,* In consideration that such officer hath given any vote, opinion, judgment or decision, in any particular manner, upon any particular side, or more favorable to one side than the other, *or* [on] any matter, question, cause or proceeding, or hath omitted to perform any official act or duty, or hath performed such act or duty with partiality or favor, or otherwise contrary to law, shall, on conviction, be adjudged guilty of bribery, and be punished by imprisonment in the penitentiary for a term not exceeding seven years.

It is plain that there is nothing in this section especially applicable to Judges. It was intended by it to provide a punishment for the man or person who bribes a Judge, rather than to the Judge. It applies to the man who gives a bribe—not to the man who takes it. But here is the section that follows:

SECTION 2. Every such officer who shall, directly or indirectly, accept or receive any gift, consideration, gratuity or reward, or any promise or undertaking to make the same: *First*, Under any agreement that his vote, opinion, judgment or decision, shall be given in any particular manner, on any particular side, or more favorably to one side than the other, in any question, matter, cause or proceeding, which may be pending, or be brought before him in his official capacity, or that he shall neglect or omit to perform any official duty, or perform the same with partiality or favor, or otherwise than according to law; or, *Second*, In consideration that he hath given his vote, opinion, judgment or decision, in any particular manner, on any particular side, or more favorably to one side than the other, of any question, matter, cause or proceeding, or hath neglected or omitted to perform any official act or duty, or performed such act or duty with partiality or favor, or otherwise contrary to law, shall, on conviction, be adjudged guilty of bribery, and shall be punished by imprisonment in the penitentiary for a term not less than two years.

That section, now, applies to Judges, as well as to other officers. Read it,—look at it yourselves,—and say if you could take cognizance of an offense of this kind before there was a regular trial and conviction in a regular criminal court. You couldn't do it. You couldn't think of doing it. If a Judge has been bribed, he is thereby disqualified for his office. But that part of his punishment is not administered by the court which tries the fact of the bribery, but is administered by the Court of Impeachment, which can only inquire if there has been a conviction.

The next section of this article applies to persons using bribes to procure offices and appointments. And so on with the twelve sections which follow. They fix penalties for the various forms that bribery and corruption in office may assume. None of them apply to Judges in the corrupt discharge of their duties,—except the second, which I have read. But the law goes on, pointing especially at Judges first, and then on down, and after enumerating almost every kind of officer, or the form that corruption would assume in almost every kind of office, we have the sixteenth section, which I will read:

SECTION 16. Every person exercising or holding any office or public trust, who shall be guilty of willful and malicious oppression, partiality, misconduct or abuse of authority in his official capacity, or under color of his office, shall, on conviction, be punished by imprisonment in a county jail for a term not exceeding one year, and [by] fine, not exceeding one thousand dollars.

Here is the great thing upon which they rely in this case. Under this section I have been arraigned before you, and I hold that there is nothing in the section having a more direct application to me than to any one of you. If my office is one of public trust, yours is also. If I am responsible under this section for a mistake as to my authority and of the law, you are equally responsible for mistakes in your legislation. How does it stand with you when you pass an unconstitutional law? You do that occasionally, you must admit, and when you do, are you individually and collectively indictable? I hold that an office of public trust,—such a one as is meant by this statute,—does not include either a Judge or you. It refers to ministerial officers. I am as clearly exempted from the special operation of that statute as you are. If I could be indicted under this section for official acts, you could also, and then how would it be? According to Mr. Knott,—that is, if Mr. Knott's notion of this section is correct,—you could be indicted for almost every and any official act in which you participate. You may vote for railroad bills. The opponents of these bills say it is high-handed oppression in office, and indict you for it. You may vote against them, and the friends of the roads indict you for willfully and maliciously neglecting and refusing to advance the best interests of the State. Mr. Knott's construction of this statute would lead to this with you. With me it would be worse, because the instances when people are dissatisfied with decisions against them by Judges are more frequent, perhaps, than with laws.

But, even if I am indictable for my official acts, by this section, that does not make it right to impeach me for them. And if I am impeached for them, it doesn't dispense with the necessity of having a record of a conviction for them in the impeachment court. The law does not stop at this point exactly. I will read the seventeenth and eighteenth sections:

SECTION 17. Every officer or public agent of this State, or of any county, who shall commit any fraud in his official capacity, or under color of his office, shall be adjudged guilty of a misdemeanor, and punished by imprisonment in the county jail for a term not exceeding one year, or by fine, not exceeding one thousand dollars, or by both such imprisonment and fine.

SECTION 18. Every person who shall be duly convicted of any of the offenses mentioned in the preceding sections of this article, shall be forever disqualified from holding any office of honor, trust or profit, under the constitution or laws of this State, and from voting at any election.

The twenty-third section also has some bearing on this point, and I will here read it:

SECTION 23. Every officer who shall be convicted of any official misdemeanor or misconduct in office, or who shall be convicted of any offense which, by this or any other statute, is punishable by disqualification to hold office, shall, in addition to the other punishments prescribed for such offenses, forfeit his office.

From all these sections it is very plain that those who hold me, or any Circuit Judge, amenable for any alleged offenses under these sections, are mistaken as to the meaning of the sections; and if they are not mistaken about that—if Circuit Judges are meant—the only or first thing to be done, is to indict and procure a record of conviction, to be used in divesting the Judge of his office. So far as that is concerned, however, as I have before said, I would waive the necessity of an indictment if there was any plainly stated and specific charges brought against me. In this sixteenth section, we read the punishment of an offense styled "willful and malicious oppression" in an official capacity. Now, how can that apply to a Judge? It is the duty of a Judge to declare the law —not to execute it. If he declares the law to be so and so, that cannot be oppression in the Judge. If the effect is oppressive, it is the oppression of the law—not of the Judge. The consequences of the law being declared and ruled in a certain way, are not to be reckoned back to a Judge in that way, surely. When a Judge sentences a convicted criminal, it is not the personal, individual act of the Judge. No strictly official acts are personal acts. And when an instance of oppression comes up, it is the oppression of the law, and cannot be of the Judge. A Constable, Jailor, or other ministerial officer, may act very oppressively under color of discharging his duty; but it is absurd to say that a Judge, whose province it is to say what the law is, can be oppressive in declaring that law to be in a certain case as he conceives it to be. When he enforces a decision, he enforces the law. When his decision is oppressive, the law is oppressive. Now, it is against the theory of our government, and against common sense, to call law oppressive. It might do in some particular instances to say that certain enactments of law were unwise, and had an oppressive tendency. But the law cannot be willfully and maliciously oppressive. You cannot impute malice to law. If, then, it is the province of the Judge to declare the law, and his decisions are law, his decisions are no more oppressive than the law. The only way to avoid this conclusion is, to deny that the decisions of a Judge are law, and that would not help the matter for the prosecutors in this case; for when a Judge of the Circuit Court declares the law in a case to be so and so, who can review his decision, and say it is not law? Who can overrule the decisions of a Circuit Judge? No earthly power but the Supreme Court. The constitution and laws of this State give *you*—gives this Senate—no such power; and I will not suppose that it seeks to exercise it by usurpation.

But, gentlemen, so much for the law of this case. I will now advert to the facts. I hold that neither in the constitution, nor laws, nor even in the celebrated section paraded here by Mr. Knott, is there any ground for this proceeding against me. But that is not all. Even the facts don't make out any case. I propose now, gentlemen, to run over, as briefly as I can, the facts elicited from the State's witnesses that have been examined, and, in doing so, I shall detain you but a short time.

Mr. Knott objected that this was not the proper time for the respondent to comment upon the evidence adduced by the State, and that he could now merely state the grounds of his defense.

Mr. Hardin supported the position of his colleague by a reference to several authorities, and argued the impropriety and illegality of the course proposed by the respondent.

Senators Parsons, Watkins, Scott, Goodlett, and Wilson, stated the practice of the courts with which they were respectively familiar in regard to this point; and an animated discussion was going on, when

Judge Jackson said: I have no wish to comment upon the evidence any further than is necessary in stating the grounds of my defense. I will endeavor not to violate the rule as it seems to be understood by the Senate, and, if I do so, let me be stopped.

I now propose to look at the articles of impeachment in this case first, and in connection with my comments upon them, to state such facts as I deem material to my defense. In doing this, I will allude to the nature and quality of the language in which the charges against me are dressed, and also to the nature of the acts imputed to me. I shall endeavor to show that these articles of impeachment have been got up in a manner which ought not to have been exhibited.

Now, it is almost the universal opinion,—it is the belief and opinion of the whole State, and perhaps of the whole United States,—that when a Judge is impeached, his own personal, individual character goes in with it; in other words, that to attack a Judge by impeachment is to attack his character. Yet it is obvious from an examination of our law that an impeachment in this State does not involve character at all. The article of the constitution providing for impeachments provides simply and only for misdemeanors. Now, there is nothing dishonorable or infamous in these misdemeanors. It is a misdemeanor for which a Judge can be impeached to practice law. Yet is not dishonorable to practice law. It is a misdemeanor for a Judge to be under thirty years of age. Yet there is nothing disreputable about that. And it is certainly not discreditable or dishonorable to be over sixty-five. I have heard it said, on the contrary, that gray hairs were as good as curls. Yet a Judge is not permitted to be over sixty-five, and if he acts as such after he has attained that age, he commits a misdemeanor for which he can be impeached. There is nothing dishonorable if a person doesn't take an oath to faithfully do so and so. Yet a Judge can be impeached for that. There is nothing criminal about any of these things—nothing involving character. So it is if a Judge doesn't reside in his circuit. Suppose the Judge of the Fifteenth Judicial Circuit chooses to live in St. Louis or Jefferson City; they are pleasant enough places, and it is not disreputable to live in either place. Yet the Judge could be impeached for it. This is the entire list of impeachable misdemeanors in office. I leave the other class of impeachable offenses out of view, now, because none of them are alleged against me. In this whole list there is not one act dishonorable or disreputable in itself. Would it not have been easy enough, then, to have stated the charges against me in temperate language, without reflecting upon my character as a man. These articles do reflect upon my character in a most unwarrantable manner. It may be said that they have attempted to charge me with other acts than those I have named, but still I think that the charges might have been and should have been put in dignified, respectful language. It is nothing to me that I may be at liberty to reply in the same tone and style. There is no use in my showing how bad the House acted in the matter, and how they were all led away from reason and law by a few interested men, who had managed to get themselves on the Judiciary Committee. These things may be so, but really I don't like to be arraigned on such charges, and dislike to make such a defense to any charge.

Look at the beginning of this thing. At first it is the act,—the solitary act of one man,—and that man one who it is notorious was my competitor for the position which I hold. When that man failed to turn me out of the office by producing dissatisfaction among the people of my circuit,—when my circuit refused to be dissatisfied with me,—and he could not effect his object in that way, then he appeals to the Legislature to do it. The General Assembly is called upon to do what the people have had an opportunity of doing, and what they would not do. It does seem to me that the Legislature, in considering this matter, ought to have looked at it like other sensible men are bound to do. If the complaint comes only from one man, they should weigh that complaint more. The fact that there is now and has been no general complaint is a material fact for you to notice. By looking over the business of the House you will see that the petition of Solomon G. Kitchen alone started this whole proceeding. I believe you all want to do me justice. I believe there isn't a Senator here, but that would rather I should be able to maintain my rights than that I should fail of doing so. Then, I say, if you have doubts on the score of my guilt or innocence, let your minds revert to the origin of this matter. Reflect that it is a notorious fact, that a single citizen of my circuit, and that one a notoriously embittered personal enemy, has instituted these proceedings, and evidently not because he believes or can establish the fact that the people of the circuit will support him in it, but because as a Judge and man I have acted in such a way as did not suit him or his purposes.

But you can look at this point in another light. Now, then, let me suppose that you take it for granted that this single citizen of my circuit had a right to institute these proceedings against me. Let it be assumed as a *prima facie* case that this citizen is honestly of opinion that I ought to be impeached for the good of my country, and not to gratify his personal enmity, and that he came here in all honesty and sincerity, and did this thing out of respect for his country's laws. Now, then, if this is the *prima facie* state of the case, most certainly I have a right to show that that is not the fact, and that the proceedings against me were conceived and brought forth by malice alone. And to do this, I have only to point out the petition with which the thing was done, and ask you to compare it with the articles of impeachment. The petition contains almost an entirely different set of charges from that set out in the articles. After he got here, and was fully counseled and advised about the matter, he concluded to abandon the charges on which he came here, and substitute new ones. This, of itself, is a very significant circumstance. There is one instance particularly, to which I must direct your attention. In the petition, at one point, I am charged with a great outrage in refusing a trial to a man, and it was alleged that I thereby caused his death. This was a great thing, and much parade was made of it in the petition. Well, now, look through the articles of impeachment and you will see that that great charge has entirely disappeared. It seems they couldn't get this charge that I had killed a man through the committee. Now, what was the reason? When it came up in the committee room there was considerable discussion over it.

Mr. Knott. Mr. President: No testimony has been offered in relation to this matter. None can be offered, because it is a wholly outside matter. With what propriety, then, can the respondent go on in this style, with assertions about the committee of the House which he cannot substantiate with proof, and which the rules of evidence would not permit us to contradict? I certainly think it is out of order.

Judge Jackson. Never mind, Mr. Knott. Wait till I get through, and you will see that what I say is material enough. It may interest you more than you think for now. It seems that the committee had got hold of my reason or excuse for not trying the man, and it affected some of them more closely than they expected. I did not know what the jury law for that county was, because, although one had been made for it, I had received no copy of it, as I should have done, and the fault lay near the doors of the committee itself. One of the committee who was familiarly designated as Charley was quite anxious to put this killing charge in. But another said, "Now, Charley, you know that won't do. You know who is to blame for his not getting the jury law, and at last that will come out; and who will be sued, if it does come out?" And there was something about a squib which settled the matter.

Senator Thompson said that he thought the respondent was now clearly out of order. He had expected him to confine himself, in his remarks at this time, to the law and the evidence upon which he expected to base his defense; and he had no desire to hear the strictures upon the committee which the respondent was now uttering.

Judge Jackson. I was only illustrating the grounds of my defense. If it is wrong in me to defend myself from these charges in this way, it was wrong ever to make them. I was only stating this circumstance to illustrate how it was—

Senator Richardson, (in the chair.) This matter of which you have just been speaking, has certainly nothing to do with the case, Judge Jackson, and I think, it would be much better for you to drop it, and continue your remarks upon topics which you can discuss with more propriety.

Judge Jackson. Well, it seems this squib case is ruinous to some of the committee, and I will pass it for the present. I will go now to the articles of impeachment. I will read the first article:

Article I. That, unmindful of the sacred obligation by which he stood bound to discharge the solemn duties of his office faithfully, impartially, and consistently with the dignity and importance of the trust reposed in him, as Judge of the Fifteenth Judicial Circuit, in the State of Missouri, the said Albert Jackson, at a Circuit Court begun and held at the town of Bloomfield, within and for the county of Stoddard, in the State of Missouri, on the third Monday in May, A. D. 1858, (whereat the said Albert Jackson, by virtue of his office aforesaid, did preside as

Judge,) did willfully and maliciously conduct himself in a manner highly oppressive and unjust to one Jonas Eaker, viz:

First. The said Albert Jackson, desiring to harrass and oppress the said Jonas Eaker, did, at the Circuit Court aforesaid, whereat he, the said Albert J·ckson, presided as Judge, as aforesaid, cause an attachment to issue against him, the said Eaker, as for a criminal contempt, because said Eaker did not make return to a writ of mandamus, which writ had never been delivered to said Eaker, but of which a *copy* had been delivered to said Eaker; by virtue of which attachment the said Jonas Eaker was arrested and held in custody for several hours, and released finally by said Albert Jackson, on condition that he, the said Jonas Eaker, should make return to the copy that had been delivered to him, said Jackson well knowing that said writ had never been legally served upon him, the said Eaker, and that he was not in contempt for not answering thereto.

Second. In refusing to permit counsel for said Eaker to speak in his behalf, when they proposed to show to the court that said writ of mandamus had never been properly delivered to, or served upon him.

Third. In peremptorily, and in an oppressive, angry, and insulting manner, ordering the counsel of said Eaker, to wit, Solomon G. Kitchen and William G. Phelan, *to shut their mouths and sit down*, when they, in behalf of their said client, attempted to suggest an insufficiency in the service of said writ of mandamus.

Fourth. In depriving said Jonas Eaker of the benefit of counsel, and of the privilege of speaking through such counsel in his own defense, as he had a lawful right to.

I had intended to take up the articles one at a time as they come in order. But for want of time I will limit myself to a brief notice of the four or five different classes of charges without regard to the number of the articles in which they are contained. I will allude to this charge in the first article, and then notice all the charges belonging to the same class.

The gist of this charge is that I told two attorneys to shut their mouths and sit down, upon a certain occasion, and that the whole transaction constitutes an instance of oppresslon towards individuals and lawyers. I believe this is the only instance in which I am charged with any oppression of any individual other than a lawyer. Now, it is useless for me to tell you what the law is about such cases as these, and I think you will see from the nature of the transaction, as it has been and will be detailed in evidence, independent of any reference to the strict rules of law, that there was no oppression in this whole transaction. I contend that a Judge has a right to enforce order in his courts, and to compel refractory parties to submit to the process issued from his courts. I read from the statute in relation to courts:

Each court may enforce, by attachment, the return of any writ or process sent out of the same court.

Now, it is not only the right of a court to do this, but it is the duty of the court to do so, whenever a case of the kind arises. And such a case was here. A mandamus had issued from my court. The party was not in attendance; he conceived that he had a defense which he could keep all to himself; he has a reason for making no return and he keeps that reason to himself. Now, I could do nothing but issue an attachment under the circumstances. I told him when he was brought in that he could not pursue that course, and that if he had a reason for not answering, he must state what it was, and that was all that was necessary. As to the attorneys, they claimed to be the next friend of the court. I thought they had no right to appear in that capacity, and they thought they had, or seemeed to think so; and were importunate about it. Now, when there is a difference of opinion between the Judge and the lawyers, who is to decide? I didn't think they had anything to do with it. They thought they had. I decided against them, and for myself, and that was my offense. Their pertinacity may have ruffled me for a moment, and I may have been compelled to speak to them decidedly to make them desist. But in all that I cannot conceive that I was out of the line of my duty; and if I were mistaken as to my right or duty, who but the Supreme Court can overrule my decision? But I will leave that and go on to the next article.

In this next article I am charged with secretly advising a Mr. Walker as to the best course for him to pursue in regard to a suit against him by a Mr. Moore. I believe there are three or four cases of this kind where they have attempted to make a charge against me out of my conversations with parties to suits. In regard to this Moore and Walker case, I believe it will turn out in the testimony that the conversation alluded to took place after a change of venue had been taken in the case, which sent it out of my circuit; and that I spoke of the suit only as an individual and not as a Judge. When a man becomes a Judge, he still has feelings and interests in common with his neighbors,—the same feelings and passions that he had before; and a suit likely to affect his own rights or property would be a subject on which he might very safely converse with a neighbor. I know of no law forbidding a Judge to take a part in the general concerns of his town and community. I think it will appear from the evidence that this conversation between Walker and myself was a merely casual one, and that I did not give him any advice; and that I was not stirring up strife or litigation, or anything of that kind. I think Mr. Walker's statement of the affair will bear me out in representing these facts to you. I will read the specification in this article:

First. During the Circuit Court aforesaid, whereat said Albert Jackson presided as aforesaid, there was pending before said court the cause of Matthew H. Moore *vs.* James Walker, and the said Albert Jackson, corruptly, partially, and to the utter degradation of the solemn and important functions of his said office, secretly advised the said James Walker, defendant in said cause, not to compromise the same; that the field notes by which the property in dispute between him and the said Moore could be identified, were lost, and that said Walker would be successful in said cause, if he would refuse to compromise the same; and that, in consequence of the prejudice of the said Albert Jackson, the said Moore was compelled to have the venue in said cause changed.

My answer to this, gentlemen, is simply that I did not secretly advise Mr. Walker not to compromise, or give him any other secret advice whatsoever; and that our conversation was a casual one, in which there was no departure from my duty as a Judge and as a citizen. I think you will see that the charge is not true in fact and ought not to have been made.

I will now turn your attention to the next three articles all together:

Article III. That, actuated by a spirit of arbitrary despotism and wanton injustice, totally repugnant to the sacred duties pertaining to his office, and highly dangerous to the rights of the citizens of the State, the said Albert Jackson, Judge of the Fifteenth Judicial Circuit, at a Circuit Court begun and held within and for the county of Wayne, in the State of Missouri, at the town of Greenville, in said county, on the last Monday in September, A. D. 1858, whereat said Albert Jackson, by virtue of his office aforesaid, presided as Judge, was guilty of willful and malicious oppression, misconduct, and abuse of authority in his official capacity:

First. During the Circuit Court aforesaid, at the time and place aforesaid, David M. Fox, one of counsel for plaintiff, in the cause of ——— Limbarger *vs.* ——— Power, then and there pending before said court, presented a petition to said Albert Jackson, then and there presiding as Judge of said court aforesaid, to change the venue of said cause to some other court, because of the prejudice of the Judge, and informed him, the said Albert Jackson, that both parties and their counsel had agreed that said cause might be sent to either the county of Madison or the county of Iron, as either of said counties would be convenient and easy of access; but the said Albert Jackson, Judge as aforesaid, utterly unmindful of the rights of the parties and counsel in said cause, and totally disregarding the provisions of the statute in such cases made and provided, and willfully and maliciously intending to harrass and oppress the parties aforesaid, and their counsel, awarded a change of venue in said cause to *Mississippi county*, well knowing said county to be remote, difficult of access, and inconvenient to all the parties, counsel, and witnesses in said cause.

Second. When counsel engaged in said cause, to wit, David M. Fox and Philip Pipkin, attempted then and there to prevail upon him, the said Albert Jackson, to change the venue to some other county more convenient to all parties, and informed him that by sending said cause to Mississippi county he would deprive them of the privilege of attending to their clients' cause, as they had been employed to do, he, the said Jackson, replied to each of them in an oppressive, inselent and insulting manner, highly shameful and derogatory to the dignity of the important position he occupied as Judge, as aforesaid.

ARTICLE IV. That, influenced by a similar spirit of injustice and tyrannous disregard for the rights of the citizens of the State, the said Albert Jackson, at a Circuit Court begun and held within and for the county of Dunklin, at the town of Kennett, in said county, on the second Monday in May, A. D. 1858, whereat he, the said Albert Jackson, presided as Judge, did conduct himself, in his official capacity, in a manner highly oppressive, unjust, and tyrannical, viz:

First. During the sitting of the Circuit Court aforesaid, at the time and place aforesaid, counsel for the defendant, in the cause of —— Smith *vs.* —— Cude, then and there pending before said court, whereof said Albert Jackson was Judge, presented to said Albert Jackson, Judge of said court, a petition to change the venue of said cause to some other court, on account of prejudice on the part of the Judge; whereupon said Albert Jackson, willfully and maliciously intending to harrass and oppress the parties and counsel in said cause, awarded a change of venue in said cause to the *county of Pemiscot*, notwithstanding he was then and there assured by counsel for both parties in said cause, that said county was difficult of access, and inconvenient to both parties and witnesses; that both parties to said cause had agreed that the venue of said cause should be changed to Bollinger or Scott county, either of which would be much more convenient to all parties than the county of Pemiscot, and that if said cause should be sent to the county of Pemiscot, counsel for both parties would be compelled to abandon it; and to the earnest entreaties of counsel for both parties in said cause, that a change of venue therein might be awarded to some other county where it would be possible for them to attend to it, and that would not be so difficult of access, and inconvenient to the parties therein, he, the said Jackson, angrily, rudely, and insultingly replied, in a manner indicating a total disregard for that courtesy toward counsel, and respect for the rights of parties, that common decency and the duties of his office required.

ARTICLE V. That said Albert Jackson, Judge as aforesaid, has, in numerous other instances, been guilty of willful and malicious oppression, misconduct, and abuse of authority, in awarding changes of venue in causes pending before him as Judge as aforesaid, to counties remote, inconvenient, and difficult of access, intending thereby to harrass and oppress counsel and parties, and to deter others from availing themselves of their right to a change of venue under the law; particularly at a Circuit Court begun and held at the town of Kennett, within and for the county of Dunklin, on the second Monday in May, A. D. 1858, whereat said Albert Jackson presided as Judge:

First. In awarding a change of venue in the cause of the Point Pleasant and Dunklin County Road Company *vs.* Moses Farrar, then and there pending, to the county of *Pemiscot*, well knowing said county to be inconvenient and difficult of access to the parties to said cause, and contrary to the earnest request of both parties to [have] said cause [removed] to some more convenient county.

Second. In awarding a change of venue in the cause of said Road Company *vs.* Nathaniel G. Murphy, then and there pending, to the said county of *Pemiscot*, well knowing the same to be difficult of access and inconvenient to both parties and counsel.

My action in four cases is here complained of, and the principle is the same in all. Now, when an application for a change of venue is made by either party to a suit, the law is that the Judge shall send the case to some convenient county,—to a county as convenient as may be to the opposite party. I think I will be able to prove that I have done this in these cases, or at least that I have done so according to the best of my judgment. But as you do not and cannot know the state of the business in the surrounding counties, and are not, perhaps, acquainted with that country, I do not see how you can decide that matter. It isn't always the nearest county that is as convenient as may be to the opposite party. And sometimes it is hard to say which would be the most convenient county. In such cases, who is to decide the question? Evidently it is not the counsel who presents the application. He can have nothing to say in the matter. And it is not the duty of the court to consult the convenience of the attorneys on either side, as they have no rights in regard to the matter to be consulted. If any such case as is here stated were to arise, where both parties desired a case sent to a certain county, nothing is easier than for them to take the case to that county by agreement, and the Judge's notion about it need not be consulted. That such is the law, no one will dispute, and it is a fact which shows that there was no such agreement in any of these cases. Then, again, if the Judge is in error about which is the proper county to send a case to on change of venue, and is obstinate in supporting his error, what is the remedy? The Supreme Court, of course. This Court certainly has no power to review my official acts in connection with cases like these. If I, by any mental or physical defect, could not decide correctly in these cases as to my duty, and such instances were of frequent occurrence, it is possible that a proceeding by address might be made to remove me from office. But if I was simply in error, and there was no corruption about it, nothing but the Supreme Court could set me right. But, gentlemen, I was not in error about these cases. You should have my experience in such matters in that country. You should understand the efforts of these lawyers at such times to have cases sent to such places as would give them undue advantages,—places where they reside themselves, and where, however inconvenient it might be to the parties, they would have things their own way. If you could see and know all these things as I have seen and known them, you could then say whether I was right or wrong, and I would not fear your judgment. So far from there being anything oppressive, wanton, corrupt, malicious, or tyrannical, in my conduct, (I believe those are the principal adjectives used to describe my course,) you would say I did my duty.

In the next article, article six, a case tried at Poplar Bluff, Gibson *vs.* Dunn, is rehearsed, and I am charged with an offense belonging to another class. I am charged here with oppressing a lawyer. What I have to say to this, applies to all the instances of the kind, and I will try to notice them all together. The charge is, speaking to lawyers in an oppressive and harsh manner. Now, then, gentlemen, I will endeavor to make the evidence show you under what circumstances every instance of this kind occurred. It is true, that when I am exasperated and excited, I sometimes use violent expressions. In this Gibson and Dunn case, I don't think I used the language imputed to me. My recollection is, that I asked him, on this or some other occasion, if he didn't think it was possible for him to keep his mouth shut a moment. Many times I have been much troubled and annoyed by the pertinacity and importunity of this Mr. Phelan, and would have to speak to him in this style to get him to stop something which I conceived he had no right to do or say. Surely I had a right to do this, and it was my duty to do it. Wouldn't it be a ridiculous thing to impeach the Lieutenant-Governor for calling me to order in this Court where he presides, even if he found it necessary to speak to me in a peremptory and decided manner? These charges against me are no less ridiculous. It was my duty to keep order in my courts. That was one of the solemn duties incumbent upon me, which have been paraded before you so much. Am I to be turned out of office, and held unworthy of the trust reposed in me by the people, for discharging this solemn duty according to the best of my ability? I think not. I take it that a Judge is not impeachable for any thing of the kind. There is no court in which some unpleasant occurrences of this nature are not witnessed. Until lawyers and Judges become angels, such occurrences always will be witnessed, and it is folly to arraign a Judge for doing, at such times, what he conceives to be his duty. It is worthy of remark, that only four or five such cases are set down here against me, although my whole course as a Judge has been carefully scrutinized to find similar charges. And in the few instances cited, there is not the smallest circumstance to indicate, even if I were in error at the time, that my error was the result of, or grew out of corruption. They have not even attempted to show that I acted corruptly in a single instance. All I ask of you in regard to these charges, is this: Remember that when there was a difference of opinion, it was my province to decide, and place yourselves in my circumstances, and see if you would not have decided as I did.

There is another matter that I may notice in the same way, and that is in regard to those bills of exceptions, and the differences of opinion between the court and lawyers as to what they should be made to show. In regard to them I will ask, is it possible that the statements of these very lawyers as to my action is the evidence upon which you are to try me? The Supreme Court tries the validity of my ruling by the record I make. Should you not do the same? Nothing can be more unfair than to take away from me in this manner my own record of my official acts, and try me by a record made by my enemies. My record may be a bad one, but as it presents my official action, I wish to be tried by it. I would not be tried in the fearful manner which Mr. Knott has detailed to you. He says that if I have caused the scales of justice to vary in a single solitary cause but the estimation of a hair, I must be amenable to this Court. I shuddered when I heard it. Who can stand such a trial? What infallible Judge is there on the earth that can stand such a trial? It is but reasonable to suppose that in some cases I have been wrong in my ruling and judgments, and the same may be said of any Judge, not even excepting those on the Supreme Bench. But I hope, gentlemen, that you do not consider that the imperfection which must exist in all human tribunals, is in my case a matter of impeachment. Imperfection, irregularity, error—you have nothing to do with such things. You must look for fraud and corruption; and for nothing else, for you have no jurisdiction of anything else. If you will try me by my record, bearing that in mind, it is all I ask, gentlemen.

You all, doubtless, recollect the substance of the testimony in regard to this charge about my ordering Mr. Phelan to shut his mouth and sit down, and the matter about the grand jury, and it is not, therefore, necessary for me to detail the facts now. I pass it with the remark, that if I did treat Mr. Phelan in the manner here charged, I was for once wrong, though not criminally so, and no proof has been or can be adduced to establish any corruption or criminality on my part with reference to this matter.

In the seventh article, which is the next, I am charged with publicly accusing Mr. Fox, a lawyer, with lying and perjury. As this is a proceeding in the nature of an action for slander, I suppose I would not be prevented from justifying myself by giving in evidence the truth of the alleged slanderous words. It matters not, however. I expect it to appear in the evidence before you that my treatment of Mr. Fox in the instances mentioned in these articles was about this: On one occasion, when he was in a very extraordinary manner arguing a case, and was severely reflecting upon the court in the course of his remarks, I stopped him; he did not heed my calling him to order; I stopped him again and again; and finally, when it was evident that he would not pay attention to my orders, and when his client had in vain attempted to get other lawyers to stop him, I ordered him to sit down. On another occasion, when he had proposed an amended or supplemental answer for a client which palpably and flatly contradicted the matter previously sworn to by his client, I then told him that if the one was true, the other was false. I might have used the word *lie*, and it would not have been misplaced, though I do not think I did. I could find no better explanation of his conduct than that he wished to get the young man to swear to facts under such circumstances as would bring about a prosecution for perjury, when he would have an opportunity of defending him for a fee from the charge. Am I guilty of an outrageous offense because I happened to look at the matter in this light? I suppose not.

I will now read the eighth article:

ARTICLE VIII. That said Albert Jackson, Judge as aforesaid, forgetting the dignity of his office, and regardless of his sacred obligation to demean himself faithfully and impartially therein, did, on the trial of one Green DePriest, on an indictment for resisting an officer in the exercise of his official duties, had at a Circuit Court begun and held at the town of Thomasville, within and for the county of Oregon, on the third Monday in April, A. D. 1858, whereat he, the said Albert Jackson, presided as Judge, conduct himself willfully *partial* and corrupt, and highly unbecoming and disgraceful to his high official position:

First. In privately advising one James V. Odell, a lawyer, to procure said DePriest to employ him, the said Odell, as his counsel, and to take a contingent fee to defend him; that said DePriest could not be convicted on the indictment pending against him for resisting the officer, because he had already been convicted of disturbing the peace of a family, which was charged to have been done at the same time he resisted said officer.

Second. In officially and voluntarily advising said James V. Odell, as counsel for said DePriest, to plead a former conviction; which said advice said Albert Jackson, presiding as Judge, gave said Odell in open court, upon the trial.

Third. In partially and corruptly transcending his duties as Judge, on the trial of said DePriest, to such an extent that the Circuit Attorney, prosecuting for the State, abandoned said cause, and entered a "*nolle prosequi.*"

Now, the facts in regard to this case are about these: I happened to be acquainted with the fact, that this man DePriest was indicted twice for the same act. First there was an indictment for resisting an officer, and it was true that in doing this he made some noise, which was the basis for another indictment for disturbing the peace of a family. I told this to the young man, Odell. The law in the case was plain enough. I should not have permitted the man to be twice convicted for the same offense, even if no attorney had appeared for him to represent the fact to the court. I cannot conceive that there was anything improper in my conversation with young Odell in regard to the matter. I simply told him what the law was, and if I added that he might take a conditional fee in the case, what harm or what corruption would anybody see in that? It is my opinion, that it was a very a little business to send up such things as that, and allege them against me as grounds of impeachment, and I shall let it go for what it is worth.

Let us turn now to these celebrated habeas corpus cases, as they come next in order. Mr. Knott was very felicitous in his great spread about this habeas corpus act—this great bulwark of the liberties of the people. From the state of the pleadings it was necessary for him to prove that this act was a bulwark, and the redoubtable gentlemen went at his task with avidity. In charity I gave him that opportunity of displaying and exercising his rampant rhetoric, and the result has justified my expectations. He embraced the opportunity, and has introduced as backers Mr. Hallam and Mr. Blackstone. Well, as I am still charitable, I will not close the discussion here, but leave the point as a controverted one, and Mr. Knott may have still another opportunity for a big spread. But here is a question: How have I acted about these habeas corpus writs? In the first case I refused to grant a writ. Now, a good and sufficient answer to the allegation that I refused this writ maliciously is found in the very petition for the writ itself. My conduct is fully justified when you look at the petition, and remember the testimony concerning it, including the fact that the accused was not in confinement at the time. I knew when the petition was presented that the attorney wanted the man brought to that county, so that he could go his bail, and thereby get possession of his property. But let the matter stand upon the simple fact that I decided the petition insufficient and refused to issue a writ. Whose business is it to decide upon the sufficiency of petitions for writs of this kind? When I decide that a petition is not sufficient, and does not comply with the law, who can overrule my decision and review my action in the premises? Certainly this Court could not undertake to do anything of the kind. With regard to the other cases, in them I had nothing to go by but the returns of the officers, who had the men in custody. When it appeared that there was no reason for holding either of them in confinement, I discharged them as I was bound to do. If those officers made false returns, I knew they could be indicted for it, and I did not suppose that they would subject themselves to such a punishment. When one returned that he had the prisoner in custody by virtue of nothing more nor less than the verbal orders of a Justice of the Peace, I discharged him; and if there was a good reason for holding him before that verbal order was made, it was no fault of mine if that was not set out in the order of commitment. At the time of the hearing of this case, I would not have been allowed to hear outside statements as to the guilt or innocence of the accused. I had to pass upon the question as to the legality of this confinement without any light, except that afforded by the return. How can you, here in this Court, have more? And in the other case it was the same way. The return of the officer showed that a mittimus had been lodged in his hands, but there was no statement of any reason for confining the prisoner, and I simply did my duty in discharging him. In connection with these cases, I demand a trial upon my record; and if any error is pointed out in my action, to make it available for the purposes of this prosecution, I demand proof of fraud or corruption in that error.

But without dwelling upon this part of the case, I will now pass to the eleventh article, and notice it briefly. I am here charged with calling the attention of the grand jury, at the November term of the Stoddard Circuit Court, to a particular offense, which I had some reason to believe had been committed. I am at a loss to know why this accusation was brought against me. It is my duty to instruct the grand jury as to the law of particular offenses, and if I didn't do it, for such a neglect of duty I might be arraigned. No personal considerations, of friendship or enmity, could or ought to make me neglect this duty. And I am not done with it when my public charge is given, for if, at any time during court, the grand jury wants instructions as to the law of any particular case, it is my duty to give them the instructions, and I shouldn't hesitate to do so, whatever might be the result to my friends or enemies. As to what has been said about my following the grand jury to their room and giving them instructions, I have already expressed my views. I have nothing to retract or take back in that connection. I have honestly thought it my province to instruct the grand jury as to what offenses were indictable, and if they were to disregard my instructions, and there was no better method of enforcing my decisions as to the law, I would send every member of such a jury to jail without hesitation. As to my instructions concerning indictments against myself, it is strange, indeed, if I was not right. I make a decision in court; some bystander says it is wrong and oppressive, and goes to the grand jury and presents me for it; now isn't it ridiculous to say that that grand jury can then indict the Judge for his decisions? I say again, that if a grand jury in one of my courts were to persist in an attempt to indict me under such circumstances, I would send every one of them to jail. They have no right to find indictments in defiance of my instructions, and they cannot review my decisions and pass upon their legality or illegality.

There is another case which I may mention here. When a Judge is interested in any case, he cannot try it, of course, and he cannot make any order concerning it. In this instance when I was indicted for gaming jointly with three others, though the testimony plainly showed that I did not participate in the act which was called gaming, and refused to participate in it, although I knew it was not gaming, yet as it was an indictment against myself, so far as it related to myself, I could make no order concerning it—neither to remove it, quash it, nor dispose of it in any manner. There it must lay until it is taken up under the provisions of the law for such cases. Mr. Bartlett was one of the parties indicted, and was put upon his trial separately. I could not refuse to try him, and if I did not refuse, there was no reason why I should not declare the law of the case as I had always understood and declared it. I stated then as I had stated to the grand jury, and on many other occasions, that betting was the thing known to the law as gaming; that if men should bet whisky,—even if it were not more than a thimble-full,—that would be gaming. I stated that the law was so framed that it could not be evaded by any trick, and that whenever there was a bet, though it was nothing more than coffee-grains, it was just as much gaming as if dollars had been staked. Then I explained the difference between betting and competing for a prize or other thing, whether it was valuable or not. I told them that the State was laid off into various agricultural districts, and that in each district premiums were virtually given by the State to the men who would produce the best hog, or calf, or horse, or goat. I showed that this competition for a premium or given thing could not be gaming, and explained how a game of euchre might be played merely in competition, or to see who should pay for a given thing, and that on the same principle this could not be gaming. I declared the law to be thus in the case of Mr. Bartlett. In view of the law and the facts of the case, the attorneys would have asked that the indictment be quashed; but I wouldn't do that, as it would be an order affecting me as well as the other defendants. The Circuit Attorney entered a *nolle prosequi* as to Bartlett, and I said then that I would not make any order which would affect me as one of the defendants in the indictment. I will read you the law which says that a Judge shan't make any order in his own case:

> Whenever any indictment or prosecution for a criminal offense shall be pending in any court against the Judge thereof, the same shall be removed to the Circuit Court of some county in a different circuit, upon the order, in writing, of the Circuit Attorney prosecuting for the circuit, or upon the order of any Judge of the Supreme Court.—Rev. Stat., p. 1183.

Under this law, there the case against me stands yet. I have not heard of any order removing it, and I don't think any has been made.

Now, then, gentlemen, these are all the facts in regard to that case. Is there anything wrong in all that? There is the whole matter. Was my decision of the law, or any step I took, wrong? and if it was, is there even the shadow of proof that the error was through corruption? It was not wrong to try Mr. Bartlett separately. Although there were four persons named in the indictment, the act of each one was the act of himself, and the parties would be separately answerable for their respective acts.

If it were admissible, it would be easy enough for me to prove by Mr. Bartlett that so far as I was concerned with the card-playing, I was neither competing nor betting. Since I have been on the bench, I have perhaps occasionally, and for amusement, played a game of euchre; but it has been very seldom, and never for the smallest stake. And I could show outside matters which would leave no doubt on your minds that this thing was got up, not because any one thought I had been guilty of gaming or any other breach of the criminal code, but wholly and simply out of personal enmity to me. I expect to show a personal matter in connection with this thing, and that by testimony the strongest that can be produced, which shows that this was but a part of a combination against me, as hellish as ever was a conspiracy against any mortal man.

[The respondent here commenced reading fragmentary sentences from a letter which he held in his hand. Mr. Knott objected to the reading of the letter, and considerable confusion ensued, during which Judge Jackson, Mr. Knott, and one or two Senators were all speaking at the same time. A report of what was said would not be intelligible, and could not be made. When order was restored, Judge Jackson proceeded as follows:]

I have had no person to defend me in this trial for reasons which I will take the liberty of stating here. It is because I have been conscientious about it, and not because I was not able to employ counsel who would have defended me with much more ability than I possess. But I am conscious of having done nothing worthy of the reprobation of this Court. I had nothing to palliate or excuse or justify, and I supposed it would be a virtual admission that there was something of the kind to be done if I were to employ counsel for my defense. I have no admissions to make. I can't promise that if you'll let me off, I'll do differently from what I have done heretofore. I'll do exactly the same things, in the same way, under the same circumstances. I admit that there may be found, in my conduct, errors and mistakes, but I must be convinced of the existence of those mistakes and errors before I will change my course in a single case; and the Supreme Court is the only tribunal competent to point out such things in my official action.

I will turn now to the twelfth article. This is the one in which I am charged with certain irregularities in holding a court in Butler, when it is said the Clerk was drunk, and I discharged the grand jury, and so on. Now, in regard to all these things I have to say, simply, that I did as near right as I could. I expect it to appear in evidence before you that the Clerk was there on the first day, and that every thing went on as usual. On the morning of the second day the Clerk was not present, and I was told that he was sick. It wasn't told to me by any person that I now remember that the Clerk was drunk. Now, without knowing anything of the kind of my own knowledge, or having any legal information of the fact, what was my course? The law does not empower me to appoint a Clerk except upon the happening of a certain contingency. I did not know of my own knowledge that such a contingency had happened in this case. And even if I had appointed a Clerk, what good would it have done? There is a provision for Clerks appointing deputies and the court approving the appointment; but there was no provision for my appointing a deputy. You may have noticed that the paper presented here was not an appointment of a deputy by the Clerk requesting me to approve the same, but was a request that I would appoint the deputy myself. This is not the law. The Clerk must select the man, and appoint him, and the court can then approve or disapprove the appointment as it sees proper. Here this man Donaldson was not appointed, but he requested me to appoint him, or, rather, the paper presented to me was of that purport. Now, if I had done so, they would have given it as an instance of usurpation of authority. But more than this, I'll prove to you by incontestible evidence that Blount, the Clerk, never signed that paper, and never had anything to do with it, and that it was a forgery of an attorney, made for the purpose of getting to make up the record in his own cases. But I thought I had no discretion in the matter, and I took the course which the law pointed out as my duty. In regard to the papers, it is true that they were scattered about, and that I took it upon myself to collect them together and preserve them. I expect it to appear in evidence that I staid till the next day after the grand jury was discharged, took the papers and assorted them, put them in the office, instructed a person who could subsequently communicate with the Clerk as to the manner in which I had disposed of them, locked the door of the Clerk's office, and gave the key to this person. For all my steps at this court I had good reasons, which I expect you will see as the evidence comes before you. I believe that my punctuality in holding courts will bear the closest scrutiny. How often it is that Judges do not even go to the place for holding their courts at all! Yet it is worthy of notice that I have never missed but one court since I have been Judge, and then it was no fault of mine.

Now for the charges with regard to my not signing bills of exceptions. In regard to these things, I repeat that I hold it wholly incompetent for you to examine into the validity of the acts of a Judge in such matters. In the Griffiie case, you have heard the testimony given in relation to it, and it is not necessary for me to detain you with any remarks upon it. With regard to the Moore and Eldridge case, I do not remember that any record has been introduced here showing that any such case was ever tried by me, and if so, the presumption would be that there was no such case. If there is no record evidence in this case, there need be none in any of the others, and in this way I might be called upon to defend my action in every case I ever tried from aspersions of bystanders, who know nothing of the condition of the record, and cannot say what I really did do. But if you could examine into such things at all, even when you have the record, and you wanted to know what I did and why I did it, you should call the witnesses in each case before you, and have the pleadings before you, and have every thing done before you the same as it was done before me, and then you might decide understandingly as to the propriety and legality of my acts.

About that instrument of writing in the Moore and Eldridge case, if the record was here I presume that you would have no difficulty in understanding what they charge about the date, or the erasure of the date. The facts were that there was an erasure on the date which was matter of inspection. Some read it with one date, and some with another. The witnesses at the trial had no need to speak of this erasure, as the instrument itself was handed around and inspected by the jurors. To simply give a copy of it in the bill of exceptions would not have answered, because then the fact of the existence of the erasure could not be known. I may have been wrong about the witness Kittrell making any statement in regard to it at the time of the trial, but I can hardly think I was wrong in fixing the bill of exceptions so as to show the facts passed upon by the jury. If I did wrong in refusing to sign that bill of exceptions, they had a remedy, and as they did not resort to it, it is but fair to conclude that they consented to the arrangement I made. At worst it could be nothing but an irregularity, which no testimony would prove to have originated in malice.

This, now, will bring me to the eighteenth article, and I will now notice the case of Mrs. Buckner. In this case the record shows the facts as they appeared upon the trial, and it is not necessary for me to go into a defense of that record. All that about calling the lawyer to order does not go upon the record, I know, but the objection to my doing that is too trivial for argument. Such things a Judge is bound to do,—every Judge does them,—and I think the proof will show that he was only called to order when he commenced to comment upon what was not testimony as if it were testimony, and when he was commenting upon what Mrs. Buckner said her daughter had said, which had been declared inadmissible testimony. I think I shall be able to prove that Mr. Davis himself said that he stopped his speech, and behaved as he did on that occasion for effect on the jury, and that he thought it was about the best way he could take to clear his client.

Senator Rains announced that the hour of adjournment had arrived, and asked Judge Jackson to give way for the present for a motion to adjourn.

Judge Jackson said he would conclude his remarks during the evening session.

The Court then adjourned.

EVENING SESSION.

Thursday, June 16, 1859.

The Court met pursuant to adjournment.

The managers and responded attended.

Judge Jackson arose and resumed his opening speech, as follows:

Gentlemen, when the Senate adjourned this morning, I was proceeding to review the eighteenth article of impeachment. This article cuts quite a conspicuous figure in this case, and has made a considerable handle for harangues. I have thought it better to read the article here now:

Article XVII. At a Circuit Court begun and held at the town of Bloomfield, within and for the county of Stoddard, in the State of Missouri, on the third Monday in November, A. D. 1857, whereat the said Albert Jackson, by virtue of his office of Judge of the Fifteenth Judicial Circuit, presided, and before which one Sarah Buckner was arraigned for trial on an indictment for murder in the first degree, the said Albert Jackson, maliciously and corruptly intending to procure the conviction of said Sarah Buckner, was willfully and maliciously guilty of the most shameful oppression, partiality, misconduct, and abuse of authority in his official capacity.

First. In preventing William C. Grimsley, a witness introduced on the part of the State, who had testified to a certain conversation on the part of the prisoner, from detailing such portions of said conversation as tended to extenuate the crime charged against her; which he, the said Jackson, did on his own motion, without the Circuit Attorney having made any objection thereto.

Now, without saying whether this is true or false, I hold that this Court cannot overrule one of my decisions as to the admissibility of certain evidence. If such evidence as is here spoken of was offered, and ruled out by the Court, the presumption is that it was illegal and inadmissible. If it were right for you now to pass upon these questions of evidence, you could not tell whether the portions of the conversation alluded to should have been admitted unless you heard them yourselves as I did, and altogether it was foolish and idle to make such a charge against me here. But I read on:

Second. In privately advising the Circuit Attorney to withdraw the evidence of said Grimsley, and in permitting the Circuit Attorney to withdraw said evidence from the consideration of the jury, and preventing the counsel for the prisoner from cross-examining said witness Grimsley.

About this I simply say, that, if the testimony is gone into, it will show that no part of Grimsley's testimony was withdrawn by the Circuit Attorney, either upon my suggestion or anybody else's. I will read on:

Third. In allowing his partiality and solicitude for the conviction of said prisoner, Buckner, to extend so far as to induce him, the said Judge, to take the examination of the witnesses, and the management of the cause, almost entirely out of the hands of the attorney prosecuting for the State, although counsel for prisoner repeatedly and earnestly protested against such gross abuse of official authority and unprecedented oppression.

Fourth. In refusing counsel for the prisoner any of the usual courtesies due from the bench to the bar, but attempting to oppress, harrass, and annoy said counsel during said trial, by making use of the most rude, insolent, contemptuous, and insulting expressions towards them.

Fifth. In refusing to allow said prisoner's counsel to advert to, or speak of, the testimony of said witness Grimsley, in their arguments to the jury, even to correct any impression said testimony might have made upon the minds of said jury.

Sixth. In refusing to allow counsel for the said prisoner to make use of illustrations in their arguments in said cause, and by repeatedly and vexatiously interrupting the said counsel for said prisoner, during their arguments to the jury, and so harshly and insultingly as to compel one of said counsel to abandon the defense of said prisoner in the midst of his argument.

Seventh. In imposing such wanton and tyrannical restrictions upon counsel, in arguing said cause for said prisoner, as to effectually defeat her constitutional guaranty of being heard by herself or counsel, and preclude the possibility of her having a fair trial by an impartial jury, which is the ultimate and strongest protection of the rights and liberties of the people.

Eighth. In unjustly, corruptly, and cruelly refusing to sign a bill of exceptions, legally tendered to him by counsel for said prisoner, until said bill of exceptions was made to contain the testimony of said William C. Grimsley, notwithstanding he had refused counsel for the prisoner the privilege of cross-examining said Grimsley, and had suffered his testimony to be *withdrawn*, and had refused to allow counsel for prisoner to advert to, or comment on, said testimony, in their arguments to the jury.

Ninth. In many other corrupt and oppressive acts, indicating a degree of indecent solicitude on the part of said Jackson for the conviction of said Sarah Buckner, unbecoming even a public prosecutor, but highly disgraceful to the character of a Judge, as it was contrary to the spirit of our laws and subversive of justice, and tending to bring the judiciary of the country into utter abhorrence and contempt.

If there is testimony to support all these charges, you have it before you. How far they are sustained, and whether, if they all took place, it is matter of impeachment, are questions which I submit for your consideration and decision. After the testimony which I shall offer on these points, I think you will easily see that nothing improper is attributable to me. The Circuit Attorney who conducted the case will be here, and I depend upon his giving a true statement of the facts.

In reviewing the whole case, it seems to me impossible that my official conduct can be the subject of censure here. It is not so much that there may not be irregularities in it, but the impossibility of showing the faintest trace of any malice. The record shows that the very things of which complaint is made were not objected to at the time of the trial; and if there was irregularity or illegality in the course pursued by the prosecution, it certainly was not my peculiar province to interfere unless there were objections or exceptions. But there seems to be a singular feature in the case. It seems that the attorneys wanted to comment upon the testimony of the witness which they say was withdrawn, yet there was no objection to the withdrawal of the testimony itself. The only objection is in the ruling about the commenting. They don't want it to go to the Supreme Court, however, that they objected to this ruling. By comparing the record and the testimony together, you will see that after the trial, when the motion for a new trial was made, nothing is said in the reasons for the new trial about the testimony of Grimsley. You will notice that there is nothing of the kind in the motion for a new trial; and the first time you see anything about there being only the testimony of one witness is in the motion in arrest of judgment. I always looked upon it as true that the testimony of one witness alone, uncorroborated by circumstances, was not sufficient to support a conviction for a capital offense. It seems that the woman's attorneys, judging by their own story, were willing that she should be convicted upon the evidence of but one solitary witness, and that one the boy, because they say they objected to the withdrawal of the only other witness. They were so anxious to have the other witness in and to have a chance to cross-examine him, that what they ought to have known would have been much better for their client was objected to,—so they say now,—but there is no objection on the record. They profess to have been willing to let the Circuit Attorney get in illegal testimony, because they were so anxious to get out of the same witness hearsay evidence for them to hang a speech upon. It does seem to me that the account given of this trial by Mr. Phelan before you is preposterous and contradictory. The facts are, that after the trial the case was continued two or three weeks. In the meantime I heard of the statement of defendant's counsel that the testimony of Grimsley had been wholly withdrawn. One of them, Mr. Phelan, who will talk at a round rate whether or no, I understood reflected severely upon the course I pursued in connection with the trial. Hearing of this, and under such circumstances as were very well calculated to excite me somewhat, I stated that if what Mr. Phelan said about my ruling the testimony of Grimsley out entirely were true, that he ought to be hung instead of the woman, for he failed to present the very fact which would have acquitted her, and then stated the principle about a single uncorroborated witness which he afterwards claimed great credit for suggesting. But I will have an opportunity of noticing this whole case more particularly hereafter, and I will now leave it with this single observation. It is very difficult for a Judge who necessarily tries a great many cases to remember distinctly the minutiæ of every case, and hence it is very difficult for him to defend his action in any case, let alone a large number of cases, from the aspersions of bystanders who do not speak by the record. No Judge in the State of Missouri can sustain himself in an impeachment proceeding if he is called upon to defend his manner of trying cases without the record. That is the thing you must go by, and that I must be tried by.

There is one or two small matters which I believe have escaped me. One is this case where I am charged with giving a Mr. Ringer advice about his county warrants. With regard to that matter it may be or it may not be that I had some conversation with him on the subject, but

I am certain that I shall be able to show you that he does not state it correctly, and that his statements are not to be relied upon. He states emphatically that this occurred in Stoddard county, in the month of October. Now I am very able to prove that never since I have been a Judge have I been in that county in the month of October in any year. You may notice that he was very particular to place it after the August election in 1857. Now why was that? It was because I was elected in August of that year for six years, and they have been particular in all the charges against me not to go beyond that election. But the truth is that I never since that time have been in Stoddard in October, and am always off on the circuit at the time he has fixed.

But another matter. In regard to the appointment of a Circuit Attorney, *pro tem.*, at the term when he was himself indicted, I hold that the happening of such a circumstance could not affect me. After I had once made an appointment, I had no more power to revoke that appointment without cause, than I would have to turn the regular Circuit Attorney out of his office. I knew nothing about the indictment till it was all over. As to the quashing of the indictment, I can only leave that to be explained by the record. I have no recollection about it. This is certain, that if I had permitted the defendant to be tried upon a defective indictment, when a conviction would have amounted to nothing, that would have been a more serious charge against me than this, and my enemies would have attributed such a course to my friendship for Hicks.

Now, gentlemen, I believe I have gone, in a very desultory style, over the principal authorities, principles, and facts upon which I expect to rest my defense,—except one thing, which I will now barely mention in conclusion. I think that if I can show that my course as a Judge has been acceptable to the people who elected me, and that no general dissatisfaction exists among them, it ought to go a great ways in my favor. Isn't it singular that there are no witnesses, no jurors, and no parties litigant, here complaining of my course as Judge? To me it is a singular and a significant fact. It is only a few,—a very few,—who are dissatisfied, and they are lawyers who are excited against me simply because I have not been the pliable tool in their hands which they hoped to find me. Errors I may have committed—wrongs I may have done,—but there is not a solitary item of proof to show any corruption or malice in any official act; and that you will patiently listen to the proofs of these facts, is all I ask of you in this case.

The opening speech of the respondent being now concluded, the President of the Senate inquired of Judge Jackson whether he was ready to proceed with the testimony in his behalf, and after some little delay, he announced that he was ready.

TESTIMONY OF GEORGE W. CREATH.

GEORGE W. CREATH called and examined by Judge Jackson.

Q. Which county do you reside in, Mr. Creath?

A. I reside in Wayne county.

Q. Do you hold any office in that county?

A. Yes, sir.

Q. What is it?

A. I am Clerk of the Circuit and County Courts.

Q. Were you present at the September term, 1858, of the Wayne Circuit Court? Do you recollect an application for a change of venue in the case of Limbarger *vs.* Powers?

A. Yes, sir. There was a case of that style on the docket. There was a petition presented by Mr. Fox, for a change of venue, which was granted.

Q. Did you hear anything about an agreement as to where the case should be sent, on the day it was presented?

A. Yes, sir. I heard him ask the Judge to send it to Madison county.

Q. Where was it sent to?

A. To Mississippi county.

Q. Did you hear Mr. Fox say anything the next day in regard to it?

A. I heard him remark that he believed he would rather have the case where it was, than to have it sent to Mississippi; and I understood him to make application to have the case rescinded. The Judge said the order had already been made, and that he had no right to make the change to suit him. Mr. Fox made some reply, and the Judge told him that if he wouldn't consider it a personal matter, he would fine him for contempt. This is what occurred, as near as I can state it. I don't recollect precisely the conversation.

Senator Watkins. Was this the next day after the change was awarded?

A. Yes, sir.

Q. Was it in court?

A. Yes, sir, court was in session.

[Senator Watkins asked the witness to repeat his statement, which he did, and then Judge Jackson resumed his examination.]

Q. How long have you been Clerk of the courts in Wayne county?

A. Better than seven years. Ever since you have been Judge, and longer.

Q. What has been Judge Jackson's general bearing towards lawyers and parties litigant?

[Mr. Knott objected to this question, and it was waived.]

Q. If you know how the citizens of the Fifteenth Judicial Circuit look upon my course of conduct as Judge of the Circuit Courts, you will please state it.

Mr. Knott. May it please the Court, we have raised no issue as to the general course of the respondent. He is on trial for particular and specified crimes and misdemeanors. Whatever may be the answer to this question, it cannot affect the case at bar, and hence I object to it as immaterial and irrelevant.

Judge Jackson said that his general character as a Judge had been assailed, and he had a right to defend it by such evidence as this question would elicit. He insisted upon his question.

The question for the action of the Court then being, shall the respondent be permitted to ask the question? it was decided in the negative by the following vote:

Ayes—Messrs. Hedgpeth, and Morris—2.

Noes—Messrs. Brown, Byrne, Churchill, Fox, Frazier, Goodlett, Gullett, Halliburton, Harris, Horner, Hyer, Jones, McFarland, McFerran, McIlvaine, Newland, O'Neil, Parsons, Peyton, Rains, Richardson, Robinson, Scott, Thompson, Vernon, Watkins, Wilson, and Wood—28.

Absent—Mr. Johnson.

Excused from voting—Messrs. Coleman and Wright.

Senator Goodlett then proposed the question given below, to which the managers objected, the objection being overruled by the following vote:

Ayes—Messrs. Brown, Byrne, Churchill, Coleman, Fox, Goodlett, Gullett, Harris, Hedgpeth, Hyer, McFerran, Morris, Newland, Peyton, Richardson, Robinson, Scott, Watkins, Wilson, Wood, and Wright—21.

NOES—Messrs. Frazier, Halliburton, Horner, Jones, McFarland, McIlvaine, O'Neil, Parsons, Rains, Thompson, and Vernon—11.
Absent—Mr. Johnson.

Q. Do you know of Judge Jackson being guilty of innumerable instances of oppression, and contumelious, insolent and insulting expressions; and did or not the Judge habitually indulge in such in the exercise of his official functions?
A. I never knew him to be guilty.
JUDGE JACKSON. You have been at the courts regularly since I have been Judge. You will state whether I have regularly attended the courts.
A. Yes, sir.

CROSS-EXAMINED BY MR. KNOTT.

Q. What is your understanding of contumelious conduct?
A. I don't know as I could give the exact definition.
Q. You don't know then what contumelious conduct means?
A. Well, I don't know whether I understand it or not.
Q. You can stand aside then.
JUDGE JACKSON. It is usual and right, then, to have the word explained to the witness.
MR. KNOTT. Never mind; he has answered, and can stand aside.

JUDGE JACKSON here announced that the absent witnesses for the State were present. The taking of the testimony for the respondent was then suspended, and Mr. C. A. Davis, witness on the part of the State against whom an attachment had issued, appeared, was sworn and charged under the rule, and on motion of SENATOR WATKINS was discharged from any further proceeding under the attachment.

TESTIMONY OF MATTHEW H. MOORE.

Mr. MATTHEW H. MOORE, witness on the part of the State for whom an alias subpena had issued, also appeared, was sworn, called, and examined by Mr. Knott.
Q. Where do you reside, Mr. Moore?
A. I reside in Cape Girardeau City, Cape Girardeau county, Mo.
Q. Within which circuit?
A. The Tenth Judicial Circuit.
Q. What is your profession?
A. That of a lawyer.
Q. Have you practiced any in the Fifteenth Circuit?
A. I have attended the courts of two of the counties of that circuit. I had been practicing in them before it was formed.
Q. Were you plaintiff in a cause entitled M. H. Moore *vs.* James Walker?
A. Yes, sir. I brought the suit in the fall term. There was a change of venue in the case awarded to Scott county.
Q. Previous to the taking the change of venue do you know of any expression of opinion as to the merits of the cause,by Judge Jackson?
A. Of my own knowledge, I do not.
Q. Had you been informed that such a thing had occurred?
A. Yes, sir. As to the day, I can't state when that information reached me. It was before the petition for the change of venue was presented. I had prepared a petition, and left it with Mr. Tyrell the night previous to leaving, not being able to stay myself to attend to the

matter; and I recollect telling Mr. Tyrell that Mr. Eaker had told me that Mr. Walker had told him—

[Judge Jackson objected to the hearsay statement coming in as evidence. The witness proceeded.]

Well, I had received information, and that information was to the effect that the Judge had expressed an opinion as to the merits in the cause. It is but justice to state that I had previous to that time determined upon taking a change of venue; but it is also true that this information came before any application was made for the change.

SENATOR PARSONS. What cause was assigned in the petition?

A. The cause was prejudice in the mind of the court against me. In talking to Mr. Tyrell, I spoke about what I had heard concerning the Judge's expression of opinion, and perhaps said that it would be an additional ground for change of venue. But I don't recollect that anything of the kind was mentioned in the petition. It was merely a general averment of prejudice against myself.

Q. Were you at Dunklin court, May, 1858?

A. Yes, sir, I was.

Q. Were you counsel in the case of Smith *vs.* Cude, pending in that court at that time?

A. Yes, sir, I recollect the case. There was an application made by Cude, and a change of venue awarded.

Q. What were the reasons assigned for this application?

A. I don't recollect of anything more than prejudice.

Q. You will please go on and state what were the wishes of the parties concerning the removal of the case; who were counsel; and what representations were made to the court in relation to the change.

A. I do not recollect all the counsel engaged in the cause. The defendant's counsel were, I think, Mr. Davis and H. H. Bedford. I am not certain whether Kitchen and myself were in the cause with them. Upon consultation it was determined to take a change of venue, and an application was made, and an affidavit and petition were prepared. I think Dr. Horner, and perhaps Mr. Phelan, and I don't recollect who else, were for the plaintiff. Dr. Horner lives in Hornersville, in Dunklin county. They were consulted, and from my recollection of the conversation, I understood them as agreeing that the case should be sent to either Bollinger or Scott county, as the most convenient to the parties and witnesses. The court ordered it to Pemiscot. Objection was made, and the reason assigned, that it was the nearest point, and objection was then urged on both sides that it would be impossible to go through the swamp; and besides this the inability of counsel on both sides was urged on account of a conflict of courts in the two circuits. In the upper counties the times of holding the courts did not interfere with the courts of this circuit. The Judge answered that the order was made, and he would not change it.

Q. What was his manner towards counsel, when they were bringing these facts to his notice?

A. He was what might be termed pert or short, in answer to expostulations touching the inability of counsel to follow the case to Pemiscot. He made some short, impetuous reply, to the effect that he didn't have their convenience to consult, and that he would not hear anything more on the subject.

Q. Were you at Bloomfield during the trial of Sarah Buckner?

A. I was there the first week of the court when she was tried, and was present at her trial.

Q. Were you connected with the cause?

A. Not by employment—that is, I had no fee in the case. I was requested by one of the attorneys to take part in the case, and afterwards the defendant when in court requested me to assist in her defense. Remarking that I would not take an active part, I agreed to assist in doing the writing, and to make suggestions, and thus to assist generally.

Q. You will please go on and state what you observed during the progress of that trial.

A. My recollections of the trial are, that a son of the defendant, a small boy, perhaps about fourteen years of age, was introduced upon the part of the State, and in his examination, as he was manifesting a considerable degree of hesitancy, the Judge observing it, commenced asking questions. After that he asked most of the questions on the part of the State. Afterwards, William C. Grimsley, ex-Sheriff, was examined in chief. He gave confessions of the defendant—confessions as to the part she had taken in causing the death of the deceased. While making these confessions, I understood that she had been speaking of her own and her daughter's connection with the transaction. The witnes being turned over to the defense, was asked by defendant's counsel if in the same conversation, or during the same confessions, the defendant had stated that her daughter had done the killing. The witness answered that she did. The defendant's counsel then asked for the whole of this conversation, to which the State objected, and the objection was sustained. The cross-examination was here suspended, and the court took a recess for dinner. Very soon after dinner, the Circuit Attorney asked leave to withdraw the witness. Defendant's counsel objected, and a bill of exceptions was drawn at the time and presented to the court for signature. The Judge refused to sign at that time. When the case came to argument—

Q. What was the purport of the question asked by defendant's counsel, which was overruled by the court?

A. It was propounded with a view of getting out acknowledgments of Buckner concerning a rape or seduction of the daughter, which had either been perpetrated or attempted. David R. Conran was called to the stand, and questioned upon this point concerning the statement of the deceased to him. The Circuit Attorney objected, and the objection was sustained, and his testimony was not given. A female witness was called for the same purpose, and the same question propounded and overruled as before. In the argument of the case, Charles A. Davis alluded to this testimony, not as testimony, but as a supposed state of facts. As well as I recollect, he called one of the jurors by name, and addressed him thus: "Mr. A. B., what would you have done under such circumstances?" At that point the Judge stopped him, telling him he must confine himself to the testimony. Mr. Davis stopped his argument. He said that if he couldn't argue the case as he wished, he would abandon it. His remark was, as well as I can recollect, that he wouldn't stand by and see a client "Jeffreyized."

Q. Did the court, when application was made to withdraw the testimony of Grimsley, tell the jury it was excluded?

A. Yes, sir. Leave was granted by the court, and he then addressed the jury, saying that testimony was withdrawn. Mr. Phelan, the other counsel for the defense, commenced an argument. He perhaps referred to what they had expected to prove upon the cross-examination of Grimsley, and what they wished to prove by the other witnesses. He was here stopped by the Judge, who told him that he knew, or ought to know, that that testimony was not before the jury, and if he did not confine himself to the testimony, he would make him sit down.

Q. You say that during the examination of the boy, the Judge asked most of the questions for the State. Did he in like manner conduct the examination of Grimsley?

A. I don't recollect that the Judge put any questions to Grimsley, but as to the boy, the Circuit Attorney asked one or two preliminary questions, and then asked the general question, letting him go on and relate all he knew about the matter. The boy seemed to hesitate a good deal, and it is my impression that the Judge asked the boy the most of the questions asked for the prosecution.

Q. Who drew up the bill of exceptions to save the points taken during the trial?

A. I did. I drew up several during the progress of the trial.

Q. I understood you to say that there was one of the bills that he refused to sign?

A. Yes, sir. There was an exception saved to the questions propounded by the court, and also to a withdrawal of the witness, Grimsley, and that bill he refused to sign.

Q. Was Mr. Davis interrupted more than once during the progress of his argument?

A. I don't recollect that he was interrupted more than once. He may have been, but the only time that I now remember, was the final interruption, when Mr. Davis quit the case.

Q. What was the Judge's manner, in this case, towards the counsel for the defense?

A. He seemed to be in ill-humor, and treated them quite contemptuously, at least so far as I could judge, and as far as any applications for any ruling of the case were concerned.

Q. Did you make any argument in the cause?

A. I did not, sir.

Q. At what time did you leave the court?

A. Well, sir, I couldn't say. I think it was on Saturday or Sunday. It was the last of that week, or first day of the next. Court had adjourned over to some day in the next week, or the week following, to give an opportunity, a chance, to prepare a bill of exceptions.

Q. How long have you practiced in Judge Jackson's circuit?

A. Since its organization in 1855, or 1856.

CROSS-EXAMINED BY JUDGE JACKSON.

Q. What time did you say you left the Circuit Court at Bloomfield?

A. I think it was on Saturday or Sunday.

Q. At the time your case against Walker was pending, did you say you presented your application for a change of venue yourself?

A. No, sir. I prepared the petition and gave it to Mr. Tyrell.

Q. What time did you leave there?

A. It was one day during the latter part of the week.

Q. Do you remember the day?

A. I can't say. I think it was on Thursday or Friday. I was in court but little that week, because I had made a sale of lots in May preceding, and I was out trying to collect most of the time.

Q. Had you given any notice of the application for a change of venue before you left?

A. I don't think I had. If any notice was given, it was by Mr. Tyrell.

Q. Don't you think you had this conversation with Mr. Tyrell about your case after you had presented your petition for a change of venue?

A. I think not.

Q. Had there been any talk of a compromise between you and Walker?

A. Daniel Kitchen had proposed something to me at the spring term, but there was no proposition then pending. I had heard a good many threats had been made, and I would not make any proposition for a compromise for that reason. Mr. Daniel Kitchen was the party that applied to me on the subject. He had sold to Mr. Walker, and I think had probably given him a warranty deed for the property in question.

Q. How long before this term of the court had the proposition to compromise been made?

A. I think it was in March, when I was running off, with a surveyor, my addition to the town of Bloomfield, that I first discovered that Walker was on my land. That was the first I knew of it, and then I left word that Mr. Walker need not trouble himself about the matter, until I was more certain about how the lines run. We did not complete the survey then, owing to a doubt whether we had found a certain corner; and I told Mr. Miller, the County Surveyor, to get the field-notes and run off my land, and if he found that we had before begun at the proper place, to say to Mr. Walker that he need not be uneasy about it, because I wouldn't sell it over his head without first giving him a chance to pay me a fair value for my property. Mr. Miller afterwards sending me the plat, I found that the point at which we had commenced before was the correct one, and that in running off the land, it took in Mr. Walker's lot. In the April following, Daniel Kitchen wanted to buy from me, and I wouldn't sell to him then because I had not yet filed a plat, and I wouldn't sell any lots at any price until that had been done, knowing the penalty prescribed by law. I told him that after I had filed a plat, if they fixed it up that I would—

Q. What time was that?

A. That was in April.

[The witness here proceeded to detail at some length the facts in relation to his transactions, touching his town lots, surveys, etc., but as nothing was elicited in relation to the points of inquiry, his statements are here omitted.]

Q. Did you make a proposition to Mr. Walker to compromise about the land?

A. No, sir. Mr. Kitchen came to me first and last, and I treated with him alone. I did subsequently make out a written proposition in January last.

Q. Did you know that part of Walker's tract was included when you purchased?

A. No, sir.

Q. Do you know about my saying anything to you concerning it?

A. I have no recollection of anything.

Q. In this change of venue at Dunklin court, do you say the parties agreed?

A. That is my recollection. I understood that they settled upon a proposition to take the case either to Bollinger or Scott county. There was a general expression that either one would do. Mr. Horner was perhaps talking something about New Madrid county.

Q. Did they generally express themselves opposed to going to Pemiscot?

A. Yes, sir. Several expressed themselves opposed to it. Several said they couldn't go there on account of the swamp, and on account of the conflict of the times of holding court.

Q. Did they make any representations concerning their opposition before the order was made sending the case to Pemiscot?

A. As soon as you made the order there was a consultation, and a request which I understood to emanate from all parties that the order should be set aside.

Q. Were you one of them?

A. My recollection is that it didn't make much difference to me. I think, however, that I did speak of it, with a view to accommodating the other parties.

Q. Were you as verbose on that occasion as you are now?

A. I may have been. I will say that if shorter answers will suit you better, I will give them.

Q. Short answers seem to have been excepted to heretofore in that court. In the road cases against Farrar and Murphy, on which side were you?

A. I was for the plaintiff in both cases. My recollection is, that after the presentation of petitions, the same order was made in both cases. There was an objection made, but as to saying who made it, I could not.

Q. Were the objections made before or after the orders?

A. I think they were made afterwards. They were similar to those made in the other case, and were not complied with.

Q. In the Buckner case, Mr. Moore, you state that after a few questions by the Circuit Attorney, I took the examination of the witness upon myself?

A. Yes, sir. After a preliminary question or two, the witness showed a hesitancy and confusion in answering the general questions propounded by the Circuit Attorney, and my recollection is that you asked all, or very nearly all the questions for the prosecution after that. I recollect that objections were made by defendant's counsel to this course on your part.

Q. What part of Grimsley's testimony was excluded?

A. His examination in chief was completed, and the cross-examination began, and then his testimony withdrawn entirely.

Q. Wasn't it what he was going on to say that Mrs. Buckner said her daughter had said?

A. My recollection is that the witness had commenced to make a statement, perhaps of this kind. There was an articulation uttered by him, when the objection to this question was made, and the objection was sustained. I believe the first question was not objected to by the State, and that it was whether there had been, in the conversation between the witness and the defendant, any reason assigned for the commission of the acts in which she had confessed she participated. This being answered affirmatively, he was then directed to go on and state what those reasons thus assigned were. If he answered, I am not prepared to say what the answer was. The question being objected to and overruled, defendant's counsel objected, and excepted to the ruling of the court, and presented a bill of exceptions, which was not signed. At the meeting of court after dinner, the motion was made to withdraw the witness, and leave was granted; and then the court instructed the jury that the testimony of this witness was not before them.

Q. Did you say that a bill of exceptions was made at this time?

A. A bill was drawn, but none presented. A preliminary exception had been saved, and I do not know now why the bill was not signed.

Q. Who made the motion to withdraw the testimony of Grimsley?

A. The prosecuting attorney.

Q. When the court announced that the testimony was withdrawn, was there any objection to that?

A. Yes, sir. Defendant's counsel objected to the withdrawal of the witness.

Q. For what reason?

A. They wanted the benefit of his cross-examination. They were apprised of the nature of the conversation which they wished to draw out, and they wished to get before the jury the exculpation of the defendant, appearing from that conversation.

Q. Do you know what occurred when the motions in arrest and for a new trial were determined?

A. No, sir. That was at the adjournment. I can speak of it only from hearsay.

Q. Who prepared the bill of exceptions in this case, which was finally signed?

A. The defendant's counsel. I suppose Mr. Phelan was one.

Q. Had Mr. Kitchen anything to do with it?

A. Mr. Kitchen was not there at the trial. He had been employed to assist in a previous trial as prosecutor.

Q. You are sure that when I stopped Mr. Davis he was commenting on Grimsley's testimony?

A. My recollection is that he didn't refer by name to the witness, but was going on making a supposed case, and commenting on the facts supposed, and in doing so he appealed to a juror, an old gentleman, wanting to know what he would do upon being thus informed concerning the perpetration of outrages upon a member of his family, when he was stopped.

Q. How long have you been practicing law?

A. I obtained license from Judge Hough, in 1853, and went around the circuit then.

Q. Have you followed the business of an attorney ever since?

A. I have had a good many different occupations. Previous to commencing the practice in this State, I was keeping a hotel, and prior to that I was on a farm, and sometime before that I practiced law in Kentucky.

Mr. Knott. What time do you say the testimony of the witness Grimsley was withdrawn in this Buckner case?

A. The court had adjourned for dinner just after the refusal of permission to examine him as to the reasons assigned for the conduct of defendant, and immediately after dinner Mr. Woodsides moved to withdraw the testimony. The cross-examination had proceeded no farther than to the point where the question I have stated was objected to, and overruled.

Q. Was it upon that account that the defendant's counsel objected to the withdrawal of the witness?

A. It was upon the ground that the testimony elicited on the examination in chief had already gone to the jury, and could not be entirely effaced. Defendant's counsel insisted upon having the benefit of a cross-examination, but the court instructed the jury that the testimony was withdrawn. There were various remarks made, and a good deal of excitement prevailed, during which the Judge stated some reasons why he refused to let the witness answer.

The examination of this witness was here closed.

George W. Creath, witness on behalf of the respondent, was discharged by consent of parties.

On motion of Senator Halliburton, the Court adjourned.

ELEVENTH DAY.

FRIDAY, June 17, 1859.

The Court met pursuant to adjournment, and was opened by proclamation.

The managers and respondent attended.

The examination of witnesses for the State was resumed.

TESTIMONY OF CHARLES A. DAVIS.

CHARLES A. DAVIS called and examined by Mr. Knott.

Q. Where do you reside?

A. In Jackson, Cape Girardeau county, Missouri.

Q. What is your profession?

A. I am a lawyer by profession.

Q. Are you engaged in the practice at this time?

A. No, sir. At present I am Register of the Land Office at Jackson.

Q. In the year 1857, were you practicing in the Fifteenth Judicial Circuit?

A. I was.

Q. Please state whether you were at the trial of Sarah Buckner, in the Stoddard Circuit Court, November, 1857.

A. I was. I appeared as an attorney for the defendant in that case, at the request of Gen. Watkins, who had been employed, and was unable to attend, and asked me to appear for him.

Q. Do you remember whether a witness named Grimsley was introduced by the State in the trial of that case?

A. Yes, sir.

Q. Please state whether his testimony was withdrawn, and upon whose motion.

A. His testimony was withdrawn upon the motion of the Circuit Attorney.

Q. Did you participate in the argument of the case?

A. Yes, sir.

Q. Please state what occurred while you were making your argument.

A. After the testimony in the case was closed, I undertook to argue the defense. After making an exordium, I was about to rehearse the testimony of Grimsley, when Judge Jackson stopped me. I then went on to some other part of the order of my speech, and came back again after a while to the point. I undertook to suppose a case which involved the points in Grimsley's testimony, and the Judge stopped me again. I asked if I could not be permitted to argue a supposed case; and being told that I could not, I remarked that if I was to be Jeffreyized in that manner, I would abandon the case. I then left.

Q. Did you hear the Judge make any remark, when you quit the case?

A. I didn't hear but one remark as I went out of the door.

CROSS-EXAMINED BY JUDGE JACKSON.

Q. Was Mr. Grimsley cross-examined any?

A. My recollection is that some questions were asked him by defendant's counsel, before dinner. I don't state it with any confidence. There was no cross-examination of any consequence.

Q. You say Mr. Grimsley's testimony was withdrawn. In what way?
A. By the Circuit Attorney.
Q. Did he propose withdrawing the testimony or the witness?
A. I don't remember. I suppose he withdrew the witness. I know we considered him withdrawn, and when the motion was sustained by the court, I requested Mr. Moore to draw up a bill of exceptions.
Q. Did the Judge tell the jury that the testimony was withdrawn?
A. Yes, sir, I remember that he did.
Q. When you were making your speech, how did you come to want to comment on what was known to you to be withdrawn?
A. I suppose I was governed by the same principle on which I had sometimes before acted. I don't mean any disrespect, but I must say that I didn't think your decision correct, and hoped that the jury would differ with you, as had been the case in other trials, and that I might operate upon them for that purpose.
Q. Mr. Davis, when Grimsley went to state what Susan Seabaugh had said to her mother, wasn't that what was excluded?
A. When Grimsley got through his relation as to the mother's confession, we got it out that the girl had killed Buckner, and you stated that what Grimsley had stated as a confession, and the part of her confession which tended to exculpate her, was not testimony. I then drew up a bill of exceptions, contending that we had a right to bring out the whole of the confession. We presented that bill, and you refused to sign it. It was drawn up about as soon as we could draw it up.
Q. When did you leave that court?
A. I left the day the trial was consummated.
Q. Was any instruction asked to exclude the testimony of Grimsley?
A. I remember no written instructions. After representing Gen. Watkins up to the time my speech was stopped, I delivered myself of the case, and had nothing more to do with it.
Q. Do you remember what was said the first time I stopped you, when you were making your speech?
A. I have no distinct recollection of it.
Q. Didn't you manifest a good deal of ill-will in regard to the interruption, and didn't I have to speak to you two or three times before you heeded me?
A. I think you did. I remember your saying you had stopped me two or three times, but I don't remember that such an occurrence took place but twice.
Q. Do you remember saying that it was about the best way you could conclude your speech, and that you thought that would have a better effect than if you had gone on?
A. Yes, sir. A number of persons asked me why I didn't continue my remarks, and I was joked about it a good deal. In reply to what was said about the abrupt manner in which I had abandoned the case, I said that I thought it was about the happiest termination that could have been given to my speech, and that I thought if anything would produce an effect upon the jury, favorable to the defendant, your conduct throughout the trial certainly would.
Q. Did you say that you were glad that it happened just as it all did?
A. I may have said that I was glad because of the effect I thought it would have, and that it had relieved me from the necessity of making a speech.
Q. Don't you think you might have said you stopped on purpose?
A. I cannot recollect. I would not exaggerate by saying that as many as thirty or forty persons spoke to me about it, and asked me why I had abandoned the cause. I might have said in joking with them about the matter, that I stopped on purpose.

Q. Did you think it was a joking matter?
A. Which do you mean, the case, or your conduct?
Q. The question is the whole affair.
A. No, sir, I didn't. I characterized it by a different name.
Mr. Knott. I understand you to say that in the examination of Grimsley in the forenoon, you had just reached the cross-examination, and after dinner the Circuit Attorney was allowed by the court to withdraw the witness?
A. Yes, sir.
Senator Parsons. What was the Judge's demeanor towards the counsel of the prisoner?
A. Well, sir, in that case, I don't think I can state. I have no recollection of anything offensive up to the time I offered to file the bill of exceptions, and I don't know then that there was anything objectionable in his demeanor. The most offensive demeanor towards the counsel was when he interrupted them in their speeches.
Mr. Knott. Were you in court during the delivery of the argument of Mr. Phelan?
A. No, sir. After I abandoned the case, I was not in at all when Mr. Phelan's argument was going on.

The testimony on the part of the State here closed, and the respondent proceeded to call the witnesses for the defense.

TESTIMONY OF FRANCIS LAWSON.

Francis Lawson called and examined by Judge Jackson.
Q. In what county do you reside?
A. I reside in Butler county.
Q. Were you at the Circuit Court in that county at the term when the Clerk was reported sick?
A. No, sir.
Q. What term were you there?
A. At the last term in that county, 1858.
Q. Have you been in court in Butler county frequently?
A. Yes, sir. I have been there about court pretty frequently.
Q. Do you know of Judge Jackson being guilty of innumerable instances of oppressive, contumelious, insolent, and insulting expressions towards lawyers and parties litigant; and did or not the Judge habitually indulge in such in the exercise of his official functions?
A. It looks to me like I would have to answer the first part in the negative, and the latter part in the affirmative.
Q. Perhaps you don't understand the question?
A. I mean to say that I never saw anything wrong in the Judge's manner of conducting business.

CROSS-EXAMINED BY MR. KNOTT.

Q. You have had no more business in court than would keep you there half a day occasionally?
A. Sometimes I staid two or three days about court.
Q. Well, you were just going in and out incidentally,—you didn't take a seat or remain in court all the time, did you?
A. No, sir; I was just in occasionally.
Judge Jackson. Have you not been on juries frequently?
A. Yes, sir; I have been on a good many juries.
Mr. Knott. How many juries did you ever serve on?
A. In the last six years I suppose I have served on half a dozen.

TESTIMONY OF DR. J. W. SOUTHER.

Dr. J. W. SOUTHER called and examined by Judge Jackson.
Q. In which county do you reside?
A. I reside in Ripley county.
Q. In what place?
A. In Doniphan, the county seat.
Q. Have you been about court much for the last three or four years?
A. Yes, sir. I have been about court some little.
Q. Do you know of Judge Jackson being guilty of innumerable instances of oppressive, contumelious, insolent, and insulting expressions towards lawyers and parties litigant; and did or not the Judge habitually indulge in such in the exercise of his official functions?
A. I do not. He did not.

CROSS-EXAMINED BY MR. KNOTT.

Q. What is your profession?
A. I practice medicine.
Q. How often are you present in court? You are not in the habit of taking a seat in the court room, and paying close attention to the manner of doing business there?
A. No, sir.
Q. Then, I will ask you if you are prepared to say what Judge Jackson's manner of doing business is?
A. I only speak from what I have seen.
Q. Well, you set by and look on occasionally?
A. I am generally close about, during court week.
Q. Well, you practice medicine—and are only in court casually, I suppose?
A. Yes, sir.
SENATOR JONES here propounded to the witness the next question given below, to which the managers objected as irrelevant, the objection being overruled by the following vote:

AYES—Messrs. Brown, Churchill, Coleman, Fox, Harris, Hedgpeth, Hyer, Jones, Morris, Newland, Parsons, Peyton, Rains, Richardson, Robinson, Scott, and Wilson—17.
NOES—Messrs. Byrne, Frazier, Goodlett, Gullett, Halliburton, Horner, McFarland, McFerran, McIlvaine, O'Neil, Thompson, Vernon, Watkins, Wood, and Wright—15.
Absent—Mr. Johnson.

Q. What has been the general demeanor of Judge Jackson towards the members of the bar practicing in his circuit since he has been Judge of that circuit?
A. His conduct has been good and courteous so far as I know.
Mr. KNOTT. Did you say that you had often been in court?
A. Yes, sir. I have been there pretty often.
Q. What was done while you were there? Do you know any case that was tried while you were present?
A. I was in when Kinsey was tried for hog stealing,—not during the whole of the trial, but a part of it. I was in while they were trying a bond case; they had sued a parcel of securities on a bond; and I was in while they tried the case of Sickles *vs.* McMinn.
Q. What lawyers have you seen in court?
A. I have seen Mr. Kitchen, Mr. Bedford, and Mr. Woodsides.
Q. What do you understand by contumelious conduct?
A. I suppose it means obstinate, contrary, probably.

Q. If a man were to tell you that you had sworn a lie, or made another man swear a lie, wouldn't you think that insulting?

A. Yes, sir. I would.

TESTIMONY OF PINCKNEY POWERS.

PINCKNEY POWERS called and examined by Judge Jackson.

Q. Were you at Wayne Circuit Court, September, 1858?

A. Yes, sir.

Q. Were you one of the parties in the case of Limbarger *vs.* Powers?

A. Yes, sir.

Q. State, if you please, what took place in court in connection with the change of venue in that case.

A. Me and Mr. Limbarger had a suit then, and there was some talk going on about it between the attorneys. I was sitting by Mr. Bedford. Mr. Pipkin was sitting on the opposite end of the table. Mr. Bedford was on my right, Mr. Pipkin on my left. I saw Mr. Pipkin write a notice, that they would take a change of venue. I turned around and told Mr. Bedford what he was doing. "Oh! no," said Mr. Bedford, "I reckon they won't do that," and when I told him that I seen Mr. Pipkin writing the notice, he said, "Well, I will oppose its going to Fredericktown." Mr. Pipkin handed over the notice, and asked us to acknowledge the service of this. Mr. Bedford said, "certainly," and Mr. Pipkin went on writing the petition. When he was through, he beckoned to Mr. Limbarger, and he signed it, and he handed it over to the Clerk, and made affidavit. Mr. Fox picked it up, and presented it to the Judge. All this occurred in a few minutes.

Q. Did you agree that the case should go to any particular county?

A. No, sir.

Q. Did you want the case to go to Madison or Iron county?

A. No, sir.

Q. Who were your attorneys?

A. Mr. White and Mr. Bedford.

Q. Do you know of Mr. Bedford having agreed with other counsel to take the case to Madison or Iron?

A. I do not.

Mr. KNOTT. Where was the case sent to?

A. To Mississippi county.

TESTIMONY OF JOSEPH WHITE.

JOSEPH WHITE called and examined by Judge Jackson.

Q. Where do you reside?

A. In the town of Greenville, in Wayne county, in this State.

Q. Were you present at the Wayne Circuit Court, September, 1858?

A. I was, sir.

Q. Were you an attorney in the case of Limbarger *vs.* Powers?

A. Yes, sir. I was for Powers.

Q. State if you know what took place at the Wayne court when the cause was pending there.

A. I know the plaintiff applied for a change of venue, and the court ordered the case sent to Mississippi county.

Q. At the time the application was made, did you make known that you were willing for the case to go to any particular county?

A. I did not. I was willing that the case should be tried there.

Q. How far from Greenville to Charleston, Mississippi county?

A. Somewhere between sixty and seventy miles.

Q. Which would be the most convenient to go to, Iron, Madison, or Mississippi?

A. If the swamp is up, at across Nigger Wool, the distance would be a little more to Charleston, and upon condition that you would have to cross the swamp, it would be more convenient to go to one of the upper counties.

Q. Which would be the most convenient, going from Bloomfield?

A. Mississippi.

Q. Were you present at Ripley court, at the April term, 1858?

A. Yes, sir.

Q. Were you connected with the Kinsey trial?

A. Yes, sir. I was associated with the Circuit Attorney in the argument of the case. It was a case of larceny, and was tried twice at the same term.

Q. Do you remember what was said about taking down the testimony in that case,—about my not letting them have time to take it down?

A. I know there was something said about it. Mr. Tyrell, I think, took the evidence. I recollect that you said that what was evidence after the witness was through could be taken down. I recollect that Mr. Tyrell agreed to take it down.

Q. Do you recollect any interruption of Kinsey's counsel?

A. I recollect when Mr. Fox was speaking he made a comparison. I believe he was comparing the court to the Spanish Inquisition, and I recollect your asking him what he meant, and that his reply was, "if the shoe fits you, you can wear it."

Q. What was the nature of the comparison you speak of?

A. To the best of my recollection he said he would as soon be tried by the Spanish Inquisition, or be guillotined, as to be tried in that style. I couldn't tell whether he meant the court or the jury, or what. I was mad at the time. Mr. Fox made assertions about me and acted insultingly towards me. I spoke very harshly to him. I abused him just as much as I could.

Q. Do you recollect my stopping Mr. Fox?

A. Yes, sir. It was at this time. Mr. Fox was using very improper language, and you stopped him.

Q. How long have you been practicing in the Fifteenth Judicial Circuit?

A. I have lived in the Fifteenth Circuit since 1849, and been practicing law a great portion of the time.

Q. Do you know of Judge Jackson's being guilty of innumerable instances of oppressive, contumelious, insolent, and insulting expressions towards lawyers and parties litigant; and did or not the Judge habitually indulge in such in the exercise of his official functions?

A. I don't know of Judge Jackson being guilty of the like of that. He sometimes acted, I thought, a little crudely; but he never treated the lawyers as severely as I would have done if I had been in his place.

CROSS-EXAMINED BY MR. KNOTT.

Q. You would consider it "crude" to tell a man in court that he lied wouldn't you?

A. I think I would. I don't know that I ever seen the Judge do that, however.

Q. Did you ever see the Judge act "crudely" towards Mr. Phelan and Mr. Fox?

A. I never seen more on his part than on theirs.

Q. In this case of Kinsey, at the time the Judge stopped Mr. Fox while he was speaking, do you recollect whether he was saying anything that applied to you?

A. At the first of the allusion, he said something in relation to my volunteering, and I thought he alluded to me until the court asked him what he meant, and he replied that "if the shoe fits you, you can wear it."

Q. When Mr. Fox spoke about the Inquisition, did he particularize or make his comparisons so pointed that you were confident he didn't mean you?

A. I don't think he did.

Q. Wasn't he speaking about your volunteering in the case, and wasn't he playing upon your name, Joseph, by a reference to Joseph of old?

A. I think he did make use of something of that kind.

Q. When the Judge asked him to explain, didn't he say, "if you will deduct from my time, I will do so?"

A. I think he did.

Q. Why did you afterwards think that he alluded to the court, when you say that at first you thought he alluded to you?

A. I thought so from the course he took, and from the rough manner in which he replied to the court.

Q. Was any of this roughness exhibited before he was interrupted by the court?

A. I thought it rough treatment from the word go.

Q. How far is it from Greenville to Ironton?

A. I can't tell you the exact distance. It is about forty or forty-five miles.

Q. This swamp—Nigger Wool—isn't it generally up in the winter and spring?

A. Yes, sir; I believe it is.

Q. Do not the courts set there in the spring and fall?

A. Yes, sir.

Senator Goodlett. Were you in court all the time when the application for a change of venue, in this case of which you have spoken, was up?

A. I would make this concession: I am satisfied that I never heard any agreement entered into, and I think I was present when application was made to the court. If any statement was made to the court that there was an agreement, I never heard it.

Mr. Knott. How far is it from Greenville to Fredericktown?

A. It is forty-five or fifty miles.

Q. Whereabouts does Mr. Powers live?

A. About half way between Greenville and Fredericktown.

Q. From where he lives, which is the nearest point, Ironton or Charleston?

A. Ironton.

Q. Don't you have a good deal of business at Ironton? Isn't it the shipping point for that part of country?

A. Yes, sir. There is some business of that kind done.

Q. How far is it from eighteen or twenty miles from Greenville, the neighborhood where Powers lives, to the county seat of Mississippi county?

A. I do not know the distance. It is nearer to Mississippi county at Powers' than at Greenville. They live in the northern part of the county, a little east of north, and Charleston, I think, is a little north of due east, mighty near due east.

Q. Do you think you were in all the time pending the discussion of the matter as to where the case should be sent?

A. I think I was.

Q. Do you know which one of the attorneys wrote the petition?

A. I can't be certain which it was.

Q. Where was Mr. Bedford when it was presented? In what part of the court house?

A. I don't recollect.

Q. Did you see where your client was setting?

A. Yes, sir. He was sitting by me. I conversed with him on the subject.

Q. Were you not willing that the case should go to Bollinger?

A. I was disposed to let it go there without objection.

Q. Had your client any objection to the case going there?

A. None that I know of.

SENATOR McILVAINE. How far is it from the residence of these parties to Ironton?

A. I don't know that I can answer precisely. It is called some forty-five or fifty miles from Greenville to Ironton, and they live about eighteen miles north of Greenville. I suppose Ironton is twenty, twenty-five, or thirty miles from where they lived at that time.

JUDGE JACKSON. Do either Mr. Fox or Mr. Pipkin reside in the Fifteenth Circuit?

A. No, sir; they do not.

Q. Do not the courts at Ironton interfere with the courts in the Fifteenth Circuit?

A. I forget at what time the courts are held.

TESTIMONY OF MILES PONDER.

MILES PONDER called and examined by Judge Jackson.

Q. In which county do you reside?

A. In Ripley.

Q. Do you hold any office there?

A. Yes, sir; I am Clerk of the Circuit Court in Ripley county.

Q. State if you recollect what occurred at the trial of the State *vs.* Kinsey in that court.

A. Yes, sir; I was present.

Q. Well, if you recollect any interruption in the progress of that trial, state it if you please.

A. The only interruption I saw was between Judge Fox, defendant's counsel, and the court. To the best of my recollection the time for the speeches of the attorneys in this case was limited. I think that half an hour was allowed to each attorney to speak. That is my impression, although I am not certain. Mr. Fox spoke on that length of time, when the Judge stopped him and informed him that his time was up. He turned around and made some remarks, and asked for a longer time, and the court granted him ten minutes. He proceeded till after the lapse of the ten minutes, when he was informed by the court again that his time was out. I don't remember precisely about the time, but I think he then asked to be allowed to speak longer, and his request was granted. He proceeded only a few minutes, and just after he proceeded, the Judge stopped him and said, "you must address yourself to the case if you wish to proceed." Mr. Fox thanked him, and went on until the court again informed him that his time was up, and he contended a few minutes about speaking longer, and the court told him to take his seat. There may have been other things passed, but there was nothing else that I saw.

Q. Do you recollect the circumstance that occurred about taking down testimony? Do you recollect any difficulty about the time for taking down the testimony?

A. I have no recollection of anything of the kind.

Q. Do you recollect at the October term, 1857, anything that occurred in the case of Lacey and Gale *vs.* Powers and Ponder, between Mr. Fox and the court?

A. I remember an answer or an amended answer, or something that required to be sworn to, any how. You told him he couldn't make that answer.

Q. Do you recollect my taking it up in my hands?

A. I only recollect a remark that you made, that the defendant couldn't take that affidavit.

Q. How long have you been Clerk of the court there?

A. I entered on the discharge of my duties—well, it will be six years ago next January. I have been Clerk of the court ever since you have been Judge.

Q. Do you know of Judge Jackson being guilty of innumerable instances of oppressive, contumelious, insolent, and insulting expressions towards lawyers and parties litigant; and did or not the Judge habitually indulge in such in the exercise of his official functions?

A. No, sir, I don't know that I have. If I am to confine the answer to lawyers, I wouldn't so consider it.

Q. Have you known such conduct towards parties?

A. No, sir.

Senator Jones. Were you in court when Judge Jackson and Mr. Fox had the difficulty about the answer?

A. I was close by.

Q. What reason did the Judge assign in this conversation why Mr. Fox could not file that answer?

A. I could hardly say. He wanted me to qualify the defendant to the answer, and I think he asked leave to file the answer, or he wanted to be qualified to it, or something of that kind. I don't remember.

Judge Jackson. Do you remember my asking him if he had written the answer?

A. I don't remember it distinctly.

Q. Do you recollect my telling him that he lied, or that he caused his client to lie?

A. No, sir, I don't.

Q. Do you recollect that I said anything about perjury?

A. I do not.

Q. What was the general bearing of the Judge towards lawyers practicing in his courts?

[This question was objected to by the managers, but the objection was waived after a short debate.]

A. It was generally courteous and kind, according to my view. After parties sometimes disobeyed his ruling, he would sometimes speak very positively and harsh to them, but not at first.

Q. Do you mean parties to suits or attorneys? Do you know of any instance in which I have ever spoken harshly to the parties themselves?

A. Well, to the parties themselves I think you was always kind and courteous, and you was kind and courteous to the lawyers generally.

Senator Fox. Did you ever know the Judge to speak harshly to an attorney without first receiving some harsh treatment from that attorney?

A. I don't think I ever did.

Q. Were you by all the time during the disturbance between Mr. Fox and the Judge?

A. Yes, sir. My attention was called to the circumstance, and I was there to swear the defendant to the answer. The court told him the defendant couldn't make that answer, for some reason. I couldn't say what it was.

Mr. KNOTT. In this conversation, you say that Mr. Fox proposed to have the defendant himself sworn?

A. Yes, sir.

The examination of witnesses here ended for the forenoon.

J. W. Souther, Francis Lawson, Dr. Russell, and Pinckney Powers, witnesses, were discharged by consent of parties.

Mr. KNOTT, on behalf of the managers, called the attention of the Court to the law regulating costs in cases of impeachment, and suggested the propriety of some action on the subject.

SENATOR GOODLETT then, to test the sense of the Senate, offered the following resolution:

Resolved, That the Chairman of the Committee on Accounts be instructed not to issue certificates to defendant's witnesses until the final decision of this cause, when, if the defendant is acquitted of the charges against him, said certificates shall issue according to law.

To this resolution, SENATOR WILSON offered the following amendment, by way of substitute:

Resolved, That the Committee on Accounts be instructed to audit and allow the witnesses summoned by the State and respondent in the impeachment case now pending, for mileage and attendance in said cause, as said witnesses may be discharged by the Court.

This amendment was agreed to by the following vote:

AYES—Messrs. Byrne, Churchill, Coleman, Gullett, Harris, Hedgpeth, Horner, Hyer, Jones, McFerran, McIlvaine, Morris, Newland, O'Neil, Peyton, Rains, Robinson, Scott, Vernon, Watkins, Wilson, and Wood—22.

NOES—Messrs. Brown, Fox, Frazier, Goodlett, Halliburton, McFarland, Parsons, Richardson, Thompson, and Wright—10.

Absent—Mr. Johnson.

The question then being on the adoption of the substitute, it was adopted by the following vote:

AYES—Messrs. Byrne, Churchill, Coleman, Gullett, Harris, Hedgpeth, Horner, Hyer, Jones, McFerran, McIlvaine, Morris, Newland, O'Neil, Peyton, Rains, Robinson, Scott, Vernon, Watkins, Wilson, and Wood—22.

NOES—Messrs. Brown, Fox, Frazier, Goodlett, Halliburton, McFarland, Parsons, Richardson, Thompson, and Wright—10.

Absent—Mr. Johnson.

On motion of SENATOR HORNER, the Court adjourned.

EVENING SESSION.

FRIDAY, June 17, 1859.

The Court met pursuant to adjournment.
The managers and respondent attended.
The examination of witnesses for the defense was resumed.

FRANCIS LAWSON recalled and examined by Judge Jackson.

Q. Are you acquainted with the handwriting of Jacob C. Blount?

A. Yes, sir. I have frequently seen him write his name.

Q. From your knowledge of his handwriting, would you say that was his signature? (showing witness a paper.)

A. I don't think it is his handwriting.

CROSS-EXAMINED BY MR. KNOTT.

Q. What is the material difference between that signature and Mr. Blount's usual manner of writing his name?

A. There is a material difference in the way he forms his *J*.

Q. Did you ever see Mr. Blount write when he was so drunk he couldn't stand up?

A. No, sir, I never did.

MILES PONDER recalled and examined by Judge Jackson.

Q. Do you recollect the case of Moore *vs.* Eldridge, the administrator of Parker, in the Ripley Circuit Court?

A. Yes, sir, I recollect the case.

Q. State what you know of a paper before the jury, and any difficulty that may have occurred about it.

A. In the trial of that case, the defendant, Moore, wished—well there had been a firm of Moore and Parker, and Parker was dead and Eldridge was his administrator. When the suit was pending he wished to introduce the article of agreement for carrying on the business as partners. The court refused to allow that paper to be introduced, because,—well, I couldn't tell what was the reason, but I think it couldn't be ascertained what the date of the paper was. The court refused to allow that paper as evidence, and Moore wanted to use it as evidence.

Q. How did it affect the suit?

A. Well, I don't know exactly how it affected the suit.

Q. Hadn't the suit been spoken of pretty generally?

A. Yes, sir. It was talked about a good deal. The suit was about a note, and the articles were important to show whether the note was given in accordance with the articles. That is the reason why the paper was material in this suit, and it is necessary to have the articles in to show something about these—

Mr. KNOTT objected to the witness giving an opinion as to the effect of the instrument as evidence in the case.

Q. What was the nature of the suit?

A. The suit was on a note. Moore had refused to pay the note, because he said it was given through a mistake. He wanted to introduce the articles to show that the note was given to Parker through a mistake.

Q. Do you recollect in making up a bill of exceptions any difficulty about this article. That is what we want now.

A. They moved an arrest of judgment from the fact they were not allowed to introduce their instrument. The only way I know—

Mr. Knott. If you were present when the bill of exceptions was presented, say so, and tell what occurred, and if you were not present you need not make any statement about it.

A. I don't remember what passed between them when the bill of exceptions was made up. They excepted because they hadn't been allowed to introduce this article.

Judge Jackson. Was this instrument to go into the bill of exceptions?

A. I don't remember.

Q. Do you recollect any difficulty about the instrument in preparing the bill of exceptions?

A. I don't remember any difficulty. I don't recollect whether he wanted to have it in the bill of exceptions, or not. It strikes me that it was not. The date couldn't be made out from being defaced or erased. It seemed to have been altered. I couldn't make out the date.

TESTIMONY OF CHARLES F. HENDERSON.

Charles F. Henderson called and examined by Judge Jackson.

Q. In which county do you reside?

A. In Butler county.

Q. Were you there at the Circuit Court, November term, A. D. 1857, when Blount was so he couldn't be in court?

A. Yes, sir. I was living there at the time.

Q. Do you know anything about a suit pending against you then by Ewing & Co.?

A. I think there was a suit commenced. However, I don't recollect what was done with it, or what could be done with it then. I don't know much about the suit, or what become of it.

Q. Had process in the case of Ewing & Co. *vs.* Henderson been served in time for any steps to be taken in the case at that term of the court?

To this question the managers objected on the ground that it could only elicit the opinion of the witness upon a matter of law.

Judge Jackson contended that the evidence of Mr. Phelan had made it proper to ask the question.

The question for the action of the Court being, shall the respondent be permitted to ask the question? it was decided in the negative by the following vote:

Ayes—Messrs. Goodlett, Gullett, Harris, Hedgpeth, Morris, Parsons, Peyton, Robinson, and Wood—9.

Noes—Messrs. Brown, Byrne, Churchill, Coleman, Fox, Frazier, Halliburton, Horner, Hyer, McFarland, McFerran, McIlvaine, Newland, O'Neil, Richardson, Thompson, Vernon, and Wright—18.

Q. How long have you been living in Butler county?

A. About nine years, I think.

Q. Do you live in the town of Poplar Bluff?

A. I lived there until last year.

Q. Do you know of Judge Jackson being guilty of innumerable instances of oppressive, contumelious, insolent, and insulting expressions towards lawyers and parties litigant; and did or not the Judge habitually indulge in such in the exercise of his official functions?

A. Not to my knowledge. I have been but very little in court, though I have been living there.

Q. What has been the general demeanor of Judge Jackson towards lawyers practicing in his courts, and towards witnesses and parties, so far as you know?

A. I can't say I have seen anything amiss in him. So far as I know there has been nothing amiss.

Mr. Knott. I understand you to say you have been very little in court?

A. Yes, sir. Very little.

Mr. Knott. You can stand aside then.

TESTIMONY OF ALEXANDER SLOAN.

Alexander Sloan called and examined by Judge Jackson.

Q. In which county do you live?

A. In Wayne county.

Q. How long have you been living there?

A. Twenty-six years.

Q. Have you been in court during the last three or four years much?

A. Yes, sir. I think I have attended all the courts two or three days each, for the last four or five years.

Q. Do you know of Judge Jackson being guilty of innumerable instances of oppressive, contumelious, insolent, and insulting expressions towards lawyers and parties litigant; and did or not the Judge habitually indulge in such in the exercise of his official functions?

A. No. I never recollect seeing anything of that kind.

Q. What has been the general demeanor of Judge Jackson towards lawyers practicing in his courts, and towards witnesses and parties, so far as you know?

A. It has been respectful; as much so as usual. I never saw any thing wrong.

CROSS-EXAMINED BY MR. KNOTT.

Q. You say you have been at court one or two days each term. You mean, I suppose, that you have been there incidentally, going in and out, as your business calls you?

A. Yes, sir.

Judge Jackson. You have been on juries frequently, haven't you?

A. Yes, sir. Both grand and petit juries.

Mr. Knott. When you have been on the grand jury, you have been pretty much confined to the jury rooom while court was in session, haven't you?

A. Yes, sir.

Q. How often have you been on the grand jury for the last three or four years?

A. Once, I believe.

Q. How many times have you been a petit juror.

A. I don't recollect but one or two times.

TESTIMONY OF JAMES A. ATKINS.

James A. Atkins called and examined by Judge Jackson.

Q. In which county do you reside?

A. In Wayne county.

Q. How long have you been living there?

A. Thirty years.

Q. Have you been about the Circuit Court any for the last four years? Have you been a juror occasionally?

A. Yes, sir.

Q. Do you know of Judge Jackson being guilty of innumerable instances of oppressive, contumelious, insolent, and insulting expressions towards lawyers and parties litigant; and did or not the Judge habitually indulge in such in the exercise of his official functions?

A. I have never known anything of the kind.

Q. What has been the general demeanor of Judge Jackson towards lawyers practicing in his courts, and towards witnesses and parties, so far as you know?

A. I don't know much about it. I haven't heard any but a few complain.

CROSS-EXAMINED BY MR. KNOTT.

Q. You say you have been at court more or less for the last three or four years. You mean that you were there incidentally, passing in and out, and that you did not set there all the time noticing the manner of doing business?

A. Yes, sir. That is what I mean.

Q. What is your business?

A. That of a farmer.

TESTIMONY OF LEMUEL KITTRELL.

LEMUEL KITTRELL called and examined by Judge Jackson.

Q. Were you present at the Circuit Court in Ripley county when the case of the State *vs.* Kinsey was tried?

A. Yes, sir.

Q. If you noticed anything peculiar between the court and Mr. Fox, state what it was.

A. Mr. Fox was employed by Mr. Kinsey. The lawyers in this case were limited as to how long they should speak. Mr. Fox went on with his speech, and the court stopped him, and reminded him that his time was near out. Mr. Fox thanked him, and went on. He run over his time fifteen minutes. The court stopped him again, and he asked for more time, and the court still gave him more time, and when that was out, says he, "Mr. Fox, set down." Mr. Fox did set down. He appeared to be speaking in a peculiar way.

Mr. KNOTT. Never mind stating anything about that. Mr. Fox's peculiarities are not under investigation.

A. Well, when I came in he was speaking in a powerful way, and if you must know, I thought it was a little too much whisky. He wasn't speaking to the *pint* or subject at all, according to my judgment.

Mr. KNOTT. We don't want your judgment.

JUDGE JACKSON. How long have you been living in Doniphan?

A. I have been living at Doniphan ever since it was born, as the saying is.

Q. Do you know of Judge Jackson being guilty of innumerable instances of oppressive, contumelious, insolent, and insulting expressions towards lawyers and parties litigant; and does or not the Judge habitually indulge in such in the exercise of his official functions?

A. No, sir. I don't.

Q. What has been the general demeanor of Judge Jackson towards lawyers practicing in his courts, and towards witnesses and parties, as far as you know?

A. So far as I know, it has been all right, except that some times the lawyers got so troublesome that he couldn't do much with them. I thought his general course towards the lawyers was tolerable loose.

SENATOR JONES. What is the general character of Judge Jackson in the Fifteenth Judicial Circuit for honesty and integrity in the discharge of his official duties?

[Mr. Knott objected to this question, and after discussion it was withdrawn.]

TESTIMONY OF DABNEY S. COOPER.

Dabney S. Cooper called and examined by Judge Jackson.

Q. In which county do you live?

A. I live in Stoddard county.

Q. Were you on the jury in the case of the State *vs.* Sarah Buckner?

A. Yes, sir.

Q. Do you recollect the testimony of Grimsley in that case?

A. No, sir. I can't recollect.

Q. Do you recollect whether it was withdrawn?

A. I cannot recollect whether it was withdrawn or not.

Q. Do you recollect any instructions that were given to the jury in relation to that matter?

A. Not now. It has been too long ago.

Q. Do you recollect any difficulty taking place between the court and Charles Davis?

A. I recollect of his setting down, and leaving the case.

Q. Do you know what made him set down?

A. No, sir; I don't.

TESTIMONY OF JAMES DENNIS.

James Dennis called and examined by Judge Jackson.

Q. In which county do you reside, Mr. Dennis?

A. I live in Butler county, Missouri.

Q. State if you were at the court when Mr. Blount didn't work.

A. Yes, sir; I was there. It was the November term, 1857.

Q. How long did court hold at that time?

A. I think it held one day, all day Monday, and adjourned Tuesday, about 12 o'clock.

Q. Was it Tuesday or Wednesday?

A. I am not certain whether it was Tuesday or Wednesday.

Q. Do you recollect what was the matter with the Clerk?

A. On Monday night Blount was either drunk or sick. I am not certain whether it was Monday or Tuesday night. I know no Clerk was appointed. I think it was about 12 o'clock the court adjourned.

Q. Do you recollect any attempt to go on with the business?

A. Yes, sir. You said that we could take judgments on plain notes of hand if we wished. You said you thought that could be done.

Q. What became of the papers belonging to the cases then in court?

A. You took them into the Clerk's office, and separated the papers belonging to the criminal cases from the papers belonging to the civil cases, and then put them away. You took me into the Clerk's office, and showed me where you put them, and then you locked the door, gave me the key, and I went down and gave it to Blount.

Q. Were you present in court when the case of Gibson *vs.* Dunn was called?

A. Yes, sir; I was.

Q. State, if you please, if any thing unusual occurred between the court and Mr. Phelan, while we were trying that case.

A. I cannot recollect what occurred then. I didn't observe anything unusual. At another term of the court, I witnessed a difficulty between the Judge and Mr. Phelan.

Q. Well, go on and state what was said and done.

[The witness was proceeding to narrate some circumstances which had no connection with the case in hand, when he was stopped by Mr. Knott, and his statements on this point excluded.]

Q. Mr. Dennis, were you one of the attorneys in the Sarah Buckner case?

A. I was. I helped to take down the evidence in the case. I wasn't employed, but was only assisting Mr. Phelan. I don't recollect much about the case. I had the chills then, and had taken quinine that day. I didn't charge my mind with what occurred. I made the opening speech in the case.

Q. Were you present when Mr. Davis made his speech?

A. Yes, sir. He got to commenting on some evidence, and the Judge called him to order, and told him "that evidence is not in the case." Mr. Davis then said, "if you won't allow me to draw figures and comparisons, I shall abandon the case." Then he stopped.

Q. How long have you lived in the Fifteenth Circuit?

A. Over three years.

Q. Have you attended all the courts in the circuit?

A. Yes, sir. I have been in all the nine counties.

Q. Do you know of Judge Jackson being guilty of innumerable instances of oppressive, contumelious, insolent, and insulting expressions towards lawyers and parties litigant; and does or not the Judge habitually indulge in such in the exercise of his official functions?

A. No, sir. I can't say that I do.

Q. What has been the general demeanor of Judge Jackson towards lawyers practicing in his courts, and towards witnesses and parties, as far as you know?

A. As far as I have seen, you have treated the bar with respect and courtesy. I can speak for myself, and I haven't seen you mistreat any body else.

Q. Did you ever see Jacob Blount write his name? Are you acquainted with his handwriting?

A. Yes, sir; I am.

Q. From your knowledge of his handwriting would you say that was his signature? (showing him the paper.)

A. I don't think it looks like his signature. His *J*'s always come below the line.

Mr. Knott. Did you ever see him write his name when he was so drunk that he had to be held up to do it?

A. No, I never saw him do that, though I have seen him write when he was pretty tight.

Mr. Knott. Well, then, you may stand aside.

TESTIMONY OF ALEXANDER WARD.

Alexander Ward called and examined by Judge Jackson.

Q. In which county do you reside, Mr. Ward?

A. I live in Wayne county.

Q. How long have you lived there?

A. About fourteen years, last fall, since I came to Missouri.

Q. Are you frequently at Circuit Courts?

A. Yes, sir; I am.

Q. Do you know of Judge Jackson being guilty of innumerable instances of oppressive, contumelious, insolent, and insulting expressions towards lawyers and parties litigant; and does or not the Judge habitually indulge in such in the exercise of his official functions?

A. I never saw anything of it, at our court. I always have seen you courteous.

Mr. Knott. What is your business?

A. Farming.

Q. You are merely incidentally at court, I suppose?

A. That is all, sir.

JUDGE JACKSON. You have served on juries?

A. Yes, sir.

TESTIMONY OF A. LOWE.

Mr. A. LOWE called and examined by Judge Jackson.

Q. In which county do you live?

A. I reside in Ripley county.

Q. What is your occupation?

A. I have been following surveying and writing in the Clerk's office some four years.

Q. Do you recollect anything concerning the case of the State *vs.* Kinsey?

A. I was not in court at the trial of that case.

Q. Do you recollect anything about the Judge saying anything about some one being guilty of perjury or subornation of perjury?

A. I do not.

Q. Do you recollect the case of Lacey and Gale *vs.* Powers and Ponder?

A. Yes, sir.

Q. Do you recollect anything said to Mr. Fox during the pendency of that case?

A. No, sir.

Q. Do you recollect anything in the case of Moore *vs.* Eldridge?

A. I recollect an instrument of writing offered by Moore, and the court overruled its being evidence. He didn't permit it to be introduced as testimony.

Q. Do you recollect whether that instrument was used in another case?

A. No, sir; this is the case that they offered to introduce the instrument in.

Q. Was there any other case except this one between Eldridge and Moore in which this paper came up?

A. I think this case that we have spoken of was an appeal from the County Court. In the trial in the County Court, I suppose they had the paper.

Q. Well, was it in this case of Moore *vs.* Eldridge that this question about the erasure came up?

A. Yes, sir. I think so.

Q. Have you generally been in the Circuit Court for the last three or four years?

A. I have been in every court more or less for that time.

Q. Do you know of Judge Jackson being guilty of innumerable instances of oppressive, contumelious, insolent, and insulting expressions towards lawyers and parties litigant; and does or not the Judge habitually indulge in such in the exercise of his official functions?

A. I do not, sir.

Q. What has been the general demeanor of Judge Jackson towards lawyers practicing in his courts, and towards witnesses and parties, so far as you know?

A. So far as I know, it has always been courteous.

TESTIMONY OF JAMES DOWDY.

JAMES DOWDY called and examined by Judge Jackson.

Q. In which county do you live?

A. I live in Stoddard county when at home, in this State.

Q. What do you do there?

A. I ain't doing anything there just now. I have been acting Sheriff of that county some three years. It will be three years next August since I got the appointment.

Q. Were you present at the time when there were some proceedings in the Stoddard Circuit Court about a mandamus against Judge Eaker?

A. Yes, sir. I saw the writ.

Q. Did you offer to deliver the original writ to Mr. Eaker?

A. Yes, sir, I did, and when I carried it to him, he said he was too old for King Wasson. I told him the service of my deputy wasn't legal, and he would have to answer, and there was the original writ and he could answer on that; but he turned off, telling me what I have said.

Q. Who is Wasson?

A. Mr. Wasson lives down in Stoddard county and professes to be a lawyer.

Q. What became of the writ?

A. It was returned into the court. When the matter came up into court my understanding was that it was decided that the Deputy Sheriff hadn't served the writ right, and it was handed to me, and I went to him and told him what the decision was about the way of serving the writ, but he wouldn't have anything to do with it. I turned round and went back, and went in and handed the writ to the court, and I stated that Mr. Eaker wouldn't have anything to do with the writ.

Q. Do you know what my reply was when you told me Mr. Eaker had refused to have anything to do with the original writ?

A. No, sir. I don't recollect. I don't recollect whether you made any reply.

Q. Do you know when he did answer?

A. I think it was that evening.

Q. Didn't he ask until next morning to make his return?

A. I don't know. It is likely he might have asked that, though I don't recollect anything about it.

Q. What has been the demeanor of Judge Jackson towards members of the bar practicing in his courts?

A. I always thought he allowed them to do pretty much as they pleased.

Q. Do you know of Judge Jackson being guilty of innumerable instances of oppressive, contumelious, insolent, and insulting expressions towards lawyers and parties litigant; and does or not the Judge habitually indulge in such in the exercise of his official functions?

A. No, sir; I don't.

CROSS-EXAMINED BY MR. KNOTT.

Q. Where was Judge Eaker when the difficulty came up in court about the service of the writ of mandamus?

A. I don't recollect.

Q. Was it the return day of the writ when you say you took the original to Judge Eaker?

A. I took the writ to him the same day they had the difficulty about service. Afterwards he wrote his return.

Q. Where was Judge Eaker when you took the writ to him? Was he in or out of the court house?

A. He had gone out; and when I had spoke to him, he turned off and went into Miller's store.

SENATOR PARSONS. Was this offer of the original before or after he was attached?

A. It was before.

Q. How long?

A. Some little time. It was long enough for me to go back into court. I think the attachment was issued after I went back and made a report of what he wouldn't do.

Mr. HARDIN. Did you make any statement under oath, or any affidavit to these facts?

A. No, sir. I just made that statement.

The examination of witnesses was here suspended.

The following named witnesses were discharged by consent of parties:

For Respondent—Charles Henderson, Dabney S. Cooper, Alexander Ward, Lemuel Kittrell, Miles Ponder, Alexander Sloan, A. Lowe, James Dowdy, and James A. Atkins.

For the State—Washington Carlisle.

On motion of SENATOR NEWLAND, the Court adjourned.

TWELFTH DAY.

SATURDAY, June 18, 1859.

The Court met pursuant to adjournment, and was opened by proclamation.

The managers and respondent attended.

The examination of witnesses for the defense was resumed.

TESTIMONY OF JAMES A. WALKER.

JAMES A. WALKER called and examined by Judge Jackson.

Q. In which county do you live?

A. In the county of Dunklin.

Q. Were you an attorney in the case of Smith *vs.* Cude?

A. Yes, sir, I was.

Q. Were you present when an application for a change of venue in that case was made?

A. I was not in the court house at the time the application was made.

Q. Did you consent that the case should be sent to either Cape Girardeau, Scott, or Bollinger county?

A. I don't think I was consulted. It was my understanding that Dr. Horner arranged that matter.

Q. How do the citizens of Dunklin county generally go to Pemiscot county?

A. Generally by water. One can go by keel-boat, canoe, pirogue, to Portage, and there get a horse for the balance of the distance. In a dry time you can go on horseback. When the water is very high you can't go at all. We had no Circuit Court in Pemiscot this time, on account of the water. The water was under the court house I understood.

Q. How far is it from the county seat of Dunklin to the county seat of Pemiscot?

A. In a dry time it is fifty miles. We have to go by water seventy-five or eighty miles. The way you go from Pemiscot to Dunklin depends entirely upon the stage of the water.

Q. Don't the people living in that country go through from county to county at all seasons of the year?

A. We go there at any time, wet or dry.

Q. Is it usual to go around by way of Cape Girardeau?

A. No, sir. We don't usually go way around by way of Cape Girardeau. We hardly ever go that way.

Q. Where do the parties in this case of Smith *vs* Cude live?

A. The plaintiff lives in Dyer county, Tennessee. The defendant in Dunklin county, in this State. The witnesses, I believe, live in Dunklin, also.

Q. Which is the most convenient county to these parties, Cape Girardeau, Scott, Pemiscot, or Bollinger?

A. Pemiscot, I should think, was the most convenient. It might happen that either of the others would be more convenient.

Q. What are the facilities for going across the swamp?

A. There are plenty of canoes, keel-boats, and pirogues.

Q. Are not the goods to supply the stores of that county taken across there?

A. Yes, sir. The goods are most all landed at Point Pleasant, hauled to Portage, and then shipped in keels. There are men who hold themselves in readiness to take travelers across the swamp. They usually charge about five dollars. If there is more than one it costs less.

Q. What is your profession?

A. I practice law some.

Q. Do you know of Judge Jackson being guilty of innumerable instances of oppressive, contumelious, insolent, and insulting expressions towards lawyers and parties litigant; and did or not the Judge habitually indulge in such in the exercise of his official functions?

A. I must answer that question in the negative. I have known hard feelings to exist between members of the bar and Judge Jackson, and I have at times heard him use insulting language to them. Sometimes I thought that they were to blame, and sometimes I thought that he was wrong.

Q. Well, what has been the general demeanor of Judge Jackson towards lawyers practicing in his courts, and towards witnesses and parties?

A. Sometimes it has been very courteous and affable, and at other times not so much so.

Q. Well, let us have the general demeanor.

A. Well, for the last three or four courts there has always been something wrong between the court and the bar. I can't say that the court has been to blame for it, however. I was never involved in anything of the kind myself, and I never looked into the matters of others.

SENATOR WATKINS. Do you practice throughout the circuit?

A. No, sir. My practice is principally confined to Dunklin county.

CROSS-EXAMINED BY MR. KNOTT.

Q. How long does it take to go across this swamp that you speak of when you go by water?

A. Generally a day and a half or two days. It is about fifteen miles from Hornersville to Portage. There you have to hire a horse in going on to the county seat of Pemiscot.

Q. What did you say the expense would be in going by this route?

A. It would be five dollars and something more for a horse.

Q. Is it possible to travel in this way at all seasons of the year?

A. No, sir. When the water is very high you would have to take some other route.

Q. Can you go horseback at any season of the year?

A. It is very difficult. It sometimes happens that it could be done, but usually it would be very difficult.

Q. How would it do to go in a buggy?

A. It could hardly be done.

Q. Do you know whether the courts in Pemiscot have been held regularly of late?

A. I have understood that they have had no court there for some time on account of the high water.

Q. Did you say that Mr. Horner was your associate counsel in this Smith *vs.* Cude case?

A. Yes, sir.

JUDGE JACKSON. How long does it take to go from Hornersville to Levee?

A. It is one hundred and fifteen or one hundred and twenty miles, and takes five, six, or seven days, owing to the conveyance used.

SENATOR WATKINS. How far is it from Portage to Gayoso?

A. About fifteen miles. That is my impression, at least. I have never been from Portage to Gayoso.

TESTIMONY OF WILLIAM H. HORNER.

WILLIAM H. HORNER called and examined by Judge Jackson.

Q. In which county do you reside, Mr. Horner?

A. In Dunklin county.

Q. Were you one of the attorneys in the case of Smith *vs.* Cude, in the Dunklin Circuit Court?

A. Yes, sir. I was on the side of the plaintiff, Mr. Smith.

Q. Were you in court when a change of venue was awarded in this case?

A. I wasn't present when the application was made. When I was called in, Mr. Kitchen came to me and suggested Bollinger county as the most convenient. I think I suggested New Madrid county. We disagreed, he contending for one county, and I for the other. The Judge then stated that he would send it to Pemiscot county.

Q. How did that suit the parties?

A. Well, the county seat of Pemiscot is about half way between the two parties, plaintiff and defendant. Each would have to travel thirty or thirty-five miles,—about the same distance.

Q. Where do the witnesses reside?

A. I think all the witnesses are in Dunklin county, with the exception of a few, perhaps, in Dyer county, Tennessee, where the plaintiff resides.

SENATOR JONES. You say Mr. Smith was plaintiff? Did his attorneys take the change of venue?

A. No, sir; it was the defendant.

Q. When persons living in that county wish to go from Kennett to Gayoso, is it the usual way to cross at Hornersville?

A. Yes, sir.

Q. How far is it?

A. In the neighborhood of thirty or forty miles.

Q. In what counties have you been at court, Mr. Horner?

A. I have attended the courts in Reynolds, Shannon, Oregon, Stoddard, and Dunklin counties.

Q. Do you know of Judge Jackson being guilty of innumerable instances of oppressive, contumelious, insolent and insulting expressions towards lawyers and parties litigant; and did or not the Judge habitually indulge in such in the exercise of his official functions?

A. Never, to my knowledge.

Q. What has been the general demeanor of Judge Jackson towards lawyers practicing in his courts, and towards witnesses and parties, so far as you know?

A. So far as my knowledge extends it has been proper and right. I have, however, frequently seen him roused somewhat, and have known of him calling them to order and lecturing of them some.

CROSS-EXAMINED BY MR. KNOTT.

Q. What do you mean by "lecturing of them?"
A Telling them that they shouldn't and couldn't do so and so, and correcting them when they went wrong.
Q. Have you been at the county seat of Pemiscot since this Smith and Cude case was sent there?
A. I have not.
Q. Do you know whether the case has been tried there?
A. I have understood that it has not yet been tried.
Q. What has caused the delay?
A. Well, this last season the Mississippi river has overflowed most all of that country, and it was so that they couldn't hold court there.
Q. How far is it from your place to Portage?
A. It is about sixty miles to go by water.
Q. What are the facilities for travel by water?
A. Well, the people go in skiffs, canoes, keels, and pirogues.
Q. How much does that kind of traveling cost a man?
A. Between Hornersville and Portage, the fare is usually about five dollars.

Q. When the water is either low or high, isn't it impossible to go that way?
A. Yes, sir; if it is either too low or too high.
Q. Who presented the application for the change of venue about which we have been talking?
A. Mr. Kitchen, I believe.
Q. Did you hear Mr. Kitchen tell the court that the counsel in the case were willing to have the case sent to any other county than Pemiscot?
A. I don't remember it, if I did.
Q. Did you hear Mr. Phelan make any representation to the court in regard to the change of venue?
A. I don't remember any.
Q. Did you hear Judge Jackson tell Mr. Phelan or any one else to sit down while the matter was up in court?
A. I did not.
Q. You say you were not present when the application for a change of venue was presented?
A. I think I was not present when it was first presented.
Q. Why did you object to the case being sent to Bollinger?
A. I objected on the ground that the distance was so great.
JUDGE JACKSON. Did sending the case to Pemiscot drive you out of it, or prevent you from attending to it?
A. No, sir.

MR. KNOTT. Why have you not attended to it, then?
A. Because I knew the waters were so high that the Judge could not attend and hold court at the last term.

JUDGE JACKSON. Was not Pemiscot county the most convenient for your client?
A. I suppose so.

Q. Were you present when changes of venue were awarded in the two plank road cases?

A. I think not.

Q. Where does Mr. Murphy live?

A. In Dunklin county, about five miles from Hornersville.

Q. And Mr. Farrar?

A. About two and a half miles from Kennett, the county seat of Dunklin.

Mr. Knott. Did each one of the witnesses in this case keep a skiff, canoe, pirogue, or keel-boat?

A. Very likely none of them had any.

Q. It would cost each one of them at least five dollars to cross that swamp, then?

A. Yes, sir; about that amount.

TESTIMONY OF JOHN MARSH.

John Marsh called and examined by Judge Jackson.

Q. In which county do you live, Mr. Marsh?

A. In Dunklin.

Q. What is your business?

A. I am Clerk of the Circuit and County Courts, and am farming some.

Q. How long have you been in the Clerk's office?

A. About nine years as Clerk and deputy.

Q. Do you know of Judge Jackson being guilty of innumerable instances of oppressive, contumelious, insolent, and insulting expressions towards lawyers and parties litigant; and did or not the Judge habitually indulge in such in the exercise of his official functions?

A. I do not, sir.

Q. What has been the general demeanor of Judge Jackson towards lawyers practicing in his courts, and towards witnesses and parties?

A. I have always thought that he treated them a good deal better than they treated him.

Mr. Knott. You have your own standard of propriety, haven't you?

A. I speak from what I have seen.

TESTIMONY OF HENRY NOBLE.

Henry Noble called and examined by Judge Jackson.

Q. In which county do you reside, Mr. Noble?

A. In Dunklin county, Missouri.

Q. Have you been Sheriff of that county for some time past?

A. I have.

Q. Do you know anything about a certain William Atterbury being in jail in your county?

A. I don't remember much about it. I was on a trip to this city at the time I have understood he was confined there.

Q. Do you know who arrested him?

A. No, sir; not of my own knowledge.

Q. Who was your deputy at that time?

A. I didn't have any deputy.

Q. Did you arrest Atterbury?

A. No, sir; he never was in my custody.

Q. Do you know of Judge Jackson being guilty of innumerable instances of oppressive, contumelious, insolent, and insulting expressions towards lawyers and parties litigant; and did or not the Judge habitually indulge in such in the exercise of his official functions?

A. I do not.

Q. What has been the general demeanor of Judge Jackson towards lawyers practicing in his courts, and towards witnesses and parties, so far as you know?

A. So far as my knowledge goes, he has treated the bar courteously.

TESTIMONY OF ORSON BARTLETT.

ORSON BARTLETT called and examined by Judge Jackson.

Q. In which county do you reside, Col. Bartlett?

A. In Stoddard county.

Q. Were you in court at the August term, 1858?

A. I think I was.

Q. Had you a case in that court?

A. Yes, sir. There was an indictment against me in that court for card-playing.

Q. Who was your attorney?

A. Mr. Kitchen—Solomon G. Kitchen.

Q. Well, how did it turn out?

A. Well, after a good deal of talk in the court, finally the Circuit Attorney entered a *nolle prosequi.*

Q. Were there any others indicted with you?

A. Yes, sir; three others—Albert Jackson, David G. Hicks, and Isaac Brand.

Q. Do you recollect at the time of the game that you were indicted for what part I had in it?

MR. KNOTT. We object to that question. It is not material whether Judge Jackson took any part in that game of cards or not. The question is leading to a collateral issue of no importance whatever.

JUDGE JACKSON. Do you recollect, Mr. Bartlett, whether I refused to have anything to do with the game, or any part of it?

MR. KNOTT. May it please the Court, this question is clearly improper. The fact of the guilt or innocence of Judge Jackson under this indictment can make no difference in this trial. We charge him with disposing of the indictment against the Circuit Attorney and himself in a corrupt and illegal manner. Whether he protested against a participation in the gaming charged, or not, would be a material matter upon his trial under the indictment, but it is a question which cannot affect the proceedings here.

JUDGE JACKSON. I am glad, Mr. Knott, that you are so candid as to admit that by your mode of trying a man it makes no difference whether he is innocent or guilty.

MR. KNOTT. I make no such admission. But I say that your guilt or innocence of the misdemeanor charged in that indictment cannot affect the charge of usurpation of authority in telling the jury they should not find a general verdict, but should find the facts, and of permitting the Circuit Attorney to draw up an indictment against you and himself, and afterwards come into court and enter a *nolle prosequi* as to that indictment.

JUDGE JACKSON. Since it troubles you so much, I will withdraw the question and pass on.

Q. Mr. Bartlett, you will please go on and State what was done at the trial. What did I do?

A. I don't recollect much about it. I recollect of your speaking some time about the law of the case. You and the lawyers had some conversation about it.

Q. Wasn't that conversation as much or more to the lawyers than to the jury?

A. I took it to be addressed to the whole crowd, jury and all.

Q. How long have you lived in Stoddard county?

A. About twenty-two years.

Q. Have you been about the courts much since I have been Judge?

A. Well, I have been about the courts occasionally.

Q. Do you know of Judge Jackson being guilty of innumerable instances of oppressive, contumelious, insolent, and insulting expressions towards lawyers and parties litigant; and did or not the Judge habitually indulge in such in the exercise of his official functions?

A. No, sir; I don't know of innumerable instances of anything of the kind. I have sometimes seen difficulties spring up in his courts, and hard feelings excited.

Q. What has been the general demeanor of Judge Jackson towards lawyers practicing in his courts, and towards witnesses and parties, so far as you know?

A. I don't know that I am competent to answer that question. I don't know how a Judge should act in his courts. I am not acquainted with the law on the subject.

TESTIMONY OF JOHN R. WOODSIDES.

JOHN R. WOODSIDES called, sworn, and examined by Judge Jackson.

Q. In which county do you reside?

A. In Oregon.

Q. Were you at the Circuit Court in Stoddard county, November term, 1857, at the trial of Sarah Buckner?

A. I was, sir.

Q. You will please state what occurred in court during that trial.

A. I don't remember anything unusual.

Q. Do you know anything about the Judge taking the prosecution into his own hands?

A. I do not.

Q. What part did you take in the trial of that cause?

A. I was the Circuit Attorney. My recollection is that I examined the witnesses and managed the prosecution myself.

Q. Do you remember anything unusal occurring during the examination of a witness named Grimsley?

A. I remember that Grimsley was a witness, but I don't remember with any distinctness what questions were asked him or what he said. I think he commenced by giving her admissions in a conversation with him.

Q. Do you recollect objecting to any portion of his testimony?

A. I think it is likely I did object to some parts of a conversation detailed by the witness; and if I remember correctly, something then passed by way of discussion between me and the lawyers engaged for the defense.

Q. Do you recollect whether the court gave any instruction as to the evidence of this witness?

A. I don't recollect.

Q. If any had been given, wouldn't you recollect it?

A. I cannot say positively. I suppose I would. It would probably have made an impression on my mind.

Q. Do you recollect anything about the testimony of Grimsley having been withdrawn from the jury?

A. Well, sir, I have an indistinct recollection that after I objected to some statements made by the witness as illegal testimony, and when the court met after dinner, I asked leave to discharge the witness. The court assented, and I discharged him then, perhaps.

Q. Do you recollect whether there was any objection to this from the other side?

A. There may have been objections made at the time. So much was said upon the trial of the case that I do not remember any one thing distinctly.

Q. Did the Judge give the jury any instructions concerning the testimony of Grimsley?

A. If so, I don't remember them.

Q. Did you attend the courts throughout the circuit in the fall of 1857?

A. Yes, sir.

Q. From your knowledge of the respective times of holding the courts, state whether I was or could have been in Stoddard county in the month of October.

A. I don't think you could have been there during that month.

Q. Mr. Woodsides, you have been a good deal on the circuit. Do you know of Judge Jackson being guilty of innumerable instances of oppressive, contumelious, insolent, and insulting expressions towards lawyers and parties litigant; and did or not the Judge habitually indulge in such in the exercise of his official functions?

A. No, sir.

Q. What has been the general demeanor of Judge Jackson towards lawyers practicing in his courts, and towards witnesses and parties, so far as you know?

A. Well, sir, as to your general demeanor, it is somewhat diversified. Towards the younger members of the bar, so far as I have observed, it has been uniformly kind. Towards some of the older members, it would be difficult to describe it, exactly. I think for the last year or so there has not been as much harmony and good feeling between the court and Messrs. Phelan, Kitchen, and others, perhaps, as there ought to have been so as to get along pleasantly. I may say, however, that you have treated the members of the bar generally with kindness.

Q. Do you know of any circumstances which lead you to conclude that there was a conspiracy among some members of the bar to interfere with my progress with business in the courts, and to get me out of office?

Mr. Knott. We must make at least a formal objection to this question. It does seem to me that it is entirely too latitudinous, and must lead to an investigation of a wholly collateral issue.

Senator Parsons. I would suggest to the respondent that he had better inquire first whether any conspiracy existed, and if the witness answers affirmatively, he can then with more propriety go into the detail of the facts connected with that conspiracy.

Judge Jackson. That is it. I propose to show that there was a conspiracy to interfere with the discharge of my duties, and to get up this prosecution.

Mr. Hardin. We object merely to the legality of this course, being willing for the question to be answered, and the answer to be subjected to the rules of evidence.

Judge Jackson. I repeat, then, Mr. Woodsides, do you know of any facts or circumstances which led you to infer that there was a combination among some of the members of the bar on the circuit to interfere with the discharge of my duties, and to get up this prosecution?

A. I know of no combination; and I know of but one circumstance from which I could possibly infer that any disposition to get up one existed. I had a conversation with one member of the bar from which such an inference might, perhaps, be drawn.

Q. What was that conversation?

Mr. Hardin. May it please the Court, it is evident that this question is but following up one immaterial point to introduce many others.

Testimony on this subject here is clearly inadmissible, and it is useless to take up the time of the Court with such an investigation. We object to the question.

JUDGE JACKSON. I insist upon the question, and will reduce it to writing, so that it can be passed upon by the Court:

[The question was then reduced to writing by Judge Jackson as follows:]

Q. What was the conversation to which you allude as being a circumstance to show a conspiracy to get up this prosecution?

The question for the action of the Court being, shall the respondent be permitted to ask the question? it was decided in the negative by the following vote:

AYES—Messrs. Fox, Goodlett, Gullett, Harris, Hedgpeth, Jones, McIlvaine, Morris, Newland, Rains, Robinson, Scott, Wilson, and Wood—14.

NOES—Messrs. Brown, Byrne, Coleman, Frazier, Halliburton, Horner, Hyer, McFarland, McFerran, O'Neil, Parsons, Peyton, Richardson, Vernon, Watkins, and Wright—16.

Absent—Messrs. Churchill and Johnson.

Sick—Mr. Thompson.

The examination in chief then closed.

CROSS-EXAMINED BY MR. KNOTT.

Q. Mr. Woodsides, were you a witness before the Judiciary Committee of the House of Representatives last winter?

A. I was.

Q. Did you write out your statement of the facts within your knowledge in relation to this Sarah Buckner trial?

A. I believe I did write out a part of it.

Q. Is that your statement, signed by yourself? (showing witness a paper.)

A. That is my signature.

Q. In your statement, used as evidence before the committee, didn't you state that you were the Circuit Attorney, and that in that capacity you asked leave of the court to withdraw the testimony of Grimsley, and that it had been granted? Didn't you state those facts substantially?

A. I presume that I did, for that is and was my understanding of the facts. The court took a recess while Grimsley was under examination, and when the court met again, I asked the court to permit me to withdraw that witness or to withdraw his testimony—I don't remember distinctly how it was stated—and the request was granted.

Q. Was there any objection to this movement from the attorneys on the other side?

A. It is likely there was. I don't remember.

Q. Didn't the other party insist upon the right to cross-examine this witness?

A. I think I can now remember that they did, and that there was considerable contention over the point.

Q. Did they cross-examine any?

A. Not much, if any.

Q. Was it your understanding that the testimony of the witness was entirely withdrawn from the consideration of the jury?

A. I believe I can say that it was.

Q. I didn't get a fair understanding of your statement in relation to Judge Jackson's treatment of Messrs. Kitchen and Phelan. You will please state the nature of that treatment again.

A. Well, sir. I stated that his treatment of those gentlemen has not been uniformly kind. I couldn't, however, go so far as to say that it has been uniformly oppressive. At the commencement of Judge Jackson's term as Judge, everything seemed to go off pleasantly. But for a year or so back, his demeanor towards those two gentlemen, and probably towards others, has changed considerably.

Q. Is he not in the habit of giving you greater liberties and latitude than he gives to either of those gentlemen, in the trial of a cause?

A. As to that, I make it a point never to ask for anything to which I do not conceive I am clearly entitled, and he generally gives me all I ask.

Q. Do you say that you have ever seen Judge Jackson treat either of these gentlemen oppressively?

A. At times, had I been treated as they were, I should have considered it very oppressive. I have noticed a good deal of harsh treatment on both sides. I have said, and may here say again, that I could never treat any court as I have seen Mr. Phelan treat Judge Jackson, and I would not practice in a court where the Judge treated me as Judge Jackson has treated Mr. Phelan.

Q. When you have noticed this harsh treatment of the court by these gentlemen, were they not merely retorting?

A. I don't know. When the first difficulty that I noticed sprung up, in Butler county, I was not present—that is, I was not present when the difficulty commenced.

Judge Jackson. You stated that when I first went on the bench, you noticed no difficulty, but that afterwards there was a change in my demeanor towards Mr. Phelan and Mr. Kitchen. When did you first discover the difference?

A. I first discovered it at Butler court, in the spring of 1857. I have no recollection of any difficulty or change in demeanor before that spring, in the month of May.

Q. Previous to that time, hadn't you heard those gentlemen express themselves highly favorable to me as Judge?

A. I think I have.

Q. Wasn't the election for Judge held the next August?

A. It was.

Q. Did you notice any difficulty except this one that you speak of before the election?

A. No, sir.

Mr. Knott. Did you ever hear Mr. Kitchen speak in a harsh manner to the court without observing that it was provoked by harshness coming from the court?

A. I cannot say that I have. I spoke more particularly of Mr. Phelan. I believe now that I remember but the one instance before the election, at the May term, 1857, of the Butler court. Mr. Phelan then made some remarks such as I had never heard addressed to a court before, and that struck me as quite harsh; and the court in reply came down tolerably rough upon Mr. Phelan.

Judge Jackson. Let me understand about that that you said concerning practicing in courts where you were treated as I treated Mr. Phelan. Was my conduct oppressive, or do you mean that it would have been oppressive if you had been treated so after treating me as *you* did? Was it oppressive in view of the provocation which I received?

A. I do not mean to say that you had not provocation. I mean that I would not practice in a court where my feelings and relations to the Judge were such as Mr. Phelan's evidently were.

Q. What were the remarks which you say were addressed to me by Mr. Phelan, and which you say you never heard the like of before?

Mr. Knott. I will call the attention of Senators to the fact, that this conversation or occurrence is dated at a period prior to the date of any specification in the articles of impeachment, and hence that it is useless and improper to go into these details. If this witness is permitted to state this conversation, we may call Mr. Phelan to give his version of the affair, its origin, and so on; and thus it opens a door for collateral issues and investigations which can serve no purpose but to delay this trial, and spin it out indefinitely. In all our charges we have never gone behind the first of August, 1857, and the respondent cannot make an issue of this kind with any propriety. We object to the question.

Judge Jackson said he believed he would submit the question to the Senate, and reduced it to writing, as follows:

Q. What were the remarks you heard Mr. Phelan make to the Judge at Butler court, in May, 1857, such as you say you had never before heard addressed to a court, and which induced him to retort in what you call tolerably strong language?

The question for the action of the Court being, shall the respondent be permitted to ask the question? it was decided in the negative by the following vote:

Ayes—Messrs. Fox, Goodlett, Gullett, Hedgpeth, Jones, Morris, Newland, Robinson, Scott, and Wilson—10.

Noes—Messrs. Brown, Byrne, Churchill, Coleman, Frazier, Halliburton, Harris, Horner, Hyer, McFarland, McFerran, McIlvaine, O'Neil, Parsons, Peyton, Rains, Richardson, Vernon, Watkins, Wood, and Wright—21.

Absent—Mr. Johnson.

Sick—Mr. Thompson.

Judge Jackson. I have a few other questions to ask this witness which I had forgotten. Mr. Woodsides, were you present at the Bluff, at May court, 1858?

A. I think I was.

Q. Do you recollect the case of Gibson *vs.* Dunn, and what occurred between the court and Mr. Phelan while it was being tried?

A. I was not present at the time.

Q. Were you at the Butler court at the term when Blount, the Clerk, was incapacitated for his duties by sickness or a reported drunkenness?

A. Yes, sir.

Q. Do you remember what time the court adjourned?

A. I don't remember precisely. I believe the court was in session two days. Mr. Blount was in court the first day, and everything went on as usual until Tuesday morning, when the Clerk being absent very little more business was done.

Q. Do you recollect when the grand jury was discharged?

A. No, sir.

Q. Did you write any indictments at that term?

A. Yes, sir; several. I think I wrote five or six on Monday night or Tuesday.

Q. Do you remember what business was transacted on Tuesday?

A. Well, several things were done, but I couldn't now state what they were with any certainty. I remember that some person sent to the court a request for the appointment of a Deputy Clerk, and I afterwards learned that the court refused to make the appointment.

Q. Who sent it in?

A. I understood that Mr. Phelan presented such a request to the court; but I didn't see the document, and I do not know of my own knowledge what was done with it.

Mr. Knott. What length of time is allowed for holding that court?

A. A week, commencing on the first Mondays in May and October.

Q. Had the grand jury finished their business when they were discharged?

A. I think not.

Q. Were there any cases of considerable importance under investigation by the grand jury?

A. I think there was at least one very important case.

Q. On what day were they discharged?

A. It is my impression that it was Tuesday.

SENATOR CHURCHILL. I did not get a perfect understanding of the account which this witness gives of the trial of Mrs. Buckner, and would like him to repeat some portions of his testimony.

SENATOR PARSONS. I have some few questions to ask concerning that trial, which may, perhaps, cover the points relative to which the gentleman from St. Louis desires a better understanding, and with his permission I will ask them now.

[Senator Churchill consenting, Senator Parsons proceed to ask the questions given below:]

Q. Did Grimsley testify to any facts other than the confessions of the prisoner?

A. Yes, sir. He stated that he knew the prisoner and her daughter, and that they had been confined in his custody. I don't remember that anything else was said before I propounded a general question as to his knowledge of any facts in connection with the murder, when he went on to state the substance of the prisoner's confessions.

Q. In your remarks to the jury, did you comment upon the testimony of this witness, or any portion of it?

A. My impression is that I did not.

Q. What was your reason for omitting to comment upon it?

A. I considered it withdrawn.

Q. When you speak of withdrawing oral testimony already before the jury, what do you mean?

A. Well, sir, I am not certain that my language was correct. Speaking from my best recollection, I will say that at the time it is likely that I considered the testimony of Grimsley illegal, and for that reason wished to withdraw the witness. When I applied to the court for permission to do this, the Judge seemed to give an affirmative reply,—seemed to assent to the withdrawal. Grimsley knew no material facts other than the confessions, and I supposed it right to withdraw them. In my argument to the jury, I may have stated the action of the court, and—

Q. When you applied to withdraw the witness, did you intend to withdraw his testimony—every thing that he said—wholly from the consideration of the jury?

A. Yes, sir. I intended to withdraw his testimony, and I suppose my motion was so understood.

SENATOR SCOTT. Had Grimsley been subpenaed by both parties?

A. I don't know. It has, perhaps, been so stated in my presence, but I have no personal knowledge of the fact.

SENATOR PARSONS. Was Grimsley cross-examined at all, or offered as a witness for the defense?

A. He was not offered as a witness for the defense, and my impression is that he was not cross-examined.

SENATOR PEYTON. You say that the whole of Grimsley's testimony was taken away from the jury?

A. Yes, sir. I treated the whole of it as a nullity. All that he knew consisted of declarations of the prisoner, which I supposed inadmissible. I didn't comment upon them for that reason.

The testimony of this witness being here ended, the President of the Senate inquired what action would be taken upon the writ of attachment issued against him by the court. The witness stated his reasons for not obeying the subpena served upon him, and thereupon he was discharged without the payment of costs, by unanimous consent.

TESTIMONY OF DAVID G. HICKS.

DAVID G. HICKS called and examined by Judge Jackson.

Q. Where do you reside, Mr. Hicks?

A. I live in Stoddard county, Missouri.

Q. Were you present at the Ripley Circuit Court when a person named Kinsey was tried for hog stealing?

A. Yes, sir, I was present.

Q. Do you remember anything unusual occurring during that trial?

A. I remember that when one of the witnesses was on the stand, one of the attorneys, Mr. Fox, after he had spoken three or four words, wished him to stop so that he could write them down. Judge Jackson told the witness to go on, and said that he was brought there for the benefit of the court and jury. A person who was there, Mr. Tyrell was his name, while there was some talking about taking down the testimony, he remarked, "let him go on," and said he could take it down. Mr. Tyrell did take down the testimony I presume. The court told them they should have ample time after the trial was over to take down the testimony, and that the witness was here for the benefit of the jury and not for the attorneys.

Q. Do you remember any interruption in Mr. Fox's speech?

A. Yes, sir. After the witnesses were all examined, Mr. Fox was the first to argue the case for the defense. He commenced his speech against Joe White, and went on speaking of him about fifteen minutes. I must say that I thought Mr. Fox was partly or tolerably "tight," and he run on at a great rate. He come to a part of his speech when his words were, as nearly as I can recollect them, "Joe, Joe, thou renegade from thy father's house!" and just here Judge Jackson called him to order, and told him to confine himself to the law and the testimony in the case. Mr. Fox then pulled out his watch, and remarked that he hoped the court would deduct the time of this interruption from the time to which his speech was limited. He then went on with his speech, and while he was closing up what he had to say of Mr. White, the Sheriff or his deputy, passing by where he was, brushed against his coat, when he threw up his hands in affectation of terror, and called out, "Oh! Judge, protect me from assault!" The Judge again remarked, "Mr. Fox, you must confine yourself to the law and evidence of the case." Mr. Woodsides, I think it was, timed him. He went on in the same strain for some time. I believe he run over his time. Finally the Judge said to him, "Mr. Fox, take your seat." Says he, "very well," and then he sat down. That is about all I remember about it.

Q. Did you at this court hear me tell Mr. Fox that he lied, or that he had made his client lie?

A. No, sir. I believe it was at that court I saw you examine a paper, and you called to Mr. Fox and asked him if he wrote that. Mr. Fox said it was his writing. You had two papers, I think, and pointing to them you said, "one or the other of these is false," and you pointed out how it was that one was in conflict with the same person's sworn statement made previously.

Q. Were you present, Mr. Hicks, when the case of Moore *vs.* Eldridge was tried?

A. Yes, sir.

Q. Please state the facts connected with any difficulty about an instrument of writing which you may have heard.

A. Well, there was a jury sworn, and the case came on to be tried. A paper was introduced before the jury—I believe it was the articles of partnership. Mr. Parker died, and the suit was between Moore and his administrator. There was a dispute about the paper. The date of the instrument was crossed out, and a date some two years later written over it. The ink of the last date was of a different color from that of the first. Upon the date of the instrument rested the issue of the trial. They introduced their witnesses, and, after the evidence was through, the jury gave in their verdict, and the parties losing took an appeal. They filed a bill of exceptions, and one reason alluded to this erasure of the date. When they presented the bill of exceptions to the Judge he wouldn't sign it without an alteration. They didn't agree to the alteration which he suggested, and he then picked up the paper and showed them the erasure, and then he wrote in the bill of exceptions, where there was mention of the paper, the words, "upon which there is an erasure in the date." He then signed it that way; whether they sent the case up or not I don't know.

Q. Did the erasure affect the date of the instrument? did it change it?

A. Yes, sir; it would have been two or more years later if another date had not been interlineated.

Senator Watkins. Was the old date rubbed out?

A. Yes, sir, but it was still perceptible. You could tell the year, month, and day. I stated that the ink of the last date was of a different color, but I am not sure that such was the case. I may have got that idea from hearing it mentioned in the argument of the case.

Q. Which party wanted to use the instrument as evidence?

A. I believe it was Moore—he was the plaintiff.

Q. Which party drew up the bill of exceptions?

A. I don't remember; I think it was Mr. Moore's attorneys.

Judge Jackson. Were you at the Stoddard Circuit Court in August, 1858?

A. Yes, sir.

Q. Do you recollect the trial of Mr. Bartlett? If you do, state to the court fully the facts in relation to that trial.

A. At this court I was acting as Circuit Attorney. Col. Bartlett was indicted for playing cards, or betting five cents' worth of whisky on a game of cards. The jury heard the evidence. It was to the effect that they played for whisky. I don't now know whether I wrote out any instructions, but I wanted the court to instruct the jury that playing cards for whisky, watermelons, and so on, was gaming. The court said that he didn't think either was indictable. He said that there must be a bet, else there was no offense known to the law, and went on at some length to explain the law. He said that if it was no more than one cent that was played for, it was indictable if it was a bet; but unless it amounted to a bet it was not indictable. He told me that if I wanted the point settled, the jury could find the facts, he would declare the law, and then I could file a bill of exceptions and take the case to the Supreme Court. Then I entered a *nolle*. Judge Jackson and myself were included in the same indictment, and I asked leave to enter a *nolle* as to all the persons included except myself. But the Judge said that the law provided another mode of disposing of the case against himself, and I only entered a *nolle prosequi* as to Bartlett. There the case remains yet.

Mr. Hardin. Do you say you entered a *nolle* as to all the parties but yourself?

A. No, sir. I asked leave to enter a *nolle* as to all except myself, but the Judge said he could not permit such an entry in his own case, and that when the proper order was made he would remove it. It was neither dismissed nor acted upon in any manner.

JUDGE JACKSON. You will please state further, Mr. Hicks, the facts concerning an indictment against yourself at the November term of the court.

A. I was at the August term indicted for an assault. At the November term I was appointed Circuit Attorney, *pro tem.*, and on the second day an attorney, one Mr. Miller, presented a motion to quash this indictment against me. I didn't know any one had appeared for me, but the first thing I knew he had the motion ready. The Judge wanted to know the reason for the motion, and some little was said about it, but the motion was not filed, and nothing was done in the case then. If the indictment against me was ever quashed, I don't know it. The next thing I knew about it I went back and examined the record, and saw that on the last day an entry appeared, which said that the indictment was quashed for reasons filed, but I could find no motion or reasons. There was nothing of the kind on file. I hunted for them, but could not find them. I never talked to Mr. Miller on the subject, and don't know whether the record was made up that way on his motion or not. It was not with my knowledge or consent. The indictment was found at the special August term, and in November—

SENATOR GOODLETT. Who drew up this indictment against you?

A. I did it myself. I told the grand jury that I would go to the Judge and get him to appoint some one else. One of them told me he had already informed the Judge, and that it was unnecessary.

JUDGE JACKSON. Do you know whether Mr. Davis remained any length of time in Bloomfield after the Buckner trial?

A. I think he went away the next day.

Q. Were you at Butler court at the time Mr. Blount was unable to attend to his duties?

A. No, sir.

Q. Were you present at Bloomfield when the mandamus case against Jonas Eaker was tried?

A. Yes, sir.

Q. State what occurred there—what you saw of that case.

A. When the case came up, Mr. Kitchen and Mr. Phelan appeared for Mr. Eaker. Mr. Eaker was in the house at the time, setting not far from me. Something was said about the service of the writ, when the Judge remarked that a writ of this kind was of the same nature as a writ of habeas corpus, and required the respondent himself to make a return, and told Mr. Dowdy to go to Judge Eaker and offer him the original writ. About this time Judge Eaker got up to leave the house, and in about five minutes afterwards I saw Mr. Dowdy go to Mr. Eaker and speak to him a moment. I heard Mr. Eaker reply that he was too old for that, and he turned and went off. The Sheriff came back and informed the court that Mr. Eaker refused to be served with the original writ. The Judge spoke to the Clerk to issue an attachment, and in a little while after this Mr. Eaker was brought in, and the Judge asked him if he didn't know he was in contempt of court. Mr. Eaker said he didn't intend any contempt. The Judge said he supposed it was the fault of his attorneys, and said, "if I thought you were your own adviser in this matter I would inflict a penalty upon you." The Judge imposed no fine.

Q. Do you say that Mr. Kitchen and Mr. Phelan appeared as the attorneys of Mr. Eaker?

A. Well, Mr. Kitchen said he did not appear as an attorney, but as a friend of the court, and said Mr. Eaker had not been served. The court said the reason for making no return should be explained, and that he ought to make the return and let that show that there had been no service. He further said that Mr. Eaker was aware of the existence of the writ, and had sufficient notice to place him in contempt if he did not make some return, and that if he didn't he would proceed against him as if he were in contempt. Mr. Kitchen kept contending that Mr. Eaker was not in court, and said he did not appear for him, but as the friend of the court. Judge Jackson remarked that the court would take care of itself, and added something to the effect that he didn't want his friendship. Mr. Phelan came in and kept talking and apologizing for Mr. Eaker making no return, and the Judge turned to him and asked him if it wasn't possible for him to keep his mouth shut. I ain't sure but he put his hand up to his mouth and held it shut a moment, and then said he could. After not a great while, court adjourned. When the Judge came down from the bench, Mr. Kitchen approached—

Mr. KNOTT. Stop, sir! You have not been asked as to anything that occurred after court adjourned.

JUDGE JACKSON. State, Mr. Hicks, if you heard Mr. Phelan apologize, and say he was to blame, and that he wouldn't do so again.

Mr. KNOTT. We object. You needn't answer, Mr. Hicks, until directed to do so by the Court.

JUDGE JACKSON. I'll have to write out the question, then, I suppose. I'll put the question thus: "Did you hear Mr. Phelan, after the court adjourned, apologize to me, say he was to blame, and promise not to offend that way again?"

Mr. KNOTT. The question is so extremely illegal, in both form and substance, that I will not make a single argument upon the question of its admissibility.

JUDGE JACKSON. It will be remembered by the Court that I asked Mr. Phelan this very question, and he stated that he did not apologize. Now, if I can contradict him upon this point, I have a right to do so.

Mr. HARDIN. May it please the Court, this question could not have been constructed in a more leading form. But this is not the only objection to it. If it is asked in order to contradict our witness, it must be refused for two reasons. First, it is not a material question; and no principle of evidence is better settled than that you cannot contradict a witness upon an immaterial question. It is true that Judge Jackson asked Mr. Phelan some question of the same general nature as this, but we objected to it at the time as immaterial. In the second place, to contradict a witness, even upon a material question, a foundation must have been laid by asking the witness sought to be contradicted the same question, with all the accompanying circumstances of time, place, and connection.

JUDGE JACKSON. I'll save the question and not put it now. I'll pass to another matter. Mr. Hicks, were you present when it is said I accused Mr. Phelan of tampering with the grand jury?

A. I was not.

Q. Were you in court during the Buckner trial?

A. I was, most of the time.

Q. Do you recollect how many witnesses were examined for the State?

A. I believe there were but two witnesses examined in regard to the murder.

Q. State all you know in regard to that trial.

A. All I know about it I will state. Mr. Woodsides conducted the prosecution, and things went on very smoothly till they got to arguing the case. Mr. Davis, Mr. Phelan, and Mr. Dennis were for the defense. Mr. Davis, I think, made the first speech on his side. He was going on with it, and had been speaking fifteen minutes, perhaps, when the Judge stopped him. I think the first time the Judge stopped him, he remarked that he (Mr. Davis) should not draw conclusions from what was not evidence. Mr. Davis went on for some time, when the Judge said to him, "Mr. Davis,—Mr. Davis,—Mr. Davis,—you must confine yourself to the law and evidence." Mr. Davis did not notice him till he had spoken the third time. The Judge told him he couldn't be allowed to go on in that way. Mr. Davis's precise words in reply, I can give partly. He said, "don't you allow me to suppose a case? I'll have nothing more to do with this trial then." He said something more, but I cannot give his exact words. It was to the effect, however, that he would not be Jeffreyized. He then walked out. I think I asked him if he didn't wish to finish his speech, or something of that kind, and he said, "it was ended just as I wanted it; it will have a better effect with the jury, than if I had gone on and finished my speech." That was his remark to me.

Q. Do you remember whether the witness, Grimsley, was cross-examined?

A. Yes, sir. Mr. Grimsley was cross-examined; I am sure of it; I both saw and heard the attorneys for the defense cross-examine him.

Q. Were you in court at the time when the bill of exceptions was presented?

A. I was not in the court house all the time. Court adjourned that evening—no, you adjourned over one week to give Mr. Phelan time to prepare a bill of exceptions. He, in the meantime went to Cairo to attend a railroad meeting,—a meeting for something in regard to the Cairo and Fulton Railroad,—and he was taken sick. The Judge adjourned the court again a time or two. I was not present when the bill of exceptions was finally presented. I only know from rumor what took place then. I can't even say I was in Bloomfield at the time.

Q. Do you know of Judge Jackson being guilty of innumerable instances of oppressive, contumelious, insolent, and insulting expressions towards lawyers and parties litigant?

A. I can't say I do.

Q. And did or not the Judge habitually indulge in such in the exercise of his official functions?

A. No, sir; I believe he did not.

Q. What has been the general demeanor of Judge Jackson towards lawyers practicing in his courts, and towards witnesses and parties?

A. He generally got along very well with all of them except Mr. Phelan, Mr. Fox, and Mr. Kitchen. With Mr. Kitchen I know he had some difficulty on but one occasion. But with Mr. Phelan and Mr. Fox, I think I recollect several occasions when there were harsh things said on both sides.

CROSS-EXAMINED BY MR. KNOTT.

Q. Mr. Hicks, do you pretend to give the precise words of the conversations you heard during the Buckner trial?

A. Yes, sir; in part.

Q. I believe you stated that you were in and out of the court house incidentally, and were not interested in the trial?

A. Yes, sir.

Q. Do you remember the day of the week when this mandamus case was taken up? Was it the second or third?

A. I don't remember.

Q. Was it during the first or the latter part of the week?

A. I can't say. My impression is that it was about the middle of the week.

Q. What time of day was it?

A. I can't relate that either.

Q. When Mr. Dowdy and Mr. Eaker walked out of the court house as you have told us, where did they meet? Where was Mr. Eaker when you say Mr. Dowdy offered to serve him with the original writ?

A. He was leaning on a bench outside. Either Mr. Dowdy offered him the writ, or told him what the Judge said, when he made the remark I repeated and walked off. I don't remember whether I heard what Mr. Dowdy said or not.

Q. Where were you when this happened?

A. Not a great ways off,—near the gate which entered the enclosure. I don't remember my exact position.

Q. How long was this after the court directed the Sheriff to take Mr. Eaker the original?

A. Not a great while.

Q. How far were you off at the time?

A. About as far as from here to that chair, (pointing to a chair in the room.)

Q. And you say positively, that you heard Mr. Eaker say "I'm too old for that?"

A. I did hear him say that he was "too old."

Q. How did you know the Sheriff had the original writ? Did you see it?

A. Yes, sir. I saw it, together with the copy which had been served, lying on the stand in the court house.

Q. What did Mr. Dowdy say when he presented the writ?

A. I can't give his exact words, and do not know that I heard them all. But he told him that the service of Mr. Jackson, his deputy, was wrong, and offered him the original. Mr. Eaker said he was "too old," and I understood the balance of the sentence to be "for King Wasson."

Q. Did Mr. Kitchen or Mr. Phelan suggest to the court the failure of the service of the writ?

A. Yes, sir; and the Judge told them that Mr. Eaker had sufficient notice to make him aware of the existence of such a writ, whether it was properly served or not, and that if he did not make a return he would attach him for a contempt.

Q. And you say the court refused to permit Mr. Kitchen to appear as *amicus curiæ*, and enforced a return by attachment?

A. Well, it appeared so to me.

Q. Were you in court when Mr. Eaker was brought in under the attachment?

A. Yes, sir.

Q. What was it you heard the Judge say then?

A. I heard him say that Mr. Eaker was in contempt, but he supposed it was the fault of his attorneys.

Q. You say also that you heard the Judge tell Mr. Kitchen that he didn't want his friendship, when Mr. Kitchen suggested the failure of service?

A. Yes, sir.

Q. Do you recollect whether anybody else was present at the interview between Mr. Dowdy and Judge Jackson concerning Mr. Eaker's refusal of the original writ? Was Mr. Charles A. Davis present?

A. I don't think he was there. In fact I am sure he was not there at that time—and believe he was not at that court. Others were present, but I don't recollect any particular one at this moment.

Q. In this case of Moore *vs.* Eldridge, how many witnesses were examined?

A. I think I can name but two,—Lemuel Kittrel and Dr. Russell. There may have been others.

Q. Where were the Judge and the parties when the bill of exceptions in this case was tendered?

A. I don't know where the bill was tendered. The first I knew about it, there was a squabble about it which attracted my attention.
Q. Did you read the bill of exceptions?
A. I did not.
Q. Who was present at the time?
A. I think, Mr. Kitchen, Mr. Phelan, the lawyer for Mr. Eldridge, and Mr. Bedford, were there. I don't remember any others.
Q. Do you say that you could distinguish the two dates on the instrument of writing about which there was a controversy?
A. Yes, sir.
Q. What were they?
A. I think one was 1854. I don't remember the date under the other, though it was later I think.
Q. What do you say was the controverted point concerning this instrument?
A. The squabble was about the erasure. The Judge picked up the bill of exceptions and interlined a statement of the fact that an erasure existed.
Q. Are you sure the erasure affected the date?
A. I am sure the erasure affected the year. I have since had occasion to examine it.
Q. Did you say that the two dates were written with different ink?
A. Well, I don't know whether it was a different color, but I think there was a difference.
Q. Are they in the same handwriting?
A. I don't know.
Q. How far apart were they?
A. One was immediately by the other.
Q. In the case where you say Mr. Fox was abusing Mr. Joseph White, wasn't Mr. Fox speaking generally of the character of circumstantial evidence, and didn't he in this connection merely allude to Joseph of old by way of illustration?
A. I don't think he was.
Q. Didn't he allude to the circumstance of Joseph of old being the victim of circumstantial evidence?
A. He frequently does such things, but I heard nothing of the kind then.
Q. In this case which you relate of an altercation between Judge Jackson and Mr. Fox, are you sure that the Judge had two papers when he spoke to Mr. Fox?
A. Yes, sir. I am sure he had two papers.
Q. Do you pretend to give the exact language of the Judge upon that occasion?
A. Well, I think I can give his exact language. Says he, "Mr. Fox, is this your handwriting?" Mr. Fox said it was. "Then," said the Judge, "you have certainly made your client swear falsely; one of these papers contradicts the other."
Q. Mr. Hicks, I will ask you whether it did not occur thus: The Judge asked Mr. Fox if that was his handwriting, or if he wrote that, and then told him that he either lied or caused his client to lie.
A. I can say positively that the Judge did not use the expression "you have either lied or caused your client to lie."
Q. What was the character of the paper alluded to?
A. I think it was an answer.
Q. And you are positive that the assertion of the Judge upon that occasion was, "you have made your client swear falsely?"
A. Yes, sir.
Q. Well, you have stated that at the August term, 1858, of the Stod-

dard Circuit Court you were indicted for an assault. Had you been under recognizance to answer for that offense at the November term following?

A. I do not know now whether I was or not.
Q. Did you enter into recognizance in court?
A. I can't answer. I don't recollect.
Q. Was there any *capias* ordered in your case?
A. I think I entered into a bond in some case,—whether it was in this or not I can't say. I don't know whether the Sheriff had any *capias* for me or not.
Q. Was any order made for issuing a *capias?*
A. I believe the court made a general order for the issuing of *capiases* in all the State cases requiring them.
Q. At the November term you were again appointed Circuit Attorney?
A. Yes, sir.
Q. On what day of that term was the indictment against you quashed?
A. The record shows that it was the last day, and for reasons filed. It reads on, "now at this day comes the defendant by his attorney, etc., and the indictment in this case is quashed for reasons filed."
Q. Did you make any order to have that case, or the other in which you were indicted jointly with the Judge, removed to another court?
A. No, sir; I was only acting Circuit Attorney *pro tem.*, and I thought it was not necessary for me to take that step.
Q. Did you make any application to the Judge to appoint some one else to draw up the indictments against yourself?
A. No, sir. I told the grand jury that I would do so, but one of them told me that he had himself informed the Judge of the facts, and it was not necessary.
Q. Who was it told you this?
A. It was James L. Hale, foreman of the grand jury, I think.

The cross-examination of this witness being here concluded, on motion of SENATOR WATKINS the Court adjourned.

EVENING SESSION.

SATURDAY, June 18, 1859.

The Court met pursuant to adjournment.
The managers and respondent attended.
The examination of respondent's witnesses was resumed.

TESTIMONY OF REUBEN P. OWEN.

REUBEN P. OWEN called and examined by Judge Jackson.
Q. In which county do you live?
A. In Stoddard county.
Q. Do you hold any office there?
A. Yes, sir. I am Clerk of the Circuit and County Courts.
Q. How long have you held that position?
A. About twelve years. I was Deputy Clerk five years.
Q. Do you know of Judge Jackson being guilty of innumerable instances of oppressive, contumelious, insolent, and insulting expressions

towards lawyers and parties litigant; and did or not the Judge habitually indulge in such in the exercise of his official functions?

A. Well, I can't say that I do know of innumerable instances of occurrences of that kind. I have seen some difficulties and sparring between attorneys and the court; but I never saw anything of the kind towards parties to suits.

Q. What has been the general demeanor of Judge Jackson towards lawyers practicing in his courts, and towards witnesses and parties, so far as you know?

A. At times it has been kind, and at other times I have thought him a little cross.

Mr. Knott. Did you never notice that he was a little partial to David G. Hicks?

A. I don't know as to that. I know that he and Mr. Hicks are very friendly.

TESTIMONY OF WILLIAM NORMAN.

William Norman called and examined by Judge Jackson.

Q. Where do you reside, Mr. Norman?

A. In Stoddard county, Missouri.

Q. How long have you been living there?

A. Nearly nine years.

Q. Have you been much about the courts?

A. Not a great deal.

Q. Do you know of Judge Jackson being guilty of innumerable instances of oppressive, contumelious, insolent, and insulting expressions towards lawyers and parties litigant; and did or not the Judge habitually indulge in such in the exercise of his official functions?

A. No, sir; I can't say that I do.

Q. What has been the general demeanor of Judge Jackson towards lawyers practicing in his courts, and towards witnesses and parties, so far as you know?

A. I can't say that I have ever seen anything myself that I regarded as seriously wrong.

Mr. Knott. You are only casually in court, I suppose?

A. Only so, sir.

TESTIMONY OF DR. JOHN D. SMITH.

Dr. John D. Smith called and examined by Judge Jackson.

Q. In which county do you live?

A. In Stoddard county.

Q. How long have you been living there?

A. I will have been living there ten years next July.

Q. Have you been about in the courts much during that time?

A. Some little.

Q. Do you know of Judge Jackson being guilty of innumerable instances of oppressive, contumelious, insolent, and insulting expressions towards lawyers and parties litigant; and does or not the Judge habitually indulge in such in the exercise of his official functions?

A. I do not.

Q. What has been the general demeanor of Judge Jackson towards lawyers practicing in his courts, and towards witnesses and parties, so far as you know?

A. So far as I know, it has been gentlemanly.

CROSS-EXAMINED BY MR. KNOTT.

Q. How far do you know?
A. I don't know very far, I suppose.
Q. You are only casually in court?
A. Yes, sir; only casually.
Q. From what you have seen, could you form an opinion as to the general conduct of Judge Jackson towards lawyers practicing in his courts?
A. I don't know what you mean by generally.
Mr. KNOTT. You can stand aside then.

JUDGE JACKSON here offered as evidence the following documents, being the original papers of the causes in which they are respectively entitled; and, at the suggestion of SENATOR PARSONS, they were read from the stand:

IN THE MATTER OF THE STATE OF MISSOURI *vs.* CHARLES RUSSELL.

State of Missouri *versus* Charles Russell. } In vacation. Petition for Habeas Corpus.

To the Honorable Albert Jackson, Judge of the Fifteenth Judicial Circuit in the State of Missouri:

Your petitioner, the undersigned, Charles Russell, respectfully shows that he is restrained of his liberty by William F. Crjts, in the town of Bloomfield, in the county of Stoddard, and State of Missouri: That, on the 4th day of January, 1859, your petitioner was arrested upon a warrant or process issued by Jonas Eaker, a Justice of the Peace in Stoddard county, and charged with passing a counterfeit half dollar to one Thomas Jackson, and ever since the day aforesaid your petitioner has been, and still is, restrained of his liberty by said Cryts. That, on the 6th day of January, 1859, the said Jonas Eaker, Justice of the Peace aforesaid, examined witnesses touching the matter charged in said warrant or process, but the said Justice of the Peace did not examine nor take the statement of your petitioner touching said matter, and commanded said Cryts to take your petitioner into custody, and in want of bail in the sum of three hundred dollars, your petitioner to keep in custody until the next term of the Circuit Court of said county. That the said restraint is illegal, because the said magistrate, the said Jonas Eaker, Justice of the Peace aforesaid, who issued said warrant or process, and committed to custody your petitioner as aforesaid, did not, at any time, take the examination of your petitioner, in relation to the offense charged, as provided by law. That your petitioner has demanded a copy of the warrant, order, or process, by virtue of which he is restrained as aforesaid of said Cryts, and such copy was refused by said Cryts.

his
CHARLES ⋈ RUSSELL.
mark.

Charles Russell, petitioner above named, makes oath that the foregoing petition and the matters therein are true to the best of his knowledge and belief.

his
CHARLES ⋈ RUSSELL.
mark.

Subscribed and sworn to before the undersigned, Clerk of the Circuit Court of Stoddard county, this 6th day of January, 1859.

REUBEN P. OWEN, *Clerk*,
by his Deputy, VAN W. HALE.

State of Missouri, County of Stoddard, } *ss.* "By the Habeas Corpus Act."

The State of Missouri to William F. Cryts, Constable of Castor township, Stoddard county, Greeting:

You are hereby commanded that the body of Charles Russell, under your custody detained as it is said, under safe and secure conduct, together with the day and cause of his being imprisoned and detained, by whatsoever name the said Charles Russell may be known, you have before me, Albert Jackson, Judge of the Fifteenth Judicial Circuit of the State of Missouri, at the court house in the town of Bloomfield, in said county, on the — day of January, 1859, to do and receive what shall then and there be considered concerning the said Charles Russell, so imprisoned and detained as aforesaid; and hereof fail not at your peril.

Witness my hand this 6th day of January, A. D. 1859.

ALBERT JACKSON, *Judge.*

I do hereby certify and return that I have in custody the above named Charles Russell, by virtue of a verbal order of Jonas Eaker, a Justice of the Peace in and for Stoddard county, Missouri, and that no certified copy of said examination has been delivered to me.

W. F. CRYTS, *Constable.*

State of Missouri *versus* Charles Russell.

The defendant being brought before me by the said William Cryts, and he showing no authority, or mittimus, or warrant, for holding in custody, it is ordered that the said Charles Russell be discharged from the custody of said William Cryts.

January 7th, 1859.

ALBERT JACKSON.

IN THE MATTER OF THE STATE *VS.* JOHN R. MAIN.

State of Missouri *versus* John R. Main. } In vacation. Petition for Habeas Corpus.

To the Honorable Albert Jackson, Judge of the Fifteenth Judicial Circuit in the State of Missouri:

John R. Main, the undersigned petitioner, humbly shows, that he is restrained of his liberty by one John J. Jackson, at the town of Bloomfield, in the county of Stoddard, in the State of Missouri. That on or about the 5th day of January, 1859, he was arrested on a warrant or process issued by one James Cravey, Justice of the Peace in the county of Stoddard, aforesaid, charged with grand larceny, and taken before the said Justice, who made and issued the warrant or process, a copy of which is hereto annexed; and by virtue of which your petitioner is restrained of his liberty as aforesaid. That the property charged as having been stolen by your petitioner, your petitioner held in possession by reason of a contract made with the owner thereof. That the said restraint is illegal in that the said magistrate who made the said warrant, by virtue of which your petitioner is restrained of his liberty, did not at any time before committing your petitioner as aforesaid, take the examination of your petitioner, in relation to the offense charged, as provided by law; but when your petitioner asked leave to make a statement in relation thereto, said magistrate refused to hear the same, and told your petitioner that what your petitioner could say would make no difference. That the said warrant of commitment is insufficient and defective, and the said magistrate has not certified the examination of your petitioner as by law commanded, and there is no testimony to warrant such restraint. Therefore your petitioner humbly prays that your honor will inquire respecting said restraint, and your petitioner as in duty bound will ever pray, &c.

JOHN R. MAIN.

John R. Main, petitioner above named, makes oath that the above petition and the matters therein are true to the best of his knowledge and belief.

JOHN R. MAIN.

Subscribed and sworn to before the undersigned, Clerk of the Circuit Court of Stoddard county, Missouri, this 7th day of January, 1859.

REUBEN P. OWEN, *Clerk*,
by VAN W. HALE, *Deputy*.

State of Missouri,
County of Stoddard, } *ss.*

The State of Missouri to the Constable of Richland Township and the keeper of the jail of said county of Stoddard, Greeting:

These are to command you, the said Constable, forthwith to convey and deliver into the custody of the keeper of the jail of the county of Stoddard aforesaid, the body of John R. Main, taken and brought before me, a Justice of the Peace within and for the county aforesaid, and charged before me, upon the oath of Robert Whitehead, of Stoddard county, with grand larceny; and you, the said keeper of the said jail, are hereby required to receive the said John R. Main into your custody into the said jail, and him there safely keep until he shall thence be discharged by due course of law.

Given under my hand this 5th day of January, A. D. 1859.

JAMES CRAVEY, *Justice of the Peace.*

A true copy of the original mittimus in my hands.

JAMES DOWDY, *Sheriff*,
by his Deputy, JOHN J. JACKSON.

State of Missouri,
County of Stoddard, } *ss.* "By the Habeas Corpus Act."

The State of Missouri to John J. Jackson, Deputy Sheriff of Stoddard county, Greeting:

You are hereby commanded that the body of John R. Main, under your custody detained as it is said, under safe and secure conduct, together with the day and cause of his being imprisoned and detained, by whatsoever name the said John R. Main may be known, you have before me, Albert Jackson, Judge of the Fifteenth Judicial Circuit of the State of Missouri, at the court house in the town of Bloomfield, in said county, on the —— day of January, 1859, to do and receive what shall then and there be considered concerning the said John R. Main, so imprisoned and detained as aforesaid; and hereof fail not at your peril.

Witness my hand this 7th day of January, 1859.

ALBERT JACKSON, *Judge.*

I do hereby certify and return that the above named John R. Main is in my custody, by virtue of a warrant made and issued by James Cravey, Justice of the Peace in the county of Stoddard, a copy of which is hereto annexed and filed. That I have not in my possession, and never had, any certified examination of said John R. Main, in relation to the offense stated in said warrant, and no testimony in relation thereto.

JAMES DOWDY, *Sheriff*,
by his Deputy, JOHN J. JACKSON.

The State of Missouri
versus
John Main. } Charged with Grand Larceny.

The defendant being brought before me in obedience to the within writ, and there being no charge brought against him, nor any evidence produced against him, and there being no evidence that he had been legally arrested and tried before a committing magistrate, or before any one having authority to commit him to the custody of the Jailor of Stoddard county, and the paper herewith presented as a mittimus not being sufficient in form and substance to authorize the Jailor of Stoddard county to hold him, the said John Main, in custody, it is ordered that he be forthwith discharged.

January 7th, 1859. ALBERT JACKSON.

During the reading of the foregoing documents, Mr. David G. Hicks came into the Senate Chamber, and stood near the Secretary's desk until the reading was concluded. He then addressed the President, and asked permission to correct some statements made by him in his examination during the forenoon session. An assent being signified, he said that upon reflection since he was examined, he wished to retract two statements. The first was that he had been told by Mr. James L. Hale, foreman of the grand jury at the August term of the Stoddard Circuit Court, that the fact of a charge being under investigation against himself (Hicks) had been communicated to the Judge. He was, he said, informed by Mr. Hale that no such conversation had taken place, and he was now satisfied that he had been mistaken as to the man. The second was an answer to a question by Mr. Knott, whether Mr. Fox was commenting on circumstantial evidence when he was interrupted by Judge Jackson, in the Kinsey case. In his examination he had given a negative answer, and he now remembered that Mr. Fox *was* commenting in that way. He therefore wished these two statements stricken out of his testimony by the reporter.

TESTIMONY OF WILLIAM H. BUFFINGTON.

William H. Buffington called, sworn, and examined by Judge Jackson.

Q. Mr. Buffington, have you any papers in your office containing the signature of Jacob C. Blount, former Clerk of Butler county?

A. At your request, Judge Jackson, I have looked over the files of returns in my office, and have selected four specimens of Mr. Blount's signature, which I have here with me.

Q. From a comparison of this signature with those attached to the papers, would you pronounce it genuine?

[Witness was here shown, by Judge Jackson, the paper purporting to be a request by Mr. Blount for the appointment of Mr. Donaldson as Deputy Clerk of the Circuit Court of Butler county.]

A. In reply I will state that I suppose no man, with my knowledge of the handwriting of Mr. Blount, would swear positively that this is not a genuine signature. But I will say that this does not resemble the signatures in these specimens, nor others in my office; and basing my judgment on the signatures which I suppose to be genuine, I should say that this was not Mr. Blount's writing. This (pointing to the request for the appointment of the deputy) is a rounder, smoother hand. The *J* is written differently from the invariable manner of writing it in all the other signatures I have seen, and there are other points of dissimilarity which any one can notice by inspecting and comparing it with the specimens which I have here.

[The papers were here handed around among the Senators for examination.]

Senator Parsons. Mr. Buffington, did you say you had never seen Mr. Blount write his name?

A. If I did not, I say now that I never saw him write, and my knowledge of his handwriting has been acquired solely from papers sent from him to my office. I presume that the returns from his office were written by himself, from the fact that they have been uniformly in the same handwriting.

Mr. Knott. I will ask you, Mr. Buffington, what effect the knowledge of the fact that a man was probably drunk at the time of writing his name,—so drunk that he had to be held up for the purpose,—would have upon your judgment as to the genuineness of that particular signature? Would it do to apply the usual rules for determining the genuineness of a signature in such a case?

A. I do not think it would.

TESTIMONY OF HENRY MILLER.

HENRY MILLER called and examined by Judge Jackson.

Q. In which county do you live?

A. In Stoddard county, Missouri.

Q. How long have you been living there?

A. Ever since and before the county was organized. About thirty-six years.

Q. Have you been much about the courts in that county?

A. Ever since I have lived there I have been off and on at every court, I reckon.

Q. Do you know of Judge Jackson being guilty of innumerable instances of oppressive, contumelious, insolent, and insulting expressions towards lawyers and parties litigant; and does or not the Judge habitually indulge in such in the exercise of his official functions?

A. No, sir; I don't.

Q. What has been the general demeanor of Judge Jackson towards lawyers practicing in his courts, and towards witnesses and parties, so far as you know?

A. So far as I have any knowledge, I don't know that he has treated them wrong in any way.

TESTIMONY OF THOMAS J. WALKER.

THOMAS J. WALKER called and examined by Judge Jackson.

Q. In which county do you live?

A. In Stoddard county.

Q. How long have you lived there?

A. Fifteen years last March.

Q. Have you been about courts much for the last three or four years?

A. Yes, sir. I am pretty generally about the courts.

Q. Do you know of Judge Jackson being guilty of innumerable instances of oppressive, contumelious, insolent, and insulting expressions towards lawyers and parties litigant; and did or not the Judge habitually indulge in such in the exercise of his official functions?

A. No, I don't.

Q. What has been the general demeanor of Judge Jackson towards lawyers practicing in his courts, and towards witnesses and parties, so far as you know?

A. It's my opinion you give them rather too much latitude.

Mr. KNOTT. We don't want your opinion; we want facts.

JUDGE JACKSON. What is the opinion of the lawyers themselves, generally?

A. Well, for the first eighteen months they praised you, and they began to grumble and complain then.

Mr. KNOTT. What is your occupation?

A. I am a farmer.

TESTIMONY OF JOHN R. DILLON.

JOHN R. DILLON called and examined by Judge Jackson.

Q. Where do you live, Mr. Dillon?

A. In Ripley county.

Q. Have you held any office in that county?

A. I have been the High Sheriff of that county for several years.
Q. How many years?
A. Four.
Q. Do you know of Judge Jackson being guilty of innumerable instances of oppressive, contumelious, insolent and insulting expressions towards lawyers and parties litigant; and did or not the Judge habitually indulge in such in the exercise of his official functions?
A. No, sir; not in my presence.

TESTIMONY OF THOMAS L. MOORE.

Thomas L. Moore called and examined by Judge Jackson.
Q. Do you know anything about one William Atterbury being in custody about the first of February, 1858?
A. Yes, sir; I was helping to guard him about that time, a day and a night, in Kennett.
Q. What became of him?
A. On Sunday night, while he was in charge of Mr. Parish, he got away, and I don't know what became of him after that.
Q. Was he ever in jail?
A. No, sir. The jail was out of fix; the key was at the shop, I believe, and we couldn't put him in jail.

CROSS-EXAMINED BY MR. KNOTT.

Q. In what county was this?
A. In Dunklin county.
Q. What time was it?
A. I think it was in February, though I don't remember the day of the month.
Q. Who arrested this man Atterbury?
A. Davy Hicks fetched him there,—him and another man.

Judge Jackson. On what day of the week did they arrest him?
A. They brought him there on a Saturday, and on Sunday night he broke custody, as well as I recollect.

[Judge Jackson here announced that he was through with his testimony, but in a few minutes afterwards said he had one more witness to examine, who was accordingly called.]

TESTIMONY OF JAMES L. HALE.

James L. Hale recalled and examined by Judge Jackson.
Q. Did you ever inform me that the grand jury, at the August term, had under investigation a charge against me, or one against David Hicks?
A. No, sir, I didn't. I didn't know whether it was right to do so or not. There was some talk about it, but I didn't tell you.
Q. Wasn't it a conversation as to what they would do if they had a charge against the Judge or the Circuit Attorney, and did any one say they had consulted me about it?
A. I don't remember.

Judge Jackson here announced that he was through.

The managers asked a short time in which to consult as to what rebutting testimony they should offer, which was granted.

SENATOR PARSONS then offered the following resolution:

Resolved, That the Committee on Accounts allow William Vanover and Eugene Donnelly, special messengers employed in this cause, the sum of five dollars per day and ten cents per mile for their services,—mileage to be computed as is provided for witnesses.

SENATOR GULLETT offered the following amendment to this resolution:

Amend by striking out "five dollars" and inserting "three."

This amendment was rejected by the following vote:

AYES—Messrs. Fox, Frazier, Goodlett, Gullett, McFerran, McIlvaine, Richardson, Thompson, and Wright—9.
NOES—Messrs. Brown, Byrne, Churchill, Coleman, Halliburton, Harris, Hedgpeth, Horner, Hyer, Jones, McFarland, Morris, Newland, O'Neil, Parsons, Peyton, Rains, Scott, Vernon, Watkins, Wilson, and Wood—22.
Absent—Messrs. Johnson and Robinson.

The question then being upon the adoption of the original resolution, it was adopted by the following vote:

AYES—Messrs. Brown, Byrne, Churchill, Coleman, Goodlett, Halliburton, Harris, Hedgpeth, Horner, Hyer, Jones, McFarland, Morris, Newland, O'Neil, Parsons, Peyton, Rains, Scott, Thompson, Vernon, Watkins, Wilson, and Wood—24.
NOES—Messrs. Fox, Frazier, Gullett, McFerran, McIlvaine, Richardson, and Wright—7.
Absent—Messrs. Johnson and Robinson.

The following named witnesses were discharged by consent of parties:
For the State—James Cooper, C. A. Davis, David Manning, N. W. Sitz, W. F. Cryts, William Ringer, James Walker, —— Whitehead, J. J. Jackson, J. A. Walker, William O. Hull, D. McCloud, James Hale, Moses Harvey, and W. G. Harty.
For the Respondent—Isaac Hobbs, William B. Cone, C. M. Dowdy, H. A. Shook, Robert Miller, Jacob Miller, William Morgan, John Gallaway, James Hodges, W. B. Howell, and John R. Woodsides.

On motion of SENATOR WATKINS, the Court adjourned.

THIRTEENTH DAY.

MONDAY, June 20, 1859.

The Court met pursuant to adjournment, and was opened by proclamation.

The managers and respondent attended.

HENRY MILLER, witness on the part of the respondent, was recalled to the stand, and the question given below was proposed by the respondent, which was objected to by the managers, and decided to be legal and proper by the following vote:

AYES—Messrs. Churchill, Coleman, Fox, Goodlett, Gullett, Harris, Hedgpeth, Jones, McIlvaine, Morris, Newland, Peyton, Rains, Richardson, Robinson, Scott, Watkins, Wilson, and Wood—19.

NOES—Messrs. Brown, Byrne, Frazier, Halliburton, Horner, Hyer, McFarland, McFerran, O'Neil, Thompson, Vernon, and Wright—12.

Absent—Messrs. Johnson and Parsons.

Question. What was it that influenced the jury in the case of Berry *vs.* Griffie to render a verdict for more than the petition asked for?

[The answer of the witness was to the effect that the jury had given the excessive verdict owing to the fact that they gave the plaintiff the amount of damages sued for, and then computed interest upon that amount.]

The respondent here announced that he had no further evidence to offer, and the witnesses on both sides were, by consent, discharged.

SENATOR JONES then moved to adjourn until two o'clock, P. M.

SENATOR PARSONS, by way of amendment, moved to adjourn until three o'clock, P. M.

The question being upon adjourning until three o'clock, P. M., it was decided in the negative by the following vote, the ayes and noes being demanded by Senator Goodlett:

AYES—Messrs. Byrne, Gullett, Halliburton, Harris, Hedgpeth, McFarland, Parsons, and Rains—8.

NOES—Messrs. Brown, Churchill, Coleman, Fox, Frazier, Goodlett, Horner, Hyer, Jones, McFerran, McIlvaine, Morris, Newland, O'Neil, Peyton, Richardson, Robinson, Scott, Thompson, Vernon, Watkins, Wood, and Wright—23.

Absent—Messrs. Johnson and Wilson.

The question then being upon adjourning until two o'clock, P. M., it was decided in the negative by the following vote, the ayes and noes being demanded by Senator Halliburton:

AYES—Messrs. Byrne, Churchill, Fox, Gullett, Halliburton, Harris, Hedgpeth, Hyer, Jones, and Rains—10.

NOES—Messrs. Brown, Coleman, Frazier, Goodlett, Horner, McFarland, McFerran, McIlvaine, Morris, Newland, O'Neil, Parsons, Peyton, Richardson, Robinson, Scott, Thompson, Vernon, Watkins, Wood, and Wright—21.

Absent—Messrs. Johnson and Wilson.

[The foregoing account of the proceedings of this day is extracted, (with the exception of the paragraph included in brackets,) from the journal kept by the Secretary, an accident having prevented the reporter from being present, and he being, on this account, unable to present a more full report.]

[Reported by George C. Stedman.]

MR. HARDIN'S ARGUMENT.

The managers and respondent having announced themselves ready to proceed with the argument of the cause,

Mr. HARDIN rose and said:

Mr. PRESIDENT: It becomes my duty to open the argument in this cause; and in doing so I must confess that I feel sensibly the responsibility resting upon me. This arises from two considerations,—the serious character of the charges, and the position I hold, representing as I do the people of the State. It is due to them, and to this Senate, that the law and the evidence should be presented in as clear and forcible a manner as possible. I regret my great inability to come up to this standard; yet, having accepted the responsibility and honor of the position, I will now present an argument upon the charges before this Court.

It is the history of our race that persons in power are oppressive, tyrannical, partial, corrupt; not all, but many. It is also a part of that history that, by these means, the liberties of the people are, more or less, destroyed. Sensible of these truths, the founders of our State government, desiring to obtain for themselves and their posterity the greatest happiness possible, and believing that liberty, entire liberty, was the means of that happiness, sought to establish the one in order to attain the other. They were also sensible of another truth, that if persons in office were faithful and impartial in the discharge of duty, the happiness and liberties of the people might be preserved. Apprehensive that this would not always be the case, the founders of the State government seemed to have framed our constitution and laws with an eye indicating extreme jealousy of persons in authority. For instance, they established a Legislative department, and yet the Representatives are allowed to serve but one term of two years, and Senators but one term of four years, before they shall account, as it were, to the people, for the fidelity of their acts. They established an Executive department; but the incumbent is ineligible for reëlection on the expiration of his term of office. They established a Judiciary department; and yet all those portions of the constitution and laws providing for it, show that they were extremely jealous of those who were to wear the ermine of the bench. To preserve the independence of the judiciary, the Judges were appointed during good behavior, subject, however, to removal by address and impeachment. In addition to this, they might for misdemeanors in office be punished by fine and imprisonment. It so happened, however, that the people thought that the tenure of good behavior was too long, and the Judges too far removed from proper accountability. The constitution was, therefore, reformed, and the tenure limited to six years. Notwithstanding this limitation, and early reckoning with the Judges, those checks upon their conduct already mentioned were still retained. This, sir, is a part of our constitutional history, and it shows that the people were jealous of the power and influence of position to their injury. It was never taken for granted that because a man was Judge he could not err; it was never supposed that he could not be corrupt; it was never regarded as an office wherein no partiality could exist, or that authority could not be abused.

Again, ours was modeled after the Federal constitution in almost every principle. The provisions of the two in providing for the impeachment of the Judges of the respective jurisdictions seem to be the same.

There is no power in the Federal constitution for removing Judges by address. Such a provision was proposed in the constitutional convention, but was not adopted. For this reason, Judges of the United States are exempt from accountability for causes for which our Judges may be removed. Notwithstanding this, the jurisdiction of the two constitutions upon the subject of impeachment seems to be the same. If this be so, the precedents and adjudications of the Senate of the United States as a court of impeachment will aptly apply here. Although the term "high crimes and misdemeanors" is the special language of the constitution of the United States, and the term "misdemeanor in office" that of ours, we shall maintain that they have the same force and signification, since we have Mr. Blackstone for authority that the words "crimes" and "misdemeanors" are synonymous. If there be any difference, the term "misdemeanor in office" comprehends greater latitude of signification than the term "high crimes and misdemeanors." The word "misdemeanor," as rendered by the best authorities, means evil intent, ill conduct, fault, and mismanagement. We maintain, therefore, that where the conduct of the Judge arose from ill intent, whether to gratify malice or serve friendship, he is guilty of a misdemeanor in office. But, sir, it has been said upon this occasion that a Judge is not impeachable for any act, the commission of which has not been previously prescribed by positive law to be an offense. This is not a new position. It was taken at an early day in the Senate of the United States, and found to be untenable. As a full answer to the argument used in support of that position, I will read to the Senate the views of Mr. Story:

There is also much force in the remark, that an impeachment is a proceeding purely of a political nature. It is not so much designed to punish an offender, as to secure the State against gross official misdemeanors. It touches neither his person nor his property; but simply divests him of his political capacity.—1 Story's Com. p. 560.

The offenses to which the power of impeachment has been and is ordinarily applied, as a remedy, are of a political character. Not but that crimes of a strictly legal character fall within the scope of the power, (for, as we shall presently see, treason, bribery, and other high crimes and misdemeanors are expressly within it;) but that it has a more enlarged operation, and reaches what are aptly termed political offenses, growing out of personal misconduct, or gross neglect, or usurpation, or habitual disregard of the public interests, in the discharge of the duties of a political office. These are so various in their character, and so indefinable in their actual involutions, that it is almost impossible to provide systematically for them by positive law.—Ibid. p. 532, § 764.

Again, there are many offenses, purely political, which have been held to be within the reach of parliamentary impeachments, not one of which is in the slightest manner alluded to in our statute book. And, indeed, political offenses are of so various and complex a character, so utterly incapable of being defined, or classified, that the task of positive legislation would be impracticable, if it were not almost absurd to attempt it. What, for instance, could positive legislation do in cases of impeachment like the charges against Warren Hastings, in 1788? Resort, then, must be had either to parliamentary practice, and the common law, in order to ascertain what are high crimes and misdemeanors; or the whole subject must be left to the arbitrary discretion of the Senate, for the time being. The latter is so incompatible with the genius of our institutions, that no lawyer or statesman would be inclined to countenance so absolute a despotism of opinion and practice, which might make that a crime at one time, or in one person, which would be deemed innocent at another time, or in another person. The only safe guide in such cases must be the common law, which is the guardian at once of private rights and public liberties. And however much it may fall in with the political theories of certain statesmen and jurists to deny the existence of a common law belonging to and applicable to the nation in ordinary cases, no one has as yet been bold enough to assert that the power of impeachment is limited to offenses positively defined in the statute book of the Union, as impeachable high crimes and misdemeanors.—Ib. p. 555, § 797.

Congress have unhesitatingly adopted the conclusion, that no previous statute is necessary to authorize an impeachment for any official misconduct; and the rules of proceeding, and the rules of evidence, as well as the principles of decision, have been uniformly regulated by the known doctrines of common law and parliamentary usage. In the few cases of impeachment which have hitherto been tried, no one of the charges has rested upon any statutable misdemeanors. —Ib. p. 566, § 799.

It is, therefore, not necessary to prescribe previously, by positive law, what conduct of the Judge shall be deemed misdemeanors in office,—it is impossible, there being so many ways to exhibit corruption, so many ways of exercising partiality, so many ways of abusing authority. Precedent and common law are the intelligent guides, and they teach us that Judges may be impeached for personal misconduct, abuse of authority, oppression of a citizen, be he an attorney, litigant, or spectator; or for any violation of law, or rules and practice in courts of justice. As illustrative of this position, and to show how far the power of impeachment extends, I propose to read several precedents, many of which are quite the same, in fact, as many of the charges now under consideration before this Court. In 1804, John Pickering, a Judge of the District Court of the United States, was impeached for misbehavior, and found guilty of all the charges by a constitutional majority of the Senate. The charges were founded on the conduct and rulings of Judge Pickering in only one case, and are as follows, as seen in Sargeant's Constitutional Law, page 376:

First. For misbehavior as a Judge, in ordering the delivery to the claimant of goods seized by the Collector without requiring security. *Second.* In refusing to hear evidence, offered on the part of the United States, to show the forfeiture of said goods. *Third.* In refusing to allow the United States to appeal from his decree, in a case of admiralty and maritime jurisdiction, where the matter in dispute exceeded three hundred dollars. *Fourth.* For appearing on the bench, for the purpose of administering justice, in a state of total intoxication, produced by the free and intemperate use of inebriating liquors, and then and there frequently, in a most profane and indecent manner, invoking the name of the Supreme Being. He was found guilty on all these charges, by a constitutional majority of the Senate, and a sentence of removal from office was passed on the 12th of March, 1804.

In 1805, Judge Chase was impeached on the following charges, but was acquitted by the Senate of the United States:

ARTICLE I. That, unmindful of the solemn duties of his office, and contrary to the sacred obligation by which he stood bound to discharge them "faithfully and impartially, and without respect to persons," the said Samuel Chase, on the trial of John Fries, charged with treason, before the Circuit Court of the United States, held for the district of Pennsylvania, in the city of Philadelphia, during the months of April and May, one thousand eight hundred, whereat the said Samuel Chase presided, did, in his judicial capacity, conduct himself in a manner highly arbitrary, oppressive, and unjust, viz:

First. In delivering an opinion, in writing, on the question of law, on the construction of which the defense of the accused materially depended, tending to prejudice the minds of the jury against the case of the said John Fries, the prisoner, before counsel had been heard in his defense.

Second. In restricting the counsel for the said Fries from recurring to such English authorities as they believed apposite, or from citing certain statutes of the United States, which they deemed illustrative of the positions upon which they intended to rest the defense of their client.

Third. In debarring the prisoner from his constitutional privilege of addressing the jury (through his counsel) on the law, as well as on the fact, which was to determine his guilt, or innocence, and at the same time endeavoring to wrest from the jury their indisputable right to hear argument, and determine upon the question of law, as well as the question of fact, involved in the verdict which they were required to give.

In consequence of which irregular conduct of the said Samuel Chase, as dangerous to our liberties as it is novel to our laws and usages, the said John Fries was deprived of the right secured to him by the eighth article amendatory of the constitution, and was condemned to death without having been heard by counsel in his defense, to the disgrace of the character of the American bench, in manifest violation of law and justice, and in open contempt of the rights of juries, on which, ultimately, rest the liberty and safety of the American people.

ARTICLE II. That, prompted by a similar spirit of persecution and injustice, at a Circuit Court of the United States, held at Richmond, in the month of May, one thousand eight hundred, for the district of Virginia, whereat the said Samuel Chase presided, and before which a certain James Thompson Callender was arraigned for a libel on John Adams, then President of the United States, the said Samuel Chase, with intent to oppress and procure the conviction of the said Callender, did overrule the objection of John Basset, one of the jury, who wished to be excused from serving on the said trial because he had made up his mind as to the publication from which the words charged to be libelous in the indictment were extracted; and the said Basset was accordingly sworn and did serve on the said jury, by whose verdict the prisoner was subsequently convicted.

ARTICLE III. That, with intent to oppress and procure the conviction of the prisoner, the evidence of John Taylor, a material witness on behalf of the aforesaid Callender, was not permitted by the said Samuel Chase to be given in, on pretense that the said witness could not prove the truth of the whole of one of the charges contained in the indictment, although the said charge embraced more than one fact.

ARTICLE IV. That the conduct of the said Samuel Chase was marked, during the whole course of the said trial, by manifest injustice, partiality, and intemperance, viz:

First. In compelling the prisoner's counsel to reduce to writing, and submit to the inspection of the court, for their admission or rejection, all questions which the said counsel meant to propound to the above named John Taylor, the witness.

Second. In refusing to postpone the trial, although an affidavit was regularly filed, stating the absence of material witnesses on behalf of the accused; and although it was manifest, that, with the utmost diligence, the attendance of such witnesses could not have been procured at that term.

Third. In the use of unusual, rude, and contemptuous expressions towards the prisoner's counsel; and in falsely insinuating that they wished to excite the public fears and indignation, and to produce that insubordination to law to which the conduct of the Judge did, at the same time, manifestly tend.

Fourth. In repeated and vexatious interruptions of the said counsel, on the part of the said Judge, which at length induced them to abandon their cause and their client, who was thereupon convicted and condemned to fine and imprisonment.

Fifth. In an indecent solicitude manifested by the said Samuel Chase for the conviction of the accused, unbecoming even a public prosecutor, but highly disgraceful to the character of a Judge, as it was subversive of justice.

ARTICLE V. And whereas it is provided by the act of Congress, passed on the 24th day of September, 1789, entitled, "an act to establish the judicial courts of the United States," that for any crime or offense against the United States, the offender may be arrested, imprisoned, or bailed, agreeably to the usual mode of process in the State where such offender may be found: and whereas it is provided by the laws of Virginia, that upon presentment by any grand jury of an offense not capital, the court shall order the Clerk to issue a summons against the person or persons offending, to appear and answer such presentment at the next court, yet the said Samuel Chase did, at the court aforesaid, award a *capias* against the body of the said James Thompson Callender, indicted for an offense not capital, whereupon the said Callender was arrested and committed to close custody, contrary to law in that case made and provided.

ARTICLE VI. And whereas it is provided by the thirty-fourth section of the aforesaid act, entitled "an act to establish the judicial courts of the United States," that the laws of the several States, except where the constitution, treaties, or statutes of the United States shall otherwise require or provide, shall be regarded as the rules of decision in trials at common law, in the courts of the United States, in cases where they apply; and whereas, by the laws of Virginia, it is provided that, in cases not capital, the offender shall not be held to answer any presentment of a grand jury until the court next succeeding that during which such presentment shall have been made, yet the said Samuel Chase, with intent to oppress and procure the conviction of the said James Thompson Callender, did, at the court aforesaid, rule and adjudge the said Callender to trial, during the term at which he, the said Callender, was presented and indicted, contrary to law in that case made and provided.

ARTICLE VII. That, at a Circuit Court of the United States for the district of Delaware, held at Newcastle, in the month of June, one thousand eight hundred, whereat the said Samuel Chase presided, the said Samuel Chase, disregarding the duties of his office, did descend from the dignity of a Judge, and stoop to the level of an informer, by refusing to discharge the grand jury, although entreated by several of the said jury so to do; and after the said grand jury had regularly declared, through their foreman, that they had found no bills of indictment, nor had any presentments to make, by observing to the said grand jury, that he, the said Samuel Chase, understood "that a highly seditious temper had manifested itself in the State of Delaware, among a certain class of people, particularly in Newcastle county, and more especially in the town of Wilmington, where lived a most seditious printer, unrestrained by any principle of virtue, and regardless of social order; that the name of this printer was"—but checking himself, as if sensible of the indecorum he was committing, added, "that it might be assuming too much to mention the name of this person, but it becomes your duty, gentlemen, to inquire diligently into this matter," or words to that effect; and that, with intention to procure the prosecution of the printer in question, the said Samuel Chase did, moreover, authoritatively enjoin on the District Attorney of the United States the necessity of procuring a file of the papers to which he alluded, (and which were understood to be those published under the title of "Mirror of the Times and General Advertiser,") and, by a strict examination of them, to find some passage which might furnish the ground-work of a prosecution against the printer of the said paper; thereby degrading his high judicial functions, and tending to impair the public confidence in, and respect for, the tribunals of justice, so essential to the general welfare.

ARTICLE VIII. And whereas mutual respect and confidence between the government of the United States and those of the individual States, and between the people and those governments, respectively, are highly conducive to that public harmony, without which there can be no public happiness, yet the said Samuel Chase, disregarding the duties and dignity of his judicial character, did, at a Circuit Court for the district of Maryland, held at Baltimore, in the month of May, one thousand eight hundred and three, pervert his official right and duty to address the grand jury then and there assembled, on the matters coming within the province of the said jury, for the purpose of delivering to the said grand jury an intemperate and inflammatory political harangue, with intent to excite the fears and resentment of the said grand jury, and of the good people of Maryland, against their State government and constitution, a conduct highly censurable in any, but peculiarly indecent and unbecoming in a Judge of the Supreme Court of the United States; and moreover that the said Samuel Chase, then and there, under pretense of exercising his judicial right to address the said grand jury, as aforesaid, did, in a manner highly unwarrantable, endeavor to excite the odium of the said grand jury, and of the good people of Maryland, against the government of the United States, by delivering opinions, which, even if the judicial authority were competent to their expression, on a suitable occasion and in a proper manner, were at that time, and as delivered by him, highly indecent, extra-judicial, and tending to prostitute the high judicial character with which he was invested, to the low purpose of an electioneering partizan.

The precedents which I have read, show the jurisdiction, as claimed by the House of Representatives of the United States, in cases of impeachment. They also afford us much light as to the rights and duties of the court, as well as those of attorneys, jurors, and others. To my mind there was ample evidence to justify the conviction of Judge Chase; but I shall not now undertake to sustain this opinion. To do so, would necessarily incur the reading of the evidence, and a full commentary of the case. But it cannot be admitted that, because he was not convicted upon these charges, that the accused in this case cannot be convicted here on similar charges. Many men are indicted for, and convicted of murder, whilst, upon like charges and like evidence, others are acquitted.

I propose now to show, by precedent, what jurisdiction our own House of Representatives have claimed. I read from the Legislative Journals, 1826, page 352, articles of impeachment against Judge Thomas, as follows:

ARTICLE I. That, unmindful of the solemn duties of his office, and contrary to the sacred obligation by which he stood bound to discharge them faithfully and impartially, the said Richard S. Thomas, in the month of April, in the year one thousand eight hundred and twenty-three, at the county of Cape Girardeau, at a Circuit Court holden for the said county, whereat the said Richard S. Thomas presided, did, in his judicial capacity, conduct himself in a manner highly arbitrary, oppressive, and unjust, and against the known and established law of the land:

First. In refusing to recognize John Juden, junior, Clerk of the said Circuit Court for Cape Girardeau county, as Clerk of the said court, and attempting to deprive him of his said office, under pretense that the said office was vacated by the amendments to the constitution of this State, made in the year 1822; whereas the said Richard S. Thomas was in truth actuated by the corrupt desire of removing the said John Juden, in order to confer the said office upon his own son Claiborne S. Thomas, and although the said Richard S. Thomas, in his official capacity, hath always recognized, as legal, the acts done by the Clerks of the other circuits in the Fourth Judicial District since the passage of the said amendments to the constitution, he, the said Richard S. Thomas, well knowing that the said Clerks derived their authority from commissions issued to them previous to the passage of the said amendments, and from none other.

Second. In declaring, in pursuance of the aforesaid corrupt design, the said Claiborne S. Thomas to be Clerk of the aforesaid Circuit Court, and as such entitled to the possession of the papers appertaining to the said office of Clerk, and in demanding the same to be delivered up to the said Claiborne S. Thomas; whereas the said Juden was then in fact the Clerk of the said court, appointed and commissioned according to law.

Third. In ordering upon the first day of the said April term the said court to be adjourned until court in course, and in refusing to transact the business of the said court under the pretense that the office of the said Juden had been vacated as aforesaid, that he had refused to deliver up to the said Claiborne S. Thomas the records of the said court, and that the question, who was the Clerk, must be determined by the Supreme Court of this State, whereas, in fact, the said Juden was the Clerk of the said court, and entitled to the custody of the said records, and the said Richard S. Thomas, Judge as aforesaid, had full power and authority to compel, by due process, the said Juden to deliver up the said records, if, in fact, his said office had been vacated by law.

ARTICLE II. That, prompted by the aforesaid corrupt motive in favor of his said son, the said Richard S. Thomas, in the vacation succeeding the said April term, persisted in refusing to acknowledge the said Juden as Clerk of the said court, by means whereof, and of the above mentioned illegal conduct of the said Judge, at the said April term, the said Juden was afterwards, to wit, in the month of June, in the said year, compelled to resign his said office of Clerk.

ARTICLE III. And whereas, a certain Charles G. Ellis did, on the nineteenth day of April, in the year 1823, obtain, before David Armour, a Justice of the Peace within and for the county of Cape Girardeau, a judgment against the said Claiborne S. Thomas, son of the said Richard S. Thomas, for the sum of fifty-seven dollars and thirty-six cents, together with the costs of suit, and the said Claiborne prayed for an appeal, and was desirous of removing the said suit to the Circuit Court for the said county, whereof the said Richard S. Thomas was Judge; yet the said Richard S. Thomas, corruptly intending to protect the said Claiborne, and deprive the said Ellis of his right to a speedy and impartial administration of justice, did conduct himself, in his official capacity, in a manner highly partial, oppressive, and unjust:

First. In becoming security in an appeal bond for his said son, in the said suit, upon the 22nd day of April, in the said year, and thereby voluntarily acquiring an interest in a cause about to be removed to the said judicial tribunal over which he, the said Richard S. Thomas, then presided.

Second. In refusing, at the August term, in the year 1823, of the Circuit Court of the county of Cape Girardeau, to which the said suit had been removed by appeal, to try the same, and ordering a change of venue therein, to the county of St. Francois, in the Third Judicial Circuit, although no application, according to law, had been made therefor, by either of the parties, nor did the said parties consent thereto.

Third. In refusing, at the last August term of the said court, wherein the said cause was then depending, it having been sent back by the Judge of the said Third Judicial Circuit, for want of jurisdiction to try the same, and in ordering the same to be continued, because his said son was interested therein, although the said Ellis had neither applied for, nor consented to, the said continuance.

Fourth. In refusing, at the last August and December terms of the said court, to try said cause, and ordering the same to be continued, for the reason above assigned, although the said Ellis neither applied for, nor assented to, the said continuances.

ARTICLE IV. And whereas the said Richard S. Thomas did, in the month of April, 1824, issue a warrant directed to the Sheriff of Cape Girardeau county, commanding him to take the body of Ezekiel Fenwick, charged with the murder of William R. Bellamy, and the said Fenwick could not be found by the said Sheriff in obedience to the said warrant; yet the said Richard S. Thomas, unmindful of his duties, and to the great scandal of public justice, did agree with John D. Cook, counsel of the said Fenwick, that if the said Fenwick would surrender himself upon the said warrant, no further testimony should be heard, and that the said Fenwick should be admitted to bail upon the charge aforesaid; that the said Fenwick, relying upon the said promise, did surrender himself to the said Judge upon the 24th day of the said month, at the said county; whereupon the Judge inquired if there was no testimony present, and being answered in the negative, discharged the said Fenwick on bail, declaring it was not his business to procure the attendance of witnesses, although he well knew that several witnesses acquainted with the circumstances of the said supposed murder, resided in the adjoining county of Perry, at a distance not exceeding thirty miles, and their attendance could be procured within a short period of time.

Judge Thomas was convicted on all the charges, and removed from office. These precedents establish clearly, that for any character of offense, showing corruption, oppression, partiality, or other abuse of authority, the Judge may be impeached therefor. And besides, a close analogy may be observed between the charges now under consideration and those which have been read.

It has been claimed here, Mr. President, that great latitude of discretion is allowed to a Judge, and that many of the offenses charged in the articles of impeachment before the Senate were matters of judicial discretion, and although however wrong the motive, still the act cannot be questioned here. We aver that there is no discretion left to the Judge; that the common law and practice of courts declare his whole duty,—define his powers and jurisdiction in almost every particular. Discretion in a Judge has ever been reprehended by Judges themselves, and by the people. Their duty is to pursue the law. They cannot, more than any other officer, depart from it. Lord Mansfield said:

But discretion, when applied to a court of justice, means sound discretion, guided by law. It must be governed by rule, not by humor. It must not be arbitrary, vague, and fanciful, but legal and regular.—Case of John Wilkes, How. State Trials, p. 1089.

The discretion of the Judge, (says Mr. Gibbon, very truly,) is the first engine of tyranny. To this I will add the memorable words used by Lord Camden, in the case of Haidson and Kersey, in the Court of Common Pleas, when he was Chief Justice of that court: "The discretion of a Judge is the law of tyrants; it is always unknown; it is different in different men. It is casual, and depends upon constitution, temper, passion. In the best it is oftentimes caprice; in the worst it is every vice, folly, and passion, to which human nature is liable."—8 Ibid. p. 56, note.

It is, perhaps, a popular opinion, that there must be some special consideration to make the act corrupt. This is not the case, however. Corruption embraces bribery, but has a more general signification. It is defined by Mr. Bouvier, in his Law Dictionary, to be a wrongful act, done with the intention to give some advantage inconsistent with official duty and the rights of others.

Ordinarily, malice is understood to be wickedness, depravity, a heart bent on mischief. But this is not its legal signification. It means, in its legal sense, a wrongful act, done knowingly, without just cause or excuse.

This has been classed as a criminal case, and much argument used to give it that character. There is nothing in the nature of the case to make it such. Neither the articles of impeachment, nor answer, are formally drawn. No *capias* issued for the body of the accused; nor has any jury been sworn to try the facts adduced in evidence. The accused is only present at his pleasure; there is no law requiring his presence, as in criminal cases. Besides, if convicted, there is no corporal punishment, no fine, no imprisonment. There is, therefore, no analogy between this and a criminal case. In the case of Judge Pickering, the articles of impeachment do not so much as charge him with having acted with corrupt intent. They allege that he is impeached for high crimes and misdemeanors, and the specifications set forth the facts. That is all; that is sufficient; and it is for the court, after hearing the evidence, to say whether the charges contain proper grounds for impeachment, and whether the evidence would sustain them.

With these remarks, I now propose to enter upon the consideration of most of the articles.

The first article charges respondent with oppression, corruption, and partiality in his conduct towards Judge Eaker and his attorneys. The members of the Senate will remember that a writ of mandamus was issued by Judge Jackson against Jonas Eaker, as Judge of the County Court, returnable on the first day of the May term of the Stoddard Circuit Court—being the 17th day of May. The Sheriff served the writ by delivering a copy, and made his return accordingly. On the 20th day of May the case was called, and Messrs. Kitchen and Phelan, attorneys for Eaker, informed the court that as the writ had been served by the delivery of a copy, there had been no legal service. The Judge refused to hear them, stating that it was not a case for counsel. They then, as friends to the court, desired to present the facts, which was peremptorily refused, and they ordered to shut their mouths and take their seats. In the meantime, the Sheriff, with the writ that had been returned into court, went in search of Judge Eaker, and on finding him, offered it to him, which he refused to receive. The Sheriff reported these facts to Judge Jackson, who forthwith ordered an attachment to issue against Eaker, who was arrested and detained in custody for an hour, and released upon his promise to make his return to the copy on the next day. The conduct of the Judge towards the attorneys was stormy and offensive. He refused to hear them either as attorneys for Eaker, or as friends of the court, but compelled them to sit down and be silent. The writ run out on the 17th May; after that date it could not reissue. The Judge knew both from the return endorsed on the writ, as well as by special information of the attorneys, that the writ in the first instance was served by the delivery of a copy. The writ cannot be served by copy. (Mo. Rep., 159.) An attachment will not issue where there has not been proper personal service. (Tapping on Mandamus, p. 456–7.) The evidence sustains the entire charge, and I trust it may not be esteemed a small matter for a Judge to imprison, without authority of law, a citizen and an officer of the State. The principle involved is the pure administration of justice, and the rights and liberties of the people; a principle too momentous not to attract the attention of this Court. Why, sir, the brightest pages of our history are but records of the blood and treasure exhausted by our country in resisting the unlawful imprisonment of our citizens by a foreign nation. Indeed, we remember but recently the universal acclaim that went up from the hearts of our countrymen, at the magnanimous and courageous conduct exhibited by a distinguished officer of our naval service, in successfully resisting an hour's unlawful imprisonment of a person whose citizenship was but imperfectly declared. That which has been so successfully maintained against foreign nations, we trust is, and ever will be, maintained between our own citizens. It is the principle, the due administration of law, that we plead for. The Judge who will knowingly violate the law in one instance, will at his pleasure do so in a dozen. If he would wrongfully imprison one, the same tyrannical disposition and ungovernable temper will compel the imprisonment of the many. The hour's loss of time is nothing; but the infraction of law, the violation of the sacred liberty of the subject, is all. The respondent pleads not ignorance of his duty; nor is there any pretense that such was the case. The evidence fully convicts him of a wanton violation of every duty and principle of law in relation to the trial of the cause, and it is for this Senate to approve or reprobate his conduct.

The evidence adduced in support of the second article is, that during the pendency of an action of ejectment of Moore against Walker, in the Stoddard Circuit Court, for the recovery of the possession of certain lots in Bloomfield, the respondent, Judge of such court, advised Walker not to compromise the case with Moore, and gave as a reason that the field notes of the town were lost, and that Moore could not recover in the action. Walker immediately made this advice known to his friends, and it reached the ears of Moore, who soon thereafter applied for, and obtained, a change of venue of his case from the circuit, because of the prejudice of respondent against him. Moore had determined on making this application before this information came to his hearing. Moore and respondent were not on friendly terms. This is substantially the evidence. Is it competent for a Judge to give advice in private to parties litigant in his court? Is it wrong, or right? Is it probable that he could discharge impartially his official duties, and act thus? The Judges who are to pass sentence ought not to deliver their opinions before the case comes immediately before them, because they will not fail to support those opinions which they have prematurely exposed. (1 Chitty's Crim. Law.) There is a statute which prohibits a Judge from being counsellor in any cause. (Rev. Stat., p. 541, sec. 58.) And it is generally admitted as a principle of law, that no Judge shall give, extra-judicially, opinions in a cause pending in his court, or which might probably come before him. The respondent in this instance has violated a most sacred principle of law; degraded the dignity of his position, by encouraging the prosecution of law suits before him, when the parties were in the way of amicable adjustment of their differences. Instead of cultivating, as it were, impartiality, he is found encouraging the growth of further animosity in society, and all perhaps to gratify a personal malice against Moore. To approve his conduct by an acquittal, will be to arm him afresh for those secret and private thrusts, which he seems to be so capable of making against parties in his court who are found to be subjects of his enmity and hatred.

Article three charges respondent with misdemeanor in office in directing a change of venue from Wayne to Mississippi county, in the Tenth Judicial Circuit. The application was made by Mr. Fox, attorney for plaintiff, in the case of Limbarger against Powers. The cause alleged was prejudice of the Judge against plaintiff. Mr. Fox and the Judge were not on amicable terms. The parties and witnesses lived in the same neighborhood—in the northern part of Wayne county—and quite as convenient to the county seats of Bollinger and Iron counties, as to that of Wayne. The county seat of Mississippi is about twenty-five miles from the county seat of Wayne, and on the east side of the swamp, which is always difficult to cross, but quite impassable during the rainy season of the year. When the waters are up, this swamp is crossed by means of various kinds of craft, attended with expense; when dry, it is crossed on horseback; but when the waters have measurably subsided, they are too shallow for craft, and too deep for crossing on horseback. Near three days are occupied generally in crossing in craft. Around the swamp, by the usual traveled route, it is some two hundred miles. The attorneys in the case do not attend court in Mississippi county. They agreed that the case should go to the county of Madison or Iron, because of the convenience of either to them and the parties and witnesses. To travel by land from where the parties lived to Mississippi county, a person would have to pass through the counties of Bollinger, Scott, and Cape Girardeau. On the next day after the order was made for the removal of the cause to Mississippi county, Mr. Fox asked the court to rescind the order, alleging as a reason that he would rather have the case tried there than that it should go to Mississippi county. The Judge replied that if he would not take it as a personal offense, he would fine him for contempt. Upon this state of facts, we claim that respondent was guilty of oppression and misconduct. The statutory rule is, (Rev. Code, 1855, p. 1559, sec. 4,) that the case should be removed to the county outside of the circuit most convenient to Powers, the adverse party. This was not done; nor was the convenience of the attorneys or witnesses consulted. But, disregarding the letter and spirit of the law, and that just rule of practice so often pursued by upright and impartial Judges, that of looking as far as possible to the convenience of counsel and witnesses, this respondent removed the case to a court beyond the swamp, with the apparent purpose of punishing Judge Fox and others for their temerity in making the application. No justification or excuse for this conduct can be found in the evidence. That he was operated upon by some motive of evil intent, may be seen in the unfriendly relations existing between him and Judge Fox, and in the harsh and unbecoming language used towards the counsel in relation to the application.

Article six charges respondent with gross and malicious oppression and misconduct in publicly charging William G. Phelan, Esq., whilst court was in session, with the disgraceful and criminal act of tampering with the grand jury. The facts seem to be that Mr. Phelan, an attorney in the cause, was in the act of submitting an argument to the jury empanneled in the case of Gibson against Dunn. Without any provocation on the part of Phelan whatever, respondent made the declaration. Phelan undertook to deny, and exculpate himself from, the charge. Respondent peremptorily required him to shut his mouth and sit down. The manner of respondent was angry and severe. Phelan was not permitted at any time to deny the charge, or vindicate himself against it. The respondent has not undertaken before this Senate to aver and substantiate the truth of his accusation; nor is there any pretense that he could do so. Instead of cultivating order and harmony in his court, and so demeaning himself as to win the love and respect of the bar, the respondent himself, whilst occupying the bench, affords ample cause for personal violence and breaches of the peace, by villifying and uttering foul slanders against those whom he may regard as his enemies, In law, he is a conservator of the peace; in practice, what? a relentless persecutor of those who have not his friendship. As he does not excuse or justify his conduct, is there any one so indifferent to the harmony and good order of our courts of justice as to find no words of condemnation for such acts? Will not this Senate reprobate severely such tyrannical and abusive conduct towards attorneys found to be quiet and respectful in deportment, and faithful in the discharge of duty. Not to do so, would in effect place those officers of our courts beyond the pale of protection, and license a malignant Judge to inflict upon them every character of tyranny, abuse, and oppression that his low and grovelling nature might originate.

Article seven contains a kindred charge to the last. It is, that whilst the Ripley Circuit Court was in session, the respondent, without any provocation, but in a spirit of vindictive persecution, charged Judge Fox, an attorney of the court, with being guilty of the *crime of perjury*, or *subornation of perjury*, and *of lying*, and *causing his client to lie*. The gist of the evidence is, that the client had sworn to the original, and Judge Fox to the amended answer. Court was in session, the respondent occupying the bench; Fox was quietly engaged in writing at a table within the bar. Holding up to view one of the answers, respondent asked Fox whose writing that was. The reply was, I can't say till I see it. Respondent then said *you have sworn to a lie*, or *caused your client to swear to one*. The words proven to have been used by respondent are not the exact words set forth in the article. In impeachment cases this is not necessary. Lest it may be so contended, I will read an authority. In the case of De Sacheverell, impeached for high crimes and misdemeanors, and convicted by the House of Lords, the defendant moved in arrest of judgment upon the ground of a variance between the proof and charge. After argument, the Lord Chancellor delivered the opinion of the House of Lords, as follows:

That by the law and usage of parliament, in prosecutions by impeachment for high crimes and misdemeanors, by writing or speaking, the particular words supposed to be criminal are not necessary to be expressed in such impeachments.—15 How. State Trials, p. 473.

The proof is ample and sustains the charge. The words proven are the import and substance of what was said by respondent on that occasion. If there was a variance between the two answers, it was the duty of the adverse party to have moved the objection, and made the fact apparent. If, however, it was proper for the Judge to announce the variance, it could and ought to have been done in very different language. The use of the very offensive and slanderous words employed would lead us to believe that he was moved to make the charge by no other feelings than those of malice and revenge. Public and stinging exposure of Judge Fox was doubtless the sole object, and not that the ends of justice required it. To approve of such malicious persecution and oppression in our courts, is to give license to the exhibition of the worst passions, and allow no protection to character or good conduct. Was there any occasion for such language? Will any state of facts justify it? I answer no; and if not, is the character of Judge Fox to be thus publicly maligned, and the Judge be held to no account? If so, then our courts will become, instead of sanctuaries of justice and forums for the highest dignity of character and the liveliest expression of personal and professional friendship, places where slanders and assaults, vituperation and calumny, will hold sway.

In article eight the respondent is charged with partial and highly unbecoming conduct at the April term, 1858, of the Oregon Circuit Court. An officer, in attempting to arrest one DePriest, whilst disturbing the peace of a family, was resisted by him. A true bill was returned against DePriest for each offense. He was convicted of one offense in the forenoon of the day of trial. During the recess of court, respondent advised an attorney, Mr. Odell, that the two indictments were for the same offense, and that DePriest would be acquitted on the charge yet to try upon a plea of former conviction; and further advised him to hunt up DePriest and take the case upon a contingent fee. Mr. Odell was employed as advised, and moved to quash the indictment, giving as a reason the former conviction. Respondent overruled the motion to quash, and advised Mr. Odell of his error, and that a plea in bar was the proper practice. A *noll. pros.* was thereupon entered by the Circuit Attorney, and the fee paid by DePriest. Was the conduct of respondent proper and right? Did he not prejudge the case? and that, too, wrongfully. He gave his opinion, and the case resulted as he advised. The evidence fully sustains the charge; and upon principle it does not seem admissible that a Judge should be admitted with impunity to thus express his opinions, and exhibit partiality.

Respondent is charged in article ten with having illegally and corruptly discharged from the custody of the Deputy Sheriff, one John R. Main. He was in custody of this officer by virtue of a writ to commit him to jail. No examination, if any, had been given by the Justice with the mittimus. Main presented to respondent a petition to be discharged under the habeas corpus act. Respondent denied the sufficiency of the petition, and suggested certain amendments, which were interlined in the petition. The evidence taken before the magistrate, if any, was not presented; nor was this officer called; nor was any rule made upon him to produce the evidence. Respondent directed the release of Main, and gave as his reason that the Justice did not insert in the commitment that he had good cause to believe that Main was guilty of the offense charged. Upon examination, I find that this warrant follows strictly the forms that have been in use since this became a State. Nor have I discovered by any authority that such a requisition has ever been, or should be, used in such warrant. The reason given, is, therefore, a gratuity, and intended, doubtless, to cover a worse one. He fixed his own justification on that particular reason. Its sufficiency is not admitted by any usage or authority known to me. Our statutes provide that if the commitment be informal, insufficient, or irregular, the prisoner shall give bail, if it appear from the examination taken, or, if there be none, from the testimony of the magistrate, that there is sufficient legal cause of commitment. As the warrant conforms to the forms in use, I hold it to be formal, sufficient, and regular. If in this I am in error, respondent should have ascertained from the legal sources of information, whether there was a sufficient legal cause of commitment. He made no rule for the presence of either. It was his duty to have done so. In not doing so, he screened the offender from punishment which perhaps justly awaited him. We claim that the offense was clearly and specifically set forth in the warrant. Where that is the case, the law is that the prisoner shall not, in the absence of the evidence, be discharged. If this latter position be true, respondent grievously abused his authority in discharging the prisoner because no evidence was adduced. If not true, our other position must be true. The warrant was either informal, insufficient, and irregular, or *vice versa;* if the latter, as there was no evidence adduced, the prisoner should have been bailed or remanded; if the former, he was guilty of a misdemeanor in not requiring the production of the evidence. He suggested, and permitted to be corrected, deficiencies in the petition; but, although his prescribed duty, he had no care for the State. At the same time, upon a like proceeding, respondent discharged Russell, another offender against the laws. Although different in fact from Main's case, respondent's omission of duty was quite as obvious. As respondent has been for several years a Judge, and long time a practitioner, I will not presume so much as to suppose that he was ignorant of the law, or his duty, in relation to these cases. Not being ignorant, he must therefore have knowingly inflicted upon society a grievous wrong in refusing to enforce the laws made for its protection. In the articles of impeachment against Judge Thomas, he was charged among other things with having discharged a prisoner, alleging that it was not his duty to hunt up the witnesses, well knowing that there were witnesses in an adjoining county who, if present, would establish the charge. Upon this he was convicted. Is there a shade of difference between the conduct of Judge Thomas and that of respondent in the Russell case? He well knew the offense charged against Russell; that he had had an examination before a Justice; that he was not acquitted, but held for further trial; that he had been granted the customary indulgence to get bail; that though the commitment was not in the hands of the Constable when his return was made to the writ of habeas corpus, yet it came to the hands of, and was presented to, respondent, before the prisoner was discharged. Of course, Russell was in the custody of the Constable under the original warrant, till a commitment came to hand. It is neither the law, nor the practice, that the issuance of the commitment should follow the announcement of the judgment of the Justice. The court said in the case of Still *vs.* Walls, 7 East, 536:

> It never could be doubted but that a magistrate might, by parol, order an offender to be detained in custody until he could make out his warrant of commitment, and this court were in the constant habit of directing commitments verbally, which were afterwards recorded.

It is also the constant practice, doubtless, of the magistrates and courts, to grant the accused time to obtain bail. The Constable was allowed to amend his return to the writ of habeas corpus, after it was presented to respondent. Should he not have directed a further amendment when the commitment came to the Constable? To have done so, would have thwarted his purpose to discharge Russell. In presenting the commitment to respondent, the Constable in effect claimed the custody of Russell under it, and also that he ought not to be discharged. To break the force of this, respondent warned him, "if you don't mind, you will contradict your return." This alarmed him, as his return was that he held Russell under a verbal order of the Justice, and he abandoned the case to such rulings as respondent should make.

Again, Solomon G. Kitchen, at the special instance of the sole Judge of the County Court of Stoddard county, came to this place for certified lists of the swamp lands of that county. The fees alone were sixty-five dollars. Upon his return the court audited his claim for those fees and services at about one hundred and seventy dollars. These are the facts; yet respondent charged the grand jury as alleged in article eleven. Were the facts as represented by respondent, still it would not be allowable, by any authority or practice known to me, for him in his charge to the grand jury to bias the public mind against the supposed offender. It is the duty of the Judge to instruct the grand jury as to their powers and duties, limited, according to practice, to a brief synopsis of the statutory provisions. To attempt to fix public prejudice against an unoffending citizen, by presenting a false statement of facts, and by using the influence of position, is too truly a flagrant breach of the trust reposed in a Judge. You will remember from the articles I read to you this morning against Judge Chase, that he was impeached for a like breach of duty. This we urge as a prominent instance of the reprobation that such an abuse of authority has received at the hands of an intelligent assembly. It is a fair deduction to assert that such charges to grand juries are violative of the common law as administered in the United States, and of the practice as known to the courts thereof, since the House of Representatives of the United States, made up as it was and is from every section of the Union, voted the impeachment against Judge Chase. That vote is the evidence of their opinion. But the subject of Judge Chase's charge was a total stranger, against whom he could have had no personal malice. The present is the reverse of that. Respondent regarded Mr. Kitchen as his personal enemy at the time, made so, as Mr. Kitchen testifies, by the harsh and unfeeling conduct of respondent whilst on the bench towards him. Out of court they had had no issue, not an unkind word; in court, Mr. Kitchen had been repeatedly the subject of his tyranny, abuse, and malignant remarks. Nor does it appear from the evidence that Mr. Kitchen had ever given him cause, or been other than respectful and courteous. As the facts did not justify, nor the law nor the practice in the courts authorize, the character of the charge to the grand jury, his course must be traced to low, personal malice, and relentless persecution. This is further confirmed by the testimony of Mr. Ringer, who represents that, in the fall of 1857, being about one year before the charge was given to the grand jury, respondent sought him out, inquired into his accounts with Kitchen, then Court House Commissioner, and advised him to sue and hold Mr. Kitchen personally responsible for the unpaid balance due him on the contract to build the court house; and further advised Mr. Ringer that he could recover. Such a suit would have to be instituted in the Circuit Court of the county of Stoddard, as both Ringer and Kitchen reside there; of that court respondent was and is Judge. There is further evidence of his persevering pursuit of Kitchen. Doubting whether his public charge had or would influence the grand jury to indict Mr. Kitchen, respondent, transcending every official duty,—dishonoring the ermine of his office,—appeared before the grand jury in their retirement, and repeated his public charge, with this, that Mr. Kitchen was the person referred to. These are the facts, substantially. They convict respondent of sacrificing the sacred character of his position to destroy the character and fortunes of his neighbor. Such conduct in a private individual would be treated with loathing and contempt. What words will suitably characterize it, when found in a Judge? I have them not. Protection against such vile persecution is due the citizen. May the judgment of the Senate afford it. Such a judgment would receive the applause of our people.

Article fifteen charges respondent with willful and corrupt abuse of authority in the case of Moore against Eldridge, administrator, tried at the Ripley Circuit Court. The case was called for trial, a jury ordered, and the court took a recess for dinner. The case had, for some reason, excited much attention and discussion among the people. During recess, respondent fell in with a few persons, among them was Mr. Kittrell, a very intelligent witness, who were speculating as to the final result of the case. Mr. Kittrell brought the subject of their conversation to the attention of respondent, who expressed the opinion that Moore ought not to recover of Eldridge. Mr. Kittrell controverted the opinion expressed, and he and respondent had some discussion about it. We maintain it as an indisputable principle of law, that a Judge should not declare his mind as to any case pending, or which might thereafter come before him. To do so obliges him for the sake of consistency to maintain them. Upright and honorable Judges will not and do not do so. Whenever done it is a flagrant abuse of authority, and evidence of a partizan mind. Before such a Judge the rights of parties are uncertain, and dependent more on his will than the law. Often, yea, too often, does the least intimation, either of word or act, from the Judge, determine the mind of the jury. In this particular instance his conduct was improper in the highest degree, as the officer was then collecting a jury from the people, of whom respondent's auditory was a part, and for aught we know the jury may have been made up in part from that auditory. Can such unbecoming conduct and abuse of authority pass unrebuked by this Senate? But, again: At the trial Mr. Kittrell testified *only* as to the execution of an instrument of writing offered in evidence. The verdict of the jury was for Eldridge, and Moore sought a review of his case by the Supreme Court. The bill of exceptions was prepared, and the counsel for both parties informed respondent that it embraced all the evidence, at least satisfactorily so. Respondent refused to attest the bill of exceptions, because it did not set forth that Kittrell testified before the jury that there was an erasure or alteration of the date of the instrument. The attorneys denied that Kittrell had made such a statement. He was called, and stated to respondent that he did not make that statement, but only testified as to the execution. Respondent asked him then if there had not been an erasure or alteration of the date. Witness said he did not know; the writing was as he had always seen it. Respondent thereupon inserted the controverted statement in the bill of exceptions, in brackets, as a part of the testimony of Kittrell, and signed it. Messrs. Kitchen, Bedford, and Kittrell, have testified before this Senate that Kittrell did not make the statement alleged; yet it is a part of the record of that case that he did, made so by respondent in the face of their denials. What more glaring abuse of authority could be desired to support this impeachment? The corrupt motive is to be found in his favoring the cause of Eldridge. To effect this he expressed his opinions for him publicly and without reserve. Judgment being for Eldridge, he shaped the record, in violation of every principle of justice, to secure its affirmation. There is no dispute as the facts; nor can there be any as to the motive that operated upon respondent. Can any intelligent, virtuous mind hesitate to remove a Judge whose conduct is so flagrantly subversive of the rights of the people? I trust not, and believe not.

Article sixteen charges respondent with gross oppression, partiality, and abuse of authority, at the trial of Berry against Griffie, in the Stoddard Circuit Court. The principal facts are, that at the trial, the respondent, as Judge, made some remarks, in the presence and hearing of the jury, in relation to the merits of the case, that Mr. Tyrell, attorney for defendant, deemed prejudicial to the rights of his client, and at the time "objected to an instruction from the court in that manner and form, as improper and unfair." The jury rendered a verdict for plaintiff for more than was prayed for in his petition. Defendant, by his attorney, moved for a new trial on the following reasons:

First, on the trial plaintiff totally failed to prove any cause of action alleged in the petition. Second, the jury were misled by testimony to prove who was the owner of the land in question at the time of trial. Third, the testimony introduced which tended to prove who was the owner of the land in question at the time of trial should have been excluded. Fourth, the jury were misled by the opinion of the court, that defendant had no interest susceptible of conveyance in the land mentioned in the petition. Fifth, plaintiff on the trial proved no damages. Sixth, on the trial defendant proved performance of the contract alleged in petition. Seventh, the verdict is greater than the testimony warrants.

This motion was overruled and exceptions saved. Defendant also moved to arrest the judgment on these reasons:

First, the verdict is inconsistent with the plaintiff's demand of relief, in that it is greater in amount than the relief demanded. Second, the jury gave damages for an item in plaintiff's account, which the plaintiff was not allowed to prove, to wit: the item of rails, for which plaintiff claimed one hundred dollars.

This motion was also overruled and exceptions saved. Subsequent to these rulings of the court, plaintiff, on leave, entered a remitter.

Defendant tendered his bill of exceptions for the signature of respondent, who refused to sign it unless the causes set forth in the motion for a new trial, and the cause in the motion in arrest, were stricken out. Not being able to obtain respondent's attestation without, it was done. Respondent refused to and did not attest the evidence at all, giving as a reason that he did not know what the evidence was, because of the noise that prevailed in the court room at the time it was delivered. Mr. Bedford, attorney for plaintiff, concurred with Mr. Tyrell that the whole evidence was truly written. Respondent still peremptorily refused to attest the evidence, and the case was taken to the Supreme Court without it. Either practice prevails in that circuit, at the pleasure of the party appealing, to embrace the evidence in the bill of exceptions, or to have a separate attestation for the evidence unexcepted to. These, I believe, are the main facts, substantially. We aver that respondent endeavored corruptly to prevent defendant from getting this cause fairly before the Supreme Court. We aver that he favored the cause of Berry, and used his influence with the jury for his success. This position is supported by his verbal remarks and comments to them. Having once committed his feelings, his purpose was to work out favorably the final result. The verdict, though for a larger amount than claimed by the petition, was allowed to stand. He refused to hear affidavits that the jury did not found their verdict solely upon the evidence, but were influenced by the opinions he expressed. Such a refusal is but evidence of the effect that those intimations and insinuations were intended to have. If it is proper for a Judge to comment, at his pleasure, before the jury, and thus determine their verdict, why longer retain this boasted tribunal? A party demands a jury only when he is not willing to trust the Judge; if, however, these special efforts of the Judge to control the verdict are to be deemed proper, he has gained nothing by the choice, and the supposed benefits of the system. It may be said there is an appellate jurisdiction, for the correction of errors, intentional or otherwise. 'Tis true; but where the respondent is Judge, that is only a theory, not a practical benefit. Taking the evidence before this Senate as authority, he does not intend, if he can prevent it, that his judgment shall be reversed. The records for the Supreme Court contain no impartial history of the case. His will and pleasure is the rule. He concedes to no law, to no right, if in the way of his purpose. Of all Judges, none but he has been so bold as to claim to prescribe the causes set forth for new trials, or in arrest. Excepting the instance before us, where in the history of the judiciary has a Judge dared to say that he would not attest the exceptions unless specified causes in the motion papers were stricken out? These motions had already been overruled, and were a part of the proceedings in the cause, and what effect, therefore, it may be asked, would an erasure of specified causes have? Motions are no part of the record, and consequently the Supreme Court could not review the action of the inferior court upon them, unless they should be preserved by a bill of exceptions. (10 Mo. Rep., p. 457.) This respondent well knew, and hence his proscriptive conduct. To lessen the causes would lessen the chances of a reversal of his judgment. The right to prescribe one cause, is, in principle, the right to prescribe the motion, as well as the right to make it, which would be subversive of the law. The powers of the Judge, and the rights of the pleader, are at law perfectly consistent. The latter may assign causes at his pleasure; the former sustain or overrule; and the appellate court is the arbiter between them. It is, therefore, an inevitable conclusion that respondent by this reckless and proscriptive act, not only grossly abused the rights of the pleader, but the clear and well defined rights of the Supreme Court—that of reviewing the acts of the court below and thereby directing the due administration of justice. If this position be indisputable, then the Senate has this pointed issue before it: either to approve of this bold subversion of the law, or to remove respondent from office, and maintain the rights and powers of that court which was organized as the supreme protecting power to society, the State, and the citizen. But it may be said that the causes stricken out were frivolous. Whether so or not, does not affect the principle. The pleader had the right to assign causes without limit, and no power known to the law can take it from him. That a corrupt motive controlled respondent is further evidenced by the fact that he refused, absolutely, to attest the evidence. The statute is, that if truly written, the Judge shall sign it. (Rev. Code, 1855, p. 1264.) The question is, was it truly written, and not whether respondent believed or knew it to be so. Messrs. Tyrell and Bedford testify that it was true; nor did respondent then or now claim that it was not. He based his refusal on the statement that there was so much noise at the time that he was unable to hear the evidence. But if untrue, it devolved upon him to certify this as the cause. (Rev. Code, 1855, p. 1265.) Failing to do so, Griffie could not procure the certificate of bystanders, as they can certify only where the Judge has endorsed his refusal. The defendant was, therefore, left unprotected, and the right of appeal, in effect, denied him. For of what value is the right, if he could not avail himself of its benefits? With such uncontroverted evidence before the Senate, can it hesitate to convict and remove? Can it hesitate to take from respondent that authority which, though given to him for the sacred purposes of right and justice, he has so vilely abused?

The material facts adduced in support of the charges alleged in article eighteen are as follows: At the trial of Sarah Buckner, charged with the murder of her second husband, her son by the first husband, about fourteen years old, was introduced as a witness on behalf of the State, and proved the murder to have been committed by his mother, and a sister older than himself. The State further introduced Grimsley, the Sheriff, who testified as to confessions made by defendant, at the time of her arrest. Whilst this witness was on the stand, respondent said, "Mr. Circuit Attorney, I would withdraw that witness," who not taking the hint, the witness proceeded. On cross-examination, counsel for defendant undertook to elicit from the witness other statements, as made by defendant at the time of, and in the same conversation in which the confessions adduced were made; such as that she did not kill her husband, but that her daughter did, because of an attempt, on his part, upon her chastity. The entire defense rested upon the admission of this evidence. That it was legal and competent no one can dispute. But respondent, as Judge, refused its admission. Exceptions were saved, and a bill tendered, which he refused to, and did not, sign; nor did he endorse thereon the cause of his refusal. As soon as court opened after recess for dinner, the Circuit Attorney moved and obtained leave to withdraw from the jury the testimony of Grimsley, who was testifying at the taking of recess. Defendant by her counsel objected to the withdrawal of the testimony, insisting that the defense rested on the confessions which were for her, and had not yet been allowed to come out, and also that the entire statement should be admitted to determine the weight and construction of those confessions which had been stated, and also that, as the State had produced the testimony, which had doubtless produced a deep impression with the jury, it ought not to be withdrawn till the whole was admitted; nor then, except upon the consent of defendant. The evidence was, however, withdrawn; of this there can be no doubt, as Phelan, Moore, Davis, and others, have so testified—the jury was so instructed by the court repeatedly. Defendant offered to prove by two witnesses, that the deceased husband confessed to an attempt upon the chastity of her daughter. Respondent, as Judge, refused to admit it. In his argument to the jury, the Circuit Attorney did not comment on, or allude to the testimony of Grimsley, but treated it as having been withdrawn. In the course of Mr. Davis's argument for the defense, he undertook to allude to and comment on the testimony of Grimsley, not as evidence, but for the purpose, as it had been withdrawn, of effacing any impression it had made on the minds of the jury. Respondent forbid harshly any allusion to that evidence, as it had been withdrawn. Mr. Davis undertook, by way of effecting his purpose, to suppose a case, involving the state of facts as testified to by Grimsley. He was forbidden the use of any such supposition. After other interruptions by the court, he quit the case, saying he would not stand by and see his client Jeffreyized. Mr. Phelan, in his argument for the defense, spoke of Grimsley's testimony to divest the minds of the jury of any impression that it was testimony. Respondent directed him not to speak of it, as it had been withdrawn. Phelan endeavored to explain his purpose. Respondent seemed to get angry, and threatened him. Respondent treated Davis and Phelan with great contempt. Moore testified that respondent asked pretty much all the questions that were asked of the witnesses on behalf of the State; Phelan states that he seemed to be more the State's attorney than Woodsides. Defendant's counsel objected to respondent asking questions. Defendant was convicted, and motions for a new trial and in arrest were made, and overruled. The motion in arrest contained the reason that the defendant could not be convicted upon the testimony of one witness, without corroborating circumstances. Although respondent, in the course of this trial, claimed the credit of suggesting it, yet we shall not dispute it with him. Subsequently a bill of exceptions was tendered respondent for his signature, not embracing the testimony of Grimsley, or the action of the court in relation to it. Respondent insisted that there were two witnesses on behalf of the State, Grimsley being one of them. Mr. Phelan assured him that the testimony of Grimsley was withdrawn from the jury. Respondent insisted that it was not withdrawn, and thereupon wrote the testimony himself, at large, in the bill of exceptions; and, what is more, put in as a part of the testimony of Grimsley, that which defendant made every effort to call out on cross-examination, and which respondent refused to admit. Upon this state of facts, we charge respondent with a corrupt intent to procure the conviction of said Sarah Buckner, and with most shameful oppression, partiality, and abuse of authority at her trial. No fact enumerated is consistent with the due administration of justice. Nothing like it has ever been observed in our favored land, beyond the limits of his circuit. There it has, to our disgrace, been oft repeated, as the evidence, before the Senate, establishes beyond controversy. Does not the most unlettered citizen in the law know that the whole confession, both that which is for, as well as against, the party confessing, must go to the jury? Is there a magistrate in office so stupid that does not know it? Are not all the authorities uniform in maintaining this rule of evidence? Respondent has not, and does not controvert it. Why, therefore, were his rulings, upon so important an occasion, so much at war with law and humanity? Can there be any other conclusion than he had a cruel purpose to procure her conviction? This is strengthened by other facts in the history of this strange trial. A bill of exceptions, recording the outrage which he had perpetrated, was promptly presented for his signature. This he as promptly refused, although it was his lawful duty to give it. Apprehending, as it might be supposed, that this flagrant act might, in some form, develop a happy effect for defendant, and thinking also, perhaps, that the impression the confessions admitted had made could not be effaced from the minds of the jury, he advised the Circuit Attorney, by a hint, to withdraw the evidence. The hint was not then taken. After recess, however, it was acted upon. Whether a private conference transpired does not appear in evidence; but this we do know, that respondent advised it before noon, and after recess it was withdrawn. Why it was withdrawn does not appear in evidence. No reason was given. Nor can it be supposed that if there was one, it was favorable to the defense, since the respondent, who sought her conviction, as every fact shows, and the Circuit Attorney, whose duty it was to effect it, concurerd in, and the counsel for defense objected to, its withdrawal. As further evidence that respondent was controlled by corrupt motives on that occasion, he used the influence of his position against defendant, in conducting mainly the examination on behalf of the State; in other words, was "more the State's attorney than Woodsides." The counsel for the defense saw and felt, from the character and manner of the examination had by respondent, that he was using it as a weapon against their client, and were, therefore, forced to object to any further examination by him. There was a Circuit Attorney present, and competent to discharge his duties. Why, therefore, should this respondent elbow him aside, unless perchance he believed that his efforts would be the most effective? There are other links in the chain of evidence that support the charge. At best it was but an innocent and very natural caution in the counsel of defendant to impress upon the jury the fact that Grimsley's testimony was withdrawn. I claim that it was their right and duty to do so, and it seems to me that no upright and just Judge would have denied it to them. They explained their purpose, but to no effect. For the sake of their cause, they endeavored to do by indirection what they were not allowed to do by direct words. The same tyrannical mandate fell from the bench, and crushed every hope of service to a client that seemed to be marked as a victim by that Judge, to whom she looked for mercy and an impartial trial. So unjust and unfeeling were his commands, so severe and contemptuous his manner, that the proud spirit of Mr. Davis could no longer endure it. He would no longer witness at the shrine of public justice the immolation of those sacred rights which the law had so faithfully guarantied to his client, his associate, and himself; but indignantly abandoned the cause to such fortunes as might attend it. Mr. Phelan counted on more success; but he had not gone far on the line of strict duty, before, under threats of severe punishment, he made it convenient to suit his argument to the latitude that had been prescribed. Under the force of such rulings, such manner, and such influences, it is needless to repeat that this wretched old woman was convicted. Did respondent, on that occasion, discharge his duty? Did he administer faithfully and impartially the law? That he did no intelligent and unbiased mind can or will admit. The thrilling horror of the crime does not enter into the question. Possibly, in point of fact, conviction was her just desert. But these things ought not to justify or excuse the conduct of respondent, or influence deliberation on the charge under consideration. As it is proper to adduce subsequent acts to show the intent with which a deed has been committed, we claim, as decisive evidence of the corrupt motives that governed respondent at the trial, that, without authority of law or usage, or the plainest dictates of natural justice to sustain him, he inserted in the bill of exceptions the testimony of Grimsley as having been given to, and considered by the jury, when in truth it had been withdrawn. No fact has been more satisfactorily established at this trial than that. He that would seek by such shameful conduct to unbalance the scales of justice in another court ought not and cannot be trusted in his own. He that would impose a false record on the Supreme Court, will, without remorse, sacrifice the noblest principles of the law for the accomplishment of such purposes as so depraved a being may in his pleasure originate.

I have now, Mr. President, considered as many of the articles as it was my purpose at the beginning to do. If I have presented the facts fairly, and drawn just conclusions therefrom, I am satisfied. I might have elaborated the argument more, but have not deemed it necessary. The case is one of great breadth, but not complex; the evidence, though voluminous, is clear, and without material discrepancy. With a proper appreciation of the duties of a Judge and the rights of attorneys and parties of his court, no one can hesitate to visit upon respondent the award which the enormity of his conduct so justly deserves. I venture the opinion that the evidence discloses a more flagrant abuse of authority and duty, than was ever shown in any impeachment trial in our beloved republic. The impeachments of Judges Pickering and Thomas were confined to a very limited number of acts of misbehavior. This, however, covers a period of eighteen months, and almost every character of official duty. He is found to have repeatedly used his authority to punish those he regarded as his personal enemies, and to screen those admitted to be friends. He has played a bolder part still; he has used the same authority to protect his official acts from the scrutiny of the grand jury, and to prevent the most glaringly unjust adjudications from an investigation by the appellate court. All these acts were, beyond dispute, governed by corrupt motives. In most of the charges, it is obvious from the acts themselves; in others, such conclusion is readily drawn from the attending circumstances. He does not claim, nor could it be admitted from his reputation for learning in the law, that his behavior under investigation was the result of ignorance of his duty. If not founded in ignorance, his conduct is most reprehensible, and he the proper subject of punishment. If not so founded, it is due to those who have so long and so often suffered the severity of his tyranny, and to the honor and fidelity of the judiciary of our State, that one who has proven himself so grossly recreant to the sacred principles, moral and legal, of his position, should not only be removed, but disqualified from again holding office. Whatever, however, may be the action of this Senate, I trust it will be such as will meet the approval of the people of the State.

The argument of Mr. Hardin having been concluded, on motion of SENATOR JONES the Court adjourned.

EVENING SESSION.

MONDAY, June 20, 1859.

The Court met pursuant to adjournment.
The managers and respondent attended.

[Reported by George C. Stedman.]

ARGUMENT OF JUDGE JACKSON.

JUDGE JACKSON arose and addressed the Court as follows:

MR. PRESIDENT: In what I have to say further I shall not go over a part of the law I did the other day in presenting my case. I shall barely allude to certain parts of it. As I still entertain the views I then took, with regard to the constitution of the State of Missouri, and the constitution of the United States, in cases of this kind, and as to what is to govern in cases of impeachment in this State. I hold you cannot go outside of the laws and the constitution of the State of Missouri. There is hardly a provision made in that to meet any case which may arise there, however illegal, however unjust a Judge may act. There is no method upon it by which he may be got rid of. And in doing that, I hold, as I did then, there are two classes of impeachment. Now, there can be nothing more plain and distinct, and it is for the safety of the citizens of the State, that these provisions are made in the constitution. I could not help noticing a certain provision, and that was that a person shall not be deprived of life, liberty, and property, except by the judgment of his peers, or the law of the land. That a person cannot be preceeded against by information for an indictable offense; and I simply allude to it again for a moment or two. During one of the discussions that was going on here a gentleman of the Senate said they had duties to perform as Senators to their consciences and to their country. That is the whole doctrine. How can you try a person according to the laws of the State of Missouri, if, when you are trying that person not as a citizen you have your Senatorial influence, and proceed as Senators and not as citizens? Now, the constitution provides that when a person has violated the laws of Missouri, he must be tried by his peers—that is, persons standing just precisely as he does. He is a citizen, having the same rights and privileges, and no others. Now, as Senators you have your opinions of the rules of the Senate, and the propriety of Senators, and how they should act. That upon a jury is a different matter. But the constitution says that no man shall be tried for an offense by persons acting in any other capacity than that of a common citizen.

I will direct the attention of the Senators to these provisions of the constitution of the State of Missouri. The constitution provides that there are three distinct departments, which combined constitute the magistracy. No person belonging to one department shall exercise powers properly belonging to another. Now, gentlemen, in trying this case, what do you do? You exercise the powers of the judiciary. Do you not take upon you to discharge and decide in this case? and in doing that you have to decide, whether decisions made by the Supreme Court were right or wrong. In order to convict me of these charges here, you must have a case before you which I had before me in the Circuit Court, and you have then to decide whether the decisions I made were right or wrong. Now, gentlemen, is that your province as Senators? Can you exercise that power and control over the judiciary? Must not they be separate and distinct? If a Judge of the Circuit Court commits an offense, he must be indicted and tried by a jury; and if convicted, then it is for a felony, and then it is not impeachable under the law. The Legislature may turn a Judge out of office, but in doing that they cannot examine into his guilt or innocence, but simply into the fact whether he has been convicted or not. The fact of his having been convicted being ascertained, it is sufficient for the Senate to dismiss him from office,—if it is for a misdemeanor in office, and he be guilty of any offense.

The only misdemeanors a Judge can commit under the constitution, or under the law, I have noticed. The constitution provides that he shall reside in the circuit; he shall be thirty years of age and not over sixty-five, and shall take the oath to support the constitution. If a person undertakes to exercise the duties of Judge, and does not reside in the circuit, it is not crime that renders him ineligible; but if he resides outside the circuit, persons interested may petition the Legislature and state the fact,—that a Judge of such circuit does not reside in the circuit,—and they may impeach. And what does the Senate do? Not to inquire if that Judge is guilty of crime or not, but simply, has he done something which the constitution or the law forbids. And so, too, if a Judge practices law while he continues to hold office,—that is impeachable. It is, however, no crime. But he cannot do the two together. If he has a partner practicing in his own court, that is no crime, but it is what the law forbids the Judge to do. If he will persist in having a partner, he cannot hold an office, and he is dismissed.

The General Assembly can impeach, or exclude from office, persons convicted of bribery, perjury, and other infamous crimes. Page 67, article third, sections fourteen and fifteen of the constitution says this: Before a person can be impeached for committing an offense, he must be indicted and convicted, and then all the Senate will do will be to inquire into the fact of conviction. And there too is another provision of the constitution—"trial by jury shall forever be inviolate"—"no person shall be deprived of life, liberty, or property, but by the judgment of his peers and the law of the land"—"no person, for an indictable offense, can be proceeded against by information," etc.

Now as to the constitution of the United States, to which these precedents all refer, there is not the exception there. The provision is, that all trials shall be by jury, except in cases of impeachment. The constitution of Missouri does not make that exception in any case, for in no case whatever can a person be proceeded against except by indictment. But that makes the difference, and that is where all these precedents which are read here to-day comes from, that the managers do not notice the distinction.

The constitution of the United States also provides that persons may be indicted for treason, bribery, and high crimes and misdemeanors; but in the constitution of the State of Missouri, the Judges and other officers may be impeached for misdemeanors in office. There is all the difference in the world. They can be impeached for felonies or any other offenses. Under the constitution of the State of Missouri, it cannot be done. It is only for misdemeanor in office; and misdemeanor and malfeasance, though for the latter a person cannot be impeached. It must be for misdemeanor,—for doing something which the law provides he must not do, and leaving undone something which the law provides he shall do. And I hold that these distinctions are important. I think where they do not involve crime, they involve official misconduct. Now, a Legislature cannot inquire into the misconduct of Judges.

If a Judge of the inferior courts decides wrong, if he commits error, if he makes mistakes, it must be rectified in the superior court, and not by the Legislature. Giving the Legislature this power over the judiciary is putting it completely under the control of the Legislature. Why, in making a decision, if this rule is to govern, if the course which the managers defend in this manner, the Judge must make his decision of what he thinks will be the opinions of the majority of the Senate. If he makes a decision, though he may be honest in it, and conceives it to be the law, a bystander takes exceptions to it. The attorney on one side comes up and goes to trial, and a point is decided against him which he thinks is right; he ascertains whether a majority of the Senate thinks the same way with him. If they do, they impeach the Judge, and bring him publicly before the Senate; and if he has committed error, he is guilty of crime.

Now, gentlemen, is that fair? Is that the law of Missouri? If I thought it was, indeed I would not wish to hold a judgeship one single solitary day. No Judge would be safe; his character would always be in the hands of the Legislature; his conduct would always be subject to investigation; and for error, and misconduct, and mistakes, he would be held up before the world, and his conduct treated as criminal.

Now, Mr. Hardin argues here, from beginning to end, that the Judge has no discretion. If, in conducting his court, he acts contrary to the law, he may be impeached. Who has to decide whether he acts contrary to the law? If the courts are not to decide, who is to decide according to law? Mr. Hardin's notion is, as expressed by himself, that it is the Legislature only. Now, Mr. Hardin says the constitution guards the liberties of the people. So it does, and in guarding the liberties of the people, it provided three separate and distinct parts of government. And Mr. Hardin says, persons entrusted with power are apt to become oppressive. Is it any more dangerous in the hands of the Judiciary than in that of the Legislature? Are not members of the Legislature just as liable to be oppressive? Are not they just as much so as the Judges of the courts? But who, if Judges do wrong,—who are the persons to rectify them? I ask him where, in the constitution or laws, he finds that authority, that the Legislature may set in judgment upon the acts of the Judiciary. If the Representatives of the people, they are elected only two years. If the Senators, they are elected for four years. The Judges are elected for six years. If either of these persons act oppressively, and not right, who are they responsible to? Is it not to their constituents? If a man violates the law which his constituents may not, can they have him indicted for it? Is it any opportunity to get clear of him, except when the next election comes around, not to vote for him? If these officers do not discharge their duties faithfully and honestly, the only way you can get clear of them is by the poll books.

It did not, when the constitution was passed, and when this law was acknowledged, regulating impeachments,—it was not the case with Judges. They must hold it by life tenure; they could hold it until sixty-five years of age. If they got a Judge, it was impossible, if they were displeased with him, to get clear of him. Now people choose their own Judges, and if they choose to put up with a person who cannot be as courteous as some others, there is no injustice done to any person or laws. It is their business.

Now, the constitution, as Mr. Hardin says, of the State of Missouri was modeled after the constitution of the United States. That is not so. The constitution of the United States was made for one purpose, and the constitution of the State of Missouri was made to govern the people in all their domestic relations and civil affairs. The constitution of the United States is limited in its operation and for particular purposes. The constitution of the State of Missouri is to govern in all particulars. Now, in referring to Judge Thomas, because as Mr. Hardin said, you will notice, gentlemen, in that case the cause of impeachment against Judge Thomas, was for violating a particular provision of that law. It is found now in the statute—the law about disposing of offices. It will be found in volume 1, page 613:

Every person holding or exercising any office of public trust under the constitution or laws of this State, who shall for any reward or gratuity, or any valuable consideration, paid or agreed to be paid, directly or indirectly, grant, bargain, or sell such office, or any deputation thereof, or grant the right or authority to discharge any of the duties thereof to another, shall, on conviction, be punished by imprisonment in the penitentiary, not exceeding five years, or by imprisonment in a county jail, not exceeding one year, or by fine, not exceeding one thousand dollars, or by both such fine and imprisonment.

Under this preceding section, in looking into that, you will find it was said,—Colburn Thomas it is said had agreed to give Washington (or) the General-Adjutant four thousand dollars for the circuit. The clerkships were filled by appointment. It was after the violation of that law he was accused. He was probably impeached for some of these, and may be found guilty, but was the punishment for the illegal offense and illegal act? Now, in the articles of impeachment, two thousand things may be omitted. They may be expressed, and they may find a person to say the Judge did it; but are they of such a nature he may be dismissed from office for having done so? For a violation of that law,—in turning back the law at that time was nearly the same as it is now,—for violating a law in that particular, in helping to sell or make a bargain about selling the office, and buy it as the Judge did, and making his son fill it,—that was an express violation of the statute.

In another cause decided for allowing illegal testimony to be introduced in a cause. If a Judge is influenced, and permits illegal testimony to go before a jury, that is not impeachable; but if he did it for the express purpose, and with an understanding that it was to acquit or convict a person, for that he would be impeachable. It is corruption, and not for errors and mistakes.

Now, gentlemen, I propose to go through these articles and examine the principal testimony as applied to them; and in doing so, I shall not violate the chronological order in which the testimony was given in, but take each witness's testimony and apply it to each article, as I am going along. There are two, three, or four witnesses whose testimony is of much importance, as connected with these articles. Now, the first article of impeachment,—it is upon a mandamus case:

That the said Albert Jackson, desiring to harrass and oppress the said Jonas Eaker, did, at the Circuit Court aforesaid, whereat he, the said Albert Jackson, presided as Judge, as aforesaid, cause an attachment to issue against him, the said Eaker, as for a criminal contempt, because said Eaker did not make return to a writ of mandamus, which writ had never been delivered to said Eaker, but of which a *copy* had been delivered to said Eaker.

Now in order to examine into this and establish this, what course has been pursued? Now I hold in no court could the records be departed from, and the official acts of any Judge must be known from the act, and nothing else. If you introduce oral testimony to establish a record, what use is any copying records, if no record is made up? If this is not to be a proof of the action of a Judge, what use are they? If a bystander is to be called in to establish records, of what use are the records? And what protection has a Judge for his acts and doings, if a bystander or any person who may be interested may be called in to contradict that record? Now the law is here plain, even if there had been no decision upon it. It is so plain in that matter, I do not think it could be misunderstood. I will read first from a part of the decision in the case of Medlin *vs.* Platte county, where it was attempted to offer the verbal testimony of a person. But hear what was done in court. I will only read that part of it. It is the 8th volume, at the commencement of the case, page 235; I read on page 238:

With regard to the instructions charged to have been erroneously given by the Circuit Court, it may be observed, that, like other bodies corporate, and also like persons, it will be presumed to accept whatever is for its interest to receive, until it in some way signifies its dissent; but it will be presumed to part with none of its rights till it has expressed its will on its records: the evidence then offered, *i. e.*, the testimony of one of the Judges, to prove that the several members of that court, while in session, assented to the erasure of Johnson's name, &c., was inadmissible. The Judges of the County Court could express their assent to such an act on their record only; and it will then only be in season for this court to decide whether such an entry of assent can be made *nunc pro tunc*, when such an entry shall have been made by the County Court, but no such entry being now made, this court must proceed as if it had never heard anything of the assent of the Judges in open court.

There, one of the Judges offered to swear such a thing was done in court, and the Supreme Court decided if it was not upon the record, the word of the Judge itself was not sufficient. Here it is brought in,—just a bystander,—to contradict the record of what a court of record does. His opinion only of deeds of law it is judging by. The proceedings cannot be established by oral testimony. I refer also to the 12th vol. Mo. Reports, case of Milan, administrator, *vs.* Pemberton, p. 598:

From the testimony in this case, it is apparent that the plaintiff relied upon what was done by him under the last cited clause of the statute. He proved before the court, that he had offered this claim for allowance in the County Court at July term, 1845, and that the defendant waived the notice in open court. That the claim was not sufficiently proved and was withdrawn. There was an objection to this proof by parol; there was no trace of any such proceeding on the record of the County Court. The testimony was offered before the court, and as there was no jury, it was right and proper for the court to hear the testimony first before it could determine upon its legality. The effect of this testimony, its admissibility, its competency, were brought before the court by the plaintiff's instruction. We have no doubt that such evidence was improper; it was entirely inadmissible. No case has been found, where a party has been permitted to prove before one court of record what he did, what proceedings were had and done before another court of record in a judicial investigation, by mere parol testimony. The acts, doings, judgments, and proceedings of courts of record is known by the records of these courts. Such proceedings may often be amended; may be altered to suit the true state of facts; but there is always something to alter or amend by. Here there is an attempt not to alter or amend, but to make out a new subject matter altogether, and that, too by the testimony of witnesses. It is admitted that there is no trace of any such proceeding as the one here proved by witnesses upon the records of the County Court.

I refer also to volume 7, page 600, and to volume 4, page 228.

These decisions all go to show that the record of the doings and proceedings of a court of record must be established by the record itself, and oral testimony cannot be introduced to establish what was done in court. Now in these articles of impeachment, it is the testimony of persons who stood by and saw what was done, and were present when the record was being made up. Now the result of what is done, the result of proceedings in court, the motions, all motions and decisions, all that are made, goes upon the record; and the action of the Judge must be proved by the record. If his official acts are to be inquired into, either to sustain a seat, or for any purpose,—for an indictment,—it must be proved by that record; and if it is there, he cannot dispute it. Now, in this mandamus case, the record is here, and shows all that was done by the court in that case. There was, during the progress of that matter, an attachment issued; and, before it was served, and directly after, were proceedings that have nothing to do with this. It does not govern the conduct of the court, for all he did officially was upon the record. A mandamus had been applied for, and had been issued, sometime before the setting of the Circuit Court. It was made returnable to the first day of that term. In the case there called, there had been no return made by the person upon whom it was served. Now what was the course to pursue in that case? What could the Judge of the Circuit Court do? All that he could do about the matter was—all that he could see was—that he issued a writ, and there was no return to it to him. Was he to look to the bystanders? He had no more right to look to the Sheriff than any body else; the information could come from no person but the person through whom it was served. If it had never been served at all, what could the Circuit Court do? All it could do would be this: knowing the writ had issued, the next step would be, to bring in the person to show cause why it had not been returned to him. And was the Circuit Court to compel him? Must the Judge, after issuing the writ himself, go about personally and see whether it was served or not, and see whether the person had a good excuse for not answering it? Everything, I take it, must be done regularly and in order; and if a writ was issued, and if the Sheriff had served it, or had served it by any other person. This could be delivered by any person; it did not require an officer to do it; he had nothing to do with returning it to the court; it is not that kind of writ. It is like a writ of habeas corpus. If there is no return to it in twenty-four hours, the Judge must issue an attachment upon the person upon whom it was served. There was nothing improper in this case.

But it seems Mr. Eaker, judging from what he says, thought there was going to be a difficulty. He employs attorneys to keep from answering. All he had to do was to tell it to the court, and not to bystanders. How could he do it in court, except by making a return? And you cannot help from gathering from the testimony of the witnesses so far, it was not my intention to oppress and harrass him. I intimated to him before the attachment, you must make that excuse in court in the proper manner. That thus being served by copy it is not necessary for him to answer. Then if that return is good, there would be an end to it. The question was, how would he meet that in court? That is all about it.

The law provides that a Judge of our court may enforce by attachment any writ or process sued out of the same court. It was not for the court to step aside, and go and ask Mr. Eaker, "has this been served upon you?" and if he tells you "no," that would be a personal matter,—it would have nothing to do with the court. It must go to the ears of the crowd, and not to the ears of the Judge, and that was the difficulty in this matter.

But in this case the charge is that I caused attachment to issue for a criminal contempt. "Of which a copy only had been delivered to said Eaker." Now how was all this known? not how was the Judge to know, but how was the court to know that except by return in court?

But I read on:

—Well knowing that said writ had never been legally served upon him, the said Eaker, and that he was not in contempt for not answering thereto.

***Second.* In refusing to permit counsel for said Eaker to speak in his behalf, when**

they proposed to show to the court that said writ of mandamus had never been properly delivered to, or served upon him.

Third. In peremptorily, and in an oppressive, angry, and insulting manner, ordering the counsel of said Eaker, to wit, Solomon G. Kitchen and William G. Phelan, *to shut their mouths and sit down,* when they, in behalf of their said client, attempted to suggest an insufficiency in the service of said writ of mandamus.

Fourth. In depriving said Jonas Eaker of the benefit of counsel, and of the privilege of speaking through such counsel in his own defense, as he had a lawful right to.

Now, I would like to know how Mr. Eaker could have had counsel when he had no case in court. If it was not served upon him, he was not there. How could he have counsel in court? Yet it is really, I suppose, that case was confined to certain lawyers in the Fifteenth Judicial Circuit. This idea of being a friend to the court and claiming it as a right. Now, it seems from the learned Mr. Hardin, that it is a right. I never heard it contended for as a right, except from these two gentlemen in the management of the case. An attorney may simply suggest a fact to the court. But the fact didn't exist. For instance, if a Judge be about to render a judgment, by additional punishment, a summons on a note, and the summons was returned into court, and the petition had been filed, and the summons issued and returned, and it turned out the return, the notice hadn't been served in time, and the attorney supposes so; and here is the person,—he makes no defense, and does not appear; the Judge says there must be a judgment given against him. He may not like to say the return was not served in time; a bystander says I do not appear, but simply suggest there is no service. Now, that is acting as *amicus curiæ,*—as Mr. Knott's learned friend calls it, *ameecus cureea.* Now, who contended that it gave a lawyer a right as an attorney to do that? Not only is it a friend of the court, but it is the "next friend,"—such as infants have appointed to defend them. I think the Legislature should provide that particular officer, and let the people say who they want to act as next friend to the Judge; and not let any person claim as a right to appear and advocate a cause as though they were another court. Now, Mr. Hardin I take to appear as the next friend—the friend—of the court. There could be no appearance, except such an appearance through which there could be a judgment rendered. And whoever heard of such a thing as a judgment being rendered upon a friend of the court? This is what these men contended for, and I intended to instruct them. Mr. Kitchen calls it "squabble." I tried several times to ascertain if they had been employed to attend. I told them that it could not be that they were friends and counsel; and they said they were the next friends of the court. Mr. Phelan says he was surprised that he had no right to appear as next friend of the court. And when he went into court and appealed, he found out he was not allowed to appear as next friend, and then, after repeatedly urging me about it, when I told them I did not want their friendship, they come up here and reproach me because they were not allowed to act in this unheard of way. Mr. Phelan says, "when spoken to by Judge Eaker, I told him there was no service, and he requested me to attend to the matter in court." Now, what business had he (Eaker) in court if he was not served? Mr. Phelan further says:

I concluded the only way to get at it was to appear as the friend of the court, and not as an attorney, and suggest the failure of the service. You will recollect, Judge Jackson, that you picked me up on that point once at Butler Court, and I knew you too well to take a course for which you had once, as it were, reprimanded me. I didn't want you to get me again in a matter of that kind, and I thought the course I did pursue was the only one you would regard as proper. Mr. Eaker asked my opinion as to the matter prior to this term of the court.

Now he says that was the only way he got out of it, not merely to make a suggestion, but actually to appear for the defendant, and that is the way. That was his opinion; that was the only way he could get out, and when Mr. Kitchen told him he couldn't do it, he was taken by surprise. And he supposed whenever he was a mind to he could appear and instruct the court, and if the court didn't go according to his instructions, he could have it impeached for it. I supposed Mr. Eaker ought to make return to the court and not to the bystanders—and he thought not,—so he concluded he would get these lawyers. Mr. Kitchen talks about a great deal of "jabbering." It may be so on his part; I had nothing to do with it. I told him I would hear no more of it, and got tired of it, and issued an attachment; and when Mr. Eaker came in he was not put in custody. He then concluded he would do what I intimated ought to be done. And he said he wanted to write it, that this was served by a copy, and did not make any further answer. I thought so, and when it came to the court, I acted upon it. When it only came to me as an individual, I had nothing to do with it. But as to my acts as a court, when it came in that way, I was satisfied and thought it was a proper course. And what does Mr. Eaker say of it? Did he find fault with it? He said here upon the stand, there was nothing unfriendly, and he had no hard feelings—and I think something about not speaking to me last spring. It was not that Judge Eaker thought himself oppressed, but some other person told Judge Eaker he was oppressed and badly treated, and he came to think he was; and then comes up here and tells the Legislature it was him that was aggrieved. And there was no difficulty in the court; but some persons who wanted to act as Judge themselves come and tell him they were oppressed, and annoyed, and tyrannised over, and therefore it was a case of impeachment.

But there is something behind all this, gentlemen, that might be shown. I may mention it here, that you certainly would not make up your opinion in this case on illegal testimony; you would require legal testimony in every part and stage of the proceedings; you would require legal testimony to show I was Judge of the Fifteenth Judical Circuit Court; you would require testimony to show that the counties in this case were part of that circuit. Do you know Stoddard county is in the Fifteenth Judicial Circuit? Where has the law been read showing it was ever in that circuit? I am charged with doing acts in the Fifteenth Judicial Circuit. Has there been any evidence brought to show that either of these counties composes part of the Fifteenth Judicial Circuit? Though you were trying a common criminal, for a crime charged to have been done within the limits of a certain county, would it not have to be proved that it was done in that county? Now, there has never been a solitary person that has had a case in court there, that has been a Clerk, or Sheriff, or person who has served upon a jury, who comes forward and finds fault with my acts. It has all been by some person or other through their attorneys. And now, gentlemen, would you not require there should be some proof that they were attorneys? Has there the least proof of that ever been introduced? What does Mr. Phelan say about it? When he found there was a question about it, and he was intimating he thought there was such proof and it could not be produced, he treated it as though it was a matter he did not pay attention to,—having his name enrolled and taking the oath, or anything of the kind. He thought it was a matter rather unimportant. Hear what the law says about it:

SECTION 1. No person shall practice, as an attorney or counsellor at law, in any court of record, unless he be a free white male, and obtain a license from the Supreme Court or Circuit Court, or some one of the Judges thereof in vacation.

SECTION 2. Every appliant for license to practice law, shall produce satisfactory testimonials of good character, and undergo a strict examination as to his qualifications, by one of the Judges.

SECTION 3. Every person obtaining a license, shall take an oath or affirmation to support the constitution of the United States, and of this State, and faithfully to demean himself in his practice, to the best of his knowledge and ability. A certificate of such oath shall be endorsed on the license.

SECTION 4. Each Clerk shall keep a roll of attorneys, which shall be a record of the court.

SECTION 5. If any person shall practice law in any court of record, without being licensed, sworn, and enrolled, he shall be deemed quilty of a contempt of court, and punished as in other cases of contempt.

Now in all these cases where they represent themselves as attorneys, they were liable to be fined for contempt of court. And Mr. Phelan admits the fact. Now, I take it, you can hardly convict a person of these serious charges unless they are properly made out. But I care nothing about these assertions. It is the main facts themselves, these articles here that are alleged, these accusations you are about to make against me—I deny they exist. Those that do exist—those facts that do exist—I admit, and every act I did do, gentlemen—every act of my office —I still stand by. Wherever it is alleged here that these acts were done, and it is proved that they were done, I say I admit them. Wherever I told these men they were out of order, and told them to take their seats, I would do it again, under similar circumstances. It was my duty to keep order in court; and when they undertook to usurp that authority, and to tell me I was out of order, I did try to make them conduct themselves in a proper manner. I think I did my duty. I should do so again, under similar circumstances.

In all the decisions I made, take the record—take the records of my court—go back to the first case I ever tried; then take all, up to the last, every one that is upon record, and as I did, so I will do again, under similar circumstances. I acted at the time I entered these judgments,—at the time I made these decisions,—at the time I enacted these rules,—I did it with the best lights I had before me. I have seen no reason to change them. If oppressive,—if any man had to suffer an injury,—it is not my fault, but the fault of the law. I simply carried out the law as I conceived it to be. If I committed errors, take it to the Supreme Court, and have those errors removed, and do not hold me up as a criminal. And if I did these things, they may be right, just, legal. If I did it from unholy purposes,—if I did it through a corrupt motive,—if I did it for the objects of gratifying a malicious disposition, then turn me out. But let, I say, that fact be proved. If the facts that exist prove my corrupt motives; and if you find it exists, then turn me out to wander, and show I am not worthy to hold the office of Judge, and I won't complain; but not because you find the testimony of witnesses—and these witnesses who are they? Witnesses who stand up here and acknowledge themselves bitter enemies! Here is Mr. Tyrell, who testifies—what does he tell you? In words, that his testimony is false! He told you that up to within a few months, he thought highly of me; and when, as he says, he was dissatisfied with me, he admits and confesses he had thought I got no justice from that committee. But since then, he says he thought they were doing right, but simply because he is questioned about it. He said I had accused him of swearing falsely, not because I had acted wrong as Judge, but he says because I had accused him wrongfully. Then it was, he says, he comes up here and tells this tale. I hadn't done anything wrong up to that time! He comes in now and testifies I have been guilty of these charges.

Now as to the mandamus case, gentlemen, there is the testimony of Mr. Eaker, the testimony of Mr. Tyrell, and the testimony of Kitchen, Phelan, and Bedford. They all testify, except Messrs. Tyrell and Bedford. They didn't say much about it. It is mostly hearsay with them; but it simply amounts to the same thing. The facts are got out. There is no proof,—there is nothing oppressive, nothing! The Judge of the court comes up and tells you, up to this last spring there was no unkind words thought of, or unfriendliness between us. He has been told he was oppressed, not because he thought so, but because he has been told so. With regard to the mandamus being issued, all these three trials have been had, and the counsel all fail to show anything oppressive or wrong in issuing the attachment. Then all present could not acquit the attorneys of anything of that kind towards the court.

The next article is in these words:

ARTICLE II. That said Albert Jackson, Judge as aforesaid, regardless of the sacred obligation resting upon him to administer justice faithfully, impartially, and without respect to persons, was, at a Circuit Court begun and held at the town of Bloomfield, in the county of Stoddard, on the third Monday in November, A. D. 1858, whereat he, the said Albert Jackson, presided as Judge, willfully and maliciously guilty of the grossest *partiality* and injustice, to wit:

First. During the Circuit Court aforesaid, whereat said Albert Jackson presided as aforesaid, there was pending before said court the cause of Matthew H. Moore *vs.* James Walker, and the said Albert Jackson, corruptly, partially, and to the utter degradation of the solemn and important functions of his said office, secretly advised the said James Walker, defendant in said cause, not to compromise the same; that the field notes by which the property in dispute between him and the said Moore could be identified, were lost, and that said Walker would be successful in said cause, if he would refuse to compromise the same; and that, in consequence of the prejudice of the said Albert Jackson, the said Moore was compelled to have the venue in said cause changed.

Well, look at the testimony to support that. There is but one witness. I will read the testimony of Mr. Walker:

Me and Mr. Moore was disputing about some property. He was claiming my lots in Bloomfield. I thought he had no right to them; and that was the matter that the suit was to be about. Me and Mr. Jackson talked about it. He asked me how had we come out with our difficulty, if we had fixed it up, or something like that. I told him we hadn't fixed it up, and I didn't know as we would. Then he told me it didn't matter; that the field-notes of Bloomfield had got lost, and, says he, they can't hurt you anyhow. I told him that I thought not, and he said, that's my opinion about it. That was about all there was of it.

He says they were about to compromise before the suit was brought, and that I told him I thought he could get it. Well, now, that is the substance of the conversation. There is no matter in it. He evidently thinks the conversation was before he was sued. I presume the conversation was after the suit, whether it is in proof or not. I will state a fact: I never knew about the suit until Moore got up and said he intended to apply for a change of venue. Day after that I happened to meet Walker, and had this conversation. And there was another matter. I was interested about changing the lines. Had I not told it, it would have been ground for impeachment; but because I did tell it, I have been impeached for doing so. And if I had gone on and tried the cause, it would have been in such a way,—it would have affected my own rights—that would have been impeachable. "You say it was last week." Mr. Moore says it was last week. He went away about Thursday. He left a petition to be presented; consequently it was the intention to take the change of venue, and probably the notice was given a day or two, or three days, before it was noticed. The first I knew about the suit was from the notice of the change of venue. And he, Moore, said he would have taken the suit away anyhow, it was no consequence. Now what is there corrupt in all that? It was a matter of general conversation, and I think I remarked to him that the field notes of the town could not be found, and they could not establish their lines; and that was all about it. If that is an impeachable matter, I cannot help it. I do not think I did wrong. I never thought about it until I found it brought up here against me. If you think I was acting corruptly in that matter—that I did it for the purpose of betraying Mr. Moore—it is right for you to take it into consideration; but I think the motives should be proved—in particular the effect of the act, and whether it was from a bad motive I did it.

The third article charges:

ARTICLE III. That, actuated by a spirit of arbitrary despotism and wanton injustice, totally repugnant to the sacred duties pertaining to his office, and highly dangerous to the rights of the citizens of the State, the said Albert Jackson, Judge of the Fifteenth Judicial Circuit, at a Circuit Court begun and held within and for the county of Wayne, in the State of Missouri, at the town of Greenville, in said county, on the last Monday in September, A. D. 1858, whereat said Albert Jackson, by virtue of his office aforesaid, presided as Judge, was guilty of willful and malicious oppression, misconduct, and abuse of authority in his official capacity:

First. During the Circuit Court aforesaid, at the time and place aforesaid, David M. Fox, one of counsel for plaintiff, in the cause of ——— Limbarger *vs.* ——— Powers, then and there pending before said court, presented a petition to said Albert Jackson, then and there presiding as Judge of said court aforesaid, to change the venue of said cause to some other court, because of the prejudice of the Judge, and informed him, the said Albert Jackson, that both parties and their counsel had agreed that said cause might be sent to either the county of Madison or the county of Iron, as either of said counties would be convenient, and easy of access; but the said Albert Jackson, Judge as aforesaid, utterly unmindful of the rights of the parties and counsel in said cause, and totally disregarding the provisions of the statute in such cases made and provided, and willfully and maliciously intending to harrass and oppress the parties aforesaid, and their counsel, awarded a change of venue in said cause to *Mississippi county*, well knowing said county to be remote, difficult of access, and inconvenient to all the parties, counsel, and witnesses in said cause.

Second. When counsel engaged in said cause, to wit, David M. Fox and Philip Pipkin, attempted then and there to prevail upon him, the said Albert Jackson, to change the venue to some other county more convenient to all parties, and informed him that by sending said cause to Mississippi county he would deprive them of the privilege of attending to their client's cause, as they had been employed to do, he, the said Jackson, replied to each of them in an oppressive, insolent and insulting manner, highly shameful, and derogatory to the dignity of the important position he occupied as Judge, as aforesaid.

Now, merely for awarding that case to Mississippi county, am I guilty of these outrages against parties, and this tyranny? Now, gentlemen, what are the facts in the case in proof of these charges? The simple fact is, as Mr. Bedford's testimony shows, that Mr. Fox presented a petition for a change of venue, without saying one word to me where he wanted it; and I am bound to say I could not notice what he said to me. I will reverse the argument. Suppose Mr. Fox had told me he wanted to send it to Madison, or Iron, and I had done so, it would have been tyrannous, and they would have charged me with partiality. Mr. Fox applied for a change of venue, and wanted me to send it to a certain county, and had I done so, that same thing would have been a pretty good case for impeachment. It would have shown I had done what was not to the interest of the parties, if he had presented a petition. After I had ordered the change, they come here and complain about it. What does Mr. Hardin say? He reads the statute and he tells you the statute says he shall send it to some county as convenient as may be to the opposite party. I want to know if Mr. Hardin was in earnest about that? Suppose that party lived in the north-west county of this State,—suppose the defendant, Limbarger, the opposite party, had lived in the north-west corner of this State,—could you have sent it up there to where he was? and would not that have been an outrage? A Judge is made a judge of that matter. He must exercise his discretion. He ought to be honest in it,—in exercising that discretion. But in doing this thing,—in sending it to Mississpipi county,—why, after I have done it, Mr. Tyrell comes up here, and shows his spite against me. In his testimony he tells you he was present when this was done. He says Mr. Pipkin and Mr. Fox were the attorneys, and they wanted to go to another county; and when Mr. Fox and Mr. Bedford come, they say Mr. Fox and Mr. Pipkin were attorneys on the same side, showing Mr. Tyrell did not know anything about it. He ought to have said nothing about it, if he did not know the facts. He should have said nothing about it. He sees these two attorneys,—one on one side, and the other on the other side,—recommending me to send the case up to these counties. In this conversation there is not a word said about the party. Now, I hold the Judge is not to be governed by an attorney. An attorney will take a change of venue to suit his convenience.

As to Mr. Fox and Mr. Pipkin, one lives in Iron county, and the other in Madison county; the others did not attend courts in either of the other counties. For me to be sending it there would have been to send it away from Limbarger's attorneys. Mr. Fox and Pipkin may think so. And what does Mr. Limbarger say? Mr. Bedford tells you he was attorney for Limbarger, and he says that he thinks it was recommended to me that either of these counties would do, and he was was willing I should send it to either. You will notice, gentlemen, there was not a word said; I made no reply until after the order was made. I consider that after the Judge has made an order, it must stand there, unless there has been some mistake. Otherwise it must not be changed during that term of the court. It must be shown to be a mistake in making out the testimony; because, I hold, when a decision is once made, it should stand. Because if you cannot change it within five months afterwards you cannot change it within five days. Mr. Bedford says he agreed, and when it come out after examining two other persons, Mr. Limbarger and Fox did not find fault Mr. Limbarger says he started home after the case had been continued, when some one told him there was going to be a change of venue. He went back to the court house, and saw Pipkin writing a notice, and Mr. Fox writing a petition, and he set down by Bedford and told him "they are going to take a change of venue in this case." "No," said Bedford, "that is not the case." I see he objected to going to Fredericktown, Madison county. He shows that remarkable paper. Fox in a minute or two threw his paper on the Clerk's desk. He handed it to me, and I ordered it to be sent to Mississippi county. Not a word was said to me. Then Mr. Fox got up and said it didn't suit him to go over there. The Clerk was sworn here. He said next day Mr. Fox said again he had rather the case would be left in Wayne, than be sent to Mississippi county, and this is what it is. After Mr. Fox had been urging it some little I told him, says I, "Mr. Fox, if you would not take it as a personal matter, and say it was to mortify you, I would fine you." It was no interest to me to make that change. After it was made, I told him I would fine him for contempt, for importuning me on the subject. Now is there anything oppressive in all that? In sending it to Mississippi county? It was a little further than sending it to Iron, but there was only one county to go through in either case, and it was more convenient to the attorneys on the other side—more convenient for Bedford to go to Mississippi, because he never attends the Circuit Courts of Iron and Madison. The proof is before you that it was impossible to try it in Madison, because the Phillips case tock up the time of the court, and if the suit had been sent to Bollinger, it wold have been three years before they would have reached the case. Now, was not I taking proper notice of the convenience of all parties when I sent it to Mississippi county? Now, I think I exercised a most judicious care in the matter.

Now, let us look at this matter about oppression to attorneys, and see what it is. Bedford thought the facts that make it so did not exist. I merely exercised what I conceived to be a proper care in the matter, and acted accordingly. I do not think there is anything like corruption; but taking all the circumstances together, I think I find I fixed the most convenient place under the circumstances, that it could have been sent to. Now, where is the proof in the matter of the charge for officicial misdemeanor?

In regard to these other three cases of change of venue to Pemiscot county, the testimony is by these same persons that testified before. Here is Mr. Moore. He testified they went together up to Cape Girardeau and Bollinger counties, eighty or a hundred miles. This other county was the most convenient county, for the attorneys had rather it would go up there. The witnesses had rather it would go to Pemiscot, as Phelan, Bedford, and Moore testified. Now, what was the testimony of all the persons residing there? Marsh, Clark, and Horner, practicing attorneys, on one side, say they could cross there all the time. If it is up, they could go in boats; if it is down, they go on horseback; it requires no steamboat at all. Now, with regard to what took place, see how these men swore here about it. What takes place at the time of the order for a change of venue? See how they say it was presented to me. Because they wanted it to go up to Bollinger county, and because I did not send it up there, this is oppression and misconduct! Mr. Horner says he was present, representing the plaintiff in that case, and when the petition was presented, he says that though one party was willing for it to go to Cape Girarneau or Bollinger, he wanted it sent to New Madrid county. That is one of the next above Pemiscot, and still across the swamp. He wanted it to go there. He says, as they could not agree, then I told them I would send it to Pemiscot, and that was the county he said he really wanted it to go to. He did not mention it, because after the others mentioned one, and I did not send it to that one, he mentioned another county as near as he could. But this is the place he wanted it to go. He says the parties and witnesses live across in Tennessee, and in Dunklin and Pemiscot. It was much more convenient than to attend those counties above. Where, then, is this corruption? Where is any ground of complaint in granting these changes of venue? Is there anything more than exercising a sound discretion upon my part? I do not think there is any bad motive shown. I did it for no end but to discharge what I conceived to be my duty. That will apply to a similar case—this Point Pleasant and, Dunklin County Plank Road; and the Dunklin County Plank Road against Murphy was sent to the same county. It is proved the parties live in Madison, Dunklin, and Pemiscot counties, except the parties interested, and they live in Tennessee, and this county is between their residence and the other parties. Where is misconduct in all that? Now, Mr. Murphy was a member of the Legislature, and from that county. They did not notice him last winter, when they had him here as a witness. Mr. Murphy would not so testify, and they knew it. But those outside persons, who have no interest in the case, come up and say they have been oppressed and mistreated, because they were attorneys, and not a single one of them has shown but what he, being an attorney, was guilty of contempt of court. They have not shown they were licensed, nor taken the oath; and if they do not show that, they are guilty of contempt of court in getting up to speak. They may call themselves attorneys, but the law don't; and if I do not take that advantage, or if they are proceeding against me criminally, let them pursue the law, and let me be convicted by legal, competent, and fair testimony. In the third article is the case of Limbarger *vs.* Powers, in Wayne county; and then article four is a case from Pemiscot county. They are all on the same footing, and all alike, and what is proper in one is proper in another. I'll read the sixth article:

ARTICLE VI. That at a Circuit Court begun and held at the town of Poplar Bluff, within and for the county of Butler, on the first Monday in May, A. D. 1858, whereat said Atbert Jackson presided as Judge, the said Albert Jackson was willfully guilty of gross and malicious oppression, misconduct, and abuse of official authority, not only unbecoming his high position as Judge, but disgraceful to his character as a man, to wit:

First. During the sitting of the Circuit Court aforesaid, whereat said Jackson presided as Judge as aforesaid, one William G. Phelan, a regularly licensed lawyer, practicing in said court, arose to address a jury that had been empanneled and sworn to try an issue joined in a cause then and there pending, to wit, the cause of Gibson *vs.* Dunn, in which said Phelan had been employed and was acting as counsel; whereupon said Albert Jackson, maliciously intending to oppress said Phelan, and to injure his reputation as a citizen, and diminish his success as a lawyer, in an angry, oppressive, insolent, and insulting manner, ordered him to sit down, and then and there publicly, and in an insulting and contemptuous manner, accused said Phelan of having been guilty of a disgraceful and criminal act, to wit, *tampering with the grand jury*, and that said Phelan was in criminal contempt of court, together with other shameful and insulting expressions.

Second. When said Phelan immediately offered to defend himself against said disgraceful accusations and insulting expressions, said Albert Jackson, under color of his authority as Judge, in an angry, insolent, and oppressive manner, peremptorily ordered said Phelan to shut his mouth and sit down, (or words of that import,) and refused to permit said Phelan to say anything by way of denial, excuse, explanation, palliation, or in any manner to vindicate himself against the disgraceful, criminal charge, thus publicly alleged against him by said Judge in open court.

Now then, gentlemen, we will look at the testimony of Mr. Phelan in that matter:

A. I noticed nothing unusual in the trial of this cause—nothing that had any particular connection with it. The trial of the cause was commenced in the forenoon, and I cannot tell the exact stage of the case when the court took a recess for dinner. After dinner, Judge Jackson came in apparently very much excited. I made a motion—I am unable to say now what it was, whether it was addressed to the court, or whether it was the commencement of my argument of the case before the jury: I am inclined to think it was the latter. The Judge stopped me. He said that I couldn't go on; that I was in contempt of court, and that I had been tampering with the grand jury. I don't recollect what my reply was, though I recollect being astonished at the manner in which the charge was brought against me. I think I said, "I believe not, Judge," and I wished to defend myself. I cannot state exactly what occurred. There were some little altercations between us, and I demanded to know what the charge was. The Judge told me to sit down. I did sit down, but got up again directly, and he told me to go on with the case, but he wished me to understand that I was in contempt of court, and that I would have to answer for it—understand me that I do not pretend to give his exact phraseology. I was under the impression at the time that a certain man who was a particular friend to the Judge had betrayed the secrets of the grand jury, and I still think he did. I proposed to myself to take some steps in regard to the matter; however, that leads me into outside matter, and it is not necessary to mention it further here.

Q. When you attempted to rebut the charge brought against you, did you succeed in getting an opportunity?

A. I endeavored to do so, but I never got leave to say a single word. His reply to my inquiries concerning the charge, and to my offers to exculpate myself, was, in effect, that I might go on with the case then on hand.

Q. What was the character of his address to you?

A. It was very severe, very severe, indeed, and his manner showed much excitement.

Q. Were you excited yourself at the time?

A. I was not excited at that moment. Afterwards I was, when he told me to "sit down," to "hush up," "take your seat." I do not pretend to give the words exactly, though it was one or the other, and made an impression upon me as very severe and insulting.

Now let me tell what Mr. Kitchen said. But first, you recollect Mr. Phelan contends, and he tells you in his testimony, that he never gets excited; he was "annoyed" once or twice, but never excited! But here he says he was excited,—not only annoyed but was excited. Mr. Kitchen testifies to the same point, and says he said it was a lie! and what was it for? Now, gentlemen, I will admit that of all these charges and proceedings brought against me, this is the only instance in which I manifested any excitement. I will admit I have been annoyed and aggravated; but this is the only instance in which I was excited. Now I was not permitted to go on and tell all I could that caused that excitement. But what did I do that should induce Mr. Phelan to tell me, as I sat upon the bench, "it was a lie and false." I should have thought that would have excited almost any Judge. I was doing that which, if I hadn't done it, would have been good cause of impeachment; and it is the very kind of act upon which one of these articles is founded, for not giving information to be brought against the Clerk. Here when I did do the very thing which the law requires me to do,—to inform him he was in contempt,—then I am impeached for that! I did inform him, to give him notice that he might have time to answer. They say I insulted the man. I do not think there was a Judge in the State that had a harder time than the Judge of the Fifteenth Circuit. The law provides a person shall be informed of a charge, and shall have time to make a defense; and here, when I did that, I got insulting langage. Suppose I had fined him without informing him of it—I would have been impeached then. Let me proceed either to the right or to the left, I am still impeached. Now, here I come in and say, "Mr. Phelan, you must answer for contempt of court. You have been interfering with the grand jury in the discharge of its duties," and gave him time; well, he then boldly says it is a lie,—that it is false, He then wants to make an explanation and defend himself. I say "no, go on, we will examine into this matter when you get through with the case." He insists. I tell him several times to proceed in the case. Here, then, for that—doing just what the law says shall be done, that he shall have a reasonable time to make his defense,—I am impeached for acting in accordance with it! What shall I do? What shall I do? In what way can I discharge my duties? If I had fined him I would have been impeached, because he would not have had time to make a defense. "Here was some little altercation between us. He told me to go on with the case, but that he wished me to understand I was in contempt of court, and would have to answer for it," &c. Now, was not that a proper way to do it? I found that he was in contempt of court, and to purge him of that contempt, I wanted him to go on with the case and finish it. Certainly this was not an improper course of policy. The law required me to inform him beforehand.

There is nothing in this charge. I assert that in the whole of my official career, this is the only time I ever was excited on the bench; and if permitted, I could give my reasons for it. He says there was something he believed. Mr. Bedford testified that he got up, and appeared excited also. I say I was excited and do not believe there was a man in the State of Missouri but what would have been excited under the circumstances. Notwithstanding I cannot explain it here, such was the fact. Phelan says I came from the direction of the grand jury room. I only told him to give him a chance to exculpate himself, and then there occurred what Kithcen terms "jabbering," and Tyrell, "squabbling." But I was never excited except on this occasion. These polite terms they used, I suppose, because I am, as Mr. Phelan says. When I make a decision it cannot be changed. If I make a decision that don't please them and won't change it, then it is obstinacy. If it pleases them to let the decision stand, then it is firmness; and according to their feelings in the matter, I am as obstinate as a mule if I won't alter things that they want altered, but am as firm as a Judge when I stick to a thing they believe to be right. This is their phraseology.

Q. What was the character of his address to you?
A. It was very severe, very severe, indeed, and his manner showed much excitement.

His expression to me, that it was a lie—that it was false, was not very severe and insulting at all! But if I tell him to take his seat, that was very severe and insulting!

Q. Had you done anything to excite the Judge in the manner that you speak of, in the trial of this case?
A. I think not. I think his excitement proceeded from another matter.

That was the fact. He tells you there was another matter. You cannot get information of it out of his testimony. And so there was something behind to excite, and all they proved I did, was merely to inform him he was in contempt which it was my duty to do. And this, too, is charged in the language of the articles of impeachment as corrupt, and gross, and malicious oppression, and misconduct, and abusing official authority. And that publicly and in an insulting manner, &c.

Now then, gentleman, I submit it. Suppose I told him to shut his mouth and set down. Suppose I used these expressions. I do not think they are very proper and better language might be used by a Judge, even under excitement; but when they come to the proof, they do not prove I said these words, but only words to that effect. Look at the testimony of Mr. Tyrell, or Mr. Phelan, or Mr. Bedford, or Mr. Kitchen. When I ask them the question directly, what it is I said, they can never come exactly at it. I asked them to describe some so very sharp, some harsh, and some severe, but not a single time will they tell an expression used; but not any time will they fail to say, it was a harsh expression. They won't give the points, but they come to the conclusion, and swear positively to the fact. But I hold it, if I spoke in what is called harsh language, what may be harsh to one is not to another; and so it is not so much what he speaks, as the motive from which he acts, that you are to look at. If I did these things with the intention to discharge my duties, and to get along with the court, all is right. They might not have been in as courteous language as others have used, but does that show dishonesty and corruption? Most certainly not. I think, gentlemen, you will be particular to require the testimony to prove, not so much what was done, as the motive with which I acted. If there is not conclusive testimony to show I have acted corruptly in these things, either in receiving pay, gratifying a malicious disposition, or doing injustice in gratifying that disposition, you will not certainly find me guilty of these charges. I may not get along as smoothly, and speak as courteously as other Judges, but does it show I have been corrupt in the matter?

ARTICLE VII. That said Albert Jackson, Judge as aforesaid, influenced by similar spirit of malicious persecution, was, at a Circuit Court begun and held at the town of Doniphan, within and for the county of Ripley, on the 4th Monday in October, A. D. 1857, whereat said Jackson presided as Judge, guilty of other and similar acts of willful and malicious oppression, misconduct, and abuse of authority:

First. In wantonly, insolently and insultingly accusing one David M. Fox, a regularly licensed lawyer, practicing in said court, of being guilty of the *crime of perjury*, or *subornation of perjury*, and of *lying*, and causing his client to lie; all of which said Albert Jackson, without any provocation, but in a spirit of vindictive persecution, did charge upon said Fox, in open court, whilst he, the said Albert Jackson, was exercising the functions of Judge of said court; tending by these, and innumerable other instances of oppression, contumelious, insolent and insulting expressions towards lawyers, and parties litigant, which he, the said Jackson, almost habitually indulges in the exercise of his official functions, to bring the high and important office he holds into utter degradation and contempt.

I have not the testimony here of some of the witnesses that testified on that point. Mr. Fox, in testifying about that, states that the words were something similar to that. He says nothing about the "perjury," or the "lie," or "causing his client to lie," but words similar to that. That is what they all will testify when it comes to these harsh words, put down here as having been used. None will swear positively to the fact, but words similar to that. Now, instead of telling a person he lies, to tell him he has been mistaken, and it is a mistake in this matter, some persons would say it was tantamount to telling a lie. Now, they want us to infer they believe this word "lie" was used, though none of them will state the exact language. Mr. Fox told you it was in the case of Lacey *vs.* Gale. The Clerk says he was in court during the time, and he did not hear any such words. Mr. Fox says it was in that case. Mr. Ponder, the Clerk, says he was there during the trial, and no such words were passed—he did not hear them. Mr. Hicks tells you as Mr. Fox. I had the paper in my hand. Mr. Fox tells you he had been offering an additional answer or affidavit, and I held the paper in my hand; and Bedford testifies to that too, and I asked Mr. Fox if this was in his hand writing, and he says it may be. Then they say I told him he lied, or caused his client to lie; but they won't say that it was those words, but only to that effect. I said to Mr. Fox, of these two things you have written, both cannot be true; one must be false. They want to make it out, "if you signed this paper, you either lied, or caused your client to lie."

Now, it seems there was some business going on in connection with the paper I had, and Mr. Fox had drawn up another answer. The paper I held in my hand was an answer drawn in a former action upon a note,—wherein the answer stated the note was given for a certain consideration, on the payment of goods or something of the sort,—filed at this term of the court. He had failed to get judgment. He dressed up an answer, and makes a man swear he never gave the note. The former answer contradicted this. I had that in my hand as he was preparing the new one, and as he was about to swear this young man to it, it being drawn to my attention that he was just going to swear so as to contradict the other—says I, "Mr. Fox, one or the other of these is false. If you make him swear to that, you make him contradict this." Was there anything improper in that? I saw it going on before my face. Was there anything wrong then, if I had spoken in harsh terms to Mr. Fox about it? You all know the immense influence an attorney exercises over his clients. They will do anything their attorneys tell them and think there is nothing wrong in it. I saw what Mr. Fox wanted to do, and I had time to anticipate and prevent that young man from making a false affidavit. I used the language, that "if he made him swear to that, one of them was false." The testimony does not extend any further than that, and shows just about that state of facts. Was there anything criminal in what I did there? And then, too, "guilty of perjury and subornation of perjury." They use two terms without any need for either.

ARTICLE VIII. That said Albert Jackson, Judge as aforesaid, forgetting the dignity of his office, and regardless of his sacred obligation to demean himself faithfully and impartially therein, did, on the trial of one Green DePriest, on an indictment for resisting an officer in the exercise of his official duties, had at a Circuit Court begun and held at the town of Thomasville, within and for the county of Oregon, on the third Monday in April, A. D. 1858, whereat he, the said Albert Jackson, presided as Judge, conduct himself willfully *partial* and corrupt, and highly unbecoming and disgraceful to his high official position:

First. In privately advising one James V. Odell, a lawyer, to procure said DePriest to employ him, the said Odell, as his counsel, and to take a contingent fee to defend him; that said DePriest could not be convicted on the indictment pending against him for resisting the officer, because he had already been convicted of disturbing the peace of a family, which was charged to have been done at the same time he resisted said officer.

Second. In officially and voluntarily advising said James V. Odell, as counsel for said DePriest, to plead a former conviction; which said advice said Albert Jackson, presiding as Judge, gave said Odell in open court, upon the trial.

Third. In partially and corruptly transcending his duties as Judge, on the trial of said DePriest, to such an extent that the Circuit Attorney, prosecuting for the State, abandoned said cause, and entered a "*nolle prosequi.*"

Now, here in this case, gentlemen, there is this about it. There is no evidence that there was such a case ever tried there. Most certainly the record should be here to show the fact, at least, as to what was done upon that suit, and whether there was a *nolle prosequi* entered or not. Here you take the testimony of witnesses that such proceedings were had in court. I have no objection to what I said outside of the court being testified to orally. But if there was a *nolle prosequi* against De Priest, the record ought to show that, or at least there ought to be no evidence about it. To get up a case which there is no record of, and then get up certain facts to agree with it, is an improper course of proceeding. Well, we will see what Mr. Odell says about that:

Q. Were you in court during the trial of the case of the State *vs.* DePriest?

A. Yes, sir. I was counsel for the defendant.

Q. Mr. Odell, did you have any conversation with Judge Jackson in regard to that case?

A. Yes, sir, I had a conversation. I don't know that I had a conversation with the Judge about it, but he had with me.

Q. Well, what was it? what was said?

A. Mr. DePriest had been convicted of disturbing the peace of a family; well, I don't know, he was either convicted or plead guilty, and at the same time was indicted for resisting an officer. The conversation the Judge had with me was this: He observed to Mr. Hull, or myself, that we could safely take a conditional fee in the case; that there were two distinct indictments, and only one offense, and that that would be a good plea. I did take the case, but being quite young in the practice, I didn't make a plea of a former conviction, but moved to quash the indictment, giving the former conviction as a reason for the motion. The motion to quash was overruled, and the Judge said that was not the way to do it. The Circuit Attorney entered a *nolle prosequi*. I got the fee.

Q. Were you employed at the time of the conversation?

A. No, sir. DePriest came to me afterwards. It was his son that employed me. Solomon DePriest, the old man, was not there.

Q. You took the case then after this conversation with the Judge?

A. Yes, sir. I took it, as the doctors say, on the principle of "no cure no pay."

Q. Was the Circuit Attorney by at the time the Judge had this conversation with you?

A. I don't remember.

Q. Did the Judge make that remark, that you could safely take a conditional fee, when the Circuit Attorney was not present?

A. Yes, sir. I recollect now that he was not there.

Q. Who was the Circuit Attorney?

A. John R. Woodsides.

Q. After your motion to quash was overruled, did the Judge advise you to plead a former conviction?

A. Yes, sir, I think he did.

Q. Who was in the case with you?

A. I was alone.

Q. How did the conversation with the Judge come up?

A. Mr. Hull, and the Judge, and I were in a room, and I don't know how it came up.

Q. Did you suggest the facts to the Judge, or did you commence the conversation about the case?

A. No, sir, I did not.

Q. Was the nature of the two offenses charged in the two indictments the same?

A. I don't remember much about that.

CROSS-EXAMINED BY JUDGE JACKSON.

Q. Was that the first court you attended? Did we get together there the first time?

A. No, sir. We got together first at Greenville.

Q. Was not Mr. Hull with you when we met at Greenville?

A. No, sir. Mr. Hull joined us at Eminence. We then went with you through to Thomasville.

Q. Was not Woodsides in the company going from Eminence to Thomasville?

A. I do not remember.

Q. Well, at the time the conversation occurred, were not you and Mr. Hull talking and complaining that business was dull, and then didn't I say, "now, young men, here is Green DePriest is indicted twice for the same offense, and you might get a fee from him?"

A. I don't know that the conversation came up that way. It might have been so.

Q. Didn't I tell you my impressions were that the two indictments were for the same offense, and that if I was correct in my impressions about the facts, you might safely take a fee in the case?

A. It is likely you are right, Judge.

Q. Didn't you say DePriest wouldn't employ you, and wasn't it then I told you you might take a conditional fee?

A. We had a long conversation about it, and it may be as you say, though I don't remember.

Q. Didn't you make a motion to quash on the ground that there was no legal offense charged, or something of that kind?

A. I don't recollect.

Q. Was not Mr. Hull with you in the case?

A. That was not my understanding.

Q. How much did you charge him?

A. I charged him five dollars, but it was not enough.

Q. Didn't you divide the fee with Mr. Hull?

A. No, sir. He claimed the right to half of it. He pretended like I agreed to divide with him, because he was present when the conversation took place; but I told him it was not enough to divide, and that if I had to give any of it to him, I would give it all.

Q. Well, when you made your motion to quash on the ground that there was a former conviction, was it not then that I suggested that that would be a good ground of acquittal?

A. Yes, sir, you did say that that would be a good ground of acquittal.

Q. When we were talking about it, didn't I tell you that if my impressions about the facts were correct, you might go into the case whether you got a fee or not, and that you would get the glory of acquitting him, which would be worth as much as the fee?

A. I think you did tell me something like that.

Q. And you did get the fee?

A. Yes, sir. I know I got it, and Hull raised a fuss with me because I wouldn't divide. [Laughter.]

Mr. Knott. Was it in consequence of advice given you by the Judge that you undertook the defense of the case?

A. Yes, sir; it was.

Now, there is no evidence of any such case at all. If a person was up on an indictment for perjury, must not the case in which he was sworn,—would not the record of that court have to be introduced? He gives testimony about a case in which I am impeached, and without a record to show there was any such a case. Presumptions are always against the party that might make use of anything. If there is a record, and they do not produce it, the presumption is that it makes against them. That's the law.

Was there anything wrong in telling young Odell that? Certainly, when that case came up, if the man had already been convicted for an act, and the last indictment was based upon the same act charged as a different offense, I should have ordered the attorney to enter a *nolle prosequi*, and would not have allowed the man to be convicted twice for the same offense. This I hold would have been my duty under the statute, which expressly provides that a person shall not be convicted twice for the same offense. And the constitution also makes that provision. Would it not then be the duty of the Judge to state that fact, and not permit him to be convicted twice? I should do it. I do not think I ought to be impeached for doing so. It is the duty of the Judge to point out the law, and to appoint attorneys, and tell them what to do. Now, gentlemen, the law provides that when a person has no attorney, the Judge shall appoint an attorney. If the Judge shall happen to tell the person himself there is a certain matter in that case, and if you cannot employ an attorney, you need not employ one, what wrong is it? How often I have attended court in that circuit when there was not a single lawyer in his seat! How could I dispose of the business except by taking it upon myself to act the part of an attorney? I was at court at Eminence when there were three State cases on the docket. There was no Circuit Attorney or other attorney there. I had to make an order the same as though there was an attorney there, and I suppose I ought to be impeached for that! It may be a Judge acts differently from what you members of the Senate would, but if he did not do it from a corrupt motive, it is not impeachable. In this case I would not sit by on the bench and see a Sheriff, or Circuit Attorney, or other man, get a conviction against a man twice in the same case. And in this case, if there was such a case, and there is no evidence of that, I did not think Mr. Woodsides would do it. I think when he saw it was the same case, he entered the *nolle* of his own accord. The record is not here, and we can tell nothing about it. What corruption is there in that? Even if it is as he says, and there was such a case, I told him merely to look into it, and if it does exist, take advantage of it on the trial. Was there anything corrupt in that?

The hour for adjourning having arrived, Judge Jackson announced that he would conclude his argument in the morning.

On motion of SENATOR GOODLETT, the Court then adjourned.

FOURTEENTH DAY.

TUESDAY, June 21, 1859.

The Court met pursuant to adjournment, and was opened by proclamation.

The managers and respondent attended.

JUDGE JACKSON, resuming his argument, said:

GENTLEMEN: I presume in what further I shall have to say, I shall occupy your time at farthest not more than hour. With regard to articles nine and ten, three cases of habeas corpus, I can only say, my acts in those cases are fully shown upon the papers themselves. The petitions and returns of the officers to my order are before you, and that is all I have to do with it. There was some outside testimony with regard to what was done in the Main case; and in the Russell case it has been testified that particular papers were brought in and handed to me. The testimony shows very clearly that the witnesses, at least Mr. Tyrell and Mr. Jackson, are mistaken. They say of the papers that the Constable brought them in, and laid them down on the table before me. They said I told him these papers would contradict his return. His return then had been made to the writ, and that is all I had to decide from. There was no contest about the returns, and it was simply presented to me that he had Russell in custody by virtue of a verbal order. Now, if he held them by any other authority, my discharge did not affect that. But they are mistaken about this. Look at what Mr. Tyrell says about it. He says when this came in it alarmed him. He knew they were in existence. He says he was alarmed when they were laid before me. And Mr. Eaker says the papers were just then written. What becomes of the assurance that Mr. Tyrell knew these papers were in existence? And moreover, Mr. Eaker tells you when he handed the papers to Cryts, Cryts told him the defendant was already discharged. And so Mr. Tyrell comes in and says he was alarmed when these papers came in, because he knew they were in existence, and he was afraid his man would not get clear! If I was going to discharge the fellow anyhow, it would not affect him. Why should he be alarmed? He knew they might come in, and at the time when he says he knew they were in existence they hadn't been written; and then undertakes to say further, that I knew all about it. And the testimony of Eaker is, that he did not deliver them. Now, why does he say that he never thought I had done wrong until after this matter started? I recollect upon his testimony he got mad, and said I was disposed to injure him; but it did not affect me any way. I could only act upon the return of the officer.

In this Atterbury case—that is for not granting a writ when it should have been granted. Now, gentlemen, what I have to say is, just take that paper for yourselves and read it. It is signed by William M. Atterbury:

To the Honorable Albert Jackson, Judge of the Fifteenth Judicial Circuit in the State of Missouri:

The undersigned, your petitioner, respectfully makes known to your Honor, that one William W. Atterbury is restrained of his liberty at this time by, he believes, Henry Noble, Sheriff of Dunklin county, and *ex officio* Jailor of said county; and he believes that said Atterbury is imprisoned in the jail of said county; that said Atterbury was taken and delivered to said Jailor by one David G. Hicks, on the pretense that he had a capias for him on the charge of embezzlement, which petitioner well knows said Hicks never had, though he believes that said Atterbury is indicted in the Circuit Court of said county for embezzlement; that he prays your Honor to issue a writ of habeas corpus to bring said Atterbury before your Honor, that he may give bail, which he is able and willing to give in Bloomfield, as two good and solvent men will go his bail, but is unable to do so in Dunklin county. Petitioner does not present a copy of the cause of detention, from the fact that he has had no opportunity to apply for the same.

And, in duty bound, he will ever pray.

WILLIAM M. ATTERBURY.

[The 5th section of article 1st is not complied with sufficiently.]

William M. Atterbury, the above named petitioner, makes oath, and says that the foregoing petition, and the matters therein, as stated, he believes to be true.

WILLIAM M. ATTERBURY.

Sworn to and subscribed before me, this first day of February, 1858.

REUBEN P. OWEN,
Clerk Circuit Court of Stoddard county, Missouri.

The very man who says he did not know whether he was in the custody of the Sheriff or not, and signs the petition that he believes he is, and does not know whether he is or not! Was there ever such a petition ever presented for a writ? And this I refused to grant. Then what was the outside circumstances of the case? Why, Mr. Noble comes in here and tells you that Atterbury was not in his custody, and that he was here in Jefferson City, and he had no deputy in Dunklin county. And further testimony is before you showing that Atterbury was never in jail, but that he was brought there on one afternoon, and the next night but one he broke away, and that was the last of it. A man breaks custody, goes up there in Bloomfield and gets this petition out, and don't know whether he was in custody or not! Now have I ever refused improperly to grant a writ? What does the statute provide? Now if they believed I laid myself liable, would not they have proceeded against me as provided by statute? Mr. Phelan's testimony is that I refused to issue it because Mr. Hicks was improperly inserted there. I think I might have stated that "the fifth section is not complied with sufficiently." I believe this is the reason I refused to grant it, and no one will say I improperly refused to issue a writ of habeas corpus on that petition. You can only say I was mistaken. If there was injury done to the prisoner who made application, he could have proceeded against me under the statute.

The writ of Main, and return, shows that he was discharged because the mittimus was not sufficient authority for detaining him in custody. Now, if there is anything improper in all that, I do not see where it exists. It was my duty to act upon it, and I did it to the best of my ability. In the Russell case, the evidence is clear about that, even if this discharge paper has anything to do with it. Mr. Eaker himself says he never made it out until after the prisoner was actually discharged. There was a conflict about the discharge before the papers came. I had acted upon Russell's just as upon Main's, and had discharged them, and I wrote out the orders sometime afterwards. I did not write the discharge of Russell until after I disposed of the other case. I may have been writing the orders when these papers were laid down on the desk. What had I to do with the papers? The prisoners were discharged then.

The eleventh article is about instructing the grand jury with regard to a certain matter. I will read it:

ARTICLE XI. That at a Circuit Court, begun and held at the town of Bloomfield, within and for the county of Stoddard, on the third Monday of November, A. D. 1858, whereat the said Albert Jackson presided as Judge, the said Albert Jackson, disregarding the duties of his office, did descend from the dignity of a Judge, and stoop to the level of a common informer, by calling the attention of the grand jury, empanneled and sworn for that county, at said court, during his public charge to them, to the fact that he, the said Jackson, had understood that a certain citizen of said county had gone to Jefferson City and pretended to transact some business for said county, in relation to obtaining some certified lists of swamp lands; that he had obtained a warrant upon the County Treasury for one hundred and seventy or seventy-five dollars, and that if the facts were as he understood them, they constituted the crime of obtaining money under false pretenses, which was punishable by imprisonment in the penitentiary, and that it was the duty of said grand jury to make diligent inquiry of said case; that the man to whom he alluded was a lawyer, and that they, the grand jury, could find out who it was by asking the County Treasurer who had obtained a warrant for a hundred seventy or seventy-five dollars; whereby everybody there, and those present, understood him, the said Judge, to mean Solomon G. Kitchen, a citizen of said county.

And by appearing before the said grand jury, in their room where they had retired to consider of presentments, and then and there again telling them it was their duty to make diligent inquiry of said facts; and that if they found the facts to be as he had understood them, they should find an indictment against the person who had obtained the warrant, and that Solomon G. Kitchen was the man who had procured the said warrant; thereby rendering his high functions as a Judge subservient to a low personal malice, and seeking, under color of his official duties, to wreak his own private vengeance, by affixing to the reputation of a personal enemy the imperishable disgrace of a public prosecution for a felonious offense.

Now, what was the testimony to sustain that? It is, that in my charge to the grand jury I directed their attention to certain facts which I understood existed, and directed them to inquire into and see if they did exist; and said if they existed, that the person, whoever it was, ought to be indicted. If he obtained that warrant under false pretenses, it was an indictable offense. As in all this I did nothing more than discharge my duty, I cannot admit that I did wrong. I would have to do the same thing under similar circumstances, let who would be the object or subject of my remarks. It is my duty to instruct the grand jury. If I know of any particular offenses in that county, it is my duty to direct the attention of the jury to them, and state what the law is in regard to them; and I would not discharge my duty officially if I did not. Because the person should happen to be so designated that there was no mistaking as to who it was, is no evidence that I had any personal malice against Mr. Kitchen, and it would be a singular state of things if a Judge must refrain from charging a grand jury because the person against whom he charges is his enemy. It would look as if he was making a personal matter of it. A Judge that would refrain from discharging his duty under such circumstances, would be unworthy of being a Judge. Because a person is an enemy of the Judge, he should not set a jury upon him; but to refrain because he was an enemy, for fear persons would say he was trying to wreak his private vengeance upon the man, all sensible persons know to be wrong. Now, if the Senate feels any interest about the matter, let the Senators go down and ask the Secretary of State to say if what he said was right and coincided with the fact. He said he had paid money before he got the warrant. The Secretary will tell you, and did state, that if he ever paid the money at all, it was not paid until the next winter. This was a matter the county was interested in. I supposed there had been a violation of the law, and told the grand jury to inquire into and ascertain the facts. And that is all I have to do with it.

Article twelve reads thus:

ARTICLE XII. That the said Albert Jackson, Judge as aforesaid, at a Circuit Court, begun and held at the town of Poplar Bluff, within and for the county of Butler, on the first Monday in November, A. D. 1857, whereat said Albert Jackson presided as Judge, was willfully and maliciously guilty of gross misdemeanors and abuse of official authority:

First. In refusing to suspend the Clerk of said court and appoint a temporary Clerk thereof, although he well knew that said Clerk was guilty of a misdemeanor in office, in not being present and attending to the duties required of him by law, and should therefore be suspended, and although he was earnestly requested by nearly all of the lawyers present to appoint a temporary Clerk, in order that the business of the court might go on.

Second. In refusing to try any cause pending in said court, civil or criminal, at said term, regardless of the consequences upon the rights of parties litigant, and attorneys.

Third. In taking possession of the papers pertaining to causes triable and amenable at said term, and arbitrarily refusing parties and lawyers access thereto.

Fourth. In peremptorily discharging the grand jury, which had been empaneled, sworn and charged to inquire, in and for the body of said county, at said term, notwithstanding members of said grand jury informed said Judge that they had a large amount of business before them; that they had sent out subpenas for witnesses to appear before them, in relation to various matters of which they were inquiring, and did not desire to be discharged; and notwithstanding this was but the second day of the term, and said court was allowed a whole week in which to hold said term. All of which misdemeanors were intended to oppress and harrass the parties and lawyers, and calculated to impair public confidence in the efficacy of the constitutional guaranty "that justice shall be administered without sale, denial, or delay."

This shows what influence lawyers have, and what the law is. It was my duty to appoint a temporary Clerk, and they undertake to say that if I did not obey the law in this matter, I am to blame. Then it is to be looked into, to see if I lawfully did it. Now, I would like to see the law. The testimony is this: that on the first day of the Court, the Clerk was there discharging his duties. Business went on; cases were decided; Mr. Woodsides was there; a jury trial comes on and lasts till dark; on the second day of the term the Clerk is not present. They then undertake to say he was drunk. It may be that I understood that it was so at the time, though no person had told me who had seen him so. At any rate, he was not there discharging his duties. He had been there the day before. Now, what is the law for the court to pursue in a case of that kind?

SECTION 23. If any Clerk shall, knowingly and willfully, do any act contrary to the duties of his office, or shall, knowingly and willfully, fail to perform any act or duty required of him by law, he shall be deemed guilty of a misdemeanor in office.

SECTION 24. When any court, or the Judge or Judges, or a majority of them, in vacation, shall believe, from their own knowledge, or from the information of others, on oath or affirmation, that the Clerk of the court in which they preside, has been guilty of a misdemeanor in office, they shall give notice thereof to the

Attorney General, stating the charges against such Clerk, and requiring him to prosecute the same; and they may suspend such Clerk from office until a trial can be had, and appoint a temporary Clerk, who shall possess the same qualifications, take the same oath, and give the like bond as other Clerks, and who shall possess the same power, perform the same duties, and receive the like fees, as other Clerks, and shall continue in office until the regular Clerk shall resume his office, or a successor shall be elected.

Then I should have had information that he committed a misdemeanor. All that I knew about it was he was not there. There was no notice given to me that he had been guilty of a misdemeanor. I did not know it of my own knowledge, and there was no charge exhibited against him, and there was no request made for me to do so. It was simply this: As far as I knew, the Clerk had been there on the day before and discharged his duties. On the second day, he did not come. To be sure he might have been drunk. That I knew nothing about. There was nothing said to me about it though. Mr. Phelan says he told me he was drunk. "If there is any particular business which you want presented," I said, "I will keep the minutes and make them up." The next thing Mr. Bedford came in and asked for the ruling upon the Clerk for papers, as though I could do it. The court finally adjourned. Mr. Phelan says he lost three or four hundred dollars, at least. He had a claim for thirteen hundred dollars. What a percentage would he have had! I wonder if the merchants of St. Louis give that percentage on notes. But let us examine a little further. From Mr. Henderson's testimony, we learn that there was a mistake; he had not brought the suit right. He didn't insert the names of the parties, and consequently could not have got a judgment in that court. He had a mind to insert the names of the parties, but he only put it Ewing & Co. And this Mr. Henderson lets out the fact that Mr. Phelan's clients wrote to him not to pay Mr. Phelan, as he was not the man to do it. Now, what becomes of this loss?

I never suspended this Clerk, because there was no information against him. Mr. Phelan says he did come and tell me himself. Now, about Mr. Phelan's testimony; he says that up to the time of the last County Court, throughout to the end, no cause of suspension existed. Now, what becomes of all these charges of neglecting to suspend him, and of having notice of his misdemeanor, when Phelan swears there had never been notice of his misdemeanor up to this day, or up to the time he left the State? There is another little article connected with this. Mr. Phelan swears positively in this matter; and now they say I was applied to to appoint. Now, what is the law in that particular?

SECTION 22. Every Clerk may appoint one or more deputies, to be approved by the Judge or Judges, or a majority of them, in vacation, or by the court, who shall be at least seventeen years of age, and have all other qualifications of their principals, and take the like oath, and may, in the name of their principals, perform the duties of a chief Clerk; but all Clerks and their sureties shall be responsible for the conduct of their deputies.

Now, then, the Clerk may appoint a deputy, and that deputy must be approved of by the court. No court has a right to appoint a deputy over the Clerk. He is responsible for the duties of his office. The court cannot appoint a deputy without his consent. That is what they attempt to make me liable here for, because that application was made to me to appoint a deputy, and I refused to do it. Now, we will read this document:

To the Honorable Judge of the Fifteenth Circuit:

The undersigned being unable to act as Clerk at this time, would respectfully recommend to your Honor, Donaldson S. Walker, as a fit person to represent him.

[Signed,] JACOB C. BLOUNT.

I do not suppose any person could go into the office of the Clerk and transact business of importance. They could probably get along better than without any Clerk, but what good would it have done to appoint a Clerk at that time, to assist in the business of the court? Now, Mr. Phelan says he took this down. I thought at the time this document was the best evidence of the Clerk being drunk. I didn't think a sober man would have signed such a document, asking me to appoint a deputy. I took it for granted Blount must be drunk to ask me to appoint a deputy. Now see just what kind of a man Phelan is to swear,—how reckless he comes in here and tells you this is his handwriting, and that Blount signed this himself, and his wife held him up in bed while he put his name to it. Here is Bedford, well acquainted with Blount's handwriting, and Lawson, who knows his handwriting, and they swear they do not believe that is Blount's handwriting. Buffington comes up here and swears he does not believe this is Blount's handwriting. You can see that the man that executes this must handle a pen better than Blount could, and yet he swears Blount was so drunk he could not sit up in bed! Now, what is the testimony of such a man worth? I am going to go through it a little, to show, not what it proves, but the manner of getting it in. But here is the fact. I never thought of it that day until he was swearing that Blount had signed his name to it. I supposed it was about this way: that Blount told some person to sign his name to it. It was the body of this instrument I was going by. I supposed Blount was so drunk he could not write, and he told some bystander, and it would have all been right hadn't Phelan sworn so positively that Blount did it with his own hand. It excited suspicion. I inquired into that matter, and found that all acquainted with Blount's handwriting swear he never did sign it. That goes only to Mr. Phelan's testimony, not to the facts of it.

Well, so much about that matter. I do not see that I have been criminally negligent of any duty with regard to that transaction. You have heard the testimony of Mr. Dennis about it,—that I gathered up the papers, and had them a while under my arm, and finally, when I went away, when court was adjourned, I took Mr. Dennis into the office, separated the civil actions from the criminal, sorted them as well as I could, told him when Blount came to show them to him, locked the door, and gave him the key to give to Mr. Blount, and he did so. And if that was not doing all I could, I am at a loss to know what more could be expected. I do not think it was criminal in anything, with regard to my duty, though it is brought up here as a charge of official corruption in office.

ARTICLE XIII. That the said Albert Jackson, unmindful of the dignity of his position as a Judge, and disregarding the restraints imposed by his said office, did, in the month of October, A. D. 1857, privately counsel and advise one William Ringer to sell all the county warrants that should be issued, in payment of a contract which said Ringer had with Stoddard county for the building of a court house, and put the money in his pocket, and then bring a suit for damages against Solomon G. Kitchen, the commissioner, and assured him he could recover in such suit; endeavoring thereby to incite a vexations and expensive suit in the court of which he was himself Judge, for the purpose of annoying, harrassing, and oppressing said Solomon G. Kitchen.

Well, I think that would have been a singular kind of suit, to be brought after he had been paid; after he had got his pay in warrants. If a person cares to turn around and sell them, and then bring an action against another man for them, it would be but frivolous. How the conversation affected Mr. Kitchen I can't see. The testimony of Ringer amounts to little. He said I said something about the warrants. He says I might have asked him if he hadn't some warrants. I knew while he was telling me I did not recollect anything about the conversation, and could prove it was not in October. I only did that to prove the fact that if he is mistaken in one thing, he is in another. I can prove I was not that year in Stoddard county during the month of October, and very little in November. I left the county on the last Monday in September, and did not go back until the second Monday in November. Woodsides testified to that fact. Now if Mr. Ringer is mistaken in this matter, he may be mistaken about the conversation, and in the very material parts of it. I do not think it amounts to anything one way or another.

The fourteenth article reads thus:

ARTICLE XIV. That the said Albert Jackson, Judge as aforesaid, was, at the Circuit Court begun and held at the town of Doniphan, within and for the county of Ripley, on the fourth Monday in April, A. D. 1858, and on the trial of one William Kinsey, for grand larceny, which trial was had at said court, whereat said Albert Jackson presided as Judge, willfully and maliciously guilty of great oppression, misconduct, and abuse of official authority, corruptly intending thereby to embarrass and oppress the counsel of said Kinsey, and procure his conviction:

First. By arbitrarily refusing to allow said Kinsey's counsel time to take down the testimony of the witnesses introduced on said trial.

Second. By repeated interruptions of the counsel for said Kinsey during said trial, tending to harrass and embarrass them.

Third. By the frequent use of rude, insulting, insolent, and discourteous expressions towards said Kinsey's counsel during the trial.

Fourth. By peremptorily stopping one of said Kinsey's counsel in the midst of his argument to the jury, and ordering him to take his seat, although said counsel (David M. Fox) was in the discharge of his proper and lawful duties.

Now, with regard to the first head,—the refusal to allow the taking of testimony,—it was simply this: The witness was going on to make his statement, and they stopped him to take down his testimony. That I deem was the usual way. I thought it was perplexing the witness, and had announced a different rule,—that a witness might go on to make his statement of his testimony until he got through, and then if counsel wished time to take down the testimony, they might have the time, and the witness should stay there to take down his testimony. I think this is the better way. It embarrasses the witness to stop every minute or two to say a few words. I thought the best way was to take the statement, and if the lawyers could not take it down as fast as he made it, the rule operated on one side as well as the other. It operated on the counsel for the plaintiff as well as on the counsel for the defendant, and on the defendant's counsel as well as the counsel for the plaintiff. There was no partiality in the matter.

The only proof of any interruption of attorneys in that case is with regard to Mr. Fox. You have heard the testimony in that, and what it was—that I told him to take his seat, and not interrupt me in that way. It is not alleged or proved that it occurred with any other attorney. Now what is the proof—what is the testimony in that case?

Upon this second trial of the Kinsey case, Mr. Joseph White volunteered to prosecute. The evidence in the case was altogether circumstantial. In my argument for the defense, before the jury, I took occasion to comment or reflect upon Joseph. It had leaked out during the progress of the trial that this Joseph had volunteered his services in the prosecution. In my remarks I played upon the name of Joseph some. I said that I supposed that he was named after Joseph of old, and that out of respect for his great prototype, who was himself the victim of circumstantial evidence, he ought not to undertake to forward the perpetration of a similar wrong. I carried this allusion to some extent; spoke of the fact that the father of Joseph the prototype, when he heard that his son was in Egypt, could not believe that it was true; and in some manner which I am not now able to detail, I instituted a comparison between the father of the prototype Joseph and the prosecutor in the case, saying that as the one could not believe in the existence of his son, so the other, when he heard of his hog, would not believe it to be the same. In my further remarks I spoke in an ironical strain of a grand inquisitorial body sitting in judgment upon this hog matter, and in this connection I did refer to Judge Jackson. Before this, however, I should have observed that my time had been limited to an hour and forty-five minutes. When I came to speak, in the ironical strain that I have mentioned, of the grand inquisitorial body, the Judge interrupted me and asked me to explain myself, and say whether I meant him. I replied that if he would not discount or offset my time, I would not explain. Afterward,—I don't know what gave rise to it,—he abruptly told me to sit down. Whether this grew out of what I had been saying in my speech I will not undertake to say, but he did order me to sit down. I then told the jury to see what a poor chance my unfortunate client had, and that my only dependence for getting justice was in them, and complied with the order of the court by taking my seat. And, gentlemen, I believe it was the best speech I ever made in my life.

Now here is Mr. Fox's statement. He tells you he spoke ironically, alluding to the Judge as an inquisitor. He says I asked him if he alluded to me. He replied that he would make no explanations unless I deducted the time out of his speech. From his own words we see he was certainly acting improperly in court, to announce before a jury that the Judge was acting corruptly on the bench. Could any Judge submit to it without calling him to order? Now, what does Mr. Kittrell, and the Clerk, and Mr. Hicks, say about it? The statement of Mr. Kittrell is, substantially, that Mr. Fox was exceeding his time. He would talk about this Joseph in Egypt instead of talking about the case. I told him to confine his argument to the case. He went on, and I gave him some minutes longer,—gave him all the privilege a lawyer could have, and he exceeded that time, and did not progress any in his argument. He was still dwelling upon Joseph. I again directed his attention to the case, and extended the time a few minutes longer. He still alluded to Joseph in Egypt. I told him to sit down. That is what Mr. Kittrell says. He says, moreover, he thought Mr. Fox was a little intoxicated, and Mr. Fox himself says he did not know what he was doing. Go on further and look at the Clerk's testimony. He is more minute than Mr. Kittrell. He says he had been limited. He was called,—his attention was directed to it, that he was exceeding his time, and still I was disposed to let him go on, and at last he made use of such expressions, and in such a way, that I told him he must stop. And, says Mr. Ponder, "he was under the influence of whisky." Mr. Hicks was a young man whose memory is pretty good. He mentioned an instance about the Sheriff rubbing against him, and the assaults of the Sheriff, and he represents how he was going on. Now was not he certainly out of order, and was it not my duty to call Mr. Fox, under these circumstances, to order? Was I acting harshly? Was not I forbearing towards him? And he says he was making the best speech he ever made in his life! If that was his best speech, what have I not been subjected to in listening to him make other speeches! What have I been subjected to in setting on the bench, and listening to him go on in that way! Now, was I guilty of what is said here,—of "repeated interruption of said counsel?" Mr. Fox states that at one time it was harsh, rough language, and manner. I will allude here to a little incident about Mr. Fox,—about his good speeches, and good conduct. What was his manner in addressing the court? "It was the same style of coolness, candor, and respectful address in which I am now speaking." Those are his words. Any person acquainted with Mr. Fox would know he was doing the best in the world he was capable of, and that even then, when he was speaking "in the same style of coolness and respectful address," he was out of order.

So when Mr. Fox is doing his best, he is out of order. But for doing this, I am charged with peremptorily stopping counsel and ordering him to take his seat, "although said counsel was in the discharge of his proper duties"—I was wrong. Mr. Fox, during this course,—was *he* in the discharge of his proper duties? Now these are frivolous charges, and this is one of the particular charges against me of abusing attorneys. And in all these they have not proved an attorney was in court. Suppose it was an indictable offense, and the statute provided that if a Judge shall speak insultingly and disrespectfully to an attorney, he shall be fined and imprisoned,—suppose he should be indicted for it, should not the indictment state that such a person, being a regularly licensed attorney, in the discharge of his duties, was then and there insulted by the Judge? Would he not have to prove he was an attorney by producing his license, and by producing a copy of the record to show that he was enrolled, and had taken the oath of an attorney? They simply come in here and say "I was an attorney in such a case," and it seems there is not a case they would not testify to before they were attorneys in the case. There is no evidence but their say-so. I believe there is nothing further about the interruption and disrespect, and insulting and tyrannous manner.

About that Mr. Phelan complains, I investigated that yesterday afternoon. I was informing him of a fact that he was not advised of. I proceeded as I conceived according to law.

Now here is another series of offenses of which I am accused of being guilty,—for not signing bills of exceptions. There is the case of Moore against Eldridge. There is the Buckner case, and the Griffie case, and the Whitehead case, and one case in Ripley county. The charge is here:

In refusing to sign a bill of exceptions duly tendered to him by counsel for the said Moore, unless it was made to show that certain facts were proven that were not proven on said trial."

Now the record of that case is not here, as it should be, to show there was any such a case. Don't you see their witnesses do not know there was any such case there? And what was the fact? There was a case of Eldridge against Moore, at that term of the court, but not a case of Moore against Eldridge. There were two different suits against the same parties relating to the same matter, and that celebrated instrument of writing was in both cases. Now Mr. Kittrell said that case of Eldridge against Moore was tried in that term of the court. He was mistaken. Mr. Ponder, the Clerk, and Mr. Lowe, Deputy Clerk, both tell you the case in this court was Eldridge against Moore, and not Moore against Eldridge, and there was no such case as the latter in court. It had been disposed of before, a court or two. This was on a note, and was George T. Moore and James Moore *vs.* John Eldridge. There was never an attempt to take a bill in a case of Moore against Eldridge. In this, they tell you, I refused to sign a bill of exceptions unless certain facts were proven. Now the testimony in the case is this: When they came to make up the bill of exceptions, there was a difficulty about it with regard to what should go in the bill of exceptions. They say I said that Mr. Kittrell testified about this instrument of writing, and they said he did not. That issue may be between us. It was a difficulty, and Mr. Kittrell was called in to decide it. Mr. Kittrell says, as they did that, I pressed the matter further. If that is the case the fact exists, and it must go in the bill of exceptions. Mr. Kittrell tells you that paper was testimony before the jury. Mr. Kitchen tells you I put it in the bill of exceptions. It will take but a moment to show about that paper. I am obliged to remember all the cases I disposed of, instead of going to the record. I can only quote from memory. Look at the records; if they are wrong, condemn me for them. But this outside matter,—what attorneys say, I cannot remember that. Now this was a note upon which Eldridge sued Moore. Moore had given a note to the firm, which he thought had gone to the firm, but which had gone to Parker alone. It was necessary to say whether this note was given before the date of the articles of agreement or not. If the note was given afterwards, it would be like as if it was a matter they knew about, and had no connection with the partnership business. Then it was material to see what was the date of this instrument of writing. It was produced, and the testimony is that there was an erasure, which was a matter of inspection, to say whether the instrument was dated the same day with the note. One of the dates would and one would not correspond. I told them to state the fact, just merely to keep that instrument of writing to its proper office. The erasure could not be copied, and it would go up with a certain date, and the Supreme Court could not see there was that blot. They all admit the fact was in proof before the jury, whether Mr. Kittrell did or did not testify to it. I am charged with inserting testimony which was not proven, and then Mr. Kitchen tells you I put it in brackets to show that it was not Mr. Kittrell that said it. Didn't I do just what I ought to have done?

Then in the same article is the charge of this conversation I had about the Moore case. I contend, gentlemen, that a Judge is like any other man. He takes an interest in the affairs of the community. He is presumed to. In all matters he is like other persons. In becoming a Judge he does not separate from society. Suppose this murder that occurred in St. Louis,—suppose the Judge of the Criminal Court expressed himself thus: "That man ought to be hung," in the excitement of the moment; would you say he was guilty? In this Walker case, it was a public case. I had a talk about it. I was giving my opinions about the instrument of writing,—whether Moore should receive his pay from the firm. They had a good deal of talk, and I mentioned that it came to the ears of Moore, and he did not think I had so expressed myself. He permitted the trial to go on, and did not apply for a change of venue. He said if that is the case, I shall not gain it; it will be the same thing in court; and he was perfectly willing for a trial under the circumstances. It was an incidental matter. It happened to be spoken of as I came out. I was not going to pry into the matter, and ascertain, and give advice.

The sixteenth article is upon this case of the bill of Griffie. Now, Tyrell tells you that in that case the trial was had, and the jury rendered a verdict against the defendant for a larger amount than was claimed in the petition, and I believe that was the fact. That was the act of the jury, but my conduct in the case is what they censure. He says when they came to make up bills of exceptions, I would not sign until parts of the motion papers were stricken out. He could not give his testimony on parts that were material. I suppose he did not know the whole matter was here, and it would be seen then whether it was proper to do so. Now, Bedford testifies Mr. Tyrell was not in the case until after the trial was over. Mr. Miller says Mr. Tyrell was not about until the trial was over. And the pleading in the case was all done by Wasson. Miller says Wasson conducted the case. Tyrell comes in and testifies about this matter, and says I intimated to the jury (and brings it up as an instruction) that if the defendant had no interest in the land, he could not recover. In making up the bill of exceptions, I would not let that go in, and a few words will explain that. In making motions for a new trial they generally assign the reasons for a new trial. If there have been instructions given, they number the instructions given. If a party moves for a new trial, then there is the erroneous instructions. They say the court erred in giving the second instruction, and it is numbered.

These instructions are all on a paper filed in the cause, and then when they make a motion for a new trial, and they number the instructions properly, and refer to it that way, and when it comes to the Supreme Court that instruction, thus objected to, is considered, and then the instruction is examined into. Here was a dodge attempted to be practiced by Mr. Tyrell. I suppose he wanted to get the paper in there so it would look as though the instruction had been given, in order to show the court erred in giving the fifth or second instruction. When he came to make up the bill of exceptions, I told him, "if you put that in there it looks as if that instruction had been given, when it really was not. When you let it go up to the Supreme Court, if it comes up there you show it was an instruction." But the observation I made he incorporates as an instruction. And if I had signed the bill of exceptions that way, it would have gone up to the Supreme Court as if that instruction had been given. You may say, "because a Judge gave an erroneous instruction," and if you don't show that instruction has been given, the Supreme Court will do nothing with it. But if you put it in as an erroneous instruction, why, it looks as if it had actually been given. That, I told him, he must strike out. And then, too, he says there was improper evidence given, and comes and sets out what that evidence was. I don't remember any such evidence having been given. The evidence that was given in the case should be taken down. If such evidence was given in the case, the Supreme Court would act upon it, and he wanted to incorporate it in the motion for a new trial. If I had signed that bill of exceptions, it would have been as much as to show this evidence was in. It was for attempting to get in evidence that was not evidence, and I do not blame lawyers for that. You know lawyers will do their best. If I can get a thing in,—if a Judge permits it,—it shows I am pretty smart, and can get a Judge to do things others cannot. I am sure I did nothing wrong in that. You will find that I can refer to it in a moment. Now here is the motion for a new trial:

Defendant moves for a new trial in this case, because, first, on the trial plaintiff totally failed to prove any cause of action alleged in the petition.

Second, the jury were misled by testimony to prove who was the owner of the land in question at the time of trial.

I did not know there was any such testimony as that, and would not sign it.

Fourth, the jury were misled by the opinion of the court, that defendant had no interest susceptible of conveyance in the land mentioned in the petition.

Now, that is what he wanted to put in. He says I had given that opinion. He brings it in here that it was an instruction. "The jury were misled by the opinion of the court that the defendant had no interest." If he had excepted to the opinion of the court, and was giving instructions to cover that point, it would have been all right. That would have been evidence. He was not there at the trial, and knew nothing about it. He wanted to get up an embarrassment in the case afterwards. This is the first motion. The other is about the testimony, and this is about the instruction. If there is anything wrong in that, is it not an error of the judgment, and not corruption or fraud in office? I will read here a part of article sixteen:

ARTICLE XVI. That said Albert Jackson, at a Circuit Court begun and held at the town of Bloomfield, within and for the county of Stoddard, on the third Monday in November, A. D. 1858, whereat said Albert Jackson presided as Judge, was willfully and maliciously guilty of much gross oppression, partiality, misconduct, and abuse of authority in his official capacity:

First. In expressing opinions and making assertions relative to the cause of Gustavus Berry *vs.* John Griffie, then and there pending, unbecoming his position as Judge.

Second, In expressing opinions and making assertions relative to the merits of said cause in open court, in the presence and hearing of the jury empanneled and sworn to try said cause, calculated to influence the minds of the jury against the defendant.

Third. In corruptly endeavoring to prevent the defendant in said cause from getting the same fairly before the Supreme Court on appeal, by refusing to sign a bill of exceptions, properly tendered to him by counsel for said defendant, until a large portion of the motion papers had been stricken out, so that a large number of material reasons urged for a new trial in said cause did not appear in said bill.

Fourth. In corruptly refusing to examine and sign the testimony preserved in the bill of exceptions in said cause, although counsel for both parties agreed that all of said testimony was correctly set forth therein, alleging as a reason that there was so much noise in court during the trial of said cause that he did not know what testimony had been given; corruptly intending, by such refusal, to prevent said defendant from getting said cause fairly before the Supreme Court.

Now, you have all the testimony of Bedford, and Tyrell himself said that during the progress of that trial, Bedford was sitting in such a position with regard to myself, I could not hear, and I asked him to sit out one or twice, so I could hear the responses. Mr. Tyrell attempts to insinuate that it was because I kept such bad order, and allowed so much noise. That is not the case. Nobody complains I kept such bad order. Now it was under these peculiar circumstances that Bedford tells you I told him two or three times to sit out so I could hear him, and then, when they want me to certify to the testimony, as an honest man I could not do it and say what it was. And for that I am arraigned! Under that state of circumstances it was impossible for me to know the case. I would not certify to it. They say because they took it,—because both parties agreed to it,—I ought to have certified to it. If I certify it must be from my own knowledge. They could have put that in. It didn't hinder them from taking it to the Supreme Court, and so both parties heard the testimony. This is the substance of it. It was not necessary to have me certify to it. They could have done so if they chose. No doubt the Supreme Court would have acted upon it. It was not my fault. I did not hinder them from making a statement. They could have done that if they chose. "In corruptly refusing to sign a bill of exceptions in the case of Daugherty against Whitehead." Now, what they were I do not remember. The case is not here. I really do not remember how it was.

Now then for the seventeenth article. That is in regard to those gaming cases. and my conduct in that matter. There was one indictment also pending against me for the same offense. That I cannot say about. That is, you have heard the testimony and can say whether I acted corruptly in that matter. The jury were sworn and heard the testimony on that matter, and saw whether it was sufficient to sustain the indictment. My opinion then was, and is yet, that it was not; and cases of that kind are not indictable under our statute. It must be for betting. If circumstances amount to a bet, if it is only a thimble-full of whisky, it is indictable. If otherwise, it is not, and these are my opinions as a Judge; and that law came to me to be administered. I gave my opinion about it, and they undertake to say I influenced the jury. Now, that prosecution came up because the difficulty had never been decided, and I wanted to determine it. And Mr. Tyrell says if that indictment had not contained my own name I would have quashed it. But I did not think I had a right to quash my own indictment. I would make no order whatever in my own case. I could not quash and could not enter a *nolle prosequi* in it. Mr. Bartlett chose to have his case tried, and when that point came up before me to decide from the testimony there introduced, there was something mentioned on the part of the attorney for defendant. The attorney probably believed that they would like to hear the opinion of the court upon the testimony. I went on by argument to show the reason I came to that conclusion. If the jury took the case and found the defendant not guilty, I did not want that done. After they found him not guilty, I could do no more in the case. The same difficulty would occur again in any other court. I told them they could find a special verdict, and I would deliver my opinion, and then the matter could be sent up to the Supreme Court, and could be finally adjusted and settled. If the Supreme Court decided it was indictable, I should be forever bound by it. Now, that is the whole matter. I was delivering my opinion as a Judge on the bench. If they had brought in a verdict of guilty I would have had to set it aside. It would have laid over until the next term of the court. It would have been tried again with the same results. There would have been no end to it. Now, the Circuit Attorney, seeing this was the opinion of the court, entered a *nolle prosequi.* He wanted it to include all cases in that indictment except against himself. I told him he could not do it against or for myself. I could do nothing. And the one against myself stands there yet, unless the Circuit Attorney or Judges of the Supreme Court has given an order sending it away. "Then permitting David G. Hicks to enter a *nolle prosequi.*" Now, this is intended to show that the Circuit Attorney entered a *nolle prosequi* in my own case. Now, that was not done; it was in Bartlett's case and in Brand's, but in Hicks's case, and my own, it was not done. No such thing. It was intended to make it appear I had done it in my own case. I did not think I would have been doing so much wrong, but having no right to meddle in my own case, I let the matter stand. In the other cases, I gave my opinion. In my own I did nothing. They wanted to make it appear that I dismissed my own case in dismissing Bartlett's. It was their indictment,—several persons in the same indictment,—but it was not a general indictment. The indictment was against either one or against all of them. That is my view of it. I don't think any lawyer would undertake to contradict it.

Now comes the celebrated Sarah Buckner case. If you can conceive, gentlemen, in that what these persons are driving at, most certainly you can do more than I can. If what they say is true,—for they say, as Mr. Davis says, as Mr. Moore says, as Mr. Bedford says, as Mr. Phelan, and Bartlett, and others say,—I have acted exactly right in that matter. And why is it they impeach me for this case? I do not say but Mr. Byrne's (?) view of the case is different from what they say. They say that Grimsley's testimony was withdrawn. Mr. Bedford testifies about that, but the most he knows about it is what Mr. Davis said, and what Mr. Davis understood,—which was that Grimsley's testimony must have been withdrawn, and that it had been excluded. Mr. Davis tells you that it was withdrawn, and that the bill of exceptions was taken to it and it was excluded. Mr. Moore says the same thing, but he does not remember whether the bill of exceptions was signed or not. Mr. Phelan does not remember that, and swears that Grimsley was not cross-examined. They wanted to except to it, but could not. To use his own language, they did their best, but did not have a chance to say a word in the matter.

Mr. Moore says I would not allow them to allude to Mr. Grimsley's testimony. If the testimony was withdrawn and excepted to, was it not my duty to prohibit them from commenting upon it? But then a great fault they find is this: That when they came to make out the bill of exceptions, I refused to sign the bill of exceptions unless Grimsley's testimony was incorporated. How could the Supreme Court decide whether Grimsley's testimony was withdrawn or not? If they say it was withdrawn, and excepted to, would not it have to go up to the Supreme Court for it to decide whether it was Grimsley's testimony or not? They have fallen into a trap if they did so. Now, gentlemen, I simply tell you what I conceive to be the facts, and refer to Phelan's testimony, and he will bear me out. Mr. Phelan tells further, Grimsley was not cross-examined. They say he was cross-examined and for some time. Now it shows how hard it would be for you to decide upon a case against me, upon testimony of this kind—matters which are not upon the record,—or one recollects it one way and another a different way. There is a strange discrepancy. Mr. Phelan cannot be right, because in the detail of his testimony he goes on and says:

There were but two witnesses examined for the prosecution in this case. One was defendant's son, and the other William C. Grimsley, ex-Sheriff of Stoddard county. Mr. Grimsley went on to give in his testimony at considerable length. He was under examination two or three hours. Mr. Woodsides, the Circuit Attorney, finally asked leave to withdraw the witness, which was granted, and the trial went on.

Q. Did you object to the withdrawal of the witness?

A. We made what objection we could. I cannot say whether any exception was entered of record. We were not allowed to speak of Grimsley's testimony, and when Judge Jackson announced that the testimony of the witness was withdrawn, we knew well enough it was useless to make objection. He is very decided. When he has once made a decision, it is impossible to get him to review it. You may talk of the laws of the Medes and Persians, but they were not more unalterable than Judge Jackson's decisions. Mr. Davis alluded to the statements of Grimsley not as testimony, but by way of illustration. He was stopped in his argument by the court. I being the oldest attorney in the cause, tried to conclude the argument for the defense; and in my argument before the jury, I wished to allude to the statements of Grimsley for the purpose of removing any impressions they might have made on the minds of the jury. The Judge stopped me, also, and reiterated that the evidence of Grimsley was withdrawn from the jury. I was not willing that the verdict of the jury should stand, and wished to have a chance to take the case to the Supreme Court; but I had not time then to prepare a bill of exceptions. In this matter the Judge treated me with more than kindness. However, I am anticipating; I will come to that directly. I filed a motion for a new trial, and Judge Jackson adjourned the court to a day one or two weeks subsequent. I was compelled to leave the place, and while I was gone, I was taken sick and was unable to attend on the day to which Judge Jackson had adjourned the court. He continued his kindness to me, however, and adjourned the court a second time to a day perhaps three weeks subsequent to the day of trial. After I returned home, on the day appointed I presented a bill of exceptions. In making out the bill of exceptions, I believe I put in the motion for arrest of judgment (I inserted it then, because it was the first time I thought about it,) the point that the testimony of one witness, uncorroborated, was not sufficient to support a conviction for a capital offense. In discussing this, the Judge persisted in saying that the testimony of Grimsley was not withdrawn. When I adverted to the fact that I was not permitted to comment upon the testimony of Grimsley, and that we had not been allowed the benefit of a cross-examination, the Judge took offense, and made some threat. He said that he was going to do something. I asked him was it fine? He said, "no, worse than that." I asked him was it go to jail? He said, "no, worse than that," again. "Then," I said, "I suppose you mean to strike me from the roll?"

Q. When did this occur?

A. I have not, perhaps, made myself understood. This was in my argument of the cause before the jury. I adverted to these facts and others, but the Judge persisted in saying th t the testimony had not been withdrawn, and refused to sign the bill of exceptions until it was incorporated.

Q. Did you say that Grimsley was a witness on the part of the State?

A. Yes, sir. While he was on the stand under examination, the Judge observed, "Mr. Circuit Attorney, I would withdraw that witness." He made use f some expression tantamount to that, if it was not those very words. The Circuit Attorney did not seem to take the hint given him, and the examination continued until the adjournment at noon. As soon as court convened after dinner, the Circuit Attorney asked leave to withdraw the testimony of this witness. The Judge said "well," and the testimony was accordingly withdrawn. When Mr. Davis, my associate in the case, spoke of it by way of illustration, and not as testimony, the conduct of the Judge was then harsh in the extreme, so much so that Mr. Davis gave up the case, saying that if he could not act for the defendant without the dictation of the court, he would abandon his cause. As I said before, when I came to argue the case, I spoke of Grimsley's testimony to divest the minds of the jurors of any impression that it was testimony. The Judge told me I must not speak of it—that it was not testimony. I endeavored to explain to him my purpose. He seemed to get angry, and threatened me. Then it was that I asked would he fine? and he told me "worse than that;" was it go to jail? and when he told me it was worse than that, I said, "I reckon you intend to strike me from the roll." The point about the testimony of one witness, uncorroborated, not being sufficient, never struck me until I came to prepare the motion in arrest of judgment. It is proper to observe that the prosecution rested the case on the testimony of the prisoner's son alone, after the testimony of Grimsley was withdrawn. When I presented the bill of exceptions, as I before stated, he refused to sign the bill until Grimsley's testimony was incorporated.

Q. Was Mr. Grimsley examined in the presence of the jury?

A. Yes, sir. The examination lasted an hour or two; and his testimony was withdrawn from the consideration of the jury as I have stated.

Now, why did they object to it if Grimsley's testimony was withdrawn? and if they wanted to comment on that testimony, why did they wish to have it withdrawn? The facts are these: Mr. Phelan tells you that he wanted to get that witness to state what Mrs. Buckner told him that Susan told her. That is the part he wanted to get out. That is the part I thought ought to be excluded, and that is the part where the difficulty arose. If there was anything withdrawn, it was because he had got it out, and that part of the testimony was withdrawn. "We relied upon the cross-examination to bring out the facts of the admission of the daughter." That leaves no doubt as to what they were contending for. I decided in that matter that the statements of hearsay would not be testimony. If it was testimony for Mrs. Buckner to give her own version, certainly it was not right for her to tell what other folks said who were not there to testify in the matter. Thus it was proper for me to prevent the attorneys from commenting on the case, when the testimony was withdrawn. When they wanted to comment on it, didn't I do right to prevent them? When Mr. Davis went on, and spoke, and insisted upon speaking, and commenting upon Grimsley's testimony, I stopped him. He says further he undertook merely to illustrate by supposition. But his supposition was to suppose a case like this testimony, and I would not permit him. It was merely a dodge to get in what he had no right to do. And Mr. Davis tells you himself that he tried two or three times. He heard me calling to him to tell him he was out of order. Mr. Hicks said I had to speak two or three times, and he turned around and said if he could not conduct the case he would give it up. He admits it was just done for effect. Mr. Davis admits that himself. Now, if I committed wrong, what harm is there in all this about that case? There was a woman on trial for having perpetrated one of the most disgusting murders that was ever perpetrated. So far as I was concerned, I was willing to give her a fair trial. Phelan says I took more interest in the case than he did, and trying to make out I was trying to prosecute that wretched woman, when it was the fault of her attorneys she was convicted. Now, Phelan tells you he never thought to ask that instruction. I asked him in his testimony, "Phelan, why didn't you ask for instructions from the court that the testimony of one of the witnesses was not sufficient to convict?" and he says he did not think of it then. Is it possible that persons who pretend to take upon themselves to defend a person from a charge of murder, in a case of that kind, should be so negligent of their duties not to think of that important matter? And so angry was he that he could not get in this matter about attempted rape, that he lost his case! And now he wants me to be impeached for his bad conduct! Now, gentlemen, that matter,—the whole of it,—is before you.

The charges are of four or five different kinds, several contained in each. Here is another one here that is included in the sixteenth article:

Sixth. In hearing and determining a motion to quash an indictment then and there pending, against one David G. Hicks, who was then and there acting as Circuit Attorney, *pro tem.*, without having first appointed some other attorney to represent the State in that behalf.

Here is the indictment against Hicks, and it is quashed. Now, gentlemen, see if it was not proper to quash that indictment. The circumstances I do not recollect much about. The testimony was detailed by young Miller. He tells you he had a motion drawn up, and was going to move to quash, and Mr. Hicks told him not to, and he did not file his reasons. Afterwards though,—he says that was about the second day of the term,—at the last day of the term, he asked the court to quash that indictment; and when he did so he moved to quash that indictment, and it seemed there had been others of the same kind of assault with intent to kill. It left out the words "with malice aforethought." Mr. Hicks drew all these indictments up the same way as in drawing an indictment for himself. I knew nothing about it. The grand jury did not tell me they wanted another Circuit Attorney. It comes out there is an indictment against Hicks drawn up by himself—there are others in the same fix, and when Miller presents this, I asked the question if the same fact existed as in the others, and he told me yes; I quashed it then, because I had quashed all the others for the same defect. What corruption is there in that? They undertake to say I did it because I was friendly to David Hicks. What evidence is there of it? They undertake to introduce testimony about that. I am friendly to David Hicks,—more so than I am to a good many others. Is it a crime for one person to be friendly to another person? Who would be fit for a Judge if he has no more partiality for an honest man and gentleman than he has for a horsethief and scoundrel? Gentlemen, I ask any of you if you do not feel a warmer feeling of friendship and more partiality towards an honest man and gentleman in every respect, than you do for a dishonest man and a scoundrel? I do not think a person ought to be a Judge if he had just as much respect and just as much esteem for a dishonest man as for an honest man. I do not think that man would be fit for a Judge. In regard to Mr. Hicks, I like the young man. I believe he is a general favorite. From what acquaintance I have had with him for three or four years, I think him a promising young man, and would do anything to assist him. But that I would act dishonest to befriend Mr. Hicks or any other man, is an insinuation which I repel with scorn. They have tried to insinuate it that way, and to rake up everything against me in my private relations. If they succeed in it, it is for you to decide how far it is their province to act in this direction.

I want to allude to a few points in Phelan's testimony, to show the state of his feelings, and see his statement, and his swearing to the writing; and so, too, about Tyrell. How they swear when it comes against me! When they say I have acted harshly, and spoken harshly, and "severe in the extreme," to use Phelan's term, and when you ask them the question directly what was said, these very gentlemen cannot give the words, but they are willing to swear to their conclusions that it was "harsh in the extreme." To give the words—they can't do it. I tried in every way, but they would not do it. And in speaking to Mr. Phelan—

Q. Was I excited, and do you think my manner betrayed this excitement?
A. I have no earthly doubt of it, on that occasion more particularly.
Q. Which, Mr. Phelan, do you think it was: was I acting oppressively in the matter, or was it that you thought you had a right to do so something, and that I thought you had no right to do it, and you wanted your way, and I wanted mine? Wasn't that what was the matter?
A. In that respect there might be a difference of opinion.
Q. Well, when there is a difference of opinion occurring in court, between lawyers and the Judge, whose province is it to decide?
A. The Judge's, of course.
Q. Might not the Judge make a wrong decision honestly? Couldn't he be honestly mistaken, and do you think such a mistake would be a fraud?
A. No, sir; there can be no question on the point whether an honest mistake is a fraud.
Q. Didn't you get excited on that occasion, and talk a good deal, as you are apt to do?
A. Annoyed is the utmost term I can use to express my feelings at the time. There was a good deal of hard feeling excited by your course.

Before, he said he did get excited a little, and more particularly when he says that in that case at Butler, when I announced to him he was in contempt of court, he was a little excited, and says, "I rather think not, Judge!" Kitchen says his expression's stronger—that it was a "lie" and "false."

Mr. Fox, if you will notice his testimony about that, expresses it as Mr. Kitchen did, but not in as strong language. And see what Mr. Phelan here says about the excitement. He says the utmost he can ever admit was he was "annoyed." How was he annoyed? When he wanted to be the "next friend." It was annoying to think he could not be Judge. It was very annoying.

Mr. Fox, as mild as he is, and speaking so little and pleasantly, as he was going on, was thought by Senators to be out of order.

Q. Well, Mr. Phelan, you informed us that you were an attorney. Where do you practice?
A. In the Fifteenth Circuit. I cannot say that I am enrolled in all the courts in that circuit. I have never taken the trouble to attend to the matter. In fact I cannot say that I ever thought about it.
Q. Is your name enrolled as an attorney in any county?

He thinks he is an attorney, but don't know whether he is an attorney or not, and has not taken pains to have his name enrolled, though the law says if he does not do it, he is in contempt. He thinks it a very simple matter, and wants to claim the rights and privileges of an attorney, though the law requires it positively, and says he is contempt of court if he don't do it. It is for you to say how far such testimony will go to establish facts. The first charge is issuing an attachment which I ought not to have done. Gentlemen, a similar thing was done here—here you had a right to issue attachments, though there were persons here offering excuses at the time, saying the persons would be here. They did not come in obedience to the writ, neither had any return been made in obedience to the writ. I had issued a writ, and all I could do was to issue an attachment, and see what was the matter. Was there anything oppressive in that? And even if it was so, whose fault was it? Not the fault of the Judge, but the fault of the law allowing such things. Then the one of talking out of the court to Walker, Odell, and Ringer, and in that case of Moore. Now, what would that amount to, gentlemen? Do you think I ought to be turned out and thought not worthy of holding office in the State again? Was there any evil intention, and if there was an evil intention was there anything evil in the act or in the intention either? And then as to this insulting expressions and manner towards attorneys. Now, gentlemen, in every case where it has been done, it was where I conceived the attorneys needed it,—as they did. Your Speaker here has a gavel or hammer, and can rap. The Judge has to sing out at the top of his voice, as in the case of Fox, when I had to call out three times before he heard me. Perhaps a rap on a sounding-board would have caused him to hear me the first time. Suppose a Judge calls a crowd to order when they are not out of order? It would be ridiculous. He must decide as he thinks—according to the best of his ability. So in this case, when these lawyers were out of order, I endeavored to put them in a way of discharging their duties. They say I did it with harsh, abusive, and insulting language. But when you come to ask them about these insulting expressions, they cannot tell what they were. They only say it was harsh, and abusive. With regard to signing the bills of exceptions. I think in these cases I did not do wrong. I can admit I was mistaken. I can admit I should have signed them. What were the facts? Are they really as they say? Do they show I did anything corruptly? Am I to have no allowance for errors or mistakes, in the discharge of my duty? Am I to be held strictly answerable for every error I commit—that it is no mistake or error, but crime? I think you will take it fairly into consideration, and give me the advantage of that. If it is error, or if it is mistake or irregularity, with no bad intention about it, why of course it was not impeachable. Here is another class of accusations which I do not conceive it is your duty to pass upon, and that is whether I have made right or wrong decisions. Now, I think if a Judge decides wrong in a case, if he is mistaken, exceptions must be taken, and the case must be carried to the Supreme Court and there rectified. If it is acquiesced in, it stands that the Judge was right in his decision. But if he makes a mistake, the law provides it must go to the Supreme Court. And I do not think that this Court has a right to investigate these matters and say whether my decisions were right or wrong. If there was corruption attending them, you may examine them, but I still hold, as before, it must be upon conviction for an indictable offense, before you can convict. A Judge is as liable to be indicted as any other person, though for a matter not connected with his office. If convicted he can be turned out, because Judges cannot hold office if they commit offenses and violate the law. Now, all I ask is that you examine the testimony and give it an impartial hearing, and I shall be bound to be satisfied about it.

The argument of Judge Jackson having been concluded, on motion of SENATOR RAINS, the Court adjourned to 2 o'clock, P. M.

EVENING SESSION.

TUESDAY, June 21, 1859.

The Court met pursuant to adjournment.
The managers and respondent attended.

[Reported by George C. Stedman.]

ARGUMENT OF MR. KNOTT.

Mr. KNOTT, having announced himself ready to proceed with his concluding argument, rose and said:

MAY IT PLEASE THE COURT—MR. PRESIDENT: I regard the cause now about to be submitted to your final adjudication, as one of the most stupendous that can be submitted to a human tribunal. The interests involved, and the consequences to be anticipated from trials of the nature of the present one, are of a magnitude that cannot pertain to any other. The State upon one hand, pointing to her violated laws and polluted Judiciary, appeals to her highest tribunal, demanding that the great and plenary power with which it is endowed may be exerted to drag corruption from the high places in which it has perched, and save her institutions from the foul contamination of its baleful presence; while upon the other, a distinguished recipient of popular favor, protesting his innocence, implores the Court not to pronounce against him a judgment that will not only remove him from his place, but forever stigmatize him as being unworthy of public confidence and unfit to be entrusted with any office of honor, trust, or profit. I am aware, too, that every member of this honorable Court has, in the presence of his country, and in the most solemn manner, called upon his God to witness his determination to try this cause according to law and justice; and while this solemn obligation rests upon you, I feel there is one of no less solemnity devolving upon myself.

The House of Representatives, with a unanimity before unknown to the annals of this or any other State,—a unanimity clearly evincing the deep and earnest interest excited in them by the alarming spectacle of corruption and wrong exhibited in the official conduct of this respondent,—preferred this accusation and sent me here to make good the same before this bar; and to them I am sensible I owe the strictest accountability for the manner in which I discharge the grave and important duties they have entrusted to me. I know, too, that although my voice may be circumscribed by these walls, the inspection of my participation in this trial will not be limited to this occasion or confined to this capitol. The dark picture of judicial crime upon which I shall ask this Court to look, will be contemplated in every avenue of life, in every neighborhood throughout the State. The farmer in his rural retirement, the artisan in his workshop, the lawyer at his desk, and the merchant in his counting-house, each having an interest in the issue of this trial, will examine and pass upon the action of every one connected with it. And, sir, long after you and I shall have left the busy arena of life, should official corruption rear again its horrid head in our beloved State, legislators and statesmen, recurring to this case as a precedent, will scrutinize our actions and criticise the manner in which we discharge our several duties, with judgments unbiassed by any consideration that may influence the opinions of those contemporary with these proceedings.

I need not therefore assure this Court that, while I invite their attention to an application of the facts developed by the testimony to the law that must govern in the adjudication of this cause, I shall "nothing extenuate, nor aught set down in malice." I will endeavor to confine myself strictly to the law as I find it in the books, and the facts detailed by the witnesses who have been sworn upon this stand; and in the deductions I shall seek to draw therefrom, I will not intentionally deviate from the rigid requirements of truth and justice "even in the estimation of a hair." I will not give myself the latitude the respondent has seen proper to assume. I will not give wings to my imagination and soar beyond the confines of the evidence, to decoy your minds from a calm and close investigation of the facts disclosed, and a proper application of the law, as the respondent has deemed it wisest to do. There is no necessity for any such excursions of fancy on my part; the case itself affords a field far too extensive for my physical strength or inteltectual powers to explore, without seeking to venture beyond its boundaries. I will not suppose a state of facts that has no existence, as he has done, and ask the Court to regard the case supposed as being proved; for, sir, rather than seek thus unjustly to prejudice the safety of a single hair of his head, my tongue should rot, nerveless and palsied, within my speechless lips. Nor shall I in any particular undertake to emulate the manner in which the respondent has conducted his defense throughout. He has exhausted the whole range of histrionic art, from the lowest comedy to the heaviest tragedy; but, sir, I possess no such dramatic versatility. I cannot one moment assume the supercilious haughtiness of a dictatorial despot, and sneer upon all around me with an air of supreme contempt, and the next melt into tears under the overwhelming power of my own pathos. Nor are my powers of sarcasm so brilliant as those from time to time exhibited by the respondent. I promise no polish in my discourse, except what may be imparted to it by an honest conviction that I am in the discharge of a high and sacred duty.

It will be remembered that in the commencement of these proceedings, and indeed frequently during the preliminaries to this trial, the respondent not only poured upon the House of Representatives all the vials of his wrath, because they, in the proper discharge of what they conceived to be an indispensable duty they owed to the State, preferred these accusations against him; but treated the accusations themselves, as well as those who were delegated to present them here, with the most supreme contempt. Such, sir, was the arrogance of his manner that I was frequently almost constrained to exclaim as Cassius does of Cæsar:

"Why, man, he dost bestride the narrow world
Like a Colossus; and we *petty* men must
Walk under his huge legs, and peep about
To find ourselves dishonorable graves."

In the opening of this trial even the Senate was scarcely up to the dignity of his contempt. When honorable gentlemen sought to interchange opinions upon the best method of proceeding, he haughtily denounced this Court as the most disorderly jury he had ever seen. When he came to state his defense, he not only advertised himself as the idol of the Fifteenth Judicial Circuit before whom that entire community deemed it an honor to bend the knee in the humblest reverence, but informed the Court that he was going to show that the charges brought against him were not only trivial, contemptible, and insufficient in law, but unfounded in fact; that he was the object of a blind, fanatical persecution,—sought to be made the victim of a horrible conspiracy, concocted by his deadly foes to evict him of his office, and blast his reputation, for no crime, no shadow of wrong upon his part, but that he would cause the fiendish machinations of these remorseless enemies to recoil upon them with such accumulated force that they would only be saved from annihilation to become the "hiss and by-word" of all good men, the synonym of all that is low, mean, and demoniac. I do not pretend that such was the language used by the respondent at any time, but that such was the idea he intended to convey. Yet, when the State supports her cause by an array of testimony rendering it as clear and palpable as yon sun in his meridian splendor,—so irrefragable that even *he* had not the effrontery to deny that the case was made out; when he is confronted here by an array of gentlemen as respectable as any in the State, I care not where they may be sought,—gentlemen whose reputation he dared not assail,—gentlemen who detailed their testimony with a calmness and candor that carried with it an irresistible conviction of its truth,—all this boasted defense, this horrid conspiracy, this planned system of persecution, upon the altar of which he claimed to be an unoffending sacrifice, "vanishes into thin air," and he seeks to escape your just condemnation, and the punishment due to his crimes, because a number of gentlemen did not know that he was habitually guilty of offenses, a single one of which would be sufficient, not only to hurl him in disgrace from his high position, but ought to fix upon him the scorn and detestation of every good man in the State. I need not remind this Court, that all the respondent seemed to try to establish by his great retinue of witnesses was, that *they* were ignorant of the truth of the charges alleged against him; for even that defense, discreditable to his character as a jurist, and insulting to the common sense of this Court, has been abandoned by him in disgust; and finally exchanging the supercillious airs of arrogance and sarcasm, with which he has given variety to the manner of conducting his defense, for the piteous tones of the profoundest humility, he presents the revolting spectacle of a man high in office, and hitherto high in public confidence, pleading his mental imbecility, ignorance, and incapacity, in extenuation of a long and damning catalogue of crimes alleged against him. Having failed to establish a single circumstance he promised in his defense, he stultifies himself by saying, that notwithstanding we may have proven every charge against him, it was only a mistake in judgment, an error of the head, not resulting from any corrupt intention; and triumphantly calls upon the prosecution to explore the recesses of his hidden heart, and drag forth the evidences of corruption lurking there,—to anatomize his secret soul, and point out the very chamber where lurked the evil motive for each disgraceful act of official violence we have fixed upon him. Very well, I shall do so when I come to analyze the evidence and apply it to each particular charge; but I must defer the dissection until I shall have examined some of the astounding positions the respondent has assumed in relation to the provisions of the constitution and the law involved in this cause. But, sir, I do not advert to the doctrines advanced by the respondent because I believe they have made an impression, or can excite any feeling but pity, or ridicule. I do so for the purpose of showing the people of Missouri what kind of material a Circuit Judge may be made of,—what amount of intellect and legal acumen is possessed by some who hold in the hollow of their hands the most important interests of the State, and the dearest rights of the citizen; and I have no doubt they will say the respondent has at least succeeded in establishing his plea of ignorance, if he *has* failed to show his innocence.

In the first place, sir, this learned Judge states, without any qualification, that the House of Representatives in presenting these articles, and the Senate in sitting here to try them, are each guilty of a violation of the constitution, because the second article of the constitution provides that "the powers of government shall be divided into three distinct departments, each of which shall be confined to a separate magistracy; and that no person charged with powers belonging to one of these departments, shall exercise any of the powers properly belonging to either of the other departments." He contends that the Judiciary is independent of the Legislature, and that whatever may have been his crimes, whatever may have been his official misconduct, the House of Representatives had no right under the constitution to prefer these articles; and that you, sir, in setting here to pass upon them, violate your obligation to support the constitution, because such action would be an infringement of the rights and privileges of the Judiciary, whose sole province he claims it to be, to make inquiry into, and properly punish such conduct. I will venture to say, sir, there is not another man in Missouri, learned or unlearned, who would hazard the expression of such an opinion. Explain to the most illiterate man in the limits of the entire State the fact, that the powers of government are distributed among three separate and distinct departments, and that neither is absolute, but all are accountable for the proper and lawful discharge of their respective duties, and ask him whether it would be proper to permit each one of these magistracies to be the judge of its own official demeanor, and he will unhesitatingly tell you, no! that if you make each department the tribunal to determine upon the propriety of its own conduct, you would soon have no restriction upon the abuse of power save the conscientious compunctions of the official, with no criterion of rectitude save his own inclination. No proposition can be more self-evident than that as the Judge is made an officer by the people, and for their benefit, he should be made answerable to them for the fidelity of his deportment in office; and if made responsible to them they have a right to accuse him through their immediate representatives, and to have him tried before a tribunal of a character not likely to be swayed by the might of popular feeling, or the influence usually pertaining to elevated positions, either political or social. But, sir, the provisions of the constitution are too plain to justify an argument. To state the position the respondent assumes is all that is necessary to show its absurdity; and besides, sir, the respondent himself, strange, inconsistent and contradictory as it is, presently assumes the equally ridiculous position that there are "*two kinds of impeachment!*" In the one kind the House of Representatives may, for certain things which *he* is pleased to call misdemeanors, of which I shall speak presently, prefer articles of impeachment, the accused may be confronted by his witnesses and have a fair trial; that in the other class he must be first indicted, tried by a jury, and *convicted* by a jury, and the Senate upon the record of that conviction, and that alone, may impeach and evict him of his office; and the only authority he cites for this remarkable position is the fourteenth section of the third article of the constitution:

> The General Assembly shall have power to exclude from every office of honor, trust, or profit, within this State, and from the right of suffrage, all persons convicted of bribery, perjury, or other infamous crime.

Now, sir, let us see whether this doctrine is sustained by this law, or any principle of reason. What, then, does this clause in the constitution mean? It simply means that the right of suffrage, and the right to hold any office of honor, profit, or trust in the Commonwealth, are franchises inherent in every citizen, and that to deprive him of either of those rights requires an exertion of sovereign power; that sovereignty could not in the narrow limits of the constitution specify every offense for which the citizen should be disfranchised, nor provide the means by which it should be done; and that the Legislature is the agency selected by the sovereign power for the accomplishment of these objects. It merely means to confer upon the General Assembly the power to pass a law declaring that all persons convicted of bribery, perjury, and other infamous crimes, should be disqualified from holding any office within the State, and deprived of the right of suffrage; and wherever the Legislature has included disfranchisement in the penalty affixed to any crime, it is one of the inseparable incidents to a conviction for that crime. Turn to page 608 of the Revised Statutes of Missouri, 1855, and you will find the Legislature, acting upon this view of this provision of the constitution, has enacted that

Every person who shall be convicted of any perjury, or subornation of perjury, punishable by any of the provisions of this article, shall thereafter be incompetent to serve as a juror, testify as a witness in any case, civil or criminal, and shall be disqualified from voting at any election, or holding any office of honor, trust, or profit, within this State.

And besides, I expect to show that under the denomination "*other infamous crimes*," the Legislature has included the very offenses of which the respondent here stands impeached; and has affixed to them the penalty of perpetual disfranchisement. But, sir, let us make a practical application of the doctrine of the respondent. The House of Representatives presents to this honorable Court articles of impeachment, charging some Judge with the commission of an infamous crime. The accused is brought before this bar,—granting such a thing possible after he has been tried by a jury, convicted and sentenced. The managers appear, and everything being ready for trial, they present the record of the conviction of the accused by the jury, and tell you that is all the evidence you are to examine as to the guilt of the party. You protest that you are under the obligations of a solemn oath to try the cause according to law and justice, and you cannot consent to give your consciences into the keeping of twelve other men. Perhaps they may have been bribed; perhaps the witnesses upon whose testimony the verdict was founded may have been hired to swear falsely. You would prefer to see the witnesses face to face,—to see how they deport themselves,—or you would at least like to know upon what grounds the jury predicated an opinion you must be forced to adopt as your own. But no, you have nothing to examine but the record of conviction. And what next? Convict him? He has already been convicted. Disfranchise him? His disfranchisement is an inseparable incident to his conviction. That was accomplished when the jury pronounced him guilty, and the court passed the sentence of the law upon him. This grave and dignified body, then, has been sitting here to enact one of the silliest, flattest farces imaginable,—to do a thing that has already been fully accomplished! I appeal to this honorable Court, if in all their experience they have ever known a position so palpably absurd, so utterly devoid of the slightest trace of common sense, to be assumed before? He protests against this Court trying his cause. He invokes the constitution, and demands a trial by his peers, by a jury of his country. Ah! sir, he has a high appreciation of the trial by jury now; but when a victim of his persecution goes before a grand jury of his country, and tells them 'the Judge of the Circuit Court has singled me out as the object of his vindictive malice, he has violated my liberty, he has outraged my rights, he has willfully, corruptly, and brutally oppressed me, I demand at your hands the protection guarantied by the laws of my country,' he goes privately before that grand jury in their retirement, and instructs them they cannot indict *him* for anything of which he may be guilty in his office! You have not forgotten, sir, that the respondent in opening his case the other day, when he came to speak of the seventeenth article, said expressly, "I *did* tell the grand jury they could not indict me; I told them, too, I would fine them for contempt of court if they persisted in it;" and in the very next breath he claims the privilege of being indicted by a grand jury; and even goes so far as to say that the constitution precludes a trial without it.

Again, sir, he tells you, notwithstanding every fact charged has been incontrovertibly established, they only amount to errors of judgment, for which the proper remedy would be by appeal to the Supreme Court. Yet one of the gravest charges alleged against him is for having on repeated occasions falsified the records of his courts, refused to sign bills of exceptions, and prevented in various ways the taking of cases fairly, fully, and properly before the Supreme Court. He tramples our laws under his feet, violates every principle of human right and justice, effectually thwarts the citizen's right to an appeal to the Supreme Court, claims to be independent of the Legislature, and supreme in his own courts. A pillar and support of the law, he claims a chartered privilege of immolating upon the altar of his vengeance the rights and interests of all who may incur his hate. If consistency is a jewel, what a wonderfully rich lapidary he must be!!

And now, sir, pray what are the offenses for which the respondent admits he *may* be impeached? What are the things and the only things for which he says the constitution authorizes the House of Representatives to prefer charges against him, or justifies the Senate to set as a Court of Impeachment? *First*, The crime of being over sixty-five years of age! *Second*, That of being under thirty! *Third*, Residing out of the circuit over which he claims to preside! He avers that these three cases embrace all the causes for which he can be impeached; but I appeal to the distinguished lawyers I recognize in this Court to tell me if he can be impeached at all for any of these things. Besides, sir, out of his own mouth I will refute him. In his answer, the respondent lays it down as the very corner-stone of his defense, that "by the constitution of Missouri, a Judge can only be impeached for misdemeanors in office, and those misdemeanors must first be declared, and the penalty affixed therefor, by an act of the Legislature." I quote his very language. Now, sir, where has the Legislature declared either of these things misdemeanors in office? and what is the penalty affixed thereto? Sir, the Legislature could never be guilty of such a puerile absurdity. I grant, sir, that no man has a right to exercise the functions of Judge of the Circuit Court if he is under thirty years of age, or over sixty-five, or if he reside out of the circuit over which he claims to preside; but, sir, under our statute, requiring that every Judge within thirty days after his election shall file with the Secretary of State a statement of his age under oath, and since the people of any circuit would hardly elect a man as a Judge who resides somewhere else, such a thing can scarcely happen; but if it should happen, it would not be a misdemeanor in office. On the contrary, the official conduct of the party thus unlawfully in possession of the office, might not deviate a single hair's breadth from the line of perfect rectitude. Sir, I will insult no member of this Court by insinuating that it is possible for him to endorse this silly doctrine of the respondent, for I know it is a fact with which you are every one familiar, that there is another method, in no particular resembling this proceeding, by which a man must be turned out of an office into which he has obtruded himself while under legal disability. But in order to demonstrate fully and effectually the extreme absurdity of his position, I ask to apply his doctrine to the present case. Suppose this impeachment is sustained, and the respondent disqualified from holding any office of honor trust, or profit in this

State. So far as the Judgeship is concerned he is in the same predicament he would be if over sixty-five years of age. Now suppose, notwithstanding this fact, he should be again elected Judge of the Fifteenth Judicial Circuit, and by some means obtain a commission to discharge the duties pertaining to that office, According to the respondent's position, he should be impeached. What for? Why for obtruding himself into an office he had no right to hold under the law. Why has he no right to hold it? Because he had been impeached and disfranchised. Well, what penalty do you or can you expect to inflict in this second impeachment? You can't disfranchise him; that has already been done. You had as well talk of killing a man after he is dead!

I have bestowed thus much attention upon the positions assumed, and the general principles laid down by the respondent, merely to show, Mr. President, what amount of legal knowledge, what degree of ordinary reason it is thought necessary by some to qualify a man for one of the most important positions in the government,—an elevated place in the judiciary of the country. And I must be permitted to say, sir, that I am confident the people of the Fifteenth Judicial Circuit, whom the respondent has so frequently represented, with perhaps as much modesty as truth, as holding him in such profound veneration, will consider themselves happily rid of such a Judge when they have seen how illy capacitated he is to preside over their most vital interests; for I am happy to have the occasion to say that, from my intercourse with those of them whom I have had the pleasure to meet as witnesses here, the State cannot produce a more intelligent community, nor one more worthy of her protection.

But, sir, let us inquire for what causes a Judge *may* be impeached. The constitution, twenty-ninth section, third article, provides that "the Governor, Lieutenant-Governor, Secretary of State, Auditor, Treasurer, Attorney-General, and all Judges of the courts of law and equity, shall be liable to impeachment for any misdemeanor in office." Hence the inquiry becomes pertinent, what will constitute a misdemeanor in office, within the meaning of this provision of the constitution? The respondent has repeatedly claimed, that to constitute an offense impeachable, it must be declared so by the constitution; but I entertain a different opinion. I think if the framers of the constitution had undertaken to define all the offenses for which an officer should be impeached in that instrument, it would have been more voluminous than this statute book, and hence they used one general term applicable to every variety of misbehavior calculated to lessen the adaptation of the office to the purposes for which it was designed, whether that misbehavior amount to a crime or even an indictable offense or not. Like many other words, the term misdemeanor has a general and a technical meaning. Technically, it is defined by Mr. Blackstone, in the fourth book of his Commentaries, page five, to be a gentler name than crime for the smaller faults and omissions in violation of law. I will read what he says: "A crime or misdemeanor is an act committed or omitted in violation of a public law, either forbidding or commanding it. This general definition comprehends both crimes and misdemeanors, which are synonymous terms, though in common usage the word 'crimes' is used to denote such offenses as are of a deeper and more atrocious dye; while smaller faults and omissions of less consequence, are comprised under the gentler name of misdemeanor only." In its ordinary, general sense, the term misdemeanor is defined by our best lexicographers to mean, "ill-behavior," "evil conduct," "fault," "mismanagement," and includes every species of misbehavior of which a man can be guilty, that can tend to bring disgrace upon himself, and diminish the respect due to his position, from murder and treason, down to the numerous vices that so frequently mar the purity of the social circle. It is in this sense I think it is used in the constitution. I think it was the intention of the framers of that instrument to provide that any person entrusted with any of the distinguished positions enumerated in the twenty-ninth section of the third article of the constitution, who should, during his continuance therein, be guilty of any conduct calculated to disgrace that high office, should be impeached and disfranchised, whether that conduct were indictable or not.

In support of this view, my learned colleague, Mr. Hardin, on yesterday, read to you the opinions of Mr. Story and others, who express themselves clearly and unequivocally in favor of it. Besides, he demonstrated to you that the Congress of the United States has unhesitatingly acted upon the conclusion, that the offense for which an officer may be impeached need not be such as would subject him to indictment. And here is another American authority upon the same subject, in addition to those cited by my colleague:

> The causes for impeachment, as stated in the Federal constitution, are treason, bribery, and other high crimes and misdemeanors, and in most of the State constitutions, misdemeanors in office. The meaning of both is probably the same. A violation of official duty, whether criminal or not, is a subject of impeachment.—Walker's Introduction, page 90.

But, sir, if the other view of the subject be preferred,—if it be thought that the term misdemeanors in office is used in the constitution in a circumscribed, technical sense, and that the word misdemeanors is there used to denote indictable offenses, of what may such offenses consist? Our statute provides that the common law of England, when the same does not conflict with the constitution of the United States or of this State, or any statute in force, shall be the rule of action and decision in this State. Permit me to read, then, some common law authorities by which such offenses are defined:

> The *oppression* and tyrannical partiality of Judges, Justices, and other magistrates, in the administration and under color of their offices, may be punished by *impeachment in Parliament*, or by information or *indictment*, according to the rank of the offenders, and the circumstances of the case.—1 Russell on Crimes, page 136.

From this authority we see that *oppression* and *partiality*, by a Judge, is not only indictable, but impeachable.

But I will read another author upon the same point:

> There is yet another offense against public justice which is a misdemeanor of deep malignity; and so much the deeper, as there are many opportunities of putting it in practice, and the power and wealth of the offenders may often deter the injured from a legal prosecution. This is the *oppression* and *tyrannical partiality* of *Judges*, Justices, and other magistrates, in the administration and under color of their office. However, when prosecuted either by *impeachment* in Parliament, or by information in the court of Queen's Bench, according to the rank of the offenders, it is sure to be severely punished with forfeiture of their offices, (either consequential or immediate,) fines, etc.—4 Stephen's Commentaries, page 272.

Judge Bouvier, in his excellent Law Dictionary, defines a misdemeanor to be "a term used to express any offense inferior to a felony, punishable by indictment or particular prescribed mode." We find from the authorities I have read, that any act of oppression, partiality, abuse of authority, or official misconduct on the part of a Judge, is indictable; and hence a misdemeanor in office, an offense answering exactly to the terms of the constitution subjecting him to impeachment.

I am willing, however, sir, for the accommodation of the respondent, to come even to the terms he has prescribed himself, that to render an offense impeachable, it must be defined, and a penalty affixed by statute; for as I have before assured you, this case is abundantly provided for. The Legislature of our State, well knowing the natural proneness of some classes of men when "clothed with a little brief authority," to domineer over their fellows, and override their rights and liberties; and knowing, too, that just such characters would claim to be independent of all law not laid down within the lids of the statutes, with a sagacity and foresight worthy of American statesmen, has enacted that

Every person holding or exercising any office or public trust, who shall be guilty of willful and malicious oppression, partiality, misconduct, or abuse of authority in his official capacity, or under color of his office, shall, on conviction, be punished by imprisonment in the county jail for a term not exceeding one year, and fine not exceeding one thousand dollars.—1 Revised Statutes Missouri, page 613.

Now, here is any kind of willful and malicious misconduct on the part of a Judge made indictable, and the penalty affixed by express statutory enactment; and hence, according to the most rigid requirements of the rule laid down by the respondent in his answer, sufficient to subject him to impeachment.

The respondent, sir, knows and feels that he cannot escape the force of this statute, and so completely overwhelming was this conviction upon him when he came to advert to it in his argument, he had no way to evade it but by totally denying that it had any application whatever to a Judge. To prove that it does not apply to a Judge, he had recourse to an argument that would have wreathed tbe countenance of every member of this Court with a smile of ridicule, had not pity for his miserable confusion repressed it. Says he, this cannot apply to me, for a Judge cannot be guilty of oppression; he may be guilty of an act the *consequences* of which may be oppressive, but the act itself cannot be so! What a wonderfully nice distinction this is, indeed! Why, sir, he rivals the celebrated Hudibras:

He can distinguish and divide
A hair 'twixt south and south-west side!

I suppose, sir, in carrying this newly discovered and truly wonderful principle into practice, he would say, if I were to raise my gun and fire it in the direction of your body, whereby you are slain, I would be guiltless of your murder, because it would not be the act of firing, but the *consequences* of it that deprived you of life! He forgot to say in the same connection that a Judge could not be guilty of *partiality!* That was too much for even *his* effrontery. But, sir, I will not insult the common sense of this Senate by further noticing a quibble so pitiful that the most contemptible pettifogger that ever exercised his professional chicanery in a Justice's court, would feel himself disgraced to resort to it; for it is a proposition upon which no one here will require an argument, that of all others the office of Judge of the Circuit Court may be and frequently is exercised most injuriously to the rights and liberties of the people; that of all others it may be most easily perverted to the vilest oppression, is most liable to be polluted by partiality, and subject to the greatest abuse; and that every person exercising its functions should be held to the strictest accountability for all his acts of willful official misconduct.

Again, sir, I hold that a Judge is impeachable, not only for what he may do in contravention of law and the duties of his office, but for neglecting or refusing to do what is enjoined on him by law. You will remember that in Mr. Blackstone's definition of the terms "crimes" and "misdemeanors," I just now read to the Court, he includes *omissions* as well as *commissions*. But, sir, I will read another authority upon this point:

Where an officer *neglects* a duty incumbent upon him either by common law or by statute, he is indictable for his offense.—1 Rus. on Cr. p. 135.

Again, on page 138 of the same volume, the same subject is more elaborately discussed:

It has already been stated that an officer *neglecting* the duties of his office is guilty of an indictable offense.

But I am not forced to rely upon the common law authorities, of which an abundance might be produced to sustain this position. Turn to the twenty-first section of the sixth article of the act respecting crimes and punishments:

Every officer or person holding any trust or appointment who shall be convicted of any willful misconduct or misdemeanor in office, or *neglect* to perform any duty enjoined on him by law, when no special provision is made for the punishment of such misdemeanor, misconduct, or negligence, shall be punished by fine not exceeding five hundred dollars, or by imprisonment in the county jail not exceeding one year, or by both such fine and imprisonment.

Here, sir, a willful neglect to perform any duty enjoined by law is a misdemeanor; and statutable misdemeanors being, according to the respondent's own demand, impeachable under the constitution, the conclusion is unavoidable, that a Judge may be impeached for willful neglect of duty.

But, sir, how has the Legislature classified such offenses as oppression in office, partiality, abuse of authority, and other official misconduct? It has not only declared them indictable, and affixed a punishment to them, but justly and properly placed them in the category of *infamous crimes*. The constitution of the State, in the fourteenth section of the third article, confers upon the General Assembly the power to exclude from every office of honor, profit, or trust within this State, and from the right of suffrage, every person convicted of bribery, perjury, or other *infamous crimes;* and the General Assembly in pursuance of this power, after denouncing the offense of oppression, partiality, and general misconduct, upon the part of those entrusted with power, in the sixteenth section of the sixth article concerning crimes and punishments, in the eighteenth section of the same article declares that

Every person who shall be duly convicted of any of the offenses mentioned in the preceding sections of this article shall be forever disqualified from holding any office of honor, trust, or profit, under the constitution or laws of this State, and from voting at any election.

And truly, sir, what can render a man more deserving of the lowest depths of infamy, than the betrayal of such distinguished confidence as is reposed by a generous, unsuspecting, honest people, in the person whom they elevate to the position of Circuit Judge? It seems to be an instinct almost universal in the human mind, and certainly, sir, it is a redeeming trait in our nature, to hold the treacherous betrayal of confidence in the utmost loathing, abhorrence, and detestation. Judas Iscariot and Bendict Arnold will stand the despised and execrated monuments of more than fiendish depravity, as long as treachery has a signification in human language; but deeply stained as they were by the crime of treason, they are no more entitled to the universal abhorrence and execration of which they are so justly the objects, than he who, called by his country to administer her laws, protect her citizens, and maintain her institutions in their purity and integrity, ignominiously betrays the confidence of the generous, confiding people, who have delighted to honor him, and perverts the power with which they have entrusted him to the advancement of his own private interests, and the gratification of his own licentious passions. It was just and wise in the Legislature to exclude from office and from all participation in the rights of government all who should betray her most sacred trusts.

With these general principles before you, these plain, unmistakable landmarks, by which your judgments may be unerringly guided in the law, that law by which you have sworn to be governed in deciding this cause, I will undertake to demonstrate that the respondent is guilty of almost every variety of official crime that diabolical ingenuity could devise, or human depravity perpetrate.

I have shown that every offense charged against the respondent is a statutable misdemeanor in office, coming within the strictest technical construction of the constitutional provision conferring jurisdiction in this case; and now I shall show that every one of those charges is true!

In doing so, sir, the means I shall employ will be the testimony of the witnesses introduced upon this stand, and the records offered in evidence; and upon these proofs I shall demand by authority of law that your judgment shall be predicated, for there is not a single circumstance that can diminish their weight, or cloud their character. It is true, the respondent has frequently denounced them as his enemies, intending unquestionably to prejudice the minds of this Court against the testimony they should give; but I appeal to all who have listened to the evidence in this cause, if in all their experience they ever heard so much testimony given with so little indication of personal feeling. Who, I demand, was the witness testifying upon this stand, who seemed to be actuated by improper motives, or exhibited in his testimony anything like the influence of a personal bias? You saw them subjected to the most harrassing, and frequently insulting, cross-examination by the respondent, without betraying the slightest disposition to do him the most trifling injustice. No fact was withheld that could possibly be construed by the respondent into an extenuation of his conduct; no indecent forwardness to disclose what might tend to convict him, was manifested by any witness introduced by the State; but in the spirit of honorable, dignified gentlemen, they detailed their testimony with an appearance of calmness, candor, sincerity, and truth, but rarely exhibited in any court.

That some of the witnesses introduced by the prosecution may entertain feelings of bitterness towards this respondent, I will not deny; they would be less than human not to do so, after the deep and deadly wrongs the evidence shows he has inflicted upon them,—the settled plan of vindictive, relentless, untiring persecution, with which he is proven to have sought for months to ruin them in their social and business relations. But be that as it may, he has attempted by no legal means to assail their testimony; he has not attempted to show to this Court that they are men unworthy of belief,—he dared not do it; he knew that such an attempt would recoil upon his own head with overwhelming, crushing weight. He has not attempted to show that the facts detailed by them are inconsistent with each other, or with the charges, for he knows that every witness is corroborated by the testimony of others and the records filed in the case. By such proofs, admitted by the respondent himself to be irrefragable, I propose to show that he was willfully and maliciously guilty of every charge alleged against him at this bar.

The respondent is charged first with a misdemeanor in office, in being guilty of willful and malicious oppression, exhibited in the unjust and illegal imprisonment of Jonas Eaker, because Mr. Eaker failed to make return to a writ of mandamus that had not been served upon him. The points made by the State are, that Mr. Eaker had not been served with the writ, and hence, was under no obligation to pay any attention to it; that the respondent knew this, and yet for the purpose of harrassing him, or to establish the supremacy of his own opinion, right or wrong, he, in defiance of every principle of law, issued an attachment, had Eaker seized and held in custody, and compelled him to answer, notwithstanding no process had been served upon him,—an act of high-handed, disgraceful, and dangerous tyranny, I boldly pronounce unheard of before in the judicial history of the American government.

It is proper, sir, for me, before proceeding to an investigation of the facts proven in relation to this charge, to apprise the Court, by exhibiting the law, what is the proper and legal manner of serving a writ of mandamus. In order to do so, I will not trouble you to advert to the numerous authorities I have at hand,—one shall suffice. The Supreme Court of our State, the grand centre of our judicial system, the great luminary from which our lesser tribunals derive so much of their legal light, with a precision and accuracy that has ever distinguished that learned body, has decided in the case of Ladue *vs.* Spaulding, (17 Mo. Rep., p. 139,) that a writ of mandamus must be served by delivering it to the person to whom it is directed, and he makes his return to it; that it is no service for the officer to read it to him, and make his return upon it, as he would an ordinary summons; that the original writ must be delivered to the person required to answer.

Now, sir, what are the facts in this case? The record which has been read to the Court shows that upon a certain day the respondent issued a writ of mandamus to Jonas Eaker, Judge of the County Court, directing him to make return thereto on the first day of the next ensuing term of the Circuit Court of Stoddard county. This writ was placed in the hands of John J. Jackson, Deputy Sheriff of the county, who delivered a copy of it to Mr. Eaker, as he and Eaker both testify, and returned the original to the Clerk, with a certificate of that fact endorsed upon it, as also appears by the copy of the record here produced. On the fourth day of the term the case was called. Mr. Kitchen, who had been employed, as he and Eaker both tell you, to represent Mr. Eaker in the matter, attempted to suggest to the respondent that there had been no service, and consequently there was no such case properly before the court. There was the original writ, too, with the endorsement of the officer upon it, showing there had been no service, in court, and offered by Mr. Kitchen for his inspection. Mr. Phelan, who had also been engaged by Mr. Eaker to assist in the matter, likewise attempted to obtain a hearing, in order to explain that his client was under no obligation to appear; but the respondent, after peremptorily closing the mouth of Eaker's counsel, arbitrarily demands of Mr. Eaker himself that he shall enter an appearance and answer to the writ, notwithstanding its defective service. Mr. Eaker declines to do so, and the respondent issues an attachment, has the Sheriff seize him and bring him into court, where he is only released from custody upon the condition that he will the next morning answer to the copy. These facts are established beyond any kind of controversy, by the testimony of Mr. Tyrell, Mr. Jackson, Mr. Kitchen, Mr. Phelan, and Mr. Eaker. And how, sir, does he attempt to escape the just consequences of an act of high-handed oppression they indisputably fix upon him? He attempts to show that the defective service by Mr. Jackson was cured before the attachment was issued. You, perhaps, observed the smile of triumph that illumined his countenance when he thought he had succeeded in palming that trick upon you. But how, pray, does he seek to make this appear? He introduces Mr. Dowdy, the Sheriff, and proves by him, that upon the case being called, and when it was suggested that the original had not been handed to Mr. Eaker, the respondent ordered him to take the original and deliver it to him, and tell him to make return to it; that he did so; that Mr. Eaker refused to receive it, and then the respondent caused an attachment to be issued, and Eaker to be arrested. He proves the same thing by Mr. Hicks, who stands in the court house door, hears the court tell Dowdy to take the original and deliver it to Eaker, and hears Eaker refuse to take it when offered to him at the gate of the court house yard. Unfortunate was it for him, sir, that he offered such proof, for it shows clearly and incontrovertibly that he *knew the service by copy was void and worthless*; for otherwise he would not have sent Dowdy to Eaker with the original. But "he that diggeth a pit shall fall into it;" and this unfortunate proof places the respondent in a still more unenviable dilemma, as I shall show. I hold in my hand a copy of the writ, which commands Eaker to appear and answer on the *first* day of the next term of court, which was the 17th day of May. This record also shows that the case was called and the attachment issued on the *twentieth*, at which time Mr. Dowdy and Mr. Hicks swear the original was offered to Eaker. So, sir, the respondent has shown, either that he was guilty of the ridiculous absurdity of having a man summoned on the 20th of May to answer on the 17th of the same month, three days after the time mentioned in the writ for answering had elapsed, or of the perfidy of attempting to deceive Mr. Eaker, and induce him to appear and answer to a writ that had not been served upon him. I am perfectly willing that the respondent may explain the ridiculous predicament he has placed himself in as he best can; but I feel compelled to think he has himself afforded us one of the strongest proofs of an ignominious and corrupt determination upon his part to make Eaker answer to that writ of mandamus, right or wrong!

But what else, sir, does he urge as a defense to this charge? I blush for the reputation of my State, but it is true,—a Judge of a Circuit Court in Missouri contends that it was Mr. Eaker's duty to come into court and inform him that this writ of mandamus had not been served! What an extremely ridiculous position for any sensible man to assume, let alone a distinguished member of the judiciary of an enlightened State! Why, sir, according to this doctrine, if Mr. Eaker had never *heard* of the writ of mandamus, he would have been liable to arrest and imprisonment for not going into court and informing the respondent that it had not been served upon him. And so, sir, I suppose that every citizen in the State, in order to save himself from being confined in jail for contempt of court, or at least to keep out of the clutches of the Sheriff, must go to the Circuit Court and tell the Judge that no writ has been served upon him.

If I could assemble around me in one vast audience the honest and intelligent people of the Fifteenth Judicial Circuit, and tell them their Judge had expressed, before this learned Court, an opinion so utterly devoid of the least scintilla of common reason, exhibiting such gross and palpable ignorance of the most obvious principles of law, not a face in all that assembly but would burn with shame and indignation that he had so stultified himself, and them.

It is apparent, sir, that the respondent, in causing Mr. Eaker to be arrested, acted in violation of law, and further, when he refused to hear the counsel of Mr. Eaker speak in his behalf. It is a constitutional privilege that every man enjoys of being represented by counsel if he desires it. Had Mr. Eaker been properly served with process, it was entirely optional with him whether he would have spoken a single word to the court, or whether he would have left it to his counsel to represent him; and more than that, if it was proper or necessary for Mr. Eaker to suggest, when the case was called, that he had not been served with process, his employed counsel had a constitutional right to make that suggestion for him, of which no court could deprive them without an arbitrary abuse of official power. Yet, sir, it seems that constitutional guaranties are mere gossamer when interposed between this Judge's whims and their gratification. When a regularly licensed attorney presumes to make a suggestion for his client, he is peremptorily ordered to take his seat, and shut his mouth. When he attempts to make a respectful remark, as "*amicus curiæ*," he is insultingly and harshly told that his friendship is not desired by the court. The lawyers at his bar must be so many dumb dogs, or make their every sentence conform to the humor of his caprice.

But this respondent not only acted wrong in imprisoning Eaker, but he knew it at the time, and did it to oppress Eaker, to injure Kitchen and Phelan, and to establish his own supremacy at the sacrifice of every opposing obstacle. Grant him all the mental imbecility he claims, and still he knew that the manner in which the mandamus was served gave him no jurisdiction over the person of Eaker, no right to have him arrested,—or why did he send Dowdy to serve the writ over again? Why did he discharge Eaker from imprisonment when he simply wrote upon the copy that John J. Jackson had handed him, what he and his lawyers had both previously told him, namely, that the writ had been served by a copy, and he was not bound to answer? Think of that, sir. When the case is called, he is told by Kitchen and Phelan there has been no service, and he merely insults them for their pains. He inspects the writ, finds himself there is no service, and sends Dowdy out to deliver the original to Eaker, and thus decoy him into an appearance. Mr. Eaker is attached, and when he simply writes upon the copy of the writ what the court already knew, that he had not been served, he is discharged. He had taken it into his head that Eaker should yield to him, and he determined that he should do so at all hazards, regardless of law, regardless of right, and regardless of his oath of office. He knew that Kitchen and Phelan had told their client that there was no difficulty in his cause,—that there had been no sufficient service of the writ; and he determined if possible to let Judge Eaker know, and to let all that audience know, that the opinions of Kitchen and Phelan were not to be relied upon. Mr. Hicks gives us the key to this in his testimony. He says, when Mr. Eaker was brought into court upon the attachment, the Judge said to him, "I don't suppose you meant to be in contempt; I suppose it was the fault of your lawyers; they didn't know their duty." There it is, sir. There's a splendid opportunity to give the professional success of Kitchen and Phelan a stab; and the respondent eagerly availed himself of it. He bullies them when they dare arise to speak for their client. He pursues a course toward them calculated to make all believe they do not know their duty. He then makes an example of Eaker, to show what difficulties their ignorance brings upon their clients; and when he is dragged before the court, he takes occasion to tell the community through those present that Jonas Eaker has been brought into trouble through the unreliable advice of his counsel, Kitchen and Phelan.

It is a principle well established in the law, that every sane man is conclusively presumed to intend the probable consequences of his own act. I shall show the authority for this before I conclude. Therefore, if you believe the respondent to be a sane man, and that it is oppressive to a man to be imprisoned unlawfully, or to be insulted and brow-beaten when he offers to speak to a court, you are bound to conclude that this respondent intended to oppress Eaker and his counsel. Ah! but says the respondent, "Mr. Eaker did not think my conduct oppressive." Sir, have you forgotten the evidence of Washington Carlisle? Did he not tell you that Mr. Eaker presented this respondent to the grand jury for this very act of oppression? If he did not think it oppressive, why did he make the affidavit he did, and cite the sixteenth section of the sixth article of the act concerning crimes and punishments? Has the respondent forgotten that little slip of paper that caused such a trepidation in him when it fell into the hands of the grand jury? I will remind him of it before I get through. If he intended to oppress Eaker, or Kitchen, or Phelan, and willfully did any act tending so to oppress either of them, he is guilty of a misdemeanor in office; and for every misdemeanor in office he is liable to impeachment. There is no evading this conclusion. It will force itself upon you. It is the evil intent you are to punish, not the amount of damage done.

Now, sir, the proof upon this article plainly shows the respondent willfully and maliciously guilty of three distinct offenses: disgracing the bench by a hectoring, contumelious, and insulting demeanor towards members of his bar, who were in the respectful and proper discharge of their duties; peremptorily and tyrannically depriving a citizen of the right guarantied to him by the constitution, of being heard by his counsel; and of violating the sacred right of personal liberty, in open contempt of every safeguard the constitution and laws of our country have sought to throw around it. And to you is submitted the question, whether such conduct, such open, gross, and infamous acts of unrestrained tyranny, shall be permitted to pollute your judiciary, destroying its efficacy, defeating all the beneficent objects for which it was established, and rendering it an engine of oppression to our citizens of the most dangerous and despicable character; or whether the majesty of law shall be vindicated, and the purity and dignity of our institutions protected.

You must go home and tell your constituency that you have licensed the courts to insult, abuse, and brow-beat any counsel whom they may employ to represent their interests; that you have licensed them to compel the citizen to answer to process whether it has been served upon him or not; that you have given them permission to drag the citizen away from the demands of his business, however urgent, from the bosom of his family, however much they may require his presence, and compel him to answer to a process that has never been served upon him: or you must tell them we have established the subordination of official authority to the law of the land; we have set the seal of condemnation upon judicial oppression; we have taught all whom the people have entrusted with power that they cannot render that power subservient to the gratification of their own passions without expecting certain and just retribution.

I cannot, sir, consistently with what yet remains for me to do in connection with this cause, dilate elaborately upon the character of the conduct of which the respondent is proven to have been guilty in this instance, nor upon the consequences that must inevitably result from permitting it to be indulged in without restraint by the courts of the country. I must leave it to those who have inherited the priceless legacy of freedom from the battle-beds of revolutionary sires, to determine whether it is worth the protection of the law, or is to be surrendered to the caprice of every petty despot who may be disposed to lord it over them:

for the field yet remaining for me to explore is far too wide; subjects demanding the scrutiny of this Court, and the condemnation of every patriotic citizen of the country, and remaining to be considered, are too numerous and too execrable in their natures to justify me in lingering upon the threshhold of the case. I must proceed to the next charge exhibited against the respondent, and request the Court to apply the facts disclosed by the evidence to the accusation; and if I am not much mistaken in the effect of plain, unequivocal testimony, upon honest and intelligent minds, I will be sustained in the assertion that no case was ever more clearly and fully established.

By the record, sir, which I hold in my hand, and which has been read as evidence to the Court, it is shown that at the November term, 1858, of the Stoddard Circuit Court, there was pending the case of Matthew H. Moore against James Walker, instituted by Mr. Moore for the purpose of obtaining possession of certain lots in the town of Bloomfield, where both the respondent and Mr. Walker reside. The second article charges upon the respondent an exhibition of willful and corrupt partiality in this case, utterly inconsistent with the duties of his position as Judge of the court in which the cause was pending, disgraceful to the character of the judiciary of the State, and in direct violation of the law it was his most sacred duty to maintain and uphold; and the evidence proves the charge true to the very letter. He is charged with advising Mr. Walker not to compromise this suit, assuring him that the field-notes of the town were lost, and that he would be successful. And Mr. Walker tells you in his testimony that there had been overtures of compromise made to him by Mr. Moore, but not being acceded to by him, were withdrawn; that one evening during the November term, 1858, of the Stoddard Circuit Court, the respondent came to him, near his stable in Bloomfield, and asked him if he and Moore had settled their difficulty about these lots; he told the respondent they had not, and he didn't know that they would; and that the respondent said to him, "I would not do it; the field-notes of the town are lost, and he can't hurt you." Here, sir, it is shown that he not only advised Walker not to compromise, but gives him his opinion upon the merits of the case; or rather assures him he will gain it, and gives him one of the best reasons for that opinion in the world, namely, that the field notes are lost and Moore can't identify his property. It is a matter of no kind of consideration with this immaculate Judge how justly Mr. Moore may have been entitled to the property in question, how much he had paid for it, or how unjustly Walker may have been keeping him out of it; he discovers a defect that must necessarily exist in Moore's proofs, and fearing that Mr. Walker is an honest man,—for this Court will say he *does* carry the very index of honesty in his face,—and will make a compromise in which justice may be done to both parties, he descends from the bench, finds Mr. Walker out, and officiously sets himself to work to fortify his mind against any such compromise, and gives him such assurances of success as to insure his not accepting Moore's proposition for an adjustment of the difficulty existing between them.

What a splendid example of judicial purity and impartiality is here presented! I challenge the world for a production of its parallel since the days of the illustrious Jeffreys, whom this Judge so successfully emulates! How the world will admire, and our own citizens venerate, a system that permits the Judge to act as counsellor for any party he may feel disposed to favor! How we should congratulate ourselves that it has been reserved for a Missouri Judge, with a single exertion of his towering genius, to make a discovery in the science of jurisprudence that the long succession of ages required for the perfection of the common law was inadequate to develop! How little our Legislature understood of the natural prerogatives,—"the divine right,"—of the judiciary, when they declared by statute that no Judge should act as counsellor in any case, and that for any willful partiality he should be fined a thousand dollars and imprisoned in the county jail for twelve months!

But the respondent says he gave this advice to Walker after the case had been removed by change of venue! Then why did he ask Walker if he had settled it? If he had just before made an order moving it out of the circuit, it is but reasonable that he should have known it was not settled, without asking. But unfortunately for the respondent, sir, Mr. Walker says he made no secret of what the Judge had advised him; he went straight and told several that he was safe; the Judge had told him he could gain his case. And Mr. Moore tells you he heard of the Judge having given this advice before he filed his petition for a change of venue.

The respondent then shifts his ground, and says the advice was given after the notice was given that a petition would be presented for a change of venue! But this won't do; for it is not in evidence that any notice of the kind was given. On the contrary, Mr. Moore tells you he prepared a petition and swore to it, and left it with Mr. Tyrell to obtain the change of venue for him, and went home without doing anything more. Sir, the respondent is forced to try another defense, and he does so; but what is it? Why, that this suit of Moore against Walker affected his interests incidentally, or collaterally; that he was the owner of lands somewhere contiguous to Bloomfield, the title to which was in some manner connected with the matter in controversy between Moore and Walker. I don't know whether this is true or not, sir. Mr. Tyrell, Mr. Bartlett, Mr. Kitchen, Mr. Phelan, Mr. Bedford, Mr. Miller, Mr. Hicks, and Mr. Owen, the Recorder, all live in Bloomfield, but you hear a syllable of no such thing from any of them. But suppose it *is* true: it only shows the conduct of the respondent to be if possible more corrupt and perfidious,—springing from motives of selfish interest. Let the respondent reflect for a single moment upon the unhappy predicament in which this wonderful defense places him, and he will see that he has exhibited himself to the world in the attitude of a Judge sacrificing the interests of a private party to the preservation of his own,—the meanest act, the basest tyranny of which he could have been guilty had he put his invention on the rack to produce the sublimated essence of corruption. My God! what a spectacle! A Circuit Judge, holding in one hand the law which was intended to protect alike the humblest citizen and the highest official in the State, and which he has sworn to apply faithfully to the protection of all; while with the other he ruthlessly seizes upon the rights of the defenseless private citizen, and immolates them upon the altar of his own self-aggrandizement! Can anything be more horrible or terrifying to the patriotic citizen? No matter how just Moore's claim to the property in question may have been, the establishment of it would have interfered with the interests of the Judge; and therefore the Judge may justify himself in violating the law and his oath of office, and in bringing disgrace upon the judiciary, by descending from the bench and taking upon himself the burden of his adversary's defense! The law, I suppose, is not made for the private citizen; it is only to enable the pampered despot, mantled in judicial robes, to sacrifice the rights of all around him to the preservation and advancement of his own interests! "Oh! shame, where is thy blush!"—when a Judge can resort to such a plea as this!—when he can ask this Court to tell the citizens of Missouri that, when their rights conflict with the interests of a Circuit Judge, the law affords them no protection!

It is established by the evidence beyond the power of controversion, that the respondent did act partially in this case; that he prejudged it, and apprised one of the parties of his judgment. Now, had he a right, or was it proper for him to have expressed an opinion in relation to it to anybody, let alone one of the parties? One of the most celebrated of the English Judges refused to express an opinion out of court upon a case likely to come before him for adjudication, even when specially solicited to do so by the king himself, upon the grounds, that if a man express an opinion in one place, the pride innate in every human bosom would influence him to make good that opinion anywhere else. So that if a Judge should give an opinion when off the bench, he would at least be tempted to support that opinion when on the bench, although wrong.

But, sir, if a Judge may be permitted to advise a party litigant before him in one case, he may in every case; and if he is permitted to espouse the cause of any party he may select in every case, the inquiry becomes pertinent, at what stage of the proceedings the privilege attaches, and at what stage he must cease its exercise. Can there be any restriction to the exercise of such a privilege by a Judge, unless it is prohibited entirely? What is to prevent him from giving his friend the advantage of his counsel, from the drafting of the declaration to the levying of his execution? Sir, establish this doctrine, and no man will appeal to the laws of his country until he has secured the good will and advice of the Judge; and to obtain this he would bring to bear upon him every appliance that can possibly tend to influence his feelings, so that a thousand avenues will be opened at once, through which corruption in as many insidious forms may invade the judiciary and effectually annihilate its efficacy, before any adequate remedy can be applied. The rich suitor, by means of his wealth, will procure a speedy promotion of his interests, at the expense of law and justice, while the squalid victim of "chill penury" will die at the gates of the temple of justice ere his cause is reached, through the immense accumulation of more favored causes in which the Judge is interested as counsellor. The friendless child of poverty will be permitted to rot in the suffocating vapors of the dungeon for a crime of which he is perhaps innocent, while red-handed murder will walk abroad at noonday arm in arm with the powers of the law and the administrators of justice.

Sir, it was wrong—common sense says it was wrong—for this respondent to act as he is proven to have done in this instance; and the statute not only plainly forbids a Judge to act as counsellor in any case, but provides that he shall be fined a thousand dollars and confined in jail for a year for any exhibition of willful partiality. Was he willfully partial? Was his advice voluntary or involuntary? Did he go to Walker of his own accord and in his sane mind give him this advice, or was he compelled to do it? If he was in his proper senses and under no compulsion, the act was willful; there is no escape from it. He tells you himself he did it because he had an interest in the matter; that it either directly or remotely involved the title to his own land. But, sir, there is another motive developed by the evidence. Mr. Moore tells you the respondent was unfriendly to him; and in consequence of this prejudice he was compelled to take a change of venue. Here, then, are sufficient incentives upon a will ready to be influenced to do wrong,—personal aggrandizement, and vengeance upon an enemy, hand in hand, both to be accomplished by one bold stroke of official crime!

I will dwell no longer upon this charge. The offense it alleges has been clearly proven. This Court will stamp it indellibly with the seal of indignant condemnation, and a virtuous, intelligent, and patriotic constituency will affirm the judgment.

I will now request the Court to turn their attention to the facts developed by the testimony in relation to the third article, in which the respondent is charged with willful and malicious oppression in sending the case of Limbarger *vs.* Powers from Wayne to Mississippi county, upon a change of venue. Mr. Fox and Mr. Bedford tell you that they were the counsel for the two parties,—Mr. Fox acting for Mr. Limbarger, and Mr. Bedford for Mr. Powers. That when Mr. Limbarger had determined to have the cause removed to another circuit, on account of the prejudices of the Judge being arrayed against him, there was a consultation between them as to the proper county to which the case should be sent. Mr. Fox proposed Madison, but Mr. Bedford objected to that county because Mr. Fox resided there. Iron and Bollinger were then mentioned, and it was agreed that either of them would be suitable. Whereupon Mr. Fox presented his petition to the Judge for a change of venue; the Judge examined the petition, and in a tone of voice betraying considerable feeling, ordered the change to Mississippi county. Mr. Fox instantly arose to expostulate against the cause being sent to so remote a county, and assured the court he had consulted Mr. Power's counsel, and they had agreed the case should be sent either to Iron or Bollinger. Mr. Powers, and Mr. Bedford, his counsel, were both present and tacitly assented to Mr. Fox's representations of the agreement. But the respondent in a harsh and insulting manner orders Mr. Fox to shut his mouth; "the order has been made and shall not be changed." Mr. Pipkin, who was associate counsel with Mr. Fox for Mr. Limbarger, arose, and in a respectful manner called the attention of the court to the fact that either of those other counties would be suitable, but that sending the cause to Mississippi would drive him out of the case. To Mr. Pipkin the respondent replied in a rude and insulting style, that it was no concern of his if he *was* driven out of the case; and when Mr. Fox requested him to rescind the order entirely, and informed him he would rather the case should remain where it was than to follow it to Mississippi, the respondent told him he would fine him if he thought it would not be construed into a personal matter. That these are the facts, sir, there can be no possible dispute. No witness he has introduced controverts any of them. Mr. White merely states he was not consulted at all about it, but it was never pretended by any one that he had been. Mr. Powers was introduced, but he merely states that Mr. Bedford objected to the case going to Madison, as Bedford says himself.

Now, sir, was this conduct proper, or was it oppressive? Examine the fourth section of the statute regulating changes of venue, and you will find the duty of the court under the circumstances clearly defined. It was simply to ascertain what county would be most convenient to Mr. Powers under all the circumstances, and to award a change of venue to that county. But does he do so? Mr. White, Mr. Fox, Mr. Bedford, and others I believe, testify that from Greenville, the county seat of Wayne, where this cause was pending, it is by the usual route over a hundred miles to the county seat of Mississippi; while from the residence of both parties to Ironton, the county seat of Iron, it is only about twenty or twenty-five miles, and about twenty-five to the county seat of Bollinger, from the same point.

The parties are therefore compelled to travel four times as far, and subjected to four times the expense; while there is not a single advantage insured to either. On the contrary, the trouble and expenses of both parties are not only multiplied to a grievious and burdensome extent, but the chances of a speedy trial are very materially diminished; for it is hardly to be presumed that all the witnesses on both sides of the case could find it convenient to leave their families and business and go upon a journey of over a hundred miles, while there would be but comparatively little difficulty in procuring their attendance upon a court within twenty or twenty-five miles of them. And more than that, sir, every single lawyer engaged in the cause is compelled to abandon it! Ah! but says the respondent in his answer to this article, with a recklessness characteristic of him, "I supposed good lawyers could be obtained in Mississippi." I have no reason, sir, to suppose otherwise myself; there may be, and no doubt are, learned and talented lawyers there; but I ask if that fact justifies the respondent in tyrannically snatching business out of the hands of Fox, Bedford, Pipkin, and White? The respondent intended that portion of his answer as a witticism, and I am quite content he shall have the benefit of a sarcasm purchased by a forfeiture of the respect of every good man that will read it. Had he a right to compel Limbarger and Powers to resort to counsel they had perhaps never seen, although they *might* have been learned and talented?

But, sir, did the respondent willfully intend to act oppressively in this instance? If the probable and reasonable consequences of his act were grievous and oppressive, you are compelled by the law under your oath to conclude that he maliciously did it for that purpose. If I deliberately fire a pistol in the midst of this audience without any assignable motive, and a man is thereby slain whom I have never seen before, it is a conclusion of law—an inevitable, conclusive presumption—that I maliciously intended to take that man's of life, and I will be held guilty of murder. And, sir, the same principle applies to every variety of voluntary human action. If a man do any wrongful act whatever, by which any injury accrues to another, he is conclusively presumed by the law to do the act for the purpose of inflicting the injury naturally resulting from it. Now, sir, was it likely to be any more oppressive to Limbarger and Powers to be compelled to undergo the hardship of over four times as much travel as was necessary? Was it right, or would you consider it oppressive, to quadruple the costs, and diminish the chances of a speedy trial, by sending their cause over a hundred miles away,—where, sir, you are informed it has not been tried to this day,—while there were three courts within twenty or twenty-five miles of the parties where no obstacle to the proper administration of justice existed? Will you entertain no suspicion of oppressive, malicious intent upon the part of this man, when you see him sending a case *through* three counties,—Cape Girardeau, Bollinger, and Scott,—either of which would have been much more convenient to all concerned than the county of Mississippi? Was it no oppression to Mr. Fox, Mr. Pipkin, or Mr. Bedford to be driven out of their case, when there was not the slightest necessity for it? He cannot plead ignorance of the probability that all these consequences would result from his unprecedented order in this cause, for he was told earnestly and repeatedly by counsel at the time that it would be so, and on the next morning was requested to rescind the order and leave the case there, subject as it was to be biased by his prejudices, rather than that the parties and witnesses should be subject to such unheard of inconvenience and hardship; but, sir, these expostulations are only answered by contumely and insult.

We are not, however, left to a presumption of malice only; the circumstances attending the case, every one, tend to show he was acting directly under the influence of that passion; for, sir, if he was actuated by no bitterness of feeling, if he intended to do the parties or counsel no wrong, why did he, when they attempted to address him in a respectful manner, answer them with an insult? If there was any valid reason why the cause should not have been sent to Iron, Bollinger, Cape Girardeau, or Scott, why did he not with that politeness always characteristic of a gentleman point out the obstacle? Or if Mississippi was the only county to which it was proper to send the case, why did he not gentlemanly and courteously suggest the reason? If he did not intend to oppress the lawyers engaged in the case, why did he manifest such a brutal disregard for their feelings as well as their interests? Why did he persist in a course that he was assured would drive them out of the case, if he did not intend they should be driven out? And why, sir, I ask, does he claim in his answer to these articles the despotic prerogative of sending a case to any county, however remote? Because, sir, a habitual course of reckless disregard to the rights and interests of all others had induced in his mind the idea that he was supreme, sovereign in his own courts. He is actuated by no bad motive, although when a petition for a change of venue is presented to him, he imposes grievances of the most unprecedented character, and when respectfully requested to mitigate the consequences of his order by selecting a more convenient county, he insults and abuses all concerned by an outburst of angry passion disgraceful to himself and disgusting to others. But pardon me, sir; I forgot that he never becomes disturbed or excited! The current of his feelings is as gentle as the breath of evening's zephyr kissing the violet's closing eyes. His temper is as placid as sleeping infancy, as harmless as the dimpled smile of the new-born babe. The milk of roses runs through his every vein. *He* never says anything that will wound a lawyer's feelings!

I need not, Mr. President, enter upon a minute examination of the evidence to demonstrate that almost a precisely similar course of unjust and unwarranted oppression was pursued by the respondent, as charged in the fourth and fifth articles. The three cases mentioned in these articles are sent to Pemiscot county, in spite of the protestations of Mr. Phelan and Mr. Bedford, and I believe some others of the lawyers engaged in them, that it was the most inconvenient and inaccessible county that could be selected, and would effectually drive them out of the cases. But the defendant comes in, and in his defense to these two articles admits the correctness of the principle laid down by the House of Representatives, that it was his duty to send these cases to the most convenient county, by contending that he did so,—that Pemiscot was most convenient to all parties. This I do not believe; the respondent don't believe it; and no sensible man can believe it from the testimony.

It is true, sir, as Mr. Bedford tells you, that Dunklin and Pemiscot counties are geographically contiguous, but there is between them an almost impassable swamp. Mr. Walker, one of the respondent's witnesses, tells you that at certain seasons of the year, when the water is too low to be navigated in boats or dug-outs, and the mud too deep for horseback travel, it is entirely impassable; and he is corroborated by Mr. Bedford and Mr. Phelan, Dr. Horner, and perhaps others, when he says that communication between the two counties is carried on by means of dug-outs or skiffs, or other small craft. He also tells you that from the point of embarkation in Dunklin to Portage, in Pemiscot, is about sixty-five miles, and from Portage to Gayoso, the county seat, about fifteen, making about eighty miles' travel for the parties and witnesses by the dug-out and skiff route; while Mr. Bedford, as well as Mr. Walker, tells you that in order to go from one county seat to the other, by land, you would be compelled to travel over two hundred miles, and that through Scott and New Madrid. Dr. Horner tells you that he thinks Pemiscot is the most convenient county; but although the Doctor honestly thinks so, you do not, I am confident, even from the facts exhibited in his own testimony. He tells you that this swamp must be crossed in boats of some kind. He tells you in answer to a question propounded by myself, that but few, if any, of the witnesses or parties in these cases, keep dug-outs or boats for the purpose of crossing the swamp; that in order to cross, each party must pay five dollars ferriage, and hire a horse or other conveyance to travel the remaining fifteen miles over land, which would cost an additional dollar, whilst the distance from one county seat to the other, and the average distance traveled by the witnesses, according to his testimony, would be about thirty-five miles. Now, sir, here is an expense incurred by each witness in going to and returning from the place of trial, of twelve dollars for traveling expenses alone, without his board-bill; and what, according to the Doctor's estimate of the distance, will he get in fees? Why, sir, five cents a mile, each way, making three dollars and fifty cents, which, taken from his traveling expenses, leaves each witness minus eight dollars and fifty cents of his own money, granting that the dollar a day he receives for each day's attendance at court will pay his board-bill. Yet, sir, there is no hardship, no oppression in forcing these witnesses to incur this expense, or, rather, in depriving the parties of the benefit of their testimony, for you very well know not one of them would attend court under such circumstances.

But the respondent contends that, as the defendants in each of these cases took the change of venue, he was bound to send the causes to the county most convenient to the plaintiffs. This is very true, but what county would be most convenient? Why, manifestly, that county in which the speediest trial can be obtained, with the least expense; for it behooves a plaintiff, when he is compelled to resort to the law, to have the earliest determination possible of his rights. Now, sir, how does Pemiscot county suit the plaintiffs in this particular, according to the evidence of Dr. Horner, the respondent's main witness? He tells you that the county seat of this county is extremely liable to inundation, particularly in the spring of the year, and that in consequence of the high waters there has been no court in that county for the last two springs! So that, although he is counsel in all three of these cases, he has not been in Pemiscot county since they have been sent there, nearly two years ago. Mr. Walker, another one of the lawyers in these cases, says he has not been there. Mr. Phelan, Mr. Bedford, and Mr. Kitchen have not, and never expect to be. The Judge of the Circuit Court has not even been there. So the cases have not yet been tried, and the Lord knows when they will be! Yet the plaintiffs can be kept out of their rights for years, witnesses and parties be subjected to an enormous traveling expense, lawyers driven out of the cases and deprived of business, and still there is nothing wrong or oppressive in all this!

I think this Court is fully prepared to appreciate the motives that actuated a course of conduct unjust, arbitrary, and oppressive, as this must surely be regarded by every honest man. Here are Kitchen, Phelan, and Bedford, all of whom the respondent dislikes, and holds himself prepared to annoy and harrass whenever a convenient opportunity is presented. They assure him that by sending these cases to Pemiscot, he will deprive them of the right and privilege of attending to their clients' causes. His evil nature prompts him, and he says in his heart, "Ah ha! I have now a chance for vengeance, and I will embrace it by using my official power to diminish the business of these loathed objects of my hate. I will compel them to try all their causes before me, or they shall not try them at all. I will send them to the utmost parts of the State, or I will drive them out of their cases."

He was fully apprised of all the evil and oppressive consequences that would result from his action in these cases; he was assured that the counsel for the parties had, in all the cases, agreed upon a county where such difficulties did not exist; and there is no escaping the conviction that he deliberately and maliciously intended that the oppressive and burthensome consequences should result from the changes of venue that have been proven to exist in these cases.

Now, sir, I presume that the statute allowing changes of venue was enacted for the best of purposes. It was, sir, that the stream of justice, emanating from a fountain of crystal purity, might be preserved from even a suspicion of contamination. It was, sir, that society might be enabled to comply with its compact with each of its constituents with the utmost fidelity, and that the law might in every instance be administered without the possibility of injustice; and it is for you to say whether this beneficent object shall be defeated, and the means ordained for its accomplishment made a machine for the oppression of those it was designed to protect; or whether it shall be carried out in good faith. Your duty, sir, is too plain for further argument or comment. If the citizen who sees proper to avail himself of his legal right to have his cause sent for trial to a court where he can obtain justice is subjected to insult, abuse, and oppression, for claiming that privilege, and there is no redress for the wrong, it is a disgrace to the character of the State to allow that provision to remain in the statute a single day longer. It is a deceitful promise of a privilege to the honest citizen that is impossible to be observed in good faith.

The respondent has said, with his usual regard for his legal reputation, that however wrong and injurious his conduct in these cases may have been, the proper remedy was by appeal to the Supreme Court; that there the party injured can get full redress for any oppression to which he may be subjected in having his case sent to a remote and inconvenient county.

I will not insult the good sense of this Court by asking you to seriously notice for a single moment a position so extremely ridiculous, for every one must see at a glance that the Supreme Court could only say what the statute itself says, that cases must be sent upon changes of venue to the most convenient county; and besides, the order changing the venue of a cause confers upon the court to which the cause is sent complete jurisdiction over it, and if that court is guilty of no error after the cause comes within its jurisdiction, the order sending it there would be no grounds for reversing the judgment, simply because the county was remote and inconvenient. A lawyer that would express such an opinion ought to have his license taken from him; but even if correct, this proceeding is not intended to redress private grievances. It is to punish a public outrage, and prevent a recurrence of such dangerous and disgraceful offenses in future.

But, sir, I must proceed to the consideration of the charge contained in the sixth article, which, I must say, sir, sustained, as I shall show it is, by the most irrefragable evidence, is well characterized in the article itself, as not only unbecoming the position of this respondent as a Judge, but disgraceful to his character as a man. No man of proper feelings, no man whose bosom is animated by the noble sentiments that give the human being preëminence in the scale of created beings, can contemplate the facts developed by the witnesses in relation to this and the succeeding charge, without a thrill of indignant horror.

There is a degree of magnanimity in an open foe, who places himself upon an equality with his adversary, who would scorn to avail himself of a mean advantage over his enemy, and who would spurn with indignation a revenge to be obtained by ignoble means. Even the deadly rattlesnake that coils in our path is entitled to a portion of our respect, because he gives us warning ere he strikes his venomed fangs into our flesh. But here, sir, we have a Judge of the Circuit Court, sheltering himself under the panoply of his office, making use of the power incidental to his position to glut a fiendish vengeance, by affixing to the reputation of a lawyer practicing in his courts a foul and damning slander, that must haunt him like an unquiet spirit through his whole life. Here we see a grave and dignified Judge, seated upon the bench for the administration of justice, in open court, in the presence of a large concourse of citizens from all parts of the country, deliberately accusing a lawyer at his bar of a disgraceful crime; and when that lawyer offers to repel the charge, his foul traducer locks his mouth, that the crowd, infected by the poison of his slanderous breath, might spread it far and wide,—that the current of base detraction his malice had set in motion might grow into a resistless tide of calumny, whose remorseless waves would forever swallow up the fair fame of his unhappy victim.

Sir, there is no escaping the weight, the force of the facts we have proven. Mr. Bedford and Mr. Kitchen, as well as Mr. Phelan himself, tell you that while the case of Gibson *vs.* Dunn was on trial in the Butler Circuit Court, Mr. Phelan, being one of the counsel in the case, arose to address the jury, when the respondent accused him from the bench of tampering with the grand jury; that Mr. Phelan offered to say something in reply, but was told by the court he should not,—that he should go on with that case, and explain afterwards; and that Mr. Phelan replied, "I think not, Judge," and sat down.

Now, sir, here it is plainly proven that this Judge, without any apparent cause, charges Mr. Phelan with the crime of *embracery*, tells him he is in contempt of court, and refuses to allow him to utter a single syllable by way of denial or palliation of the charge; and the respondent, feeling the overwhelming weight of this proof, pretends that he merely intended to notify Mr. Phelan that he was in contempt! Is that the way such notice should have been given, sir, by enunciating a foul slander against him, to be scattered by that crowd far and wide through the country? I must be permitted to say, sir, that this excuse, in my opinion, is an after-thought; that such an intention had no existence in the mind of this respondent at the time he made the ignominious assault upon Mr. Phelan's character, because we hear nothing more of this alleged contempt after the slander is perpetrated. This immaculate court makes no further attempt to vindicate its wounded dignity. Mr. Phelan is never called to the bar, notified explicitly of what his offense consisted in, and permitted to defend himself. None of these things were done, because this Judge knew that Phelan was innocent of any wrong. He had accomplished his design, and sated vengeance, like the gorged lion, slumbered in its lair.

But what had Phelan done to call this storm of judicial wrath upon his head? Let us probe this matter to the bottom, and see whether this respondent's conduct upon that occasion was actuated by such a tender regard for the peace and dignity of the State as he would fain make you believe, or whether it sprung from other motives.

It seems, sir, that the respondent had been guilty, or at least supposed to be guilty, of some kind of oppression or other misdemeanor in office, for which Mr. Phelan, the injured party, had, as every other citizen of the State who feels himself called upon has, a right to make complaint to the grand jury. It is also in evidence that this respondent was boarding with one William Henley, a bosom friend and crony, who was a member of the grand jury; that during the recess for dinner on the day in question the respondent and Mr. Henley had a private interview, in which Mr. Henley informed the respondent that Mr. Phelan was about to prefer a charge against him for official misconduct, oppression, or some abuse of official power. This intelligence, while it excites his fears of personal disgrace, and arouses his invention to devise means of escape, calls out all the envenomed feeling that rankles in his bosom, all the malice that belongs to his revengeful nature. He fears he will be indicted, and he seeks to forestall public opinion by laying it all to the malignity of Phelan. He desires to create the impression in advance that the indictment against him was obtained through the criminal interference of Phelan with the grand jury. He intends, too, to ruin Phelan's character. He therefore selects the moment when all eyes are upon him, when he is just in the act of addressing a jury, knowing that if he does not succeed in blasting his reputation he will so discompose him that it will be impossible for him to acquit himself with credit in his case. I ask every reasonable mind if these conclusions are not legitimate from the evidence?

But, sir, the testimony gives this dark picture of official corruption a still more revolting feature. Mr. Phelan tells you that, when he found he was not to be permitted to vindicate himself, he sat down and drew up an affidavit accusing Mr. William Henley with having disclosed the secrets of the grand jury; and you are told by members of that grand jury that, when this presentment was made by Mr. Phelan, Judge Jackson came into the grand jury room and told them they could not indict Henley for what he had done; that a member of the grand jury had a right to tell the *Judge* anything that transpired before them in their retirement; that it took the grand jury, the Judge, and Circuit Attorney to constitute the court! What makes the Judge any more the repository of the secrets of a grand jury than the Clerk, or Sheriff, or any private citizen, I can't see; nor can I divine why they should be instructed that they could violate their oaths by telling one man the secrets of their deliberations and not another. But, sir, let the honest, intelligent constituencies of Missouri contemplate this disgusting spectacle of judicial corruption; let them behold one of their Circuit Judges guilty of the grossest acts of oppression and misconduct, brutally tyrannizing over an unoffending citizen because he has dared to appeal to the powers of the law for protection, and then descending from the bench, obtruding upon the privacy of the grand jury, and there using the influence of his official position to shield a bosom friend from justly merited punishment, because he had warned him that an inquiry had been instituted before the grand jury as to the propriety of his official conduct; and if there is an honest heart that will not revolt at the loathsome, disgusting sight, my imagination can conceive of no exhibition of abject, foul, fiendish depravity that could excite its condemnation.

But, sir, the respondent seeks to palliate this charge because Mr. Kitchen tells you that, after the respondent had refused to permit Phelan to defend himself against the accusations he there publicly alleged against him, Phelan remarked that the charges were *false* or a *lie*, which expression he did not recollect. Ah! sir, how greedily the respondent caught at that morsel of evidence! How he clung to it! But I appeal to you—I appeal to every member of this Court—I appeal to every one whose bosom heaves with the emotions of a human heart, if you had been thus assailed,—if a disgraceful criminal charge had been brought against you in the presence of hundreds, who would scatter it among the community from which you draw your support,—if your lips had been sealed, and all opportunity of self-defense denied you,—had it been the last act of your life, would you not have hurled the lie into the teeth of your vile accuser, with an indignant, scornful defiance that would have transfixed the foul tyrant upon the spot? If there is one here who claims the name of an American freeman that would not, let him seek another land,—let him go to climes where the very air he breathes will awaken no noble, no manly emotion in his soul!

The next article, sir, contains a charge of a kindred nature, but of even more atrocity, and is as unequivocally sustained by the proof. It is here charged, sir, that without provocation even, much less legal cause, this respondent from the bench, in open court, accused David M. Fox of the crime of perjury or subornation of perjury! Mr. Fox, Mr. Bedford, and Mr. Kitchen, all tell you plainly and emphatically that the respondent called the attention of Mr. Fox to a piece of paper which he held in his hand and asked him if he wrote it, or if it was in his handwriting. Mr. Fox replied that it was. The respondent then said to him, "sir, you have either *sworn to a lie yourself*, *or made your client do so.*" It did not escape your observation how the respondent hung out for the *exact* words when the witnesses were testifying, nor how he prevaricated when he came to speak of the testimony upon this point yesterday. Nor, sir, have you forgotten how clearly all the witnesses corroborated each other as to the exact words used by the respondent. Had a meteor exploded in the court room at the time of which they spoke they would have been as likely to have forgotten it as the remarkable language used by the respondent on that occasion. Mr. Bedford says, "for some reason there appeared to be a hiatus in the business of the court, and Mr. Fox and myself were seated at a table close together,—Mr. Fox was perhaps writing when the Judge called his attention to the paper, and asked him if he wrote it," &c. No one was looking for such an extraordinary outburst. It was like a startling peal of thunder in a clear sky; it made an impression never to be effaced. That he used the identical language they swear to, there can be no particle of doubt. True, Mr. Hicks in his testimony says, that his recollection is distinct that the language of the Judge was, "one of these must be false;" but it is clear that he alludes to an entirely different case. Mr. Fox tells you the paper (and at the time the Judge had but the one paper in his hand) was an amended answer in a case in which the original answer had been stricken out; that his client had made affidavit to one and he to the other; hence the expression "you have sworn to a lie yourself, or made your client do so." Mr. Bedford and Mr. Kitchen both say the Judge had *one* paper in his hand, but know nothing of the case to which it related, but distinctly remember the expression. Now Mr. Hicks don't recollect the term of court nor the case, but remembers that Fox's client, whoever he was, had sworn to *two papers*, and whilst one of these papers was under discussion the Judge had both in his hand, and remarked that one of them must be false. So it is plain that Mr. Hicks's testimony, so far from conflicting with that of the other witnesses, only shows another case in which the Judge was guilty of unbecoming language. He was not speaking of the same case; and there can be no doubt, sir, that this respondent whilst seated upon the bench was wilfully and deliberately guilty of the vilest calumniation of Mr. Fox. After it is proven upon him he can make no excuse, nor offer any palliation. He don't even pretend that it was true that Fox was guilty, but seeks to show by Mr. Hicks that he was not guilty of speaking the words.

And now, sir, I ask in the name of the people of my State, in the name of all they hold dear, in the name of all for which the protection of the law has been promised, if such conduct as this shall be tolerated?—if our Circuit Courts, instead of being examples of virtue, the dispensers of justice, and the means of protection to the citizen, are to be converted into engines of iniquity and oppression?—if our Judges are to entrench themselves behind their official power and heap such damning slanders as this upon the members of the bar, and the private citizen, and be held guiltless?

It was a favorite remark of President Jackson, and one which he desired might be written in letters of gold upon the walls of our national capitol, that "the slanderer is worse than the murderer;" and I believe, sir, with Fielding, that vice has no more abject slave,—society produces no more odious vermin,—nor can the devil receive a guest more worthy of him, nor possibly more welcome to him, than the slanderer. No fiend in human shape can inflict a wrong more deadly. The ruthless hand of robbery may deprive you of your gold, but industry will replace it; the incendiary's torch may lay your dwelling in ruins about you, but upon the ashes of your home the skillful architect will rear a more splendid edifice; the assassin may plant his thirsty dagger in your heart, yet while your loving wife and little ones weep around your early grave, they can rejoice in the rich heritage of a spotless name you have left behind you, and as they come year by year to strew around your tomb affection's offering of vernal flowers, you will look down and beckon them to the happiness of your bright abode. But who shall replace the gem of character the slanderer's thievish hand has snatched from its casket? Who shall extinguish the embers of scorn and suspicion that ever linger upon the site of ruined hopes destroyed by the baleful fires of calumny? Where, oh! where is the hand to close the gaping wounds the murderer of your reputation makes? Who would dry the widow's tear that she might gaze upon a dead husband's blasted name? Who will avert the glance of scorn from the homeless orphan, when the nightshade springs rankly upon the grave of his dishonored sire?

"The purest treasure mortal times afford
Is spotless reputation; that away,
Man is but gilded loam, or painted clay."

Living, you can cherish no jewel more rare; dying, you can leave no legacy more rich. Yet, sir, a Judge of the Circuit Court can trample this priceless pearl beneath his feet, and when appeal is made to the authorities of the State to tear from him the ermine he thus disgraces, he will ask you to say he has been guilty of no wrong! I know not, sir, whether I should have waited for the slow interposition of the law or not; but had you been placed in Mr. Fox's situation, you would have throttled the tyrant in his seat,—you would have dragged him from the bench, and choked his slanderous tongue from his lying throat, had he not instantly retracted the foul aspersion upon your character.

But, sir, I do not ask that this case shall be viewed through the distorting medium of passion. Look at it in the calm, clear light of reason, law, and justice. Suppose the respondent had inflicted an enormous fine upon Mr. Fox, or sent him to jail, or shot him down in the bar without any provocation, is there a sane man in the Union that would say he should not be impeached and hurled headlong into infamy and disgrace? Well, sir, turn to the seventh section of our bill of rights, and you will find your character placed side by side with your person and your property, and declared equally entitled to protection; and the respondent, when he took upon himself his oath of office, swore he would protect it with the same fidelity that your life, liberty, or property should be. Yet, he perpetrates one of the most outrageous slanders upon the fair fame of a citizen that malignity can invent, and does so, too, in open court, whilst sitting as the impersonation of justice, and without a shadow of provocation; and still would have you believe he is one of most amiable characters, one of the most angelic creatures in the world! Oh! no! *he* never indulges in an expression that can touch the most exquisite sensitiveness! His temper is as smooth and placid as a summer lake ere the evening breeze wreaths its tranquil face with tiny wavelets! He never *can* be excited—"*annoyed*," perhaps, is the utmost term that can be applied to him! Oh! he *is*—

"As mild a mannered man as ever scuttled ship or cut a throat,"

—there is no doubt of it.

So far as the eighth article is concerned, sir, inasmuch as the respondent objects to any adjudication upon it in the absence of the record, I will pass it over, notwithstanding he has, on more than one occasion during this trial, expressly admitted every fact it contains. In his answer to this article he has denied the existence of the case, which made it incumbent upon us to produce the record; but in his address to the Court he has repeatedly admitted it, and not only that, but detailed every circumstance connected with it. But as the record has been unfortunately mislaid, I will not ask you to believe the evidence he has given himself upon the article, but proceed to consider what I esteem a palpable violation of his oath of office.

The constitution, sir, guaranties to every citizen the privilege, whenever his liberty is restrained illegally or otherwise, of having a writ of habeas corpus issued by some competent authority, and an inquiry instituted as to the cause of his confinement, and for the purpose of having such relief afforded to him as the circumstances of his case might show him entitled to.

The Judges of the Circuit Courts throughout the State are made by law, with others, the proper authority for carrying this provision of the constitution into effect. They are made the agencies by which this beneficent provision may be applied to the protection of the citizen; and whenever a proper state of facts is presented to a Judge of the Circuit Court showing a necessity for the issuing of a writ of habeas corpus, he is bound under his oath of office to issue it, unless the privilege has been suspended by the Legislature, in consequence of invasion or rebellion. It is a right that every citizen has of demanding this writ, and that no Circuit Judge has a right to refuse,—for, sir, it is nonsense to provide in the constitution that this privilege shall never be suspended, if a citizen may be deprived of it by a stubborn or corrupt Judge. And more, sir, being a duty especially incumbent upon a Judge of the Circuit Court, if he neglect or refuse to issue a writ of habeas corpus when properly applied for, he is liable to indictment and impeachment for a misdemeanor in office, in not discharging the duties enjoined upon him by law. I have read to you not only common law authorities, but the statute in relation to such offenses, and it is unnecessary to do so now.

It is charged, sir, that the respondent, without any justifiable excuse, refused to issue a writ of habeas corpus, notwithstanding there was a petition therefor, proper in every particular, duly presented to him. I will read the petition. [Mr. Knott here read the petition of Atterbury for writ of habeas corpus.] The facts connected with this transaction as detailed by Mr. Phelan are substantially these: Wm. W. Atterbury was under indictment in Dunklin county for some offense, but had never been arrested. Coming, however, into Stoddard county, David G. Hicks, without any warrant or authority of law whatever, arrested him and took him to Dunklin. Being a comparative stranger in that county, it was impossible for him to procure bail, but he could do so in Stoddard county, where he was acquainted. In this emergency his son, William M. Atterbury, presented to the respondent the petition for a writ of habeas corpus that I have just read; but the respondent refused to issue the writ, not because Atterbury was not entitled to it, but because David G. Hicks was charged with having taken Atterbury without a regular warrant. He told Phelan he suspected it was a trap set for Mr. Hicks in order to get him into a difficulty, and he would not issue the writ; but seeing upon reflection the difficulty this would lead him into, he writes upon the petition 'the fifth section not complied with.' But will this after-thought relieve him? What does the fifth section require? Simply that a copy of the cause of commitment shall accompany the petition, unless the prisoner has been removed, or a copy has been requested and refused.

Now, sir, in this instance it is apparent to every member of this Court that this section of the habeas corpus act could not be complied with. The petition itself shows there *was* no warrant or process of any kind, and alleges that very fact as a reason why the imprisonment was illegal. Was it not adding insult to injury to require this man to file with his petition a copy of what he had just sworn had no existence? If Hicks had arrested this man, and held him in custody without a *capias*, or warrant of any kind, as was sworn to in the petition, how in the name of reason could this section have been complied with? But even had there been a warrant of any kind by virtue of which Atterbury was held in custody, the petitioner was excused from presenting a copy of it because the prisoner had been removed to Dunklin county, some sixty or seventy miles distant.

But, sir, seeing that this pitiful quibble will not avail him, he resorts to another. He says that before Atterbury's petition was presented, he had escaped from custody. It was fortunate for him, perhaps, that he had escaped; but does that excuse the respondent? That was no part of the reason why he refused the writ, for Atterbury was sixty or seventy miles away, and he knew nothing of his escape at the time; and, besides, had his escape been known, there would have been no necessity for presenting the petition.

But he urges, again, that Atterbury was never in jail. Grant he never was; does that constitute an excuse for the respondent? He did not know when he refused the writ but what he was in a dungeon. But, sir, we are not here asking this Court to avenge Atterbury's wrongs, but we are asking you to maintain the supremacy and authority of the constitution. We are demanding that when an officer takes upon himself an oath to support that constitution, he shall be made to support at least its most vital provisions,—that he shall not be permitted to deprive the citizen of one of his most inestimable privileges,—his right to the writ of habeas corpus.

I will ask the Court to contrast the rigid, technical adherence to the very letter of the statute to which the respondent pretends in this instance, with his utter recklessness and disregard for the rights of the State, exhibited in the outrageous and disgraceful abuse of official authority of which he was guilty in turning loose upon the community in which he lives a couple of felons, in direct and open contravention of law.

In this instance, Atterbury admits he is under indictment in Dunklin county; but while he alleges his imprisonment to be without warrant or authority of law, he merely claims the privilege of giving bail, and urges upon the Judge that he can, if permitted, procure bail in Stoddard county, where he is acquainted. He intimates no desire to escape the operation of the law, but that whilst he is held to answer for a bailable offense, he merely wants the constitutional right of bail. Yet, sir, his petition is spurned, his constitutional rights are disregarded by the officer whose sworn obligation it is to guard and protect them, because an adjudication of the matter may possibly implicate the special object of his partiality,—Mr. Hicks,—in the false imprisonment of a citizen. But how different is his conduct in relation to John R. Main and Charles Russell, two felons recently brought before him and claiming and obtaining their discharge upon a flimsy technicality.

This record, sir, which I presume it is not necessary for me to read now, as you have already heard it, shows that Main had been arrested, and examined before Mr. Cravey, a Justice of the Peace of Stoddard county, on a charge of grand larceny; that Mr. Cravey had found from the evidence that there was probable cause to believe him guilty, and in default of bail, had committed him to jail, and delivered him into the custody of John J. Jackson, Deputy Sheriff of Stoddard county. These facts appear upon the face of the petition sworn to by Main himself. This record, together with the testimony of Mr. Jackson and Mr. Tyrell, shows also that while Main was in the custody of John J. Jackson, who was preparing to take him to jail, Main preferred his petition to the respondent for a writ of habeas corpus, setting forth that he was illegally restrained of his liberty, because the Justice had not taken *his* statement according to law. The respondent issued the writ; it was served upon the Deputy Sheriff, and he made return that he held the prisoner by virtue of a warrant of commitment signed by James Cravey, Justice of the Peace, and exhibited a copy of the warrant with his return. This warrant, sir, which has been read to the Court, clearly and specifically set forth that Main was held in custody to answer to a charge of grand larceny. It is plain and unequivocal in its language. Yet, sir, the respondent, with this warrant before him, discharges Main; and what for, pray? Because there is no reason to believe he should be held to answer for a felony? By no means. Because he had reason to believe him innocent of any crime? Not at all. But foul with crime as he had every reason to believe him, he liberated him on account of an informality—and an immaterial one at that, sir—in the warrant of commitment. Permit me to read the order discharging him:

The State of Missouri *versus* John Main. } Charged with Grand Larceny.

The defendant being brought before me in obedience to the within writ, and there being no charge brought against him, nor any evidence produced against him, and there being no evidence that he had been legally arrested and tried before a committing magistrate, or before any one having authority to commit him to the custody of the Jailor of Stoddard county, and the paper herewith presented as a mittimus not being sufficient in form and substance to authorize the Jailor of Stoddard county to hold him, the said John Main, in custody, it is ordered that he be forthwith discharged.

January 7th, 1859. ALBERT JACKSON.

There, sir, the only pretext for discharging this man is a pretended informality in the warrant of commitment; but suppose there had been a real insufficiency in the warrant of commitment, would he have been justified in discharging him? Let us recur to the statute and see thirteenth section, third article, of the habeas corpus act:

When the imprisonment is for a criminal or supposed criminal matter, the court or magistrate before whom the prisoner shall be brought, under the provisions of this act, *shall not* discharge him for *any informality, insufficiency, or irregularity* of the commitment.

Sir, the originators of that section were men of thought, of wisdom, of observation. They were sensible of the fact that by far the largest proportion of our committing magistrates are men of but little experience in drafting legal documents, from the fact that they are generally selected from among the various industrial avocations of life, and are precluded by their business engagements from devoting that degree of time and attention to such matters as is necessary to insure perfect accuracy. They were aware too, sir, that it might possibly happen that a magistrate authorized to issue a writ of habeas corpus would abuse that power, and turn loose upon the State every malefactor brought before him, simply on account of a technical defect in the mittimus authorizing his confinement. To guard against such an evil,—just such an one as is complained of in this instance,—they enacted that clause I have just read. For fear that some Judge might be tempted to claim and exercise a power so repugnant to reason, and so dangerous to the well-being of the community, they circumscribed their duties in this respect, as you see from this statute, in terms so plain that the "wayfaring man, though a fool, need not err therein." Yet, sir, vain and nugatory is this barrier to the improper exercise of power by the Judge, if it is to be beaten down and trampled under foot with perfect impunity, as has been done by this Judge in this very case. He may stultify himself; he may plead ignorance; he may tell you as much as he pleases that he did not know this section was in the statutes, but you will never believe that a man who had the *fifth* section so ready at his fingers' ends when Atterbury was imploring bail, was not aware of the existence of another section of the same act last January.

I confess, sir, there might be some force in the respondent's plea of ignorance, were it not for the more infamous case of Russell, that occurred about the same time,—indeed, I believe the very same day.

In this case, it appears from the testimony of Mr. Tyrell, Mr. Jackson, Mr. Cryts, and Mr. Eaker, who all corroborate each other, that a man calling himself Charles Russell was arrested and taken before Jonas Eaker, a Justice of the Peace of Stoddard county, on a charge of passing counterfeit money. Mr. Eaker examined the witnesses, and finding there was probable cause to believe him guilty, held him to bail in the sum of three hundred dollars, and allowed him until ten o'clock the next morning to procure securities. William F. Cryts being the Constable of the township, Russell was placed in his custody as the proper ministerial officer of the Justice's Court, for safe keeping until the designated hour next morning. But before that hour arrived, the respondent issued a writ of habeas corpus for the body of Russell, had him brought before him, and discharged.

Mr. Tyrell, when he presented Russell's petition, explained to the respondent the circumstances of his imprisonment; the petition itself showed the circumstances of arrest under a proper warrant, examination before a court of competent jurisdiction, and the order of that court placing him in the custody of the Constable. Yet, because the Constable states in his return that he held him by virtue of a verbal order of Jonas Eaker, under all these circumstances, he immediately discharges him. Cryts held Russell legally in custody, and all the circumstances showed it. In proof, I will call your attention to a case in 7 East's T. Reports, directly in point:

It never could be doubted but that a magistrate might by parol order an offender to be detained in custody until he could make out his warrant of commitment; and this court were in the constant habit of directing commitments, verbally, which were afterwards recorded.—Still *vs.* Walls, p. 536.

Now, sir, what was this Judge's duty under the law, and the facts shown by the petition itself? No man, sir, who has the least regard for his reputation for common sense, will pretend to say that he had anything to do but send the prisoner back to Justice Eaker, to give bail in the amount fixed. But even granting, sir, that it was necessary for

Mr. Cryts to have had in his possession the examinations and warrant to justify him in holding the prisoner, we learn from the testimony of Mr. Cryts, Mr. Tyrell, and Mr. Jackson, that before the Judge had discharged Russell, Mr. Cryts went and procured these papers, and brought them and laid them down upon the table before the Judge. But what does the Judge do then? Does he manifest the slightest care or regard for the welfare of that community, or the majesty of the criminal code? Does he exhibit that strict impratiality that should ever characterize a Circuit Judge? Granting that the petition itself did *not* put him fully in possession of the fact that the prisoner was in custody for a felony, what does he do when the papers are presented to him to satisfy him of that fact? He does not even deign to look at them, except to ascertain what they are; but with a sneer tells Mr. Cryts "he had better be careful or he would contradict his return;" and went on and discharged the prisoner, with full evidence of his guilt and the legality of his imprisonment lying there upon the table before him. No wonder he quibbled so upon the introduction of the record in this case, for he was sensible that it would fix upon him the most detestable guilt. No wonder he kept the original in his possession, and refused to produce it until we had established clearly our right to introduce a copy. But I want to remind the Court of an admission made by the respondent in this Court, that affords a key to this whole matter.

When John J. Jackson was on the stand, the respondent, in cross-examining, asked him whether, when Cryts was elected, Isaac Brand was not his opponent for the office of Constable; if Mr. Brand wasn't declared elected, and if Cryts didn't contest the election successfully; and if Mr. Brand wasn't Jonas Eaker's son-in-law. I thought this rigmarole had proceeded far enough, and objected to its being carried any further, when the respondent replied to my objection, that he wanted to show the relationship between Eaker and Brand, because, when Russell was brought before him, and Cryts stated he merely held him by virtue of a verbal order of Eaker's, he thought it was a scheme concocted by Eaker and Brand to get Cryts into a difficulty, by getting him to contradict his return to the writ of habeas corpus; and hence, it was to save Billy Cryts (knowing him to be young and inexperienced) from being entrapped by Eaker and Brand, that he refused to examine the papers that Cryts brought and laid before him. If he dare deny making this statement, the reporter's notes will show it. I arose at the time to expose the dilemma in which it placed him, but he withdrew the question. But see what a defense, what an excuse this is for a learned Judge. A felon is brought before him. Evidence is exhibited conclusively showing that he has been tried and found guilty by a magistrate of competent jurisdiction of one of the most heinous crimes known to the calendar. The prisoner even admits these facts in his petition. Yet the law that declares him legally in custody must be blindly overridden, the safety of community that required his punishment must be jeopardized, and a villain turned loose to curse the country by a repetition of his crimes, all to save the reputation of Billy Cryts from the blighting mildew,—nay, the faintest breath of suspicion! But who asked him to violate his oath of office, to trample under his feet the laws of the land and the rights of an entire community, merely for Mr. Cryts's benefit? Who asked him to assume a guardianship over Mr. Cryts at such enormous sacrifices? Mr. Cryts did not I am sure. This Court is satisfied that he is abundantly able to take care of himself, and that he will go through life respectable and respected, notwithstanding all the diabolical machinations of Jonas Eaker and Isaac Brand, which the wonderfully magnifying properties of the respondent's imagination have enabled him to discover.

Now, sir, there is not one particle of sincerity, not one syllable of truth in this flimsy excuse; but it shows one thing,—it shows that this respondent did not like Eaker. He perhaps thought of the time he wrongfully and corruptly imprisoned him for daring to assert his privileges as a freeman; or perhaps he thought of the time Eaker presented him to the grand jury for oppression in office, when he violated his oath and the law, and degraded his position by going to that grand jury privately and telling them he was above the law when mantled in his official robes. I think it likely he thought of all these things, and said in his heart, 'I'll show this community that although they have elected Eaker Judge of the County Court, and Justice of the Peace, he is a poor illiterate fool, that doesn't know how to keep a prisoner when he gets him. I've got a good chance to disgrace him, and I'll do it, if Cryts *has* presented me with conclusive evidence that this felon is justly, legally, and properly in custody.'

I will not now consume the time of the Court by reading the numerous cases, both in England and in this country, in which magistrates have been held guilty of misdemeanor in office for taking inadequate bail, in order to show how much graver the offense would be to send adrift upon the community without any bail at all every villain that may see proper to ask to be discharged under a writ of habeas corpus; for if the circumstances of these cases do not themselves suggest sufficient reasons for the condemnation of a Judge that would be guilty of them, I despair of any power of mine to represent them in the light best calculated to exhibit the hideous moral turpitude and monstrous official corruption they involve. If this respondent shall be held worthy still to occupy a high place in the judiciary,—shall still be permitted to hold the sceptre of the law, after such conduct as the evidence in relation to these two cases shows him guilty of,—I am confident that every citizen who is conversant with the facts attending these cases will shudder when he sees what cobwebs manacle the hands of crime,—when he sees that murder may drink the blood of his victim in the streets; that the incendiary may bask in the blaze of his victim's dwelling, and gloat over the charred and blackened bones of his wife and little ones; and that all the shackles the law can impose upon him are but as gossamer, to be swept away by the breath of a Circuit Judge.

The hour of adjournment having arrived, Mr. Knott rested his argument; and on motion of SENATOR PARSONS, the Court then adjourned.

FIFTEENTH DAY.

WEDNESDAY, June 22, 1859.

The Court met pursuant to adjournment, and was opened by proclamation.

The managers and respondent attended.

Mr. KNOTT resumed his argument as follows:

I am aware, Mr. President, that from the great number of charges alleged in the articles of impeachment under consideration, and the almost infinite variety of facts and circumstances adduced in evidence to establish the respondent's guilt of each one of them, the remarks I had the honor of submitting to the Court on yesterday, as well as such as I deem it incumbent upon me still to offer, must necessarily appear, as they really are, illy digested, hurried, and imperfect. The field is too extensive to be thoroughly explored by a single intellect in one excursion, without wearying in the task.

The great picture of judicial crime presented in this case does not consist of a single master-stroke of guilt; but is made up of a series of individual instances of official corruption, each of which is possessed of features sufficiently revolting, not merely to afford ample employment to an intellect superior to my own, but to insure the heart that conceived it an immortality in the annals of human depravity.

I hope, therefore, it has not been and will not be expected that I should linger upon each particular offense of which we have shown the respondent guilty, until I shall have adverted to every single fact that can bear upon the question of his guilt,—until I shall have dissected his heart, and exhibited to the sickened and disgusted gaze of the Court every black and rotten recess from which corruption could have crept. I could not so trespass upon the patience of this honorable body, which has already been so fully exercised, even had I the physical and mental capacity to do so. I must rely upon your own appreciation of the revolting nature of crimes, which under the most auspicious circumstances I would be unable properly to discuss, and your ability to make a proper application of the numerous facts proving conclusively the perpetration of such crimes by the respondent. And, sir, while you make this application of the facts exhibited in the evidence to the question of the respondent's guilt, I will ask you to keep in view the fact, that notwithstanding we have frequently proved facts and circumstances showing beyond any possible doubt the unmistakable motive of revenge underlying the respondent's repeated acts of gross misconduct in office, the law by no means requires us to show the malicious intent, the unlawful design that actuated the perpetration of any offense charged in these articles. The rule of law by which you are to be governed in this particular is, that the commission of an unlawful act by a sane man carries with it a conclusive presumption that he did the act with malicious and unlawful intent. I will read you 1 Greenleaf's Evidence:

SECTION 18. "Every sane man is conclusively presumed to contemplate the probable *consequences* of his own act."

So, if the consequences of a Judge's conduct will probably operate oppressively, the conclusive presumption of law is that he willfully intended to oppress. Again, sir, I will read from the same volume:

SECTION 39. "As men seldom do unlawful acts with innocent intentions, the law presumes every act unlawful in itself to be *criminally* intended, until the contrary appear; thus on a charge of murder malice is presumed from the fact of killing unaccompanied with circumstances of extenuation, *and the burden of disproving the malice is thrown upon the accused.*"

So, sir, when we establish that the respondent unlawfully imprisoned Eaker, sent cases to remote and inconvenient counties when there existed no earthly necessity for it, outraged the characters of Phelan and Fox in open court, refused a writ of habeas corpus to Atterbury, or violated the statutes of the State in turning loose upon the people of Stoddard county a thief and a counterfeiter, the law under which you have sworn to try this case requires you to presume that he did these things with a criminal intent, until he himself shows to the contrary. "The burden of disproving the malice is thrown upon the accused;" and if he folds his hands and makes no effort to rid himself of the consequences of this legal presumption, he cannot expect this Court to close their eyes upon the law and reason and pronounce him innocent, when all the world besides will say he is guilty.

I need not remark that he has made no effort to show any other than the unlawful, malicious, criminal motive, which the law attaches to his conduct, and of which he must divest it or be held guilty.

Instead of doing so, I say boldly he has not dealt fairly with the evidence of a single witness. He has interpolated, misstated, and distorted it in every manner of which he was capable; while he never dared to allude to the overwhelming array of authorities my learned colleague produced against him in making his able argument in this case. Oh! no! he expects to override law, evidence, common sense, and justice, with his *towering position!* He has been *elected*, forsooth, and that has placed him upon a pinnacle inaccessible to law or justice, from which he can look down with serene indifference upon all created things! Yes, sir, he has attempted frequently to frighten this Senate out of their propriety by parading his *immense popularity* before their eyes! It would seem, sir, from his vaunting, that he could take a stand in the centre of the Fifteenth Judicial Circuit, and sing as Selkirk did:

"I am monarch of all I survey;
My right there is none to dispute."

I will not undertake to demonstrate that there is as much modesty as truth in this gratuitous self-advertisement of the gentleman's standing at home, but I will say he places a very flattering estimate upon this Court. According to his view, you will pronounce him "*not guilty*" for fear of offending some of those whom he would have you believe prostrate themselves in servile obeisance beneath his autocratic scepter. He says, 'if you convict me, you'll lose votes in the Fifteenth Judicial Circuit.' How complimented and how grateful that intelligent and high-minded people will feel to the respondent, when they learn he has asserted such a dictatorial sway over them! But, sir, as it seems gratifying to the respondent to entertain this vain illusion of personal popularity, I will not be so cruel as to disturb it. I will concede to him, to save his feelings, that every man in the Fifteenth Judicial Circuit holds him in the highest possible esteem, except one. Yet, if he corruptly and maliciously use the authority of his office to persecute that man in a single instance, he is as amenable at this bar as if ninety-nine out of every hundred were the victims of his malice. And, sir, I care not what may be his position in society, even if he "dress in purple and fine linen," and hold subject to his will the very thoughts of thousands; yet, if he has closed the gates of justice upon one single man, though clothed in the rags of extremest poverty, his influence will not save him from being dismissed in disgrace from the distinguished place he has dishonored.

But, sir, I must resume the examination of the charges in the order in which they are preferred; and in doing so, will invite the attention of the Court to a consideration of the eleventh article.

Mr. Tyrell and Mr. Kitchen tell you, that at the November term, 1858, of the Stoddard Circuit Court, the respondent, in his public charge to the grand jury, told them he had understood that a citizen of that county had gone to Jefferson City ostensibly on business for the county, but in reality upon his own business; that he had procured a warrant upon the County Treasury for a hundred and seventy-seven dollars, for his pretended services; that they must investigate these facts, and, if true, prefer an indictment against the party, for he was as guilty as if he had stolen that much money; that the facts constituted the crime of obtaining money under false pretenses; and that they could ascertain who the man was to whom he alluded, by inquiring of the County Treasurer who had presented a warrant for one hundred and seventy-seven dollars. Mr. Tyrell tells you the Judge, in this charge, so accurately described a transaction of Mr. Kitchen's, that he knew at the time he referred to Mr. Kitchen. Mr. Kitchen tells you that the County Court, desiring to dispose of the swamp lands belonging to that county, employed him to visit Jefferson City for the purpose of procuring a certified list of such lands; that in order to save his own business from suffering for want of attention during his absence, he employed Mr. Phelan to attend to it, before he would make the contract with the County Court; and to pay Mr. Phelan, agreed to give him half he should receive from the county for obtaining the lists; that he proceeded to this city at his own expense, and, in order to get the lists in time, he paid out over sixty dollars of his own money for the hire of an extra Clerk for the Secretary of State; that upon his return, the County Court, to reimburse him for his expenses, and to pay him for his time and trouble, drew a warrant in his favor for one hundred and seventy-seven dollars, or, rather, in his and Phelan's favor, for he shared half in it for attending to Mr. Kitchen's business while he was gone. He also tells you that while the Judge was giving this charge to the grand jury, several spoke to him to the effect that "the Judge was after him," showing clearly that it was generally understood he was speaking of him. And more, sir; Kitchen and Tyrell both tell you he said the man to whom he alluded was a lawyer, indicating him not only by the transaction, but by his profession.

Such, sir, are the facts; and to disprove them, the respondent has offered you no scintilla of evidence; on the contrary, so far from there being the slightest palliation for this unheard-of conduct, it is in evidence that for months he had harbored toward this victim of his persecution the most malignant feelings of revenge; that he had taken every opportunity to oppress him; that he taxed his ingenuity for obstacles to throw in the way of his success. And besides, sir, you have not forgotten that when this same victim of his malice was the other day confined to a bed of sickness, and the opinion of his physician was that his removal from his room would endanger his life, when the proposition was made to take his testimony at his bedside, this immaculate respondent, this embodiment of mercy, this pure minister of pity, who melts at every sight of sorrow, or sound of woe,—flushed with anger, with every feature gleaming with passion, said, "no, he shall come here if it costs him his life!" The law gave him "the pound of flesh," and he exacted it with an avidity that would have shamed Shylock himself.

Sir, had I been the victim of the wrongs that have been inflicted upon that man; had I been hunted down with an insatiate, tireless hate, for months, as he had been; had I been singled out and foully branded with a felony, as he had been, in the presence of hundreds, and by the very court who holds the guardianship of my fair fame, I would have come here *at the risk of my life!* Worn down by disease and anguish, I would have dragged my emaciated body to this bar, and with the last feeble gasp for life, poured into my country's ear the story of my wrongs, and demanded vengeance upon the tyrant's head!

I need not tell this Court, that of all the rights the human being can hold dear and sacred, that of having his reputation kept pure and spotless is most important. Man is preëminently a social being. He was never created to live independent of the good opinion, respect, and friendship of his fellow creatures. All his hopes, all his aspirations, all his acts are intimately and inseparably associated with the esteem of others. Whatever may be his disposition, inclinations, or aspirations; whatever may be his sphere or avocation in life, the approbation of his fellows is his guiding star through time. Upon that star, through the clash, the jars, the turmoil of life's great battle, his eye is fixed; and when that eye glazes beneath the icy touch of death, it turns still to catch its last lingering beams.

> "On some fond breast the parting soul relies;
> Some pious drops the closing eye requires."

For reputation, the hero treads the stormy path of war and toil; the poet tunes his sweet-toned lyre; the scholar trims the midnight lamp; the peasant toils through summer's heat and winter's cold;—and to purchase reputation, the miser "heaps the shining ore." So rich, so priceless is this gem, that statesmen have placed it in the same casket with life and liberty,—have made its protection a special subject for constitutional enactment. Yet, sir, I appeal to you in the name of virtue, and of justice; in the name of every right held sacred by the human heart; in the name of our outraged laws and sullied institutions, to contemplate the appalling picture of judicial crime presented in this case! I ask you to behold a Judge of your Circuit Court, under the solemnities of his oath of office, perverting the duties of his post, and making his official power an engine of iniquity and oppression; breathing upon the character of an unoffending citizen the blighting mildew of a damning slander that will poison his happiness through life, go with him to a dishonored grave, and cling to his wife and children long after he has mouldered into dust. I ask you to look at this Judge deliberately robbing a harmless, defenseless man of this invaluable gift, more priceless far than gold or diamonds; stealing from him the precious talisman that secures the only joys that linger about his path through life, and tell me, tell your constituents, he is guilty of no crime!

The law very wisely provides that the deliberations of grand juries shall not only be had secretly, but forever kept secret. It makes this beneficent provision out of tenderness to the character of the citizen; to save his reputation from unjust aspersion, injurious remark, or even suspicion, until at least twelve men, acting under oath, upon sworn testimony, shall say there is probable cause to believe him guilty of a crime.

It is the duty of the Judge to instruct them upon the law in the abstract; to tell them what facts constitute the various offenses of which they are to inquire; but not to single out a citizen, and forestall the action of the grand jury by an expression of his own opinion, or make him an object of public suspicion by even hinting at his guilt, until the constitutional authority—the grand jury—says he should be put upon his trial. The grand jury, in their retirement, take up the facts detailed by witnesses legally sworn; and if, after applying these facts to the law they have received from the court, they find any party innocent, there is no harm done. They are under an oath never to divulge the fact; no one else knows that his conduct was ever under investigation; and so he goes forth with his character unsullied by even the breath of public suspicion, pure and spotless.

But, sir, permit a Judge to single out any man he may see proper, whether charged with a crime or not, and, under pretext of charging the grand jury, perpetrate any slander upon him that his fiendish malice may dictate, and whose reputation will be safe? Having a grudge against any citizen, he may, from the bench, in the presence of hundreds, describe him by his avocation, residence, age, dress, and personal appearance, so exactly that all present can easily distinguish whom he means; and then inform the grand jury he has heard that such a person has committed a burglary, larceny, forgery, arson, or any other infamous crime. It avails nothing, sir, that the grand jury find the base insinuation utterly without foundation. The concourse present think the Judge would not make such a charge without just grounds; so it is taken up, discussed, and reiterated and rehashed with as many shades and variations as there are auditors present, accumulating horrible details, until at last it becomes a fixed, proven fact, in the estimation of a large portion of community. The poor man, though innocent as the unconscious babe, is ruined. Like the beauteous flower over which the deadly sirocco has poured its poisonous fires, his reputation, blasted by the baleful breath of damning slander, withers, droops, and dies. Weeping pity will water it with her tears in vain; the tender plant is dead; and all the showers that can be distilled upon it cannot awake it again to life and beauty. Vengeance is glutted; and malice, mantled in judicial robes, smiles upon the desolation it has sent upon a peaceful, unoffending, happy family. "Back-wounding calumny the *whitest* virtue strikes." So you, sir, may be a victim, too.

I will attempt no further to portray the terrible consequences of permitting such monstrous iniquity to go unrestrained, for I know it is far beyond my feeble powers. I have no language adequate to the task. But I thank God I am addressing a Court composed of pure-minded, upright men, who will appreciate and punish the loathsome, disgusting, and dangerous wrong fixed indelibly upon the respondent in this instance.

I have only known these crimes historically. I have never seen them in court. It has been my good fortune, during the very limited time I have been at the bar, to appear before a gentleman distinguished by every virtue that can ennoble man. Honest, learned, and just, he inscribed his name in imperishable characters upon his country's brightest page; and has at length retired, after a long career of usefulness, respected, honored, and beloved by all who know him. I repeat, sir, I have only known such offenses as are proven upon this respondent as matters of history, and I would to God it had never been our lot to turn this dark page of Missouri's annals. I would it might now be blotted out forever; that the Leathean waters of eternal oblivion might hide the fact that a Missouri Judge was guilty of such foul and damning crimes!

I have already shown to the Court that, both at common law and by the statute of this State, a Judge, neglecting or refusing to discharge any duty incumbent upon him by law, is guilty of a misdemeanor in office; and that for misdemeanors in office, particularly statutable misdemeanors, he is liable to impeachment, and should be dismissed from office. I have also shown you that it is the duty of a Judge, when he has reason to believe, from his own knowledge, or legal information from others, that the Clerk of his court has been guilty of any misdemeanor in office, to give information of such misdemeanor to the Attorney-General, and suspend the Clerk from office, and appoint a temporary Clerk in his stead. I furthermore showed you, by the very same statute, that any willful neglect of the Clerk to discharge any of the duties of his office should be deemed a misdemeanor in office.

Now, sir, I propose to show you from the testimony that the respondent was willfully guilty of a criminal neglect of duty in refusing to suspend the Clerk of the Butler Circuit Court, and appoint a temporary Clerk in his place, when he knew, not only from his own knowledge, but from universal outcry, that the Clerk was drunk and neglecting every duty of his office; and that he did this as an act of kindness, a special mark of favor to the Clerk, to save him from punishment and disgrace.

Mr. Phelan, Mr. Bedford, Mr. Ruff, and Mr. Vandiver and Mr. Scott also, I believe, tell you that at the November term, 1857, of the Butler Circuit Court, on the first day the Clerk was in court and attending to his duties. The grand jury was sworn and empanneled, and perhaps a case tried. On the second day, however, they tell you the Clerk was absent, and reported drunk,—too drunk to attend to business. Mr. Phelan and Mr. Bedford tell you that the lawyers requested the Judge to appoint another Clerk, that the business of the court might proceed; and so solicitous was Mr. Phelan that he offered to keep the minutes himself. The Judge refused to permit this, unless he would abandon all his cases at that term. This Mr. Phelan could by no means afford to do, but proposed to procure a competent man. He did so. He brought Donaldson Walker into court, but the Judge refused to allow him to do anything, unless requested by Mr. Blount, the Clerk. Mr. Phelan then went to Blount's house, where he found him in a condition of almost total inebriety, and he and Mrs. Blount held him up in bed while he signed a written request that Donaldson Walker should be installed as his deputy. This document was presented to the Judge, but he still refused to appoint even a deputy, or, rather, to approve the appointment of one by Blount. On the contrary, he takes all the papers pertaining to cases answerable and triable at that term, rolls them up in a newspaper, places them under his arm; and, when Bedford and Phelan apply to see some of them, they are insultingly told that some of the papers had been purloined, and he was afraid to trust them. He finally locked them up in the Clerk's office, and gave the key to Mr. Dennis; and that evening had the grand jury called into court and peremptorily discharged, although, as Mr. Ruff, who was a member of that grand jury, tells you, they had very important business on hands, and objected to being discharged. Mr. Bedford tells you the same thing, and that this was upon the second day of court, while there was a whole week in which to hold the term. And Mr. Phelan tells you that the respondent afterwards told him that the reason he didn't suspend Blount, or appoint another Clerk, was that "Blount was a clever fellow."

When all these things are proven plainly and beyond any kind of question by the witnesses against him, and more than corroborated by his own witness Dennis, he finally comes out in his address yesterday and whiningly asks to be excused because he didn't *know Blount was drunk!* Ah! sir, that won't do. He knew he was not in court attending to the duties of his office, and do you find him inquiring the reason? I suppose it would be natural that he should do so when he missed him at his desk, and Scott, Ruff, Vandiver, Phelan, Dennis, and Bedford, all tell us it was a notorious fact that he was drunk. Phelan says he told the Judge himself that Blount was drunk, and that he heard a number of others tell him the same thing. But more than that, sir, the other day while Mr. Scott was under examination, when I asked him if Blount was drunk, the respondent admitted that he knew he was drunk. Look at the printed report of Scott's testimony, and if the reporter has kept the remark of the respondent as well as the question and answer of the witness, you will find that open admission of the respondent as I have stated it. It is not my duty to reconcile these two statements. He may do it at his leisure after the termination of the trial if he sees proper.

The respondent labored hard to show that Blount never signed this appointment of Donaldson G. Walker. But I'll venture to say, when you take into consideration the fact that Blount was so drunk when he signed it that he had to be held up by his wife and Phelan, you will say his signature to it is in the very same handwriting as the other papers exhibited to you, although several witnesses have sworn that they don't look alike.

But, sir, I appeal to you in the name of common reason and candor, do you believe that Phelan would go to Blount's house, forge Blount's name to a paper that was to be filed in Blount's own office, and that was designed for the very purpose of placing another man in that office,—that he would do all this in the open face of day and openly avow it as his own act? Sir, you are bound to believe either that Phelan was utterly demented, that he was entirely deprived of every spark of reason, or you must believe his testimony is true, and that Blount signed that paper. In favor of the former hypothesis there is not a single fact before you; on the contrary he details his testimony with the candor and honesty of a perfect gentleman, and indicates a far more than ordinary degree of intelligence. No man ever saw evidence given with more ease, candor, sincerity, consistency, and intelligence than Phelan detailed his; and besides here were a hundred of his neighbors who had known him for years; why didn't the respondent introduce *them* to attack his evidence? But alas! for the poor, weak old man! The Court remembers that when Mr. Phelan was upon the stand, the respondent himself said he knew him to be an honorable, highminded gentleman. The fact is clear, sir; it cannot be disputed. Blount appointed Walker deputy, as this paper which the respondent himself offered in evidence shows, and he refused to ratify the appointment. And why? He astonished you yesterday by saying that the reason he did not appoint another Clerk was, the papers belonging to the office were in such a condition, scattered around and lost, that no other Clerk could have done anything had one been appointed. Why, in the name of sense, what sort of a reason is this, sir? The Judge is applied to to suspend a Clerk for misdemeanor in not attending to his duty, and he says 'oh! it's no use, he has been guilty of so many misdemeanors it won't do any good to turn him out of office!' Whose duty is it, sir, to keep the papers in order? The Clerk's. Suppose the Clerk fails to do so, what is the consequence? He is guilty of a misdemeanor in office, and it is the Judge's duty to prefer charges against him, and suspend him from office until they are determined.

But this Clerk permits the papers belonging to his office to become scattered around and lost during vacation; gets drunk during court; absents himself from the court; neglects every duty belonging to his office; clogs every wheel of business—suits must be continued at any sacrifice, the grand jury discharged and the court adjourned in the commencement of the term, and still he must not be indicted or suspended from office because he is a *clever fellow!*

It is no difference, sir, how many distressed suitors eagerly throng the vestibule of the court, in the vain hope of warding off impending ruin by a speedy determination of their legal rights,—let them wait. Let squalid poverty make its cheerless nest upon their hearthstones; let the fruits of honest toil they have for years slowly accumulated to gladden the dreary evening of life be snatched from them by the remorseless hand of debt; let ruin and misery invade the joyous precincts of their happy homes, and make their horrid dens in the bright abodes of domestic bliss—Blount is a *clever fellow*, and must not be suspended from office! Let the poor prisoner rot amid the filth and vermin of the loathsome dungeon; let him vainly rave, as the jail fever consumes his burning brain, that the constitution promises him "a speedy trial, without sale, denial, or delay;" let him die; let his bones bleach forgotten on the slimy floor of the noisome prison vault—*Blount is a clever fellow*, and it would be a pity to suspend him from office! Throw wide the gates of vice; let loose upon the country all the hellish brood of crime; let arson light up the midnight sky with the lurid flames of burning dwellings; let the warm life-blood of the unoffending citizen slake the assassin's fiendish thirst; let murder's bloody dagger gleam in the sunbeams of noonday; let prowling rapine desolate the bright habitations of innocence and peace—the grand jury shall be discharged, the court shall be adjourned, crime shall go unrestrained, because *Jacob C. Blount is a clever fellow*, and it would be a pity to suspend him from office for a misdemeanor!

Perhaps John R. Main and Charles Russell, the two felons he turned loose in open violation of the statutes of the State, were *clever fellows!* Perhaps he thought Mr. Hicks a *clever fellow* when he quashed an indictment against him for an assault with intent to kill! Perhaps it was because Col. Bartlett was a *clever fellow* that he usurped the province of the jury, denied them the right of finding a verdict according to the law and the evidence, and finally procured a *nolle prosequi* for him. But there is one thing certain,—he didn't think Mr. Kitchen a clever fellow when he sheltered himself behind the duties of his office to make a mean, cowardly attack upon his character, or when he attempted to hound the grand jury upon him for having made a fair and honorable contract with the County Court of his county.

Is there no partiality, no wrong, no corruption in all this? Oh! no, certainly not. Don't you know Blount is a *clever fellow!* And now, sir, that this word corruption occurs to my mind, let us see what it means in law. Mr. Bouvier defines it thus in his Law Dictionary: "Corruption—an act done with intent to give some advantage inconsistent with official duty, or the rights of others." So, sir, when the respondent triumphantly tells you to prove the corruption in his demeanor, tell him his refusing to suspend a drunken Clerk, who was palpably guilty of misdemeanors in office, and to appoint a temporary Clerk was inconsistent with his sworn duty; inconsistent with the rights of parties; inconsistent with the rights of the bar; inconsistent with the rights of the whole community, and intended to give an advantage to the Clerk,—intended to save him from punishment and disgrace because he was a clever fellow, and hence was under the law *corrupt.*

But, sir, we not only find the respondent guilty of this instance of partiality,—this instance of corruption,—in directly conferring an advantage inconsistent with his official duty and the rights of others, but prove as charged in the very next article that he is guilty of similar misconduct at a different place and under entirely different circumstances.

You are told by Mr. Ringer that he had undertaken to build a court house in Bloomfield, in pursuance of a contract he had made with Mr. Kitchen, who was commissioner for Stoddard county; that in October, 1857, the respondent came to him, took him to one side, and asked him if he had any county warrants for building the court house; he told the respondent he had not, but that Kitchen had; the respondent then advised him to get the warrants, sell them, put the money in his pockets, and then sue Kitchen, and assured him he could recover, because Judge

Eaker's court was not a legal court, and Kitchen was individually liable upon the contract.

And how does he seek to evade this plain, unequivocal testimony of Mr. Ringer? He feels the force of it; he knows it establishes against him a crime for which he should instantly be hurled from office; and how does he seek to avoid its just and inevitable consequences? By showing any inconsistency in it? By showing or attempting to show by any of Mr. Ringer's numerous and respectable acquaintances here that he is unworthy of belief? No! but by attempting to prove that he was not in Stoddard county during the month of October, 1857. I will not say, sir, how well he has succeeded in proving a negative in this particular, nor will I pretend to say he *was* in Stoddard county during that month,—perhaps he was not; but I do say it by no means follows, that because Mr. Ringer may have mistaken the latter part of September or the first of November for a portion of October, in fixing the time of this interview, the interview never occurred. Nor will any member of this Court hold him less guiltless for this flimsy plea,—this slight mistake in point of time, which may or may not be so.

Here, sir, he is exhibited, by the evidence, descending from the bench, and notwithstanding it is his peculiar province, his sworn duty under the law, to dispense even-handed justice to all,—notwithstanding there is a statute expressly forbidding his acting as counsellor in any case,—privately advising one citizen to bring a suit against another, and even assuring him he will recover judgment.

But who is this other? Why has he such a lively solicitude for the welfare of Mr. Ringer? Why does he take such a deep and abiding interest in the private affairs of another, that propriety, justice, official obligation, and plain statute law all cannot repress? Is it because he is overflowing with the "milk of human kindness?" Does his conduct well up like the sparkling waters of the crystal fountain from a pure heart, full of tender sympathy, kind emotions, and generous impulses? Or is it the venom distilled beneath the adder's tongue, the poison gall oozing from a mean, revengeful soul, surcharged with hate and malice?

Mr. Kitchen is the man against whom he wishes to incite a vexatious suit. It is Kitchen from whom he would snatch the hard earnings of long years of honest toil to pay the county's debts,—so you may guess the kind of spirit that dictated his gratuitous advice to Ringer. But wherefore should Kitchen pay this debt more than Jackson? He had been guilty of no wrong. He had been guilty of no bad faith. Why should *he* pay the county's debt? Ah! sir, it seems to me that human depravity can get no lower,—that man can never approximate nearer the nature of the arch enemy of Heaven and earth,—than has been done in this instance. The respondent sees the man against whom he has long entertained the deadliest hate selected for his probity and capacity to superintend the erection of a public building. He beholds him discharge the duties incumbent upon him with an honest fidelity that secures the approbation of all. The prosperity of the unoffending object of his malice becomes an eye-sore to him; galls him; goads him on to fury. Envy takes possession of his entire soul. He thinks,—he dreams of vengeance. He pants for the destruction of his enemy's happiness; he longs to see his wife and children stripped of the appliances of comfort and elegance that industry, frugality, and honesty have accumulated around them; he craves to see them exiled from the home endeared to them by all the ties of nativity, and the sweetest reminiscences of affection; he wildly prays to see them the beggared pensioners upon a heartless world's precarious sympathy. To bring all this woe upon the victim of his envious rage, he seeks to crush him with the overwhelming weight of a public liability he is under no moral obligation to discharge. He seeks out Ringer. He endeavors to influence him to institute proceedings against Kitchen. He assures him he can recover. He gives his reasons why. Already his eye glitters with the strange, wild light of exulting vengeance, as he imagines the success of his malicious schemes. But Ringer, like an honest man, spurns the fiendish counsel. He knows that Kitchen is under no obligation to pay the debt of a wealthy county, even if some lame provision of law does make him personally liable, and he scorns such mean advantages. Well was it perhaps for Kitchen that he did, for although he may not have been liable personally, there is no calculating the annoyance and perplexity to which he might have been subjected by a vexatious suit.

But, sir, this Judge can commence at the very inception of a case; he can advise how the suit should be brought, how it shall be managed, and what judgment will be rendered; the opinions he expresses in private he will make good upon the bench; he will effectually destroy public confidence in the purity and efficacy of the judiciary; he will make the temple of justice a huckster's stall for retailing favors to litigants; and when brought before the bar of his country to answer to the law he has outraged, and meet the justice he has trampled under his feet, he would fain make you believe he is a poor, miserable, buffeted, persecuted, martyred victim of a horrible conspiracy; that he is

"As pure as the ice that's curded by the frost
From purest snow, and hangs on Dian's temple."

But, sir, I think as I remarked on yesterday, if Lord Coke could not trust himself to give the king advice, our courts should not be permitted to advise parties litigant, though they are as immaculate as the respondent has shown himself to be.

If you have never actually witnessed such a calamity, Mr. President, you have no doubt frequently exercised your imagination upon the various exciting incidents that attend the wreck of a gallant ship. The whole of the dreadful panorama is perhaps before your fancy as soon as mentioned; you hear the dull crash of the fatal concussion; you see a hundred faces, pale with consternation, hurrying to an fro; you hear a hundred voices mingling in one wild shriek; you see the noble vessel go down to the unknown realms of silence beneath the wave; you see the hundred struggling victims sink forever in the boiling vortex. And you see the last survivor of the terrible catastrophe clinging to the life-boat, and battling for existence with the raging elements around him. Buoyed by his faithful craft above the treacherous flood, he valiantly buffets the tumbling billows that rear their heads like hungry monsters round him. In vain the waters boil beneath him; in vain the tempest eddies around him,—he is master of the storm. So, sir, is it with him who is sustained by truth and right,—he proudly outrides every storm of persecution or distress that beats upon him. But let him lack these sure supports,—let him be clogged with guilt, burdened with crime,—like the shipwrecked galley-slave with his fetters on, he struggles a moment with the yielding tide, clutches the little straw that's wafted near him, and sinks into eternal infamy. And so, sir, I might say, were the respondent in this case sustained by truth, right, and conscious innocence, there would be no necessity for the course he has found it necessary to pursue. He would not be compelled to attempt to cover up the gross outrages of which he stands impeached in these articles, and convicted by the evidence adduced in this trial, by distorting the testimony, and shutting his eyes to the overwhelming array of authority my learned colleague produced against him. He would not have felt himself compelled to glide as hastily as possible over the incontrovertible array of facts establishing every other charge against him, and predicate his whole defense upon the shade of palliation the testimony gives to the offense charged in the next article. He would never have passed so hurriedly the imprisonment of Eaker, his defamation of Phelan and Fox, his partiality to Walker and Ringer, his abuse of the privilege of the writ of habeas courpus, his persecution of Kitchen, and all the other crimes of which he stands charged, and bestowed so much eloquence upon his conduct in the case of the State *vs.* Kinsey,—the most trivial charge in the whole catalogue,—had there been no tinge of guilt upon him. He would have taken up each charge; he would have shown triumphantly by the evidence that he was as innocent as the unborn babe. He would have dwelt upon each allegation until he had rid his reputation of the least trace of suspicion. But, sir, the truth is, he was overwhelmed by the facts in the case. He felt himself sinking irretrievably under the immense weight of the evidence, and like the poor drowning mariner he catches at every straw.

You remember how he dwelt upon the evidence offered in support of the fourteenth article, and no doubt wondered that he would linger so long upon a charge comparatively trivial, whilst there was such an accumulation of proof establishing conclusively the perpetration of so many more heinous offenses. And, sir, I can account for it upon no other hypothesis, than that he desired if possible to divert the attention of the Court from the contemplation of the darkest features of his case.

But, sir, with all his labor upon this part of the case, he merely pretends that there was some excuse for his tyrannical conduct on the trial of Kinsey; that the conduct of Mr. Fox justified his harshness and oppression in that particular case. This I deny. I hold that whatever may have been the conduct of Mr. Fox, it would not justify the course of conduct pursued by the court in reference to the rights of Kinsey. I maintain, sir, that whilst Mr. Fox was acting as an attorney and counsellor at law, Kinsey had a right to his services after he had employed him, that no court under the constitution of this State could deprive him of. It is true that the court had a right to fine Fox, and to imprison him for contempt of court if he was out of the line of his duty, and persisted in remaining so after having been called to order by the court; but, sir, whenever he sealed that advocate's mouth, and made him take his seat, he snatched away from Kinsey a constitutional right, the right to be represented by counsel, and the right, as a freeman, of selecting what counsel he saw proper.

But I deny that Mr. Fox was out of the strict line of his duty. True, Mr. Hicks says he was drunk; but whether Mr. Hicks knows more about that than Mr. Fox does himself, who swears he was perfectly sober, I won't pretend to determine. Perhaps he does; but be that as it may, what are the facts as to his conduct? It seems from the testimony that the court had restricted the time that Mr. Fox should occupy in addressing the jury. That Mr. Fox after his exordium, in which he had perhaps spoken of the fact that the prosecution was predicated entirely upon circumstantial evidence, took occasion to animadvert upon the fact that Joseph L. White had volunteered his services in behalf of the prosecution. It seems he then proceeded to show the extreme unfitness in Mr. White's volunteering, not merely because the State was ably represented, but because Mr. White was a gentlemen of talent and influence which could have been more mercifully bestowed upon the unfortunate and indigent defendant, and besides that, of all men in the world, *Joseph* should be the last to volunteer in the prosecution of a case resting upon circumstantial evidence; because Joseph of old, to whom all other Josephs are indebted for a name, was himself a victim of circumstantial evidence. While thus playing upon Mr. White's given name, perhaps by way of apostrophising him ironically, he calls out "Joseph! Joseph! Joseph!" Here he is stopped by the Judge and asked to explain. Explain what? Was he not in the discharge of his duty? Had he not a right to obliterate from the minds of that jury the effect of Mr. White's speech, by argument, by irony, by ridicule, or by an appeal to their sympathies, if he should think proper? Was there anything so criminal in a little good-natured ridicule of a talented opponent whose influence upon the jury he desired to counteract, that his mouth must be closed for it? Oh! but says the respondent, he had spoken of a *grand inquisitorial body!* Well, pray, sir, is not the grand jury a *grand inquisitorial* body? And is there any harm in alluding to it by its right name? But if it was this expression that stung his Honor, it was really a long time getting through to the quick. He had made use of this expression in opening his remarks. He had told them, and he had a right to tell them, that the cause they were called to try had been taken before a grand inquisitorial body, where the accused could not defend himself, which was strictly true; but the respondent never thought of the vulnerable nature of his dignity until Mr. Fox had almost completed a satire of some length upon Mr. White. It won't do, sir; it wasn't for that he made Fox stop. But perhaps it was because he appealed to the court to protect him from the assaults of the Sheriff, for I know he did, in an ironical style, as he says himself, appeal to the court for that purpose. Yet that had transpired sometime before, according to the statement of Mr. Hicks, and nothing was thought of it. Then why did he interrupt him whilst apostrophising "Joseph?" My opinion is he did so to annoy Fox, to break the thread of his discourse, to ruin its effect with the jury, and to provoke a reply that would afford a pretext for preventing him from proceeding. I arrive at this conclusion from what had already transpired and what immediately followed. There had been one mistrial in the case before, and something that then transpired, induced the counsel for the prisoner to take down the testimony. This the respondent would only permit under such restrictions as I'll venture to say no lawyer here ever heard of before. He then assumed the right to limit Kinsey's counsel in their arguments. At a moment when there was no occasion for it in the world, he interrupted Mr. Fox and demanded an explanation; and because Mr. Fox declined complying with a request he had no right to make, he peremptorily and unlawfully made him take his seat. All these things, sir, taken in connection, show a settled determination that Kinsey should be convicted; and, sir, they were done to bring about that end.

I don't pretend to say Mr. Fox did exactly as I would have done in the reply he made to the court, nor that he was strictly in the line of his duty in that particular. If he was not, it was the prerogative of the court to fine him for contempt of court; but, sir, he had no right to deprive Kinsey of the privilege promised him by the constitution of being heard by his counsel. He had no right to limit that counsel. If he had, he had the right to deprive Kinsey of the benefit of counsel altogether, which no one will affirm. The right of being heard by counsel, means the right of being fully heard; and no court can constitutionally deprive you of it by gagging your advocate in the middle of his speech. If Fox was in contempt, he should have been fined; but in the name of God Almighty secure to the citizen his constitutional right of being heard in court. It is of a violation of this right by the respondent that we complain, and the closing remark of Mr. Fox's speech to the jury gives you the key to the reason of it. "Gentlemen of the jury, you see what a chance my poor man has. Take his case." Could anything be more eloquent, more touching, or more appropriate?

"You see what a chance my poor man has,—the victim of circumstantial evidence, deprived of his constitutional right of being heard in court, by judicial tyranny; my mouth is sealed; take his case." I think with Mr. Fox, sir, that he never made a better speech in his life. No lawyer ever did. It is what would have gushed up from the heart of every just man.

There is scarcely a single provision in the Bill of Rights that this respondent is not proven to have violated. There is scarcely a constitutional guaranty he has not broken. He has trampled the inalienable right of personal liberty under his feet. Clothed in the armor of official authority, he has assassinated private character with a treachery and cowardice only equalled by the frenzied malice that instigated the disgraceful crime. He has denied to the citizen the privilege of the writ of habeas corpus. He has deprived him of a speedy trial without delay. He has closed the mouth of his counsel. He has descended from the bench and participated in the litigation before him. He has brought disgrace, obloquy, and contempt upon the judiciary of the State in every manner that infernal ingenuity could devise; and when arraigned before the bar of his country, and all these disgraceful and dangerous malversations proven clearly and indisputably upon him, he points triumphantly to the Supreme Court, and says, "there's the tribunal to correct all the wrongs I have done." I will not do the respondent the injustice to say I believe he is sincere in this opinion. I am confident he knows better; but I do believe he entertains so contemptible an opinion of the intelligence of some members of this Court as to think he can induce them to adopt a doctrine so absurd.

My opinion is, sir, he desires to escape conviction on any terms, even at the sacrifice of legal reputation, and every thing else that can save him from the imputation of insanity; and hence I have no idea he believes that the Supreme Court has any more jurisdiction in this case than I have myself. It is true, sir, and I see now that I and every other citizen of the State have reason to rejoice at the fact that we have a Supreme Court, composed of gentlemen selected on account of their learning, wisdom, and purity of character; and that to that distinguished tribunal every citizen in the State has a right to appeal. But for what purpose? Merely to have the errors of an inferior court corrected, and not to punish the Judge for the malice with which he committed the error, and brought all the evil consequences of that error upon the aggrieved party. This is the tribunal provided by the constitution for the accomplishment of that object. The Supreme Court is designed to protect the individual parties in each case from the effects of the errors of the inferior court, whilst it is the province of this Court to prevent the recurrence of such errors as result from a bad intention, by removing from office and disfranchising the party guilty of their commission.

But let us suppose for a moment that the Supreme Court should have been appealed to in each one of these cases. Let us suppose that the Supreme Court is the only tribunal to which the citizens of the State can look for protection against all the oppression, partiality, abuse of official authority, and misconduct of which the Judges of our Circuit Courts may be guilty in their offices. What security has any one in a single right he claims as a citizen under the constitution, if such conduct is to be tolerated as this respondent was guilty of in the cases of Moore *vs.* Eldridge, Griffie *vs.* Berry, and Daugherty *vs.* Whitehead?—which have been selected and presented to you as examples out of the numerous instances in which he has effectually defeated a fair adjudication of causes by the Supreme Court, by falsifying the records of his court, and refusing to sign bills of exceptions, unless they were made to omit the very errors he was charged of committing. I would ask the Court to take the case of Moore against Eldridge; examine the conduct of the respondent in relation to it, and tell me what benefit any citizen can hope to derive from an appeal to the Supreme Court, if that conduct is all proper and right. I would submit that conduct to a candid world, and challenge the production of its parallel in the annals of American jurisprudence.

At the April term, 1858, of the Ripley Circuit Court, there was pending the case of James Moore *vs.* John Eldridge, administrator of the estate of a deceased Mr. Parker, formerly a partner in business with the plaintiff, Moore. On a certain day during the term the case was called, a jury ordered, and the court took a recess for dinner. During this recess, Mr. Kittrell tells you he found the respondent here, Judge of the court as he was, upon his (Kittrell's) wood pile, discussing the merits of the case in the presence of a group of some five or six who were standing around him. Mr. Kittrell took up the opposite side from the respondent, and each argued his views at considerable length,—Kittrell contending that Moore should recover, and the respondent contending that the estate of Parker was not liable, and hence, of course, that Moore could not recover. Mr. Kittrell is presently met by Mr. Moore, who tells him he is sure to lose the case, for the Judge has already decided against him. Now, sir, in the name of virtue and of justice, look at that conduct! The Judge orders a jury in a case, and while the Sheriff is summoning it, he descends from the bench, collects a crowd of citizens about him, decides upon the merits of the case, maintains his view with zeal in a long argument. The community all become apprised of the Judge's decision. The parties come into court satisfied of the pre-adjudication of the case; and the Judge, well prepared to sustain his argument upon the wood pile by a decision upon the bench, takes his seat with the gravity of a Hale, to go through the mockery of trying a cause that everybody knows he has already determined!

But, sir, shameful as this conduct is,—disgraceful as it is to the judicial character,—dangerous as it is to the interests of the citizens of this State,—it is by no means the most reprehensible that we find the respondent guilty of in this very case. Having decided the case against Moore in the streets, it is not difficult to imagine that he would use every effort to effect his defeat in court; but we find him going even further than that. We find him effectually defeating his right to a fair trial in the Supreme Court.

Upon the trial of the case, Lemuel Kittrell was the only witness introduced, and he was introduced I believe to prove that Parker had executed an instrument of writing produced as evidence of the fact that Parker's estate was liable to Moore for the amount claimed. The case went against Moore; and desiring to take it up, he presented his bill of exceptions, embodying the testimony of Mr. Kittrell, to the respondent for his signature. The respondent refused to sign the bill of exceptions, because the evidence of Kittrell set out in it did not state that the date of the instrument had been altered. Mr. Kitchen, who was Moore's lawyer, told him Kittrell had never sworn to any such thing. Mr. Bedford, counsel for Mr. Eldridge, told him also that Kittrell had not sworn to any such thing. Not satisfied with the statements of both parties, Mr. Kittrell is called and asked if he had testified to anything concerning the alteration of the date of the instrument? He said that he had not; that the instrument was as he had always seen it; that he had given no such testimony as the Judge had said he had. Yet, sir, in spite of what Kitchen, Bedford, and Kittrell all tell him, he interlined the testimony of Kittrell with his own hand, so as to make it appear that Kittrell had sworn to a fact that he had not,—

namely, that the date of the instrument had been altered,—and signed the bill after he had thus falsified it. There can be no mistake in these facts, sir. Kitchen, Bedford, and Kittrell all swear to them. He refused to sign a bill of exceptions embodying all the facts, until he had falsified it,—until he had made it so as almost to insure an affirmance of his judgment by the Supreme Court. And Moore, finding he was not to be permitted to present his case to the Supreme Court as it had been tried, abandoned his appeal, and, as you are told, compromised the case.

It is true, sir, the witnesses all tell you there was a blot, or some kind of an apparent obliteration of the date; and Mr. Hicks even states that there was a new date in different ink discernable. But that was a matter of inspection. If it was a fact material in the case, Kittrell had not sworn to it, and this respondent had no right to falsify his testimony and make it appear that he did. He had no right to put into a witness' mouth words he never thought of uttering.

Why, sir, look at the difference this little interlineation in that bill of exceptions makes in the case! Here Moore presents a paper purporting to be signed by the deceased, showing clearly that the deceased promised to pay him so much for his services during the succeeding year. The date then becomes material, and if the fact be established that so material a portion as the date has been altered, and no explanation of the alteration appearing, the whole paper upon which Moore predicates his case is vitiated. This material point the defendant fails to make, and the Judge takes it upon himself to make it for him in the bill of exceptions. The truth is, sir, he had expressed an opinion in public, and argued it zealously off the bench; he had sustained it in court upon the trial; and to prevent that opinion from being reversed by the Supreme Court, no means were so base that he would not resort to them.

But again, sir, take the case of Berry against Griffie, pending in the Stoddard Circuit Court, at the November term, 1858. I learn from this record that this case had been brought to recover back a certain sum of money paid by Berry to Griffie, for Griffie's claim upon a piece of land, and a lot of rails he was to make. In the instrument upon which the suit is founded it is not pretended that Griffie had any interest in the land more than a mere claim upon government land; and from anything I can see in these papers the sale of Griffie's interest to Berry was a fair and valid transaction, showing no design upon the part of Griffie to overreach Berry, who made the contract with his eyes open. But be that as it may, during the trial of this cause the respondent turned to the jury and told them that "Griffie had no interest in the land susceptible of conveyance, at the time he made the contract." Now, sir, what right had he to make any such assertion, even if true, to that jury? That was the very question they were trying; and was it fair, was it just, was it even necessary that he should interfere with the discharge of their duties under their oath, to the prejudice of either party? You know very well, sir, the influence a Judge's position necessarily gives him over the minds of the jury. They not only conclude from his position that he is an honest, just, unprejudiced man, but that he knows the law and desires to see it fairly administered; hence they listen attentively, and in ninety-nine cases out of a hundred believe every syllable he utters, never suspecting the slightest bias. I appeal to you then, sir, to know if it is right,—if it is lawful,—if it is consistent with the right of the trial by jury, for a Judge to forestall the judgment of a jury by expressing to them his own opinion upon a matter of fact submitted to them?

Suppose you were plaintiff in an action of ejectment, and the Judge should tell the jury you never had any title to the land in question, irrespective of the evidence before them,—suppose he should take it upon himself in an action of trespass, to tell the jury that the plaintiff never had any title to, or possession of the premises,—would you not consider him far beyond the line of his duty? Sir, it is the right of every citizen to have the facts connected with any case in which he may be interested tried by an unbiassed jury of his country; and so careful is the law that the minds of that jury shall be kept free from any prejudice whatever,—so careful is the law that the jury shall decide upon the facts from the evidence, and that alone, that it prohibits the juror after he is sworn from conversing with any one, or from permitting any one to express an opinion, or even to talk to him about the case, until after he shall have delivered his verdict in court. Yet it is proven that this respondent, whose sworn duty it is to see that the trial by jury is maintained inviolate, is himself the first to violate it,—that seated upon the bench for the administration of justice between his fellow men, he so far forgets the solemn obligations of his office as to publicly espouse the cause of one of the parties, and attempt to forestall the action of the jury by an unqualified expression of his own opinion.

Sir, if such conduct as this is tolerated, the trial by jury, upon which the sages of the law have bestowed so many encomiums, is a mere farce,—a contemptible cheat,—a mean fraud upon the honest citizen. Establish a doctrine that a Judge has the right to bring the whole weight of his influence to bear directly upon the jury in favor of any party he may select, and you make our court houses mere market places for the retailing of judicial favors.

Of this conduct the House of Representatives complain. They contend that in thus interfering with the proper administration of justice, he exhibited a degree of partiality inconsistent with his position as Judge, injurious and oppressive to the opposite party, and sufficiently disgraceful to the judiciary of the State to demand the dismissal of the respondent from office.

But this is by no means the worst feature in his behavior in this case of Berry *vs.* Griffie, as the evidence clearly shows. After the respondent had turned to the jury and told them the defendant never had any interest in the land susceptible of conveyance, they retired, and after some deliberation brought in a verdict for eleven dollars more than the plaintiff had demanded. Mr. Tyrell, the attorney for the defendant, filed a motion for a new trial, setting out among other reasons "that the jury were misled by testimony to prove who was the owner of the land in question at the time of the *trial;*" "that that evidence ought to have been excluded;" and "that the jury was misled by the opinion expressed by the court that the defendant had no interest in the land susceptible of conveyance." These three reasons inserted in the motion for a new trial were regarded by Mr. Tyrell as valid, and argued by him before the court. He urged very properly that it was not right that a Judge should bias the minds of a jury by expressing his own opinion as to the merits of the case in their hearing, and offered the affidavits of some of the jurors that it was upon that very expression of his that the verdict was predicated; but the respondent overruled his motion. Mr. Tyrell then filed a motion in arrest of judgment, which was also overruled; whereupon he drew up a bill of exceptions embodying these three reasons to which I have just called your attention as having been urged for a new trial and overruled, and tendered it to the court for his signature; but the Judge refused to sign it unless these three reasons were stricken out; nor would he sign it until Mr. Tyrell had stricken them out.

Now, sir, there can be no doubt of these facts. Here I have in my hand the motion for a new trial itself, with all three of these reasons in it, and here is a certified copy of the bill of exceptions, with all of them stricken out; and Mr. Tyrell tells you on his oath how it came to be done, and not only that, but that he urged them as grounds for a new trial, and relied upon them as grounds for a reversal of judgment. That he did act as he is charged in this instance there can be no shadow of doubt; but why did he do so? It is but just to presume that no rational man ever acts without some motive. His will must be and is concerned in, and consents to all his voluntary acts; and from the circumstances surrounding, and the consequences resulting from his actions, we must infer the intent by which he is actuated. Judging, therefore, from the partiality he exhibited in favor of Berry upon the trial, and from the fact that the inevitable consequence of striking out the reasons relied upon for a new trial would be to deprive Griffie of a fair trial in the Supreme Court,—we are forced to the conclusion that his conduct was shaped with that view, particularly when the still darker circumstance of his refusing to examine and sign the testimony taken in the case is taken into consideration.

Mr. Tyrell tells you he presented a fair and full statement of all the evidence given in the case, and desired the respondent to examine and sign it, that it might go with the bill of exceptions; but this he utterly refused to do, pretending that there was so much noise in court during the trial he could not hear what the evidence was. Mr. Tyrell then went to Mr. Bedford, who was the opposite counsel, and got him to assure the court that the evidence was properly set forth; but he still refused to sign, or even to look at it. Such is the testimony of both Bedford and Tyrell.

Now, may it please the Court to review these two cases for a single moment. In each of them the respondent selects his party, and shamelessly exhibits his partiality for him to every spectator present; in each of them his favored party is successful; in each of them he falsifies the records, and utterly precludes the unsuccessful party from all possibility of a fair trial in the Supreme Court; and yet, sir, he claims that the Supreme Court alone should review his official conduct. These two cases, sir, and the case of Daugherty *vs.* Whitehead, tried at the same term with the case of Berry *vs.* Griffie, sufficiently demonstrate the fact that a Judge of the Circuit Court is not only endowed with sufficient powers to effectually defeat the right of the citizen to an appeal to the Supreme Court, but that, possessing like frailties, acted upon by the same impulses, influenced by the same passions that others are liable to, they may exercise that power to the destruction of the interests of all they may desire to oppress, and that they will do so unless restrained by the proper authority. And to you is submitted the important question whether they shall be permitted to force all cases coming before them to conform to their Procrustean beds; whether they shall be permitted to espouse the cause of a favorite party, win public favor to his cause by discussing its merits in the streets, forestall the judgments of the jury by an unqualified expression of their opinions from the bench, and then cover up their base partiality and ignominious tyranny by refusing the unsuccessful party the benefit of an appeal to the Supreme Court, unless such parts of the record as expose their perfidy are suppressed. It is now submitted to you whether our Circuit Courts, instead of being the beneficent protectors of the rights and interests of all, may remorselessly prey upon the objects of their sacred guardianship, and then withhold from the victims of their unjust and arbitrary tyranny the remedy guarantied to them in the constitution. You are now asked whether liberty and justice, outraged by our judiciary, shall veil their beauteous faces forever from our view, and their sacred shrines become the loathsome, putrid dens of foul corruption. You are now asked, sir, whether our courts shall be an honor and a blessing to our country, or whether, by such a course of unheard of corruption as the respondent is proven to have been guilty of in these three cases, they shall clothe themselves in the same immortal infamy that makes the names of Star Chamber and High Commission, after the lapse of more than two centuries, still the abhorrence of an enlightened nation. And these questions you must answer to your consciences and your constituents.

But, sir, in your just execrations of the highly disgraceful conduct of the respondent in connection with these cases, let me ask you not to forget another charge alleged against him of a very serious character for misconduct of another variety at the same term of court. The testimony develops the fact that at the August term, 1858, of the Stoddard Circuit Court, there was an accusation pending before the grand jury against one David G. Hicks, for an assault with intent to kill. Whether Mr. Hicks was under recognizance or not I will not say; but one thing is certain,—the respondent knew this accusation was pending against him. Mr. Hicks, when upon the stand the first time, told you that Mr. Hale told him he had told the Judge so himself. After dinner, Mr. Hicks was called to the stand again, for what purpose I will not undertake to say; but while upon the stand then, he took occasion to say he had been mistaken; that Mr. Hale had not told him that he told the Judge of the accusation pending against Hicks. But Mr. Hale himself being recalled, tells you it is true *he* did not tell the respondent there was an accusation pending against Mr. Hicks for shooting at Mr. Conran, but that several *others* told him so in his hearing. Yet, notwithstanding this knowledge, the respondent, in the absence of Mr. Woodsides, the Circuit Attorney, appointed David G. Hicks Circuit Attorney *pro tem.* The grand jury found a true bill against Hicks, notified the Judge of the fact, as Mr. Hale tells you, and asked him to appoint some attorney to prepare an indictment. This, however, the Judge failed to do. So Mr. Hicks, acting as Circuit Attorney, prepared the indictment against himself, and it was returned to the court "*a true bill.*" The respondent *then* knew—of course, he was bound to know—that there was an accusation pending against Mr. Hicks; but, sir, this record shows no order for a *capias*, no voluntary appearance at that term, nor that any *capias* issued for Mr. Hicks in vacation. He goes upon his "parole of honor"—a process unknown, sir, to any of our courts, I believe, except those over which this respondent has the honor to preside—until the next November term. At that term the case of the "State of Missouri *vs.* David G. Hicks, indicted for assault with intent to kill," is entered in full upon the Judge's docket and stares him plainly in the face, so that he could not avoid seeing it but by shutting his eyes. Woodsides, the regular Circuit Attorney, is again absent; and, as this record shows you, sir, Mr. Hicks must again be appointed to prosecute the pleas of the State, notwithstanding the pendency of this indictment against him. Whether this case was placed on the first-day's docket or not, I will not undertake to say; but it is in evidence that this escaped the general massacre of indictments which occurred on that day. Mr. Hicks did not weep, I presume, like Niobe, over the indiscriminate slaughter of his numerous progeny, which, we are told, the lawyers made on that occasion, but probably, desiring to prolong the sport, told Mr. Miller, his counsel, not to file a motion to quash the indictment against him for several days, until the grand jury should be discharged; and so we don't hear of his case being called even until after the grand jury is discharged. Mr. Miller then comes into court and asks the court to quash the indictment against Mr. Hicks—files no motion, assigns no reason, but simply asks that it be quashed; and the respondent, without looking at the indictment, without appointing any attorney to represent the State, without even waiting for reasons to be filed,—so eager was he to discharge his friend,—quashed the indictment, as is shown by this record. The grand jury had been discharged; there was no one there to say a single word for the State,—to ask that Mr. Hicks be secured by recognizance until another grand jury could pass upon the case, which, indeed, under the circumstances, would have been proper in the Judge to do upon his own motion. So there is no atonement for violated law,—no vindication of justice and the dignity of the State; but Mr. Hicks, through the reprehensible lenity of the court, goes thereof without day.

Now, sir, contemplate the spectacle presented in these facts, in all its horrible deformity,—see the rights of every citizen in the State prostrate at the mercy of the Judge and Circuit Attorney; and if you are powerless to correct an evil so gross, so glaring, and so dangerous, in the name of justice,—in the name of all that man can hold dear,—I implore you to go back to those who sent you here and tell them what you have seen and know,—tell them a Circuit Attorney may imbrue his hands in the innocent blood of an unoffending citizen; that he may prepare the indictment against himself; that he may stalk abroad among community without even the restraints of bail; that at the ensuing term of court his case may be passed over until the grand jury has been discharged, and then he may come into court in person or by his counsel and ask that the indictment drawn against himself, by his own hand, and made defective on purpose, may be quashed; and that the Judge of the court, coming in as the great actor in the last scene of this grand drama of corruption and wrong, may quash the indictment without even looking at it, without even waiting to have a reason filed, and without appointing any one to protect the interests of the State,—tell them that a Circuit Attorney may commit any crime known to the code, and, if he is a pet of the court, the court may save him from punishment; and that for such outrages upon justice and the security of the private citizen, there is no power that can reach him; and let them in the name of God fortify themselves against an evil that may prove destructive to their most sacred rights,—let them repair a breach in the fortifications they have sought to erect around their rights, ere it let in upon them a thousand monstrous wrongs for which they have no remedy. Ah! but perhaps Mr. Hicks was a *clever fellow!*

It does really seem to me, sir, that this respondent, in his official career, has endeavored to bankrupt an invention of boundless fertility in the production of iniquity and wrong. His conduct, since he has been Judge, is a sort of kaleidoscope, exhibiting corruption in every conceivable variety of form. He seems to have permitted no occasion, no circumstances, and no place to check the black drippings of depravity perpetually distilling from him. He makes an open exhibition of his partiality upon the street; he converts the bench into a theatre for the enactment of the most disgraceful oppression in every shape that malice can conceive; and not yet content, he explores the privacy of the grand jury room in search of a new field for the display of a new variety of official iniquity.

I maintain, sir, that the Judge of the Circuit Court has no more right to visit a grand jury in their retirement for the purpose of instructing them as to their duties, than I, or any other private citizen has, and if he presumes to do so, I hold him guilty of a violation of law as well as propriety.

The constitution and the statute law of the State both provide that the proceedings of courts of justice shall be public. Read the thirty-fifth section of the act establishing courts of record: "The sittings of every court shall be public, and every person may freely attend the same."

Does this mean that a Judge may discharge one portion of his functions publicly, and another privately? if so, how do you ascertain which are his public, and which his private, inquisitorial duties? If you grant that he may exercise *any* portion of his functions in private, have you any other statute than the one I have read to justify the conclusion that he may not take his seat and merely open court in public, and then retire to a private chamber and transact all the other business under the secrecy of lock and key, if so disposed? Can you find any more authority either in reason or law for a Judge going to a grand jury room and instructing them in their duties, than he has to invade the privacy of a petit jury room, and there instruct them in relation to a case they may have under consideration? Can you cite a sentence of law, or show a particle of reason, that will justify a Judge in claiming the privilege this respondent has shamelessly usurped,—of giving the grand jury private instructions? Sir, you cannot. But, inasmuch as he is the guardian of the interests of the whole community,—inasmuch as he holds in his hands the law designed for the protection of the life, liberty, property, and reputation of every citizen; and inasmuch as the interests of every citizen are immediately involved in the manner in which his duties are discharged, the law requires him to discharge those duties under the supervision of his employers,—under their immediate inspection,—in full view of the whole community; nor does it make any distinction in those duties.

Suppose a Judge should claim the prerogative of trying a man for murder with closed doors—with no one present but the accused, his counsel, the State's attorney, Clerk, jury, and the witness under examination; or suppose that, after the jury in any case of felony had retired to consider of their verdict, the Judge should claim and exercise the right of going into the privacy of their room, and there instruct them upon the case,—who would not feel a thrill of horror at such a gross and daring usurpation? Who would consider himself safe if such a thing were permitted to be done?

Yet, sir, dangerous and reprehensible as such a usurpation would be, the prerogative of instructing the grand jury privately would be a thousand fold more disastrous and execrable. Clothe a Judge with this extraordinary privilege, and mark the terrible train of tremendous consequences that must inevitably result. The Judge himself may be guilty of innumerable crimes, or his friends may have, with a high hand, rioted over the outraged rights of their fellow-citizens, and the down-trodden laws of the State, through a long career of crime; and yet he sets at the head of the grand jury, and, as they inquire of each particular case, he can instruct them that such is not an indictable offense under the law, which they are sworn to receive at his hands. I need not remind you how he screened Henley, his bosom crony, from indictment in this very way, for having revealed the secrets of the grand jury, at the Butler Circuit Court, in May, 1858; but I will presently show you how he endeavored to screen himself and others.

And besides, sir, see what a terribly fearful engine of tyranny he would thus be enabled to wield to the utter and irretrievable demolition of all upon whom he might be disposed to wreak his vengeance. Using the influence of his position, he may procure a distorted statement of facts against an unoffending citizen, who has been so unfortunate as to provoke his ire; pervert the law in his private instructions to the grand jury; procure an indictment against him, and chain his devoted victim down to suffer for months, and perhaps for years, all the horrors incidental to an unjust imprisonment. The poor man is finally dragged forth, declared guiltless by a jury of his country, and restored to liberty merely to linger through a few years of pain and sorrow, his constitution broken by imprisonment and preyed upon by disgrace, his hopes ruined, and his reputation forever blasted by the imperishable odium of a prosecution for an infamous crime, until, relieved by the friendly hand of death, he sinks into a welcome grave, "unwept, unhonored, and unsung;" whilst the fiend in human shape, whose poisonous breath wrought all this piteous desolation, is caressed upon the bosom of society, unsuspected of a crime that would make the devil himself hang his head in shame. Ah! yes, he chuckles over the ruin his diabolical malice has effected, and says, "I'm safe; the grand jury were sworn never to divulge what transpired in their room; my victim rots in disgrace, and his orphan children wander friendless and homeless through a pitiless world, but my secret is safe; my official position is the 'open sesame' to the best society; my revenge is sated; I'll roll in luxury now, until my 'eyes stand out with fatness.'"

But, sir, palpable as these considerations are, the respondent has the effrontery to admit that he has committed so gross a violation of the law, and claims that he did right in doing it. He has told you he visited the grand jury during their retirement at the August term, 1858, of the Stoddard Circuit Court. And why does he say he did it? Because David G. Hicks was a young and inexperienced lawyer, and was unable to give the information they needed. Is that an excuse? Why did he appoint this callow fledgeling of the law, knowing he was incompetent? There were Bedford, Kitchen, Phelan, Tyrell, and Davis, all able and experienced lawyers. Or, if the court must give the instructions, why not have the grand jury brought into court, as required by law? Why not transmit to them through Mr. Hicks the opinion of the court? It is presumed that he could understand and remember it, at least until he reached the grand jury room.

Sir, this excuse is too flimsy and transparent. There is no sincerity or truth in it, as the facts clearly show. Mr. Jackson tells you that he and the Judge were in conversation, when Mr. Hicks came and told the Judge that the grand jury had in their possession a piece of paper citing a certain section in the statute,—Mr. Jackson did not know what one; that the Judge instantly went off in the direction of the grand jury room, and presently returned with a paper, which Mr. Hicks identified as the one of which he had spoken. When the Judge entered the grand jury room, Mr. Carlisle, who was a member of the grand jury, tells you there was complete silence for some moments. As soon as the anger of the Judge would give him tongue, he says, "some body has been tampering with the grand jury; there is a paper here I want." Now, sir, why did Mr. Hicks come so straight and notify the Judge that that paper was in the grand jury room? Why should the Judge become so agitated about it? Why did he rush to the grand jury room so impetuously and demand it? Perhaps that paper is the key to the appointment of Mr. Hicks Circuit Attorney *pro tem.* You will remember, sir, that a short time previous the respondent had imprisoned one Jonas Eaker, and compelled him to answer to a writ of mandamus that had not been served upon him. Mr. Eaker considered this an act of willful and malicious oppression, or, to say the least of it, misconduct; and Mr. Carlisle tells you he presented the respondent to the grand jury for it, and to show them that it was indictable, handed them this famous slip of paper, citing page 613 of the Revised Statutes of Missouri:

SECTION 16. Every person exercising or holding any office or public trust, who shall be guilty of willful and malicious oppression, partiality, misconduct, or abuse of authority in his official capacity, or under color of his office, shall, on conviction, be punished by imprisonment in the county jail for a term not exceeding one year, and by fine not exceeding one thousand dollars.

The reason is obvious, then, why his Honor was so wrought upon by that little piece of paper. It concerned his own security, and he intended to suppress it at all hazards,—the law, reason, and right to the contrary notwithstanding.

But, sir, how does he behave after he gets the paper? Is he content with securing that merely? No, sir. He turns to this sixteenth section, and instructs them that it does not apply to *him*,—that it will apply to Judge Eaker of the County Court, but not to him!

Here, sir, is the very climax of corruption. See the regular gradations in this deliberate career of official crime. He first willfully and maliciously oppresses Eaker,—he knows he has violated the law; he is conscious of guilt, and expects to be presented to the grand jury. He appoints Mr. Hicks Circuit Attorney, knowing there was an accusation pending against him, in order to have the means of being kept advised as to the action of the grand jury. He tolerates in Hicks a disclosure of the secrets of the grand jury. Availing himself of that disclosure, he violates the law again, by invading the precincts of the grand jury room; and there he puts the finishing touch upon this panorama of official iniquity by deliberately misdirecting them in the law, in order to screen himself from indictment! In the name of God Almighty, I ask if corruption ever exhibited its hideous, disgusting features so shamelessly or so boldly before?

But, sir, he was not guilty of this double crime only once. He again visited the grand jury during their sitting at this same term of court. Why he did so I will not now undertake to determine; but it will certainly strike most minds as a remarkable coincidence that, at the very moment he entered the grand jury room, they had under consideration a charge against himself and Mr. Hicks for gambling. Whether Mr. Hicks again apprised him of the business before the grand jury, or whether he was appointed Circuit Attorney *pro tem.* for that purpose, is, perhaps, unnecessary to inquire; but certain it is, that whilst on this visit to the grand jury the respondent told them that playing cards for whisky, oysters, and such things, was not an indictable offense; and it is also certain that the grand jury found an indictment against the respondent, David G. Hicks, Isaac Brand, and Orson Bartlett, for gaming for these very articles, and at that very term of court.

It is entirely immaterial, in my estimation, whether the facts of which the respondent was guilty amounted to betting, in law, or not. That was a question of fact for the jury to determine, and with which the Judge had no right to interfere, either in or out of the grand jury room; and the respondent was willfully and maliciously guilty of gross official misconduct in endeavoring to force their opinions upon this point of fact to conform to his own, right or wrong. The grand jury, however, it seems withstood the influences of the Judge, and found an indictment against him, and Mr. Hicks, and Mr. Brand, and Col. Bartlett, for gambling for whisky. Col. Bartlett pleaded "not guilty," and claimed a separate trial; and, sir, upon this trial the respondent—as if determined not to be out done,—determined that the parties to that indictment should escape the penalty of the law, right or wrong—was, if the evidence you have before you is true, guilty of one of the most shameful exhibitions of willful partiality—one of the most daring and outrageous abuses of his official authority—the judicial history of this or any other country affords.

Review for a single moment the facts connected with this trial. A jury is empanneled and sworn to try the cause; the State introduces her evidence, and proves that the respondent, David G. Hicks, Isaac Brand, and the defendant, Bartlett, did, at a certain time in Stoddard county, play at a game of cards, and that it was made to depend upon the issue of that game who should pay for the whisky to be drank by the four. After the State had proven these facts, the respondent, upon the bench, took it upon himself to tell the jury that these facts did not constitute a betting, and were not indictable under the statute against gambling. Not content with merely enunciating this view of the case, he proceeded to enforce it by a zealous and labored argument,—he brought forward a great variety of examples to prove his position correct. Not yet content, he told them they should not find a general verdict,—if they did, he would set the same aside; that they should find the facts, and he would take it upon himself to say under the law whether the defendant was guilty or not. Such are the facts, sir, established by an array of testimony impregnable as the rock of Gibraltar,—such are the facts that the respondent, after flatly denying in his answer, is now forced to admit. And I submit to the wisdom and intelligence of this honorable Court,—I submit it to the candor of the people of an enlightened State,—if the annals of American jurisprudence afford a case of parallel atrocity to the one they exhibit.

The Legislature of our State, sensible of the undue influence a Judge may exercise over the minds of a jury,—knowing the impression sometimes made by a tone of voice, a look, or gesture,—conscious of the natural proneness of the human heart to partiality, and aware that, if permitted at all to sum up or comment on the testimony before a jury, the Judge might at least be tempted to unsettle the seals of justice,—has, by special statutory enactment, expressly prohibited the exercise of such a privilege.

They were also satisfied that, if permitted to instruct a jury orally as to the law, a court could mislead them with perfect impunity,—obtain just such a verdict as it might desire,—and then so modify the coloring of its instructions in the record submitted to the inspection of the Supreme Court, on appeal, as to present entirely a different aspect to the one before the jury; and in the very same act provided that the court shall not instruct the jury orally, unless both parties consent to it. In order to prevent a court from giving instructions in any case, and then denying that any such instructions were given, the law requires that they shall be in writing. I will not attempt to comment upon the wisdom and propriety of this provision of law,—for such must be apparent to even the most casual thinker,—but merely read the act. Section thirty-one, article six, practice and proceedings in criminal cases, Revised Statutes, page 1195:

The court shall not, on the trial of the issue on any indictment, *sum up or comment upon the evidence*, or *charge the jury as to matter of fact*, unless requested so to do by the prosecuting attorney and the defendant or his counsel; but the court may instruct the jury on any point of law arising in the cause, *which instructions shall be in writing.*

Now, sir, from the evidence of Mr. Bedford, Mr. Tyrell, Mr. Kitchen, and others, you find the respondent, in utter contempt of this plain requirement of the statute, without the solicitation of any one whatever, taking it upon himself to comment at great length before the jury, in this trial of Col. Bartlett, upon the facts adduced. He taxes his ingenuity for illustrations to impress upon the minds of that jury the idea that the facts proven do not constitute an offense indictable under the statute. He charges them that, although the facts detailed by the witnesses may have been true, that the defendant is not guilty. He not only violates this plain statute in the manner of giving his instructions, but the instructions themselves were wrong, and he knew it. What was that jury summoned for, sir? Manifestly to determine whether or not the defendant was guilty as charged. But why go through with so ridiculous a formality, if they are to set there as twelve senseless blocks merely to echo the opinion of the Judge? The question, sir, as to whether the facts proven constitute the crime charged, was clearly one, and indeed the only one, for the jury to decide; and the respondent either knew it, and willfully transcended his duty, or he was so shamefully ignorant of the duties pertaining to his position that he should not longer be permitted to disgrace himself and his office, and endanger the rights of community, by occupying it. I will not presume to advise him which horn of this unenviable dilemma to take.

But, sir, I do not execrate the offense of which this respondent acknowledges himself guilty in this instance,—I do not hold it up to your abhorrence as one of the most despicable crimes with which he could have polluted the "judicial ermine,"—I do not invoke upon it the fullest vengeance of the law merely because it is a violation of the statutes,—statutory provisions, to the whims of his corrupt passions, are like dry stubble before a hurricane of fire,—you have seen him violate them and trample them under his feet with a facility and an indifference that no longer excites your surprise; but I denounce it as a crime that should hurl him from his office, bring upon him the loathing and contempt of all good men, and embalm his name in eternal infamy, because it strikes at the very vitality of one of the most invaluable privileges,—one of the most cherished rights of every freeman,—the trial by jury.

I would not, sir, were I even less exhausted than at present, attempt a dissertation upon this glorious right of every human being under the operation of the beneficent institutions of our beloved country. Statesmen, taught by the experience of ages its inestimable value, have made it a subject of constitutional enactment; and sages, imbued with a burning eloquence that I can never hope to emulate, have portrayed its beauties, and commended its preservation to the jealous vigilance of freemen, in strains of impassioned eulogy that I have no power to imitate. I simply ask you to behold a Judge of one of your Circuit Courts, under a solemn oath to support the constitution of your State,—under every obligation that can be supposed to bind a human being to a strict discharge of a high and solemn trust,—striking this sacred right of the citizen into the dust. I ask you to hear him tell a jury in a criminal case, "you may find the *facts*, but I will determine whether the defendant is guilty or not under the law;" and if the daring and outrageous innovation upon the right of the trial by jury does not thrill you with horror, I must confess my utter inability to conceive any public calamity that could excite your alarm.

There is no evading the facts, sir. All the witnesses who testified upon this point tell you unmistakably, and the respondent himself admits, that he told the jury "they might find the facts, but he would determine whether the defendant was guilty or not;" and even threatened to set aside their verdict if they should find the defendant guilty. These facts are so, without the slightest variation, or attempt to palliate them. And will this honorable Court tell the constituency of Missouri that a Circuit Judge may throttle a jury, and compel them to bring in a verdict such as he desires?—that he may gag them in the midst of their duties?—that, by the potency of judicial magic, he may convert them into twelve insensate tools,—a set of senseless automatons,—to act as he acts upon them, and to echo merely the sentiments of the court, right or wrong? Will you tell them, sir, that a Judge may preside at a trial in the issue of which he has himself an indirect interest, and command the jury to find a particular kind of verdict, and still be held guilty of no wrong, no corruption? Will you tell them that it is perfectly right when a citizen is under trial for treason, murder, or any other felony, for the court to invade the province of the jury, and claim the right to determine the question of his guilt? Will you endorse the doctrine that in any criminal case the jury may be compelled to find a special verdict as to the facts, under a threat that the court will set aside any other verdict they may bring in?—that the jury may only find the facts, and that the court must say guilty or not guilty under the law? Will you tell them that the glorious privilege of being tried by your equals,—by twelve honest and unprejudiced men,—sanctified by constitutional enactment, and venerable from the use and approbation of ages, has dwindled to this poor, contemptible, disgusting farce?

I regret, sir, that I have not the strength to make an extended application of the monstrous doctrine acted upon by the respondent in this case, in order to exhibit it in all its horrible deformity. But I will ask you to suppose just one case. A man is arraigned for murder. A jury is sworn, and witnesses are introduced who relate all the sickening details of the horrible transaction. The length and depth and situation of each ghastly wound is minutely described. The demoniac oath of the fiendish murderer, as he plunged the glittering steel to the heart of his helpless victim, and that victim's dying shriek, are each detailed. The bloody knife, and the shirt stiff with gore, are both exhibited. The remorseless felon sets sullenly by, whilst the Judge instructs the jury that "they may find the *facts*, but he will say whether the prisoner is guilty or not under the law." The jury retire, and soon return with a recital of the sickening details of the horrible tragedy, which the Judge himself has just heard from the lips of the witnesses. The jury is discharged, and the Judge concludes the disgusting farce by saying, "it is the opinion of the court that the facts do not constitute an offense; the prisoner is a '*clever fellow*,' and may go hence without day." So the villain is turned loose to butcher somebody else; and every sensible, thinking man concludes, very justly, that all the boasted protection of the law is a disgraceful cheat.

I will not trespass upon the attention of the Court to show that a Judge, clothed with the absolute power claimed by the respondent in this case, could as easily pronounce an enemy guilty as he could a friend innocent; but I must request the Court to look at the system this immaculate respondent has been seeking to inaugurate in the Fifteenth Judicial Circuit. I would to God, sir, I could exhibit to every citizen of that intelligent community, to-day, the studied system of petty but complete despotism this respondent has deliberately attempted to fix upon them. Look at it, sir.

He tramples upon the liberty of a citizen,—imprisons him without authority of law; and when that citizen complains to the grand jury of his oppression, he goes before the grand jury and tells them he is above the law,—they can't indict him. He singles out his victim in his charge to the grand jury; publicly charges him of a crime; follows the grand jury to their room; insists upon, and by perverting the law, obtains an indictment; and having in his charge to the grand jury prepared the public mind in his favor, upon the trial of the indictment he instructs the jury that they may find the facts, and he will say whether the accused is guilty or not. The jury report the facts; he pronounces the man guilty; and the public mind, already poisoned by himself for the purpose, approves the verdict; and finally, when the victim of his vengeance would seek redress at the hands of the Supreme Court, he is denied the right of a fair trial before that tribunal; the records are falsified, and his doom rendered certain by that distinguished court. On the other hand his friend is presented to the grand jury. Through his Circuit Attorney he ascertains the fact,—goes to the grand jury room, and tells them they cannot find an indictment. If, however, they do, he bullies the jury upon the trial, compels them to find a special verdict; and outrages law, reason, and justice, by pronouncing him not guilty, in spite of the evidence.

Let no man say this system of tyranny has no existence except in my imagination. He has been proven guilty of every fact going to establish it. Revert to his dastardly attempt to procure an indictment against Kitchen, when he had been guilty of no wrong. See him follow the grand jury even to their retirement and insist upon it; think of his going to the grand jury of Butler county and telling them that Wm. Henley could not be indicted for revealing the secrets of the grand jury; see him in the grand jury room in Stoddard county trying to shield himself and David G. Hicks from indictment for playing cards for whisky; see him upon the trial of that indictment taking the consciences of the jury into his own hands, and compelling them to find a verdict to suit himself; see him refusing to sign and allow proper bills of exceptions, and thus effectually defeating the right of appeal; see him compelling parties to try their causes before him, or to follow them upon change of venue to counties so remote as to utterly preclude a fair or speedy trial; and you will be satisfied that he has deliberately inaugurated a system of oppression and despotism over his circuit, as complete, as perfect, and as well planned and fortified at all points, as any that ever rioted over the fallen freedom of mankind. I know, sir, it must almost stagger credulity itself, that such a state of affairs exists in the midst of an enlightened State, boasting of the purity and efficacy of its institutions; but, alas! the evidence in this cause proves beyond a doubt that it is as true as it seems incredible. Whether this foul blot shall be permitted longer to stain the fair escutcheon of our State is for you to determine. It has been exhibited to you in a light by no means sufficient to expose all its hideous deformity, but strong enough to enable you to discern its diabolical blackness; and it is with you to apply the remedy for its obliteration with which the sovereignty of your State has invested you.

I come now to call your attention to a feature of this case that I cannot contemplate without a thrill of the most intense horror. It has been reserved till the last because it exhibits the very achme, the summit and perfection, of cold-blooded atrocity,—the grand master-piece of a genius prolific in deeds of iniquity, that should secure to its author an immortality of infamy. But I feel my incapacity to do justice to the subject. The horrible picture of depravity, cruelty, and wrong it presents is far beyond my limited powers of expression, if even within the compass of human language. I know not what passion of the human soul the dreadful spectacle would soonest excite, if presented in terms suited to its perfect portrayal; nor would I appeal to anything save your sense of right and justice. But hear a short and simple story of wrong and misery, which, if told aright, would melt the very foundation stones of this capitol to tears of pity. I would not repeat the story of Lucrece,—I would not paint her with the deadly poniard in her uplifted hand, invoking the vengeance of Rome upon the adulterous Tarquin's head; nor pale in death, with the glittering blade deep in her pulseless heart. I would not tell you of Virginius, who sheathed his poisoned dagger in the stainless bosom of his virgin daughter, ere she should fall a victim to a tyrant's lust. I would not tell you of our own distinguished countryman who struck down in the street the assassin of his honor and his domestic joys; nor of the approbation with which an entire nation recently received the verdict that he was guiltless of any crime. I would descend to the humbler walks of life,—I would tell you of a poor, defenseless widow, left by the ruthless hand of death, that struck down the husband of her choice in the full bloom of manhood, with naught to cheer the dreary desolation of her aching heart save the innocent prattle and dimpled smile of a little daughter, and the miniature of her dead companion in the bright face of her infant boy. I will not linger through the long years of poverty and wretchedness that marked that helpless family's "short and simple annals." Nor need I tell you how that little girl, like a wild vine without a dresser, grew up to womanhood rude and unpolished in all the acquirements that adorn the lady of society, but rich in the graces of purity and virtue characteristic of her sex. I need not tell you how often a mother's love had led her to weep with her beside a father's grave; how often a mother's tears bedewed her humble pillow while downy sleep nestled upon her eyelids; how all the tendrils of a mother's widowed heart twined about her; nor how the mingled emotions of pride and hope swelled that mother's bosom when she saw her eldest born, the daughter of her heart, budding into lovely womanhood, "like the beauteous rosebud bursting with its prisoned sweets." Oh! sir, who can tell the depth, the strength, the intensity of a mother's love?

> "There is none—
> In all this cold and hollow world, no fount
> Of deep, strong, deathless love, save that within
> A mother's heart."

There is no hope like that which thrills through every fibre of a mother's soul, when her eldest daughter first steps upon the threshhold of womanhood. But, alas! that hope, pure, tender, and unselfish though it is, must sometimes end in cruel, bitter disappointment.

The demon came when none dreamed of his approach. His eye of lust gleamed upon the orphan girl in her wild, uncultured beauty; and his fiendish soul panted for the destruction of her maiden purity, and longed to banquet upon the luscious sweets of her blooming loveliness. His vile approaches were repelled with indignant scorn; but brute force, raging with the fierce fires of fiendish passion, triumphed, and he remorselessly gloated over the outraged purity of the ruined girl. Ah! why did not the fragile flower wither in the bud? Why did she ripen into the full bloom of loveliness to fall before the hurricane's raging breath? With all her brilliant hopes crushed beneath the feet of beastly violence,—with all the golden dreams of her buoyant, girlish heart ended in one horrible awakening; with nothing before her but dishonor, misery, and wretchedness; with no avenger but her own frail arm, in the frenzy of vengeance, she seized a weapon and struck the destroyer dead. Her poor, wretched, widowed mother, crazed with fear and anguish, in obedience to the instincts of a mother's love, assisted in concealing the terrible vengeance of her ruined daughter; and for this she was dragged before the bar of her country. In vain did she with streaming eyes implore the protection of that tribunal in her extremity; in vain did the generous, hallowed impulses of a mother's love appeal to that court for even sympathy. His flinty eye, moistened by no tear of pity, glanced upon her not merely with indifference,—but with a heartless cruelty that might well challenge the bloodiest freak of Nero or Caligula, that court deprived her of her evidence, drove her counsel out of her cause, condemned her to death, and denied her the last resort, a fair trial before the Supreme Court! Sir, this is no fancy picture; but strange, incredible, and horrible as it is, it was a Judge of our own beloved and enlightened State that so thirsted for the blood of a poor, defenseless widow, guilty of no crime save attempting to conceal a daughter's—an only daughter's—guilt and shame. It was a Missouri Judge that thus trampled under foot every constitutional guaranty of an impartial trial when claimed by a frail, crazed old woman. Let no man gainsay this who will read the evidence concerning the trial of

Sarah Buckner, before this respondent, at the November term, 1857, of the Stoddard Circuit Court. I know, sir, I cannot relate the story of that trial as it should be told; but I will recapitulate some of the principal points in the evidence.

Upon the examination of the first witness, Mr. Moore tells you the court asked most all the questions. Mr. Phelan tells you that "the Judge upon the trial acted more as the State's attorney than the State's attorney himself." The counsel for the prisoner protested against this course of conduct by the Judge, but to no purpose; he persisted in it until the examination of the witness was concluded. The next witness introduced was Mr. Grimsley. He was permitted to detail his testimony until he came to tell what would tend to exculpate her from any crime, and there he was stopped by the court, upon its own motion. He detailed a conversation of the prisoner; he was permitted to tell all that could possibly criminate her; he was made to tell all that could fix guilt upon her, and consign her to a dishonored grave; but when he came to tell that she denied having anything to do with the killing herself,—that it was the unassisted vengeance of her daughter upon her ravisher, and that to save that daughter from an ignominious death she merely assisted her to conceal the terrible deed,—the mouth of the witness was sealed by the court. Does the Circuit Attorney ask such a sanguinary ruling at the hands of the court? No, sir; it chills the blood even of the Circuit Attorney, whilst the Judge does so upon his own motion. In vain her counsel contend that all the conversation should go to the jury; in vain they endeavor to show the cruelty and injustice of permitting only such detached portions of her confession as tend to connect her with the awful deed to go to the jury, without the explanation showing her entire innocence,—they had as well attempted to soothe the venomed rage of the deaf adder with the plaintive song of pity: he was determined that that woman should die, and that no legal barrier should stand between him and his prey. Mr. Moore tells you he prepared a bill of exceptions to this ruling of the court, and presented it to the Judge, but he absolutely refused to sign it. Seeing that the testimony of Grimsley conflicted with that of the first witness, and fearing that the discrepancy might create some doubt in the minds of the jury, he even permitted his anxiety for a conviction to extend so far as to advise the Circuit Attorney, in open court, to withdraw the testimony of Grimsley. This cannot be questioned,—Mr. Phelan testifies to it positively. The court adjourned for dinner; and upon meeting for the afternoon session, the Circuit Attorney moved the court for permission to withdraw the witness Grimsley and the testimony he had detailed, in accordance with the suggestion of the court made before adjournment. In vain did Mr. Davis and Mr. Phelan object, and claim the right to cross-examine the witness; in vain did they represent that it had wrought its deadly effect upon the minds of the jury, if left unexplained; in vain did they plead in the name of justice, mercy, and the law, that they should be permitted to obliterate the effect of Grimsley's testimony by cross-examination,—the testimony had been withdrawn, and, as Mr. Phelan tells you, the rulings of the court were, like the decrees of the Medes and Persians, irrevocable. Mr. Davis prepared a bill of exceptions to this ruling, and presented it to the court; but, determined that the prisoner should have no chance of reversal, if convicted, he refused to sign it. The respondent has asked, if he did these things, why do not the bills of exceptions show it? Mr. Davis and Mr. Moore answer the question. They tell you he refused to sign the bills when presented.

When the Circuit Attorney came to argue the case to the jury, considering the testimony of Grimsley withdrawn, he never alluded to it in his speech. You remember, when Mr. Phelan told you this, how the respondent sprang to his feet, and with what eagerness he demanded a writ of attachment for John R. Woodsides, the Circuit Attorney. He felt that his conduct in this case would damn him eternally in the estimation of every honest man, and, like a drowning man clutching at a straw, he wildly hoped that Woodsides would say something different,—something that would excite at least a shade of doubt in his favor. A special messenger was dispatched. Mr. Woodsides was brought here, and testified that the testimony of Grimsley *was* withdrawn; that he regarded it as withdrawn when he argued the case, and never spoke of it at all. His evidence in no particular conflicted with the testimony offered by the State.

Mr. Davis arose to address the jury, and in the course of his remarks, as he himself tells you, and as Mr. Bedford also states, proceeded to suppose a case of a poor, defenseless widow, whose only daughter—the jewel of her soul, the idol of her heart, the object around which all the strong tendrils of her maternal affection fondly clung, just budding into womanhood, with her pure bosom elate with hope and joy—had been ruined by the brutal violence of a fiend in human shape. But he is abruptly stopped by the Judge. Perhaps that appeal may touch some tender chord of sympathy in some bosom not sealed to all the nobler emotions of our nature,—perhaps it may moisten the eye of some juror in that box with the tear of pity. So he is stopped, and ordered not to suppose any such case, but confine himself to the facts as proven. Mr. Davis again proceeded, and presently sought to enforce some argument by the use of an illustration. Again he is interrupted by the Judge, who tells him he shall confine himself to the facts proven, and not make use of such illustrations. Again Mr. Davis attempts to suppose a case, and again he is interrupted by the court. "May it please the court," says he, "shall I not be permitted to suppose a case by way of illustration?" "No, sir," replied the Judge, "you shall confine yourself to the facts proven." "Then, sir," said Mr. Davis, "I will abandon the case, if my client is to be *Jeffreyized* in that manner."

You all know the history of the sanguinary career of the infamous Jeffreys. His name is still the synonym for cruelty, oppression, and judicial crime. But, sir, that long career of unbridled wrong and outrage that secured to him the extreme apex of ignominious fame, affords no single instance of heartless, cold-blooded cruelty, and high-handed judicial despotism, equal to this conduct of the respondent.

Mr. Davis, bullied, brow-beaten, and hampered by the court, is compelled to abandon the cause, and leave his poor old client to the mercy of a tyrannical Judge,—"in the jaws of the dragon."

Mr. Phelan then endeavored to address the jury. In the course of his argument he deemed it proper to impress upon the minds of the jury the fact that Grimsley's testimony had been withdrawn, and that they should not consider it as evidence, hoping thus to eradicate the impression that the testimony had made, as he was not permitted to do so by a cross-examination. The Judge told him to stop, and said, "I have told you that testimony has been withdrawn, and you shall not speak of it." "I merely wished, if the court please, to correct any impression that testimony may have left upon the minds of the jury," said Phelan. "You shall not speak of it, sir, it has been withdrawn," said the Judge: and threatened him with a penalty worse than fine or imprisonment if he should allude to it again.

There can be no doubt of these facts, sir. Davis, Moore, Phelan, Bedford, Thornburg, and others have sworn to them. They are as clear as the sunbeam at noonday. But why, let me inquire in the name of mercy, should this poor old woman have been subjected to such unheard of persecution? The respondent does not even claim the slight extenuation her guilt might have afforded. He turned to me the other day in the presence of this Court, and said with a sneer that I would deserve to be hung myself if I should manage a case as that was managed; that she was convicted of a capital offense, not because she was guilty, but because her counsel were too ignorant to know their duties.

But, sir, the injustice and cruelty of this respondent were not confined merely to the trial. After it had been concluded,—after a conviction had been procured through the extraordinary exertions of the court,—Mr. Phelan filed a motion in arrest of judgment, setting forth among other grounds that the uncorroborated testimony of one witness was not sufficient to warrant a conviction for a capital offense. Now, why did Phelan insert this reason in the motion? Because the testimony of Grimsley had been withdrawn, which left the case entirely upon the testimony of young Seabaugh, the only other witness introduced by the State,—showing that the understanding of Phelan was, that Grimsley's testimony had been as effectually excluded from the jury as if it had never been detailed. When this reason was inserted in the motion in arrest, it struck the respondent that there was force and validity in it; and it is evident, sir, that he yet thinks it is valid. So, when Phelan presented a bill of exceptions for his signature, he refused to sign it until he had with his own hand inserted a statement of Grimsley's testimony, as though it had never been withdrawn. He feared the force of the reason urged by Mr. Phelan in arrest; he feared to have his action a second time reviewed by the Supreme Court,—for you will perceive by this record that he had been already reversed in this very case,—and he determined to make the Supreme Court believe that the case rested upon the testimony of at least two witnesses.

Now, sir, look upon this conduct. The testimony of Grimsley is withdrawn upon his own suggestion; he refuses the prisoner the right to cross-examine him; he gags her counsel when they attempt even to advert to it, to obliterate any impression it may have left upon the minds of the jury; and finally puts the climax to his cruelty, injustice, and oppression, by totally refusing to allow and sign her bill of exceptions, until it is made to show that this testimony went to the jury without a murmur or objection of any kind, and had never been withdrawn. Sir, if the annals of human crime afford a darker and more damning case than this, oh! in the name of humanity, I pray never to look upon its horrid features. A court of justice thirsting for the blood of a poor, defenseless old woman!—pursuing her with the cruel lash of persecution even to conviction and death! My God! what a spectacle for freemen to contemplate!

The respondent has frequently during the course of this trial endeavored to excite your pity; nor have I on any such occasion sought to repress the slightest emotion of that Godlike passion in your bosoms. It is a sentiment so free from any tinge of selfishness, the human heart is always purer and better for its entertainment. It is the golden chain that binds a fallen world to the throne of a pardoning Maker, and I delight to see its precious links forever brightly burnished. And, sir, it occurs to me, if I were called upon to draw a picture of this generous emotion of the human soul,—if it devolved upon me to represent Pity in her most striking attitude, I would paint her clinging to the robes of Justice and pointing to the corse of murdered Innocence dangling at the gibbet's arm, and with streaming eyes imploring her avenging sister to tear from the judicial tyrant, who grimly smiles upon the lifeless victim of his cruelty, the ermine he has smeared with human gore, and stamp upon his name the unfading impress of eternal infamy.

Sir, I can speak no longer upon this case. I have imperfectly, but to the extent of my humble ability, discharged the duty devolving upon me; and now the responsibility of deciding this important cause according to law and justice is with you. It is neither with myself nor those who sent me here. They have impeached the respondent at your bar of a ruthless violation of almost every right held sacred by the citizen and guarantied by the constitution and laws of our State. They have accused him of wantonly trampling under his feet, without authority of law, the inalienable right of personal liberty. They have accused him of assassinating private character, in repeated instances, whilst upon the bench. They have accused him of descending from the bench and participating in the litigation transpiring in his courts, in violation of the known rules of law and the requirements of common decency. They have accused him of depriving a citizen of the privilege of the writ of habeas corpus, and again of abusing the privilege of that writ by illegally turning loose upon the country tried and convicted felons, to go forth in the perpetration of every variety of villainy and crime with which it is possible for a civilized community to be cursed. They have accused him of invading the privacy of the grand jury room, and using the influence of his position in procuring indictments where none should have been preferred, and in screening himself and his favorite friends from justly deserved accusation and punishment. They have accused him of the most alarming and unheard of innovations upon the trial by jury, calculated to deprive the citizen entirely of the inestimable right to that ancient and invaluable mode of trial. They have accused him of depriving the citizen of the right to appeal to the Supreme Court, and of attempting thereby to establish his own supremacy in the courts over which he presides. They have accused him of every variety of oppression, outrage, and cruelty that infernal malice could conceive, or human depravity execute. And having proven all, even to the minutest particular, the dark and damning catalogue of crimes they have alleged against him, they demand that you shall exercise the great and plenary powers with which you have been endowed by the framers of our government, in vindicating the character of our judiciary, and purifying that essential department of the State from the foul pollution his diversified corruption has brought upon it. Were the respondent innocent, no man could rejoice more at his honorable acquittal than myself; but guilty, he should not only be hurled from his high position, but the evidence of his condemnation be stamped in characters of fire upon his brow, that he might go forth known, detested, and despised by all, as a traitor who has polluted the purity of our institutions, and brought disgrace, obloquy, and evil of the darkest dye upon the bright escutcheon of our beloved State.

The argument of the case being concluded, SENATOR PARSONS offered the following:

Resolved, That this Court will at two o'clock this afternoon hold a private consultation as to what judgment ought to be entered in this cause.

SENATOR NEWLAND. It is now eleven o'clock, and we can spend an hour in session before the hour of adjournment arrives. I move to insert "forthwith," in lieu of "three o'clock."

SENATOR WATKINS. I would rather have an hour or two for reflection. We should not be hasty in so important a matter as this is. I therefore hope the proposition of the Senator from Cole (Mr. Parsons) will prevail.

SENATOR McFERRAN. I would ask the mover of the resolution to adjourn to withdraw it, that I may offer this as a substitute:

Resolved, That the Senate do now proceed to vote, without debate, on each article, beginning at the first and proceeding consecutively through to the last, after which a judgment of the Senate upon the whole case shall be rendered.

Mr. PRESIDENT. Will the Senator (Mr. Parsons) withdraw his motion?

SENATOR PARSONS. I cannot withdraw it. I insist upon my motion, sir.

SENATOR McFERRAN. I move my resolution as a substitute for the original resolution and amendment.

SENATOR FOX. I do not feel prepared to go immediately into voting upon the case, and shall vote in the negative when the question comes up. I have read some of the printed testimony I got last evening, and I most certainly should want to peruse the balance of that testimony, and refresh my recollection of that portion that has been detailed far back. I am not prepared to adopt the substitute.

SENATOR O'NEIL. I move that the Court adjourn until two o'clock. Carried.

The Court then adjourned.

EVENING SESSION.

WEDNESDAY, June 22, 1859.

Court met pursuant to adjournment.

The managers attended.

The question being upon agreeing to the substitute offered by Senator McFerran,

SENATOR RAINS said: Mr. President, before that question is put, I would remark that the respondent is not here. According to my view, he should have a right to address this Court further, if he choose to do so. I do not know whether he desires to do so or not. Our rules provide that "in all cases not provided for in the foregoing rules, the rules adopted for the government of the present Senate shall apply." Our rules provide that persons having spoken once, may speak again. I would like to hear from the respondent, if he has anything further to say.

In regard to this resolution, I take the liberty of stating that I shall vote to give the greatest latitude for investigation. I am, for one, disposed, sir, not to act prematurely in a matter so grave and so important as is the present. We have now heard, sir, from both sides,—from the representatives of the people, sent here by the House of Representatives as prosecutors, and we have heard from the accused. I should be pleased to hear remarks coming from any Senator in regard to this matter; and I for one shall not vote for a resolution that will compel us to act immediately, without debate. I shall give no vote that will trammel any Senator here. If there are any desires upon the part of any Senator to show why he pursued a certain course, or if he has any information more than I or any other Senator has relative to the case, I would like to avail myself of his knowledge. I am as anxious as any Senator upon this floor to get through with this case and go home; but I shall vote on all occasions to give the greatest latitude, if Senators want to discuss this matter.

SENATOR SCOTT. I shall support that motion, sir, for the reason—

SENATOR McFERRAN. Will the gentleman (Mr. Scott) allow me to withdraw that resolution and offer this one?

Resolved, That the Senate will now proceed to pronounce judgment in the case of Albert Jackson, Judge of the Fifteenth Judicial Circuit in the State of

Missouri; and that in taking the judgment of the Senate upon the articles of impeachment now depending against Albert Jackson, the President of the Senate shall state the question to be, upon each article, "Is the respondent, Albert Jackson, guilty or not guilty, as charged in the —— article?" After which the Secretary shall call the roll, and each Senator in his place shall answer "guilty" or "not guilty."

SENATOR O'NEIL. Is it not necessary that each specification should be voted on?

SENATOR MCFERRAN. Since introducing my first resolution, I have been examining some precedents, the first I have looked at in this case; and would not now have done it but from the fact of a secret session having been proposed. In the case of the United States *vs.* Chase, on articles of impeachment tried by the Senate of the United States, the vote was taken, as is proposed to be taken in that resolution, upon each article separately, and not on the specifications at all.

SENATOR PARSONS. Were there any specifications?

SENATOR MCFERRAN. Yes; numbers of them. In the Chase case the Senate did not go into secret session to make up a verdict, nor were the merits of the case discussed at all. The same rule was observed in the case of the United States *vs.* Peck.

SENATOR SCOTT. I was going to remark, I was in favor of proceeding in this case without discussion, and openly before the world. If we are to go into a discussion among ourselves in regard to this matter, it may be proper and prudent for us to have a secret session. What can be the object of any member discussing any point in any article of the impeachment, unless it be that he has formed his own opinion, and feels so deep an interest in the matter that he desires to make proselytes of others to those opinions? No necessity can arise for it, unless upon a presumption of this kind. I have mine; and I presume every Senator upon this floor has his opinion upon this subject. Perhaps I could not, if I desired, change the opinion of a single Senator; and I would not if I could. I vote for myself. It is a duty I owe to my country to vote according to what I conceive to be right and justice in this case, uninfluenced by any, and without attempting to influence any to vote as I do, for the purpose of carrying the verdict this way or that way. By pursuing this course, sir, we discharge our duty, not secretly, but publicly, in the face of the world, and conscientiously in regard to ourselves, without being subjected to the influence of this man's opinion, or that man's opinion, as he may desire to express it here. I think I should have preferred the former resolution, but I shall vote for this one. I do not, however, conceive it necessary to repeat the question to each member as his name is called.

SENATOR PARSONS. It would not be proper for me to retain my seat, Mr. President, and say nothing, after the remarks that have fallen from the lips of the Senator from Buchanan, (Mr. Scott.) He intimates the object of the proposition introduced by myself was to give some an opportunity of influencing others. I most emphatically disclaim any such object or intent; and I am sure I can convince this Senate that the gentleman from Buchanan is the only one who could possibly have put upon it such a construction. Sir, I will call his attention to the fact—if he was ever so low in the law as I have been, for I have plead before a Justice of the Peace, where I would address a jury in a cause involving five dollars—that in such cases jurymen are permitted to retire and consult together as to what they would do in the premises; and no one ever supposed the object or intent of the law was, that one juryman should be permitted to control the balance. Again, sir, in the Supreme Court of this State, in which I have had the honor to have some experience in practice, I have never yet known them to pronounce an opinion in a cause without going into a respectful deliberation. I offered that resolution out of the respect which I thought this Court owed to the people of the State, and out of respect to the rights of this respondent. Why, sir, if it was a five-dollar case before the Circuit Court of our State, they would not jump at it in a moment, and before the sound of the counsel's voice had disappeared from the walls. I did not offer the resolve for the purpose of getting up debate, but simply to give Senators time to investigate this matter; to look over the immense amount of authorities that have been brought into requisition; and to satisfy themselves what they ought to do in the premises. I confess, Mr. President, I have given careful attention to this case; but there are two or three articles about which my mind is not made up. Although I have labored to take notes of this testimony, and to examine the authorities in order to be ready to vote when the case was submitted, I supposed as a matter of course we would be entitled to some deliberation, and not deprived of the same rights which the humblest jury in the land is entitled to. I presume the object of this judgment is to render a true verdict between the State of Missouri and the accused. A Senator upon my right says he wishes to examine this matter further. Perhaps there are other Senators upon this floor who afford additional arguments in favor of my proposition.

The gentleman speaks about a secret session. Does not your grand jury secretly deliberate? Do not your petit jurors retire to a room, placed under the charge of the Sheriff, while they deliberate upon the matter under their consideration? Does not the Supreme Court deliberate in privacy before rendering a verdict? Did not the Senate of the United States, in the impeachment case of Chase, retire from the hall in which the trial had been progressing to their council chamber, and in private deliberate upon the questions of law presented in the case? It does seem to me, in view of these facts, and in view of the rights of the parties concerned, we are entitled to the privilege of giving this matter a calm and respectful consideration.

SENATOR SCOTT. I only desire, Mr. President, to reply to one position taken by the Senator. He regards this Senate as a jury sitting here to try a cause in which they must agree in their verdict, and that without consultation it would be impossible to know whether they agreed or not. Now I will admit, sir, that were we a jury, or like a jury had to agree in our verdict, without consultation it would be impossible to know whether we agreed or not. When a jury retire to consult about making up a verdict, it is impossible for them to arrive at the unanimity requisite unless they do hold a consultation. Grand juries, however, do it, not for the mere purpose of consultation, but because they are made a secret tribunal, and required by law to hold their sessions in secret. It is not necessary that we agree. Each one must, in the exercise of his own judgment, and under the dictates of his conscience, say whether he believes the defendant guilty or not guilty; and it is not necessary we should consult about and agree among ourselves what kind of verdict we will render in this case. I had no reference to the resolution introduced by the Senator. I could conceive of no object any one could have in view in holding a secret consultation in regard to this matter, unless it was to give members an opportunity, by expressing their opinions, to influence the opinions of others, and that the case might be determined differently from what it would be if Senators were to vote their independent opinions, without hearing the opinions of others expressed. This is the position I took, and I think it is a correct one.

SENATOR CHURCHILL. For one, Mr. President, I do not wish to act hastily upon this subject. This is a case of vast importance, not only to the respondent, but to the State. We have applied ourselves most industriously in the examination of this case, having since its commencement met here at eight o'clock in the morning and remained until noon, and met again at three and remained until five o'clock in the afternoon; and we should not precipitately act upon it now. A portion of the printed evidence has been put upon my table since I entered the chamber, and I should like to have a few hours to examine it. I do not think it will do any Senator harm to give one night's cool reflection to this subject. Like the Senator from Cole (Mr. Parsons) and the Senator from Jasper, (Mr. Rains,) I would not take an immediate vote on the case. I shall vote against the proposition of the Senator from Daviess, (Mr. McFerran.)

SENATOR MCFERRAN. I desire to state, that, if the Senators wish to have time to investigate the evidence or law governing this case, I have no objection, after the resolution is passed, to adjourn until to-morrow morning, to give them an opportunity for that purpose. We can then come to a direct vote upon the matter before us.

SENATOR JONES. Without debate?

SENATOR MCFERRAN. Yes, without debate. I am prepared to act now.

SENATOR RAINS. Since the Senator from Daviess (Mr. McFerran) has changed his proposition, and there is a reason for the adoption of the resolution he now offers, I feel it necessary to state a further objection I have to that resolution, which I did not think it necessary to state before. I want a little time to examine some authorities and testimony. I am now firmly of the opinion that it is our duty to vote upon each specification in place of each article. Now, I find in certain articles eight or ten different specifications. I am prepared to say that on some of these specifications I shall vote one way, and upon other specifications I shall vote differently. Some of them the testimony may fully sustain, and others it may fall far short of so doing.

SENATOR GOODLETT. I wish to say one word in reply to the gentleman from Jasper. I understand that we vote upon these articles pretty much as a jury does on a case submitted to them. For instance, an indictment is submitted to a jury, and the verdict of that jury is, whether the man is found guilty on the indictment. The mere fact that it goes on to say the prisoner did not have the fear of God in his eyes, and was instigated by the devil, does not force a juryman to believe or disbelieve it. These specifications are like different counts in an indictment. If any one specification in any one of these articles is true, and the Senate so regards it, that is sufficient in itself, as I conceive, to sustain the article itself.

SENATOR RAINS. I would like to ask the Senator from Johnson if he does not believe it possible that this Judge may be guilty of some one of these specifications, and not guilty under the article?

SENATOR GOODLETT. That may be so. The specifications may be all true, and yet not sustain the charge of the article, and herein lies the folly of voting upon the specifications.

SENATOR RAINS. I look upon it as a very different thing from a jury trial. When a jury, in deliberation as to the guilt or innocence of a person before them, once make up their verdict it is final. It does not go upon the records—it does not publish to the world any reasons. Quite different with us,—here is a record. Upon each specification I want to vote intelligibly and understandingly, so that the country will see what we consider to be criminal and what not criminal.

SENATOR GOODLETT. Is that resolution subject to amendment?

MR. PRESIDENT. It is about as far as it can go in the way of amendments already.

SENATOR GOODLETT. I only wish to amend it in order to cut off debate. I well see now, from the disposition already manifested, that there will be a heavy discussion for three or four days if the proposition prevails to discuss the case. I have not the least doubt but that every member of this body has already made up his mind from the law read and the evidence brought before us. Nevertheless, if any additional information can be obtained, I am willing to hunt for it; but I do think it useless to suffer debate from one day's end to another.

SENATOR PARSONS. Until the judgment is rendered, I suppose all proceedings that take place are part of the trial. I do not see the respondent in his place, and I doubt the propriety of taking any further steps in the case without his presence, or at least without having informed him of our proceedings. The respondent may be under the impression that we have gone into a private consultation about this matter, from what took place in the forenoon. I hold that he has a right during this discussion to make any objection, amendment, or alteration to any proposition that comes up that he may see fit.

SENATOR GOODLETT. This is a new idea, that a party has a right to go before a jury after it has retired and make suggestions to it.

SENATOR ROBINSON. I have an objection to that resolution. There are specifications in all these articles upon which I presume every member of the Senate will vote in the affirmative, and yet, taken by themselves, they are harmless. Here in article one is specification three, which simply charges that he refused to hear counsel in a certain case. In what position are we placed in voting upon this article affirmatively or negatively as a whole, contrary to the evidence? I hold there are specifications that have been and others that have not been established. It is the specifications that make out an article, and not simply the allegation. If there is no necessity for voting on these specifications, there is no necessity for having them. If we vote upon anything at all, let us vote upon the proposition, and not upon a general declaration. Yet, sir, I have little practical knowledge of any proceedings of this kind; but it seems to me the proposition of the Senator is an absurdity. He proposes to vote upon the whole article, and yet not touch one of the propositions contained in it. If the specifications were directed towards one point, the case would be different; but we have various charges under the same general affirmation. We may regard some of the charges as true, and some of them as false; yet if we vote in the affirmative upon the article itself, we vote upon the truth of the specifications, when the evidence may be insufficient on some of them. I shall vote against the resolution.

The substitute offered by Senator McFerran was agreed to by the following vote:

AYES—Messrs. Brown, Coleman, Frazier, Goodlett, Gullett, Halliburton, Harris, Hedgpeth, Horner, Hyer, Jones, McFarland, McFerran, Morris, Newland, O'Neil, Richardson, Scott, Thompson, Vernon, Watkins, Wilson, Wood, and Wright—24.

NOES—Messrs. Byrne, Churchill, Fox, McIlvaine, Parsons, Peyton, Rains, and Robinson—8.

Absent—Mr. Johnson.

SENATOR CHURCHILL. I would like the Senator to make an explanation. Suppose the respondent is guilty on some of the specifications and innocent on others?

SENATOR McFERRAN. In answer to the Senator, I would refer again to this authority,—the trial of the impeachment of Judge Chase. The fourth article of that case contained five specifications, but the vote was taken upon the entire article, and not upon the specifications. Of course Senators voting on the article believed there had or had not been enough proven under it to authorize the finding of a verdict of guilty. As in the counts of an indictment, some of the specifications may have been good and some bad; or they may have been all good or all bad. Now, we are setting here both as judges of fact and law, and I presume that as a body we pass upon the sufficiency of the articles and upon the proof to sustain them. One of the specifications may be proven to be true, and it may be sufficient to sustain the charge; another specification, although proven, may be insufficient to warrant the finding of an article against the accused. Now, I would say to the Senator from Boone, (Mr. Robinson,) that when he characterized the voting upon the articles an absurdity, he was in the teeth of authority, In the respective cases of the United States *vs.* Peck and Chase it was never proposed to vote upon the specifications. The article includes the specification in the same manner the greater includes the less; and if we find that the article is supported by the proof of one or more specifications, we are to pass upon its sufficiency.

SENATOR RAINS moved to amend the resolution by striking out the word "article" where it occurred in the question to be proposed by the President, and insert in lieu thereof the word "specification;" which amendment was lost by the following vote:

AYES—Messrs. Churchill, Fox, Harris, McIlvaine, Peyton, Rains, and Robinson—7.

NOES—Messrs. Brown, Byrne, Coleman, Frazier, Goodlett, Gullett, Halliburton, Hedgpeth, Horner, Hyer, Jones, McFarland, McFerran, Morris, Newland, O'Neil, Parsons, Richardson, Scott, Thompson, Vernon, Watkins, Wilson, Wood, and Wright—25.

Absent—Mr. Johnson.

The question being upon the adoption of the resolution, it was adopted by the following vote:

AYES—Messrs. Brown, Byrne, Coleman, Frazier, Goodlett, Gullett, Halliburton, Harris, Hedgpeth, Horner, Hyer, Jones, McFarland, McFerran, Morris, Newland, O'Neil, Richardson, Scott, Thompson, Vernon, Watkins, Wilson, Wood, and Wright—25.

NOES—Messrs. Churchill, Fox, McIlvaine, Parsons, Peyton, Rains, and Robinson—7.

Absent—Mr. Johnson.

SENATOR CHURCHILL. Since we have agreed upon the order of trying this case, I move that the Senate adjourn until 10 o'clock to-morrow morning.

SENATOR GOODLETT. In order to relieve the Senator, I move we commence at the bottom of the roll and call upward.

SENATOR CHURCHILL. I do not flinch at any responsibility, but at the same time I think a little reflection will hurt no one.

SENATOR NEWLAND. It strikes me that if we adjourn until to-morrow morning to examine the testimony already printed, the same reason would apply until all the testimony in the case was printed and examined. I think it unjust for Senators to adjourn to examine testimony that has been offered here on behalf of the State, without the possible prospect of getting the testimony printed that has been introduced on behalf of the respondent. I do not think we can accomplish anything by adjourning, and consequently I call for the ayes and noes on the motion.

SENATOR RAINS. I want to remind Senators of the courtesy they have been extending to each other during the pendency of bills in this body. Whenever a member but requested time to examine a bill, it has been granted. But here it is proposed to compel us to vote on a measure, not of minor importance, but one in which many interests and rights are involved, though we ask a little further time to examine it. Common courtesy demands that the request be complied with.

SENATOR O'NEIL. I can safely say the same thing my colleague has heretofore expressed. There are questions here upon which I am not prepared to vote; but I will say, sir, that if compelled to vote, wherever I have a doubt upon an article, that doubt shall be in favor of the respondent. This, sir, we owe the respondent, and this is the usual mode of proceeding. In addition to this, the gentleman will please to recollect that by adjourning until to-morrow morning, as has been remarked by one Senator, no opportunity will be given us of examining the testimony of the respondent, and so we shall not be in a better position to decide upon the evidence of the case than we are at the present time. It will be to the disadvantage of the respondent if we adjourn until to-morrow morning.

SENATOR GOODLETT. Mr. President, I have been here from the commencement of this trial to the present moment. I have heard every particle of the evidence, and all the arguments on both sides of the case. Knowing as I did, that one of the members of my family was lying on a bed of sickness during the time, I have staid here and attended promptly to my duties, though constantly suffering in mind on their account. And am I now to be denied the privilege of going home and attending to my family because some Senator has been too negligent to attend to the progress of the trial? There is no man more disposed to do justice to this case than myself, sir. Let those Senators who are not prepared to vote be excused until to-morrow morning, but let those who are ready to vote upon this question, vote now, so they can go home to-morrow. I feel myself prepared to vote upon each and every allegation in these articles of impeachment; and I do hope, sir, that no adjournment will take place to deprive us who are so anxious to go home of the privilege of so doing.

The motion to adjourn was negatived by the following vote:

AYES—Messrs. Byrne, Churchill, Coleman, Fox, Halliburton, Hedgpeth, Hyer, McIlvaine, Parsons, Peyton, Rains, Robinson, and Watkins—13.

NOES—Messrs. Brown, Frazier, Goodlett, Gullett, Harris, Horner, Jones, McFarland, McFerran, Morris, Newland, O'Neil, Richardson, Scott, Thompson, Vernon, Wilson, Wood, and Wright—19.

Absent—Mr. Johnson.

SENATOR PARSONS. Mr. President, I do not think it is right for us to proceed without the respondent being present.

SENATOR WATKINS. I think the proper course would be to send a messenger to inform him that he can come or not, just as he chooses.

SENATOR JONES. I don't think there is any necessity for that. The respondent is aware of his right to be present.

SENATOR BROWN. I think it due the Judge that he should have notice that we are about to pass judgment upon him.

SENATOR PARSONS moved as follows:

The respondent not being in his seat—*Ordered*, That the Sergeant-at-Arms be required to inform the respondent that we are now ready to pass judgment upon the articles of impeachment exhibited against him in this cause.

SENATOR SCOTT. I do not think the respondent has any seat in this bar. If he chooses to come and set down, I for one have no objection.

SENATOR RAINS. There is a seat assigned him by resolution.

SENATOR SCOTT. I suppose if the respondent is at home, the Sergeant-at-Arms, under that resolution, would be compelled to go to him.

SENATOR JONES. I do not suppose, sir, that the respondent considers it proper to be present when the Senate is passing sentence upon him. His non-attendance may result from motives of delicacy. I apprehend, sir, that under similar circumstance most men not altogether devoid of sensibility would absent themselves.

The motion was then rejected by the following vote:

AYES—Messrs. Brown, Churchill, Fox, Gullett, Hedgpeth, McFarland, Parsons, Peyton, Rains, Richardson, Robinson, and Watkins—12.

NOES—Messrs. Byrne, Coleman, Frazier, Goodlett, Halliburton, Harris, Horner, Hyer, Jones, McFerran, McIlvaine, Morris, Newland, O'Neil, Scott, Thompson, Vernon, Wilson, Wood, and Wright—20.

Absent—Mr. Johnson.

ARTICLE I. was then read; and the question prescribed by the resolution having been announced by the President, and the roll having been called, there appeared as voting "guilty:"

Messrs. Brown, Byrne, Churchill, Frazier, Halliburton, Horner, Hyer, McFarland, McFerran, McIlvaine, O'Neil, Parsons, Thompson, Vernon, Watkins, and Wright—16.

There appeared as voting "not guilty:"

Messrs. Coleman, Fox, Goodlett, Gullett, Harris, Hedgpeth, Jones, Morris, Newland, Peyton, Rains, Richardson, Robinson, Scott, Wilson, and Wood—16.

Absent—Mr. Johnson.

Two-thirds of the Senators present not having voted "guilty," the President of the Senate declared Albert Jackson acquitted of the charges in the first article.

On ARTICLE II., those voting "guilty" were:

Messrs. Brown, Byrne, Frazier, Goodlett, Horner, Hyer, McFarland, McFerran, McIlvaine, Thompson, Vernon, and Wright—12.

Those voting "not guilty" were:

Messrs. Churchill, Coleman, Fox, Gullett, Halliburton, Harris, Hedgpeth, Jones, Morris, Newland, O'Neil, Parsons, Peyton, Rains, Richardson, Robinson, Scott, Watkins, Wilson, and Wood—20.

Absent—Mr. Johnson.

And the respondent was declared acquitted of the charges in said article.

On ARTICLE III., those voting "guilty" were:

Messrs. Brown, Byrne Frazier, Goodlett, Halliburton, Horner, Hyer, McFarland, McFerran, McIlvaine, O'Neil, Parsons, Richardson, Thompson, Vernon, and Watkins—16.

Those voting "not guilty" were:

Messrs. Churchill, Coleman, Fox, Gullett, Harris, Hedgpeth, Jones, Morris, Newland, Peyton, Rains, Robinson, Scott, Wilson, Wood, and Wright—16.

Absent—Mr. Johnson.

And the respondent was declared acquitted of the charges in said article.

On ARTICLE IV., those voting "guilty" were:

Messrs. Goodlett, Halliburton, McFarland, McFerran, O'Neil, Parsons, Richardson, Thompson, and Watkins—9.

Those voting "not guilty" were:

Messrs. Brown, Byrne, Churchill, Coleman, Fox, Frazier, Gullett, Harris, Hedgpeth, Horner, Hyer, Jones, McIlvaine, Morris, Newland, Peyton, Rains, Robinson, Scott, Vernon, Wilson, Wood, and Wright—23.
Absent—Mr. Johnson.

And the respondent was declared acquitted of the charges in said article.

On Article V., those voting "guilty" were:

Messrs. Hyer and Thompson—2.

Those voting "not guilty" were:

Messrs. Brown, Byrne, Churchill, Coleman, Fox, Frazier, Goodlett, Gullett, Halliburton, Harris, Hedgpeth, Horner, Jones, McFarland, McFerran, McIlvaine, Morris, Newland, O'Neil, Parsons, Peyton, Rains, Richardson, Robinson, Scott, Vernon, Watkins, Wilson, Wood, and Wright—30.
Absent—Mr. Johnson.

And the respondent was declared acquitted of the charges in said article.

On Article VI., those voting "guilty" were:

Messrs. Byrne, Churchill, Frazier, Goodlett, Halliburton, Horner, Hyer, McFarland, McFerran, McIlvaine, Parsons, Richardson, Thompson, Vernon, Watkins, and Wright—16.

Those voting "not guilty" were:

Messrs. Brown, Coleman, Fox, Gullett, Harris, Hedgpeth, Jones, Morris, Newland, O'Neil, Peyton, Rains, Robinson, Scott, Wilson, and Wood—16.
Absent—Mr. Johnson.

And the respondent was declared acquitted of the charges in said article.

On Article VII., those voting "guilty" were:

Messrs. Brown, Byrne, Frazier, Goodlett, Halliburton, Horner, Hyer, McFarland, McFerran, McIlvaine, O'Neil, Parsons, Richardson, Thompson, Vernon, Watkins, and Wright—17.

Those voting "not guilty" were:

Messrs. Churchill, Coleman, Fox, Gullett, Harris, Hedgpeth, Jones, Morris, Newland, Peyton, Rains, Robinson, Scott, Wilson, and Wood—15.
Absent—Mr. Johnson.

And the respondent was declared acquitted of the charges in said article.

On Article VIII., the vote stood for "guilty:"

Mr. Thompson—1.

Those voting "not guilty" were:

Messrs. Brown, Byrne, Churchill, Coleman, Fox, Frazier, Goodlett, Gullett, Halliburton, Harris, Hedgpeth, Horner, Hyer, Jones, McFarland, McFerran, McIlvaine, Morris, Newland, O'Neil, Parsons, Peyton, Rains, Richardson, Robinson, Scott, Vernon, Watkins, Wilson, Wood, and Wright—31.
Absent—Mr. Johnson.

And the respondent was declared acquitted of the charges in said article.

On ARTICLE IX., those voting "guilty" were:

Messrs. Byrne, McFarland, McFerran, O'Neil, Parsons, Thompson, and Watkins—7.

Those voting "not guilty" were:

Messrs. Brown, Churchill, Coleman, Fox, Frazier, Goodlett, Gullett, Halliburton, Harris, Hedgpeth, Horner, Hyer, Jones, McIlvaine, Morris, Newland, Peyton, Rains, Richardson, Robinson, Scott, Vernon, Wilson, Wood, and Wright—25.

Absent—Mr. Johnson.

And the respondent was declared acquitted of the charges in said article.

On ARTICLE X., those voting "guilty" were:

Messrs. Brown, Byrne, Frazier, Goodlett, Halliburton, Horner, Hyer, McFarland, McFerran, McIlvaine, O'Neil, Parsons, Rains, Richardson, Thompson, Vernon, Watkins, and Wright—18.

Those voting "not guilty" were:

Messrs. Churchill, Coleman, Fox, Gullett, Harris, Hedgpeth, Jones, Morris, Newland, Peyton, Robinson, Scott, Wilson, and Wood—14.

Absent—Mr. Johnson.

And the respondent was declared acquitted of the charges in said article.

On ARTICLE XI., those voting "guilty" were:

Messrs. Brown, Byrne, Churchill, Frazier, Goodlett, Halliburton, Harris, Horner, Hyer, McFarland, McFerran, McIlvaine, O'Neil, Parsons, Peyton, Rains, Richardson, Thompson, Vernon, Watkins, and Wright—21.

Those voting "not guilty" were:

Messrs. Coleman, Fox, Gullett, Hedgpeth, Jones, Morris, Newland, Robinson, Scott, Wilson, and Wood—11.

Absent—Mr. Johnson.

And the respondent was declared acquitted of the charges in said article.

On ARTICLE XII., those voting "guilty" were:

Messrs. Byrne, Frazier, Halliburton, Horner, Hyer, McFarland, McIlvaine, O'Neil, Thompson, Vernon, and Wright—11.

Those voting "not guilty" were:

Messrs. Brown, Churchill, Coleman, Fox, Goodlett, Gullett, Harris, Hedgpeth, Jones, McFerran, Morris, Newland, Parsons, Peyton, Rains, Richardson, Robinson, Scott, Watkins, Wilson, and Wood—21.

Absent—Mr. Johnson.

And the respondent was declared acquitted of the charges in said article.

On ARTICLE XIII., those voting "guilty" were:

Messrs. Byrne, Churchill, Frazier, Hyer, McFarland, McFerran, McIlvaine, Thompson, Vernon, Watkins, and Wright—11.

Those voting "not guilty" were:

Messrs. Brown, Coleman, Fox, Goodlett, Gullett, Halliburton, Harris, Hedgpeth, Horner, Jones, Morris, Newland, O'Neil, Parsons, Peyton, Rains, Richardson, Robinson, Scott, Wilson, and Wood—21.
Absent—Mr. Johnson.

And the respondent was declared acquitted of the charges in said article.

On Article XIV., those voting "guilty" were:

Messrs.———0.

Those voting "not guilty" were:

Messrs. Brown, Byrne, Churchill, Coleman, Fox, Frazier, Goodlett, Gullett, Halliburton, Harris, Hedgpeth, Horner, Hyer, Jones, McFarland, McFerran, McIlvaine, Morris, Newland, O'Neil, Parsons, Peyton, Rains, Richardson, Robinson, Scott, Thompson, Vernon, Watkins, Wilson, Wood, and Wright—32.
Absent—Mr. Johnson.

And the respondent was declared acquitted of the charges in said article.

On Article XV., those voting "guilty" were:

Messrs. Brown, Byrne, Frazier, Goodlett, Halliburton, Horner, Hyer, McFarland, McIlvaine, O'Neil, Parsons, Richardson, Thompson, Vernon, Watkins, and Wright—16.

Those voting "not guilty" were:

Messrs Churchill, Coleman, Fox, Gullett, Harris, Hedgpeth, Jones, McFerran, Morris, Newland, Peyton, Rains, Robinson, Scott, Wilson, and Wood—16.
Absent—Mr. Johnson.

And the respondent was declared acquitted of the charges in said article.

On Article XVI., those voting "guilty" were:

Messrs. Brown, Byrne, Churchill, Frazier, Goodlett, Halliburton, Horner, Hyer, McFarland, McFerran, McIlvaine, O'Neil, Parsons, Peyton, Richardson, Thompson, Vernon, Watkins, Wood, and Wright—20.

Those voting "not guilty" were:

Messrs. Coleman, Fox, Gullett, Harris, Hedgpeth, Jones, Morris, Newland, Rains, Robinson, Scott, and Wilson—12.
Absent—Mr. Johnson.

And the respondent was declared acquitted of the charges in said article.

On Article XVII., those voting "guilty" were:

Messrs. Brown, Byrne, Coleman, Fox, Frazier, Goodlett, Halliburton, Horner, Hyer, McFarland, McFerran, McIlvaine, Parsons, Peyton, Rains, Richardson, Thompson, Vernon, Watkins, and Wright—20.

Those voting "not guilty" were:

Messrs. Churchill, Gullett, Harris, Hedgpeth, Jones, Morris, Newland, O'Neil, Robinson, Scott, Wilson, and Wood—12.
Absent—Mr. Johnson.

And the respondent was declared acquitted of the charges in said article.

SENATOR FOX. Mr. President, I would ask the indulgence of the Senate until morning. I would a great deal prefer having some little time to reflect upon this next proposition. It is one which to my mind has been difficult, and it would be with much embarrassment that I would vote upon it at present. I had expected, Mr. President, that the entire testimony would be printed before we voted upon any proposition. I said nothing about it in the beginning of our voting, and have submitted to some oppression of feeling in voting, because I saw there was such desire to dispose of the matter this evening. But I would insist upon indulgence on this proposition, until to-morrow morning. I have used all diligence in my power; I have been as attentive as I possibly could be in listening to the testimony and arguments in this case; but I repeat that my mind is divided on this one proposition.

SENATOR WRIGHT. Mr. President, I presume the Senate will excuse the gentleman from voting.

SENATOR FOX. I do not ask to be excused. I do not want to be excused. If I do vote now I shall most certainly adopt the rule the honorable Senator from St. Louis (Mr. O'Neil) laid down to be governed by so far as his action was concerned.

SENATOR WILSON. I hope, Mr. President, the Senate will proceed to vote.

SENATOR FOX. I move an adjournment.

The motion was negatived by the following vote, the ayes and noes having been demanded by Senator Scott:

AYES—Messrs. Churchill, Coleman, Fox, Gullett, Halliburton, Harris, Hedgpeth, McIlvaine, Parsons, Peyton, Rains, Robinson, and Wood—13.

NOES—Messrs. Brown, Byrne, Frazier, Goodlett, Horner, Hyer, Jones, McFarland, McFerran, Morris, Newland, O'Neil, Richardson, Scott, Thompson, Vernon, Watkins, Wilson, and Wright—19.

Absent—Mr. Johnson.

On ARTICLE XVIII., and last, which was then read, those voting "guilty" were:

Messrs. Brown, Byrne, Churchill, Frazier, Goodlett, Halliburton, Horner, Hyer, McFarland, McFerran, McIlvaine, O'Neil, Parsons, Peyton, Rains, Richardson, Thompson, Vernon, Watkins, Wood, and Wright—21.

Those voting "not guilty" were:

Messrs. Coleman, Fox, Gullett, Harris, Hedgpeth, Jones, Morris, Newland, Robinson, Scott, and Wilson—11.

Absent—Mr. Johnson.

And the respondent was declared acquitted of the charges in said article.

SENATOR WOOD. I move the Court adjourn until 9 o'clock to-morrow morning. Carried.

And then the Court adjourned.

SIXTEENTH DAY.

THURSDAY, June 23, 1859.

The Court met pursuant to adjournment, and was opened by proclamation.

SENATOR CHURCHILL. Mr. President, I ask leave to change my vote on the second article of impeachment.

SENATOR VERNON. I object.

SENATOR FOX. I would inquire of the honorable Senator from St. Louis if he understood the proposition at the time of voting?

SENATOR THOMPSON. I hope the gentleman will suffer the change to be made. I can easily imagine how a man would vote, or how he would like to vote after an hour's reflection on that article. I hope my old friend will withdraw his objection, if on no other ground than that of courtesy.

SENATOR VERNON. I withdraw my objection.

SENATOR GOODLETT offered the following resolution:

Resolved, That three thousand copies of the record, evidence, and arguments of the managers and respondent in the case of the State of Missouri against Albert Jackson, on articles of impeachment, be printed in bourgeois and minion type; that Thomas J. Henderson be appointed to superintend the printing of the same; and that the Committee on Accounts be required to audit and allow the expenses thereof; and that the Secretary of State be required to furnish fifty copies to the respondent and each of the managers, twenty-five copies to the State Library, one to the Recorder of each county, and to distribute the residue equally among the members of the two Houses.

SENATOR SCOTT offered the following by way of substitute:

Resolved, That the Journal of the present session of the Senate be published and distributed as provided by law in other cases, and that the evidence, both oral and record, in the trial of the Hon. Albert Jackson, be published as an appendix thereto, and no other matter connected with said trial be so published.

SENATOR SCOTT. I desire to make one or two remarks, sir, in connection with that resolution. Now, I cannot for the life of me see the propriety of making the people of the State pay the expense of publishing all the arguments, and all the debates, and all the opinions that have been made in the progress of this trial. It is a matter, sir, in which the public are not interested. If they had been, it is remarkably singular that none of the newspapers that cater to the public taste, and whose business it is to furnish matters of interest to the public, have sent a reporter here to take notes of this trial for the benefit of their readers. It is an evidence to my mind that it is not considered a matter of public interest. Now, sir, if any one has made a buncombe speech in this case that he desires to go before the public for his future benefit, let him print that speech at his own expense, as we have to do when electioneering. If no such speech has been made, why it is not necessary to publish these things in which the public are not interested. No one can be benefited by it but the individual who enunciated it; and I am not here, sir, to vote the money of my constituents to publish any such enunciation. Why, sir, just look at the amount of public printing that was done at the last session of the Legislature. We find that during the progress of the session the amount paid out for public printing was enormous. We had a large amount of public printing on that occasion, and, sir, that amount was necessary; but when we come to examine the Journal, as printed, what do we find there? We find, sir, something which, in my experience, never appeared in the Journals before. And for what? Why was it, sir, that every petition sent to the Legislature, with the signature of every man signing that petition, upon every subject, no matter how frivolous, appears printed as part of the Journal of the Senate? It has not, in my recollection, been the case before; and if it has been, it is one of the expenses that should have been curtailed, and ought ever to be properly curtailed, for it is of advantage to no human being but the public pet,—the public printer, who is to be made fat by sucking at the public teat. And, sir, this is the only object that can be effected, unless it is to publish buncombe speeches for the benefit of private individuals. Do Senators want all the arguments to go before the world as justification to them for the manner in which they have cast their votes in deciding this case? Or will they not feel prepared to stand upon their own conclusions from the testimony and the facts, uninfluenced by anything but the convictions of their own consciences in regard to what is right? Is it expected, sir, to show to the world that these arguments ought to have convinced men against their own convictions, and that the verdict upon the several articles of impeachment ought to have been different? Is it intended, sir, to make it an electioneering hobby with the people in order to justify the action of this Senate? What can be the object, sir, I cannot imagine; but whatever it may be, it is not demanded by the public good; it is not demanded by the public interest. They care nothing about the arguments; they care nothing about what was said. What was done is the question, and wherefore was it done. The testimony in the cause enlightens them upon the subject and leaves them to form their own conclusions. Now, sir, I should like for any Senator who is in favor of publishing these speeches to let us know why it is necessary to publish them. Why, many things have occurred that would come within the resolution to which I have offered a substitute, that Senators would scarcely wish to see before the world as part of their proceedings. I do not recollect all the frivolous matters, but I will call the attention of the Senate to one. A few days ago, a Senator arose from his seat and asked leave of absence for a few minutes, and he said he wanted to go out and it would not take him long. [Laughter.]

Senator Parsons. If the Senator will allow me, I will call his attention to the fact that the resolution does not provide for the printing of the arguments of any Senator, or the argument of the Senator upon my right, (Fox,) but only the arguments of the managers and the respondent.

Senator Scott. That may be the case, sir, but it is not necessary to publish the arguments of any one. If it is necessary that these arguments be published, is it not equally so that every proceeding of the Court go before the world? Why select one, two, or three of the speeches and publish them to the world for the benefit of posterity and the 'rest of mankind,' to the exclusion of other able arguments? I suppose no Senator's opinion has been changed by any argument. It was the duty of the parties to make their argument; they had a right to do it, and to undertake to influence Senators. They have discharged that duty faithfully; but, sir, it is not necessary that we publish these arguments in order that every man, woman, and child in the State of Missouri shall be able to see whether they made able arguments or otherwise. How are the public interested in these arguments? If the public was interested, the public had a right to come here and listen; and the newspapers had a right to come here and report these arguments if they thought them interesting to the reading public of the

State. I am opposed to putting my hand into the public treasury and paying to show the people whether or not able arguments, *pro* or *con*, have been made during this trial. I hope the Senate will not do it.

SENATOR McFERRAN. I am very much in hope that the articles of impeachment, the replication, and every particle of the testimony in this case will be published. I differ very much with the Senator from Buchanan, (Mr. Scott.) I believe we differ on all important cases. I think the gentleman is too far from land in his little boat; he cannot row against time as he did in days of yore. He says the people of the State are not interested in this trial. I should like to know if they are not interested in knowing what their representatives have done in this case, in view of the fact that they foot the bills. Is the gentleman afraid that the publication of the report of this trial will give an unpleasant notoriety to his actions here? The only regret I have with reference to my action is, that I did not vote "guilty" in the two instances where I voted for an acquittal.

SENATOR SCOTT. I call the gentleman to order. My point of order is that he is referring to his action in the past, in regard to a matter in which the character of a private individual is interested.

SENATOR GOODLETT. Mr. President, I must confess I am a little astonished at the vehemence and energy with which the Senator from Buchanan has opposed the printing of the records; and my astonishment is increased when I see him make an attempt to arraign an official for the manner in which the Senate Journal is printed, when such question bears not the least relevancy to the point at issue.

The very idea of publishing these proceedings was suggested to me by a gentleman opposed to the proceedings themselves. It never entered my mind until that time. I saw a desire upon the part of many that the people should know what had taken place here. I am surprised to see the gentleman oppose it. He talks about the press of this State not having taken interest in this matter. I hold in my hand the receptacle of all the Black Republican vileness of this State, in which an attempt is made to pour down upon the heads of the democratic members of this Senate the infamous and vituperative charge of having been actuated by a party spirit and partizan zeal in the prosecution of this case of impeachment.

Sir, I have endeavored as a member of this Court, acting under a solemn oath, to discharge my duty during the pendency of this trial. To-day, I stand here as the representative of a free people, democratic in principle—sent here to represent democratic principles and measures, and to sustain the party to which I belong; and when I see an effort made tending to cast calumny upon that party, I hold it due to my constituents and the intelligent people I represent, to stand upon this floor and repel the accusation, let it come from what source it may. Why, sir, but a few days ago it was published in a newspaper that the expenses of this impeachment would be forty thousand dollars, when, sir, taking into consideration everything pertaining to it, including this printing, I am informed the expenses cannot exceed fifteen thousand dollars.

SENATOR NEWLAND. I understand the expenses of this session will be fourteen thousand dollars.

SENATOR GOODLETT. If it costs fifty thousand dollars, I stand up here in favor of sending a report of it broadcast to the people! [A voice, "that's right."] Sir, we owe it to ourselves to let the people know upon what testimony we have acted, and what arguments have been brought before us. Besides this, I want the lawyers of this State to see their privileges; I want the people to see the rights they have in courts of justice; I want them to know that a Judge of the Circuit Court has a right to issue an attachment and imprison a man upon whom no previous process has been served.

SENATOR ROBINSON. I call the Senator to order. The gentleman is alluding to matters that should not now be considered. After a night of rest, some gentlemen appear to be still very restless. Now, I occupy a position in which I am perfectly collected. I feel no uneasiness about this matter, and desire no disturbance about it. If gentlemen think proper to go into a discussion of the evidence after a verdict has been rendered, I am willing to take a part with them.

SENATOR WATKINS. Has the Senator a right, Mr. President, to get up and put another gentleman down?

SENATOR ROBINSON. I am perfectly willing to hear the Senator from Johnson, (Mr. Goodlett,) but I want to inform him—

MR. PRESIDENT. The gentleman from Johnson will confine his remarks to the matter under consideration.

SENATOR PARSONS. If the Senator from Johnson will permit me, I will ask the Senator from Boone (Mr. Robinson) one question. I wish him to designate the "restless persons" of whom he spoke.

SENATOR ROBINSON. I referred to the remarks that fell from the gentleman from Johnson. He attempted to discuss a matter to justify his action. I do not know how the Senator from Cole (Mr. Parsons) may stand in regard to it. I do not presume the gentleman is restless. The remark was ironical. I did not design anything more by it than to quiet him.

SENATOR GOODLETT. I hope the conscience of the gentleman from Boone rests as easy upon this matter as mine is and has been throughout this investigation. So help me God, I have endeavored to perform my whole duty in this case, with a strict regard to the oath I took here as a member of this Court, avoiding the influence of party spirit and partizan feeling throughout the whole investigation. But, sir, we have done with the case; the respondent has been acquitted and discharged from the custody of this Court, and now, as a man, I have a right to express my opinion; and I claim the right of setting forth the reasons why I want this document published to the world. I think I have the right to say here that it is necessary for the people of this State to know their rights; and this is one of the reasons, sir, why I undertook to answer the Senator from Buchanan. I want the members of the bar and the citizens of the State to know the rights they have in courts of justice. I want them to know that upon some of these articles twenty-one Senators have voted for the rights of the people. I have a right to refer to the trial, sir, in order to give the reasons why I want these facts to go to the world. Do I understand the Chair to decide I cannot refer to the articles of impeachment by way of illustration to show why I want the matter to go before the world? I want the members of the bar in the State of Missouri to know the fact that when an attorney is in the midst of an argument before a court of justice, that a Judge from his seat on the bench may abuse him, bring charges against him, when the court room is crowded with spectators, and prohibit that attorney saying a word in his own defense, in order that these charges uncontradicted may be scattered broadcast over the country; I want the people to know that a Judge has the right to openly accuse a lawyer in court of swearing to a lie, or causing his client to swear to a lie; I want the people to know that a Judge can tamper with grand juries with impunity.

SENATOR SCOTT. I call the gentleman to order.

MR. PRESIDENT. The Senator will confine his remarks to the matter under consideration. I do not think it proper for Senators to enter at this time into an argument on the impeachability of the respondent in this case.

SENATOR GOODLETT. I was undertaking an answer to the question the Senator propounded, with respect to the necessity of publishing this trial. But if I am gagged and held down by the strict rules of this body, I cannot proceed to answer his interrogatories.

SENATOR PARSONS. I have had a little experience on this floor, and it does seem to me the Senator from Johnson (Mr. Goodlett) is in order. Now, when a question comes up about printing any document, the subject matter of that document may be referred to. When the question of printing the Governor's message arises, are not Senators at liberty to discuss matters referred to in the message, or any part of it? The same privilege exists in connection with all documents, which, by the action of this body, become part of the records of the State.

SENATOR GOODLETT. I have no disposition to inflict a speech upon the Senate in regard to this matter, but as the Senator asked me to give reasons why I desired the publication of the report, I undertook to set them forth. I state here that the newspaper press of the State has been industriously engaged in circulating it over the country that the charges preferred against the respondent in this case were absolutely ridiculous. I call the attention of the Senate to a few remarks in the St. Louis *Democrat* of yesterday:

Trial of Judge Jackson.—The Jefferson City correspondent of the *Republican* denies that the trial now in progress before the Senate is assuming a political cast. We should be gratified at this information if the writer did not mention a circumstance which contradicts it completely. He states that eighteen Senators are hostile to the accused. We maintain this impeaches the tribunal of gross partiality and prejudice. The statement could not have been made if the eighteen Senators had not betrayed themselves by partizan expressions and decisions. The close observer should not be able to tell who are for and against the Judge, because none should be either for or against him until all the testimony is given. There are but four, it seems, who lean to neither side. We can accept the statement of the writer in the *Republican*, as far as it implicates the members of the Senate who belong to the same party as the *Republican*. We can also admit that the minority may be forced into a position by the majority; that the unfriendly feeling manifested by the latter may make the former resolute in their efforts to give the victim of the impeachment fair play; but we assert that the political element must have been thrown in by the majority, who are, consequently, responsible for the demoralization with which such a movement is fraught. * * * The publication of the testimony will be necessary to the vindication of the Senate, if a verdict adverse to the Judge be rendered—otherwise it may be truly said that the will of the pro-slavery democracy in the Legislature is the tenure by which the judicial office is to be held in this State.

What was here said was the mere conjecture of a casual correspondent.

I ask the democratic Senators upon this floor which of them prejudged this case, or gave any expression before the conclusion of the evidence in the case as to the guilt or innocence of the accused? I undertake to say none. I have heard none in my conversations with all the members of the Senate. I consider myself one of the eighteen referred to in this article, and when I do so, I say the charge, so far as I am concerned, is utterly false.

Why select detached portions of the report of this trial to send out? Let the people of Missouri understand the position that this distinguished Judge occupies; let them see the arguments he made before this body; let them see the authorities he referred to in order to sustain himself in the course he has pursued.

So far as I know, sir, no member of the democratic party seeks to make political capital out of this matter; and so far as I am concerned,

I am determined that no man of the opposition shall be able to make political capital out of it. If I cannot have these facts officially published and sent forth to the people in justification of a majority of the members of this Senate, I will put it over my own signature and send it forth. They shall know the ground upon which we have acted in this case. I shall not undertake to defend myself from the charge of having been actuated in this matter by party feeling or partizan zeal; but I hold that it is due those voting *pro* and *con* in this to give the facts to the people and let them determine how we acted in this matter. Sir, I impeach no man's motives upon this floor. I have charged no Senator with having acted contrary to the strictest rules of integrity. At the same time I will not permit my motives to be impeached, either by the newspaper press or any man. I say it is necessary to the vindication of this body, that these facts go forth to the people; and also that the people be informed of the extent of their rights, and govern themselves accordingly. These, sir, are the reasons I have for wishing the publication of this matter.

SENATOR VERNON. I wish to make a few observations. We have met here, and we have been acting under the solemnity of an oath, regardless of party. I have been a democrat from my cradle up to the present time, and as such I shall oppose at all times any attempt made to deprive the public of information on all matters pertaining to the general welfare. I ask who it is wishes to conceal his official acts from the public? If it costs five thousand dollars to publish this report, let it go. Aye, sir, if the horse I ride should be taken from me to pay the taxes which the publication of the proceedings in this case would cause to be levied on my property, I would say print the report and let the people see how far we have proved true to our trust. I do not want to hide my acts or the acts of my party from public scrutiny. Let the people see whether or not we have acted in a spirit of party animosity or partizan favoritism in the course we have pursued in determining the guilt or innocence of the respondent. If my action in the case is open to censure, let my constituents know it, and have some data upon which to predicate their disapprobation, and not mere idle rumor. Whenever I desert my colors, I want my country to desert me, and lay me low. I shall vote for the resolution.

SENATOR SCOTT. I do not desire to detain the Senate. It does seem to me I have stirred up a "hornet's nest" here very unconsciously. I have heard that "the galled jade winces," and unless the apothegm is applicable at the present time, I cannot for the life of me see when it would be. I propose in my resolution not to conceal anything from the public, except the speeches, from the fact that it is alone upon the testimony we are authorized by law to render a verdict. Have we based our convictions and formed our opinions upon the arguments, aside from the law and facts? If so, I say we have perjured ourselves before the country and before God. I have listened to these speeches, and the views which each party introduced in regard to the law and the testimony; but when I act, sir, I act upon my knowledge of the law, as it has been given to me either by reading or hearing the authority announced from the Court. I act upon that, and then I act upon the testimony that has been introduced, and not upon the opinion of any other man in regard to the testimony and proofs. Why is it necessary to publish these opinions? I asked for these reasons before, but I have not been answered. Why is it necessary to publish the facts and the testimony here? "In order that the world may see the ground upon which we acted, and the people may know their rights." Will they know their rights from the opinions of the attorneys and the defendant in this case? Will they get their rights from the testimony and the specifications, and the action of the Senate upon that testimony and those specifications? I do not wish to conceal anything. I will not take the insinuation, as applied to me, that I wish to conceal anything from the public eye that the public are interested in. I ask for reasons why the argument should be published,—for reasons why the public crib should be robbed in order to publish the speeches of gentlemen that can benefit no one but the speakers. Is it necessary to show the defendant made a lame or an able argument in his defense? or do Senators wish from the character of that defense to enable the people to judge of the qualifications of the man for the high official position which he occupies? Are they to pass their judgments upon the man? If he is incapable, let them proceed against him by address. But they have proceeded by impeachment. The articles of impeachment with the replication have been published to the world. I propose to incorporate them. Let them go with the evidence upon which this Senate acted, and the public can see whether we have discharged our duties. I am not one of those, sir, that undertake to conceal my action. I am only opposed, sir, to imposing the expense upon the people of publishing the speeches that have been made here. The people will not take these speeches to determine as to the character of our action. We are responsible to the people for our action, and we are also responsible to ourselves for the faithful manner in which we have tried and determined this case upon the law and testimony, and not upon the speeches delivered by the parties on either side. Yet, sir, gentlemen have been addressing the Senate upon the presumption that some one is trying to prevent the testimony in this case from going before the country. My resolution is to publish that testimony. Then I say, sir, it is unjust to insinuate I am trying to keep back any proper information from the people. I did not act upon the speeches, and if any other has, it is with him and his conscience.

SENATOR GOODLETT. Mr. President, I believe the constitution guaranties the right of every man to be heard by himself or counsel. Now, the State and the respondent have been heard in this case, and I ask if it is not right to consider their arguments? If not, why have they a right to be heard at all?

SENATOR SCOTT. I agree, sir, that every man has a right to be heard by himself or by his counsel. Where has he that right? Betore a tribunal that is to determine his rights. He has been heard here before this tribunal, according to constitutional privileges. If the arguments of the counsel or the defendant have influenced the action of any man, it is his business, not mine. I am one of those that act upon the testimony in the case and the law in the case. I do not blame any other Senator for the manner of his action, or the motives that have influenced him. I presume these motives have all been correct. I have the kindest feelings for every Senator upon this floor, and I have the highest opinion of their honor. But, sir, I ask again and again, why publish these speeches? why take money out of the public treasury to publish the speeches that have been made here,—the speeches I am making? Why do it? I say, sir, if any speeches are published here, it is just, and nothing less than just, that all the speeches that have been made during this session, including those made on the subject now under consideration, should be published to the world. But I say it is not necessary to publish any. It is a burthensome expense that can effect no good, unless it be to render still fatter the fat officer of the government that gets more pay out of the public treasury than any other officer in the State,—and honestly gets it it may be. It may give a little *eclat* to some of those that have delivered speeches. If this is a matter of public interest, let it be urged as a reason why these speeches should be published. Let us have a reason why these speeches should be published. I go for publishing to the world the testimony in the case. Let the people see what testimony has been brought in this case, and what their rights are. Sir, I am opposed to publishing the speeches. If any are to be published, I say publish all. I want to get the speech I am making upon the record, so it shall go to the people protesting against this unnecessary expense on the part of the Senate. I say it is just to me that it shall be published.

It has been asserted by some newspapers that this trial will cost a vast amount of money. The result has proven they are mistaken. I never believed it would cost the amount predicted by some. I am happy to know it has cost less than I anticipated; but I am disposed to make it cost less if I can do it, without depriving the country or the parties of anything that is necessary for them to have, in order to enable them to form a correct judgment of the nature of our action. But the speeches do not convey such information. I presume no individual in the country will be governed by the speeches. It may be the opinion of some man that one speech would have caused him to cast his vote in one way, and another man that another speech would have influenced him differently; but let each man decide from the testimony for himself.

SENATOR WATKINS. I do not desire to discuss this subject, but I would beg leave to ask the gentleman (Mr. Scott) one question. You say there is no necessity for publishing the speeches. I ask you this question: Did you examine the law applicable to this case, or would you have known the law applicable to this case, had it not been pointed out and made known to you in these speeches? and will the people before whom you propose to lay this testimony know anything about the law applicable to this case, unless they read the record and the speeches? [A voice, "that's so."]

SENATOR SCOTT. It may be that down in the south-east the people don't know the law; but I believe in every other portion of the State of Missouri they are presumed to know the law and their rights upon every case. But are these speeches to include all the law that has been read on both sides, and all the authorities that have been quoted during the proceedings?

SENATOR HALLIBURTON. Certainly.

SENATOR SCOTT. I think then we had better collect them in pamphlet form, and publish them for the benefit of the people.

Why, sir, has it been a practice to publish the law in regard to the different cases that are brought by the country? Has it ever been done in any case before? I presume not. Has it been found necessary to publish the speeches that have been made *pro* and *con* in a case? I presume not. I admit, Mr. President, I am more familiar with the law since I have heard it expounded by the parties on each side than I was before, and was better prepared to act in the case than I would have been in the absence of any authorities. But I presume each Senator here, had he never read these authorities, in the exercise of the high functions which devolved upon him in this case, would have been under the necessity of examining the law for himself to ascertain what it was. It has been to the convenience of the Senate that the parties have read the authorities bearing upon this subject; they have enabled us to act knowingly; but I presume we scarcely would have acted when we had taken an oath to try this case, until we had acquainted ourselves with the law. Sir, I am opposed to publishing these speeches, or any other proceedings connected with this thing, excepting the testimony in the case, together with the pleadings.

SENATOR CHURCHILL. I do not pretend to say the Senate should justify all the votes I gave upon this subject. I wish to call attention to one thing. We all know a great many papers in the State have referred to this trial which we have just finished as a farce. The Senate has been abused in various papers in the country since the commencement of this trial. This impeachment was gotten up by the House of Representatives. They sent their managers here to prosecute this case, and I contend, Mr. President, that it is due to the House of Representatives and to the people that they should be enabled to see in what manner these gentlemen sent here to manage this case have conducted it, and how far they have performed their duty.

I believe this is the second trial of the kind that has occurred since Missouri became a State—a period of nearly forty years. I confess I was very unfamiliar with the law governing such cases when this trial commenced, and I take it for granted a majority of my constituents were just as ignorant of proceedings of this kind as I was. For one I wish my constituents to know what has been the evidence before us on this subject and the authorities cited by the parties, so they may understand whether we have performed the duties which we were sent here to perform.

I am sorry, Mr. President, that anything has been said here this morning that would give this thing any political character whatever. I would say that, although many gentlemen have differed with me in this matter, and though I have voted to sustain a great many of the articles of impeachment during the pendency of this trial, most of the opposition Senators I have heard say nothing about it. I believe in casting their votes they were actuated by just as conscientious motives as we upon the other side of the case were.

SENATOR WATKINS. I hope the gentleman did not pretend to say the opposition, as a party, are influenced here?

SENATOR CHURCHILL. I say the votes of the opposition will show that, as a party, they have not been influenced by party considerations. I ask to make that correction. I wished to state that fact, because, sir, since I have been here at this trial I have been struck with the evidence of fairness and of conscientious motives manifested by these gentlemen in their action upon this subject.

I believe this resolution, offered by the Senator from Johnson, (Mr. Goodlett,) ought to carry; and I think it due to the whole country it should carry. A remark has fallen from the Senator from Boone, (Mr. Robinson,) that after a night's sleep some gentlemen seem to be uneasy on account of their action on this subject. I can say that so far as I am concerned in this matter I did not give a single vote in favor of these articles I would not stand by to-day.

SENATOR ROBINSON. I had supposed my explanation of that remark was sufficient. It was predicated upon what the gentleman from Johnson was saying. I said it ironically. I thought the gentleman showed a disposition to sustain his action in the premises. I think he was conscientious in what he did. The Senator from Cole seemed to be a little anxious about it. If I had reflected, it would have been addressed to the Senator from Cole, because I know cogitation on these things influences a man occasionally.

SENATOR CHURCHILL. The proceedings of bodies of this kind are not familiar to me nor to my constituents. I wish these proceedings to be published that every man in my county may know what has been done, and the reasons influencing Senators here in casting their votes.

SENATOR THOMPSON. Mr. President, I am opposed to the amendment and am in favor of having a reasonable number of copies printed containing the entirety of the proceedings in this case.

Sir, the gentleman from Buchanan has been asking reasons for the publication of a full report of the proceedings, yet all the time failing to bring forward an argument why it should not be published. The question involved is not, as the gentleman supposes, relating entirely to the influences exerted by the arguments upon the minds of the Senators in the formation of a verdict in this case, but it comprehends a relation which exists between the House of Representatives and this body, together with important considerations disconnected with the Senate's action as a body, and transcending the contracted view which the learned gentleman has taken of the subject. The House of Representatives instituted proceedings in this case, prepared the articles of impeachment, selected two of its members to manage the case on behalf of the State; and now it is claimed by gentleman upon this floor that the action of the House through its Representatives here merits not sufficient consideration to entitle its publication as a part of the proceedings in the case! But not only so,—in their zeal to ignore the relation which the House of Representative sustains to the case, and to prevent that body knowing in what manner its representatives here have discharged the duties entrusted to them, they have overlooked the fact that the carrying out of their views would result in depriving the respondent, if not of an imperative right, of a courtesy, which, I trust, no Senatorial body in the United States under similar circumstances would be unwilling to accord to him,—namely, that of publishing his defense in connection with the testimony against him, and allowing him to show to the world wherein its invalidity exists.

Much has been said about the enormous expense of printing the arguments. I am authorized by my friend O'Neil to say that the cost of printing the entire proceedings will not exceed two hundred and fifty dollars. After having already expended fifteen thousand dollars in the examination of this case, shall we let the public remain in ignorance of our proceedings, the House of Representatives in the dark as to what their managers have done toward sustaining their action, and suppress the respondent's defense, simply because a mere pittance, compared to the amount already expended, will furnish the desired information? Why, sir, I would pay for it out of my own individual funds rather than not have the full report printed.

A debate has been going on here this morning, which I think, Mr. President, entirely out of order,—democrats and opposition, and all that sort of thing. I willingly acknowledge I am the worst partizan that ever had a head; but I hope I have sense enough not to manifest its spirit on an occasion like the present, when it is entirely uncalled for. There is no party question involved here, and why sensible men should work themselves into such a high-pressure state of party feeling, I can't imagine. I am not willing to believe my senses, even if I thought I smelt a party "mice;" for this should be the last place in the world for one to make his appearance. There will doubtless be considerable talk about what we have done here. Why, in regard to myself, it has already been said this morning by one of the Senators: "there's old Thompson, confound his old skin, he voted guilty every time—clean through." I have no objections to that; yet I do think it is nothing but justice due myself and constituents, that when such charges are made against me I may have the "documents" to show why I did thus; and so does my old friend from Andrew, (Mr. Wilson,) who voted "not guilty." I want him to have a fair shake. If ever we should go before the people, (and there is no telling but that Missouri may turn the very way I want her to go,) I don't want his friends to slander mine, nor mine to slander his.

I am in favor of printing, and I will vote against the amendment. We want to let the people know what constitutes an offense sufficient to dispossess a Judge of his office. We also want to furnish rules of proceedings for the instruction of Legislatures coming after us, before whom similar cases may arise. It may be economic policy. It may be of great benefit to the Judiciary of the State. Why the gentleman from Buchanan could ever get it into his brain that the arguments should not be published I can't see. As was said by my friend from Cape Girardeau, (Mr. Watkins,) who spoilt my speech, that was the very marrow. Why, what did I know about the law that bore on the case until it was referred to? I venture there is none here so familiar with law as not to have learned something during the progress of this trial.

Senator Parsons. Mr. President, I had supposed, sir, when this resolution offered by the Senator from Johnson was read, that he would find a hearty concurrence in it from all parts of the chamber; that the highest tribunal known to the State having rendered a most solemn verdict and judgment, one in which the people of the whole State are interested and must necessarily feel a great interest in time to come, I had supposed there would be no dissenting voice to letting them know what our opinions were and upon what they were founded. Sir, we publish documents here when in political session, many of which are of the slightest importance to the people of the State, and we send them out by thousands. But here a great rule has been established in Missouri by the decision of this honorable Court, which, for future time, must work for weal or woe. As was said by the Senator from Johnson, rules have been laid down by the judgment of this Court which authorizes Judges to take certain privileges and to do certain things, the propriety of which has been doubted heretofore—at least whether they had that power or not. We have by our solemn judgment here authorized and directed, and said to the Judiciary of the State, that it is the law of this land that you can act as counsel in a certain manner. I am not controverting the wise judgment of this Court; but I say this is a rule which this Court has adopted, and that the Judges and counsel throughout the State ought to know their rights and what are not their rights. The people of Missouri have been told by our judgment here that a Judge may make certain assertions, and it is not criminal,—it is not high misdemeanor; and if he make assertions derogatory to the character of parties litigant in his courts, this solemn judgment here sustains him. I shall not question the correctness of that judgment, but I say it is now the law of the land so far as rulings here are concerned, and our constituents ought to know it. It has been ruled here by this high tribunal, after mature deliberation and reflection, that the Judge before whom a criminal is upon trial is authorized to examine and interrogate a witness upon behalf of the prosecution, and—

Senator Fox. I arise for the purpose of calling the gentleman to order. My point of order is this: He now undertakes to determine for those who may have differed with him in judgment in casting their votes on this question, and assumes to try the conclusions which governed their action.

Senator Halliburton. I would ask, Mr. President, if the rule does not require points of order to be made in writing?

Mr. President. I do not know that it is so. I do not think the Senator from Cole (Mr. Parsons) is out of order.

Senator Parsons. I impugn no Senator's motives. No man will deny this judgment is the record of the highest tribunal of the State, that we are bound by it, and that future legislation will be bound by it. I shall not take, as did the Senator from Buchanan, a political view of this thing in the way he has taken it. I did not think about buncombe at all, and I did not suppose, in a dignified body like this, that word would ever be used. He charges that we desire to print these speeches in order that somebody may make buncombe out of it. Let us see how it will stand. I will take the gentleman upon that proposition, and let us see to what party I belong. If I would descend to the discussion of politics, what benefit would be derived from it? I believe one of the managers in this case, who made a speech, belongs to our party; I believe the other one, who laid down fully and explicitly and so clearly the law in this case, belongs to the party to which the Senator from Buchanan is attached. I am sure, in the language of my friend who is not now in his seat, that the publication of both their arguments would be dealing out even-handed justice. So far as the respondent is concerned, I confess I do not know to-day, except from rumor last night, after this case was decided, to what political party he does belong. Then, I say the argument of the Senator from Buchanan that this thing was gotten up here for the purpose of giving some particular person who made a speech, buncombe before the country, falls to the ground for the reason that, so far as we know, these speeches will go from different political parties.

SENATOR SCOTT. I desire to correct the Senator from Cole. I made no allusion to parties when I spoke of the publication of these speeches. I said they would be published only for the benefit of the parties delivering them.

SENATOR PARSONS. The gentleman has twice or thrice propounded the question, "why publish the arguments in this case?" I will answer that question for him, or, in other words, I will aid in answering it, because it has well been answered heretofore.

In the first place, sir, the managers on behalf of the State presented to this Court the points upon which they intended to rely for conviction. In the next place, the respondent presented to this Court the points he intended to rely upon for acquittal. Then, in the argument upon the case, the manager who opened the case stated to this Court the law of the case, and made his reference to it. For what purpose? So that the Court might be informed in regard to the law. He made his argument and he applied the facts to the law of the case, the respondent rebutting with his law and rebutting with his facts as far as he could, and the managers concluded. Now what is the condition of it? Why, sir, here we have the law of the case laid down to us and the points in authority in the case laid down to us, and upon them we have decided. And yet the Senator from Buchanan triumphantly asks where did you ever see such a course taken before. I have to refer him to the western end of this capitol and tell him to take up their decisions. Every decision of the Supreme Court of Missouri, from the very first to the last act, even in causes where an hundred dollars were not involved, you find the points of arguments, and you find the authorities insisted upon, both by the counsel for the plaintiff in error and for the defendant in error, and even in some cases, where the Supreme Court looked upon it as an important case, long arguments have been embodied. I think, sir, that the Senator from Buchanan had forgotten that fact, otherwise he would not have asked that question so triumphantly. In the Peck case the arguments of counsel were published, as was also the case in the Chase trial; and for the reason that the people might know the points and authorities relied upon by both parties.

But another reason, sir, for the publication of it. We know very well as a reading people in Missouri they will not undertake to go over all this evidence in detail, except as I shall show hereafter; but they will take the respondent's accusation, and the case as made out and insisted upon by each party—they will read it over, and where the respondent and managers do not agree in regard to the testimony, then the people will turn to the record and evidence, and see which party was right and which party was wrong. That, sir, is one reason why it should be published,—that is a reason why it should go to the world,—so the whole matter can be scanned in full. As I said before, this is one of the most important adjudications that has ever been had in Missouri. There is an adjudication here, according to my humble judgment,—a proposition properly adjudged (because I must respect the judgment of this Court like I would that of any other court) that authorizes a Judge of a Circuit Court to erase, and change, and underline, and supply a record in the most important cases.

SENATOR SCOTT. I call the gentleman to order.

SENATOR ROBINSON. I would ask the Senator how he comes to the conclusion that that is the law of the land. I presume the gentleman comes to it by belief in evidence that I discarded. I say he is not justifiable, and this Court is encouraging disturbances by permitting this commentary upon its action. If the gentleman insists upon this commentary, I shall insist upon my privilege to go into the ring, and when I do enter the ring I do not intend to spare him. I say the gentleman is out of order, because he is commenting upon the past action of this Court. He is going on the conclusions of his own judgment, and not the conclusions of law as established by this Court. He is giving his own construction of that law to the prejudice of those who made this decision. If the gentleman can have any object in the world, it is simply, as the gentleman from Buchanan said, to exhibit a little buncombe.

SENATOR PARSONS. I inquire who it is that rests uneasy in his seat now? [Laughter.]

SENATOR ROBINSON. I respond in this way: I am not uneasy in my seat, nor do I feel uneasy; but I am sorry to see any Senator place himself in a position of condemning or vindicating his past action when he knows very well that past action cannot be reversed. It looks to me very much as though the Senator felt very uneasy and was anxious to give to the people of the State his reasons for casting his vote on this question.

SENATOR PARSONS. I am sorry, sir, that I have disturbed the boasted equanimity of the Senator from Boone. He first attacked me this morning, rather indirectly, about my uneasiness, but I am sure the evidence exhibited in this case will require the conviction of him and the acquittal of me. The Senator further remarked in a speech here, to which I must reply, that his allusion as to uneasiness was perhaps directed more to myself than to anybody else,—that sometimes I had reacted, that sometimes I had changed my opinions, that sometimes I had followed the same course whether I was in the right or in the wrong. I must say to the Senator from Boone that from the commencement of this trial I have never discovered the slightest reaction in *him*. He has been standing to his position all the while. Not that I pretend to say, Mr. President, he thought this reaction would have been improper, but because he believed it was his honest judgment. I did, on one of the propositions, vote for the acquittal of the accused, because I deemed it right; and on other occasions I voted for his conviction, because I believed that was right. If that is reaction, I believe I reacted according to the law and the evidence in this case.

Mr. President, there is another objection I have to the amendment offered by the Senator from Buchanan. The type in which this printing is proposed to be done by the original resolution, makes the cost of publication cheaper than could be done under the substitute. The original resolution names the kind of type in which it should be printed for this reason.

I am sorry, Mr. President, I have detained the Senate so long.

SENATOR ROBINSON. Mr. President, I might perhaps be satisfied with letting this discussion pass off, but because I see a gentleman busy taking a report of it, let it go to the country for what it is worth. When it must be so evident to every one present that grave Senators have gotten up here for the purpose of reading a lecture in regard to this subject, I do not feel disposed to let the occasion pass without letting the Senate and people know what view of the subject I have, so far as the past action of this Senate is concerned. The Senator from Johnson has told us that he wishes it to go to the people that a Judge has certain powers under the decision of this Court; he wishes it to go to the people that a Judge may peremptorily order a lawyer to sit down; that he may change the record—

SENATOR GOODLETT. I call the Senator to order. I was not permitted to speak upon it, and if it was not allowed me to comment upon the facts, it is not for him to comment upon them.

SENATOR ROBINSON. There is no proposition here to keep from the people anything whatever in regard to this trial, that should be legitimately before them. The proposition of the Senator from Buchanan is simply to print the charges, the replication, and the evidence in the case. I have no objection to the printing of the speeches. I shall not vote against a proposition to that effect, since I have learned that the printing of these speeches is absolutely necessary to sustain the action of a majority of this Senate before the people. Why, the Senator from Cole regards it as a political question, and for what purpose? Does that Senator expect the people of the State will take this decision into their hands and reverse it? Why does he want it to go out to the people? This is a pretext for the purpose of reading a lecture to Senators upon this floor for their past action. As I said before, I do not envy that self-respect in a man who is disposed to rise here and read a lecture in such a case. It indicates to me very clearly that there is somewhere a doubt as to the propriety of his own action. This is all I have to say in regard to it.

SENATOR FRAZIER. I feel it due to myself to make an explanation in regard to the vote I gave. I have sat silent in my seat, and heard the whole discussion, and now that I am called upon to vote on this proposition, I will present the reasons for the vote I am going to give. In the first place, I think the people of the State should have the whole matter before them, and not a part of it. Some of the votes I gave were for the acquittal of the respondent, and some were for his conviction. In giving them I was actuated by what I conceived to be justice, according to the law and the evidence in the case. I have no doubt every other Senator acted as honestly as I did. I am surprised that any Senator should object to the full account going to the people, and be unwilling to stand or fall by the result. The Senate will bear me out in the assertion that I am as much opposed to extravagant expenditure and have voted against as many appropriations as any man upon this floor; but when the necessity of the case demands a reasonable appropriation, like the proposed one, I cannot raise an objection. I wish the people to judge of our action, not from imperfect predicates, but from a full and fair stand point, such as the entire record of our proceedings will present.

SENATOR WILSON. I should like for the Chairman on Printing to make a statement in relation to the probable costs.

SENATOR SCOTT. I find so many of the Senators anxious to have the speeches printed, that I shall withdraw my substitute.

SENATOR O'NEIL. The expense of printing the arguments will not be over $200.

SENATOR MORRIS. I will suggest to the Senator from Johnson to embrace in his resolution the articles, answer, and replication.

SENATOR WILSON. The respondent, upon his arraignment last winter, delivered a speech before this Court. I do not know whether or not it was reported. I think it should be embraced in the report, because in that speech, if I remember rightly, the respondent gave his view of the law, and the jurisdiction of the General Assembly.

MR. PRESIDENT. He traveled over the same ground in his opening speech here.

SENATOR PARSONS. I will explain. He filed a motion of the nature of a demurrer and argued the law under it, and it was on my motion it was overruled.

SENATOR RAINS. I would prefer five thousand.

SENATOR WILSON. I think one copy is sufficient for each member.

SENATOR WATKINS. I would like to have twenty-five copies. If I get three copies, what is the result? I will have one copy for myself, one for Cape Girardeau, one for Bollinger, and none for Perry. Now, my friend from New Madrid has six or eight counties, and most of them would get none. I go for printing three thousand. I look upon it as one of the most important measures ever presented here. In this case great fundamental principles have been involved. I am anxious the people shall know all about this matter. It is a little strange that all of those gentlemen who voted against these articles of impeachment seem to be opposed to letting the people know all about it.

SENATOR ROBINSON. I announce that absolutely not so; and if the gentleman chooses to make such allusions, it is not only unbecoming him, but in my estimation not becoming a gentleman.

SENATOR WATKINS. The gentleman is not to judge for me what is becoming a gentleman.

I wish to make this statement: A Senator introduces a proposition against publishing the arguments in this case. I see the Senators who voted in favor of the respondent uniformly—

SENATOR SCOTT. I call the gentleman to order. I say to him and this Senate, that I do not intend to have my action animadverted upon by any Senator upon this floor. I have acted upon the view I have taken, and no Senator shall dare to animadvert upon anything that influenced my action.

SENATOR WATKINS. I do not pretend to animadvert upon any action.

SENATOR SCOTT. I do not intend he shall comment upon the action of any one connected with the trial.

SENATOR WATKINS. I merely stated a fact which I believe exists. Every Senator who is opposed to the publication of the arguments in this case, voted against every article of impeachment.

SENATOR SCOTT. I call the gentleman to order, [advancing to the seat of Mr. Watkins,] and I will inform him that he *must not* refer to my action or votes on this trial. It is out of order. It is unbecoming to do it. The man must have acted from impure motives himself before he was prepared to impugn my motives. [Cries of "order," "order."]

SENATOR WATKINS. I have not impugned the motives of any man. I have stated a mere fact. I will stand by the record, and the world can judge of the fact.

SENATOR SCOTT. I deny the right of the Senator to state such a thing.

SENATOR WATKINS. I impute improper motive to nobody.

SENATOR SCOTT. That does not come up in this controversy; it has nothing to do with it.

SENATOR JONES. I suppose I am one of those voting in the minority. So far as I am concerned I intend to vote for the proposition of the Senator from Johnson. I suppose each Senator is very well satisfied with the vote he gave. I am satisfied with mine. I am as willing for many copies to be printed as any body on this floor. So far as the intimation goes that no one voting in the minority was in favor of the publication of his acts, it is unfounded.

SENATOR WATKINS. We are about to separate, perhaps, never to meet again. I should regret exceedingly if anything I said produced unkind feelings. I am sure I did not mean to offend. But I take back nothing I said. I merely remarked a fact that could not be controverted. I believe the gentleman from Franklin, the gentleman from Buchanan, and every gentleman upon this floor, has acted with as pure motives as I have upon this occasion. I repeat it, I did not intend to cast any slur or calumny upon any man; I merely intended to state a fact. That fact does exist, and I will not retract. I hope we shall separate with no unkind feelings.

SENATOR RAINS. Mr. President, I shall vote for the resolution. I do so, sir, from different motives, however, than those that have been assigned by Senators who have spoken. I vote for it that the people may know what the great democratic party have done here. I am sorry any allusion to partizanism was brought into the Court, because we have been recognized here as a jury, and have no right to introduce politics to influence the action of the jury. I hope partizan feeling has influenced none here in the casting of a vote. I shall vote for the adoption of this resolution for this reason, in addition to the fact that the people of Missouri are entitled to the whole—not only to the evidence, but to the speeches that have been made by both sides; by the accused and by the managers. It will be recollected these managers were elected in the House of Representatives, and have become, to a certain extent, officers sent here by the State of Missouri. They come here in the very same attitude we do, and they are responsible to the body that elected them. Shall we say, sir, to the lower branch of the Assembly, you have sent managers here to conduct a cause, and yet you shall not know how they have performed their duty? Notwithstanding it was attempted at the early part of this discussion to show that this was a party measure, and what is commonly denominated the "opposition" was afraid for this report to be printed, I am one, sir, to vote for the resolution. The charge I hurl back in the teeth of the asserters of it. I believe that under the classification recently made I am denominated one of the opposition. I am one of the opposition in so far as I am ever ready to oppose any attempt to bring a party matter into a grave decision like this. I never consult the interests of any party when I go to discharge a sworn duty.

The resolution was then adopted by the following vote:

AYES—Messrs. Brown, Byrne, Churchill, Fox, Frazier, Goodlett, Halliburton, Harris, Hedgpeth, Horner, Hyer, Jones, McFarland, McIlvaine, Morris, Newland, O'Neil, Parsons, Peyton, Rains, Robinson, Scott, Thompson, Vernon, Watkins, Wilson, Wood, and Wright—28.

NOES—Mr. Gullett—1.

Absent—Messrs. Coleman, Johnson, McFerran, and Richardson.

After some further unimportant business, on motion of SENATOR WATKINS the High Court of Impeachment adjourned *sine die.*

www.ingramcontent.com/pod-product-compliance
Lightning Source LLC
LaVergne TN
LVHW020926110826
845150LV00004B/784

* 9 7 8 1 4 2 5 5 5 3 1 9 7 *